Frh. P. Weigand

PSYCHOLOGICAL ISSUES

PSYCHOLOGICAL ISSUES

Identity and the Life Cycle

Studies in Remembering

On Perception and Event Structure, and the Psychological Environment

Cognitive Control

INTERNATIONAL UNIVERSITIES PRESS, INC.
NEW YORK

Copyright 1959, by INTERNATIONAL UNIVERSITIES PRESS, INC.

GEORGE S. KLEIN, *Editor*

Editorial Board

ERIK H. ERIKSON	GEORGE S. KLEIN
SIBYLLE ESCALONA	ROBERT R. HOLT
CHARLES FISHER	GARDNER LINDZEY
MERTON M. GILL	ROY SCHAFER

ROBERT S. WALLERSTEIN

SUZETTE H. ANNIN, *Editorial Assistant*

PART 1

IDENTITY AND THE LIFE CYCLE
SELECTED PAPERS
Erik H. Erikson
WITH A HISTORICAL INTRODUCTION BY
David Rapaport

PART 2

STUDIES IN REMEMBERING
THE REPRODUCTION OF CONNECTED AND
EXTENDED VERBAL MATERIAL
Irving H. Paul

PART 3

ON PERCEPTION, EVENT STRUCTURE,
AND PSYCHOLOGICAL ENVIRONMENT
SELECTED PAPERS
Fritz Heider

PART 4

COGNITIVE CONTROL
A STUDY OF INDIVIDUAL CONSISTENCIES IN
COGNITIVE BEHAVIOR
*Riley W. Gardner, Philip S. Holzman,
George S. Klein, Harriet B. Linton,
and Donald P. Spence*

IDENTITY AND THE
LIFE CYCLE

PART 1

IDENTITY AND THE LIFE CYCLE

Selected Papers

by

ERIK H. ERIKSON

With a Historical Introduction by
DAVID RAPAPORT

CONTENTS

Author's Preface   1

Introduction
   A HISTORICAL SURVEY OF PSYCHOANALYTIC EGO
   PSYCHOLOGY, by DAVID RAPAPORT   5

1   EGO DEVELOPMENT AND HISTORICAL CHANGE   18
    Clinical Notes

2   GROWTH AND CRISES OF THE HEALTHY PERSONALITY   50

3   THE PROBLEM OF EGO IDENTITY   101

Appendix   165

Bibliography   167

Author's Preface

The republication of selected papers usually calls for a statement of sufficient reason. This monograph contains writings which are in demand as source material—a demand so persistent and coming from such different professional quarters as to point to a live "psychological issue."

The title states the over-all issue: It is the unity of the human life cycle, and the specific dynamics of each of its stages, as prescribed by the laws of individual development and of social organization. In psychoanalysis this theme has so far not been carried beyond childhood, and a few papers cannot aim to do more than to delineate the specific psychosocial task of youth, namely, the formation of ego identity, and to outline work as yet to be done. The editor and the author are, therefore, especially grateful to David Rapaport for permitting them to publish as an introductory chapter a comprehensive paper which serves to anchor the issue in the history of psychoanalytic ego theory and in the work of my teachers. However, the reader who is not specifically prepared by previous study to follow Rapaport's treatment of the subject may do well to turn to it after having perused my less systematic papers.

The nature of these papers explains their varying commitment to theory. The first paper (a selection of clinical notes which antedated and, in fact, provided source material for my book *Childhood and Society*) illustrates that combination of therapeutic observations and impressions from "applied" work which leads a clinician to a rethinking of his premises. Application here does not mean only the use of psychoanalytic hypotheses in other fields—such as Indian education, war work, and longitudinal child study—but a sharing of the conditions of observation in these fields. The clinician approaches such episodical opportunities for communication and service with whatever theory has become implicit in his observational habits; only gradually does it become apparent that the extraclinical application suggests a new look at the clinical theory itself.

The paper "Growth and Crises of the 'Healthy Personality'" owes its existence to another challenge. A group of experts in child development, appointed by the U.S. Children's Bureau to prepare for the White House Conference in 1950 an outline of the verified facts and the promising theories pertaining to mental health in childhood, asked the writer as a clinician and citizen how, at that date and for that purpose, he could restate what in his book *Childhood and Society* had been implied regarding the development of a "healthy personality." The writer overruled his own misgivings regarding the theoretical prematurity and the possible misuses of a schema of normality, and, asking Joan Erikson (as a mother and educator) for assistance, elaborated on some clinical insights. Insight, of course, is an integral part of a clinician's work; when spelled out, however, it must include (rather than pass by) whatever verifiable knowledge, consistent theory, and therapeutic method are at the clinician's disposal (see Erikson, 1958b). The paper appears here substantially in the form in which it was presented to the study group preparing the White House Conference. However, I have put into italics certain major points which experience has shown are apt to be ignored; while a few new footnotes warn against the misuses to which this treatise has lent itself.

"The Problem of Ego Identity" was addressed to a quite different audience. The program committee of the American Psychoanalytic Association asked me to enlarge on this subject in one section of its yearly midwinter meetings. Here, naturally, references to psychoanalytic theory as well as to therapeutic technique are more numerous, although, here as elsewhere, I have left metapsychological questions to experts in this kind of thinking.

In all their differences, however, the three papers collected here describe three connected steps in clinical thinking: they gradually narrow the issue of psychosocial development from general clinical impressions, to a first outline of psychosocial stages, and finally to the more detailed formulation of one stage, namely, adolescence. Future inquiry must focus on the comparison of several life stages studied in this manner, and must eventually turn to the implications of such studies for the understanding of the whole human life cycle.

Workers from other fields will find in my bibliography references to the transcripts of a number of interdisciplinary meetings in which my concepts were presented and discussed (Erikson, 1951a, 1953, 1955a, 1955b, 1956c, 1958c; Erikson and Erikson, 1957). Nowadays, when direct oral and social communication across disciplines and continents is to a large extent replacing the solitary and detailed study of books, a certain amount of repetitiousness, with proper variations, is unavoidable. My books, *Childhood and Society* (1950a) and *Young Man Luther* (1958a), delineate how far I myself have been able to carry an integration of clinical and applied approaches. The clinical psychoanalyst, however, will note that only in more recent papers have I begun to take up in earnest the problems of clinical evidence (1954, 1958b) and of therapeutic method, in the light of our expanded historical awareness. In this respect, too, this monograph—retracing a section of one clinical worker's itinerary—presents in truth an as yet open psychological issue.

Introduction

A HISTORICAL SURVEY OF PSYCHOANALYTIC EGO PSYCHOLOGY

DAVID RAPAPORT

If there existed a systematic study of ego psychology, containing a precise definition of the ego and a full listing of ego functions, it would be relatively simple to outline the history of ego psychology. So far no such study has been published, and the survey I intend to give here may be considered as a prerequisite for such a study.

Before beginning our survey it will be worth reminding ourselves that the ego, the id, and the superego are concepts. They are abstractions which refer to certain characteristics of behavior. In contrast to the id, which refers to *peremptory* aspects of behavior, the ego refers to aspects of behavior which are *delayable, bring about delay*, or are themselves *products of delay*. The ego is a general concept: the explanation of those characteristics of behavior to which it refers requires many subsidiary concepts. Ego psychology encompasses all these concepts and its propositions state the relationships among them. Thus it is the theory of the relationships among the behavioral referents of all these concepts. In addition, however, it includes propositions coordinating ego concepts with the other concepts of psychoanalysis.

This paper, a condensation of lectures given at the Philadelphia Psychoanalytic Society and at the Department of Psychiatry of the University of Colorado, Denver, in 1954 and 1957, appeared in the *Bulletin of the Philadelphia Association for Psychoanalysis*, 8:105-120, 1958. For another survey, see Hartmann (1956b).

The first phase of the history of psychoanalytic ego psychology coincides with Freud's prepsychoanalytic theory; it ends with 1897, the approximate beginning of psychoanalysis proper (Freud, 1887-1902, pp. 215-218). *The second phase*, which ends in 1923, is the development of psychoanalysis proper. *The third phase* begins with the publication of *The Ego and the Id* (1923), and encompasses the development of Freud's ego psychology, which extends to 1937. *The fourth phase* begins with the crucial writings of Anna Freud (1936), Hartmann (1939), Erikson (1937), Horney (1937), Kardiner (1939), Sullivan (1938, 1940), and extends to the present day. The general psychoanalytic psychology of the ego based on the foundations laid by Freud began to evolve in this phase.

THE FOUR PHASES OF THE DEVELOPMENT OF EGO PSYCHOLOGY

THE FIRST PHASE

In the first phase, the main contribution to the development of ego psychology was *the concept of defense*. A subsidiary contribution was the central role attributed to *external reality*.

That conception of defense differs from the present concept. Defense was conceived of as directed against the memory and the re-encountering of certain reality experiences (Freud, 1887-1902, pp. 109-115; 1894a; 1896; Breuer and Freud, 1895). This defense concept and our present one are alike in that both imply that a quantitative factor is dammed up and displaced. But in the early defense conception this quantity was "affect" and not "drive cathexis" (1894a, p. 75). They are also alike (Freud, 1915c, pp. 177-178) in that defense, by preventing the recall and re-encounter of a reality experience, forestalls the experience of an unacceptable and thus painful affect (Breuer and Freud, 1895, pp. 26-27; Freud, 1894a, pp. 61-63).

The crucial difference between the early defense conception and the present one, however, is the setting of the former: a primitive conception of the ego. The term ego in the first phase stood either for the "person," or for the "self," or for consciousness (Breuer and Freud, 1895, pp. 122-123, 133, 225). The conception was that consciousness is commanded by "the dominant mass of ideas" (p. 116); the memories which are incompatible with this dominant mass of ideas are dissociated from consciousness by defense. Due to this separation, the affect associated with the memory cannot be dissipated—as it would be normally—over the associative network, and thus is dammed up and turns into anxiety (the toxic theory, Freud, 1894b, pp. 94, 97, 102).

The crucial similarity of this defense conception to our present concept is that reality has a central, though different, role in it (cf. Freud, 1887-1902; 1894a; 1896; and the third phase below).

THE SECOND PHASE

The theory of the first phase collapsed when Freud discovered that his patients' reports of infantile seduction were not reports of reality experiences but of fantasies (Freud, 1887-1902, pp. 215-218). Consequently, reality experience lost its central position in the theory, and only slowly regained it in the course of the next thirty years. The center of interest shifted to the agent which creates the fantasies and the processes by which this agent works: the discovery of the instinctual drive followed (Freud, 1887-1902, pp. 270-271) and its exploration dominated the second phase (Freud, 1900; 1905). Interest in defenses also declined and the conception distinguishing a variety of defenses was replaced by the global concept of repression (Freud, 1915b). Where defenses retained their individuality they were considered as various mechanisms of repression or as subsequent substitute formations (1915b, pp. 154 ff.). But the centering of interest on instinctual drives had still other effects on the conception of defenses. *First*, some defenses were treated as *instinctual vicissitudes* (1915a, pp. 117, 132). *Second*, the question arose: what is the *repressive* (defensive) *force*? This question was answered by the assumption that repression (defense) is effected by ego instincts (1905; 1914, pp. 77-78; and 1911). Thus in this phase of the theory even crucial ego functions were conceived of in terms of instinctual drives. Yet both of these conceptions contributed to the development of ego psychology: they kept alive the problem of defense mechanisms, and raised the question, "What are the 'ego forces'?" Two more conceptions of this phase are relevant to the development of ego psychology, but since *at this point* they did not directly advance it, they will be only mentioned here: *pleasure vs. reality ego* (1911, pp. 18-19; 1915a, pp. 135-136) and *narcissism* (1914).

However, the outstanding contributions to ego psychology in this phase were the conception of the secondary process (1900, pp. 598-605, 616-617), the conception of the reality principle (1911), and the analysis of the process of repression (1915b, 1915c).

Although the concept of the *secondary process* implied no genetic ego roots independent of the instinctual drives, and was conceived as imposed upon the primary process (i.e., on the instinctual drives) solely by reality experience, it is just as crucial a historical root of ego psychology as the defense conception of the first phase.[1] Although we cannot discuss the secondary process in detail, we must point out that it provided a conception of reality relations (1900, p. 574), and involved a concept of consciousness (pp. 615-616) which was independent of the topographical conception simultaneously introduced (pp. 535-542). Both the concepts of reality relations and of consciousness were crucial for the later structural concept of the ego.

The introduction of *the reality principle* (1911)—though it too implied no ego roots independent from instinctual drives—provided the secondary process with a regulation principle comparable to the pleasure principle of the primary process, and the analysis of its means of functioning (*reality testing*) provided further specifications of the conception of the secondary process (1911, pp. 14-17).

The analysis of the process of repression revealed the insufficiencies and internal contradictions of the topographic conception: the economic conception "easily defeated the topographical one" (1915c, p. 180). Repression proved to be a matter neither of topography nor of ego instincts, but of the withdrawal of hypercathexes and the establishment of permanent countercathexes (pp. 180-181). The discovery in this second phase that these countercathexes are *permanent* and that the resistances which they bring about are *unconscious* (like their antagonists, the instinctual drives, pp. 192-193) anticipated Freud's structural theory of the ego in *The Ego and the Id* (1923) which ushered in the third phase.

[1] Actually both originate in Freud's neuropsychological theory in the "Project for a Scientific Psychology" (1887-1902, pp. 347-446).

THE THIRD PHASE

The Beginning

Freud repeatedly indicated that he expected the theory of the ego to arise from the study of narcissistic neuroses (1915a, p. 125; and 1917, pp. 331-332). Yet *The Ego and the Id* and its historical setting suggest that no such new study preceded it and that it may have been written not to clarify the concept of the ego, but, by introducing the concept of the superego, primarily to explain the unconscious sense of guilt and the negative therapeutic reaction.

In *The Ego and the Id* (1923) the ego is introduced as a coherent organization of mental processes (p. 15) which arises from identifications with abandoned objects (pp. 36 ff.), is organized primarily around the system perception-conscious (pp. 27-28) but also includes the structures which are responsible for resistances and are unconscious (in the same sense as the id is, pp. 16-18), has neutral energies at its disposal (pp. 61-63), and can transform the energies of instinctual drives into energies of its own (pp. 64-65).

Thus in this conception the ego has genetic roots (Pcpt-Cs) and energies of its own. Consciousness (which in the first phase was more or less equated with the ego, and in the latter part of the second phase—as the System Cs—could account for only a small segment of ego functions) was scaled down to a mental quality, which—though exclusive to the ego—is only one of the possible qualities of ego functions and structures (pp. 16-18).

Yet this conception of the ego still had significant shortcomings: *first,* though Freud asserted that "in the ego perception plays the part which in the id devolves upon instinct" (p. 30), the ego still appears as a *resultant* of the promptings of id, superego, and reality (pp. 82-83); *second,* the ego is still the helpless rider of the id horse, "obliged to guide it where it wants to go" (p. 30); *third,* although some independent genetic roots are attributed to the ego, it is still assumed to differentiate out of the id; *fourth,* though the ego is viewed genetically, no epigenetic[2] conception of ego development, comparable to that of the phases of libido development, is postulated; *fifth,* even though the structures responsible for resistance are recognized as ego functions, no general theory of the role of defensive functions within the ego is developed; *sixth,* though the topo-

[2] For the concept of epigenesis, see Erikson (1940a, 1950a).

graphical view of consciousness is dispensed with, the structural conception of consciousness as a superordinate sense organ, developed in the early part of the second phase, is not yet incorporated.[3]

The Culmination

This conception was, however, only the beginning of the third phase, which culminated in Freud's *The Problem of Anxiety* (1926a). Here Freud repudiated the conception that the ego is totally subservient to the id (pp. 22-23). The ego autonomously initiates defense by the anxiety signal (pp. 18-19, 86-87), becomes increasingly able, in the course of development, to turn the passively experienced anxiety into a form of active anticipation (pp. 114-115), makes use of the pleasure principle in pursuing its own ends (pp. 18, 80), has a great variety of defenses at its disposal (Chs. IV, V, VI, and pp. 110-112), is ultimately concerned with reality relationships (i.e., adaptation) and therefore curbs instinctual drives when action prompted by them would lead into reality danger (pp. 18, 22, 116).

In this conception Freud finally achieved what he had previously attempted (1911, pp. 13 f.): namely, external reality is brought into the center of the theory (1926a, pp. 62, 101, 116), as it was in the first phase, but the central role of instinctual drives (p. 87), first established in the second phase, is retained. For the first time a conception of adaptation is implied: this theory of the ego provides a unitary solution for the ego's relations to reality and to instinctual drives. But this conception of adaptation is still limited in that it is developed only in reference to reality dangers.

This conception is the foundation for the concept of the autonomy of the ego, and points to constitutionally given perceptual (1926a, p. 18) and affect mechanisms (pp. 71, 75, 90, 117) as roots of this autonomy (pp. 22-23). But it does not yet achieve a concept of ego autonomy.

Finally, this theory of the ego implies an epigenetic conception —at least of that aspect of ego development which pertains to anxiety (pp. 88-92)—which involves the turning of the enforced (passive) ego responses into ego-initiated (active) processes (p. 115). But neither this conception of epigenesis nor that of passivity and

---

[3] For an attempt at such an integration see Rapaport (1951, 1956, 1957).

activity are as yet applied to the development of other ego functions or to ego development in general.

Freud's final conception of the ego includes his concepts of the secondary process and the reality principle (1932, pp. 105-108). He rounded out this final conception in a subsequent paper, making explicit the assumption of inborn ego roots, independent of instinctual drives (1937, pp. 343-344). Freud's implied conception of autonomous synthetic functions of the ego (1926a, pp. 26-44) was subsequently made explicit by Nunberg (1931) and Waelder (1936).

The third phase culminated in Anna Freud's volume (1936). By introducing the concept of defense against external stimuli she integrated two of the main themes of this phase: defense and reality relations. By systematizing the concepts of the specific defenses and by investigating the role of affects she broadened the foundations which Freud had laid for psychoanalytic ego psychology.

THE FOURTH PHASE

Preliminaries

Psychoanalysis established the first conception of reality relations in terms of the secondary process and in relation to danger situations, but did not generalize it into a concept of adaptation until 1937. Thus the theory of object relations remained outside the scope of psychoanalytic ego psychology, and the psychosocial implications of reality and object relations remained unexplained theoretically.[4] In the late 30's this gap in psychoanalytic theory apparently became so conspicuous that several simultaneous attempts to bridge it were made.[5] Some of these attempts (Erikson, Hartmann, Kris, and Loewenstein) showed a clear awareness of the foundations which existed in psychoanalysis for a theory of reality relationships in general, and interpersonal (psychosocial) relationships in particular. They also took into account the incipient theory of the ego's autonomous roots, development, and functions implied in Freud's ego psychology. Those attempts (Horney, Kardiner, Sullivan, etc.) which showed no such awareness—though otherwise their contribution to the development of psychoanalytic ego psychology was substantial—cannot be discussed here: they lead far

[4] The "theory" of object relations evolved by Melanie Klein and her followers is not an ego psychology but an id mythology.
[5] An early attempt in this direction was made by Alfred Adler.

away from the main stream of psychoanalysis. Some of the observations on which they are based have already been accounted for and some of the problems which they raised have already been solved by the recent developments in psychoanalytic ego psychology, which go a long way in demonstrating that these problems can be solved without discarding the basic theory of psychoanalysis.

The fourth phase of the development of psychoanalytic ego psychology is dominated by the contributions of Hartmann and Erikson, which are built on and complement the third phase of Freud's theory.

Hartmann and His Collaborators

Hartmann centers on those innate roots of ego development which are independent of instinctual drives; on reality relationships, that is, adaptation; and on the integration of the theory of the secondary process (second phase) with the theory of autonomous defense (third phase).

1. In the conception of Hartmann, Kris, and Loewenstein, the ego does not develop from the id but both differentiate from a common matrix: the earliest *undifferentiated phase* of postnatal development (Hartmann, 1952; Hartmann, Kris, and Loewenstein, 1946).

2. Hartmann conceived of the independent roots of ego development as *ego apparatuses of primary autonomy* (motility, perception, memory, etc.) which already exist in the undifferentiated phase and which after differentiation become the ego's major control and executive apparatuses (Hartmann, 1939).

3. These apparatuses (as well as the coordination which they effect between the instinctual drives and their objects) he recognized as the means of phylogenetically guaranteed coordination to external reality, that is to say, to an *average expectable environment*. He conceptualized this coordination as a *state of adaptedness* which is prior to conflict and not a product of conflict solution, and thus is not wrung from the instinctual drives by the exigencies of reality. Thus he provided a conceptual explanation of the relatively autonomous and adaptive character of the secondary process (1939, 1952).

4. He recognized that the conflict-born structures and functions of the ego can also attain relative autonomy from the drives. By introducing the concept of *change of function* he offered a con-

ceptual explanation of their observed relative autonomy and termed them *apparatuses of secondary autonomy*. He juxtaposed *processes of adaptation* and *states of adaptedness*, by means of these concepts laid the foundation for the psychoanalytic concept and theory of adaptation, and outlined the first generalized theory of reality relations in psychoanalytic ego psychology.

5. Hartmann's theory links the concepts *change of function* and *apparatuses of secondary autonomy* (by way of the concepts *automatization* and *neutralization*) to Freud's theories of the secondary process and of (defensive) structure formation by binding of countercathexes. The concepts *automatization* and *automatism* particularize the process of structure formation (Hartmann, 1947). Hartmann's (1950, 1955) and Kris's (1950, 1955) concept of neutralization generalizes Freud's theory of hypercathexes (1900, pp. 593-594, 599-600, 602-603, 617; 1915c, pp. 192, 193-194; and 1923, pp. 61-65), provides at least a partial conceptual answer to the question of the origin of ego energies, and clarifies the relation between *mobile* and *bound* energies by distinguishing the processes of *binding* and *neutralization* (Kris, 1950).

6. The concepts of the apparatuses of primary and secondary autonomy, automatization, and neutralization are the foundation of Hartmann's theory of the ego's relative autonomy from the id, which both generalized and particularized the conception implicit in Freud's theory of anxiety. Hartmann's theory of adaptation, however, does not fully integrate the theories of ego autonomy and reality relationships.[6]

7. Kris extended the conception of activity and passivity implied in Freud's theory of the third phase, by introducing the concept of *regression in the service of the ego* (Kris, 1952). Hartmann made an important step toward generalizing this conception by demonstrating that the ego makes use not only of the highest order secondary processes and rational regulations, but integrates and makes use both of its own archaic regulations and mechanisms and of the id's regulations and mechanisms (Hartmann, 1939, 1947). This generalization, however, does not include a systematic conception of activity and passivity.[7]

[6] For an attempt at such an integration see Rapaport (1951b, 1958).
[7] For an attempt at a systematic conception of activity and passivity see Rapaport (1953, 1958).

8. Hartmann (1939) asserted, and Hartmann and Kris (1945) elaborated on, the theoretical necessity of a concept of *autonomous ego development;* Loewenstein (1950) and Kris (1955) demonstrated its clinical necessity. Although Hartmann's concept of secondary autonomy is a powerful tool for building a theory of autonomous ego development, he did not develop such an epigenetic theory.

9. Hartmann's theory of adaptation includes a generalized theory of reality relations, which stresses the special role of social relations (1939; Hartmann and Kris, 1945; Hartmann, Kris, and Loewenstein, 1951). Yet it does not provide a specific and differentiated psychosocial theory.

Erikson

Erikson centers on the epigenesis of the ego (1937, 1940a), on the theory of reality relationships (1945), and especially on the elaboration of the theory of the role of social reality (1950b), and these are the core of his psychosocial theory of development (1950a), which complements Freud's theory of the third phase and Hartmann's elaboration of it.

1. Erikson's theory outlines *the sequence of phases* of psychosocial development, and relates these phases to psychosexual epigenesis, thereby laying the groundwork for the study of *ego epigenesis* (1950b). Thus he began to particularize Hartmann's concept of autonomous ego development, which generalized Freud's conception of the development of anxiety.

2. This sequence of the phases of psychosocial development parallels that of libido development (1950a, Ch. 2) and goes beyond it, spanning *the whole life cycle* (Ch. 7). This conception is the first in the history of psychoanalytic theory to encompass those phases of the life cycle which are customarily subsumed under the single concept of genital maturity, and to provide tools for their investigation.

3. Each phase of the life cycle is characterized by a *phase-specific developmental task* which must be solved in it (1945; 1950a, Ch. 7), though this solution is prepared in the previous phases and is worked out further in subsequent ones (1956a). Each phase is described in terms of the extremes of successful and unsuccessful solutions which can be arrived at in it, though in

reality the outcome is a balance between these extremes: (1) *basic trust vs. mistrust;* (2) *autonomy vs. shame and doubt;* (3) *initiative vs. guilt;* (4) *industry vs. inferiority;* (5) *identity vs. identity diffusion;* (6) *intimacy vs. isolation;* (7) *generativity vs. stagnation;* (8) *integrity vs. despair.*

4. Erikson's theory, like Hartmann's adaptation theory, rests on the assumption of an inborn coordination to an average expectable environment. His concept of *mutuality* (1950a) specifies that the crucial coordination is between the developing individual and his human (social) environment, and that this coordination is mutual. The theory postulates a *cogwheeling of the life cycles*: the representatives of society, the caretaking persons, are coordinated to the developing individual by their specific inborn responsiveness to his needs and by phase-specific needs of their own (e.g., generativity).

5. This theory particularizes Hartmann's theory of reality relations, in that it deals with the ego aspect and the social aspect of object relations. It conceives of the caretaking persons as representatives of their society, as carriers of its institutional, traditional, caretaking patterns, and thus it focuses attention on the fact that *each society meets each phase of the development of its members by institutions (parental care, schools, teachers, occupations, etc.) specific to it, to ensure that the developing individual will be viable in it*. The theory conceives of the sequence of epigenetic phases as universal, and of the typical solutions as varying from society to society (1950b; 1950a, Chs. 3 and 4).

6. The crucial characteristic of this psychosocial theory of ego development, and of Hartmann's adaptation theory (in contrast to the "culturalist" theories) is that they offer a conceptual explanation of the individual's social development by tracing the unfolding *of the genetically social character of the human individual* in the course of his encounters with the social environment at each phase of his epigenesis. Thus it is not assumed that societal norms are grafted upon the genetically asocial individual by "disciplines" and "socialization," but that the society into which the individual is born makes him its member by influencing *the manner in which* he solves the tasks posed by each phase of his epigenetic development.

7. Erikson introduces the concepts *organ mode* and *mode epigenesis* (1937, 1950b) and thereby specifies a major mechanism

by which society influences the solution of the phase-specific developmental tasks. These concepts constitute specific instances of Hartmann's concept *change of function*. The modes (inceptive, retentive, intrusive, etc.) in their specific phase of dominance generalize (become displaced) to organs and zones other than those of their origin, and thus can become *estranged* from their origins and can thereafter become autonomous (secondary autonomy). Erikson demonstrates that it is this change of function of these modes which is influenced by the society's caretaking institutions so that those organ modes which correspond to behavior modalities (receiving, taking, giving, letting go, making, etc.) viable in that society undergo a change of function and become ego apparatuses of secondary autonomy, that is, behavior modalities of the individual.

8. Erikson's theory (like much of Freud's) ranges over phenomenological, specifically clinical psychoanalytic and general psychoanalytic-psychological propositions, without systematically differentiating among them. Correspondingly, the conceptual status of this theory's terms is so far unclear. To systematize this theory and to clarify the conceptual status of its terms is a task for ego psychology in the future.

9. Erikson's contributions constitute an organic extension of Freud's theory and they and Hartmann's contributions are consistent with and complementary to each other. Yet Erikson related his theory in an explicit fashion mainly to the concepts of Freud's id psychology, less to the concepts of Freud's ego psychology, and only slightly to Hartmann's theory. Nor did Hartmann attempt to formulate the relation between his and Erikson's theory. Here a task of integration faces ego psychology.

Conclusion

This survey is an incomplete outline which traces only the main developments in ego psychology. Even there it understates Anna Freud's and Kris's contributions, neglects the contributions of Bibring and Fenichel, and avoids completely the relationships between the ego and the superego, and those between ego psychology and the technique of psychoanalysis. Moreover, it does not give any account of the contributions concerning self and identity (Erikson, Hartmann, E. Jacobson), values and ideology (Hartmann, Erikson), the psychosocial effects of isolation, deprivation and propaganda (Bettelheim, Erikson, Jacobson, Kris, Rapaport), nor of those arising from the direct observation of child development (Benjamin; Escalona and Leitch; Kris and collaborators; Spitz; K. Wolf), the work with autistic, delinquent, and psychotic children (Bettelheim; Mahler; Rank, Putnam and collaborators; Redl). A survey of these latter contributions, and of my few attempts to which I have referred in footnotes, must await further developments before they can be seen in proper perspective.

1

EGO DEVELOPMENT AND HISTORICAL CHANGE

CLINICAL NOTES

Men who share an ethnic area, a historical era, or an economic pursuit are guided by common images of good and evil. Infinitely varied, these images reflect the elusive nature of historical change; yet in the form of contemporary social models, of compelling prototypes of good and evil, they assume decisive concreteness in every individual's ego development. Psychoanalytic ego psychology has not matched this concreteness with sufficient theoretical specificity. On the other hand, students of history continue to ignore the simple fact that all individuals are born by mothers; that everybody was once a child; that people and peoples begin in their nurseries; and that society consists of individuals in the process of developing from children into parents.

Only psychoanalysis and social science together can eventually chart the life cycle interwoven throughout with the history of the community. To this end, the present collection of clinical notes offers questions, illustrations, and theoretical considerations concerning the relation of the child's ego to the historical prototypes of his day.

The original version of this paper appeared in *The Psychoanalytic Study of the Child*, 2:359-396, 1946.

Group Identity and Ego Identity

I

Freud's original formulations concerning the ego and its relation to society necessarily depended on the general trend of his analytic argument at the time and on the sociological formulations of his era. The fact that Freud, for his first group-psychological discussions, quoted the postrevolutionary French sociologist Le Bon has left its mark on consequent psychoanalytic discussions of "multitudes" of men. As Freud recognized, Le Bon's "masses" were society on the rebound, shiftless mobs enjoying the anarchy between two stages of society and, at their best and worst, leader-led mobs. Such mobs exist; their definition stands. However, there is a wide gap between these sociological observations and the material secured by the psychoanalytic method—namely, individual history reconstructed from the evidence of transferences and counter-transferences, in a therapeutic situation *à deux*. The resulting methodological gap has perpetuated in psychoanalytic thought an artificial differentiation between the individual-within-his-family (or seemingly surrounded by projections of his family constellation on the "outer world") and the "individual-in-the-mass," submerged in an "indistinct aggregate" of men.[1] The phenomenon and the concept of *social organization,* and its bearing on the individual ego was, thus, for the longest time, shunted off by patronizing tributes to the existence of "social factors."

[1] A psychoanalyst with an outstanding historical orientation repeated even in 1944 that "each member of a large mass of people is an individual and a non-individual, a particle of a mass subject to many psychological laws different from those under which he primarily functions when alone, at home" (Zilboorg, 1944, p. 6).
If, for the moment, we accept as representative the image of a man who is geographically completely alone (and this, of all places, at home), it is questionable that the psychological laws governing his aloneness are really different from those which guide him in a "mass." Would it not be more accurate to say: the situation differs—and with it the thresholds of consciousness and of motility, the available channels of communication and the available techniques of expression and action? That a man could ever be psychologically alone; that a man, "alone," is essentially "better" than the same man in a group; that a man in a temporary solitary condition has ceased to be a political animal, and has disengaged himself from social action (or inaction) on whatever class level; these and similar stereotypes deserve to be accepted only in order to be further analyzed.

In general, the concept of the ego was first delineated by previous definitions of its better-known opposites, the biological id and the sociological "masses": the ego, the individual center of organized experience and reasonable planning, stood endangered by both the anarchy of the primeval instincts and the lawlessness of the group spirit. One might say that where Kant gave as the coordinates of the moral burgher, "the stars above him" and "the moral law within him," the early Freud placed his fearful ego between the id within him and the mob around him.

To take account of encircled man's precarious morality, Freud instituted within the ego the ego ideal or superego. The emphasis, at first, was again on the foreign burden which was thus imposed on the ego. The superego, so Freud pointed out, is the internalization of all the restrictions to which the ego must bow. It is forced upon the child (*"von aussen aufgenötigt"*) by the critical influence of the parents, and later, by that of professional educators, and of what to the early Freud was a vague multitude of fellow men (*"die unbestimmte Menge der Genossen"*) making up the "milieu" and "public opinion" (Freud, 1914).

Surrounded by such mighty disapproval, the child's original state of naïve self-love is said to be compromised. He looks for models by which to measure himself, and seeks happiness in trying to resemble them. Where he succeeds he achieves *self-esteem,* a not too convincing facsimile of his original narcissism and sense of omnipotence.

These early conceptual models have never ceased to determine the trend of discussions and the aims of practice in clinical psychoanalysis.[2] The focus of psychoanalytic research, however, has shifted to a variety of genetic problems. From the study of the ego's dissipation in an amorphous multitude or in a leader-mob, we have turned to the problem of the infantile ego's origin in organized social life. Instead of emphasizing what social organization denies the child, we wish to clarify what it may first grant to the infant, as it keeps him alive and as, in administering to his needs in a specific

[2] In Fenichel's comprehensive volume on the theory of neurosis (1945) the subject of social prototypes is only introduced toward the end of the chapter on mental development, and then in the form of a negation: "Neither a belief in 'ideal models' nor a certain degree of 'social fear' is necessarily pathological." The problem of the superego's origin in society is not discussed until page 463, in the chapter on character disorders.

way, it seduces him to its particular life style. Instead of accepting the oedipus trinity as an irreducible schema for man's irrational conduct, we are striving for greater specificity by exploring the way in which social organization codetermines the structure of the family; for, as Freud said toward the end of his life, ". . . what is operating [in the superego] is not only the personal qualities of these parents but also everything that produced a determining effect upon them themselves, the tastes and standards of the social class in which they live and the characteristics and traditions of the race from which they spring" (1938, pp. 122-123).

II

Freud showed that sexuality begins with birth; he has also given us the tools for the demonstration of the fact that social life begins with each individual's beginnings.

Some of us have applied these tools to the study of so-called primitive societies where child training is integrated with a well-defined economic system and a small and static inventory of social prototypes.[3] Child training in such groups, so we concluded, is the method by which a group's basic ways of organizing experience (its group identity, as we called it) is transmitted to the infant's early bodily experiences and, through them, to the beginnings of his ego.

Let me first illustrate the concept of group identity by a brief reference to anthropological observations made by Mekeel and myself some years ago. We described how in one segment of the re-education of the American Indian, the Sioux Indians' historical identity of the—now defunct—buffalo hunter stands counterposed to the occupational and class identity of his re-educator, the American civil service employee. We pointed out that the identities of these groups rest on extreme differences in geographic and historical perspectives (collective ego-space-time) and on radical differences in economic goals and means (collective life plan).

In the remnants of the Sioux Indians' identity, the prehistoric past is a powerful psychological reality. The conquered tribe behaved as if guided by a life plan consisting of passive resistance to the present which does fail to reintegrate the identity remnants of the economic past; and of dreams of restoration, in which the future

---

[3] This paper is in sequence with "Childhood and Tradition in Two American Indian Tribes" (1945) and overlaps with it in this introductory part.

would lead back into the past, time would again become ahistoric, space unlimited, activity boundlessly centrifugal, and the buffalo supply inexhaustible. Their federal educators, on the other hand, preached a life plan with centripetal and localized goals: homestead, fireplace, bank account—all of which receive their meaning from a life plan in which the past is overcome, and in which the full measure of fulfillment in the present is sacrificed to an ever higher standard of living in the (ever removed) future. The road to this future is not outer restoration but inner reform.

Obviously every item of human experience as lived by a member of one of these groups, and as shared or debated by members of both groups, must be defined according to its place on the coordinates of these interpenetrating plans.

Primitive tribes have a direct relation to the sources and means of production. Their tools are extensions of the human body. Children in these groups participate in technical and in magic pursuits; to them, body and environment, childhood and culture may be full of dangers, but they are all one world. The inventory of social prototypes is small and static. In our world, machines, far from remaining an extension of the body, destine whole human organizations to be extensions of machinery; magic serves intermediate links only; and childhood becomes a separate segment of life with its own folklore. The expansiveness of civilization, together with its stratification and specialization, force children to base their ego models on shifting, sectional, and contradictory prototypes.

III

The growing child must derive a vitalizing sense of reality from the awareness that his individual way of mastering experience (his ego synthesis) is a successful variant of a group identity and is in accord with its space-time and life plan.

A child who has just found himself able to walk seems not only driven to repeat and to perfect the act of walking by libidinal pleasure in the sense of Freud's locomotor erotism; or by the need for mastery in the sense of Ives Hendrick's work principle; he also becomes aware of the new status and stature of "he who can walk," with whatever connotation this happens to have in the coordinates of his culture's life plan—be it "he who will go far," or "he who will be upright," or "he who might go too far." To be "one who can walk" becomes one of the many steps in child development which through the coincidence of physical mastery and cultural meaning, of functional pleasure and social recognition, contribute to a more realistic self-esteem. By no means only a narcissistic corroboration of infantile omnipotence (that can be had more cheaply), this self-esteem grows to be a conviction that the ego is learning effective steps toward a tangible collective future, that it is developing into a defined ego within a social reality. This sense I wish to call *ego identity*. I shall try to clarify it as a subjective experience and as a dynamic fact, as a group-psychological phenomenon and—in the bulk of this paper—as a subject for clinical investigation.

The conscious feeling of having a *personal identity* is based on two simultaneous observations: the immediate perception of one's selfsameness and continuity in time; and the simultaneous perception of the fact that others recognize one's sameness and continuity. What I propose to call ego identity concerns more than the mere fact of existence, as conveyed by personal identity; it is the ego quality of this existence.

Ego identity, then, in its subjective aspect, is the awareness of the fact that there is a selfsameness and continuity to the ego's synthesizing methods and that these methods are effective in safeguarding the sameness and continuity of one's meaning for others.

IV

While it was a step of inestimable import when Freud applied contemporaneous concepts of physical energy to psychology, the resultant theory that instinctual energy is transferred, displaced, transformed in analogy to the preservation of energy in physics no longer suffices to help us manage the data which we have learned to observe.

It is here that ego concepts must close a gap. We must find the nexus of social images and of organismic forces—and this not merely in the sense that here images and forces are, as the saying goes, "interrelated." More than this: the mutual complementation of ethos and ego, of group identity and ego identity, puts a greater common potential at the disposal of both ego synthesis and social organization.

When a Sioux Indian—at the height of his religious endeavors—drives little sticks through his breast, ties the sticks to a rope, the rope to a pole, and then (in a peculiar trance) dances backwards until the rope tightens and the sticks split his breast, so that the gushing blood runs freely down his body, we find a meaning in his extreme behavior: he is turning against himself some first provoked, then energetically frustrated infantile impulses, a "fixation" on which we found to be of decisive relevance in the Sioux's group identity and in his individual development.[4] This ritual puts "id" and "superego" in clear opposition, as do the abortive rituals of our neurotic patients. It makes similar sense when a Yurok man, having been with a woman, proceeds to heat himself by the fire of the sweathouse until he is supple enough to squeeze through an oval opening in the wall, only to jump into the cold river; whereupon he considers himself again pure and strong enough to net the sacred salmon. Here, obviously, self-esteem and inner security are restored by atonement. The same Indians, when indulging in promiscuous intercourse after having achieved the yearly communal engineering feat of bridging the river with a dam that yields a whole winter's supply of salmon, apparently experience the manic relief of orgiastic excess, which, once a year, throws atonement to the winds. But if we try to define the state of relative equilibrium between these better known extremes; if we ask what characterizes an Indian when he does not do much more than just calmly be an Indian, bent on the daily chores of the year's cycle, our description lacks a fitting frame of reference. We look for small signs of the fact that man, anywhere, anytime, betrays in minute emotional and ideational changes an ever-present conflict manifested in a change of mood from a vague anxious depression through what Freud referred to as "a certain in-between stage" to heightened well-being—and back (*"von einer übermässigen Gedrücktheit durch einen gewissen Mittelzustand zu einem erhöhten Wohlbefinden"*). But is this in-between stage dynamically so unimportant that it can be defined by pointing out what it is not; by stating that neither a manic nor a depressive trend is, at the time, clearly noticeable; that a momentary lull exists on the battlefield

---

[4] As explained in detail elsewhere (Erikson, 1945), such a collective fixation point is a meaningful part of the total instinctive self-regulation of a culture.

of the ego; that the superego is temporarily nonbelligerent and that the id has agreed to an armistice?

The necessity for defining the relative equilibrium between various "states of mind" became acute in the need to appraise morale in war. I had an opportunity to make a few observations on one of the more extreme milieus of human endeavor, namely, life on submarines (Erikson, 1940b). Here emotional plasticity and social resourcefulness are put to a high test. The heroic expectations and phallic-locomotor fantasies with which an adolescent volunteer approaches life on a submarine are on the whole not verified in the small chores and in the constricted space of his daily experience on board and in the relatively blind, deaf, and dumb role demanded of him in action. The extreme interdependence with the crew and the mutual responsibility for comfort and life under prolonged conditions of extreme hardship soon supersede the original fantasies. Crew and captain establish a symbiosis not governed by official regulations alone. With astonishing tact and native wisdom silent arrangements are made by which the captain becomes sensory system, brains, and conscience for the whole submerged organism of minutely tuned machinery and humanity; and by which the crew members mobilize in themselves compensatory mechanisms (for example, in the collective use of the generously provided food) permitting the crew to stand monotony and yet to be ready for instant action. Such automatic mutual adaptations to extreme milieus make "analytical sense" primarily where a seeming regression to a primal horde, and to a kind of oral lethargy, can be traced. Yet, if we ask why men choose such a life, why they stick to it in spite of incredible monotony and occasional nightmarish danger, and above all why they function in good health and high spirits, we do not have a satisfactory dynamic answer. In psychiatric discussions it is not infrequently suspected—on the evidence of mere analogies—that whole units, crews, and occupational groups are regressive, or motivated by latent homosexual or psychopathic tendencies.

Yet what the submarine man on the job, the Indian at work, and the growing child have in common with all men who feel at one with what they are doing when and where they are doing it is akin to that "in-between state" which we wish our children would preserve as they grow older; and which we want our patients to gain when the "synthetic function of the ego" (Nunberg, 1931) is restored.

We know that when this is achieved, play becomes freer, health radiant, sex more adult, and work more meaningful. Having applied psychoanalytic concepts to group problems we feel that a clearer understanding of the mutual complementation of ego synthesis and social organization may help us to appraise therapeutically a psychological middle range, the expansion and cultivation of which on ever higher levels of human organization is the aim of all therapeutic endeavor, social and individual.

Ego Pathology and Historical Change

I

A child has quite a number of opportunities to identity himself, more or less experimentally, with real or fictitious people of either sex, with habits, traits, occupations, and ideas. Certain crises force him to make radical selections. However, the historical era in which he lives offers only a limited number of socially meaningful models for workable combinations of identification fragments. Their usefulness depends on the way in which they simultaneously meet the requirements of the organism's maturational stage and the ego's habits of synthesis.

The desperate intensity of many a child's symptom expresses the necessity to defend a budding ego identity which to the child promises to integrate the rapid changes taking place in all areas of his life. What to the observer looks like an especially powerful manifestation of naked instinct is often only a desperate plea for the permission to synthesize and sublimate in the only way possible. We therefore can expect the young patient to respond only to therapeutic measures which will help him to complete the prerequisites for the successful formation of his original ego identity. Therapy and guidance may attempt to substitute more desirable identifications for undesirable ones, but the total configuration of the ego identity remains unalterable.[5]

---

[5] This has certain obvious implications for the "re-education" of "bad" nations. It can be predicted that no admission of having sinned and no promises to be good will make a nation "democratic" unless the new identity offered can be integrated with previous concepts of strong and weak, masculine and feminine, based on experiences in the geographic-historical matrix of the nation and in the childhood of the individual. Only a victor who demonstrates the historical inescapability of supernational aims and knows how to base them on established regional identities will make new people out of old nations.

I am thinking here of the son of an ex-German soldier who emigrated to this country because he could not accept Nazism or was unacceptable to it. His little son had hardly time to absorb Nazi indoctrination before he came to this country, where, like most children, he took to Americanization like a duck to water. Gradually, however, he developed a neurotic rebellion against all authority. What he said about the "older generation" and how he said it was clearly taken from Nazi leaves which he had never read; his behavior was an unconscious one-boy-Hitler-youth rebellion. A superficial analysis revealed that the boy in identifying with the slogans of the Hitler youths identified himself with his father's aggressors, according to the oedipal principle.

At this point, the boy's parents decided to send him to a military school. I expected him to rebel violently. Instead, a marked change came over the boy the moment he was handed a uniform with the promise of gold bars, stars, and rank. It was as if these military symbols effected a sudden and decisive change in his inner economy. The boy was now an unconscious Hitler youth wrapped up in an American prototype: the military schoolboy. The father, a mere civilian, now was neither dangerous nor important.

Somewhere, however, it had been this same father and related father surrogates who with unconscious gestures (Erikson, 1942) (especially when speaking of military exploits during the First World War) had helped establish in this boy the military prototype which is a part of many a European's group identity, and in the German mind has the special significance of being one of the few thoroughly German and highly developed identities. As a historical focus of the family's general trend of identifications the military identity continues to exist unconsciously in those who are excluded from its consummation by political developments.[6]

The subtler methods by which children are induced to accept historical or actual people as prototypes of good and evil have

---

[6] In an outstanding document, Bruno Bettelheim (1943) has described his experiences in a German concentration camp of the early days. He reports the various steps and external manifestations (such as affectations in posture and dress) by which the inmates abandoned their identity as anti-Fascists in favor of that of their tormentors. He himself preserved his life and sanity by deliberately and persistently clinging to the historical Jewish identity of invincible spiritual and intellectual superiority over a physically superior outer world: he made his tormentors the subject of a silent research project which he safely delivered to the world of free letters.

hardly been studied. Minute displays of emotion such as affection, pride, anger, guilt, anxiety, sexual tension (rather than the words used, the meanings intended, or the philosophy implied), transmit to the human child the outlines of what really counts in his world, i.e., the variables of his group's space-time and the perspectives of its life plan.

Equally undefined are the minute socioeconomic and cultural *panics* which involve the family, causing individual regressions to infantile atonements and a reactionary return to more primitive moral codes. As such panics coincide in time and in dynamic quality with one of the child's psychosexual crises, they share in the determination of his neurosis: every neurosis is shared panic, isolated anxiety, and somatic tension all at once.

We observe, for instance, that in our guilt-culture, individuals and groups, whenever they perceive that their socioeconomic status is in danger, unconsciously behave as if inner dangers (temptations) had really called forth the threatening disaster. As a consequence, not only individual regressions to early guilt feelings and atonements take place, but also a reactionary return to the content and to the form of historically earlier principles of behavior. The implicit moral code becomes more restricted, more magic, more exclusive, more intolerant, etc. What patients persistently describe as their childhood milieu often is the condensation of a few selected periods in which too many simultaneous changes resulted in a panicky atmosphere.

In the case of another five-year-old boy who produced convulsions after a number of coincidental experiences all concerning aggression and death, the idea of violence had received its problematic meaning from the following trends in the family history. The father was an Eastern European Jew whom the mild and meek grandparents had taken as a five-year-old to the New York East Side, where he could survive only by superimposing on his childhood identity that of a guy who hits first. This rule he built into our patient's identity, not without indicating how much it had cost him. Having survived with reasonable economic success, however, he then opened a store on the main street of a small Yankee town and moved into a residential neighborhood where he had to revoke his initial instructions and to impress his now cocky and inquisitive little boy, pleadingly and threateningly, with the fact that a shopkeeper's son should treat the Gentiles gently. This change of identities occurred in the midstream of the boy's phallic-locomotor stage, when he needed clear directions and new opportunities of expression—and incidentally at an age analogous to that at which the father had been the victim of migration. The family panic ("let's be gentle or else we will lose ground"), the individual anxiety ("how can I be gentle if all I have learned is to be tough and when I must be tough to feel safe?"), the oedipal problem of managing and diverting aggression against the father, and the somatic tension caused by undirected rage—these were all specific to one another, causing a short circuit instead of the mutual regulation which should dominate simultaneous changes in organism, environment, and ego. His epileptic reaction became manifest.

II

In the analysis of adults the historical prototypes which determined infantile ego-identity crises appear in specific transferences and in specific resistances.

The following excerpt from the case history of an adult illustrates the relationship of such an infantile crisis to the patient's adult life style.

A dancer, of considerable good looks (although extremely small stature), developed the annoying symptom of having to hold her torso so rigidly upright that dancing became awkward and ungainly. The analysis proved her hysterical erectness to be a break-through of a penis envy which had been provoked in childhood along with an otherwise well-sublimated exhibitionism. The patient was the only daughter of a second-generation German-American, a successful businessman given to a certain exhibitionistic individualism, which included a great pride in his powerful physique. He insisted on an erect posture (probably no longer consciously Prussian) on the part of his blond sons, but did not require the same from his dark-skinned daughter; in fact, he did not seem to see much worth exhibiting in the female body. This contributed to other motivations in the patient's dancing the overpowering wish to exhibit an "improved" posture which resembled the caricature of Prussian ancestors whom she had never seen.

The historical anchoring of such symptoms is clarified by the analysis of the resistances with which the symptom is defended.

The patient, who in her conscious thoughts as well as in her positive transference drew a parallel between the father's and the analyst's tall and "nordic" physiques, to her great dismay found herself dreaming of the analyst as a small, dirty, crumpled-up Jew. With this image of low birth and weak masculinity, she attempted to disqualify him from the right to explore the secret of her symptom, namely, the danger to her fragile ego identity emanating from the association of her sexual conflicts with an unruly pair of historical prototypes, an *ideal* prototype (German, tall, phallic), and an *evil* prototype (Jewish, dwarfish, castrated, female). The patient's ego identity had attempted to subsume this dangerous alternative in the role of the radically modern dancer: a creative gesture which in its defensive aspects constituted an exhibitionistic protest against the social and sexual inferiority of women. Her symptom betrays the fact that the father's exhibitionism, as well as his prejudices, because they were inculcated into the patient through the sensual testimony of the oedipus complex, had retained a dangerous degree of disturbing power in her unconscious.

It is usual in our culture that the unconscious evil identity (that which the ego is most afraid to resemble) is composed of the images of the violated (castrated) body, the ethnic outgroup and the exploited minority. Although it manifests itself in a great variety of syndromes, this association is all-pervasive, in men and women, in majorities and minorities, and in all classes of a given national or cultural unit. For the ego, in the course of its synthesizing efforts, attempts to subsume the most powerful ideal and evil prototypes (the final contestants, as it were) and with them the whole existing imagery of superior and inferior, good and bad, masculine and feminine, free and slave, potent and impotent, beautiful and ugly, fast and slow, tall and small, in a simple alternative, in order to make one battle and one strategy out of a bewildering number of skirmishes. In this connection, the latent image of the more homogeneous past exerts its reactionary influence in specific resistances; we must study it, so that we may understand the historical basis of the accentuated alternative the patient's ego is searching for.

Unconscious associations of ethnic alternatives with moral and sexual ones are a necessary part of any group formation. Psychoanalysis, in studying them, perfects its therapeutic methods in indi-

EGO DEVELOPMENT AND HISTORICAL CHANGE

vidual cases and, at the same time, contributes to the knowledge of the unconscious concomitants of prejudice.[7]

III

Therapeutic efforts as well as attempts at social reform verify the sad truth that in any system based on suppression, exclusion, and exploitation, the suppressed, excluded, and exploited unconsciously believe in the evil image which they are made to represent by those who are dominant.[8]

I once saw in consultation a tall, intelligent ranch owner, who was influential in Western agriculture. Nobody but his wife knew that he was born a Jew and raised in a Jewish street in a large city. His life, while outwardly successful, was made uncomfortable by a network of compulsions and phobias which, in analysis, proved to reproduce and to superimpose on his free movements in Western valleys the outline of the neighborhood in which he grew up. His friends and adversaries, his elders and his inferiors, all unknowingly

---

[7] In the inventory of our patients' ideal and evil prototypes we meet face to face the clinical facts on which Jung based his theory of inherited prototypes ("archetypes"). As for this theory, we may note in passing that the first conceptual controversies in psychoanalysis throw light on the problem of identity in the initial stages of a science. Jung, it seems, could find a sense of identity in psychoanalytic work only by a juxtaposition of his ancestors' mystical space-time and whatever he sensed in Freud's ancestry. His scientific rebellion thus led to ideological regression and (weakly denied) political reaction. This phenomenon —as similar ones before and after—had its group-psychological counterpart in reaction within the psychoanalytic movement: as if in fear of endangering a common group identity based on common scientific gains, psychoanalytic observers chose to ignore not only Jung's interpretations but the facts he observed.

Certain phenomena underlying such concepts as the "anima" and the "animus" (which I seem to recognize in my woman patient's erect image) play a dominant role in ego development. The synthesizing function of the ego constantly works on subsuming in fewer and fewer images and personified Gestalten the fragments and loose ends of all the infantile identifications. In doing so it not only uses existing historical prototypes; it also employs individually methods of condensation and of pictorial representation which characterize the products of collective imagery. In Jung's "persona" we see a weak ego sell out to a compelling social prototype. A fake ego identity is established which suppresses rather than synthesizes those experiences and functions which endanger the "front." A dominant prototype of masculinity, for example, forces a man to exclude from his ego identity all that which characterizes the evil image of the lesser sex, the castrate. This leaves much of his receptive and maternal faculties dissimulated, undeveloped, and guilt-ridden, and makes a shell of mannishness out of what is left.

[8] According to a communication by Gordon McGregor, Sioux mixed-bloods on Pine Ridge Reservation call Sioux full-bloods "niggers," only to be called, in turn, "white trash."

played the roles of the German boys or the Irish gangs who had made the little Jewish boy miserable on his daily walk to school, which led him from an isolated and more refined Jewish street through the hostile remnants of tenements and gang warfare to the shortlived haven of the democratic classroom. This man's analysis provided a sad commentary on the fact that Streicher's image of an evil Jewish identity does not surpass that harbored by many a Jew who—with paradoxical results—may still try to live it down in an area where in view of what he is, his past would be relatively unimportant.

The patient in question sincerely felt that the only true savior for the Jews would be a plastic surgeon. In the body ego of such cases of morbid ego identity, those body parts which are supposed to be of strategic importance in the characterization of the race (in the last case, the nose; in that of the dancer, the backbone) play a role similar to that of the afflicted limb in a cripple and that of the genitals in neurotics in general. The body part in question has a different ego tonus; it is felt to be larger and heavier, or smaller and disembodied; in both cases it seems dissociated from the whole of the body, while seeming to loom dominantly in the center of the attention of others. In cases of morbid ego identity and in cripples, there are dreams where the dreamer unsuccessfully tries to hide the painfully spotlighted body part, and others where he accidentally loses it.

What may be called an individual's ego space-time thus preserves the social topology of his childhood surroundings as well as the outline of his body image. To study both it is essential to correlate a patient's childhood history with the history of his family's sedentary residence in prototypal areas (East), in "backward" areas (South), or in "forward" areas (Western and Northern frontier), as these areas were gradually incorporated into the American version of the Anglo-Saxon cultural identity; his family's migration from, through, and to areas which, at various periods, may have represented the extreme sedentary or the extreme migratory pole of the developing American character; the family's religious conversions or diversions, with their class implications; abortive attempts at becoming standardized on a class level and the loss or abandonment of that level; and most of all, that individual or family segment which, whatever they were doing and wherever they were doing it, provided the last strong sense of cultural identity.

IV

A compulsive patient's grandfather, now deceased, was a business man who built a mansion in a downtown district of an *Eastern metropolis*. His will demands that the mansion should stand and remain the family's castle even though skyscrapers and apartment houses are mushrooming all around it. The mansion becomes a somewhat sinister symbol of conservatism, telling the world that the X's need neither to move nor to sell, neither to expand nor to rise. The conveniences of modern travel are accepted only as comfortably insulated pathways between the mansion and its extensions: the club, the summer home, the private school, Harvard, etc. The grandfather's picture hangs over the fireplace, a little bulb eternally lighting the rosiness of the cheeks in his generally powerful and contented countenance. His "individualistic" ways in business, his almost primeval power over the fate of his children, are known but not questioned; rather they are overcompensated for by a sensitive show of respect, scrupulousness, and thrift. The grandsons know that in order to find an identity of their own they have to break out of the mansion, so to speak, and join the mad striving which has engulfed the neighborhood. Some do, not without taking the mansion with them as an internalized pattern, a basic ego space, which has determined their defense mechanism of proud and pained withdrawal, and their symptoms of obsessiveness and of sexual anesthesia. Their psychoanalyses last inordinately long, partially because the analyst's four walls become the new mansion; the analyst's contemplative silence and his theoretical approach, a new edition of the mansion's ritualistic isolation. Further resistances become plain in dreams and associations. The curative effect of the patient's politely "positive" transference ends where the reticence of the analyst seems to resemble the restrained father rather than the ruthless grandfather. The father image, it appears (and with it the transference), is split up; the image of the weak and mild father of today is isolated from the oedipal father image, which is fused with that of the powerful grandfather. As the analysis approaches this double image, fantasies appear which make plain the grandfather's overwhelming importance for the patient's real ego identity. They betray the violent sense of power, the fury of superiority which makes it hard for these overtly inhibited people to enter economic competition except on terms of prearranged superior privileges. These men, of the once highest strata, join those from the very lowest ones in being the truly disinherited in American life; from where they are there is no admission to free competition, unless they have the strength to start all over. If not, they often resist cure because it implies a change in ego identity, an ego resynthesis on the terms of changed economic history.

The only way of breaking through this deep resignation is serious attention to memories which show (what the child knew) that the grandfather really was a simple man, and that he fulfilled his place not by force of some primeval power, but because history favored his capabilities.

For a *Western* grandfather, I refer to a previously published case (1945, p. 349). Consider a boy whose grandparents came West, "where seldom is heard a discouraging word." The grandfather, a powerful and powerfully driven man, seeks ever new and challenging engineering tasks in widely separated regions. When the initial challenge is met, he hands the task over to others, and moves on. His wife sees him only for an occasional impregnation. According to a typical family pattern, his sons cannot keep pace with him and are left as respectable settlers by the wayside. To express their change of life style in fitting slogans, one would have to state that from an existence characterized by the slogan "let's get the hell out of here," they turn to one expressing the determination "let's stay—and keep the bastards out." The grandfather's only daughter (the patient's mother) alone remains identified with him. This very identification, however, does not permit her to take a husband equal to her strong father. She marries a weak man and settles down. She brings her boy up to be God-fearing and industrious. He becomes reckless and shifting at times, depressed at others: somewhat of a juvenile delinquent now, later maybe a more enjoyable Westerner, with alcoholic moods.

What his worried mother does not know is that she herself all through his childhood has belittled the sedentary father; has decried the lack of mobility, geographic and social, of her marital existence; has idealized the grandfather's exploits; but has also reacted with panicky punitiveness to any display of friskiness in the boy, which was apt to disturb the now well-defined neighborhood.

A woman from the *Middle West,* rather unusually feminine and sensitive, uses a visit with relatives in the West to consult the writer concerning a general feeling of affective constriction and an all-pervasive mild anxiety. During an exploratory analysis she seems almost lifeless. Only after weeks, on rare occasions, is she overcome by a flood of associations, all concerning sudden, horrid impressions of sex or death. Many of these memories emerge not from unconscious depths, but from an isolated corner of her consciousness, where are boarded off all those matters which on occasion had broken through the orderly factualness of the upper-middle-class surroundings of her childhood. This mutual isolation of life segments is similar to that met with in compulsive neurotics anywhere; but in some regions it is more; it is a way of life, an ethos, which in our patient had become truly uncomfortable only because at the moment she was being courted by a European and was trying to envisage life in a cosmopolitan atmosphere. She felt attracted, but at the same time inhibited; her imagination was vividly provoked, but restrained by anxiety. Her bowels reflected this ambivalence by an alternation of constipation and diarrhea. One gained the impression of a general inhibition rather than a basic impoverishment of imagination in matters both sexual and social.

The patient's dreams gradually revealed a hidden source of unemployed vitality. While she seemed pained and lifeless in her free associations, her dream life became humorous and imaginative in an almost autonomous way. She dreamed of entering quiet church congregations in a flaming red dress, and of throwing stones through respectable windows. But her most colorful dreams put her into Civil War days—on the Confederate side. The climax was a dream in which she sat on a toilet, set off by low partitions in the middle of a tremendous ballroom, and waved to elegantly dressed couples of Confederate officers and Southern ladies who swirled around her to the sounds of powerful brass.

These dreams helped unearth an isolated part of her childhood, namely, the gentle warmth awarded her by her grandfather, a Confederate veteran. His world was a fairy tale of the past. But for all its formalism, the grandfather's patriarchal masculinity and gentle affection had been experienced through the child's hungry senses and had proved more immediately reassuring to her searching ego than either the father's or the mother's promises of standardized success. With the grandfather's death the patient's affects went dead because they were part of an abortive ego-identity formation which failed to receive nourishment either in the form of affection or of social rewards.

The psychoanalytic treatment of women with a prominent ego-identity remnant of the *Southern lady* (an identity which pervades more than one class or race) seems complicated by special resistances. To be sure, our patients are dislodged Southerners, their ladyhood a defense, almost a symptom. Their wish for treatment finds its limits in three ideas, which are all connected with the particular provisions in Southern culture for safeguarding caste and race identity by imposing the prototype of the lady on the small girl.

There is, first, a pseudoparanoid suspicion that life is a series of critical tests when vicious gossips attempt to stack up minor weaknesses and blemishes against the Southern woman—toward a final judgment: to be—or not to be—a lady. Second, there is the all-pervading conviction that men, if not restrained by the formalities of a tacitly approved double standard (which sells them lesser and darker sex objects at the price of overt respect for ladies), will prove to be no gentlemen; that they will at the very least try to blacken the lady's name and with it her claim to a socially superior husband, or to the prospect of having her children marry upward. But there is also the equally ambivalent implication that any man who does not proceed to shed his gentleman's exterior when the opportunity offers itself is a weakling who only deserves to be mercilessly provoked. The usual feelings of guilt and inferiority all exist within the coordinates of a life plan which is dominated by the conscious hope for higher social status, and made morbid by its ambivalent counterpart, the hidden hope for the man who will dissolve the woman's need to be a lady in a moment of reckless passion. In all this there is a basic inability to conceive of any area in life where the standards and the words of a man and a woman could in honesty coincide and be lifted above a certain primeval antagonism. Needless to say, such unconscious standards cause severe suffering in sincere and enlightened women. But only the verbalization of these historical trends, concomitantly with the initial analysis of the patient's character resistances, makes psychoanalysis possible.

Psychoanalysts, in their daily work, are consulted by those who cannot stand the tension between polarities, the never-ceasing necessity of remaining tentative in order to be free to take the next step, to turn the next corner. These patients repeat in their transferences and in their resistances abortive attempts at synchronizing fast-changing and sharply contrasting remnants of national, regional, and class identities during critical stages of their childhood. The patient weaves the analyst into his unconscious life plan: he idealizes him (especially if he is European-born) by identifying him with his more homogeneous ancestors; or he subtly resists him as the enemy of a brittle and tentative ego identity.

The cured patient has the courage to face the discontinuities of life in this country and the polarities of its struggle for an economic and cultural identity, not as an imposed hostile reality, but as a potential promise for a more universal collective identity. This finds its limits, however, where people are fundamentally impoverished in their childhood sensuality and stalled in their freedom to use opportunities.

In the experiences of pregenital stages the human infant learns the basic variables of organismic-social existence, before his libido becomes free for its procreative task. Child training, in creating a particular ratio of emphasis on such organismic modes as incorporation, retention, assimilation, elimination, intrusion and inclusion, gives the growing being a character basis suited to the main modes of later life tasks; if—indeed—later life tasks and early training are synchronized.

Consider our colored countrymen. Their babies often receive sensual satisfactions of oral and sensory surplus, adequate for a lifetime. It is preserved in the way in which they move, laugh, talk, sing. Their forced symbiosis with the feudal South capitalized on this oral-sensory treasure to build up a slave's identity: mild, submissive, dependent, somewhat querulous, but always ready to serve, and with occasional empathy and childlike wisdom. But underneath a dangerous split occurred. The humiliating symbiosis on the one hand and, on the other, the necessity of the master race to protect its identity against sensual and oral temptations established in both groups an association: light—clean—clever—

white; and, dark—dirty—dumb—nigger. The result, especially in those Negroes who have left the poor haven of their Southern homes, is often a violently sudden and cruel cleanliness training. This, in turn, transmits itself to the phallic-locomotor stage, in which the restrictions as to what shade of girl one may dream of and where one may move and act with abandon interfere at every moment of waking and dreaming with the free transfer of the original narcissistic sensuality to the genital sphere. Three identities are formed: (1) mammy's oral-sensual "honey child": tender, expressive, rhythmical; (2) the clean anal-compulsive, restrained, friendly, but always sad "white man's Negro"; and (3) the evil identity of the dirty, anal-sadistic, phallic-rapist "nigger."

When faced with so-called opportunities which only offer a newly restricted freedom but fail to provide an integration of the identity fragments mentioned, one of these fragments becomes dominant in the form of a racial caricature; tired of this caricature, the colored individual often retires into hypochondriac invalidism as a condition which represents an analogy to the ego-space-time of defined restriction in the South: a neurotic regression to the ego identity of the slave.

I know of a colored boy who, like our boys, listens every night to the Lone Ranger. Then he sits up in bed, dreaming that he is the Ranger. But alas, the moment always comes when he sees himself galloping after some masked offenders and suddenly notices that in his image the Lone Ranger is a Negro. He stops his fantasies. While a child, this boy was extremely expressive, both in his pleasure and in his sorrows. Today he is calm and always smiles; his language is soft and blurred; nobody can hurry him, or worry him, or please him. White men like him.

Ego Strength and Social Pathology

I

Individual psychopathology contributes to the understanding of ego identity the study of its impairments by constitutional deficiency, early emotional impoverishment, neurotic conflict, and traumatic damage. Before we turn to examples of ego-damaging social pathology we may at least state a question, although its answer will have to wait for a more systematic presentation: what factors make for a strong normal ego identity? In a general way it is plain that everything that makes for a strong ego contributes to its identity.

Freud originally stated (1914) that the sources of human self-esteem (and thus an important infantile contribution to an individual's ego identity) are

1. the residue of childish narcissism,
2. such infantile omnipotence as experience corroborates (the fulfillment of the ego ideal),
3. gratification of object libido.

Psychoanalysis came to emphasize the individual and regressive rather than the collective-supportive aspects of these statements. It was concerned with only half the story.

For if a residue of infantile narcissism is to survive, the maternal environment must create and sustain it with a love which assures the child that it is good to be alive in the particular social coordinates in which he happens to find himself. Infantile narcissism, which is said to fight so valiantly against the inroads of a frustrating environment, is in fact nourished by the sensual enrichment and the encouragement provided by this same environment. Widespread severe impoverishment of infantile narcissism (and thus of the basis of a strong ego) is lastly to be considered a breakdown of that collective synthesis which gives every newborn baby and his motherly surroundings a superindividual status as a trust of the community. In the later abandonment or transformation of this narcissism into more mature self-esteem, it is again of decisive importance whether or not the more realistic being can expect an opportunity to employ what he has learned and to acquire a feeling of increased communal meaning.

If experience is to corroborate part of the infantile sense of omnipotence, then child training must know not only how to teach sensual health and progressive mastery, but also how to offer tangible social recognition as the fruits of health and mastery. For unlike the infantile sense of omnipotence which is fed by make-believe and adult deception, the self-esteem attached to the ego identity is based on the rudiments of skills and social techniques which assure a gradual coincidence of functional pleasure and actual performance, of ego ideal and social role. The self-esteem attached to the ego identity contains the recognition of a tangible future.

If "object libido" is to be satisfied, then genital love and orgastic potency must be assured of a cultural synthesis of economic safety and emotional security; for only such a synthesis gives unified meaning to the full functional cycle of genitality, which includes conception, childbearing, and child rearing. Infatuation may project all the incestuous childhood loves into a present "object"; genital activity may help two individuals to use one another as an anchor against regression; but mutual genital love faces toward the future. It works toward a division of labor in that life task which only two of the opposite sex can fulfill together: the synthesis of production, procreation, and recreation in the primary social unit of the family. In this sense, then, ego identity acquires its final strength in the meeting of mates whose ego identity is complementary in some essential point and can be fused in marriage without the creation either of a dangerous discontinuity of tradition, or of an incestuous sameness—both of which are apt to prejudice the offspring's ego development.

The unconscious "incestuous" choice of a mate who resembles infantile love objects in some decisive feature is not to be considered as necessarily pathogenic, as writers in psychopathology seem to infer. Such a choice follows an ethnic mechanism in that it creates a continuity between the family one grew up in and the family one establishes: it thus perpetuates tradition, i.e., the sum of all that had been learned by preceding generations, in analogy to the preservation of the gains of evolution in the mating within the species. Neurotic fixation (and rigid inner defense against it) signifies the failure, not the nature, of this mechanism.

However, many of the mechanisms of adjustment which once made for evolutionary adaptation, tribal integration, national or class coherence, are at loose ends in a world of universally expanding identities. Education for an ego identity which receives strength from changing historical conditions demands a conscious acceptance of historical heterogeneity on the part of adults, combined with an enlightened effort to provide human childhood anywhere with a new fund of meaningful continuity. For this task, the systematic investigation of the following strategic points seems indicated:

1. The coherence of the body image, and its possible basis in fetal experience, with special reference to the importance of the mother's emotional attitude toward pregnancy.
2. The synchronization of postnatal care with the newborn's temperament, based as it is on his prenatal and his birth experience.
3. The sameness and continuity of the early sensual experience of the mother's body and temperament, which nourishes and preserves a lasting fund of narcissism.
4. The synchronization of the pregenital stages and of the normative steps in child development with a group identity.
5. The immediate promise of tangible social recognition for the abandonment of infantile narcissism and autoerotism and for the acquisition of skills and knowledge during latency.
6. The adequacy of the solution of the oedipus conflict, within the individual's sociohistorical setting.
7. The relation of the final adolescent version of the ego identity to economic opportunities, realizable ideals, and available techniques.
8. The relation of genitality to love objects with complementary ego identities, and to the communal meaning of procreation.

II

What has already been said concerning the collective space-time and the life plan of a society shows the necessity of studying the spontaneous ways in which segments of modern society strive to make a workable continuity out of child training and economic development. For whoever wants to guide, must understand, conceptualize, and use spontaneous trends of identity formation. Our clinical histories help in such research, where they avoid being too episodic in type, and where stereotypes, such as "the patient had a domineering mother" (which are based on comparisons with a family image implied in classical European psychiatry) are further broken down into historically significant variations. During World War II, psychiatric and psychoanalytic attempts at explaining what childhood milieus cause or do not cause a man to break down under military stress, have, on the whole, failed for lack of historical perspective.

In our work with veterans discharged from the Armed Forces as psychoneurotics before the end of hostilities, we became familiar with the universal symptoms of partial loss of ego synthesis. Many of these men, indeed, regress to the "stage of unlearned function" (Freud, 1908). The boundaries of their egos have lost their shock-absorbing delineation: anxiety and anger are provoked by everything too sudden or too intense, whether it be a sensory impression or a self-reproach, an impulse or a memory. A ceaselessly "startled" sensory system is attacked by stimuli from outside as well as by somatic sensations: heat flashes, palpitation, cutting headaches. Insomnia hinders the nightly restoration of sensory screening by sleep, and that of emotional synthesis by dreaming. Amnesia, neurotic pseudologia, and confusion show the partial loss of time-binding and of spatial orientation. What definable symptoms and remnants of "peacetime neuroses" there are have a fragmentary and false quality, as if the ego could not even accomplish an organized neurosis.

In some cases this ego impairment seems to have its origin in violent events, in others in the gradual grind of a million annoyances. Obviously the men are worn out by too many changes (gradual or sudden) in too many respects at once; somatic tension, social panic, and ego anxiety are always present. Above all, the men "do not know any more who they are": there is a distinct loss of ego identity. The sense of sameness and of continuity and the belief in one's social role are gone.

The American group identity supports an individual's ego identity as long as he can preserve a certain element of deliberate tentativeness; as long as he can convince himself that the next step is up to him and that no matter where he is staying or going he always has the choice of leaving or turning in the opposite direction if he chooses to do so. In this country the migrant does not want to be told to move on, nor the sedentary man to stay where he is; for the life style of each contains the opposite element as an alternate which he wishes to consider his most private and individual decision. For many men, then, the restraint and discipline of army life provides few ideal prototypes.⁹ To quite a few, it represents instead the intensely evil identity of the sucker; one who lets himself be sidetracked, cooped up, and stalled, while others are free to pursue his chance and his girl. But to be a sucker means to be a social and sexual castrate; if you are a sucker, not even a mother's pity will be with you.

In the (often profuse) utterances of psychoneurotic casualties, all those memories and anticipations appear associated that ever threatened or are expected to threaten the freedom of the next step. In their struggle to regain access to the nonreversible escalator of free enterprise, their traumatized ego fights and flees an evil identity which includes elements of the crying baby, the bleeding woman, the submissive nigger, the sexual sissy, the economic sucker, the mental moron—all prototypes the mere allusion to which can bring these men close to homicidal or suicidal rage, ending up in varying degrees of irritability or apathy. Their exaggerated attempt to blame their ego dilemma on circumstances and individuals gives their childhood history a more sordid character and themselves the appearance of a worse psychopathy than is justified. Their ego identity has fallen apart into its bodily, sexual, social, occupational elements, each having to overcome again the danger of its evil prototype. Rehabilitation work can be made more effective and economical if the clinical investigation focuses on the patient's shattered life plan and if advice tends to strengthen the resynthesis of the elements on which the patient's ego identity was based.

In addition to the several hundred thousand men who lost and only gradually or partially regained their ego identity in this war and to the thousands whose acute loss of ego identity was falsely diagnosed and treated as psychopathy, an untold number has experienced to the core the threat of a traumatic loss of ego identity as a result of radical historical change.

The fact that these men, their physicians, and their contemporaries in increasing numbers turn to the bitter truths of psychoanalytic psychiatry is in itself a historical development which calls

⁹ Notable exceptions are the recipients of promising commissions and members of teams in highly mechanized units. However, men whose ego identity thrives on military service sometimes break down after discharge, when it appears that the war provoked them into the usurpation of more ambitious prototypes than their more restricted peacetime identities could afford to sustain.

for critical appraisal. It expresses an increased acceptance of psychoanalytic insights in so far as they concern the meaning of anxiety and of disease in the individual case history. Yet this partial acceptance of painful unconscious determinants of human behavior has the quality of a concomitant resistance against the disquieting awareness of a social symptom and its historical determinants. I mean the subliminal panic which accompanied the large-scale testing of the American identity during the most recent period of world history.

Historical change has reached a coercive universality and a global acceleration which is experienced as a threat to the emerging American identity. It seems to devaluate the vigorous conviction that this nation can afford mistakes; that this nation, by definition, is always so far ahead of the rest of the world in inexhaustible reserves, in vision of planning, in freedom of action, and in tempo of progress that there is unlimited space and endless time in which to develop, to test, and to complete her social experiments. The difficulties met in the attempt to integrate this old image of insulated spaciousness with the new image of explosive global closeness are deeply disquieting. They are characteristically met, at first with the application of traditional methods to a new space-time; there is the missionary discovery of "One World," aviation pioneering on a "Trans-World" basis, charity on a global scale, etc. Yet there also remains a deep consciousness of a lag in economic and political integration, and with it, in emotional and spiritual strength.

The psychotherapist, in disregarding the contribution of this development to neurotic discomfort, is apt not only to miss much of the specific dynamics in contemporary life cycles; he is apt also to deflect (or to serve those whose business demands that they deflect) individual energy from the collective tasks at hand. A large-scale decrease of neurosis can be achieved only by equal clinical attention to cases and to conditions, to the fixation on the past and the emerging design for the future, to the grumbling depth and the unsafe surface.

III

In studying the ego's relation to changing historical reality, psychoanalysis approaches a new phalanx of unconscious resistances. It is implicit in the nature of psychoanalytic investigation that such resistances must be located and appraised in the observer, and in his habits of conceptualization, before their presence in the observed can be fully understood and effectively handled. When investigating instincts, the psychoanalyst knows that his drive to investigate is partially instinctive in nature; he knows that he responds with a partial countertransference to the patient's transference, i.e., the ambiguous wish to satisfy infantile strivings in the very therapeutic situation which is to cure them. The analyst acknowledges all this, yet works methodically toward that margin of freedom where the clear delineation of the inevitable makes consuming resistances unnecessary and frees energy for creative planning.

It is, then, a commonplace to state that the psychoanalyst in training must learn to study the historical determinants of what made him what he is before he can hope to perfect that human gift: the ability to understand what is different from him. Beyond this, however, there are the historical determinants of psychoanalytic concepts.

If in the field of human motivation, the same terms have been used over a period of half a century (and what a century!), they cannot but reflect the ideologies of their day of origin and absorb the connotations of consequent social changes. Ideological connotation is the inevitable historical equation in the use of conceptual tools which concern the ego, man's organ of reality testing. The conceptualizations of man's selfsame core and of reality itself are by necessity a function of historical change. Yet, here too, our search is for a margin of freedom; our method, radical analysis of resistances to insight and to planning.

As philosophers would predict, the concept of "reality" itself, while clear in its intended meaning, is highly corruptible in its usage. According to the pleasure principle, that is good which feels good at the moment; the reality principle declares that to be good which in the long run and with consideration for all possible outer and inner developments promises most lastingly to feel good. Such principles, established by scientific man, fall prey easily to economic man. The reality principle, in theory and therapy, has taken on a certain individualistic color, according to which that is good which the individual can get away with by dodging the law (in so far as it happens to be enforced) and the superego (in so far as it causes discomfort). Our therapeutic failures often define the limit of this usage: Western man, almost against his will, is developing a more universal group identity. His reality principle begins to include a *social principle* according to which that is good which, in the long run, secures to a man what feels good to him without keeping any other man (of the same collective identity) from securing an analogous gain. The question that remains is: what new synthesis of economic and emotional safety will sustain this wider group identity and thus give strength to the individual ego?

A different sort of trend in contemporary conceptualization is typified in a recent formulation, according to which "all through childhood a maturation process is at work which, in the service of an increasing knowledge and adaptation to reality, aims at perfecting [ego] functions, at rendering them more and more objective and independent of the emotions until they can become as accurate and reliable as a mechanical apparatus" (Anna Freud, 1945).

Obviously, the ego as such is older than all mechanization. If we detect in it a tendency to mechanize itself and to be free from the very emotions without which experience becomes impoverished, we may actually be concerned with a historical dilemma. Today we face the question whether the problems of the machine age will be solved by a mechanization of man or by a humanization of industry. Our child-training customs have begun to standardize modern man, so that he may become a reliable mechanism prepared to "adjust" to the competitive exploitation of the machine world. In fact, certain modern trends in child training seem to represent a magic identification with the machine, analogous to identifications of primitive tribes with their principal prey. At the same time the modern mind, already the product of a civilization preoccupied with mechanization, attempts to understand itself by searching for "mental mechanisms." If, then, the ego itself seems to *crave* mechanical adaptation we may not be dealing with the nature of the ego, but with one of its period-bound adjustments as well as with our own mechanistic approach to its study.

Maybe in this connection it is not quite unnecessary to point to the fact that the popular use of the word "ego" in this country has, of course, little to do with the psychoanalytic concept of the same name; it denotes unqualified if not justified self-esteem. Yet, in the wake of therapeutic short cuts, this connotation can be seen to creep even into professional discussions of the ego.

Bolstering, bantering, boisterousness, and other "ego-inflating" behavior is, of course, part of the American folkways. As such, it pervades speech and gesture and enters into all interpersonal relations. Without it, a therapeutic relationship in this country would remain outlandish and nonspecific. The problem to be discussed here, however, is the systematic exploitation of the national practice of bolstering for the sake of making people "feel better," or of submerging their anxiety and tension so as to make them function better as patients, customers, or employees.

A weak ego does not gain substantial strength from being persistently bolstered. A strong ego, secured in its identity by a strong society, does not need, and in fact is immune to any attempt at artificial inflation. Its tendency is toward the testing of what feels real; the mastery of that which works; the understanding of that which proves necessary, the enjoyment of the vital, and the extermination of the morbid. At the same time, it tends toward the creation of a strong mutual reinforcement with others in a group ego, which will transmit its will to the next generation.

A war, however, can be an unfair test to ego strength. During collective emergencies all resources, emotional as well as material, must be mobilized with relative disregard for what is workable and economical under more normal conditions of long-range development. Ego bolstering is a legitimate measure in such days of collective danger; and it remains a genuine therapeutic approach in individual cases of acute ego strain, i.e., wherever the individual is emotionally too young or physically too weak to meet a situation bearable to the mature and the healthy; or if a situation is too extraordinary to be met even by a relatively adequate ego. Obviously, a war increases the occurrence of both types of traumatic discrepancy between the ego and situations not included in its anticipations. The indiscriminate application of the philosophy and the practice of "ego bolstering" to peacetime conditions, however, would be theoretically unsound and therapeutically unwholesome. It is, furthermore, socially dangerous, because its employment implies that the cause of the strain (i.e., "modern living") is perpetually beyond the individual's or his society's control—a state of affairs which would postpone indefinitely the revision of *conditions which are apt to weaken the infantile ego.* To deflect energy from such revision is dangerous. For American childhood and other manifestations of the specific American freedom of spirit are but grandiose fragments striving for integration with the fragments of industrial democracy.

The effectiveness of the psychoanalytic contribution to this development is guaranteed solely by the persistent humanistic intention, beyond the mere adjustment of patients to limited conditions, to apply clinical experience to the end of making man aware of potentialities which are clouded by archaic fear.

IV

In studying his subject, the psychoanalyst (so Anna Freud [1936] points out) should occupy an observation point "equidistant from the id, the ego, and the superego"—so that he may be aware of their functional interdependence and so that, as he observes a change in one of these sections of the mind, he may not lose sight of related changes in the others.

Beyond this, however, the observer is aware of the fact that what he conceptualizes as id, ego, and superego are not static compartments in the capsule of a life history. Rather they reflect three major processes the relativity of which determines the form of human behavior. They are:

1. the process of organismic organization of bodies within the time-space of the life cycle (evolution, epigenesis, libido development, etc.);

2. the process of the organization of experience by ego synthesis (ego space-time, ego defenses, ego identity, etc.);

3. the process of the social organization of ego organisms in geographic-historical units (collective space-time, collective life plan, ethos of production, etc.).

The order given follows the trend of psychoanalytic research. Otherwise, although different in structure, these processes *exist by and are relative to each other*. Any item whose meaning and potential changes within one of these processes simultaneously changes in the others. To assure the proper rate and sequence of change, and to prevent or counteract lags, discrepancies, and discontinuities of development, there are the warning signals of pain in the body, anxiety in the ego, and panic in the group. They warn of organic dysfunction, impairment of ego mastery, and loss of group identity: each a threat to all.

In psychopathology we observe and study the apparent autonomy of one of these processes as it receives undue accentuation because of the loss of their mutual regulation and general balance. Thus psychoanalysis has first studied (as if it could be isolated) man's *enslavement by the id*, i.e., by the excessive demands on ego and society of frustrated organisms, upset in the inner economy of their life cycle. Next the focus of study shifted to man's *enslavement by seemingly autonomous ego (and superego) strivings*—defensive mechanisms which curtail and distort the ego's power of experiencing and planning beyond the limit of what is workable and tolerable in the individual organism and in social organization. Psychoanalysis completes its basic studies of neurosis by investigating more explicitly *man's enslavement by historical conditions which claim autonomy* by precedent and exploit archaic mechanisms within him to deny him health and ego strength.[10] Only the reinterpretation of our clinical experience on the basis of this threefold investigation will permit us to make an essential contribution to child training in an industrial world.

The goal of psychoanalytic treatment itself has been defined (Nunberg, 1931) as a simultaneous increase in the mobility of the id, in the tolerance of the superego, and in the synthesizing power of the ego. To the last point we add the suggestion that the analysis of the ego should include that of the individual's ego identity in relation to the historical changes which dominated his childhood milieu. For the individual's mastery over his neurosis begins where he is put in a position to accept the historical necessity which made him what he is. The individual feels free when he can choose to identify with his own ego identity and when he learns to apply that which is given to that which must be done. Only thus can he derive ego strength (for his generation and the next) from the coincidence of his one and only life cycle with a particular segment of human history.

[10] This basic plan was established, among others, in Freud's publication "Civilized Sexual Morality and Modern Nervousness" (1908) and in his habitual references to the cultural and socioeconomic coordinates of his own existence, wherever for the sake of his new science he published illustrations from his own life.

2

GROWTH AND CRISES OF THE HEALTHY PERSONALITY

The Fact-finding Committee of the White House Conference on Childhood and Youth has asked me to repeat here in greater detail a few ideas set forth in another context (Erikson, 1950a). There the matter of the healthy personality emerges, as if accidentally, from a variety of clinical and anthropological considerations. Here it is to become the central theme.

An expert, it is said, can separate fact from theory, and knowledge from opinion. It is his job to know the available techniques by which statements in his field can be verified. If, in this paper, I were to restrict myself to what is, in this sense, *known* about the "healthy personality," I would lead the reader and myself into a very honorable but very uninspiring austerity. In the matter of man's relation to himself and to others, methodological problems are not such as to be either instructive or suggestive in a short treatise.

On the other hand, if I were to write this paper in order to give another introduction to the theory of Freudian psychoanalysis, I would hardly contribute much to an understanding of the healthy personality. For the psychoanalyst knows very much more about the dynamics and cure of the disturbances which he treats daily than about the prevention of such disturbances.

I will, however, start out from Freud's far-reaching discovery

---

The original version of this paper appeared in *Symposium on the Healthy Personality*, Supplement II; Problems of Infancy and Childhood, Transactions of Fourth Conference, March, 1950, M.J.E. Senn, ed. New York: Josiah Macy, Jr. Foundation.

that neurotic conflict is not very different in content from the conflicts which every child must live through in his childhood, and that every adult carries these conflicts with him in the recesses of his personality. I shall take account of this fact by stating for each childhood stage what these critical psychological conflicts are. For man, to remain psychologically alive, must resolve these conflicts unceasingly, even as his body must unceasingly combat the encroachment of physical decomposition. However, since I cannot accept the conclusion that just to be alive, or not to be sick, means to be healthy, I must have recourse to a few concepts which are not part of the official terminology of my field. Being interested also in cultural anthropology, I shall try to describe those elements of a really healthy personality which—so it seems to me—are most noticeably absent or defective in neurotic patients and which are most obviously present in the kind of man that educational and cultural systems seem to be striving, each in its own way, to create, to support, and to maintain.

I shall present human growth from the point of view of the conflicts, inner and outer, which the healthy personality weathers, emerging and re-emerging with an increased sense of inner unity, with an increase of good judgment, and an increase in the capacity to do well, according to the standards of those who are significant to him. The use of the words "to do well," of course, points up the whole question of cultural relativity. For example, those who are significant to a man may think he is doing well when he "does some good"; or when he "does well" in the sense of acquiring possessions; or when he is doing well in the sense of learning new skills or new ways of understanding or mastering reality; or when he is not much more than just getting along.

Formulations of what constitutes a healthy personality in an adult are presented in other parts of the Fact-finding Committee's work. If I may take up only one, namely, Marie Jahoda's (1950) definition, according to which a healthy personality *actively masters his environment*, shows a certain *unity of personality*, and is able to *perceive the world and himself correctly*, it is clear that all of these criteria are relative to the child's cognitive and social development. In fact, we may say that childhood is defined by their initial absence and by their gradual development in many complicated steps. I consider it my task to approach this question from the genetic point of view: How does a healthy personality grow or, as it were, accrue from the successive stages of increasing capacity to master life's outer and inner dangers—with some vital enthusiasm to spare?

On Health and Growth

Whenever we try to understand growth, it is well to remember the *epigenetic principle* which is derived from the growth of organisms *in utero*. Somewhat generalized, this principle states that anything that grows has a *ground plan,* and that out of this ground plan the *parts* arise, each part having its *time* of special ascendancy, until all parts have arisen to form a *functioning whole*. At birth the baby leaves the chemical exchange of the womb for the social exchange system of his society, where his gradually increasing capacities meet the opportunities and limitations of his culture. How the maturing organism continues to unfold, not by developing new organs, but by a prescribed sequence of locomotor, sensory, and social capacities, is described in the child-development literature. Psychoanalysis has given us an understanding of the more idiosyncratic experiences and especially the inner conflicts, which constitute the manner in which an individual becomes a distinct personality. But here, too, it is important to realize that in the sequence of his most personal experiences the healthy child, given a reasonable amount of guidance, can be trusted to obey inner laws of development, laws which create a *succession of potentialities for significant interaction* with those who tend him. While such interaction varies from culture to culture, it must remain within the *proper rate and the proper sequence* which govern the *growth of a personality* as well as that of an organism. Personality can be said to develop according to steps predetermined in the human organism's readiness to be driven toward, to be aware of, and to interact with, a widening social radius, beginning with the dim image of a mother and ending with mankind, or at any rate that segment of mankind which "counts" in the particular individual's life.

It is for this reason that, in the presentation of stages in the development of the personality, we employ an *epigenetic diagram* analogous to one previously employed for an analysis of Freud's psychosexual stages.[1] It is, in fact, the purpose of this presentation to bridge the theory of infantile sexuality (without repeating it here in detail), and our knowledge of the child's physical and social growth within his family and the social structure. An epigenetic diagram looks like this (see Diagram A, p. 54).

The double-lined squares signify both a sequence of stages (I to III) and a gradual development of component parts; in other words the diagram formalizes a *progression through time of a differentiation of parts*. This indicates (1) that each item of the healthy personality to be discussed is *systematically related to all others*, and that they all depend on the *proper development in the proper sequence of each item*; and (2) that each item *exists in some form before "its" decisive and critical time* normally arrives.

If I say, for example, that a *sense of basic trust* is the first component of mental health to develop in life, a *sense of autonomous will* the second, and a *sense of initiative* the third, the purpose of the diagram may become clearer (see Diagram B, p. 54).

This diagrammatic statement, in turn, is meant to express a number of fundamental relations that exist among the three components, as well as a few fundamental facts for each.

Each comes to its ascendance, meets its crisis, and finds its lasting solution (in ways to be described here) *toward the end of the stages* mentioned. All of them exist in the beginning in some form, although we do not make a point of this fact, and we shall not confuse things by calling these components different names at earlier or later stages. A baby may show something like "autonomy" from the beginning, for example, in the particular way in which he angrily tries to wriggle his hand free when tightly held. However, under normal conditions, it is not until the second year that he begins to experience the whole *critical alternative between being an autonomous creature and being a dependent one*; and it is not until then that he is ready for a *decisive encounter* with his environment, an environment which, in turn, feels called upon to convey to him its *particular ideas and concepts of autonomy and coercion* in ways decisively contributing to the character, the efficiency, and the health of his personality in his culture.

It is this *encounter*, together with the resulting crisis, which is to be described for each stage. Each stage becomes a *crisis* be-

[1] See Part I of the author's *Childhood and Society* (1950a).

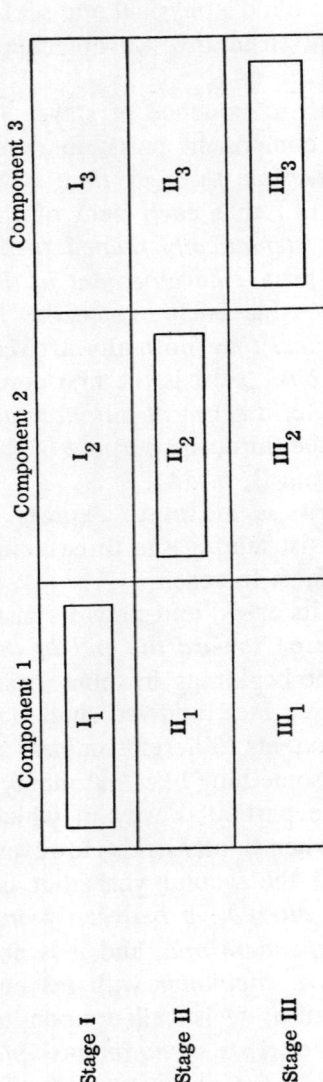

cause incipient growth and awareness in a significant part function goes together with a shift in instinctual energy and yet causes specific vulnerability in that part. One of the most difficult questions to decide, therefore, is whether or not a child at a given stage is weak or strong. Perhaps it would be best to say that he is always vulnerable in some respects and completely oblivious and insensitive in others, but that at the same time he is unbelievably persistent in the same respects in which he is vulnerable. It must be added that the smallest baby's weakness gives him power; out of his very dependence and weakness he makes signs to which his environment (if it is guided well by a responsiveness based both on instinctive and traditional patterns) is peculiarly sensitive. A baby's presence exerts a consistent and persistent domination over the outer and inner lives of every member of a household. Because these members must reorient themselves to accommodate his presence, they must also grow as individuals and as a group. It is as true to say that babies control and bring up their families as it is to say the converse. A family can bring up a baby only by being brought up by him. His growth consists of a series of challenges to them to serve his newly developing potentialities for social interaction.

Each successive step, then, is a potential crisis because of a radical *change in perspective*. There is, at the beginning of life, the most radical change of all: from intrauterine to extrauterine life. But in postnatal existence, too, such radical adjustments of perspective as lying relaxed, sitting firmly, and running fast must all be accomplished in their own good time. With them, the interpersonal perspective, too, changes rapidly and often radically, as is testified by the proximity in time of such opposites as "not letting mother out of sight" and "wanting to be independent." Thus, *different capacities use different opportunities* to become full-grown components of the ever-new configuration that is the growing personality.

Basic Trust versus Basic Mistrust

I

For the first component of a healthy personality I nominate a sense of *basic trust*, which I think is an attitude toward oneself and the world derived from the experiences of the first year of life. By "trust" I mean what is commonly implied in reasonable trustfulness as far as others are concerned and a simple sense of trustworthiness as far as oneself is concerned. When I say "basic," I mean that neither this component nor any of those that follow are, either in childhood or in adulthood, especially conscious. In fact, all of these criteria, when developed in childhood and when integrated in adulthood, blend into the total personality. Their crises in childhood, however, and their impairment in adulthood are clearly circumscribed.

In describing this growth and its crises as a development of a series of alternative basic attitudes, we take recourse to the term *"a sense of."* Like a "sense of health" or a "sense of not being well," such "senses" pervade surface and depth, consciousness and the unconscious. They are ways of conscious *experience*, accessible to introspection (where it develops); ways of *behaving*, observable by others; and unconscious *inner states* determinable by test and analysis. It is important to keep these three dimensions in mind, as we proceed.

In *adults* the impairment of basic trust is expressed in a *basic mistrust*. It characterizes individuals who withdraw into themselves in particular ways when at odds with themselves and with others. These ways, which often are not obvious, are more strikingly represented by individuals who regress into psychotic states in which they sometimes close up, refusing food and comfort and becoming oblivious to companionship. In so far as we hope to assist them with psychotherapy, we must try to reach them again in specific ways in order to convince them that they can trust the world and that they can trust themselves (Fromm-Reichmann, 1950).

It is from the knowledge of such radical regressions and of the deepest and most infantile layers in our not-so-sick patients that we have learned to regard basic trust as the cornerstone of a healthy personality. Let us see what justifies our placing the crisis and the ascendancy of this component at the beginning of life.

As the newborn infant is separated from his symbiosis with the mother's body, his inborn and more or less coordinated ability to take in by mouth meets the mother's more or less coordinated ability and intention to feed him and to welcome him. At this point he lives through, and loves with, his mouth; and the mother lives through, and loves with, her breasts.

For the mother this is a late and complicated accomplishment, highly dependent on her development as a woman; on her unconscious attitude toward the child; on the way she has lived through pregnancy and delivery; on her and her community's attitude toward the act of nursing—and on the response of the newborn. To him the mouth is the focus of a general first approach to life— the *incorporative* approach. In psychoanalysis this stage is usually referred to as the "oral" stage. Yet it is clear that, in addition to the overwhelming need for food, a baby is, or soon becomes, receptive in many other respects. As he is willing and able to suck on appropriate objects and to swallow whatever appropriate fluids they emit, he is soon also willing and able to "take in" with his eyes whatever enters his visual field. His tactual senses, too, seem to "take in" what feels good. In this sense, then, one could speak of an *"incorporative stage,"* one in which he is, relatively speaking, receptive to what he is being offered. Yet many babies are sensitive and vulnerable, too. In order to ensure that their first experience in this world may not only keep them alive but also help them to coordinate their sensitive breathing and their metabolic and circulatory rhythms, we must see to it that we deliver to their senses stimuli as well as food in the proper intensity and at the right time; otherwise their willingness to accept may change abruptly into diffuse defense—or into lethargy.

Now, while it is quite clear what *must* happen to keep a baby alive (the minimum supply necessary) and what *must not* happen, lest he be physically damaged or chronically upset (the maximum early frustration tolerable), there is a certain leeway in regard to what *may* happen; and different cultures make extensive use of their prerogatives to decide what they consider workable and insist upon calling necessary. Some people think that a baby, lest he scratch his own eyes out, must necessarily be swaddled completely for the better part of the day and throughout the greater part of the first year; also, that he should be rocked or fed whenever he whimpers. Others think that he should feel the freedom of his kicking limbs as early as possible, but also that he, as a matter of course, be forced to cry "please" for his meals until he literally gets blue in the face. All of this (more or less consciously) seems related to the culture's general aim and system. I have known some old American Indians who bitterly decried the way in which we often let our small babies cry because we believe that "it will make their lungs strong." No wonder (these Indians said) that the white man, after such an initial reception, seems to be in a hurry to get to the "next world." But the same Indians spoke proudly of the way their infants (breast fed into the second year) became blue in the face with fury when thumped on the head for "biting" the mother's nipples; here the Indians, in turn, believed that "it's going to make good hunters of them."

There is some intrinsic wisdom, some unconscious planning and much superstition in the seemingly arbitrary varieties of child training: what is "good for the child," what *may* happen to him, depends on what he is supposed to become and where.

At any rate, it is already in his earliest encounters that the human infant meets up with the basic modalities of his culture. The simplest and the earliest modality is "*to get,*" not in the sense of "*go and get*" but in that of receiving and accepting what is given; and this sounds easier than it is. For the groping and unstable newborn's organism learns this modality only as he learns to regulate his readiness to get with the methods of a mother who, in turn, will permit him to coordinate his means of getting as she develops and coordinates her means of giving. The mutuality of relaxation thus developed is of prime importance for the first experience of friendly otherness: from psychoanalysis one receives the impression that in thus *getting what is given,* and in learning to *get somebody to do* for him what he wishes to have done, the baby also develops the necessary groundwork to *get to be* the giver, to "identify" with her.

Where this *mutual regulation* fails, the situation falls apart into a variety of attempts to control by duress rather than by reciprocity. The baby will try to get by random activity what he cannot get by central suction; he will activate himself into exhaustion or he will find his thumb and damn the world. The mother's reaction may be to try to control matters by nervously changing hours, formulas, and procedures. One cannot be sure what this does to a baby; but it certainly is our clinical impression that in some sensitive individuals (or in individuals whose early frustration was never compensated for) such a situation can be a model for a radical disturbance in their relationship to the "world," to "people," and especially to loved or otherwise significant people.

There are ways of maintaining reciprocity by giving to the baby what he can get through other forms of feeding and by making up for what is missed orally through the satiation of other than oral receptors: his pleasure in being held, warmed, smiled at, talked to, rocked, and so forth. Besides such *"horizontal" compensation* (compensation during the same stage of development) there are many *"longitudinal" compensations* in life: compensations emerging from later stages of the life cycle.[2]

During the "second oral" stage the ability and the pleasure in a more active and more directed incorporative approach ripen. The teeth develop and with them the pleasure in biting *on* hard things, in biting *through* things, and in biting *off* things. This *active-incorporative* mode characterizes a variety of other activities (as did the first incorporative mode). The eyes, first part of a passive system of accepting impressions as they come along, have now learned to focus, to isolate, to "grasp" objects from the vaguer background and to follow them. The organs of hearing similarly have learned to discern significant sounds, to localize them, and to guide an appropriate change in position (lifting and turning the head, lifting and turning the upper body). The arms have learned to reach out determinedly and the hands to grasp firmly. We are more interested here in the over-all *configuration and final integration* of developing approaches to the world than in the *first appearance of specific abilities* which are so well described in the child-development literature.[3]

---

[2] My participation in the longitudinal research of the Institute of Child Welfare at the University of California (see Macfarlane, 1938; Erikson, 1951b) has taught me the greatest respect for the resiliency and resourcefulness of individual children who, with the support of an expanding economy and of a generous social group, learned to compensate for grievous early misfortunes of a kind which in our clinical histories would suffice to explain malfunctioning rather convincingly. The study gave me an opportunity to chart a decade of the life histories of about fifty (healthy) children, and to remain somewhat informed about the further fortunes of some of them. However, only the development of the identity concept (see this volume, pp. 101-164) has helped me to approach an understanding of the mechanisms involved. I hope to publish my impressions.

[3] The reader trained in child development may want to pay special attention to the fact that one can think of a stage as the time when a capacity *first appears* (or appears in testable form) or as that period when it is so well *established* and integrated (has become an available apparatus for the ego, as we would say) that the next step in development can safely be initiated.

With all of this a number of interpersonal patterns are established which center in the social modality of *taking* and *holding on to* things—things which are more or less freely offered and given, and things which have more or less a tendency to slip away. As the baby learns to change positions, to roll over, and very gradually to establish himself on the throne of his sedentary kingdom, he must perfect the mechanisms of grasping and appropriating, holding and chewing all that is within his reach.

The *crisis* of the oral stage (during the second part of the first year) is difficult to assess and more difficult to verify. It seems to consist of the coincidence in time of three developments: (1) a physiological one: the general tension associated with a more violent drive to incorporate, appropriate, and observe more actively (a tension to which is added the discomfort of "teething" and other changes in the oral machinery); (2) a psychological one: the infant's increasing awareness of himself as a distinct person; and (3) an environmental one: the mother's apparent turning away from the baby toward pursuits which she had given up during late pregnancy and postnatal care. These pursuits include her full return to conjugal intimacy and may soon lead to a new pregnancy.

Where breast feeding lasts into the biting stage (and, generally speaking, this has been the rule) it is now necessary to learn how to continue sucking without biting, so that the mother may not withdraw the nipple in pain or anger. Our clinical work indicates that this point in the individual's early history provides him with some sense of basic loss, leaving the general impression that once upon a time one's unity with a maternal matrix was destroyed. Weaning, therefore, should not mean sudden loss of the breast and loss of the mother's reassuring presence too, unless, of course, other women can be depended upon to sound and feel much like the mother. A drastic loss of accustomed mother love without proper substitution at this time can lead (under otherwise aggravating conditions) to acute infantile depression (Spitz, 1945) or to a mild but chronic state of mourning which may give a depressive undertone to the whole remainder of life. But even under more favorable circumstances, this stage seems to introduce into the psychic life a sense of division and a dim but universal nostalgia for a lost paradise.

It is against the combination of these impressions of having been deprived, of having been divided, and of having been abandoned, all of which leave a residue of basic mistrust, that basic trust must be established and maintained.[4]

II

What we here call "trust" coincides with what Therese Benedek has called "confidence." If I prefer the word "trust," it is because there is more naïveté and more mutuality in it: an infant can be said to be trusting, but it would be assuming too much to say that he "has confidence." The general state of trust, furthermore, implies not only that one has learned to rely on the sameness and continuity of the outer providers but also that one may trust oneself and the capacity of one's own organs to cope with urges; that one is able to consider oneself trustworthy enough so that the providers will not need to be on guard or to leave.

In the psychiatric literature we find frequent references to an "oral character," which is a characterological deviation based on the unsolved conflicts of this stage. Wherever oral pessimism becomes dominant and exclusive, infantile fears, such as that of "being left empty," or simply of "being left," and also of being "starved of stimulation," can be discerned in the depressive forms of "being empty" and of "being no good." Such fears, in turn, can give orality that particular avaricious quality which in psychoanalysis is called "oral sadism," that is, a cruel need to get and to

[4] One of the chief misuses of the schema presented here is the connotation that the sense of trust (and all the other *positive* senses to be postulated) is an *achievement*, secured once and for all at a given stage. In fact, some writers are so intent on making an *achievement scale* out of these stages that they blithely omit all the *negative* senses (basic mistrust, etc.) which are and remain the dynamic counterpart of the positive senses throughout life. (See, for example, the "maturation chart" distributed at the National Congress of Parents and Teachers in Omaha, Nebraska [1958], which omits any reference to crises, and otherwise "adapts" the stages presented here.)

What the child acquires at a given stage is a certain *ratio* between the positive and the negative which, if the balance is toward the positive, will help him to meet later crises with a better chance for unimpaired total development. The idea that at any stage a *goodness* is achieved which is impervious to new conflicts within and changes without is a projection on child development of that success ideology which so dangerously pervades our private and public daydreams and can make us inept in the face of a heightened struggle for a meaningful existence in our time.

Only in the light of man's inner division and social antagonism is a belief in his essential resourcefulness and creativity justifiable and productive.

take in ways harmful to others. But there is an optimistic oral character, too, one which has learned to make giving and receiving the most important thing in life; and there is "orality" as a normal substratum in all individuals, a lasting residuum of this first period of dependency on powerful providers. It normally expresses itself in our dependencies and nostalgias, and in our all too hopeful and all too hopeless states. The integration of the oral stage with all the following ones results, in adulthood, in a combination of faith and realism.

The pathology and irrationality of oral trends depend entirely on the degree to which they are integrated with the rest of the personality and the degree to which they fit into the general cultural pattern and use approved interpersonal techniques for their expression.

Here, as elsewhere, we must therefore consider as a topic for discussion the expression of *infantile urges* in *cultural patterns* which one may (or may not) consider a pathological deviation in the total economic or moral system of a culture or a nation. One could speak, for example, of the invigorating belief in "chance," that traditional prerogative of American trust in one's own resourcefulness and in Fate's store of good intentions. This belief, at times, can be seen to degenerate—in large-scale gambling, or in "taking chances" in the form of an arbitrary and often suicidal provocation of Fate, or in the insistence that one has not only the right to an equal chance but also the privilege of being preferred over all other investors in the same general enterprise. In a similar way all the pleasant reassurances which can be derived (especially in good company) from old and new taste sensations, from inhaling and imbibing, from munching and swallowing and digesting, can turn into mass addictions neither expressive of, nor conducive to, the kind of basic trust which we have in mind.

Here we are obviously touching on phenomena the analysis of which would call for a comprehensive approach both to personality and to culture. This would be true also for an epidemiological approach to the problem of the more or less malignant elaboration of the oral character in "schizoid" characters and the mental diseases seemingly expressive of an underlying weakness in oral reassurance and basic trust. A related problem is the belief (reflected in much of contemporary obstetric and pediatric concern with the methods of child care) that the establishment of a basic sense of trust in earliest childhood makes adult individuals less dependent on mild or malignant forms of addiction, on self-delusion, and on avaricious appropriation. Of this, little is known; and the question remains whether healthy orality makes for a healthy culture or a healthy culture makes for healthy orality—or both.

At any rate, the psychiatrists, obstetricians, pediatricians, and anthropologists, to whom I feel closest, today would agree that the *firm establishment of enduring patterns for the balance of basic trust over basic mistrust* is the first task of the budding personality and therefore first of all a task for maternal care. But it must be said that the *amount of trust* derived from earliest infantile experience does not seem to depend on absolute *quantities of food or demonstrations of love* but rather on the *quality* of the maternal relationship. Mothers create a sense of trust in their children by that kind of administration which in its quality combines sensitive care of the baby's individual needs and a firm sense of personal trustworthiness within the trusted framework of their community's life style. (This forms the basis in the child for a sense of identity which will later combine a sense of being "all right," of being oneself, and of becoming what other people trust one will become.) Parents must not only have certain ways of guiding by prohibition and permission; they must also be able to represent to the child a deep, an almost somatic conviction that there is a meaning to what they are doing. In this sense a traditional system of child care can be said to be a factor making for trust, even where certain items of that tradition, taken singly, may seem irrational or unnecessarily cruel. Here much depends on whether such items are inflicted on the child by the parent in the firm traditional belief that this is the only way to do things or whether the parent misuses his administration of the baby and the child in order to work off anger, alleviate fear, or win an argument, with the child or with somebody else (mother-in-law, doctor, or priest).

In times of change—and what other times are there, in our memory?—one generation differs so much from another that items of tradition often become disturbances. Conflicts between mother's ways and one's own self-made ways, conflicts between the expert's advice and mother's ways, and conflicts between the expert's authority and one's own self-willed ways may disturb a mother's trust in herself. Furthermore, all the mass transformations in American life (immigration, migration, and Americanization; industrialization, urbanization, mechanization, and others) are apt to disturb young mothers in those tasks which are so simple yet so far-reaching. No wonder, then, that the first section of the first chapter of Benjamin Spock's (1945) book is entitled "Trust Yourself." But while it is true that the expert obstetrician and pediatrician can do much to replace the binding power of tradition by giving reassurance and guidance, he does not have the time to become the father-confessor for all the doubts and fears, angers and arguments, which can fill the minds of lonely young parents. Maybe a book like Spock's needs to be read in study groups where the true psychological spirit of the town meeting can be created; that is, where matters are considered to be agreed upon not because somebody said so, but because the free airing of opinions and emotions, of prejudices and of errors has led to a general area of relative consent and of tolerant good will.

This chapter has become unduly long. In regard to the matters discussed here, it is too bad that one must begin with the beginning. We know so little of the beginnings, of the deeper strata of the human mind. But since we have already embarked on general observations, a word must be said about one cultural and traditional institution which is deeply related to the matter of trust, namely, religion.

It is not the psychologist's job to decide whether religion should or should not be confessed and practiced in particular words and rituals. Rather the psychological observer must ask whether or not in any area under observation religion and tradition are living psychological forces creating the kind of faith and conviction which permeates a parent's personality and thus reinforces the child's basic trust in the world's trustworthiness. The psychopathologist cannot avoid observing that there are millions of people who cannot really afford to be without religion, and whose pride in not having it is that much whistling in the dark. On the other hand, there are millions who seem to derive faith from other than religious dogmas, that is, from fellowship, productive work, social action, scientific pursuit, and artistic creation. And again, there are millions who profess faith, yet in practice mistrust both life and man. With all of these in mind, it seems worth while to speculate on the fact that religion through the centuries has served to restore a sense of trust at regular intervals in the form of faith while giving tangible form to a sense of evil which it promises to ban. All religions have in common the periodical childlike surrender to a Provider or providers who dispense earthly fortune as well as spiritual health; the demonstration of one's smallness and dependence through the medium of reduced posture and humble gesture; the admission in prayer and song of misdeeds, of misthoughts, and of evil intentions; the admission of inner division and the consequent appeal for inner unification by divine guidance; the need for clearer self-delineation and self-restriction; and finally, the insight that individual trust must become a common faith, individual mistrust a commonly formulated evil, while the individual's need for restoration must become part of the ritual practice of many, and must become a sign of trustworthiness in the community.

Whosoever says he has religion must derive a faith from it which is transmitted to infants in the form of basic trust; whosoever claims that he does not need religion must derive such basic faith from elsewhere.

Autonomy versus Shame and Doubt

I

A survey of some of the items discussed in Spock's book under the headings "The One-Year-Old" and "Managing Young Children" will enable those of us who, at this time, do not have such inquisitive creatures in our homes to remember our skirmishes, our victories, and our defeats:

> Feeling his oats.
> The passion to explore.
> He gets more dependent and more independent at the same time.
> Arranging the house for a wandering baby.
> Avoiding accidents.
> Now's the time to put poisons out of reach.
> How do you make him leave certain things alone?
> Dropping and throwing things.
> Children learn to control their own aggressive feelings.

Biting humans.
Keeping bedtime happy.
The small child who won't stay in bed at night.

My selection is intended to convey the inventory and range of problems described though I cannot review here either the doctor's excellent advice or his good balance in depicting the remarkable ease and matter-of-factness with which the nursery may be governed at this as at any other stage. Nevertheless, there is an indication of the sinister forces which are leashed and unleashed, especially in the guerilla warfare of unequal wills; for the child is often unequal to his own violent drives, and parent and child unequal to each other.

The over-all significance of this stage lies in the maturation of the muscle system, the consequent ability (and doubly felt inability) to coordinate a number of highly conflicting action patterns such as "holding on" and "letting go," and the enormous value with which the still highly dependent child begins to endow his autonomous will.

Psychoanalysis has enriched our vocabulary with the word "anality" to designate the particular pleasurableness and willfulness which often attach to the eliminative organs at this stage. The whole procedure of evacuating the bowels and the bladder as completely as possible is, of course, enhanced from the beginning by a premium of "feeling good" which says in effect, "well done." This premium, at the beginning of life, must make up for quite frequent discomfort and tension suffered as the bowels learn to do their daily work. Two developments gradually give these anal experiences the necessary volume: the arrival of better formed stool and the general coordination of the muscle system which permits the development of voluntary release, of dropping and throwing away. This new dimension of approach to things, however, is not restricted to the sphincters. A general ability, indeed, a violent need, develops to drop and to throw away and to alternate withholding and expelling at will.

As far as anality proper is concerned, at this point everything depends on whether the cultural environment wants to make something of it. There are cultures where the parents ignore anal behavior and leave it to older children to lead the toddler out to the bushes so that his compliance in this matter may coincide with his wish to imitate the bigger ones. Our Western civilization, and especially certain classes within it, have chosen to take the matter more seriously. It is here that the machine age has added the ideal of a mechanically trained, faultlessly functioning, and always clean, punctual, and deodorized body. In addition it has been more or less consciously assumed that early and rigorous training is absolutely necessary for the kind of personality which will function efficiently in a mechanized world which says "time is money" and which calls for orderliness, punctuality, and thrift. Indications are that in this, we have gone too far; that we have assumed that a child is an animal which must be broken or a machine which must be set and tuned—while, in fact, human virtues can grow only by steps. At any rate our clinical work suggests that the neurotics of our time include the "overcompulsive" type, who is stingy, retentive, and meticulous in matters of affection, time, and money, as well as in matters concerning his bowels. Also, bowel and bladder training has become the most obviously disturbing item of child training in wide circles of our society.

What, then, makes the anal problem potentially important and difficult?

The anal zone lends itself more than any other to the expression of stubborn insistence on conflicting impulses because, for one thing, it is the model zone for two contradictory modes which must become alternating; namely, *retention* and *elimination*. Furthermore, the sphincters are only part of the muscle system with its general ambiguity of rigidity and relaxation, of flexion and extension. This whole stage, then, becomes a battle for *autonomy*. For as he gets ready to stand on his feet more firmly, the infant delineates his world as "I" and "you," "me" and "mine." Every mother knows how astonishingly pliable a child may be at this stage, if and when he has made the decision that he *wants* to do what he is supposed to do. It is impossible, however, to find a reliable formula for making him want to do just that. Every mother knows how lovingly a child at this stage will snuggle and how ruthlessly he will suddenly try to push the adult away. At the same time the child is apt both to hoard things and to discard them, to cling to possessions and to throw them out of the windows of houses and vehicles. All of these seemingly contradictory tendencies, then, we include under the formula of the retentive-eliminative modes.

The matter of mutual regulation between adult and child now faces its severest test. If outer control by too rigid or too early training insists on robbing the child of his attempt *gradually* to control his bowels and other functions willingly and by his free choice, he will again be faced with a double rebellion and a double defeat. Powerless in his own body (sometimes afraid of his bowels) and powerless outside, he will again be forced to seek satisfaction and control either by regression or by fake progression. In other words, he will return to an earlier, oral control, that is, by sucking his thumb and becoming whiny and demanding; or he will become hostile and willful, often using his feces (and, later, dirty words) as ammunition; or he will pretend an autonomy and an ability to do without anybody to lean on which he has by no means really gained.

This stage, therefore, becomes decisive for the ratio between love and hate, for that between cooperation and willfulness, and for that between the freedom of self-expression and its suppression. From a sense of *self-control without loss of self-esteem* comes a lasting sense of autonomy and pride; from a sense of muscular and anal impotence, of loss of self-control, and of parental overcontrol comes a lasting sense of doubt and shame.

To develop autonomy, a firmly developed and a convincingly continued stage of early trust is necessary. The infant must come to feel that basic faith in himself and in the world (which is the lasting treasure saved from the conflicts of the oral stage) will not be jeopardized by this sudden violent wish to have a choice, to appropriate demandingly, and to eliminate stubbornly. *Firmness* must protect him against the potential anarchy of his as yet untrained sense of discrimination, his inability to hold on and to let go with circumspection. Yet his environment must back him up in his wish to "stand on his own feet" lest he be overcome by that sense of having exposed himself prematurely and foolishly which we call shame, or that secondary mistrust, that "double-take," which we call doubt.

Shame is an infantile emotion insufficiently studied. Shame supposes that one is completely exposed and conscious of being looked at—in a word, self-conscious. One is visible and not ready to be visible; that is why we dream of shame as a situation in which we are stared at in a condition of incomplete dress, in night attire, "with one's pants down." Shame is early expressed in an impulse to bury one's face, or to sink, right then and there, into the ground. This potentiality is abundantly utilized in the educational method of "shaming" used so exclusively by some primitive peoples, where it supplants the often more destructive sense of guilt to be discussed later. The destructiveness of shaming is balanced in some civilizations by devices for *"saving face."* Shaming exploits an increasing sense of being small, which paradoxically develops as the child stands up and as his awareness permits him to note the relative measures of size and power.

Too much shaming does not result in a sense of propriety but in a secret determination to try to get away with things when unseen, if, indeed, it does not result in deliberate *shamelessness.* There is an impressive American ballad in which a murderer to be hanged on the gallows before the eyes of the community, instead of feeling appropriately afraid or ashamed, begins to berate the onlookers, ending every salvo of defiance with the words, "God damn your eyes." Many a small child, when shamed beyond endurance, may be in a mood (although not in possession of either the courage or the words) to express defiance in similar terms. What I mean by this sinister reference is that there is a limit to a child's and an adult's individual endurance in the face of demands which force him to consider himself, his body, his needs, and his wishes as evil and dirty, and to believe in the infallibility of those who pass such judgment. Occasionally he may be apt to turn things around, to become secretly oblivious to the opinion of others, and to consider as evil only the fact that they exist: his chance will come when they are gone, or when he can leave them.

Many a defiant child, many a young criminal, is of such make-up, and deserves at least an investigation into the conditions which caused him to become that way.

To repeat: muscular maturation sets the stage for experimentation with two simultaneous sets of social modalities—*holding on* and *letting go.* As is the case with all of these modalities, their basic conflicts can lead in the end either to hostile or to benign expectations and attitudes. Thus, "to hold" can become a destructive and cruel retaining or restraining, and it can become a pattern of care:

"to have and to hold." To "let go," too, can turn into an inimical letting loose of destructive forces, or it can become a relaxed "to let pass" and "to let be." Culturally speaking, these modalities are neither good nor bad; their value depends on whether their hostile implications are turned against enemy or fellow man—or against the self.

The last-named danger is the one best known to psychiatry. Denied the gradual and well-guided experience of the autonomy of free choice, or weakened by an initial loss of trust, the sensitive child may turn against himself all his urge to discriminate and to manipulate. He will *overmanipulate himself,* he will develop a *precocious conscience.* Instead of taking possession of things in order to test them by repetitive play, he will become obsessed by his own repetitiveness; he will want to have everything "just so," and only in a given sequence and tempo. By such infantile obsessiveness, by dawdling, for example, or by becoming a stickler for certain rituals, the child then learns to gain power over his parents and nurses in areas where he could not find large-scale mutual regulation with them. Such hollow victory, then, is the infantile model for a compulsion neurosis. As for the consequences of this for adult character, they can be observed in the classical compulsive character which we have mentioned. We must add to this the character dominated by the wish to "get away with" things—yet unable to get away even with the wish. For while he learns evasion from others, his precocious conscience does not let him really get away with anything, and he goes through life habitually ashamed, apologetic, and afraid to be seen; or else, in a manner which we call "overcompensatory," he evinces a defiant kind of autonomy. Real inner autonomy, however, is not carried on the sleeve.

II

But it is time to return from these considerations of the abnormal to a study of the headings which transmit the practical and benevolent advice of the children's doctor. They all add up to this: be firm and tolerant with the child at this stage, and he will be firm and tolerant with himself. He will feel pride in being an autonomous person; he will grant autonomy to others; and now and again he will even let himself get away with something.

Why, then, if we know how, do we not tell parents in detail what to do to develop this intrinsic, this genuine autonomy? The answer is: because when it comes to human values, nobody knows how to fabricate or manage the fabrication of the genuine article. My own field, psychoanalysis, having studied particularly the excessive increase of guilt feelings beyond any normal rhyme or reason, and the consequent excessive estrangement of the child from his own body, attempted at least to formulate what should *not* be done to children. These formulations, however, often aroused superstitious inhibitions in those who were inclined to make anxious rules out of vague warnings. Actually, we are learning only gradually what exactly *not* to do with *what kind* of children at *what age*.

People all over the world seem convinced that to make the right (meaning *their*) kind of human being, one must consistently introduce the senses of shame, doubt, guilt and fear into a child's life. Only the patterns vary. Some cultures begin to restrict early in life, some late, some abruptly, others more gradually. Until enough comparative observations are available, we are apt to add further superstitions, merely because of our wish to *avoid* certain pathological conditions, without even knowing definitely all the factors which are responsible for these conditions. So we say: Don't wean too early; don't train too early. But what is too early and what is too late seem to depend not only on the pathologies we wish to avoid but also on the values we wish to create, or, to put it more honestly, on the values we wish to live by. For no matter what we do in detail, the child will feel primarily what we live by, what makes us loving, cooperative, and firm beings, and what makes us hateful, anxious, and divided in ourselves.

There are of course a few matters of necessary avoidance which become clear from our basic epigenetic point of view. It will be remembered that every new development carries with it its own specific vulnerability. For example, at around eight months the child seems to be somehow more aware, as it were, of his *separateness;* this prepares him for the impending sense of autonomy. At the same time he becomes more cognizant of his mother's features and presence and of the strangeness of others. Sudden or prolonged separation from his mother at that time apparently can cause a sensitive child to experience an aggravation of the experience of division and abandonment, arousing violent anxiety and withdrawal. Again, in the first quarter of the second year, if everything has gone well, the infant just begins to become aware of the autonomy discussed in this chapter. The introduction of bowel training at this time may cause him to resist with all his strength and determination, because he seems to feel that his budding will is being "broken." To avoid this feeling is certainly more important than to insist on his being trained just then because there is a time for the stubborn ascendancy of autonomy and there is a time for the partial sacrifice of secure autonomy, but obviously the time for a meaningful sacrifice is *after* one has acquired and reinforced a core of autonomy and has also acquired more insight.

The more exact localization in time of the most critical growth periods of the personality is becoming established only now. Often, the unavoidable cause of trouble is not one event but the coincidence in time of a number of changes which upset the child's orientation. He may have been involved in a special growth period when the family moved to a new place. Perhaps he was forced to conceive of his first words all over again when the grandmother who had taught him these words suddenly died. A trip on the part of the mother may have exhausted her because she happened to be pregnant at the time, and thus unable, on returning, to make proper amends. Given the right spirit toward life and its vicissitudes, a parent can usually handle such matters, if necessary with the help of the pediatrician or guidance expert. The expert's job, however, should be (to quote Frank Fremont-Smith) *"to set the frame of reference within which choice is permissible and desirable."* For in the last analysis (as comparative studies in child training have convinced many of us) the kind and degree of a sense of autonomy which parents are able to grant their small children depends on the dignity and the sense of personal independence which they derive from their own lives. Again, just as the sense of trust is a reflection of the parents' sturdy and realistic faith, so is the sense of autonomy a reflection of the parents' dignity as individuals.

As was the case with "oral" personality, the compulsive personality (often referred to as "anal" in the psychiatric literature) has its normal aspects and its abnormal exaggerations. If well integrated with other compensatory traits, some compulsiveness is useful in the administration of matters in which order, punctuality, and cleanliness are essential. The question is always whether we remain the masters of the rules by which we want to make things more manageable (not more complicated) or whether the rules master the ruler. But it often happens, in the individual as well as in group life, that the letter of the rules kills the spirit which created them.

III

We have related basic trust to the institution of religion. The basic need of the individual for a delineation of his *autonomy* in the adult order of things seems, in turn, to be taken care of by the *principle of "law and order,"* which in daily life as well as in the high courts of law apportions to each his privileges and his limitations, his obligations and his rights. The sense of autonomy which arises, or should arise, in the second stage of childhood, is fostered by a handling of the small individual which expresses a sense of rightful dignity and lawful independence on the part of the parents and which gives him the confident expectation that the kind of autonomy fostered in childhood will not be frustrated later. This, in turn, necessitates a relationship of parent to parent, of parent to employer, and of parent to government which reaffirms the parent's essential dignity within the hierarchy of social positions. It is important to dwell on this point because much of the shame and doubt, much of the indignity and uncertainty which is aroused in children is a consequence of the parents' frustrations in marriage, in work, and in citizenship. Thus, the sense of autonomy in the child (a sense richly fostered in American childhood in general) must be backed up by the preservation in economic and political life of a high sense of autonomy and of self-reliance.

Social organization assigns with the power of government certain privileges of leadership and certain obligations of conduct; while it imposes on the ruled certain obligations of compliance and certain privileges of remaining autonomous and self-determining. Where this whole matter becomes blurred, however, the matter of individual autonomy becomes an issue of mental health, as well as one of economic reorientation. Where large numbers of people have been prepared in childhood to expect from life a high degree of personal autonomy, pride, and opportunity, and then in later life find themselves ruled by superhuman organizations and machinery too intricate to understand, the result may be deep chronic disappointment not conducive to healthy personalities willing to grant each other a measure of autonomy. All great nations (and all the small ones) are increasingly challenged by the complication and mechanization of modern life, and are being enveloped in the problems of the organization of larger units, larger spheres, and larger interdependencies which by necessity redefine the role of the individual. It is important for the spirit of this country, as it is for that of the world, that an increased consciousness of equality and individuality may grow out of the necessity for divided function within the increasing complexity of organization; for otherwise a number of fears are aroused which find expression in anxiety on a large scale, often individually slight and hardly conscious, but nevertheless strangely upsetting to people who seemingly, on the surface, have what they want or what they seem to have a right to expect. Besides irrational fears of losing one's autonomy—"don't fence me in"—there are fears of being sabotaged in one's free will by inner enemies; of being restricted and constricted in one's autonomous initiative; and, paradoxically enough, at the same time of not being completely controlled enough, of not being told what to do. While many such fears are, of course, based on the realistic appraisal of dangers inherent in complex social organizations and in the struggle for power, safety, and security, they seem to contribute to psychoneurotic and psychosomatic disturbances on the one hand, and, on the other, to the easy acceptance of slogans which seem to promise alleviation of conditions by excessive and irrational conformity.

INITIATIVE VERSUS GUILT

I

Having found a firm solution of his problem of autonomy, the child of four and five is faced with the next step—and with the next crisis. Being firmly convinced that he *is* a person, the child must now find out *what kind* of a person he is going to be. And here he hitches his wagon to nothing less than a star: he wants to be like his parents, who to him appear very powerful and very beautiful, although quite unreasonably dangerous. He "identifies with them," he plays with the idea of how it would be to be them. Three

THE HEALTHY PERSONALITY

strong developments help at this stage, yet also serve to bring the child closer to his crisis: (1) he learns to *move around* more freely and more violently and therefore establishes a wider and, so it seems to him, an unlimited radius of goals; (2) his sense of *language* becomes perfected to the point where he understands and can ask about many things just enough to misunderstand them thoroughly; and (3) both language and locomotion permit him to expand his *imagination* over so many things that he cannot avoid frightening himself with what he himself has dreamed and thought up. Nevertheless, out of all this he must emerge with a sense of *unbroken initiative* as a basis for a high and yet realistic sense of ambition and independence.

One may ask here—one may, indeed—what are the criteria for such an unbroken sense of initiative? The criteria for all the senses discussed here are the same: a crisis, beset with fears, or at least a general anxiousness or tension, seems to be resolved, in that the child suddenly seems to "grow together" both psychologically and physically. He seems to be "more himself," more loving and relaxed and brighter in his judgment (such as it is at this stage). Most of all, he seems to be, as it were, self-activated; he is in the free possession of a certain surplus of energy which permits him to forget failures quickly and to approach what seems desirable (even if it also seems dangerous) with undiminished and better aimed effort. In this way the child and his parents face the next crisis much better prepared.

We are now approaching the end of the third year, when walking is getting to be a thing of ease, or vigor. The books tell us that a child "can walk" much before this; but from the point of view of personality development he cannot really walk as long as he is only able to accomplish the feat more or less well, with more or fewer props, for short spans of time. He has made walking and running an item in his sphere of mastery when gravity is felt to be *within,* when he can forget that he is doing the walking and instead can find out what he can do *with it*. Only then do his legs become an unconscious part of him instead of being an external and still unreliable ambulatory appendix. Only then will he find out with advantage what he now *may* do, along with what he *can* do.

To look back: the first way-station was prone relaxation. The trust based on the experience that the basic mechanisms of breathing, digesting, sleeping, and so forth have a consistent and familiar relation to the foods and comforts offered gives zest to the developing ability to raise oneself to a sitting and then to a standing position. The second way-station (accomplished only toward the end of the second year) is that of being able to sit not only securely but, as it were, untiringly, a feat which permits the muscle system gradually to be used for finer discrimination and for more autonomous ways of selecting and discarding, of piling things up—and of throwing them away with a bang.

The third way-station finds the child able to move independently and vigorously. He is ready to visualize himself as being as big as the perambulating grownups. He begins to make comparisons and is apt to develop untiring curiosity about differences in sizes in general, and sexual differences in particular. He tries to comprehend possible future roles, or at any rate to understand what roles are worth imitating. More immediately, he can now associate with those of his own age. Under the guidance of older children or special women guardians, he gradually enters into the infantile politics of nursery school, street corner, and barnyard. His learning now is eminently intrusive and vigorous: it leads away from his own limitations and into future possibilities.

The *intrusive mode*, dominating much of the behavior of this stage, characterizes a variety of configurationally "similar" activities and fantasies. These include the intrusion into other bodies by physical attack; the intrusion into other people's ears and minds by aggressive talking; the intrusion into space by vigorous locomotion; the intrusion into the unknown by consuming curiosity.

This is also the stage of infantile sexual curiosity, genital excitability, and occasional preoccupation and overconcern with sexual matters. This "genitality" is, of course, rudimentary, a mere promise of things to come; often it is not particularly noticeable as such. If not specifically provoked into precocious manifestation by especially strict and pointed prohibitions ("if you touch it, the doctor will cut it off") or special customs (such as sex play in groups), it is apt to lead to no more than a series of fascinating experiences which soon become frightening and pointless enough to be repressed. This leads to the ascendancy of that human specialty which Freud called the "latency" period, that is, the long delay separating infantile sexuality (which in animals is followed by maturity) and physical sexual maturation.

The sexual orientation of the boy is focused on the phallus and its sensations, purposes, and meanings. While erections undoubtedly occur earlier (either reflexively or in response to things and people who make the child feel intensively), a focused interest may now develop in the genitalia of both sexes, as well as an urge to perform playful sex acts, or at least acts of sexual investigation. The increased locomotor mastery and the pride in being big now and *almost* as good as father and mother receives its severest setback in the clear fact that in the genital sphere one is vastly inferior; furthermore, it receives an additional setback in the fact that not even in the distant future is one ever going to be father in sexual relationship to mother, or mother in sexual relationship to father. The very deep emotional consequences of this insight and the magic fears associated with it make up what Freud has called the oedipus complex.

Psychoanalysis verifies the simple conclusion that boys attach their first genital affection to the maternal adults who have otherwise given comfort to their bodies and that they develop their first sexual rivalry against the persons who are the sexual owners of those maternal persons. The little girl, in turn, becomes attached to her father and other important men and jealous of her mother, a development which may cause her much anxiety, for it seems to block her retreat to that selfsame mother, while it makes the mother's disapproval ever so much more magically dangerous because unconsciously "deserved."

Girls often have a difficult time at this stage, because they observe sooner or later that, although their locomotor, mental, and social intrusiveness is increased equally with, and is as adequate as, that of the boys, thus permitting them to become perfect tomboys, they lack one item: the penis; and with it, important prerogatives in some cultures and classes. While the boy has this visible, erectable, and comprehensible organ to which he can attach dreams of adult bigness, the girl's clitoris only poorly sustains dreams of sexual equality. She does not even have breasts as analogously tangible tokens of her future, her maternal drives are relegated to play fantasy or baby tending. On the other hand, where mothers dominate households, the boy, in turn, can develop a sense of inadequacy because he learns at this stage that while a boy can do well in play and work, he will never boss the house, the mother, and the older sisters. His mother and sisters, in fact, might get even with him for vast doubts in themselves by making him feel that a boy (with his snails and puppy-dog tails) is really an inferior if not a repulsive creature. Both the girl and the boy are now extraordinarily appreciative of any convincing promise of the fact that someday they will be as good as father or mother—perhaps better; and they are grateful for sexual enlightenment, a little at a time, and patiently repeated at intervals. Where the necessities of economic life and the simplicity of its social plan make the male and female roles and their specific powers and rewards comprehensible, the early misgivings about sexual differences are, of course, more easily integrated in the culture's design for the differentiation of sexual roles.

This stage adds to the inventory of basic social modalities in both sexes that of "making" in the older and today slangier sense of "being on the make." There is no simpler, stronger word to match the social modalities previously enumerated. The word suggests enjoyment of competition, insistence on goal, pleasure of conquest. In the boy the emphasis remains on "making" by head-on attack; in the girl it may change to "making" by making herself attractive and endearing. The child thus develops the prerequisites for *masculine* and *feminine initiative,* that is, for the selection of social goals and perseverance in approaching them. Thus the stage is all set for entrance into life, except that life must first be school life. The child here must repress or forget many of his fondest hopes and most energetic wishes, while his exuberant imagination is tamed and he learns the necessary self-restraint and the necessary interest in impersonal things—even the three R's. This often demands a change of personality that is sometimes too drastic for the good of the child. This change is not only a result of education but also of an inner reorientation, and it is based on a biological fact (the delay of sexual maturation) and a psychological one (the repression of childhood wishes). For those sinister oedipal wishes (so simply and so trustingly expressed in the boy's assurance that he will marry mother and make her proud of him and in the girl's that she will marry father and take much better care of him), in consequence of vastly increased imagination and, as it were, the intoxication of increased locomotor powers, seem to lead to secret fantasies of terrifying proportions. The consequence is a deep sense of *guilt*—a strange sense, for it forever seems to imply that the individual has committed crimes and deeds which, after all, were not only not committed but also would have been biologically quite impossible.

While the struggle for autonomy at its worst concentrated on keeping rivals out, and was therefore more an expression of *jealous rage* most often directed against encroachments by *younger* siblings, initiative brings with it *anticipatory rivalry* with those who were there first and who may therefore occupy with their superior equipment the field toward which one's initiative is directed. Jealousy and rivalry, those often embittered and yet essentially futile attempts at demarcating a sphere of unquestioned privilege, now come to a climax in a final contest for a favored position with one of the parents; the inevitable and necessary failure leads to guilt and anxiety. The child indulges in fantasies of being a giant and a tiger, but in his dreams he runs in terror for dear life. This, then, is the stage of fear for life and limb, including the fear of losing (or on the part of the girl the conviction that she may have lost) the male genital as punishment for the fantasies attached to infantile genital excitement.

All of this may seem strange to readers who have only seen the sunnier side of childhood and have not recognized the potential powerhouse of destructive drives which can be aroused and temporarily buried at this stage, only to contribute later to the inner arsenal of a destructiveness so ready to be used when opportunity provokes it. By using the words "potential," "provoke" and "opportunity," I mean to emphasize that there is little in these inner developments which cannot be harnessed to constructive and peaceful initiative if only we learn to understand the conflicts and anxieties of childhood and the importance of childhood for mankind. But if we should choose to overlook or belittle the phenomena of childhood, or to regard them as "cute" (even as the individual forgets the best and the worst dreams of his childhood), we shall forever overlook one of the eternal sources of human anxiety and strife.

II

It is at this stage of initiative that the great governor of initiative, namely, *conscience,* becomes firmly established. Only as a dependent does man develop conscience, that dependence on himself which makes him, in turn, dependable; and only when thoroughly dependable with regard to a number of fundamental values can he become independent and teach and develop tradition.

The child now feels not only ashamed when found out but also afraid of being found out. He now hears, as it were, God's voice without seeing God. Moreover, he begins automatically to feel guilty even for mere thoughts and for deeds which nobody has watched. This is the cornerstone of morality in the individual sense. But from the point of view of mental health, we must point out that if this great achievement is overburdened by all too eager adults, it can be bad for the spirit and for morality itself. For the conscience of the child *can* be primitive, cruel, and uncompromising, as may be observed in instances where children learn to constrict themselves to the point of over-all inhibition; where they develop an obedience more literal than the one the parent wishes to exact; or where they develop deep regressions and lasting resentments because the parents themselves do not seem to live up to the new conscience which they have fostered in the child. One of the deepest conflicts in life is the hate for a parent who served as the model and the executor of the conscience but who (in some form) was found trying to "get away with" the very transgressions which the child can no longer tolerate in himself. These transgressions often are the natural outcome of the existing inequality between parent and child. Often, however, they represent a thoughtless exploitation of such inequality; with the result that the child comes to feel that the whole matter is not one of universal goodness but of arbitrary power. The suspiciousness and evasiveness which is thus mixed in with the all-or-nothing quality of the superego, that organ of tradition, makes moralistic man a great potential danger to himself and to his fellow men. It is as if morality, to him, became synonymous with vindictiveness and with the suppression of others.

It is necessary to point to the source of such moralism (not to be mistaken for morality) in the child of this age because infantile

THE HEALTHY PERSONALITY

moralism is a stage to be lived through and worked through. The consequences of the guilt aroused at this stage (guilt expressed in a deep-seated conviction that the child as such, or drive as such, is essentially bad) often do not show until much later, when conflicts over initiative may find expression in a self-restriction which keeps an individual from living up to his inner capacities or to the powers of his imagination and feeling (if not in relative sexual impotence or frigidity). All of this, of course, may in turn be "overcompensated" in a great show of tireless initiative, in a quality of "go-at-itiveness" at all cost. Many adults feel that their worth as people consists entirely in *what they are doing*, or rather in *what they are going to do next*, and not in what they are, as individuals. The strain consequently developed in their bodies, which are always "on the go," with the engine racing, even at moments of rest, is a powerful contribution to the much-discussed psychosomatic diseases of our time.

Pathology, however, is only the sign that valuable human resources are being neglected, that they have been neglected first of all in childhood. The problem is again one of mutual regulation. Where the child, now so ready to overrestrict himself, can gradually develop a sense of responsibility, where he can gain some simple feeling for the institutions, functions, and roles which will permit him to anticipate his responsible participation as an adult, he will soon find pleasurable accomplishment in wielding miniature tools and weapons, in manipulating meaningful toys, and in taking care of himself—and of younger children.

For such is the wisdom of the ground plan that at no time is the individual more ready to learn quickly and avidly, to become big in the sense of sharing obligation, discipline, and performance rather than power, in the sense of *making things, instead of "making" people*, than during this period of his development. He is also eager and able to *make things together*, to combine with other children for the purpose of constructing and planning, instead of trying to boss and coerce them; and he is able and willing to profit fully by the association with teachers and ideal prototypes.

Parents often do not realize why some children suddenly seem to think less of them and seem to attach themselves to teachers, to the parents of other children, or to people representing occupations which the child can grasp: firemen and policemen, gardeners and plumbers. The point is that children do not wish to be reminded of the principal inequality with the parent of the same sex. They remain identified wtih this same parent; but for the present they look for opportunities where superficial identification seems to promise a field of initiative without too much conflict or guilt.

Often, however (and this seems more typical of the American home than of any other in the world), the child can be guided by the parent himself into a second, a more realistic identification based on the spirit of equality experienced in doing things together. In connection with comprehensible technical tasks, a companionship may develop between father and son, an experience of essential *equality in worth,* in spite of the *inequality in time schedules.* Such companionship is a lasting treasure not only for parent and child but for mankind, which so sorely needs an alleviation of all those hidden hatreds which stem from the exploitation of weakness because of mere size or schedule.

Only a combination of early prevention and alleviation of hatred and guilt in the growing being, and the consequent handling of hatred in the free collaboration of people who feel *equal in worth although different in kind or function or age,* permits a peaceful cultivation of initiative, a truly free sense of enterprise. And the word "enterprise" was deliberately chosen. For a comparative view of child training suggests that it is the prevalent economic ideal, or some of its modifications, which is transmitted to the child at the time when, in identification with his parent, he applies the dreams of early childhood to the as yet dim goals of an active adult life.

Industry versus Inferiority

I

One might say that personality at the first stage crystallizes around the conviction "I am what I am given," and that of the second, "I am what I will." The third can be characterized by "I am what I can imagine I will be." We must now approach the fourth: "I am what I learn." The child now wants to be shown how to get busy with something and how to be busy with others.

This trend, too, starts much earlier, especially in some children. They want to watch how things are done and to try doing them. If they are lucky they live near barnyards or on streets around busy people and around many other children of all ages, so that they can watch and try, observe and participate as their capacities and their initiative grow in tentative spurts. But now it is time to *go to school*. In all cultures, at this stage, children receive some systematic instruction, although it is by no means always in the kind of school which literate people must organize around teachers who have learned how to teach literacy. In preliterate people much is learned from adults who become teachers by acclamation rather than by appointment; and very much is learned from older children. What is learned in more primitive surroundings is related to the basic skills of *technology* which are developed as the child gets ready to handle the utensils, the tools, and the weapons used by the big people: he enters the technology of his tribe very gradually but also very directly. More literate people, with more specialized careers, must prepare the child by teaching him things which first of all make him literate. He is then given the widest possible basic education for the greatest number of possible careers. The greater the specialization, the more indistinct the goal of initiative becomes; and the more complicated the social reality, the vaguer the father's and mother's role in it. Between childhood and adulthood, then, our children go to school; and school seems to be a world all by itself, with its own goals and limitations, its achievements and disappointments.

Grammar-school education has swung back and forth between the extreme of making early school life an extension of grim adulthood by emphasizing self-restraint and a strict sense of duty in doing what one is *told* to do, and the other extreme of making it an extension of the natural tendency in childhood to find out by playing, to learn what one must do by doing steps which one *likes* to do. Both methods work for some children at times but not for all children at all times. The first trend, if carried to the extreme, exploits a tendency on the part of the preschool and grammar-school child to become entirely dependent on prescribed duties. He thus learns much that is absolutely necessary and he develops an unshakable sense of duty; but he may never unlearn again an unnecessary and costly self-restraint with which he may later make his own life and other people's lives miserable, and in fact spoil his own children's natural desire to learn and to work. The second trend, when carried to an extreme, leads not only to the well-known popular objection that children do not learn anything any more but also to such feelings in children as are expressed in the by now famous remark of a metropolitan child who apprehensively asked one morning: "Teacher, *must* we do today what we *want* to do?" Nothing could better express the fact that children at this age *do* like to be mildly but firmly coerced into the adventure of finding out that one can learn to accomplish things which one would never have thought of by oneself, things which owe their attractiveness to the very fact that they are *not* the product of play and fantasy but the product of reality, practicality, and logic; things which thus provide a token sense of participation in the real world of adults. In discussions of this kind it is common to say that one must steer a middle course between play and work, between childhood and adulthood, between old-fashioned and progressive education. It is always easy (and it seems entirely satisfactory to one's critics) to say that one plans to steer a middle course, but in practice it often leads to a course charted by avoidances rather than by zestful goals. Instead of pursuing, then, a course which merely avoids the extremes of easy play or hard work, it may be worth while to consider what play is and what work is, and then learn to dose and alternate each in such a way that *play is play and work is work*. Let us review briefly what play may mean at various stages of childhood and adulthood.

The adult plays for purposes of recreation. He steps out of his reality into imaginary realities for which he has made up arbitrary but nonetheless binding rules. But an adult rarely gets away with being a playboy. Only he who works shall play—if, indeed, he can relax his competitiveness.

The playing child, then, poses a problem: whoever does not work shall not play. Therefore, to be tolerant of the child's play the adult must invent theories which show either that childhood play is really the child's work or that it does not count. The most popular theory, and the easiest on the observer, is that the child is nobody yet and that the nonsense of his play reflects it. According to Spencer, play uses up surplus energy in the young of a number of mammalians who do not need to feed or protect themselves because their parents do it for them. Others say that play is either preparation for the future or a method of working off past emotion, a means of finding imaginary relief for past frustrations.

It is true that the content of individual play often proves to be the infantile way of thinking over difficult experiences and of *restoring a sense of mastery*, comparable to the way in which we repeat, in ruminations and in endless talk, in daydreams and in dreams during sleep, experiences that have been too much for us. This is the rationale for play observation, play diagnosis, and play therapy. In watching a child play, the trained observer can get an impression of what it is the child is "thinking over," and what faulty logic, what emotional dead end he may be caught in. As a diagnostic tool such observation has become indispensable.

The small world of manageable toys is a harbor which the child establishes, returning to it when he needs to overhaul his ego. But the thing-world has its own laws: it may resist rearrangement or it may simply break to pieces; it may prove to belong to somebody else and be subject to confiscation by superiors. Thus, play may seduce the child into an unguarded expression of dangerous themes and attitudes which arouse anxiety and lead to sudden *disruption of play*. This is the counterpart, in waking life, of the anxiety dream; it can keep children from trying to play just as the fear of night terror can keep them from going to sleep. If thus frightened or disappointed, the child may regress into daydreaming, thumb sucking, masturbating. On the other hand, if the first use of the thing-world is successful and guided properly, the *pleasure of mastering toy things* becomes associated with the *mastery of the conflicts* which were projected on them and with the *prestige* gained through such mastery.

Finally, at nursery-school age playfulness reaches into the world *shared with others*. At first these others are treated as things; they are inspected, run into, or forced to "be horsie." Learning is necessary in order to discover what potential play content can be admitted only to fantasy or only to play by and with oneself; what content can be successfully represented only in the world of toys and small things; and what content can be shared with others and even forced upon them.

What is infantile play, then? We saw that it is not the equivalent of adult play, that it is not recreation. The playing adult steps sideward into another, an artificial reality; the playing child advances forward to new stages of *real mastery*. This new mastery is not restricted to the technical mastery of toys and *things*; it also includes an infantile way of mastering *experience* by meditating, experimenting, planning, and sharing.

II

While all children at times need to be left alone in solitary play (or later in the company of books and radio, motion pictures and video, all of which, like the fairy tales of old, at least *sometimes* seem to convey what fits the needs of the infantile mind), and while all children need their hours and days of make-believe in games, they all, sooner or later, become dissatisfied and disgruntled without a sense of being useful, without a sense of being able to make things and make them well and even perfectly: this is what I call the *sense of industry*. Without this, the best entertained child soon acts exploited. It is as if he knows and his society knows that now that he is psychologically already a rudimentary parent, he must begin to be somewhat of a worker and potential provider before becoming a biological parent. With the oncoming latency period, then, the normally advanced child forgets, or rather "sublimates" (that is, applies to more useful pursuits and approved goals) the necessity of "making" people by direct attack or the desire to become father or mother in a hurry: he now learns to win recognition by *producing things*. He develops industry, that is, he adjusts himself to the inorganic laws of the tool world. He can become an eager and absorbed unit of a productive situation. To bring a productive situation to completion is an aim which gradually supersedes the whims and wishes of his idiosyncratic drives and personal disappointments. As he once untiringly strove to walk well, and to throw things away well, he now wants to make things well. He develops the pleasure of *work completion* by steady attention and persevering diligence.

The danger at this stage is the development of a sense of *inadequacy and inferiority*. This may be caused by an insufficient solution of the preceding conflict: he may still want his mummy more than knowledge; he may still rather be the baby at home than the big child in school; he still compares himself with his father, and the comparison arouses a sense of guilt as well as a sense of anatomical inferiority. Family life (small family) may not have prepared him for school life, or school life may fail to sustain the promises of earlier stages in that nothing that he has learned to do well already seems to count one bit with the teacher. And then, again, he may be potentially able to excel in ways which are dormant and which, if not evoked now, may develop late or never.

Good teachers, healthy teachers, relaxed teachers, teachers who feel trusted and respected by the community, understand all this and can guide it. They know how to alternate play and work, games and study. They know how to recognize special efforts, how to encourage special gifts. They also know how to give a child time, and how to handle those children to whom school, for a while, is not important and rather a matter to endure than to enjoy; or the child to whom, for a while, other children are much more important than the teacher.

Good parents, healthy parents, relaxed parents feel a need to make their children trust their teachers, and therefore to have teachers who can be trusted. It is not my job here to discuss teacher selection, teacher training, and the status and payment of teachers in their communities—all of which is of direct importance for the development and the maintenance in children of a *sense of industry* and of a positive identification with those who *know* things and know how to *do* things. Again and again I have observed in the lives of especially gifted and inspired people that one teacher, somewhere, was able to kindle the flame of hidden talent.

The fact that the majority of teachers in the elementary schools are women must be considered here in passing, because it often leads to a conflict with the "ordinary" boy's masculine identification, as if knowledge were feminine, action masculine. Both boys and girls are apt to agree with Bernard Shaw's statement that those who can, do, while those who cannot, teach. The selection and training of teachers, then, is vital for the avoidance of the dangers which can befall the individual at this stage. There is, first, the above-mentioned sense of inferiority, the feeling that one will never be any good—a problem which calls for the type of teacher who knows how to emphasize what a child *can* do, and who knows a psychiatric problem when she sees one. Second, there is the danger of the child's identifying too strenuously with a too virtuous teacher or becoming the teacher's pet. What we shall presently refer to as his sense of identity can remain prematurely fixed on being nothing but a good little worker or a good little helper, which may not be all he *could* be. Third, there is the danger (probably the most common one) that throughout the long years of going to school he will never acquire the enjoyment of work and the pride of doing at least one kind of thing well. This is particularly of concern in relation to that part of the nation who do not complete what schooling is at their disposal. It is always easy to say that they are born that way; that there must be less educated people as background for the superior ones; that the market needs and even fosters such people for its many simple and unskilled tasks. But from the point of view of the healthy personality (which, as we proceed, must now include the aspect of playing a constructive role in a healthy society), we must consider those who have had just enough schooling to appreciate what more fortunate people are learning to do but who, for one reason or another, have lacked inner or outer support of their stick-to-itiveness.

It will have been noted that, regarding the period of a developing sense of industry, I have referred to *outer hindrances* but not to any crisis (except a deferred inferiority crisis) coming from the inventory of basic human drives. This stage differs from the others in that it does not consist of a swing from a violent inner upheaval to a new mastery. The reason why Freud called it the latency stage is that violent drives are normally dormant at that time. But it is only a lull before the storm of puberty.

On the other hand, this is socially a most decisive stage: since industry involves doing things beside and with others, a first sense of *division of labor* and of *equality of opportunity* develops at this time. When a child begins to feel that it is the color of his skin, the background of his parents, or the cost of his clothes rather than his wish and his will to learn which will decide his social worth, lasting harm may ensue for the *sense of identity*, to which we must now turn.

Identity versus Identity Diffusion

I

With the establishment of a good relationship to the world of skills and to those who teach and share the new skills, childhood proper comes to an end. Youth begins. But in puberty and adolescence all sameness and continuities relied on earlier are questioned again because of a rapidity of body growth which equals that of early childhood and because of the entirely new addition of physical genital maturity. The growing and developing young people, faced with this physiological revolution within them, are now primarily concerned with attempts at consolidating their social roles. They are sometimes morbidly, often curiously, preoccupied with what they appear to be in the eyes of others as compared with what they feel they are and with the question of how to connect the earlier cultivated roles and skills with the ideal prototypes of the day. In their search for a new sense of continuity and sameness, some adolescents have to refight many of the crises of earlier years, and they are never ready to install lasting idols and ideals as guardians of a final identity.

The integration now taking place in the form of the ego identity is more than the sum of the childhood identifications. It is the inner capital accrued from all those experiences of each successive stage, when successful identification led to a successful alignment of the individual's *basic drives* with his *endowment* and his *opportunities*. In psychoanalysis we ascribe such successful alignments to "ego synthesis"; I have tried to demonstrate that the ego values accrued in childhood culminate in what I have called *a sense of ego identity*. The sense of ego identity, then, is the accrued confidence that one's ability to maintain inner sameness and continuity (one's ego in the psychological sense) is matched by the sameness and continuity of one's meaning for others. Thus, self-esteem, confirmed at the end of each major crisis, grows to be a conviction that one is learning effective steps toward a tangible future, that one is developing a defined personality within a social reality which one understands. The growing child must, at every step, derive a vitalizing sense of reality from the awareness that his individual way of mastering experience is a successful variant of the way other people around him master experience and recognize such mastery.

In this, children cannot be fooled by empty praise and condescending encouragement. They may have to accept artificial bolstering of their self-esteem in lieu of something better, but what I call their accruing ego identity gains real strength only from wholehearted and consistent recognition of real accomplishment, that is, achievement that has meaning in their culture. On the other hand, should a child feel that the environment tries to deprive him too radically of all the forms of expression which permit him to develop and to integrate the next step in his ego identity, he will resist with the astonishing strength encountered in animals who are suddenly forced to defend their lives. Indeed, in the social jungle of human existence, there is no feeling of being alive without a sense of ego identity. To understand this would be to understand the trouble of adolescents better, especially the trouble of all those who cannot just be "nice" boys and girls, but are desperately seeking for a satisfactory sense of belonging, be it in cliques and gangs here in our country or in inspiring mass movements in others.

Ego identity, then, develops out of a gradual integration of all identifications, but here, if anywhere, the whole has a different quality than the sum of its parts. Under favorable circumstances children have the nucleus of a separate identity in early life; often they must defend it against any pressure which would make them overidentify with one of their parents. This is difficult to learn from patients, because the neurotic ego has, by definition, fallen prey to overidentification and to faulty identifications with disturbed parents, a circumstance which isolated the small individual both from his budding identity and from his milieu. But we can study it profitably in the children of minority-group Americans who, having successfully graduated from a marked and well-guided stage of autonomy, enter the most decisive stage of American childhood: that of initiative and industry.

Minority groups of a lesser degree of Americanization (Negroes, Indians, Mexicans, and certain European groups) often are privileged in the enjoyment of a more sensual early childhood. Their crises come when their parents and teachers, losing trust in themselves and using sudden correctives in order to approach the vague but pervasive Anglo-Saxon ideal, create violent discontinuities; or where, indeed, the children themselves learn to disavow their sensual and overprotective mothers as temptations and a hindrance to the formation of a more American personality.

On the whole, it can be said that American schools successfully meet the challenge of training children of play-school age and of the elementary grades in a spirit of self-reliance and enterprise. Children of these ages seem remarkably free of prejudice and apprehension, preoccupied as they still are with growing and learning and with the new pleasures of association outside their families. This, to forestall the sense of individual inferiority, must lead to a hope for "industrial association," for equality with all those who apply themselves wholeheartedly to the same skills and adventures in learning. Many individual successes, on the other hand, only expose the now overly encouraged children of mixed backgrounds and somewhat deviant endowments to the shock of American adolescence: the standardization of individuality and the intolerance of "differences."

The emerging ego identity, then, bridges the early childhood stages, when the body and the parent images were given their specific meanings, and the later stages, when a variety of social roles becomes available and increasingly coercive. A lasting ego identity cannot begin to exist without the trust of the first oral stage; it cannot be completed without a promise of fulfillment which from the dominant image of adulthood reaches down into the baby's beginnings and which creates at every step an accruing sense of ego strength.

II

The danger of this stage is *identity diffusion*; as Biff puts it in Arthur Miller's *Death of a Salesman*, "I just can't take hold, Mom, I can't take hold of some kind of a life." Where such a dilemma is based on a strong previous doubt of one's ethnic and sexual identity, delinquent and outright psychotic incidents are not uncommon. Youth after youth, bewildered by some assumed role, a role forced on him by the inexorable standardization of American adolescence, runs away in one form or another; leaving schools and jobs, staying out all night, or withdrawing into bizarre and inaccessible moods. Once "delinquent," his greatest need and often his only salvation, is the refusal on the part of older friends, advisers, and judiciary personnel to type him further by pat diagnoses and social judgments which ignore the special dynamic conditions of adolescence. For if diagnosed and treated correctly, seemingly psychotic and criminal incidents do not in adolescence have the same fatal significance which they have at other ages. Yet many a youth, finding that the authorities expect him to be "a bum" or "a queer," or "off the beam," perversely obliges by becoming just that.

In general it is primarily the inability to settle on an occupational identity which disturbs young people. To keep themselves together they temporarily overidentify, to the point of apparent complete loss of identity, with the heroes of cliques and crowds. On the other hand, they become remarkably clannish, intolerant, and cruel in their exclusion of others who are "different," in skin color or cultural background, in tastes and gifts, and often in entirely petty aspects of dress and gesture arbitrarily selected as *the* signs of an in-grouper or out-grouper. It is important to understand (which does not mean condone or participate in) such intolerance as the necessary *defense against a sense of identity diffusion*, which is unavoidable at a time of life when the body changes its proportions radically, when genital maturity floods body and imagination with all manners of drives, when intimacy with the other sex approaches and is, on occasion, forced on the youngster, and when life lies before one with a variety of conflicting possibilities and choices. Adolescents help one another temporarily through such discomfort by forming cliques and by stereotyping themselves, their ideals, and their enemies.

It is important to understand this because it makes clear the appeal which simple and cruel totalitarian doctrines have on the minds of the youth of such countries and classes as have lost or are losing their group identities (feudal, agrarian, national, and so forth) in these times of world-wide industrialization, emancipation, and wider intercommunication. The dynamic quality of the tempestuous adolescences lived through in patriarchal and agrarian countries (countries which face the most radical changes in political structure and in economy) explains the fact that their young people find convincing and satisfactory identities in the simple totalitarian doctrines of race, class, or nation. Even though we may be forced to win wars against their leaders, we still are faced with the job of winning the peace with these grim youths by convincingly demonstrating to them (by living it) a democratic identity which can be strong and yet tolerant, judicious and still determined.

But it is increasingly important to understand this also in order to treat the intolerances of our adolescents at home with understanding and guidance rather than with verbal stereotypes or prohibitions. It is difficult to be tolerant if deep down you are not quite sure that you are a man (or a woman), that you will ever grow together again and be attractive, that you will be able to master your drives, that you really know who you are,[5] that you know what you want to be, that you know what you look like to others, and that you will know how to make the right decisions without, once for all, committing yourself to the wrong friend, sexual partner, leader, or career.

Democracy in a country like America poses special problems in that it insists on *self-made identities* ready to grasp many chances and ready to adjust to changing necessities of booms and busts, of peace and war, of migration and determined sedentary life. Our democracy, furthermore, must present the adolescent with ideals which can be shared by youths of many backgrounds and which emphasize autonomy in the form of independence and initiative in the form of enterprise. These promises, in turn, are not easy to fulfill in increasingly complex and centralized systems of economic and political organization, systems which, if geared to war, must automatically neglect the "self-made" identities of millions of individuals and put them where they are most needed. This is hard on many young Americans because their whole upbringing, and therefore the development of a healthy personality, depends on a certain degree of *choice*, a certain hope for an individual *chance*, and a certain conviction in freedom of *self-determination*.

We are speaking here not only of high privileges and lofty ideals but also of psychological necessities. Psychologically speaking, a gradually accruing ego identity is the only safeguard against the *anarchy of drives* as well as the *autocracy of conscience*, that is, the cruel overconscientiousness which is the inner residue in the adult of his past inequality in regard to his parent. Any loss of a sense of identity exposes the individual to his own childhood con-

---

[5] On the wall of a cowboys' bar in the wide-open West hangs a saying: "I ain't what I ought to be, I ain't what I'm going to be, but I ain't what I was."

flicts—as could be observed, for example, in the neuroses of World War II among men and women who could not stand the general dislocation of their careers or a variety of other special pressures of war. Our adversaries, it seems, understand this. Their psychological warfare consists in the determined continuation of general conditions which permit them to indoctrinate mankind within their orbit with the simple and yet for them undoubtedly effective identities of class warfare and nationalism, while they know that the psychology, as well as the economy, of free enterprise and of self-determination is stretched to the breaking point under the conditions of long-drawn-out cold and lukewarm war. It is clear, therefore, that we must bend every effort to present our young men and women with the tangible and trustworthy promise of opportunities for a rededication to the life for which the country's history, as well as their own childhood, has prepared them. Among the tasks of national defense, this one must not be forgotten.

I have referred to the relationship of the problem of trust to matters of adult faith; to that of the problem of autonomy to matters of adult independence in work and citizenship. I have pointed to the connection between a sense of initiative and the kind of enterprise sanctioned in the economic system, and between the sense of industry and a culture's technology. In searching for the social values which guide identity, one confronts the problem of aristocracy, in its widest possible sense which connotes the conviction that the best people rule and that that rule develops the best in people. In order not to become cynically or apathetically lost, young people in search of an identity must somewhere be able to convince themselves that those who succeed thereby shoulder the obligation of being the best, that is, of personifying the nation's ideals. In this country, as in any other, we have those successful types who become the cynical representatives of the "inside track," the "bosses" of impersonal machinery. In a culture once pervaded with the value of the self-made man, a special danger ensues from the idea of a synthetic personality: as if you are what you can appear to be, or as if you are what you can buy. This can be counteracted only by a system of education that transmits values and goals which determinedly aspire beyond mere "functioning" and "making the grade."

Three Stages of Adulthood

Intimacy and Distantiation vs. Self-Absorption

When childhood and youth come to an end, life, so the saying goes, begins: by which we mean work or study for a specified career, sociability with the other sex, and in time, marriage and a family of one's own. But it is only after a reasonable sense of identity has been established that real *intimacy* with the other sex (or, for that matter, with any other person or even with oneself) is possible. Sexual intimacy is only part of what I have in mind, for it is obvious that sexual intimacies do not always wait for the ability to develop a true and mutual psychological intimacy with another person. The youth who is not sure of his identity shies away from interpersonal intimacy; but the surer he becomes of himself, the more he seeks it in the form of friendship, combat, leadership, love, and inspiration. There is a kind of adolescent attachment between boy and girl which is often mistaken either for mere sexual attraction or for love. Except where the mores demand heterosexual behavior, such attachment is often devoted to an attempt at arriving at a definition of one's identity by talking things over endlessly, by confessing what one feels like and what the other seems like, and by discussing plans, wishes, and expectations. Where a youth does not accomplish such intimate relation with others—and, I would add, with his own inner resources—in late adolescence or early adulthood, he may either isolate himself and find, at best, highly stereotyped and formal interpersonal relations (formal in the sense of lacking in spontaneity, warmth, and real exchange of fellowship), or he must seek them in repeated attempts and repeated failures. Unfortunately, many young people marry under such circumstances, hoping to find themselves in finding one another; but alas, the early obligation to act in a defined way, as mates and as parents, disturbs them in the completion of this work on themselves. Obviously, a change of mate is rarely the answer, but rather some wisely guided insight into the fact that the condition of a true twoness is that one must first become oneself.

The counterpart of intimacy is *distantiation*: the readiness to repudiate, to isolate, and, if necessary, to destroy those forces and people whose essence seems dangerous to one's own. This more mature and more efficient repudiation (it is utilized and exploited in politics and in war) is an outgrowth of the blinder prejudices which during the struggle for an identity differentiate sharply and cruelly between the familiar and the foreign. At first, intimate, competitive, and combative relations are experienced with and against the selfsame people. Gradually, a polarization occurs along the lines of the competitive encounter, the sexual embrace, and various forms of incisive combat.

Freud was once asked what he thought a normal person should be able to do well. The questioner probably expected a complicated, a "deep" answer. But Freud simply said, "*Lieben und arbeiten*" ("to love and to work"). It pays to ponder on this simple formula; it gets deeper as you think about it. For when Freud said "love," he meant the expansiveness of generosity as well as genital love; when he said love *and* work, he meant a general work productiveness which would not preoccupy the individual to the extent that his right or capacity to be a sexual and a loving being would be lost.

Psychoanalysis has emphasized *genitality* as one of the chief signs of a healthy personality. Genitality is the potential capacity to develop orgastic potency in relation to a loved partner of the opposite sex. Orgastic potency here means not the discharge of sex products in the sense of Kinsey's "outlets" but heterosexual mutuality, with full genital sensitivity and with an over-all discharge of tension from the whole body. This is a rather concrete way of saying something about a process which we really do not understand. But the idea clearly is that the experience of the climactic mutuality of orgasm provides a supreme example of the mutual regulation of complicated patterns and in some way appeases the potential rages caused by the daily evidence of the oppositeness of male and female, of fact and fancy, of love and hate, of work and play. Satisfactory sex relations make sex less obsessive and sadistic control superfluous. But here the prescription of psychiatry faces overwhelming inner prejudices and situational limitations in parts of the population whose sense of identity is based on the complete subordination of sexuality and, indeed, sensuality to a life of toil, duty, and worship. Here only gradual frank discussion can clarify the respective dangers of traditional rigidity and abrupt or merely superficial change.

Generativity vs. Stagnation

The problem of genitality is intimately related to the seventh criterion of mental health, which concerns parenthood. Sexual mates who find, or are on the way to finding, true genitality in their relations will soon wish (if, indeed, developments wait for the express wish) to combine their personalities and energies in the production and care of common offspring. The pervasive development underlying this wish I have termed *generativity*, because it concerns the establishment (by way of genitality and genes) of the next generation. No other fashionable term, such as creativity or productivity, seems to me to convey the necessary idea.[6] Generativity is primarily the interest in establishing and guiding the next generation, although there are people who, from misfortune or because of special and genuine gifts in other directions, do not apply this drive to offspring but to other forms of altruistic concern and of creativity, which may absorb their kind of parental responsibility. The principal thing is to realize that this is a stage of the growth of the healthy personality and that where such enrichment fails altogether, regression from generativity to an obsessive need for pseudo intimacy takes place, often with a pervading sense of stagnation and interpersonal impoverishment. Individuals who do not develop generativity often begin to indulge themselves as if they were their own one and only child. The mere fact of having or even wanting children does not of course involve generativity; in fact the majority of young parents seen in child-guidance work suffer, it seems, from the retardation of or inability to develop this stage. The reasons are often to be found in early childhood impressions; in faulty identifications with parents; in excessive self-love based on a too strenuously self-made personality; and finally (and here we return to the beginnings) in the lack of some faith, some "belief in the species," which would make a child appear to be a welcome trust of the community.

[6] The same is true of "parenthood"—an all too concrete term which, in quotations from this paper, is often used as a replacement for the seemingly more obscure word "generativity."

Integrity vs. Despair and Disgust

Only he who in some way has taken care of things and people and has adapted himself to the triumphs and disappointments of being, by necessity, the originator of others and the generator of things and ideas—only he may gradually grow the fruit of the seven stages. I know no better word for it than *integrity*. Lacking a clear definition, I shall point to a few attributes of this state of mind. It is the acceptance of one's own and only life cycle and of the people who have become significant to it as something that had to be and that, by necessity, permitted of no substitutions. It thus means a new different love of one's parents, free of the wish that they should have been different, and an acceptance of the fact that one's life is one's own responsibility. It is a sense of comradeship with men and women of distant times and of different pursuits, who have created orders and objects and sayings conveying human dignity and love. Although aware of the relativity of all the various life styles which have given meaning to human striving, the possessor of integrity is ready to defend the dignity of his own life style against all physical and economic threats. For he knows that an individual life is the accidental coincidence of but one life cycle with but one segment of history; and that for him all human integrity stands and falls with the one style of integrity of which he partakes.

This, then, is a beginning for a formulation of integrity based on clinical and anthropological experience: it is here, above all else, where each reader and each study group must continue to develop in his or its own terms what I have gropingly begun in mine. But I can add, clinically, that the lack or loss of this accrued ego integration is signified by despair and an often unconscious fear of death: the one and only life cycle is not accepted as the ultimate of life. Despair expresses the feeling that the time is short, too short for the attempt to start another life and to try out alternate roads to integrity. Such a despair is often hidden behind a show of disgust, a misanthropy, or a chronic contemptuous displeasure with particular institutions and particular people—a disgust and a displeasure which (where not allied with constructive ideas and a life of cooperation) only signify the individual's contempt of himself.

Ego integrity, therefore, implies an emotional integration which permits participation by followership as well as acceptance of the responsibility of leadership: both must be learned and practiced in religion and in politics, in the economic order and in technology, in aristocratic living, and in the arts and sciences.

Conclusion

At this point, I have come close to overstepping the limits (some will say I have long and repeatedly overstepped them) that separate psychology from ethics. But in suggesting that parents, teachers, and doctors must learn to discuss matters of human relations and of community life if they wish to discuss their children's needs and problems, I am only insisting on a few basic psychological insights, which I shall try to formulate briefly in conclusion.

We have, in the last few decades, learned more about the development and growth of the individual and about his motivations (especially unconscious motivations) than in the whole of human history before us (excepting, of course, the implicit wisdom expressed in the Bible or Shakespeare). Increasing numbers of us come to the conclusion that a child and even a baby—perhaps even the fetus—sensitively reflect the quality of the milieu in which they grow up. Children feel the tensions, insecurities, and rages of their parents even if they do not know their causes or witness their most overt manifestations. Therefore, you cannot fool children. To develop a child with a healthy personality, a parent must be a genuine person in a genuine milieu. This, today, is difficult because rapid changes in the milieu often make it hard to know whether one must be genuine *against* a changing milieu or whether one may hope for a chance to do one's bit in the way of bettering or stabilizing conditions. It is difficult, also, because in a changing world we are trying out—we must try out—new ways. To bring up children in personal and tolerant ways, based on information and education rather than on tradition, is a very new way: it exposes parents to many additional insecurities, which are temporarily increased by psychiatry (and by such products of psychiatric thinking as the present paper). Psychiatric thinking sees the world so full of dangers that it is hard to relax one's caution. I, too, have pointed to more dangers than to constructive avenues of action. Perhaps we can hope that this is only an indication that we are progressing through one stage of learning. When a man learns how to drive, he must become conscious of all the things that *might* happen; and he must learn to hear and see and read all the danger signals on his dashboard and along the road. Yet he may hope that some day, when he has outgrown this stage of learning, he will be able to glide with the greatest of ease through the landscape, enjoying the view with the confident knowledge that he will react to signs of mechanical trouble or road obstruction with automatic and effective speed.

We are now working toward, and fighting for, a world in which the harvest of democracy may be reaped. But if we want to make the world safe for democracy, we must first make democracy safe for the healthy child. In order to ban autocracy, exploitation, and inequality in the world, we must first realize that the first inequality in life is that of child and adult. Human childhood is long, so that parents and schools may have time to accept the child's personality in trust and to help it to be disciplined and human in the best sense known to us. This long childhood exposes the child to grave anxieties and to a lasting sense of insecurity which, if unduly and senselessly intensified, persists in the adult in the form of vague anxiety—anxiety which, in turn, contributes specifically to the tension of personal, political, and even international life. This long childhood exposes adults to the temptation of thoughtlessly and often cruelly exploiting the child's dependence by making him pay for the psychological debts owed to us by others, by making him the victim of tensions which we will not, or dare not, correct in ourselves or in our surroundings. We have learned not to stunt a child's growing body with child labor; we must now learn not to break his growing spirit by making him the victim of our anxieties.

If we will only learn to let live, the plan for growth is all there.

3

THE PROBLEM OF EGO IDENTITY

In a number of writings (Erikson, 1946, 1950a, 1950b, 1951a) I have been using the term *ego identity* to denote certain comprehensive gains which the individual, at the end of adolescence, must have derived from all of his preadult experience in order to be ready for the tasks of adulthood. My use of this term reflected the dilemma of a psychoanalyst who was led to a new concept not by theoretical preoccupation but rather through the expansion of his clinical awareness to other fields (social anthropology and comparative education) and through the expectation that such expansion would, in turn, profit clinical work. Recent clinical observations have, I feel, begun to bear out this expectation. I have, therefore, gratefully accepted two opportunities[1] offered me to restate and review the problem of identity. The present paper combines both of these presentations. The question before us is whether the concept of identity is essentially a psychosocial one, or deserves to be considered as a legitimate part of the psychoanalytic theory of the ego.

First a word about the term identity. As far as I know Freud used it only once in a more than incidental way, and then with a psychosocial connotation. It was when he tried to formulate his link to the Jewish people that he spoke of an "inner identity"[2]

First published in *The Journal of the American Psychoanalytic Association*, 4:56-121, 1956.

The research on which this paper is based is supported by a grant of the Field Foundation to the Riggs Center.

[1] At the 35th Anniversary Institute of the Judge Baker Guidance Center in Boston, May, 1953, and at the Midwinter Meetings of the American Psychoanalytic Association, New York, 1953.

[2] "... *die klare Bewusstheit der inneren Identität* (Freud, 1926b).

which was not based on race or religion, but on a common readiness to live in opposition, and on a common freedom from prejudices which narrow the use of the intellect. Here, the term identity points to an individual's link with the unique values, fostered by a unique history, of his people. Yet, it also relates to the cornerstone of this individual's unique development: for the importance of the theme of "incorruptible observation at the price of professional isolation" played a central role in Freud's life (Erikson, 1954). It is this identity of something in the individual's core with an essential aspect of a group's inner coherence which is under consideration here: for the young individual must learn to be most himself where he means most to others—those others, to be sure, who have come to mean most to him. The term identity expresses such a mutual relation in that it connotes both a persistent sameness within oneself (selfsameness) and a persistent sharing of some kind of essential character with others.

I can attempt to make the subject matter of identity more explicit only by approaching it from a variety of angles—biographic, pathographic, and theoretical; and by letting the term identity speak for itself in a number of connotations. At one time, then, it will appear to refer to a conscious *sense of individual identity*; at another to an unconscious striving for a *continuity of personal character*; at a third, as a criterion for the silent doings of *ego synthesis*; and, finally, as a maintenance of an inner *solidarity* with a group's ideals and identity. In some respects the term will appear to be colloquial and naïve; in another, vaguely related to existing concepts in psychoanalysis and sociology. If, after an attempt at clarifying this relation, the term itself still retains some ambiguity, it will, so I hope, nevertheless have helped to delineate a significant problem, and a necessary point of view.

I begin with one extreme aspect of the problem as exemplified in the biography of an outstanding individual—an individual who labored as hard on the creation of a world-wide *public identity* for himself as he worked on his literary masterpieces.

BIOGRAPHIC: G.B.S. (70) ON GEORGE BERNARD SHAW (20)

When George Bernard Shaw was a famous man of seventy, he was called upon to review and to preface the unsuccessful work of his early twenties, namely, the two volumes of fiction which had never been published. As one would expect, Shaw proceeded to make light of the production of his young adulthood, but not without imposing on the reader a detailed analysis of young Shaw. Were Shaw not so deceptively witty in what he says about his younger years, his observations probably would have been recognized as a major psychological achievement. Yet, it is Shaw's mark of identity that he eases and teases his reader along a path of apparent superficialities and sudden depths. I dare to excerpt him here for my purposes only in the hope that I will make the reader curious enough to follow him at every step of his exposition (Shaw, 1952).

G.B.S. (for this is the public identity which was one of his masterpieces) describes young Shaw as an "extremely disagreeable and undesirable" young man, "not at all reticent of diabolical opinion," while inwardly "suffering . . . from simple cowardice . . . and horribly ashamed of it." "The truth is," he concludes, "that all men are in a false position in society until they have realized their possibilities and imposed them on their neighbors. They are tormented by a continual shortcoming in themselves; yet they irritate others by a continual overweening. This discord can be resolved by acknowledged success or failure only: everyone is ill at ease until he has found his natural place, whether it be above or below his birthplace." But Shaw must always exempt himself from any universal law which he inadvertently pronounces; so he adds: "This finding of one's place may be made very puzzling by the fact that there is no place in ordinary society for extraordinary individuals."

Shaw proceeds to describe a crisis (of the kind which we will refer to as an *identity crisis*) at the age of twenty. It is to be noted that this crisis was not caused by lack of success or the absence of a defined role but by too much of both: "I made good in spite of myself, and found, to my dismay, that Business, instead of expelling me as the worthless imposter I was, was fastening upon me with no intention of letting me go. Behold me, therefore, in my twentieth year, with a business training, in an occupation which I detested as cordially as any sane person lets himself detest anything he cannot escape from. In March 1876 I broke loose." Breaking loose meant to leave family and friends, business and Ireland, and to avoid the danger of success without identity, of a success unequal to "the enormity of my unconscious ambition." He granted himself a prolongation of the interval between youth and adulthood, which we will call a *psychosocial moratorium*. He writes: ". . . when I left my native city I left this phase behind me, and associated no more with men of my age until, after about eight years of solitude in this respect, I was drawn into the Socialist revival of the early eighties, among Englishmen intensely serious and burning with indignation at very real and very fundamental evils that affected all the world." In the meantime, he seemed to avoid opportunities, sensing that "Behind the conviction that they could lead to nothing that I wanted, lay the unspoken fear that they might lead to something I did not want." This *occupational* part of the moratorium was reinforced by an *intellectual* one: "I cannot learn anything that does not interest me. My memory is not indiscriminate; it rejects and selects; and its selections are not academic . . . I congratulate myself on this; for I am firmly persuaded that every unnatural activity of the brain is as mischievous as any unnatural activity of the body . . . Civilization is always wrecked by giving the governing classes what is called secondary education . . ."

Shaw settled down to study and to write as he pleased, and it was then that the extraordinary workings of an extraordinary personality came to the fore. He managed to abandon the *kind* of work he had been doing without relinquishing the work *habit*: "My office training had left me with a habit of doing something regularly every day as a fundamental condition of industry as distinguished from idleness. I knew I was making no headway unless I was doing this, and that I should never produce a book in any other fashion. I bought supplies of white paper, demy size, by sixpence-worths at a time; folded it in quarto; and condemned myself to fill five pages of it a day, rain or shine, dull or inspired. I had so much of the schoolboy and the clerk still in me that if my five pages ended in the middle of a sentence I did not finish it until the next day. On the other hand, if I missed a day, I made up for it by doing a double task on the morrow. On this plan I produced five novels in five years. It was my professional apprenticeship . . ." We may add that these first five novels were not published for over fifty years; but Shaw had learned to write as he worked, and to wait as he wrote. How important such initial *ritualization of his worklife* was for the young man's inner defenses may be seen from one of those casual (in fact, parenthetical) remarks with which the great wit almost coyly admits his psychological insight: "I have risen by sheer gravitation, too industrious by acquired habit to stop working (*I work as my father drank*)."[3] He thus points to that combination of *addictiveness* and *compulsivity* which we see as the basis of much pathology in late adolescence and of some accomplishment in young adulthood.

His father's "drink neurosis" Shaw describes in detail, finding in it one of the sources of his biting humor: "It had to be either a family tragedy or family joke." For his father was not "convivial, nor quarrelsome, nor boastful, but miserable, racked with shame and remorse." However, the father had a "humorous sense of anticlimax which I inherited from him and used with much effect when I became a writer of comedy. His anticlimaxes depended for their effect on our sense of the sacredness (of the subject matter) . . . It seems providential that I was driven to the essentials of religion by the reduction of every factitious or fictitious element in it to the most irreverent absurdity."

A more unconscious level of Shaw's oedipal tragedy is represented—with dreamlike symbolism—in what looks like a screen memory conveying his father's impotence: "A boy who has seen 'the governor' with an *imperfectly wrapped-up goose under one arm* and *a ham in the same condition under the other* (both purchased under heaven knows what delusion of festivity) *butting at the garden wall in the belief that he was pushing open the gate*, and *transforming his tall hat to a concertina* in the process, and who, instead of being overwhelmed with shame and anxiety at the spectacle, has been so *disabled by merriment* (uproariously shared by the maternal uncle) that he has hardly been able to rush to the rescue of the hat and pilot its wearer to safety, is clearly not a boy who will make tragedies of trifles instead of *making trifles of tragedies*. If you cannot get rid of the family skeleton, you may as well make it dance." It is obvious that the analysis of the psychosexual elements in Shaw's identity could find a solid anchor point in this memory.

Shaw explains his father's downfall with a brilliant analysis of the socioeconomic circumstances of his day. For the father was

[3] My italics.

"second cousin to a baronet, and my mother the daughter of a country gentleman whose rule was, when in difficulties, mortgage. That was my sort of poverty." His father was "the younger son of a younger son of a younger son" and he was "a downstart and the son of a downstart." Yet, he concludes: "To say that my father could not afford to give me a university education is like saying that he could not afford to drink, or that I could not afford to become an author. Both statements are true; but he drank and I became an author all the same."

His mother he remembers for the "one or two rare and delightful occasions when she buttered my bread for me. She buttered it thickly instead of merely wiping a knife on it." Most of the time, however, he says significantly, she merely "accepted me as a natural and customary phenomenon and took it for granted that I should go on occurring in that way." There must have been something reassuring in this kind of impersonality, for "technically speaking, I should say she was the worst mother conceivable, always, however, within the limits of the fact that she was incapable of unkindness to any child, animal, or flower, or indeed to any person or thing whatsoever. . ." If this could not be considered either a mother's love or an education, Shaw explains: "I was badly brought up because my mother was so well brought up. . . In her righteous reaction against . . . the constraints and tyrannies, the scoldings and browbeatings and punishments she had suffered in her childhood . . . she reached a negative attitude in which having no substitute to propose, she carried domestic anarchy as far as in the nature of things it can be carried." All in all, Shaw's mother was "a thoroughly disgusted and disillusioned woman . . . suffering from a hopelessly disappointing husband and three uninteresting children grown too old to be petted like the animals and the birds she was so fond of, to say nothing of the humiliating inadequacy of my father's income."

Shaw had really three parents, the third being a man named Lee ("meteoric," "impetuous," "magnetic"), who gave Shaw's mother lessons in singing, not without revamping the whole Shaw household as well as Bernard's ideals: "Although he supplanted my father as the dominant factor in the household, and appropriated all the activity and interest of my mother, he was so completely absorbed in his musical affairs that there was no friction and hardly any intimate personal contacts between the two men: certainly no unpleasantness. At first his ideas astonished us. He said that people should sleep with their windows open. The daring of this appealed to me; and I have done so ever since. He ate brown bread instead of white: a startling eccentricity."

Of the many elements of identity formations which ensued from such a perplexing picture, let me single out only three, selected, simplified, and named for this occasion by me.

The Snob

"As compared with similar English families, we had a power of derisive dramatization that made the bones of the Shavian skeletons rattle more loudly." Shaw recognizes this as "family snobbery mitigated by the family sense of humor." On the other hand, "though my mother was not consciously a snob, the divinity which hedged an Irish lady of her period was not acceptable to the British suburban parents, all snobs, who were within her reach (as customers for private music lessons)." Shaw had "an enormous contempt for family snobbery," until he found that one of his ancestors was an Earl of Fife: "It was as good as being descended from Shakespeare, whom I had been unconsciously resolved to reincarnate from my cradle."

The Noisemaker

All through his childhood, Shaw seems to have been exposed to an oceanic assault of music making: the family played trombones and ophicleides, violoncellos, harps, and tambourines—and, most of all (or is it worst of all) they sang. Finally, however, he taught himself the piano, and this with dramatic noisiness. "When I look back on all the banging, whistling, roaring, and growling inflicted on nervous neighbors during this process of education, I am consumed with useless remorse. . . I used to drive [my mother] nearly crazy by my favorite selections from Wagner's Ring, which to her was 'all recitative,' and horribly discordant at that. She never complained at the time, but confessed it after we separated, and said that she had sometimes gone away to cry. If I had committed a murder I do not think it would trouble my conscience very much; but this I cannot bear to think of." That, in fact, he may have learned the piano in order to get even with his musical tormentors, he does not profess to realize. Instead, he compromised by becoming—a music *critic*, i.e., one who *writes* about the noise made by others. As a critic, he chose the *nom de plume* Corno di Bassetto—actually the name of an instrument which nobody knew and which is so meek in tone that "not even the devil could make it sparkle." Yet Bassetto became a sparkling critic, and more: "I cannot deny that Bassetto was occasionally vulgar; but that does not matter if he makes you laugh. Vulgarity is a necessary part of a complete author's equipment; and the clown is sometimes the best part of the circus."

The Diabolical One

How the undoubtedly lonely little boy (whose mother listened only to the musical noisemakers) came to use his imagination to converse with a great imaginary companion is described thus: "In my childhood I exercised my literary genius by composing my own prayers . . . they were a literary performance for the entertainment and propitiation of the Almighty." In line with his family's irreverence in matters of religion, Shaw's piety had to find and rely on the rockbottom of religiosity which, in him, early became a mixture of "intellectual integrity . . . synchronized with the dawning of moral passion." At the same time it seems that Shaw was (in some unspecified way) a little devil of a child. At any rate, he did not feel identical with himself when he was good: "Even when I was a good boy, I was so only theatrically, because, as actors say, I saw myself in the character." And indeed, at the completion of his identity struggle, i.e., "when Nature completed my countenance in 1880 or thereabouts (I had only the tenderest sprouting of hair on my face until I was 24), I found myself equipped with the upgrowing moustaches and eyebrows, and the sarcastic nostrils of the operatic fiend whose airs (by Gounod) I had sung as a child, and whose attitudes I had affected in my boyhood. Later on, as the generations moved past me, I . . . began to perceive that imaginative fiction is to life what the sketch is to the picture or the conception to the statue."

Thus G.B.S., more or less explicitly, traces his own roots. Yet, it is well worth noting that what he finally *became* seems to him to have been as *innate* as the intended reincarnation of Shakespeare referred to above. His teacher, he says, "puzzled me with her attempts to teach me to read; for I can remember no time at which a page of print was not intelligible to me, and can only suppose that I was born literate." However, he thought of a number of professional choices: "As an alternative to being a Michelangelo I had dreams of being a Badeali (note, by the way, that of literature I had no dreams at all any more than a duck has of swimming)."

He also calls himself "a born Communist" (which, we hasten to say, means a Fabian Socialist), and he explains the peace that comes with the *acceptance of what one seems to be made to be*; the "born Communist . . . knows where he is, and where this society which has so intimidated him is. He is cured of his MAUVAISE HONTE. . ." Thus "the complete outsider" gradually became his kind of complete insider: "I was," he said, "outside society, outside politics, outside sport, outside the Church"—but this "only within the limits of British barbarism . . . The moment music, painting, literature, or science came into question the positions were reversed: it was I who was the Insider."

As he traces all of these traits back into childhood, Shaw becomes aware of the fact that only a *tour de force* could have integrated them all: ". . . if I am to be entirely communicative on this subject, I must add that the mere rawness which so soon rubs off was complicated by a deeper strangeness which has made me all my life a sojourner on this planet rather than a native of it. Whether it be that I was born mad or a little too sane, my kingdom was not of this world: I was at home only in the realm of my imagination, and at my ease only with the mighty dead. Therefore, I had to become an actor, and create for myself a fantastic personality fit and apt for dealing with men, and adaptable to the various parts I had to play as author, journalist, orator, politician, committee man, man of the world, and so forth. In this," so Shaw concludes significantly, "I succeeded later on only too well." This statement is singularly illustrative of that faint disgust with which older men at times review the inextricable identity which they had come by in their youth—a disgust which in the lives of some can become mortal despair and inexplicable psychosomatic involvement.

The end of his crisis of younger years Shaw sums up in these words: "I had the intellectual habit; and by natural combination of critical faculty with literary resource needed only a clear comprehension of life in the light of an intelligible theory: in short, a religion, to set it in trumphant operation." Here the old Cynic has circumscribed in one sentence what the identity formation of any human being must add up to. To translate this into terms more conducive to discussion in ego-psychological and psychosocial terms: Man, to take his place in society, must acquire a "conflict-free," habitual use of a dominant *faculty*, to be elaborated in an *occupation*; a limitless *resource*, a feedback, as it were, from the immediate *exercise* of this occupation, from the *companionship* it provides, and from its *tradition*; and finally, an intelligible *theory* of the processes of life which the old atheist, eager to shock to the last, calls a religion. The Fabian Socialism to which he, in fact, turned is rather an *ideology*, to which general term we shall adhere, for reasons which permit elucidation only at the end of this paper.

Genetic: Identification and Identity

I

The autobiographies of extraordinary (and extraordinarily self-perceptive) individuals are a suggestive source of insight into the development of identity. In order to find an anchor point for the discussion of the universal genetics of identity, however, it would be well to trace its development through the life histories or through significant life episodes of "ordinary" individuals—individuals whose lives have neither become professional autobiographies (as did Shaw's) nor case histories, such as will be discussed in the next chapter. I will not be able to present such material here; I must, instead, rely on impressions from daily life, from participation in one of the rare "longitudinal" studies of the personality development of children,[4] and from guidance work with mildly disturbed young people.

Adolescence is the last and the concluding stage of childhood. The adolescent process, however, is conclusively complete only when the individual has subordinated his childhood identifications to a new kind of identification, achieved in absorbing sociability and in competitive apprenticeship with and among his age-mates. These new identifications are no longer characterized by the play-

[4] Child Guidance Study, Institute of Child Welfare, University of California.

fulness of childhood and the experimental zest of youth: with dire urgency they force the young individual into choices and decisions which will, with increasing immediacy, lead to a more final self-definition, to irreversible role pattern, and thus to commitments "for life." The task to be performed here by the young person and by his society is formidable; it necessitates, in different individuals and in different societies, great variations in the duration, in the intensity, and in the ritualization of adolescence. Societies offer, as individuals require, more or less sanctioned intermediary periods between childhood and adulthood, institutionalized *psychosocial moratoria*, during which a lasting pattern of "inner identity" is scheduled for relative completion.

In postulating a "latency period" which precedes puberty, psychoanalysis has given recognition to some kind of *psychosexual moratorium* in human development—a period of delay which permits the future mate and parent first to "go to school" (i.e., to undergo whatever schooling is provided for in his technology) and to learn the technical and social rudiments of a work situation. It is not within the confines of the libido theory, however, to give an adequate account of a second period of delay, namely, adolescence. Here the sexually matured individual is more or less retarded in his psychosexual capacity for intimacy and in the psychosocial readiness for parenthood. The period can be viewed as a *psychosocial moratorium* during which the individual through free role experimentation may find a niche in some section of his society, a niche which is firmly defined and yet seems to be uniquely made for him. In finding it the young adult gains an assured sense of inner continuity and social sameness which will bridge what he *was* as a child and what he is *about to become*, and will reconcile his *conception of himself* and his *community's recognition* of him.

If, in the following, we speak of the community's response to the young individual's need to be "recognized" by those around him, we mean something beyond a mere recognition of achievement; for it is of great relevance to the young individual's identity formation that he be responded to, and be given function and status as a person whose gradual growth and transformation make sense to those who begin to make sense to him. It has not been sufficiently recognized in psychoanalysis that such recognition provides an entirely indispensable support to the ego in the specific tasks of adolescing, which are: to maintain the most important ego defenses against the vastly growing intensity of impulses (now invested in a matured genital apparatus and a powerful muscle system); to learn to consolidate the most important "conflict-free" achievements in line with work opportunities; and to resynthesize all childhood identifications in some unique way, and yet in concordance with the roles offered by some wider section of society— be that section the neighborhood block, an anticipated occupational field, an association of kindred minds, or, perhaps (as in Shaw's case) the "mighty dead."

II

Linguistically as well as psychologically, identity and identification have common roots. Is identity, then, the mere sum of earlier identifications, or is it merely an additional set of identifications?

The limited usefulness of the *mechanism of identification* becomes at once obvious if we consider the fact that none of the identifications of childhood (which in our patients stand out in such morbid elaboration and mutual contradiction) could, if merely added up, result in a functioning personality. True, we usually believe that the task of psychotherapy is the replacement of morbid and excessive identifications by more desirable ones. But as every cure attests, "more desirable" identifications tend to be quietly subordinated to a new, a unique Gestalt which is more than the sum of its parts. The fact is that identification as a mechanism is of limited usefulness. Children, at different stages of their development, identify with those *part aspects* of people by which they themselves are most immediately affected, whether in reality or fantasy. Their identifications with parents, for example, center in certain overvalued and ill-understood body parts, capacities, and role appearances. These part aspects, furthermore, are favored not because of their social acceptability (they often are everything but the parents' most adjusted attributes) but by the nature of infantile fantasy which only gradually gives way to a more realistic anticipation of social reality. The final identity, then, as fixed at the end of adolescence is superordinated to any single identification with individuals of the past: it includes all significant identifications, but it also alters them in order to make a unique and a reasonably coherent whole of them.

If we, roughly speaking, consider introjection-projection, identification, and identity formation to be the steps by which the ego grows in ever more mature interplay with the identities of the child's models, the following psychosocial schedule suggests itself:

The mechanisms of *introjection and projection*, which prepare the basis for later identifications, depend for their relative integration on the satisfactory mutuality (Erikson, 1950a) between the *mothering adult(s) and the mothered child*. Only the experience of such mutuality provides a safe pole of self-feeling from which the child can reach out for the other pole: his first love "objects."

The fate of *childhood identifications*, in turn, depends on the child's satisfactory interaction with a trustworthy and meaningful hierarchy of roles as provided by the generations living together in some form of *family*.

Identity formation, finally, begins where the usefulness of identification ends. It arises from the selective repudiation and mutual assimilation of childhood identifications, and their absorption in a new configuration, which in turn, is dependent on the process by which a *society* (often through subsocieties) *identifies the young individual*, recognizing him as somebody who had to become the way he is, and who, being the way he is, is taken for granted. The community, often not without some initial mistrust, gives such recognition with a (more or less institutionalized) display of surprise and pleasure in making the acquaintance of a newly emerging individual. For the community, in turn, feels "recognized" by the individual who cares to ask for recognition; it can, by the same token, feel deeply—and vengefully—rejected by the individual who does not seem to care.

III

While the end of adolescence thus is the stage of an overt identity *crisis*, identity *formation* neither begins nor ends with adolescence: it is a lifelong development largely unconscious to the individual and to his society. Its roots go back all the way to the first self-recognition: in the baby's earliest exchange of smiles there is something of a *self-realization coupled with a mutual recognition*.

All through childhood tentative crystallizations take place which make the individual feel and believe (to begin with the most conscious aspect of the matter) as if he approximately knew who he was—only to find that such self-certainty ever again falls prey to the discontinuities of psychosocial development (Benedict, 1938). An example would be the discontinuity between the demands made in a given milieu on a little boy and those made on a "big boy" who, in turn, may well wonder why he was first made to believe that to be little is admirable, only to be forced to exchange this effortless status for the special obligations of one who is "big now." Such discontinuities can amount to a crisis and demand a decisive and strategic repatterning of action, and with it, *compromise* which can be compensated for only by a consistently accruing sense of the social value of such increasing commitment. The cute or ferocious, or good small boy, who becomes a studious, or gentlemanly, or tough big boy must be able—and must be enabled—to combine both sets of values in a recognized identity which permits him, in work and play, and in official and in intimate behavior to be (and to let others be) a big boy *and* a little boy.

The community supports such development to the extent to which it permits the child, at each step, to orient himself toward a complete *"life plan"* with a hierarchical order of roles as represented by individuals of different age grades. Family, neighborhood, and school provide contact and experimental identification with younger and older children and with young and old adults. A child, in the multiplicity of successive and tentative identifications, thus begins early to build up expectations of what it will be like to be older and what it will feel like to have been younger—expectations which become part of an identity as they are, step by step, verified in decisive experiences of psychosocial "fittedness."

IV

The *critical phases* of life have been described in psychoanalysis primarily in terms of instincts and defenses, i.e., as "typical danger situations" (Hartmann, 1939). Psychoanalysis has concerned itself more with the encroachment of psychosexual crises on psychosocial (and other) functions than with the specific crisis created by the maturation of each function. Take for example a child who is learning to *speak*: he is acquiring one of the prime functions supporting a sense of individual autonomy and one of the prime techniques for expanding the radius of give-and-take. The mere indication of an ability to give intentional sound-signs immediately obligates the child to "*say* what he wants." It may force him to *achieve* by proper verbalization the attention which was afforded him previously in response to mere gestures of needfulness. Speech not only commits him to the kind of voice he has and to the mode of speech he develops; it also *defines him* as one responded to by those around him with changed diction and attention. They, in turn, expect henceforth to be understood by him with fewer explanations or gestures. Furthermore, a spoken word is a *pact*: there is an irrevocably committing aspect to an utterance remembered by others, although the child may have to learn early that certain commitments (adult ones to a child) are subject to change without notice, while others (his) are not. This intrinsic relationship of speech, not only to the world of communicable facts, but also to the social value of verbal commitment and uttered truth is strategic among the experiences which support (or fail to support) a sound ego development. It is this psychosocial aspect of the matter which we must learn to relate to the by now better known psychosexual aspects represented, for example, in the autoerotic enjoyment of speech; the use of speech as an erotic "contact"; or in such organ-mode emphases as eliminative or intrusive sounds or uses of speech. Thus the child may come to develop, in the use of voice and word, a particular combination of whining or singing, judging or arguing, as part of a new element of the future identity, namely, the element "one who speaks and is spoken to in such-and-such-a-way." This element, in turn, will be related to other elements of the child's developing identity (he is clever and/or good-looking and/or tough) and will be compared with other people, alive or dead, judged ideal or evil.

It is the ego's function to integrate the psychosexual and psychosocial aspects on a given level of development, and, at the same time, to integrate the relation of newly added identity elements with those already in existence. For earlier crystallizations of identity can become subject to renewed conflict, when changes in the quality and quantity of drive, expansions in mental equipment, and new and often conflicting social demands all make previous adjustments appear insufficient, and, in fact, make previous opportunities and rewards suspect. Yet, such developmental and normative crises differ from imposed, traumatic, and neurotic crises in that the process of growth provides new energy as society offers new and specific opportunities (according to its dominant conception and institutionalization of the phases of life). From a genetic point of view, then, the process of identity formation emerges as an *evolving configuration*—a configuration which is gradually established by successive ego syntheses and resyntheses throughout childhood; it is a configuration gradually integrating *constitutional givens, idiosyncratic libidinal needs, favored capacities, significant identifications, effective defenses, successful sublimations, and consistent roles.*

V

The final assembly of all the converging identity elements at the end of childhood (and the abandonment of the divergent ones)[5] appears to be a formidable task: how can a stage as "abnormal" as adolescence be trusted to accomplish it? Here it is not unnecessary to call to mind again that in spite of the similarity of adolescent "symptoms" and episodes to neurotic and psychotic symptoms and episodes, adolescence is not an affliction but a *normative crisis,* i.e., a normal phase of increased conflict characterized by a seeming fluctuation in ego strength, and yet also by a high growth potential. Neurotic and psychotic crises are defined by a certain self-perpetuating propensity, by an increasing waste of defensive energy, and by a deepened psychosocial isolation; while normative crises are relatively more reversible, or, better, traversable, and are characterized by an abundance of available energy which, to be sure, revives dormant anxiety and arouses new conflict, but also supports new and expanded ego functions in the searching and playful engagement of new opportunities and associations. What under prejudiced scrutiny may appear to be the onset of a neurosis is often but an aggravated crisis which might prove to be self-liquidating and, in fact, contributive to the process of identity formation.

[5] William James (1896) speaks of an abandonment of "the old alternative ego," and even of "the murdered self."

It is true, of course, that the adolescent, during the final stage of his identity formation, is apt to suffer more deeply than he ever did before (or ever will again) from a diffusion of roles; and it is also true that such diffusion renders many an adolescent defenseless against the sudden impact of previously latent malignant disturbances. In the meantime, it is important to emphasize that the diffused and vulnerable, aloof and uncommitted, and yet demanding and opinionated personality of the not-too-neurotic adolescent contains many necessary elements of a semideliberate role experimentation of the "I dare you" and "I dare myself" variety. Much of this apparent diffusion thus must be considered *social play* and thus the true genetic successor of childhood play. Similarly, the adolescent's ego development demands and permits playful, if daring, experimentation in fantasy and *introspection*. We are apt to be alarmed by the "closeness to consciousness" in the adolescent's perception of dangerous id contents (such as the oedipus complex) and this primarily because of the obvious hazards created in psychotherapy, if and when we, in zealous pursuit of our task of "making conscious," push somebody over the precipice of the unconscious who is already leaning out a little too far. The adolescent's leaning out over any number of precipices is normally an experimentation with experiences which are thus becoming more amenable to ego control, provided they can be somehow communicated to other adolescents in one of those strange codes established for just such experiences—and provided they are not prematurely responded to with fatal seriousness by overeager or neurotic adults. The same must be said of the adolescent's "fluidity of defenses," which so often causes raised eyebrows on the part of the worried clinician. Much of this fluidity is anything but pathological; for adolescence is a crisis in which only fluid defense can overcome a sense of victimization by inner and outer demands, and in which only trial and error can lead to the most felicitous avenues of action and self-expression.

In general, one may say that in regard to the social play of adolescents prejudices similar to those which once concerned the nature of childhood play are not easily overcome. We alternately consider such behavior irrelevant, unnecessary, or irrational, and ascribe to it purely regressive and neurotic meanings. As in the past the study of children's spontaneous games was neglected in favor of that of solitary play,[6] so now the mutual "joinedness" of adolescent clique behavior fails to be properly assessed in our concern for the individual adolescent. Children and adolescents in their presocieties provide for one another a sanctioned moratorium and joint support for free experimentation with inner and outer dangers (including those emanating from the adult world). Whether or not a given adolescent's newly acquired capacities are drawn back into infantile conflict depends to a significant extent on the quality of the opportunities and rewards available to him in his peer clique, as well as on the more formal ways in which society at large invites a transition from social play to work experimentation, and from rituals of transit to final commitments: all of which must be based on an implicit mutual contract between the individual and society.

VI

Is the sense of identity conscious? At times, of course, it seems only too conscious. For between the double prongs of vital inner need and inexorable outer demand, the still experimenting individual may become the victim of a transitory extreme *identity consciousness* which is the common core of the many forms of "self-consciousness" typical for youth. Where the processes of identity formation are prolonged (a factor which can bring creative gain) such preoccupation with the "self-image" also prevails. We are thus most aware of our identity when we are just about to gain it and when we (with what motion pictures call "a double take") are somewhat surprised to make its acquaintance; or, again, when we are just about to enter a crisis and feel the encroachment of identity diffusion—a syndrome to be described presently.

An increasing sense of identity, on the other hand, is experienced preconsciously as a sense of psychosocial well-being. Its most obvious concomitants are a feeling of being at home in one's body, a sense of "knowing where one is going," and an inner assuredness of anticipated recognition from those who count. Such a sense of identity, however, is never gained nor maintained once and for all. Like a "good conscience," it is constantly lost and regained, although more lasting and more economical methods of maintenance and restoration are evolved and fortified in late adolescence.

[6] For a new approach see Anna Freud's and Sophie Dann's (1951) report on displaced children.

Like any aspect of well-being or, for that matter, of ego synthesis, a sense of identity has a preconscious aspect which is available to awareness; it expresses itself in behavior which is observable with the naked eye; and it has unconscious concomitants which can be fathomed only by psychological tests and by the psychoanalytic procedure. I regret that, at this point, I can bring forward only a general claim which awaits detailed demonstration. The claim advanced here concerns a whole series of criteria of psychosocial health which find their specific elaboration and relative completion in stages of development preceding and following the identity crisis. This is condensed in Figure I.

Identity appears as only one concept within a wider conception of the human life cycle which envisages childhood as a *gradual unfolding of the personality through phase-specific psychosocial crises:* I have, on other occasions (1950a, 1950b), expressed this *epigenetic principle* by taking recourse to a diagram which, with its many empty boxes, at intervals may serve as a check on our attempts at detailing psychosocial development. (Such a diagram, however, can be recommended to the serious attention only of those who can take it *and* leave it.) The diagram (Figure I), at first, contained only the double-lined boxes along the descending diagonal (I, 1—II , 2—III, 3—IV, 4—V, 5—VI, 6—VII, 7—VIII, 8) and for the sake of initial orientation, the reader is requested to ignore all other entries for the moment. The *diagonal* shows the sequence of psychosocial crises. Each of these boxes is shared by a criterion of relative psychosocial health and the corresponding criterion of relative psychosocial ill-health: in "normal" development, the first must persistently outweigh (although it will never completely do away with) the second. The sequence of stages thus represents a successive development of the component parts of the psychosocial personality. Each part exists in some form (verticals) before the time when it becomes "phase-specific," i.e., when "its" psychosocial crisis is precipitated both by the individual's readiness and by society's pressure. But each component comes to ascendance and finds its more or less lasting solution at the conclusion of "its" stage. It is thus *systematically related* to all the others, and all depend on the proper development at the proper *time* of each; although individual make-up and the nature of society determine the rate of development of each of them, and thus the *ratio* of all of them. It is

	1.	2.	3.	4.	5.	6.	7.	8.
I. INFANCY	Trust vs. Mistrust				Unipolarity vs. Premature Self-Differentation			
II. EARLY CHILDHOOD		Autonomy vs. Shame, Doubt			Bipolarity vs. Autism			
III. PLAY AGE			Initiative vs. Guilt		Play Identification vs. (oedipal) Fantasy Identities			
IV. SCHOOL AGE				Industry vs. Inferiority	Work Identification vs. Identity Foreclosure			
V. ADOLESCENCE	Time Perspective vs. Time Diffusion	Self-Certainty vs. Identity Consciousness	Role Experimentation vs. Negative Identity	Anticipation of Achievement vs. Work Paralysis	Identity vs. Identity Diffusion	Sexual Identity vs. Bisexual Diffusion	Leadership Polarization vs. Authority Diffusion	Ideological Polarization vs. Diffusion of Ideals
VI. YOUNG ADULT					Solidarity vs. Social Isolation	Intimacy vs. Isolation		
VII. ADULTHOOD							Generativity vs. Self-Absorption	
VIII. MATURE AGE								Integrity vs. Disgust, Despair

FIGURE I

at the end of adolescence, then, that identity becomes phase-specific (V, 5), i.e., must find a certain integration as a relatively conflict-free psychosocial arrangement—or remain defective or conflict-laden.

With this chart as a blueprint before us, let me state first which aspects of this complex matter will *not* be treated in this paper: for one, we will not be able to make more definitive the now very tentative designation (in *vertical* 5) of the precursors of identity in the infantile ego. Rather we approach childhood in an untraditional manner, namely, from young adulthood backward—and this with the conviction that early development cannot be understood on its own terms alone, and that the earliest stages of childhood can not be accounted for without a unified theory of the whole span of preadulthood. For the infant (while he is not spared the chaos of needful rage) does not and cannot build anew and out of himself the course of human life, as the reconstruction of his earliest experience ever again seems to suggest. The smallest child lives in a community of life cycles which depend on him as he depends on them, and which guide his drives as well as his sublimations with consistent feedbacks. This verity necessitates a discussion of the psychoanalytic approach to "environment" to which we shall return toward the end of this paper.

A second systematic omission concerns the psychosexual stages. Those readers who have undertaken to study the diagrams of psychosexual development in *Childhood and Society* (Erikson, 1950a) know that I am attempting to lay the ground for a detailed account of the dovetailing of psychosexual and psychosocial epigenesis, i.e., the two schedules according to which component parts, present throughout development, come to fruition in successive stages. The essential inseparability of these two schedules is implied throughout this paper, although only the psychosocial schedule, and in fact only one stage of it, is brought into focus.

What traditional source of psychoanalytic insight, then, *will* we concern ourselves with? It is: first pathography; in this case the clinical description of *identity diffusion*. Hoping thus to clarify the matter of identity from a more familiar angle, we will then return to the over-all aim of beginning to "extract," as Freud put it, "from psychopathology what may be of benefit to normal psychology."

Pathographic: The Clinical Picture of Identity Diffusion

Pathography remains the traditional source of psychoanalytic insight. In the following, I shall sketch a syndrome of disturbances in young people who can neither make use of the institutionalized moratorium provided in their society, nor create and maintain for themselves (as Shaw did) a unique moratorium all of their own. They come, instead, to psychiatrists, priests, judges, and (we must add) recruitment officers in order to be given an authorized if ever so uncomfortable place in which to wait things out.

The sources at my disposal are the case histories of a number of young patients who sought treatment following an acutely disturbed period between the ages of sixteen and twenty-four. A few were seen, and fewer treated, by me personally; a larger number were reported in supervisory interviews or seminars at the Austen Riggs Center in Stockbridge and at the Western Psychiatric Institute in Pittsburgh; the largest number are former patients now on record in the files of the Austen Riggs Center. My *composite sketch* of these case histories will remind the reader immediately of the diagnostic and technical problems encountered in adolescents in general (Blos, 1953) and especially in any number of those young borderline cases (Knight, 1953) who are customarily diagnosed as preschizophrenias, or severe character disorders with paranoid, depressive, psychopathic, or other trends. Such well-established diagnostic signposts will not be questioned here. An attempt will be made, however, to concentrate on certain common features representative of the common life crisis shared by this whole group of patients as a result of a (temporary or final) inability of their egos to establish an identity: for they all suffer from *acute identity diffusion*.[7] Obviously, only quite detailed case presentations could

---

[7] It has been repeatedly pointed out to me that the choice of the term identity diffusion was not a felicitous one. At a meeting of a WHO Study Group, J. Huxley suggested dispersion instead. And indeed, the most common meaning of the term diffusion is the spatial one of a centrifugal dispersion of elements. In culture diffusion, for example, a technological item, an art form, or an idea may have been transmitted by way of migration, or excursion, or trade contact from one culture to another, often far away. In this use of the term, nothing disorderly or confused is implied; the center does not suffer from such dispersion. In identity diffusion, however, a split of self-images is suggested, a loss of centrality, a sense

convey the full necessity or advisability of such a "phase-specific" approach which emphasizes the life task shared by a group of patients as much as the diagnostic criteria which differentiate them. In the meantime, I hope that my composite sketch will convey at least a kind of impressionistic plausibility. The fact that the cases known to me were seen in a private institution in the Berkshires, and at a public clinic in industrial Pittsburgh, suggests that at least the two extremes of socioeconomic status in the United States (and thus two extreme forms of identity problems) are represented here. This could mean that the families in question, because of their extreme locations on the scale of class mobility and of Americanization, may have conveyed to these particular children a certain hopelessness regarding their chances of participating in (or of successfully defying) the dominant American manners and symbols of success.[8] Whether, and in what way, disturbances such as are outlined here also characterize those more comfortably placed somewhere near the middle of the socioeconomic ladder, remains, at this time, an open question.

Time of Breakdown

A state of acute identity diffusion usually becomes manifest at a time when the young individual finds himself exposed to a combination of experiences which demand his simultaneous commitment to *physical intimacy* (not by any means always overtly sexual), to decisive *occupational choice,* to energetic *competition,* and to *psychosocial self-definition*. A young college girl, previously overprotected by a conservative mother who is trying to live down a not-so-conservative past, may, on entering college, meet young people of radically different backgrounds, among whom she must choose her friends and her enemies; radically different mores especially in the relationship of the sexes which she must play along with or repudiate; and a commitment to make decisions and choices

---

of dispersion and confusion, and a fear of dissolution. Confusion might have been a better choice; yet a young individual may be in a state of mild identity diffusion without feeling confused. All in all, dispersion being one of the synonyms of diffusion anyway, it may not be too unfortunate to let the term stand—especially since by now it has itself become the subject of a terminological diffusion by way of quotation.

[8] See Chapters VIII (Status and Role) and XI (Social Class) in G. H. Mead (1934). For a recent psychoanalytic approach to role and status, see Ackerman (1951).

which will necessitate irreversible competitive involvement or even leadership. Often she finds among very "different" young people a comfortable display of values, manners, and symbols for which one or the other of her parents or grandparents is covertly nostalgic, while overtly despising them. Decisions and choices and, most of all, successes in any direction bring to the fore conflicting identifications and immediately threaten to narrow down the inventory of further tentative choices; and, at the very moment when time is of the essence, every move may establish a binding precedent in psychosocial self-definition, i.e., in the "type" one comes to represent in the types of the age-mates (who seem so terribly eager to type). On the other hand, any marked *avoidance of choices* (i.e., a moratorium by default) leads to a sense of outer *isolation* and to an *inner vacuum* which is wide open for old libidinal objects and with this for bewilderingly conscious incestuous feelings; for more primitive forms of identification; and (in some) for a renewed struggle with archaic introjects. This regressive pull often receives the greatest attention from workers in our field, partially because we are on more familiar ground wherever we can discern signs of regression to infantile psychosexuality. Yet the disturbances under discussion here cannot be comprehended without some insight into the specific nature of transitory adolescent regression as an attempt to postpone and to avoid, as it were, a psychosocial foreclosure. A state of paralysis may ensue, the mechanisms of which appear to be devised to maintain a state of minimal actual choice and commitment with a maximum inner conviction of still being the chooser. Of the complicated presenting pathology only a few aspects can be discussed here.

The Problem of Intimacy

The chart which accompanied the preceding section shows "Intimacy vs. Isolation" as the core conflict which follows that of "Identity vs. Identity Diffusion." That many of our patients break down at an age which is properly considered more preadult than postadolescent is explained by the fact that often only an attempt to engage in intimate fellowship and competition or in sexual intimacy fully reveals the latent weakness of identity.

True "engagement" with others is the result and the test of firm self-delineation. Where this is still missing, the young individual, when seeking tentative forms of playful intimacy in friendship and competition, in sex play and love, in argument and gossip, is apt to experience a peculiar strain, as if such tentative engagement might turn into an interpersonal fusion amounting to a loss of identity, and requiring, therefore, a tense inner reservation, a caution in commitment. Where a youth does not resolve such strain he may isolate himself and enter, at best, only stereotyped and formalized interpersonal relations; or he may, in repeated hectic attempts and repeated dismal failures, seek intimacy with the most improbable partners. For where an assured sense of identity is missing even friendships and affairs become desperate attempts at delineating the fuzzy outlines of identity by mutual narcissistic mirroring: to fall in love then often means to fall into one's mirror image, hurting oneself and damaging the mirror. During lovemaking or in sexual fantasies, a loosening of *sexual identity* threatens: it even becomes unclear whether sexual excitement is experienced by the individual or by his partner, and this in either heterosexual or homosexual encounters. The ego thus loses its flexible capacity for abandoning itself to sexual and affectual sensations, in a fusion with another individual who is both partner to the sensation and guarantor of one's continuing identity: fusion with another becomes identity loss. A sudden collapse of all capacity for mutuality threatens, and a desperate wish ensues to start all over again, with a (quasi-deliberate) regression to a stage of basic bewilderment and rage such as only the very small child knows.

It must be remembered that the counterpart of intimacy is *distantiation*, i.e., the readiness to repudiate, to ignore, or to destroy those forces and people whose essence seems dangerous to one's own. Intimacy with one set of people and ideas would not be really intimate without an efficient repudiation of another set. Thus, weakness or excess in repudiation is an intrinsic aspect of the inability to gain intimacy because of an incomplete identity: whoever is not sure of his "point of view" cannot repudiate judiciously.

Young persons often indicate in rather pathetic ways a feeling that only a merging with a "leader" can save them—an adult who is able and willing to offer himself as a safe object for experimental surrender and as a guide in the relearning of the very first steps toward an intimate mutuality, and a legitimate repudiation. To such a person the late adolescent wants to be an apprentice or a disciple, a follower, sex mate or patient. Where this fails, as it often must from its very intensity and absoluteness, the young individual recoils to a position of strenuous introspection and self-testing which, given particularly aggravating circumstances or a history of relatively strong autistic trends, can lead him into a paralyzing borderline state. Symptomatically, this state consists of a painfully heightened sense of isolation; a disintegration of the sense of inner continuity and sameness; a sense of over-all ashamedness; an inability to derive a sense of accomplishment from any kind of activity; a feeling that life is happening to the individual rather than being lived by his initiative; a radically shortened time perspective; and finally, a basic mistrust, which leaves it to the world, to society, and indeed to psychiatry to prove that the patient does exist in a psychosocial sense, i.e., can count on an invitation to become himself.

Diffusion of Time Perspective

In extreme instances of delayed and prolonged adolescence an extreme form of a disturbance in the *experience of time* appears which, in its milder form, belongs to the psychopathology of everyday adolescence. It consists of a sense of great urgency and yet also of a loss of consideration for time as a dimension of living. The young person may feel simultaneously very young, and in fact babylike, and old beyond rejuvenation. Protests of missed greatness and of a premature and fatal loss of useful potentials are common among our patients as they are among adolescents in cultures which consider such protestations romantic; the implied malignancy, however, consists of a decided disbelief in the possibility that time may bring change, and yet also of a violent fear that it might. This contradiction often is expressed in a general slowing up which makes the patient behave, within the routine of activities (and also of therapy) as if he were moving in molasses. It is hard for him to go to bed and to face the transition into a state of sleep, and it is equally hard for him to get up and face the necessary restitution of wakefulness; it is hard to come to the hour, and hard to leave it. Such complaints as, "I don't know," "I give up," "I quit," are by no means mere habitual statements reflecting a mild depression: they are often expressions of the kind of despair which Edward Bibring (1953) has recently discussed as a wish on the part of the ego "to let itself die." The assumption that life could actually be made to end with the end of adolescence (or at tentatively planned later "dates of expiration") is by no means entirely unwelcome, and, in fact, can become the only pillar of hope on which a new beginning can be based. Some of our patients even require the feeling that the therapist does not intend to commit them to a continuation of life if (successful) treatment should fail to prove it really worth while; without such a conviction the moratorium would not be a real one. In the meantime, the "wish to die" is only in those rare cases a really suicidal wish, where "to be a suicide" becomes an inescapable identity choice in itself. I am thinking here of a pretty young girl, the oldest of a number of daughters of a millworker. Her mother had repeatedly expressed the thought that she would rather see her daughters dead than become prostitutes; at the same time she suspected "prostitution" in their every move toward companionship with boys. The daughters were finally forced into a kind of conspiratorial sorority of their own, obviously designed to elude the mother, to experiment with ambiguous situations, and yet probably also to give one another protection from men. They were finally caught in compromising circumstances. The authorities, too, took it for granted that they intended to prostitute themselves, and they were sent to a variety of institutions where they were forcefully impressed with the kind of "recognition" society had in store for them. No appeal was possible to a mother who, they felt, had left them no choice; and much good will and understanding of social workers was sabotaged by circumstances. At least for the oldest girl (and this, because of a number of reasons) no other future was available except that of another chance in another world. She killed herself by hanging after having dressed herself up nicely, and having written a note which ended with the cryptic words "Why I achieve honor only to discard it. . . ."

Less spectacular but not less malignant forms and origins of such "negative identities" will be taken up later.

Diffusion of Industry

Cases of severe identity diffusion regularly also suffer from an acute upset in the sense of workmanship, and this either in the form of an inability to concentrate on required or suggested tasks, or in a self-destructive preoccupation with some one-sided activities, i.e., excessive reading. The way in which such patients sometimes, under treatment, find the one activity in which they can re-employ their once lost sense of workmanship is a chapter in itself. Here, it is well to keep in mind the stage of development which precedes puberty and adolescence, namely, the elementary-school age, when the child is taught the prerequisites for participation in the particular technology of his culture and is given the opportunity and the life task of developing a sense of workmanship and work participation. The school age significantly follows the oedipal stage: the accomplishment of real (and not only playful) steps toward a place in the economic structure of society permits the child to reidentify with parents as workers and tradition bearers rather than as sexual and familial beings, thus nurturing at least one concrete and more "neutral" possibility of becoming like them. The tangible goals of elementary practice are shared by and with age-mates in places of instruction (sweathouse, prayer house, fishing hole, workshop, kitchen, schoolhouse) most of which, in turn, are geographically separated from the home, from the mother, and from infantile memories: here, however, wide differences in the treatment of the sexes exist. Work goals, then, by no means only support or exploit the suppression of infantile instinctual aims; they also enhance the functioning of the ego, in that they offer a constructive activity with actual tools and materials in a communal reality. The ego's tendency to turn passivity into activity here thus acquires a new field of manifestation, in many ways superior to the mere turning of passive into active in infantile fantasy and play; for now the inner need for activity, practice, and work completion is ready to meet the corresponding demands and opportunities in social reality (Hendrick, 1943; Ginsburg, 1954).

Because of the immediate oedipal antecedents of the beginnings of a work identity, the diffusion of identity in our young patients reverses their gears toward oedipal competitiveness and sibling rivalry. Thus identity diffusion is accompanied not only by an inability to concentrate, but also by an excessive awareness as well as an abhorrence of competitiveness. Although the patients in question usually are intelligent and able and often have shown themselves successful in office work, in scholastic studies and in sports, they now lose the capacity for work, exercise, and sociability, and thus the most important vehicle of social play, and the most significant refuge from formless fantasy and vague anxiety. Instead infantile goals and fantasies are dangerously endowed with the energy emanating from matured sexual equipment and increased aggressive power. One parent, again, becomes the goal, the other, again, the hindrance. Yet this revived oedipal struggle is not and must not be interpreted as exclusively or even primarily a sexual one: it is a turn toward the earliest origins, an attempt to resolve a diffusion of early introjects and to rebuild shaky childhood identifications—in other words, a wish to be born again, to learn once more the very first steps toward reality and mutuality, and to acquire the renewed permission to develop again the functions of contact, activity, and competition.

A young patient, who had found himself blocked in college, during the initial phase of his treatment in a private hospital nearly read himself blind, apparently in a destructive overidentification with father and therapist both of whom were professors. Guided by a resourceful "painter in residence" he came upon the fact that he had an original and forceful talent to paint, an activity which was prevented by advancing treatment from becoming self-destructive overactivity. As painting proved a help in the patient's gradual acquisition of a sense of identity of his own, he dreamed one night a different version of a dream which previously had always ended in panicky awakening. Now he fled, from fire and persecution, into a forest which he had sketched himself; and as he fled into it, the charcoal drawing turned into live woods, with an infinite perspective.

The Choice of the Negative Identity

The loss of a sense of identity often is expressed in a scornful and snobbish hostility toward the roles offered as proper and desirable in one's family or immediate community. Any part aspect of the required role, or all parts, be it masculinity or femininity, nationality or class membership, can become the main focus of the young person's acid disdain. Such excessive contempt for their backgrounds occurs among the oldest Anglo-Saxon and the newest Latin or Jewish families; it easily becomes a general dislike for everything American, and an irrational overestimation of everything foreign. Life and strength seem to exist only where one is not, while decay and danger threaten wherever one happens to be. This typical case fragment illustrates the superego's triumph of depreciation over a young man's faltering identity: "A voice within him which was disparaging him began to increase at about this time. It went to the point of intruding into everything he did. He said, 'if I smoke a cigarette, if I tell a girl I like her, if I make a gesture, if I listen to music, if I try to read a book—this third voice is at me all the time—"You're doing this for effect; you're a phony."' This disparaging voice in the last year has been rather relentless. The other day on the way from home to college, getting into New York on the train, he went through some of the New Jersey swamplands and the poorer sections of the cities, and he felt that he was more congenial with people who lived there than he was with people on the campus or at home. He felt that life really existed in those places and that the campus was a sheltered, effeminate place."

In this example it is important to recognize not only an overweening superego, overclearly perceived as an inner voice, but also the acute identity diffusion, as projected on segments of society. An analogous case is that of a French-American girl from a rather prosperous mining town, who felt panicky to the point of paralysis when alone with a boy. It appeared that numerous superego injunctions and identity conflicts had, as it were, short-circuited in the obsessive idea that every boy had a right to expect from her a yielding to sexual practices popularly designated as "French."

Such estrangement from national and ethnic origins rarely leads to a complete denial of *personal identity* (Piers and Singer, 1953), although the angry insistence on being called by a particular given name or nickname is not uncommon among young people who try to find a refuge from diffusion in a new name label. Yet confabulatory reconstructions of one's origin do occur: a high-school girl of Middle-European descent secretly kept company with Scottish immigrants, carefully studying and easily assimilating their dialect and their social habits. With the help of history books and travel guides she reconstructed for herself a childhood in a given milieu in an actual township in Scotland, apparently convincing enough to some descendants of that country. Prevailed upon to discuss her future with me, she spoke of her (American-born) parents as "the people who brought me over here," and told me of her childhood "over there" in impressive detail. I went along with the story, implying that it had more inner truth than reality to it. The bit of reality was, as I surmised, the girl's attachment, in early childhood, to a woman neighbor who had come from the British Isles; the force behind the near-delusional "truth" was the paranoid form of a powerful death wish (latent in all severe identity crises) against her parents. The semideliberateness of the delusion was indicated when I finally asked the girl how she had managed to marshal all the details of life in Scotland. "Bless you, sir," she said in pleading Scottish brogue, "I needed a past."

On the whole, however, our patients' conflicts find expression in a more subtle way than the abrogation of personal identity: they rather choose a *negative identity,* i.e., an identity perversely based on all those identifications and roles which, at critical stages of development, had been presented to the individual as most undesirable or dangerous, and yet also as most real. For example, a mother whose first-born son died and who (because of complicated guilt feelings) has never been able to attach to her later surviving children the same amount of religious devotion that she bestows on the memory of her dead child may well arouse in one of her sons the conviction that to be sick or dead is a better assurance of being "recognized" than to be healthy and about. A mother who is filled with unconscious ambivalence toward a brother who disintegrated into alcoholism may again and again respond selectively only to those traits in her son which seem to point to a repetition of her brother's fate, in which case this "negative" identity may take on more reality for the son than all his natural attempts at being good: he may work hard on becoming a drunkard and, lacking the necessary ingredients, may end up in a state of stubborn paralysis of choice. In other cases the negative identity is dictated by the necessity of finding and defending a niche of one's own against the excessive ideals either demanded by morbidly ambitious parents or seemingly already realized by actually superior ones: in both cases the parents' weaknesses and unexpressed wishes are recognized by the child with catastrophic clarity. The daughter of a man of brilliant showmanship ran away from college and was arrested as a prostitute in the Negro quarter of a Southern city; while the daughter of an influential Southern Negro preacher was found among narcotic addicts in Chicago. In such cases it is of utmost importance to recognize the mockery and the vindictive pretense in such role playing; for the white girl had not really prostituted herself, and the colored girl had not really become an addict—yet. Needless to say, however, each of them had put herself into a marginal social area, leaving it to law-enforcement officers and to psychiatric agencies to decide what stamp to put on such behavior. A corresponding case is that of a boy presented to a psychiatric clinic as "the village homosexual" of a small town. On investigation, it appeared that the boy had succeeded in assuming this fame without any actual acts of homosexuality except one, much earlier in his life, when he had been raped by some older boys.

Such vindictive choices of a negative identity represent, of course, a desperate attempt at regaining some mastery in a situation in which the available positive identity elements cancel each other out. The history of such a choice reveals a set of conditions in which it is easier to derive a sense of identity out of a *total* identification with that which one is *least* supposed to be than to struggle for a feeling of reality in acceptable roles which are unattainable with the patient's inner means. The statement of a young man, "I would rather be quite insecure than a little secure," and that of a young woman, "At least in the gutter I'm a genius," circumscribe the relief following the total choice of a negative identity. Such relief is, of course, often sought collectively in cliques and gangs of young homosexuals, addicts, and social cynics.

A relevant job ahead of us is the analysis of snobbism which, in its upper-class form, permits some people to deny their identity diffusion through a recourse to something they did not earn themselves, namely, their parents' wealth, background, or fame. But there is a "lower lower" snobbism too, which is based on the pride of having achieved a semblance of nothingness. At any rate, many a late adolescent, if faced with continuing diffusion, would rather *be nobody or somebody bad, or indeed, dead—and this totally, and by free choice—than be not-quite-somebody*. The word "total" is not accidental in this connection, for I have endeavored to describe in another connection (Erikson, 1953) a human proclivity to a "totalistic" reorientation when, at critical stages of development, reintegration into a relative "wholeness" seems impossible.[9] We will return to this problem in the last section.

[9] *Wholeness* connotes an assembly of parts, even quite diversified parts, that enter into fruitful association and organization. This concept is most strikingly expressed in such terms as wholeheartedness, wholemindedness, wholesomeness,

Transference and Resistance

What I can say here about the therapeutic problems encountered with the patients described must be restricted to an attempt at relating to the concepts of identity and diffusion such matters of therapeutic technique as have been elaborated by workers in the field of borderline cases.[10]

On facing therapy, some of the patients under discussion here undergo a phase of particular malignancy. While the depth of regression and the danger of acting out must of course guide our diagnostic decisions, it is important to recognize, from the start, a mechanism present in such a turn for the worse: I would call it the "rock-bottom attitude." This consists of a quasi-deliberate giving in on the part of the patient to the pull of regression, a radical search for the rock-bottom—i.e., both the ultimate limit of regression and the only firm foundation for a renewed progression.[11] The assumption of such a deliberate search for the "baseline" means to carry Ernst Kris's "regression in the service of the ego" to an extreme: the fact that the recovery of our patients sometimes coincides with the discovery of previously hidden artistic gifts suggests further study of this point (Kris, 1952).

---

and the like. As a Gestalt, then, wholeness emphasizes a progressive mutuality between diversified functions and parts. *Totality,* on the contrary, evokes a Gestalt in which an absolute boundary is emphasized: given a certain arbitrary delineation, nothing that belongs inside must be left outside; nothing that must be outside should be tolerated inside. A totality must be as absolutely inclusive as it is absolutely exclusive. The dictionary uses the word "utter" in this connection. It conveys the element of force, which overrides the question whether the original category-to-be-made-absolute is a logical one, and whether the parts really have, so to speak, a yearning for one another.

There is both in individual and in group psychology a periodical need for a totality without further choice or alternation, even if it implies the abandonment of a much-desired wholeness. To say it in one sentence: Where the human being despairs of an essential wholeness, he restructures himself and the world by taking refuge in totalism.

Psychoanalysis reveals how strong and systematic are man's unconscious *proclivities and potentialities for total realignments,* often barely hidden behind one-sided predilections and convictions, and, on the other hand, how much energy is employed in inner defenses against a threatening total reorientation in which black may turn into white and vice versa. Only the affect released in sudden conversions testifies to the quantity of this energy. (See Erikson, 1953.)

[10] I owe new insights in this field to Robert Knight (1953) and to Margaret Brenman (1952).

[11] David Rapaport's (1953) ego-psychological approach to "activity and passivity" sheds new light on the ego's role in such crises.

The element of deliberateness added here to "true" regression is often expressed in an all-pervasive mockery which characterizes the initial therapeutic contact with these patients; and by that strange air of sadomasochistic satisfaction, which makes it often hard to see and harder to believe that their self-depreciation and their willingness to "let the ego die" harbors a devastating sincerity. As one patient said: "That people do not know how to succeed is bad enough. But the worst is that they do not know how to fail. I have decided to fail well." This almost "deadly" sincerity is to be found in the patients' very determination to *trust nothing but mistrust,* and yet to watch from a dark corner of their minds (and indeed, often from the corner of an eye) for new experiences simple and forthright enough to permit a renewal of the most basic experiments in trustful mutuality. The therapist, manifestly faced with a mocking and defiant young adult, actually must take over the task of a mother who introduces a baby to life's trustworthiness. In the center of the treatment is the patient's need to redelineate himself, and thus to rebuild the foundations of his identity. At the beginning these delineations shift abruptly, even as violent shifts in the patient's experience of his ego boundary take place before our eyes: the patient's mobility may suddenly undergo a "catatonic" slowdown; his attentiveness may turn into overwhelming sleepiness; his vasomotor system may overreact to the point of producing sensations of fainting; his sense of reality may yield to feelings of depersonalization; or the remnants of his self-assurance may disappear in a miasmic loss of a sense of physical presence. Cautious but firm inquiry will reveal the probability that a number of contradictory impulses preceded the "attack." There is first a sudden intense impulse completely to destroy the therapist, and this, it seems, with an underlying "cannibalistic" wish to devour his essence and his identity. At the same time, or in alternation, there occur a fear and a wish to be devoured, to gain an identity by being absorbed in the therapist's essence. Both tendencies, of course, are often dissimulated or somatized for long periods, during which they find a manifestation (often kept secret) only after the therapeutic hour. This manifestation may be an impulsive flight into sexual promiscuity acted out without sexual satisfaction or any sense of participation; enormously absorbing rituals of masturbation or food intake; excessive drinking or wild driving; or self-destructive marathons of reading or listening to music, without food or sleep.

We see here the most extreme form of what may be called *identity resistance* which, incidentally, far from being restricted to the patients described here, is a universal form of resistance regularly experienced but often unrecognized in the course of analyses. Identity resistance is, in its milder and more usual forms, the patient's fear that the analyst, because of his particular personality, background, or philosophy, may carelessly or deliberately destroy the weak core of the patient's identity and impose instead his own. I would not hesitate to say that some of the much-discussed unsolved transference neuroses in patients, as well as in candidates in training, are the direct result of the fact that the identity resistance often is, at best, analyzed only quite unsystematically. In such cases the analysand may throughout the analysis resist any possible inroad by the analyst's identity while surrendering on all other points; or he may absorb more of the analyst's identity than is manageable within the patient's own means; or he may leave the analysis with a lifelong sense of not having been provided with some essence owed to him by the analyst.

In cases of acute identity diffusion this identity resistance becomes the core problem of the therapeutic encounter. Variations of psychoanalytic technique have in common that the dominant resistance must be accepted as the main guide to technique and that interpretation must be fitted to the patient's ability to utilize it. Here the patient sabotages communication until he has settled some basic—if contradictory—issues. The patient insists that the therapist accept his negative identity as real and necessary (which it is and was) without concluding that this negative identity is "all there is to him." If the therapist is able to fulfill both of these demands, he must prove patiently through many severe crises that he can maintain understanding and affection for the patient without either devouring him or offering himself for a totem meal. Only then can better known forms of transference, if ever so reluctantly, emerge.

These are nothing more than a few hints regarding the phenomenology of identity diffusion as reflected in the most outstanding and immediate transferences and resistances. Individual treatment, however, is only one facet of therapy in the cases under discussion. The transferences of these patients remain diffused, while their acting out remains a constant danger. Some, therefore, need to undergo treatment in a hospital environment in which their stepping out of the therapeutic relationship can be observed and limited; and in which first steps *beyond* the newly won bipolar relationship to the therapist meet with the immediate support of receptive nurses, cooperative fellow patients, and helpful instructors in a sufficiently wide choice of activities.

Specific Factors in Family and Childhood

In the discussion of patients who have a relevant pathogenic trend in common, we are apt to ask what their parents have in common. I think that one may say that a number of the mothers in our case histories have in common some outstanding traits. The first is a pronounced status awareness, of the climbing and pretentious or of the "hold-on" variety. They would at almost any time be willing to overrule matters of honest feeling and of intelligent judgment for the sake of a façade of wealth, propriety, and "happiness": they, in fact, try to coerce their sensitive children into a pretense of a "natural" and "glad-to-be-proper" sociability. They also have the special quality of a penetrating omnipresence; their very voices and their softest sobs are sharp, plaintive, or fretful, and cannot be escaped within a considerable radius. One patient, all through childhood had a repetitive dream of a pair of flapping scissors flying around a room: the scissors proved to symbolize his mother's voice, cutting, and cutting off.[12] These mothers love, but they love fearfully, plaintively, intrusively; they are themselves so hungry for approval and for recognition that they burden their young children with complicated complaints, especially about the father, and they plead with the children to justify by their existence their mother's existence. They are highly jealous and highly sensitive to the jealousy of others; in our context it is especially important that the mother is intensely jealous of any sign that the

[12] This example illustrates well the balance which must be found in the interpretation given to such patients between *sexual symbolism* (here castration) which, if overemphasized by the therapist, can only increase the patient's sense of being endangered; and the *representation of dangers to the ego* (here the danger of having the thread of one's autonomy cut off) the communication of which is more urgent, more immediately beneficial, and a condition for the safe discussion of sexual meanings.

child may identify primarily with the father, or, worse, base his very identity on that of the father. It must be added that whatever these mothers are, they are more so toward the patient; the conclusion is inescapable that these patients, in turn, have, from the beginning, deeply hurt their mothers by shying away from them, and this because of an utter intolerance of extreme temperamental differences. These differences, however, are only extreme expressions of an essential affinity: by which I mean to imply that the patient's excessive tendency to withdraw (or to act impulsively) and the mother's excessive social intrusiveness have in common a high degree of social vulnerability. Behind the mother's persistent complaints, then, that the father failed to make a woman out of her, is the complaint, deeply perceived by both mother and child, that the patient failed to make a mother out of her.

The fathers, while usually successful, and often outstanding in their particular fields, do not stand up against their wives at home because of an excessive mother dependence on them, in consequence of which the fathers also are deeply jealous of their children. What initiative and integrity they have either surrenders to the wife's intrusiveness or tries guiltily to elude her: in consequence of which the mother becomes only the more needy, plaintive, and "sacrificial" in her demands upon all or some of her children.

Of the relationship of our patients to their brothers and sisters I can only say that it seems to be more symbiotic than most sibling relationships are. Because of an early identity hunger, our patients are apt to attach themselves to one brother or sister in a way resembling the behavior of twins (Burlingham, 1952): except that here we have one twin, as it were, trying to treat a nontwin as a twin. They seem apt to surrender to a total identification with at least one sibling in ways which go far beyond the "altruism by identification" described by Anna Freud (1936). It is as if our patients surrendered their own identity to that of a brother or sister in the hope of regaining a bigger and better one by some act of merging. For periods they succeed; the letdown which must follow the breakup of the artificial twinship is only the more traumatic. Rage and paralysis follow the sudden insight that there is enough identity only for one, and that the other seems to have made off with it.

The early childhood histories of our patients are, on the whole, remarkably bland. Some infantile autism is often observed early but usually rationalized by the parents. Yet one has the general impression that the degree of malignancy of the acute identity diffusion in late adolescence depends on the extent of this early autism, which will determine the depth of regression and the intensity of the encounter between new identity fragments and old introjects. As to particular traumata in childhood or youth, one item seems frequent, namely, a severe physical trauma either in the oedipal period or in early puberty—and this in connection with a separation from home. This trauma may consist of an operation or a belatedly diagnosed physical defect; it may be an accident or a severe sexual traumatization. Otherwise the early pathology conforms with that expected as typical for the dominant psychiatric diagnosis given.

The Therapeutic Design

I promised a composite sketch, and a sketch I have presented. Again, only the detailed presentation of a few cases could elucidate the relation of ego weakness to congenital proclivities, on the one hand, and to the educative deficiency of families and classes, on the other. In the meantime, the most immediate clarification of the ego's relationship to its "environment" ensues from the study of the young patient's recovery in a hospital setting, i.e., the study of his determined "oneliness" (as a young woman patient put it); of his tendency to exploit and provoke the hospital environment; of his growing ability to utilize it; and finally, of his capacity to leave this kind of institutionalized moratorium and to return to his old or new place in society. The hospital community offers the clinical researcher the possibility of being a participant observer not only in the individual patient's personal treatment but also in the "therapeutic design" which is to meet the legitimate demands of patients who share a life problem—here identity diffusion. It stands to reason that a typical problem receives elucidation as the hospital community studies what is required to treat a particular age group: in this case the hospital becomes a planfully institutionalized world-between-worlds, which offers the young individual support in the rebuilding of those most vital ego functions, which—as far as he ever built them—he has relinquished. The relationship to the individual therapist is the cornerstone for the establishment of a new and honest mutuality of function which must set the patient's face toward an ever so dimly perceived and ever so strenuously refuted future. Yet, it is the hospital community in which the patient's first steps of renewed social experimentation take place. The privileges and obligations of such a community immediately demand his subjection to and his initiation in a communal design which will also strive to meet his and his fellow patients' needs—and incidentally, also, those of the staff: for it stands to reason that a communal setting such as a hospital is characterized not only by the identity needs of those who happen to be the patients, but also of those who choose to become their brothers' (and sisters') keepers. The discussion of the ways in which the professional hierarchy distributes the functions, the rewards, and the status of such keepership (and thus opens the door for a variety of countertransferences and "cross-transferences" which, indeed, make the hospital a facsimile of a home) is entering the literature on the subject of hospital morale (i.e., Bateman and Dunham, 1948; Schwartz and Will, 1953). From the point of view of this paper, such studies also clearly point to the danger of the patient's choosing the very role of a patient as the basis of his crystallizing identity: for this role may well prove more meaningful than any potential identity experienced before (see K. T. Erikson, 1957).

Once More: the Diagram

Diagrams have a quiet coerciveness all their own. Especially does a diagram which has neither been completed nor discarded become a conceptual Harvey: one converses with it unawares. In therapeutic work, one tries to ignore the embarrassing fact that now and again the diagram looks over one's shoulder, as it were, and makes a suggestion; nor do the patients appreciate such atmospheric interferences. Only as I concluded this impressionistic survey of some of the main features of identity diffusion, did it occur to me to "locate" them on the chart: and it cannot be denied that they clarify previously vague parts of the diagram and suggest specific expansions of theory. Insisting, then, that in principle Harveys should remain expendable, we will briefly outline what this one can teach us.

The original chart showed only the diagonal, i.e., the successive achievement (or failure) of the main components of relative psychosocial health. However, it bore the legend: "Above the diagonal there is space for a future elaboration of the precursors of each of these solutions, all of which begin with the beginning; below the diagonal there is space for the designation of the derivatives of these solutions in the maturing personality."

Because all the *verticals* "begin with the beginning," one hesitates to enter even tentative terms into the top boxes. Yet, work with borderline cases (adolescent, juvenile, and infantile) suggests that the infantile frontier, to which they have all regressed, is that of a basic mistrust in their *self-delineation* and of a basic doubt in the possibility of any relationship of *mutuality*. The chart, tentatively, assumes that a successful struggle on the earliest psychosocial frontier of infancy (i.e., the trust-mistrust frontier), if well guided by a favorable maternal environment, leads to a dominant sense of Unipolarity (I, 5) by which is meant something like a dominant sense of the goodness of individual existence. This, I believe, deserves to be differentiated from the narcissistic omnipotence ascribed to this age. While still vulnerably dependent on direct, continuous, and consistent maternal support, an actual sense of the reality of "good" powers, outside and within oneself, must be assumed to arise. Its negative counterpart is a diffusion of contradictory introjects and a predominance of fantasies which pretend to coerce hostile reality with omnipotent vengeance. Once gained, however, the psychosocial foundation of unipolarity subsequently permits *Bipolarization* (II, 5) or what, in id terms, has been called the cathexis of objects. This permits an outgoing experimentation with powerful but loving individuals who retain consistent reality, even though they may go before they come, deny before they give, seem indifferent before they again become attentive. In transitory or lasting forms of autism, the child can be seen to shy away from or to despair of such bipolarization, always in search of an illusory good "oneliness."

Subsequent *Play* and *Work Identifications* (III, 5—IV, 5) with powerful adults and with older and younger age-mates need no further discussion here; the literature on the preschool and school stage amply illustrates the gains and the defeats of these more obviously psychosocial periods.

It is the horizontal (V) which contains the *derivatives of earlier relative achievements which now become part and parcel of the struggle for identity.* It is necessary to emphasize (and possible to illustrate briefly) the principle according to which early relative achievements (diagonal) when considered at a later stage (any horizontal below the diagonal) must be reviewed and renamed in terms of that later stage. Basic Trust, for example, is a good and a most fundamental thing to have, but its psychosocial quality becomes more differentiated as the ego comes into the possession of a more extensive apparatus, even as society challenges and guides such extension.

To begin, then, with the pathology just described: *Time Diffusion* (V, 1) or a loss of the ego's function of maintaining perspective and expectancy is related to the *earliest crises in life* (I, 1), and this because of the fact that the conception of temporal cycles and of time qualities is inherent in and develops from the first experience of mounting need tension, of delay of satisfaction, and final unification with the satisfying "object." As tension increases, future fulfillment is anticipated in "hallucinatory" images; as fulfillment is delayed, moments of impotent rage occur in which anticipation (and with it, future) is obliterated; the perception of an approaching potential satisfaction again gives time a highly condensed quality of intense hope and feared disappointment. All of this contributes temporal elements to the formation of basic trust, i.e., the inner conviction that—after all—sufficient satisfaction is sufficiently predictable to make waiting and "working" worth while. Whatever the original inventory of time qualities are, our most malignantly regressed young people are clearly possessed by general attitudes which represent something of a mistrust of time as such: every delay appears to be a deceit, every wait an experience of impotence, every hope a danger, every plan a catastrophe, every potential provider a traitor. Therefore, time must be made to stand still, if necessary by the magic means of catatonic immobility—or by death. These are the extremes which are manifest in few, and latent in many cases of identity diffusion; yet, every adolescent, I would believe, knows at least fleeting moments of being at odds with time itself. In its normal and transitory form, this new kind of mistrust quickly or gradually yields to outlooks permitting and demanding an intense investment in a future, or in a number of possible futures. If these, to us, seem often quite "utopian" (i.e., based on expectations which would call for a change in the laws of historical change as we know them), we must, for the moment, postpone any judgment of value. The adolescent—or some adolescents—may need, at all costs, an outlook with a perspective worth an investment of energy. The actual realizability of such an outlook may be a matter of later learning and adjusting, and often a matter of historical luck.

In the following, I shall let each step on the chart lead to a few suggestive *social considerations* which were only briefly touched on in the foregoing. To envisage a future, the young adult may also need that something which Shaw called "a religion" and "a clear comprehension of life in the light of an intelligible theory." I indicated at the beginning that we would call this something-between-a-theory-and-a-religion an *ideology*, a term highly conducive to misunderstanding. At this point let me stress only the *temporal* element in world views which might be called ideological: they are grouped around *a utopian simplification of historical perspective* (salvation, conquest, reform, happiness, rationality, technological mastery) in accordance with newly developing identity potentials. Whatever else ideology is (Mannheim, 1949; Schilder 1930-1940), and whatever transitory or lasting social forms it takes, we will tentatively view it here and discuss it later—*as a necessity for the growing ego* which is involved in the succession of generations, and in adolescence is committed to some new synthesis of past and future: a synthesis which must include but transcend the past, even as identity does.

We proceed to *Identity Consciousness* (V, 2) the ancestors of which are *Doubt* and *Shame* (II, 2). They counteract and complicate the sense of autonomy, i.e., the acceptance of the psychosocial fact of being, once and for all, a separate individual, who actually and figuratively must stand on his own feet. Here, I beg to quote myself (1950a): "Shame is an emotion insufficiently studied,[13] because in our civilization it is so early and easily absorbed by guilt. Shame supposes that one is completely exposed and conscious of being looked at: in one word, self-conscious. One is visible and not ready to be visible; which is why we dream of shame as a situation in which we are stared at in a condition of incomplete dress. Shame is early expressed in an impulse to bury one's face,

[13] See, however, Piers and Singer (1953).

or to sink, right then and there, into the ground. But this, I think, is essentially rage turned against the self. He who is ashamed would like to force the world not to look at him, not to notice his exposure. He would like to destroy the eyes of the world. Instead he must wish for his own invisibility. . . . Doubt is the brother of shame. Where shame is dependent on the consciousness of being upright and exposed, doubt, so clinical observation leads me to believe, has much to do with a consciousness of having a front and a back—and especially a 'behind'. . . . This basic sense of doubt in whatever one has left behind forms a substratum for later and more verbal forms of compulsive doubting; which finds its adult expression in paranoiac fears concerning hidden persecutors and secret persecutions threatening from behind and from within the behind" (p. 223). Identity Consciousness then is a new edition of that original *doubt*, which concerned the trustworthiness of the training adults and the trustworthiness of the child himself—only that in adolescence, such self-conscious doubt concerns the reliability and reconcilability of the whole span of childhood which is now to be left behind. The obligation now to achieve an identity, not only distinct but also distinctive, is apt to arouse a painful over-all *ashamedness,* somehow comparable to the original shame (and rage) over being visible all around to all-knowing adults—only that such potential shame now adheres to one's identity as a being with a *public history,* exposed to *age-mates* and *leaders.* All of this, in the normal course of events, is outbalanced by that *Self-certainty*, which comes from the accrued sense of an ever-increased identity at the conclusion of each previous crisis, a certainty now characterized by an increasing sense of independence from the family as the matrix of childhood identifications.

Among the societal phenomena corresponding to this second conflict there is a universal trend toward some form of *uniformity* (and sometimes to special uniforms or distinctive clothing) through which incomplete self-certainty, for a time, can hide in a group certainty, such as is provided by the badges as well as the sacrifices of investitures, confirmations, and initiations. Even those who care to differ radically must evolve a certain uniformity of differing (snobs, zoot-suiters). These and less obvious uniformities are supported by the institution of comprehensive *shaming* among peers, a judgmental give-and-take and free banding together which leaves only a few "holding the bag" in painful (if sometimes creative) isolation.

The matter of the choice of a *Negative Identity* (V, 3) as against *free Role Experimentation* has been discussed. The position of these terms on the chart signifies their obvious connection with the earlier conflict (III, 3) between free *Initiative* (in reality, fantasy, and play) and oedipal guilt. Where the identity crisis breaks through to the oedipal crisis and beyond it, to a crisis of trust, the choice of a negative identity remains the only form of initiative, complete denial of guilt or complete denial of ambition the only possible ways of managing guilt. On the other hand, the normal expression of relatively guilt-free initiative at this stage is a kind of disciplined role experimentation which follows the unwritten codes of adolescent subsocieties.

Of the social institutions which undertake to channel as they encourage such initiative, and to provide atonement as they appease guilt, we may point here, again, to *initiations* and *confirmations*: they strive, within an atmosphere of mythical timelessness, to combine some form of sacrifice or submission with an energetic guidance toward sanctioned and circumscribed ways of action—a combination which assures the development in the novice of an optimum of compliance with a maximum sense of fellowship and free choice. This ego aspect of the matter (namely, the achievement of a sense of a choice as a result of ritual regimentation) still awaits study and integration with the better explored sexual aspects of initiation rites and related rituals, official or spontaneous. Armies, of course, utilize this potentiality.

As we approach the middle region of the chart, we find that a more detailed discussion of the terms used has already been offered. Extreme *Work Paralysis* (V, 4) is the logical sequence of a deep sense of inadequacy (regressed to a sense of basic mistrust) of one's general equipment. Such a sense of inadequacy, of course, does not usually reflect a true lack of potential: it may rather convey the unrealistic demands made by an ego ideal willing to settle only for omnipotence or omniscience; it may express the fact that the immediate social environment does not have a niche for the individual's true gifts; or it may reflect the paradoxical fact that an individual in early school life was seduced into a specialized precocity which early outdistanced his identity development. All of these reasons, then, may exclude the individual from that experimental competition in play and work through which he learns to find and to insist on *his* kind of achievement and work identity.

Social institutions support the strength and the distinctiveness of work identity by offering those who are still learning and experimenting a certain *status-of-the-moratorium*, an apprenticeship or discipleship characterized by defined duties, sanctioned competitions, and special freedoms, and yet potentially integrated with the hierarchies of expectable jobs and careers, castes and classes, guilds and unions.

In Box V, 5 we again meet the diagonal, and the over-all focus of this paper; crossing it we enter the area of psychosocial elements which are not derivatives but precursors of future psychosocial crises. The first such element (V, 6) is *Sexual Identity* vs. *Bisexual Diffusion*, the most immediate precursor of *Intimacy* vs. *Isolation*. Here the sexual mores of cultures and classes make for immense differences in the psychosocial differentiation of masculine and feminine (M. Mead, 1949), and in the age, kind, and ubiquity of genital activity. These differences can obscure the common fact discussed above, namely, that the development of psychosocial intimacy is not possible without a firm sense of identity. Bisexual diffusion can lead young adults toward two deceptive developments. Induced by special mores, or otherwise seduced, they may foreclose their identity development by concentrating on early genital activity without intimacy; or, on the contrary, they may concentrate on social or intellectual status values which underplay the genital element, with a resulting permanent weakness of genital polarization with the other sex. Different mores (Kinsey, Pomeroy, and Martin, 1948) demand from some the ability to postpone genital activity, and from others, the early ability to make it a "natural" part of life: in either case, special problems ensue which may well impair true heterosexual intimacy in young adulthood.

Social institutions here offer ideological rationales for a *prolongation of the psychosexual moratorium* in the form of complete sexual abstinence, in the form of genital activity without social commitment, or in the form of sexual play without genital engagement (petting). What a group's or an individual's "libido economy" will stand for depends to some extent on the identity gain which accrues from such preferred sexual behavior.

The study of horizontal V of the chart, then, reveals certain systematic consistencies in the described elements of identity diffusion, and in those of identity formation. As pointed out parenthetically, these consistencies correspond to certain social institutions, which (in ways still to be elucidated) support the ego needs and ego functions subsumed under the term identity. In fact, the two remaining boxes of horizontal V (which at any rate are marginal to this clinical section) cannot be approached at all without a discussion of social institutions. The prime institution which awaits clarification here is that system of ideals which societies present to the young individual in the explicit or implicit form of an *ideology*. To ideology we may, in tentative summary, ascribe the function of offering youth (1) an overly clear perspective of the future, encompassing all foreseeable time, and thus counteracting individual "time diffusion"; (2) an opportunity for the exhibition of some uniformity of appearance and action counteracting individual identity consciousness; (3) inducement to collective role and work experimentation which can counteract a sense of inhibition and personal guilt; (4) submission to leaders who as "big brothers" escape the ambivalence of the parent-child relation; (5) introduction into the ethos of the prevailing technology, and thus into sanctioned and regulated competition; and (6) a seeming correspondence between the internal world of ideals and evils, on the one hand, and, on the other, the outer world with its organized goals and dangers in real space and time: a geographic-historical framework for the young individual's budding identity.

I am aware of having, in the conclusion of a pathographic sketch, "sketched in" some references to phenomena which are the domain of social science. I can justify this only with the assumption that clinical work, in cutting through the immense diversity of individual pathology in order to arrive at some workable generalities, may well come upon an aspect of matters institutional which the historical and the economic approach has necessarily neglected. Here, however, we must first attempt to bring some order into the terminological household of our own field, and this especially where it overlaps with areas of social science.

Societal: Ego and Environment

I

It has not escaped the reader that the term identity covers much of what has been called the self by a variety of workers, be it in the form of a self-concept (George H. Mead, 1934), a self-system (Harry S. Sullivan, 1946-1947), or in that of fluctuating self-experiences described by Schilder (1934), Federn (1927-1949), and others.[14] Within psychoanalytic ego psychology, Hartmann, above all, has circumscribed this general area more clearly when in discussing the so-called *libidinal cathexis of the ego in narcissism*, he comes to the conclusion that it is rather a self which is thus being cathected. He advocates a term *"self-representation,"* as differentiated from "object representation" (Hartmann, 1950). This self-representation was, less systematically, anticipated by Freud in his occasional references to the ego's "attitudes toward the self" and to fluctuating cathexes bestowed upon this self in labile states of "self-esteem" (Freud, 1914). In this paper, we are concerned with the *genetic continuity* of such a self-representation—a continuity which must lastly be ascribed to the work of the ego. No other inner agency could accomplish the selective accentuation of significant identifications throughout childhood and the gradual integration of self-images in anticipation of an identity. It is for this reason that I have called identity, at first, ego identity. But in brashly choosing a name analogous to "ego ideal," I have opened myself to the query as to what the relationship of these two concepts is.

Freud assigned the *internalized perpetuation* of cultural influences to the functions of the "superego or ego ideal" which was to

[14] I am not yet able to establish the systematic convergencies and divergencies between the work of the so-called "Neo-Freudians" and that which I am trying to formulate. It will be seen, however, that in individuals as well as in groups I prefer to speak of a "sense of identity" rather than of a "character structure" or "basic character." In nations, too, my concepts would lead me to concentrate on the conditions and experiences which heighten or endanger a national sense of identity rather than on a static national character. An introduction to this subject is offered in my book, *Childhood and Society* (1950a). Here it is important to remember that each identity cultivates its own sense of freedom—wherefore a people rarely understands what makes other peoples feel free. This fact is amply exploited by totalitarian propaganda and underestimated in the Western world.

represent the commands and the prohibitions emanating from the environment and its traditions. Let us compare two statements of Freud's which are relevant here. ". . . the super-ego of the child is not really built up on the model of the parents, but on that of the parents' super-ego; it takes over the same content, it becomes the vehicle of tradition and of all the age-long values which have been handed down in this way from generation to generation. You may easily guess what great help is afforded by the recognition of the super-ego in understanding the social behavior of man, in grasping the problem of delinquency, for example, and perhaps, too, in providing us with some practical hints upon education. . . . Mankind never lives completely in the present; the *ideologies of the super-ego*[15] perpetuate the past, the traditions of the race and the people, which yield but slowly to the influence of the present and to new developments, and, so long as they work through the super-ego, play an important part in man's life" (Freud, 1932, pp. 95-96). Freud, it is to be noted here, speaks of the "ideologies of the super-ego," thus giving the superego ideational content; yet he also refers to it as a "vehicle," i.e., as a part of the psychic system through which ideas work. It would seem that by ideologies of the superego Freud means the superego's specific contributions to the archaic, to the magic in the inner coerciveness of ideologies.

In a second statement Freud acknowledges the social side of the ego ideal. "The ego ideal opens up an important avenue for the understanding of group psychology. In addition to its individual side, this ideal has a social side; it is also the common ideal of a family, a class or a nation" (1914, p. 101).

It would seem that the terms superego and ego ideal have come to be distinguished by their different relation to phylogenetic and to ontogenetic history. The superego is conceived as a more archaic and thoroughly internalized representative of the evolutionary principle of morality, of man's *congenital proclivity* toward the development of a primitive, categorical conscience. Allied with (ontogenetically) early introjects, the superego remains a rigidly vindictive and punitive inner agency of "blind" morality. The ego ideal, however, seems to be more flexibly bound to the ideals of the particular *historical period* and thus is closer to the ego function of reality testing.

[15] My italics.

Ego identity (if we were to hold on to this term and to this level of discourse) would in comparison be even closer to *social reality* in that as a subsystem of the ego it would test, select, and integrate the self-representations derived from the psychosocial crises of childhood. It could be said to be characterized by the more or less *actually attained but forever-to-be-revised* sense of the reality of the self within social reality; while the imagery of the ego ideal could be said to represent a set of *to-be-strived-for but forever-not-quite-attainable ideal* goals for the self.

However, in using the word self in the sense of Hartmann's self-representation, one opens the whole controversy to a radical consideration. One could argue that it may be wise in matters of the ego's perceptive and regulative dealings with its self to reserve the designation "ego" for the subject, and to give the designation "self" to the object. The ego, then, as a central organizing agency, is during the course of life faced with a changing self which, in turn, demands to be synthesized with abandoned and anticipated selves. This suggestion would be applicable to the *body ego*, which could be said to be the part of the self provided by the attributes of the organism, and, therefore, might more appropriately be called the *body self*; it would also concern the ego ideal as the representative of the ideas, images, and configurations, which serve the persistent comparison with an *ideal self*; and finally, it would apply to what I have called *ego identity*. What could consequently be called the *self-identity* emerges from all those experiences in which a sense of temporary self-diffusion was successfully contained by a renewed and ever more realistic self-definition and social recognition. *Identity formation thus can be said to have a self-aspect, and an ego aspect.* It is part of the ego in the sense that it represents the ego's synthesizing function on one of its frontiers, namely, the actual social structure of the environment and the image of reality as transmitted to the child during successive childhood crises. (The other frontiers would be the id, and the demands made on the ego by our biological history and structure; the superego and the demands of our more primitively moralistic proclivities; and the ego ideal with its idealized parent images.) Identity, in this connection, has a claim to recognition as the adolescent ego's most important support, in the task of containing the postpubertal id, and in balancing the then newly invoked superego as well as the again overly demanding ego ideal.

Until the matter of ego vs. self is sufficiently defined to permit a terminological decision, I shall use the bare term identity in order to suggest a social function of the ego which results, in adolescence, in a relative psychosocial equilibrium essential to the tasks of young adulthood.

II

The word "psychosocial" so far has had to serve as an emergency bridge between the so-called "biological" formulations of psychoanalysis and newer ones which take the cultural environment into more systematic consideration.

The so-called basic *biological* orientation of psychoanalysis has gradually become a habitual kind of *pseudo biology*, and this especially in the conceptualization (or lack thereof) of man's "environment." In psychoanalytic writings the terms "outer world" or "environment" are often used to designate an uncharted area which is said to be outside merely because it fails to be inside—inside the individual's somatic skin, or inside his psychic systems, or inside his self in the widest sense. Such a vague and yet omnipresent "outerness" by necessity assumes a number of ideological connotations, and, in fact, assumes the character of a number of world images: sometimes "the outer world" is conceived of as reality's conspiracy against the infantile wish world; sometimes as the (indifferent or annoying) fact of the existence of other people; and then again as the (at least partially benevolent) presence of maternal care. But even in the recent admission of the significance of the "mother-child relationship," a stubborn tendency persists to treat the mother-child unit as a "biological" entity more or less isolated from its cultural surroundings, which then again become an "environment" of vague supports or of blind pressures and mere "conventions." Thus, step for step, we are encumbered by the remnants of juxtapositions which were once necessary and fruitful enough: for it was important to establish the fact that moralistic and hypocritical social demands are apt to crush the adult and to exploit the child. It was important to conceptualize certain intrinsic antagonisms between the individual's and society's energy households. However, the implicit conclusion that an individual ego could exist against or without a specifically human "environment," i.e., social organization, is senseless; and, far from being "biological" in its orientation, threatens to isolate psychoanalytic theory from the rich ethological and ecological findings of modern biology.

It is again Hartmann (1939) who opens the way to new considerations. His statement that the human infant is born preadapted to an "average expectable environment" implies a more truly biological as well as an inescapably societal formulation. For not even the very best of mother-child relationships could, by themselves, account for that subtle and complex "milieu" which permits a human baby not only to survive but also to develop his potentialities for growth and uniqueness. Man's ecology includes among its dimensions constant natural, historical, and technological readjustment; which makes it at once obvious that only a perpetual social metabolism and a constant (if ever so imperceptible) restructuring of tradition can safeguard for each new generation of infants anything approaching an "average expectability" of environment. Today, when rapid technological changes have taken the lead, the matter of establishing by scientific means and of preserving in flexible forms an "average expectable" continuity in child rearing and education has, in fact, become a matter of human survival.

The specific kind of preadaptedness of the human infant (namely, the readiness to grow by predetermined steps through institutionalized psychosocial crises) calls not only for one basic environment, but for a whole chain of such successive environments. As the child "adapts" in spurts and stages, he has a claim, at any given stage reached, to the next "average expectable environment." In other words, the human environment must permit and safeguard a series of more or less discontinuous and yet culturally and psychologically consistent steps, each extending further along the radius of expanding life tasks. All of this makes man's so-called biological adaptation a matter of life cycles developing within their community's changing history. Consequently, a psychoanalytic sociology faces the task of conceptualizing man's environment as the persistent endeavor of the older and more adult egos to join in the organizational effort of providing an integrated series of average expectable environments for the young egos.

III

In a recent paper which thoughtfully yet somewhat sweepingly reviews efforts at approaching the relation of culture and personality, Hartmann, Kris, and Loewenstein (1951) state: "Cultural conditions could and should be viewed also with the question in mind which and what kind of opportunities for ego functions in a sphere free from conflict they invite or inhibit." In regard to the possibility of studying the reflection of such "cultural conditions" in the psychoanalysis of individuals, the writers seem less encouraging. They state: "Analysts too are aware of differences of behavior caused by cultural conditions; they are not devoid of that common sense which has always stressed these differences, but their impact on the analytic observer tends to decrease as work progresses and as available data move from the periphery to the center, that is from manifest behavior to data, part of which is accessible only to an analytic investigation." The present paper ventures to suggest that rather central problems of ego development, which are, indeed, "accessible only to an analytic investigation," demand that the psychoanalyst's awareness of cultural differences go well beyond that "common sense" which the three authors (being themselves outstanding cosmopolitans) seem to find sufficient in this particular area of observation, while they would assuredly urge a more "analyzed" common sense in other areas.

In order to approach this whole matter psychoanalytically, it may well be necessary for the individual psychoanalyst to ask himself what particular configuration of drives, defenses, capabilities, and opportunities led him into the choice of this ever-expanding field. Some search in this area may clarify the fact that some of the most heated and stubborn answers to the question of what psychoanalysis *is* or *is not* originate in another question of great urgency, namely: what psychoanalysis *must be* (or *must remain or become*) to a particular worker because a particular psychoanalytic "identity" has become a cornerstone of his existence as a man, a professional, and a citizen. I am not denying here the necessity, in a suddenly expanding and unexpectedly popular field, to define the original sources of its inspiration and the fundamentals of its specific morality. Yet, psychoanalysis, in its young history, has offered rich opportunities for a variety of identities: it gave new function and scope to such divergent endeavors as natural philosophy and Talmudic argument; medical tradition and missionary teaching; literary demonstration and the building of theory; social reform and the making of money. Psychoanalysis as a movement has harbored a variety of world images and utopias which originated in the various stages of its history in a variety of countries, and this as a result of the simple fact that man, in order to be able to interact efficiently with other human beings, must, at intervals, make *a total orientation out of a given stage of partial knowledge*. Individual students of Freud thus found their identity best suited to certain early theses of his which promised a particular sense of psychoanalytic identity, and with it, an inspiring ideology. Similarly, overstated antitheses to some of Freud's tentative and transient theses have served as bases for professional and scientific identities of other workers in the field. Such identities easily find elaboration in ideological schools and in irreversible systematizations which do not permit of argument or change.

In speaking of scientific proof and scientific progress in a field which deals directly with the immediate needs of men, it is necessary to account not only for methodological, practical, and ethical factors, but also for the necessity of a professional identity backed by an ideological quasi synthesis of the available orientations. Sooner or later, then, training analyses must encompass the varieties of professional identity formation in candidates-for-training, while theoretical teaching must throw light also on the ideological background of principal differences in what is felt to be most practical, most true, and most right at various stages of this developing field.

IV

The discussion of "professional identities" has necessarily led us beyond identity formation proper, to its derivatives in later, truly adult stages. I will make one more step into adulthood, before returning, in conclusion, to the problem of ideological polarization as an aspect of the societal processes which meets a necessity of adolescent ego development.

I have already implied a hypothesis which goes beyond that of Hartmann, Kris, and Loewenstein (1951), who state that "cultural conditions could and should be viewed *also*[16] with the question in mind which and what kind of opportunities for ego functions in a sphere free from conflict they invite or inhibit." It may well be that the relationship between the organized values and institutional efforts of societies, on the one hand, and the mechanisms of ego synthesis, on the other, is more systematic; and that, from a psychosocial point of view at any rate, basic social and cultural processes can *only* be viewed as the joint endeavor of adult egos to develop and maintain, through joint organization, a maximum of conflict-free energy in a mutually supportive psychosocial equilibrium. Only such organization is likely to give consistent support to the young egos at every step of their development.

I have characterized the psychosocial gains of adult ego development with the terms Intimacy, Generativity, and Integrity (VI, 6—VII, 7—VIII, 8 on the chart). They denote a postadolescent development of libidinal cathexes in *intimate engagements*; in parenthood or other *forms of "generating"*;[17] and, finally, in the most *integrative experiences* and values accrued from a lifetime. All of these developments have ego aspects and social aspects; in fact, their very alternatives (Isolation, VI, 6—Self-Absorption, VII, 7—and Despair, VIII, 8) can be held in check only by the individual's fitting participation in social endeavors which "invite opportunities for ego functions in spheres free from conflict." The older generation thus needs the younger one as much as the younger one depends on the older; and it would seem that it is in this mutuality of the development of the older and younger generations that certain basic and universal values such as love, faith, truth,

---

[16] My italics.

[17] See the concern over personal children, patients, and germinating ideas in Freud's "Irma dream" (Erikson, 1954). In my psychosocial interpretation of this dream I pointed out that a dream can be seen to retrace the steps of psychosocial development at the same time that it represents a psychosexual regression to a certain infantile stage of libido development. Freud's dreams (because of the strong inner structure of his personality and maybe also because of the didactic interest with which he went about dreaming them) prove to be continuously enlightening even in regard to matters not explicitly formulated by him, such as the parallelism of psychosocial and psychosexual themes. In the Irma dream, so I showed in my paper, the theme of *phallic* intrusion can be seen to be closely associated with that of *initiative*. Similarly, Freud's dream of the Three Fates clearly points to the close relationship of *oral* incorporation and the problem of *trust*; while the dream of Count Thun strongly emphasizes themes of *autonomy* and the modes of *anal* elimination. A paper comparing these three dreams is in preparation.

justice, order, work, etc., in all of their defensive strength, compensatory power, and independent creativity become and remain important joint achievements of individual ego development and of the social process. In fact, as our clinical histories begin to reveal, these values provide indispensable support for the ego development of the growing generations, in that they give some specific superindividual consistency to parental conduct (although *kinds* of consistency—including consistent kinds of being inconsistent—vary with value systems and personality types).

The intrinsic complication and the peculiar social pathology adhering to the *verbal conventions* and *formal institutions* which communicate and perpetuate social values periodically call for special societal processes which will recreate the "average expectability" of the environments either through ceremonial rededication, or through systematic reformulation. In both cases, selected leaders and elites feel called upon to demonstrate a convincing, a "charismatic" kind of generalized generativity, i.e., a superpersonal interest in the maintenance and the rejuvenation of institutions. In recorded history, some such leaders are registered as "great"; they, it seems, are able, out of the deepest personal conflicts to derive the energy which meets their period's specific needfulness for a resynthesis of the prevalent world image. At any rate, only through constant rededication will institutions gain the active and inspired investment of new energy from their young members. More theoretically stated: only by maintaining, in its institutionalized values, meaningful correspondences to the main crises of ego development, does a society manage to have at the disposal of its particular group identity a maximum of the conflict-free energy accrued from the childhood crises of a majority of its young members.[18]

---

[18] In this paper, I cannot more than approach the possible relation of the problem of identity to ideological processes (see Erikson, 1958a), and I can only parenthetically list possible analogous correspondences between stages of psychosocial development in the individual and major trends of social organization. As pointed out in "Growth and Crises of the Healthy Personality" (pp. 65-82), the problem of Autonomy (versus Shame and Doubt) has intrinsic relations with the delineation of individual rights and limitations in the basic principles of law and justice, and the problem of Initiative (versus Guilt) with the encouragements and limitations emanating from the dominant ethos of production. The problem of workmanship critically prepares for the predominant techniques of production and their characteristic division of labor.

Before briefly applying this general assumption to ideology, I must ask the reader to take one more look at the chart. In boxes V, 6—V, 7—and V, 8 he will find whatever indication I can give of the precursors in adolescence of what later on are Intimacy, Generativity, and Integrity. The struggle for *Sexual Identity*, V, 6, while, at first, consumed with the question as to what kind of a male or female one is, through the selective search for *Intimacy*, VI, 6, approaches the problem of a choice of a future co-parent. The clarification, through a firmer identity formation, of one's status as a *follower* (of some) and a *leader* (of others), V, 7, permits the early development of a responsibility toward younger age-mates which, although an important social phenomenon in its own right, is a precursor of the sense of responsibility for the next generation (*Generativity*), VII, 7. Finally, some form of *Ideological Polarization*, V, 8, some breakdown of the multiplicity of values into a few which coerce commitment, must be part and parcel of this gradual reversal of roles, through which the "identified" individual becomes a figure of identification for the young. Such polarization, however, cannot fail eventually to become a critical part of the problem of *Integrity*, VIII, 8: a matter which we saw reflected in Shaw's statement (1952): that he "succeeded only too well" in living the public identity "G.B.S.," i.e., in the polarization of his propensities for acting like an actor on the stage of life, and for acting as a reformer in social reality.

V

Shaw, of course, was a studiedly spectacular man. But, to extend a Shavianism quoted above: a clown is often not only the best but also the most sincere part of the Great Show. It is, therefore, worth while at this point to review the words chosen by Shaw to characterize the story of his "conversion": "I was *drawn into* the Socialist *revival* of the early eighties, among Englishmen *intensely serious* and *burning with indignation* at very *real* and very *fundamental evils* that affected *all the world*." The words here italicized convey to me the following implications. "Drawn into": an ideology has a compelling power. "Revival": it consists of a traditional force in the state of rejuvenation. "Intensely serious": it permits even the cynical to make an investment of sincerity. "Burning with indignation": it gives to the need for repudiation the sanction of righteousness. "Real": it projects a vague inner evil onto a circumscribed horror in reality. "Fundamental": it promises participation in an effort at basic reconstruction of society. "All the world": it gives structure to a totally defined world image. Here, then, are the elements by which a group identity harnesses in the service of its ideology the young individual's aggressive and discriminative energies, and encompasses, as it completes it, the individual's identity. Thus, identity and ideology are two aspects of the same process. Both provide the necessary condition for further individual maturation and, with it, for the next higher form of identification, namely, the *solidarity linking common identities.* For the need to bind irrational self-hate and irrational repudiation makes young people, on occasion, mortally compulsive and conservative even where and when they seem most anarchic and radical; the same need makes them potentially "ideological," i.e., more or less explicitly in search of a world image held together by what Shaw called "a clear comprehension of life in the light of an intelligible theory."

As far as Fabian Socialists are concerned, Shaw seems fully justified in using terms characterizing an ideology of marked intellectual brilliance. More generally, an ideological system is a coherent body of shared images, ideas, and ideals which (whether based on a formulated dogma, an implicit *Weltanschauung*, a highly structured world image, a political creed, or a "way of life") provides for the participants a coherent, if systematically simplified, over-all orientation in space and time, in means and ends.

The word "ideology" itself has somewhat of a bad name. By their very nature ideologies contradict other ideologies as "inconsistent" and hypocritical; and an over-all critique of ideology characterizes its persuasive simplifications as a systematic form of collective hypocrisy (Mannheim, 1949). For it is true that the average adult, and in fact, the average community, if not acutely engaged in some ideological polarization, are apt to consign ideology to a well-circumscribed compartment in their lives, where it remains handy for periodical rituals and rationalizations, but will do no undue harm to other business at hand. Yet, the fact that ideologies are simplified conceptions of what is to come (and thus later can serve as rationalizations for what has come about) does not preclude the possibility that at certain stages of individual development and at certain periods in history, ideological polarization, conflict, and commitment correspond to an inescapable inner need. Youth needs to base its rejections and acceptances on ideological alternatives vitally related to the existing range of alternatives for identity formation.

Ideologies seem to provide meaningful combinations of the oldest and the newest in a group's ideals. They thus channel the forceful earnestness, the sincere asceticism, and the eager indignation of youth toward that social frontier where the struggle between conservatism and radicalism is most alive. On that frontier, fanatic ideologists do their busy work and psychopathic leaders their dirty work; but there, also, true leaders create significant solidarities. All ideologies ask for, as the prize for the promised possession of a future, uncompromising commitment to some absolute hierarchy of values and some rigid principle of conduct: be that principle total obedience to tradition, if the future is the eternalization of ancestry; total resignation, if the future is to be of another world; total martial discipline, if the future is to be reserved for some brand of armed superman; total inner reform, if the future is perceived as an advanced edition of heaven on earth; or (to mention only one of the ideological ingredients of our time) complete pragmatic abandon to the processes of production and to human teamwork, if unceasing production seems to be the thread which holds present and future together. It is in the totalism and exclusiveness of some ideologies that the superego is apt to regain its territory from identity: for when established identities become outworn or unfinished ones threaten to remain incomplete, special crises compel men to wage holy wars, by the cruelest means, against those who seem to question or threaten their unsafe ideological bases.

We may well pause to ponder briefly the fact that the technological and economic developments of our day encroach upon all traditional group identities and solidarities such as may have developed in agrarian, feudal, patrician, or mercantile ideologies. As has been shown by many writers, such over-all development seems to result in a loss of a sense of cosmic wholeness, of providential planfulness, and of heavenly sanction for the means of production (and destruction). In large parts of the world, this seems to result in a ready fascination with totalistic world views, views predicting milleniums and cataclysms, and advocating self-appointed mortal gods. Technological centralization today can give small groups of such fanatic ideologists the concrete power of totalitarian state machines (Erikson, 1953).

Psychoanalysis has made some contributions to the understanding of these developments especially in so far as they reflect the universal anxieties, inner dependencies, and vulnerabilities adhering to the common fact of human childhood. Psychoanalysis can also help to understand the fact that even in civilized beings the superego's paternalistic-primitive simplicity may call for an irrational trust in superpolice chiefs on earth, now that the heavenly discipline which encompassed earlier world images seems to have lost its convincing firmness. However, the application of the psychoanalytic instrument to the questions as to how man changes in his depth as he changes the expanses of his environment, and as to who is affected (and how, and how deeply) by technological and ideological changes (Erikson, 1953)—these questions must await better formulations of the ego's relationship to work techniques, to the technological "environment," and to the prevalent division of labor.

VI

In a recent seminar in Jerusalem[19] I had an opportunity to discuss with Israeli scholars and clinicians the question of what the identity of an "Israeli" is, and thus to envisage one extreme of contemporary ideological orientations. Israel fascinates both her friends and her enemies. A great number of ideological fragments from European history have found their way into the consciousness of this small state; and many of the identity problems which have occupied a century and a half of American history are being faced in Israel within a few years. A new nation is established on a distant coast (which does not seem to "belong" to anybody) out of oppressed minorities from many lands, a new identity based on imported ideals which are libertarian, puritanic, and messianic. Any discussion of Israel's manifold and most immediate problems sooner or later leads to the extraordinary accomplishments and the

[19] Organized by Professors S. Eisenstadt and C. Frankenstein of the Hebrew University. The initial impressions presented here are mine.

extraordinary ideological problems posed by the pioneer Zionist settlers (now a small minority) who make up what is known as the Kibbutz movement. These European ideologists, given—as it were—a *historical moratorium* created by the peculiar international and national status of Palestine first in the Ottoman Empire and then in the British mandate, were able to establish and to fortify a significant *utopian bridgehead* for Zionist ideology. In his "homeland," and tilling his very home soil, the "ingathered" Jew was to overcome such evil identities as result from eternal wandering, merchandising, and intellectualizing (Erikson, 1950a) and was to become *whole* again in body and mind, as well as in nationality. That the Kibbutz movement has created a hardy, responsible, and inspired type of individual, nobody could deny, although certain details of its educational system (such as the raising of children, from the very beginning, in Children's Houses, and the rooming together of boys and girls through the high-school years) are under critical scrutiny, both in Israel and abroad. The fact is, however, that in Israel a utopia was established on a frontier exposed all around, under conditions reminiscent of those faced by the Mormons. This historical fact is the only framework for judging the rationale and the rationalizations of the style of life which ensued. For no doubt, these pioneers (comparable to this country's settlers, who, in turn, utilized the historical moratorium offered by the discovery of an empty continent, for the establishment of a new "way of life") provided a new nation, sprung up overnight, with a historical ideal. A legitimate question, however, and one not too foreign to this country's historians, concerns the relationship of a revolutionary elite to those who subsequently crowd into and thrive on the lands occupied and on the gains made.[20] In Israel, the by now somewhat exclusive elite of Kibbutzniks faces that incomparably larger part of the population which represents an ideologically all but indigestible mixture: the masses of African and Oriental immigrants, powerful organized labor, the big city dwellers, the religious orthodoxy, the new state bureaucracy—and then, of course, the "good old" mercantile class of middlemen. Furthermore, the more uncompromising part of the Kibbutz movement

---

[20] We may state tentatively that the elites which emerge from historical change are groups which out of the deepest common identity crisis manage to create a new style of coping with the outstanding danger situations of their society.

THE PROBLEM OF EGO IDENTITY

has not failed to place itself between the two worlds to both of which Zionism maintains strong historical bonds: American and British Jewry (which bought much of the Kibbutz land from Arab absentee landlords) and Soviet Communism, to which the (shall we say) communalistic Kibbutz movement[21] felt ideologically close—only to be repudiated by Moscow as another form of deviationism.

The Kibbutz movement thus is one example of a modern ideological utopia which freed unknown energies in young people who considered themselves as of one "people," and created a (more or less explicit) group ideal of pervading significance—if of quite unpredictable historical fate in an industrial world. However, Israel is, undoubtedly, one of the most ideology-conscious countries that ever existed; no "peasants" nor workmen ever argued more about the far-reaching meanings of daily decisions. The subtler meanings of ideology for identity formation can probably be fathomed best by comparing highly verbal ideologies with those transitory systems of conversion and aversion which exist in any society, in that no-man's land between childhood and adulthood more or less derisively called adolescence—exist as the most meaningful part of a young person's or a young group's life, often without the knowledge, or indeed, curiosity, of the adults around them. It must be assumed that much of the spontaneous polarization of tastes, opinions, and slogans which occupy the arguments of young people, and much of the sudden impulse to join in destructive behavior, are loose ends of identity formation waiting to be tied together by some ideology.

VII

In the pathographic section of this paper I have pointed to the *total choice* of a negative identity in individuals who could achieve such escape on the basis of autistic and regressive proclivities.

The escape of many gifted if unstable young individuals into a private utopia or, as another patient put it, a "majority of one," might not be necessary were it not for a general development to which they feel unable to submit, i.e., the increasing demand for

---

[21] I.e., relative communism within the individual community, which, however, in its relation to the national economy, rather represents a capitalist cooperative.

standardization, uniformity, and conformity which characterizes the present stage of this our individualist civilization. In this country, the demand for large-scale conformity has not developed into an explicit totalitarian ideology; it has associated itself with the total dogmas of churches and with the stereotypes of businesslike behavior, but, on the whole, shuns political ideology. We appreciate as we study the capacity of our youth to manage the identity diffusion of an industrial democracy with simple trustfulness, with playful dissonance, with technical virtuosity, with "other-minded" solidarity (Riesman, 1950)—and with a distaste for ideological explicitness. What exactly the implicit ideology of American youth (this most technological youth in the world) is—that is a fateful question, not to be lightly approached in a paper of this kind. Nor would one dare to assess in passing the changes which may be taking place in this ideology and in its implicitness, as a result of a world struggle which makes a military identity a necessary part of young adulthood in this country.

It is easier to delineate that malignant turn toward a *negative group identity* which prevails in some of the youth especially of our large cities, where conditions of economic, ethnic, and religious marginality provide poor bases for positive identities: here negative group identities are sought in spontaneous clique formations ranging all the way from neighborhood gangs and jazz mobs, to dope rings, homosexual circles, and criminal gangs. Clinical experience can be expected to make significant contributions to this problem.[22] Yet, we may well warn ourselves against an uncriti-

---

[22] We may ask, for example, what inner, unconscious gain the delinquent may derive from a total choice of delinquency as a way or as a goal of life. It is possible that his radical closing up, his provocative smugness, his utter denial of remorse, may cover and counteract the anxiety of threatening identity diffusion. Are we, in turn, exposing him to this very danger as we hammer at him, offering him a "chance" at the price of remorse—the one price that he cannot afford to pay? A glance at the components of identity diffusion (column V, p. 120) will lead to these considerations:

Juvenile delinquency saves some young individuals from *time diffusion*. In the delinquent state, any future perspective, with its demands and uncertainties, is overruled by the dominant emphasis on short-range goals serving, say, a need to "get at somebody," or to just "do something," or "go somewhere." This, of course, also constitutes a simplification of social modalities, together with a primitivization of impulse life.

Identity consciousness is escaped also; or, at any rate, it is firmly hidden by the delinquent's particular identification-with-himself-in-the-role-of-delinquent, which offers such an impenetrable façade to investigator and judge. This façade—the

cal transfer of clinical terms, attitudes, and methods to such public problems. Rather we may come back to a point made earlier: teachers, judges, and psychiatrists, who deal with youth, come to be significant representatives of that strategic act of "recognition" (the act through which society "identifies" its young members and thus contributes to their developing identity) which was described at the beginning of this paper. If, for simplicity's sake or in order to accommodate ingrown habits of law or psychiatry, they diagnose and treat as a criminal, as a constitutional misfit, as a derelict doomed by his upbringing, or—indeed—as a deranged patient, a

---

outward appearance of a total choice—denies any emotional response, and prevents the emergence of any sense of shame or guilt.

Work paralysis, the painful inability to enjoy the mastery of materials and of cooperative situations, is also sidetracked in delinquency. Work mastery is in any culture the backbone of identity formation. In delinquents (often recruited from groups who are denied a meaningful work experience) there appears, instead, a perverse but deep satisfaction in "doing a job" in the destructive sense. The legal classification of such a deed may seal a young individual's *negative identity* as a criminal once and for all. This, in turn, relieves him of the necessity to search further for a "good" identity (Erikson and Erikson, 1957).

In addition, delinquent behavior saves many individuals from *bisexual diffusion.* The exaggeration of the phallic-sadistic role on the part of the boy delinquent and the careless and loveless promiscuity on the part of the girl offer an escape either from a sense of sexual inferiority or from any commitment to true intimacy.

In this connection a development highly characteristic of our time must be emphasized: I mean the new emphasis on locomotion, as provided by the machine. There is first of all what might be called the *locomotorist intoxication* of our time —the pleasure of imagining oneself to be an immensely powerful driver, while actually being moved by powers stronger and faster than those of the human body. The second intoxication (now conveniently combined with the first in drive-in shows) is the passive *intoxication by powerfully moving spectacles*—in which continuous motion is not only observed but experienced, while the organism "races its engine," as it were. Since youth is an eminently locomotor period, and since in adolescence perambulatory (as well as mental) exploration must take over much of sexual tension, the disbalance between increased passive stimulation provided by mechanical invention and decreased opportunities for vigorous action is probably a major contributor to such specific delinquencies as the appropriation of motorcars and the urge to do physical violence, and to the widespread addiction to excessive forms of dancing.

As for *authority diffusion,* it is clear that organized delinquency clearly aligns the young person with an ingroup of equals with a defined hierarchy of leadership, and clearly circumscribes outgroups such as other gangs, or all the world outside the gang. Similarly, gang ethics protect the ingroup member from a sense of *diffusion of ideals.*

It is in this way that I would approach the problem of juvenile delinquency with concepts gained from the observation of psychiatric kinds of juvenile disturbance. Such a comparison suggests that we may learn much about the dynamics of youth by juxtaposing the delinquent joiners and the schizoid isolates (even as Freud juxtaposed perversion and neurosis as the expression and the inhibition of certain impulses) (Erikson, 1956c).

young person who, for reasons of personal or social marginality, is close to choosing a negative identity, that young person may well put his energy into becoming exactly what the careless and fearful community expects him to be—and make a total job of it.

It is hoped that the theory of identity, in the long run, can contribute more to this problem than to sound a warning.

Summary

In my attempt to circumscribe the problem of identity I have been "all over the map." I do not propose to leave the matter in this condition: as far as is possible, studies taking into account the specific dynamic nature of selected media (life history, case history, dream life, ideology) will follow (Erikson, 1958a). In the meantime, and in summary: identity, in outbalancing at the conclusion of childhood the potentially malignant dominance of the infantile superego, permits the individual to forgo excessive self-repudiation and the diffused repudiation of otherness. Such freedom provides a necessary condition for the ego's power to integrate matured sexuality, ripened capacities, and adult commitments. The histories of our young patients illustrate the ways in which aggravated identity crises may result from special genetic causes and from specific dynamic conditions. Such studies, in turn, throw new light on those more or less institutionalized rites and rituals, associations, and movements through which societies and subsocieties grant youth a world between childhood and adulthood: a psychosocial moratorium during which extremes of *subjective experience*, alternatives of *ideological choice*, and potentialities of *realistic commitment* can become the subject of social play and of joint mastery.

APPENDIX

This worksheet summarizes in diagrammatic form the areas and stages of development discussed in this monograph. Being a worksheet it has undergone and will undergo both changes and expansion; being a diagram it flatly separates groupings and sequences which, under observation, prove to be overlapping. Nevertheless, it is suggested that both verticals and horizontals represent a kind of skeleton essential to whatever flesh and blood may (and must) be added by study and discussion. Such study can be enhanced by arranging each vertical along a diagonal (as in the epigenetic chart, p. 120), and by observing its inner consistency before relating it to other columns. There is no rank order; one can begin with any column for which the available data are plentiful and proceed to the next promising column.

Worksheet

	A Psychosocial Crises	B Radius of Significant Relations	C Related Elements of Social Order	D Psychosocial Modalities	E Psychosexual Stages
I	Trust vs. Mistrust	Maternal Person	Cosmic Order	To get To give in return	Oral-Respiratory, Sensory-Kinesthetic (Incorporative Modes)
II	Autonomy vs. Shame, Doubt	Parental Persons	"Law and Order"	To hold (on) To let (go)	Anal-Urethral, Muscular (Retentive-Eliminative)
III	Initiative vs. Guilt	Basic Family	Ideal Prototypes	To make (=going after) To "make like" (=playing)	Infantile-Genital, Locomotor (Intrusive, Inclusive)
IV	Industry vs. Inferiority	"Neighborhood," School	Technological Elements	To make things (=completing) To make things together	"Latency"
V	Identity and Repudiation vs. Identity Diffusion	Peer Groups and Outgroups; Models of Leadership	Ideological Perspectives	To be oneself (or not to be) To share being oneself	Puberty
VI	Intimacy and Solidarity vs. Isolation	Partners in friendship, sex, competition, cooperation	Patterns of Cooperation and Competition	To lose and find oneself in another	Genitality
VII	Generativity vs. Self-Absorption	Divided labor and shared household	Currents of Education and Tradition	To make be To take care of	
VIII	Integrity vs. Despair	"Mankind" "My Kind"	Wisdom	To be, through having been To face not being	

Bibliography

Ackerman, N. W. (1951), "Social Role" and Total Personality. *Am. J. Orthopsychiat.*, 21:1-17.
Bateman, J. F., and Dunham, H. W. (1948), The State Mental Hospital as a Specialized Community Experience. *Am. J. Psychiat.*, 105:445-449.
Benedict, R. (1938), Continuities and Discontinuities in Cultural Conditioning. *Psychiatry*, 1:161-167.
Bernfeld, S. (1944), Freud's Earliest Theories and the School of Helmholtz. *Psa. Quart.*, 13:341-362.
Bettelheim, B. (1943), Individual and Mass Behavior in Extreme Situations. *J. Abn. Soc. Psychol.*, 38:417-452.
Bibring, E. (1953), The Mechanism of Depression. In *Affective Disorders*, P. Greenacre, ed. New York: International Universities Press, pp. 13-48.
Blos, P. (1953), The Contribution of Psychoanalysis to the Treatment of Adolescents. In *Psychoanalysis and Social Work*, M. Heiman, ed. New York: International Universities Press.
Brenman, M. (1952), On Teasing and Being Teased: and the Problem of "Moral Masochism." *The Psychoanalytic Study of the Child*, 7:264-285. New York: International Universities Press. Also in *Psychoanalytic Psychiatry and Psychology, Clinical and Theoretical Papers*, Austen Riggs Center, Vol. I, R. P. Knight and C. R. Friedman, eds. New York: International Universities Press, 1954, pp. 29-51.
Breuer, J., and Freud, S. (1895), Studies on Hysteria. *Standard Edition*, 2:1-335. London: Hogarth, 1955.
Burlingham, D. (1952), *Twins*. New York: International Universities Press.
Erikson, E. H. (1937), Configurations in Play—Clinical Notes. *Psa. Quart.*, 6:139-214.
——— (1939), Observations on Sioux Education. *J. Psychol.*, 7:101-156.
——— (1940a), Problems of Infancy and Early Childhood. In *Cyclopedia of Medicine*. Philadelphia: Davis & Co., pp. 714-730. Also in *Outline of Abnormal Psychology*, G. Murphy and A. Bachrach, eds. New York: Modern Library, 1954, pp. 3-36.
——— (1940b), On Submarine Psychology. Written for the Committee on National Morale for the Coordinator of Information. Unpublished ms.
——— (1940c), Studies in the Interpretation of Play: 1. Clinical Observation of Play Disruption in Young Children. *Genet. Psychol. Monogr.*, 22:557-671.
——— (1942), Hitler's Imagery and German Youth. *Psychiatry*, 5:475-493.
——— (1945), Childhood and Tradition in Two American Indian Tribes. *The Psychoanalytic Study of the Child*, 1:319-350. New York: International Universities Press. Also (revised) in *Personality in Nature, Society and Culture*, C. Kluckhohn and H. Murray, eds. New York: Knopf, 1948, pp. 176-203.
——— (1946), Ego Development and Historical Change—Clinical Notes. *The Psychoanalytic Study of the Child*, 2:359-396. New York: International Universities Press.

BIBLIOGRAPHY

——— (1950a), *Childhood and Society*. New York: Norton.
——— (1950b), Growth and Crises of the "Healthy Personality." In *Symposium on the Healthy Personality*, Supplement II; Problems of Infancy and Childhood, Transactions of Fourth Conference, March, 1950, M. J. E. Senn, ed. New York: Josiah Macy, Jr. Foundation. Also in *Personality in Nature, Society and Culture*, 2nd ed., C. Kluckhohn and H. Murray, eds. New York: Knopf, 1953, pp. 185-225.
——— (1951a), On the Sense of Inner Identity. In *Health and Human Relations*; Report of a Conference on Health and Human Relations held at Hiddesen near Detmold, Germany, August 2-7, 1951. Sponsored by the Josiah Macy, Jr. Foundation. New York: Blakiston, 1953. Also in *Psychoanalytic Psychiatry and Psychology*, Austen Riggs Center, Vol. I, R. P. Knight and C. R. Friedman, eds. New York: International Universities Press, 1954, pp. 351-364.
——— (1951b), Sex Differences in the Play Configurations of Preadolescents. *Amer. J. Orthopsychiat.*, 21:667-692.
——— (1953), Wholeness and Totality. In *Totalitarianism*, Proceedings of a conference held at the American Academy of Arts and Sciences, March, 1953, C. J. Friedrich, ed. Cambridge: Harvard University Press, 1954.
——— (1954), The Dream Specimen of Psychoanalysis. *J. Amer. Psa. Assoc.*, 2:5-56. Also in *Psychoanalytic Psychiatry and Psychology, Clinical and Theoretical Papers*, Austen Riggs Center, Vol. I, R. P. Knight and C. R. Friedman, eds. New York: International Universities Press, 1954, pp. 131-170.
——— (1955a), The Syndrome of Identity Diffusion in Adolescents and Young Adults. In *Discussions on Child Development*, J. M. Tanner and B. Inhelder, eds. Vol. III of the Proceedings of the World Health Organization Study Group on the Psychobiological Development of the Child, Geneva, 1955. New York: International Universities Press, 1958, pp. 133-154.
——— (1955b), The Psychosocial Development of Children. In *Discussions on Child Development*, J. M. Tanner and B. Inhelder, eds. Vol. III of the Proceedings of the World Health Organization Study Group on the Psychobiological Development of the Child, Geneva, 1955. New York: International Universities Press, 1958, pp. 169-188.
——— (1955c), Discussion in *Proceedings of the International Conference on Student Mental Health* at Princeton, N. J. World Federation for Mental Health. To be published.
——— (1956a), The Problem of Ego Identity. *J. Amer. Psa. Assoc.*, 4:56-121.
——— (1956b), The First Psychoanalyst. *Yale Rev.*, Autumn, 40-62.
——— (1956c), Ego Identity and the Psychosocial Moratorium. In *New Perspectives for Research in Juvenile Delinquency*, H. L. Witmer and R. Kosinsky, eds. U. S. Children's Bureau: Publication #356, 1-23.
——— (1958a), *Young Man Luther, A Study in Psychoanalysis and History*. New York: Norton.
——— (1958b), The Nature of Clinical Evidence. *Daedalus*, 87:65-87. Also in *Evidence and Inference*, The First Hayden Colloquium. Cambridge: The Technology Press of M.I.T., 1958.
——— (1958c), Identity and Uprootedness in Our Time. Address at the Annual Meeting of the World Federation for Mental Health, Vienna.
——— and Erikson, K. (1957), The Confirmation of the Delinquent. *Chicago Review*, Winter, 15-23.
Erikson, K. T. (1957), Patient-Role and Social Uncertainty—a Dilemma of the Mentally Ill. *Psychiatry*, 20:263-274.
Federn, P. (1927-1949), *Ego Psychology and the Psychoses*. New York: Basic Books, 1952.

BIBLIOGRAPHY

Fenichel, O. (1945), *The Psychoanalytic Theory of Neurosis*. New York: Norton.
Freud, A. (1936), *The Ego and the Mechanisms of Defence*. New York: International Universities Press, 1946.
——— (1945), Indications for Child Analysis. *The Psychoanalytic Study of the Child*, 1:127-149. New York: International Universities Press.
——— and Dann, S. (1951), An Experiment in Group Upbringing. *The Psychoanalytic Study of the Child*, 6:127-168. New York: International Universities Press.
Freud, S. (1887-1902), *The Origins of Psychoanalysis. Letters to Wilhelm Fliess, Drafts and Notes, 1887-1902*. New York: Basic Books, 1954.
——— (1894a), The Defence Neuro-Psychoses. *Collected Papers*, 1:59-75. London: Hogarth, 1948.
——— (1894b), The Justification for Detaching from Neurasthenia a Particular Syndrome: The Anxiety Neurosis. *Collected Papers*, 1:76-106. London: Hogarth, 1948.
——— (1896), Further Remarks on the Defence Neuro-Psychoses. *Collected Papers*, 1:155-182. London: Hogarth, 1948.
——— (1900), The Interpretation of Dreams. *Standard Edition*, Vols. 4 & 5. London: Hogarth, 1953.
——— (1905), Three Essays on the Theory of Sexuality. *Standard Edition*, 7:123-245. London: Hogarth, 1953.
——— (1908), "Civilized" Sexual Morality and Modern Nervousness. *Collected Papers*, 2:76-99. London: Hogarth, 1948.
——— (1911), Formulations Regarding the Two Principles in Mental Functioning. *Collected Papers*, 4:13-21. London: Hogarth, 1948.
——— (1914), On Narcissism: an Introduction. *Standard Edition*, 14:73-102. London: Hogarth, 1957.
——— (1915a), Instincts and Their Vicissitudes. *Standard Edition*, 14:117-140. London: Hogarth, 1957.
——— (1915b), Repression. *Standard Edition*, 14:146-158. London: Hogarth, 1957.
——— (1915c), The Unconscious. *Standard Edition*, 14:166-215. London: Hogarth, 1957.
——— (1917), *A General Introduction to Psychoanalysis*. New York: Perma Giants, 1949.
——— (1923), *The Ego and the Id*. London: Hogarth, 1947.
——— (1926a), *The Problem of Anxiety*. New York: Norton, 1936.
——— (1926b), Ansprache an die Mitglieder des Vereins B'nai B'rith. *Gesammelte Werke*, 17:49-53. London. Imago, 1941.
——— (1932), *New Introductory Lectures on Psychoanalysis*. Lecture 31: The Anatomy of the Mental Personality. New York: Norton, 1933.
——— (1937), Analysis Terminable and Interminable. *Collected Papers*, 5:316-357. London: Hogarth, 1950.
——— (1938), *An Outline of Psychoanalysis*. New York: Norton, 1949.
Fromm-Reichmann, F. (1950), *Principles of Intensive Psychotherapy*. Chicago: University of Chicago Press.
Ginsburg, S. W. (1954), The Role of Work. *Samiksa*, 8:1-13.
Hartmann, H. (1939), *Ego Psychology and the Problem of Adaptation*. New York: International Universities Press, 1958.
——— (1947), On Rational and Irrational Action. In *Psychoanalysis and the Social Sciences*, G. Róheim, ed., 1:359-392. New York: International Universities Press.
——— (1950), Comments on the Psychoanalytic Theory of the Ego. *The Psychoanalytic Study of the Child*, 5:74-96. New York: International Universities Press.

―――― (1952), The Mutual Influences in the Development of the Ego and Id. *The Psychoanalytic Study of the Child*, 7:9-30. New York: International Universities Press.

―――― (1955), Notes on the Theory of Sublimation. *The Psychoanalytic Study of the Child*, 10:9-29. New York: International Universities Press.

―――― (1956a), Notes on the Reality Principle. *The Psychoanalytic Study of the Child*, 11:31-53. New York: International Universities Press.

―――― (1956b), The Development of the Ego Concept in Freud's Work. *Int. J. Psa.*, 37:425-438.

―――― and Kris, E. (1945), The Genetic Approach in Psychoanalysis. *The Psychoanalytic Study of the Child*, 1:11-30. New York: International Universities Press.

――――, ―――― and Loewenstein, R. M. (1946), Comments on the Formation of Psychic Structure. *The Psychoanalytic Study of the Child*, 2:11-38. New York: International Universities Press.

――――, ――――, ―――― (1949), Notes on the Theory of Aggression. *The Psychoanalytic Study of the Child*, 3/4:9-36. New York: International Universities Press.

――――, ――――, ―――― (1951), Some Psychoanalytic Comments on "Culture and Personality." In *Psychoanalysis and Culture*, G. B. Wilbur and W. Muensterberger, eds. New York: International Universities Press, pp. 3-31.

Hendrick, I. (1943), Work and the Pleasure Principle. *Psa. Quart.*, 12:311-329.

Horney, K. (1937), *The Neurotic Personality of Our Time*. New York: Norton.

Jahoda, M. (1950), Toward a Social Psychology of Mental Health. In *Symposium on the Healthy Personality*, Supplement II: Problems of Infancy and Childhood, Transactions of Fourth Conference, March, 1950, M. J. E. Senn, ed. New York: Josiah Macy, Jr. Foundation.

James, W. (1896), The Will to Believe. *New World*, 5.

Kardiner, A. (1939), *The Individual and His Society: The Psychodynamics of Primitive Social Organization*. New York: Columbia University Press.

Kinsey, A. C., Pomeroy, W. B., and Martin, C. E. (1948), *Sexual Behavior in the Human Male*. Philadelphia: Saunders.

Knight, R. P. (1953), Management and Psychotherapy of the Borderline Schizophrenic Patient. *Bull. Menninger Clin.*, 17:139-150. Also in *Psychoanalytic Psychiatry and Psychology*, Austen Riggs Center, Vol. I, R. P. Knight and C. R. Friedman, eds. New York: International Universities Press, 1954, pp. 110-122.

Kris, E. (1950), On Preconscious Mental Processes. *Psa. Quart.*, 19:540-560. Also in *Organization and Pathology of Thought*, D. Rapaport, ed. New York: Columbia University Press, 1951, pp. 474-493. Also in Kris, E. (1952), pp. 303-318.

―――― (1952), *Psychoanalytic Explorations in Art*. New York: International Universities Press.

―――― (1955), Neutralization and Sublimation: Observations on Young Children. *The Psychoanalytic Study of the Child*, 10:30-46. New York: International Universities Press.

Loewenstein, R. M. (1950), Conflict and Autonomous Ego Development During the Phallic Phase. *The Psychoanalytic Study of the Child*, 5:47-52. New York: International Universities Press.

Macfarlane, J. W. (1938), Studies in Child Guidance. I. Methodology of Data Collection and Organization. *Monogs. Society for Research in Child Development*, Vol. 3, #6, pp. 254.

Mannheim, K. (1949), *Utopia and Ideology*. New York: Harcourt, Brace.

Mead, G. (1934), *Mind, Self, and Society*. Chicago: University of Chicago Press.

Mead, M. (1949), *Male and Female*. New York: Morrow.

BIBLIOGRAPHY

National Congress of Parents and Teachers (1958), Breaking Through the Limiting Circle of Immaturity. The Headquarters of the National Congress of Parents and Teachers, 700 North Rush Street, Chicago.
Newcomb, T. M., et al., eds. (1953), *Readings in Social Psychology*. New York: Holt.
Nunberg, H. (1931), The Synthetic Function of the Ego. *Int. J. Psa.*, 12:123-140. Also in *Practice and Theory of Psychoanalysis*. New York: International Universities Press, 1955, pp. 120-136.
Piers, G., and Singer, M. B. (1953), *Shame and Guilt*. Springfield, Ill.: Thomas.
Rapaport, D. (1942), *Emotions and Memory*, 2nd ed. New York: International Universities Press, 1950.
────── (1951a), Consciousness: a Psychopathological and Psychodynamic View. In *Problems of Consciousness*, Transactions of the Second Conference, March 19-20, 1951. New York: Josiah Macy, Jr. Foundation, pp. 18-57.
────── (1951b), The Autonomy of the Ego. *Bull. Menninger Clin.*, 15:113-123. Also in *Psychoanalytic Psychiatry and Psychology*, Austen Riggs Center, Vol. I, R. P. Knight and C. R. Friedman, eds. New York: International Universities Press, 1954, pp. 248-258.
────── (1953), Some Metapsychological Considerations Concerning Activity and Passivity. Unpublished ms.
────── (1956), The Psychoanalytic Theory of Consciousness and a Study of Dreams. Unpublished ms.
────── (1957), Cognitive Structures. In *Contemporary Approaches to Cognition*. Cambridge: Harvard University Press, pp. 157-200.
────── (1958), The Theory of Ego Autonomy: a Generalization. *Bull. Menninger Clin.*, 22:13-35.
Riesman, D. (1950), *The Lonely Crowd*. New Haven: Yale University Press.
Schilder, P. (1930-1940), *Psychoanalysis, Man and Society*. New York: Norton, 1951.
────── (1934), *The Image and Appearance of the Human Body*. New York: International Universities Press, 1951.
Schwartz, M. S., and Will, G. T. (1953), Low Morale and Mutual Withdrawal on a Mental Hospital Ward. *Psychiatry*, 16:337-353.
Shaw, G. B. (1952), *Selected Prose*. New York: Dodd, Mead.
Spitz, R. A. (1945), Hospitalism. *The Psychoanalytic Study of the Child*, 1:53-74. New York: International Universities Press.
Spock, B. (1945), *The Common Sense Book of Baby and Child Care*. New York: Duell Sloan & Pearce.
Sullivan, H. S. (1938), Psychiatry: Introduction to the Study of Interpersonal Relations, I. *Psychiatry*, 1:121-134.
────── (1940), *Conceptions of Modern Psychiatry*. Washington: William Alanson White Psychiatric Foundation, 1947.
────── (1946-1947), *The Interpersonal Theory of Psychiatry*. New York: Norton, 1953.
Waelder, R. (1936), The Principle of Multiple Function: Observations on Over-Determination. *Psa. Quart.*, 5:45-62.
Zilboorg, G. (1944), Present Trends in Psychoanalytic Theory and Practice. *Bull. Menninger Clin.*, 8:3-8.

STUDIES IN REMEMBERING

PART 2

STUDIES IN REMEMBERING

The Reproduction of Connected and Extended Verbal Material

by

I. H. PAUL

CONTENTS

1 SOME GENERAL CONSIDERATIONS REGARDING LEARNING AND REMEMBERING — 1

2 EXPLICATION AND FAMILIARITY IN SERIAL REPRODUCTION OF STORIES: AN EXPLORATORY EXPERIMENT — 9

3 RETENTION STYLE AND RETENTION ABILITY — 61

4 CONCLUSIONS AND IMPLICATIONS — 137

Bibliography — 150

1

SOME GENERAL CONSIDERATIONS REGARDING LEARNING AND REMEMBERING

This monograph reports a series of experiments on how people learn and remember extended, connected, and meaningful verbal material—how they reproduce stories.[1] The major questions were: (1) What processes underlie a subject's reproduction of a story? (2) What properties of a story hinder or facilitate its recovery? (3) Are there systematic differences between subjects in the ways they retain and reproduce a story?

My study of these problems extended over four separate but interlocking experiments. The first was exploratory, the second and third were large-scale tests of the relevant variables, and the fourth was a replication and integration of the main relationships. Quasi-clinical methods (direct examination of memorial reproductions with free use of *ad hoc* hypotheses) were used in conjunction with experimental methods (control, manipulation, and measurement). Techniques for collecting, assessing, and quantifying such memory data were explored. In this monograph I will describe and discuss the methods, the experiments, and the relevant theories and concepts.

GENERALITIES, BACKGROUND, AND BARTLETT

Human learning and remembering is a vast but sparsely cultivated field of study. The rat's behavior in mazes and on jumping-

[1] The studies reported here were carried out while the writer was a Research Fellow at the Austen Riggs Center in Stockbridge, Massachusetts. He is indebted to David Rapaport for stimulation and guidance during each phase of the work. The preparation of this report was made possible in part by the grant from the Ford Foundation in support of research at the Austen Riggs Center.

stands has been extensively studied, while comparatively few experimentalists have investigated human learning, particularly the "everyday" kind, mainly because it eludes the usual laboratory methods. Methods that are subtle and supple enough for it are scarce, experimental control is difficult, and opportunities for meaningful measurement are rare. The clinical situation is still the best place for observation and the richest source of data and ideas on human learning and remembering.

The researcher who sets out to study memory faces two major problems: (1) What psychological theory will best guide his studies and lead him to worth-while observations and discoveries? A connectionist theory? A Gestalt theory? Or a functionalism rooted in clinical observation and practice? (2) What aspect of human learning and remembering should he tackle? Should he, like the majority of academic psychologists, study how people memorize lists of nonsense syllables or of unconnected meaningful material? Or should he study more complex phenomena like the assimilation and memory of emotional experiences? Is there a middle road that will combine the scientific rigor of the former with the meaningfulness of the latter?

Trace versus Schema: What Kind of Structure for Memory?

Central to any theory of learning and remembering is a conception of the process which permits a person to act on the basis of his past experience. Ever since Plato compared memory to an impression upon a wax tablet, variations on the idea of a memory "trace" have been the popular way of picturing this process.[2] Descartes' variation pictured the "pores" of the brain being widened by the passage of "animal spirits" through them; according to Sherrington, the "resistance at the synapse was lessened"; and since Thorndike, connectionist conceptions of mental functioning have been based on this neurological model.[3]

---

[2] Gomulicki (1953) has presented a comprehensive review and discussion of trace theories.

[3] Connectionism refers to those psychological theories which assume that a process of elemental association is fundamental to cognitive functioning. According to this view, held by many learning theorists, learning is basically the establishment and strengthening of bonds or connections between elementary psychological

By the early 1930's, however, this model was being sharply attacked from several directions (e.g., Lashley, 1930), the most vigorous criticism coming from Gestalt theorists. The Gestalt modification of the trace theory (Koffka, 1935; Köhler, 1929; Wulf, 1922) postulated that experience is laid down in the brain by some sort of isomorphic process. The traces which result are subject to two influences: communication with other traces (*assimilation*), and stresses inherent in the trace itself, which are expressed by the Gestalt (configurational) principles, for example, *sharpening* and *leveling* in order to achieve maximum simplicity, symmetry, and good form.

In 1932 both the connectionist and the Gestalt trace theories were challenged when Bartlett, in *Remembering,* reported the results of twenty years of research on perceiving, learning, and remembering. He erected a broad theoretical framework grounded in a vigorous functionalism that is congenial to both clinician and experimentalist.

One of Bartlett's major theses was that cognitive functioning cannot be understood unless it is studied in the light of the subject's interests, attitudes, affects, and goals. He buttressed this thesis by naturalistic observations and by experimentation—data derived from models and methods which are closer to "real life" than the usual laboratory techniques of psychology. His was "a middle road." He argued that when psychologists use meaningless and unconnected materials as stimuli (e.g., nonsense syllables), and when they force their subjects to perceive and learn in artificial or unusual ways (e.g., by means of a memory drum), they seriously interfere with their chances of understanding everyday perceiving and remembering, and their conclusions will teach us very little about how

---

units (idea and idea, or stimulus and stimulus, or stimulus and response, etc.). Retention is fundamentally due to the persisting strength and reinforcement of such bonds, and forgetting results from their weakening or destruction by interference and/or disuse. For a detailed presentation and discussion of these theories, see Hilgard (1948) and McGeoch and Irion (1952). For a critical discussion, see Koffka (1935) who, along with other Gestalt psychologists, challenged the connectionist doctrine and insisted that whatever associations manifest themselves in learning are artifacts of the truly fundamental process, which is structure formation. Learning is not a matter of the establishment and strengthening of connections, but rather represents the repatterning and reorganization of cognitive structures—of traces. Recently, Hebb (1949) has shown how Gestalt phenomena can be handled by a connectionism that is based on modern neurophysiological conceptions.

people actually deal with complex, extended, and meaningful experiences.

With his naturalistic methods, Bartlett demonstrated what psychologists, particularly clinicians, have come to accept as a fundamental fact: the perception and recollection of complex, extended experiences are rarely literal or precise, but are regularly influenced and shaped by processes like "rationalization," "effort after meaning," and "fit," directed by attitudes, interests, and affects. He did not believe that a simple trace theory could survive the complication introduced by these influences. He also thought that there are fundamental difficulties in any conception that treats the mind as a storehouse of discreet traces.[4]

What Bartlett proposed in place of the concept of trace was the concept of *schema*, a term he borrowed from neurology.[5] Head (1920), together with Holmes, had defined schema as an internal postural mode—unified, and constantly modified by every incoming sensation evoked by postural changes—which furnishes a basis for the perception and recognition of postural changes. Bartlett recognized in this concept a valuable way to picture the operation of memory and of cognition in general. Bartlett conceived of schemas as internal organizations of past reactions and experiences which function as unified and active organs. A schema is an abstraction, simplification, and articulation of experience; part and parcel of its formation and operation are the affective aspects of the experience. An experience is not the resultant of incoming stimuli impinging upon a passive "clean slate," nor of the formation of isomorphic or literal facsimiles: rather it results from the interaction of stimuli and an already-structured, active organization of schemas. An essential feature of this conception is that the mind is conceived of as made up of schemas *about* the world rather than of images or traces *of* the world.

According to this conception, recall is not a reproduction *of* a schema, it is an active construction *based upon* a schema. While some "dominant detail" does persist, the major component of the original situation that persists is the attitude which was involved in

---

[4] For a discussion of this problem see Bartlett (1932, pp. 197-202), Koffka (1935, pp. 518-519), Lashley (1930, 1952), and Hebb (1949, pp. 12-13).

[5] Brain (1950) has presented a brief and lucid discussion of the origins and properties of the schema concept. See also Oldfield and Zangwill's review (1942/43), and Oldfield's (1954) attempt to show how *schema* can replace *trace*.

it. This attitude—broadly conceived—is the major determinant of the way the person reproduces the original situation. Bartlett showed how reproduction can be understood as an attempt to "justify" this attitude. The process of justification, variously called "rationalization," "effort after meaning," or "fit," points up what is active and functional in remembering, and what is integrative and constructive. It is certainly easy to find illustrations of this process in everyday remembering, and it is especially congruent with the characteristic mnemonic phenomena encountered clinically.

Bartlett's Work Evaluated

Bartlett's work had a surprisingly light impact on psychology. This is puzzling, because even today much of his book seems fresh and pertinent—for example, his emphasis on the role of motivation in cognitive functioning anticipates the so-called "new look" by many years—and his criticisms of other theoretical and experimental approaches are still cogent. Moreover, Bartlett provided methods as well as theory to encompass a wide range of mnemonic phenomena, particularly those pertaining to extended, connected, and meaningful experiences. To anyone interested in studying human learning and remembering, his work seems still one of the best places of departure.

My studies have been influenced by the shortcomings of Bartlett's work as well as by its obvious merits. The major shortcoming is that, aside from his broad functionalistic formulations, he did not speculate about process, nor did he conduct definitive experiments (those that yield a yes-no answer) concerning the operation of schemas. He failed to delineate precisely the nature of schemas, and never suggested how we might picture the detailed workings of the processes governing schema formation and operation.

This failure had at least two important consequences: (1) It prevented him from dealing adequately with the veridical and detailed recall that people are capable of—for example, memorization by rote. (2) It led him to overlook certain parameters of individual differences which, in the final analysis, must reflect the underlying processes of schema formation and operation. True, Bartlett recognized that people differ in interests and motives, in past experiences and expectations. But he did not concern himself with differences in ability to retain, and differences in the quality and character of remembering. Such differences can, I believe, teach us a great deal about the processes of schema formation and operation. To learn about these processes is the goal of the present research project.

A Summary of the Four Experiments

The four interlocking experiments reported in this monograph are part of a larger project designed to study schema processes in remembering. A brief preview of these experiments, touching on their main goals and findings, may give the reader a useful introduction to the project and the monograph.

The first experiment was a replication of the study from which Bartlett concluded that memorial reproductions are essentially active reconstructions based on schemas. Bartlett used the serial reproduction method (transmitting a story through a chain of subjects, like the spread of gossip or rumor), a technique that speeds the course of forgetting. The story he used for one of his main stimuli is an Indian folk tale called "The War of the Ghosts" (which I will refer to as the Ghost Story). In addition to being unfamiliar in content and style to his subjects, the story has many gaps and ambiguities.

My replication was shaped by two questions: (1) Are the gaps and ambiguities of the story responsible for the conspicuous distortions and fragmentations in recall that Bartlett found? (2) What role does the unfamiliarity of the story play in this striking collapse? To answer the first question I prepared an *explicated* version of the Ghost Story, in which I tried to ameliorate and reduce many of the gaps and ambiguities by means of text changes, emendations, and clarifications. Such explications should facilitate schema formation and hence promote the retention of the story. This explicated version, however, still retained the unfamiliar quality of the original. Therefore, to answer the second question I composed a story, the Secretary Story, which is comparable in many respects to the Ghost Story but contains more familiar actors and actions. These three stories were transmitted through serial reproduction chains. This exploratory experiment (presented in detail in Chapter 2) was designed not only to verify Bartlett's thesis, but also to look for clues to underlying schema processes in the reproductions of the various stories.

The findings showed that, while the three stories underwent noteworthy collapse and numerous distortions, the explicated version of the Ghost Story was recalled better than the original version, and the Secretary Story fared better than did either version of the Ghost Story. A close examination of the reproductions highlighted the integrating and articulating role that explications played, not only those which were experimentally designed, but also the many which subjects spontaneously introduced in the course of serial reproductions. Gaps and ambiguities seemed to be crucial places for forgetting and distortion, and were the foci of schema influences; this is where much reshuffling and rebalancing of material occurred, where skeletonizations (stripping, fragmenting, and segregating) and importations (the addition of material, often extraneous but seldom conceptually unrelated) occurred. From these observations I drew tentative conclusions regarding the functioning of schemas in recall.

The most provocative conclusion was that the importations and skeletonizations reflected two basic schema processes. The complementary neurological processes of *recruitment* and *fractionation* proposed by Hebb (1949) provided, I felt, a congenial theoretical model—a useful and appropriate way of conceptualizing the reorganization and articulation of schemas as revealed in the reproductions through the operation of importing and skeletonizing.

The subsequent experiments (presented in detail in Chapter 3) took their direction from the findings of the exploratory work and continued its quest. In addition to further study of schema processes, I pursued individual differences in manner (quality) of reproduction as well as in ability (accuracy and completeness).

Importations of new material into the reproductions—largely of familiar and explicatory material—which occurred so regularly in the Exploratory Experiment occurred with noteworthy frequency in some subjects' reproductions and much less frequently in others'. Some tended to import, others to skeletonize. I systematically investigated these tendencies and found them to be stable and general individual difference parameters. I came to view them as cognitive styles (in line with Klein's conceptualization [1951]) and interpreted them as reflecting some subjects' greater reliance upon the schema process of recruitment and others' upon fractionation.

I explored and tested methods for detecting and quantifying the presence and prevalence of these styles—particularly the importing style—and investigated their consequences for various aspects of learning and remembering by examining the serial reproductions of original, explicated, and familiar stories by serial chains made up of importers and of nonimporters. One of the main findings to emerge from these studies was that explication and importation were functionally related and often showed overlapping effects. I interpreted them both as recruitment serving to integrate and consolidate schemas. Skeletonization and fragmentation, which I interpreted as fractionation, could not be studied as intensively as importing. Still I was able to show that they frequently seemed to be serving an economic function, simplifying and articulating schemas.

These four experiments are presented in detail (in Chapters 2 and 3) in a narrative manner in which the discussion of background, conceptualization, methods, and findings are intermeshed. The reader who is interested primarily in theory and only in the broad outlines of the experiments may want to skip over those sections in slightly condensed type as well as the numerous footnotes. He will find detailed discussions of theories and concepts along with the general conclusion of this research project in the *Discussion and Conclusions* sections of Chapters 2 and 3, and Chapter 4.

2

EXPLICATION AND FAMILIARITY IN SERIAL REPRODUCTION OF STORIES: AN EXPLORATORY EXPERIMENT

The story which Bartlett used so often in his memory experiments is a North American Indian folk tale called "The War of the Ghosts." Many of its episodes and themes are peculiar to Indian folklore, and to people not familiar with this folklore, the story is cryptic and the events seem unconnected. In repeated reproductions and especially in serial reproductions,[1] the story collapsed dramatically and underwent conspicuous condensation and transformation. For this reason Bartlett found it ideal for his purposes. He proposed that the distortions and elisions in the reproductions revealed the organizing influence of his subjects' schemas (their beliefs, expectations, attitudes, etc.): in so far as the subjects did not possess the appropriate schemas to deal efficiently with the story, in reproducing it they altered it in line with their available schemas.

Bartlett treated his findings in a quasi-clinical way—direct inspection of reproductions and *ad hoc* conclusions. He did not attempt objective or quantitative appraisals of the data beyond an occasional count of the number of words, nor did he attempt a further and more precise experimental analysis of the role and functioning of schemas.

[1] These methods are described and discussed below on pp. 15-17.

These two shortcomings—lack of objective methods of appraising the data, and absence of direct experimental manipulation of the relevant variables—determined the design of the present experiment. My initial plan was simply to replicate Bartlett's serial reproduction study with careful experimental controls, then to apply quantitative analyses to the results, and search for clues to the processes of remembering. However, the above considerations led me to incorporate into the experimental design two new variables—explication and familiarity—which are only implicit in the Bartlett studies.

Problem, Materials, Methods, Subjects

The Idea of Explication

Perhaps the best way to explore the hypothesis that the distortions, condensations, and losses in recall of the Ghost Story are caused by the disparity between the subjects' schemas and the story is systematically to vary the extent of this disparity and observe its effects upon recall.

One way to achieve this is to use subjects whose interests and knowledge are relevant to the story. An anthropologist familiar with Indian folklore would presumably be able to reproduce the story quite well, since he possesses appropriate schemas. We might use such experts as subjects and compare their performance with that of nonexperts. Or we might make people experts by teaching them about those aspects of a story that are strange and new—by forming the appropriate schemas in them.

Another way to decrease the disparity between schemas and story is to modify the story itself. One might systematically insert clarifying and explanatory words and passages into the text wherever it is cryptic and gappy, and thus build into it some conceptual or information bridges. This procedure facilitates schema formation in part by providing links to already existing schemas; therefore the clarifications and explanations themselves need be congruent with the subjects' knowledge and attitudes as well as their characteristic modes of explanation. For various reasons, but mainly because it is usually simplest in psychological experiments to vary the stimulus, I chose this last method.

"The War of the Ghosts" in its original form is as follows:[2]

The Ghost Story: Original Version

The War / of the Ghosts /

a) One night / two / young / men / from Egulac / went down / to the river / to hunt / seals, / *b*) and while they were there / it became foggy / and calm. / *c*) They stopped / their work / and hearkened. / *d*) Then they heard / war-cries, / and they thought: / "Maybe this is a war-party." / *e*) They escaped / to the shore, / and hid / behind a log. / *f*) Now canoes / came up, / and they heard / the noise / of paddles, / and saw / one canoe / coming up to them. / *g*) There were five / men / in the canoe, / and they said: /

"What do you think? / We wish / to take you along. / *h*) We are going / up the river / to make war / on the people." /

i) "I will not go along," / one / of the young men / said. / "I might be killed. / My relatives / do not know / where I have gone. / *j*) But you," / he said, / turning to the other, / "may go with them." /

k) So one / of the young men / went, / but the other / returned home. /

l) And the warriors / went on up / the river / to a town / on the other side / of Kalama. / *m*) The people / came down to the water, / and they began / to fight, / and many / were killed. / *n*) But presently / the young man / heard / one / of the warriors / say: / "Quick, let us go home: / that Indian / has been hit." / *p*) Now he thought: / "Oh, they are ghosts." / *q*) He did not feel sick, / but they said / he had been shot. /

s) So the canoes / went back / to Egulac, / and the young man / went ashore / to his house, / and made a fire. / *t*) He rested, / then he ate, / and he thought: / "I must tell / everybody / my adventure." / *u*) So he told / everybody / and said: / "Behold I accompanied / the ghosts, / and we went to fight. / Many / of our fel-

---

[2] The story is divided into its constituent themes and information units. The techniques for these analyses are described below on pp. 17-19. At this point I need only mention that a few objective rules of thumb were used to break the story down into its themes or episodes, and then the themes into smaller information units comparable to what others have called "idea units" (see Levitt, 1956, and also Clark, 1940). The themes are marked by letters [themes *o*) and *r*) are present only in the explicated version which is described below on pp. 33-36] and the information units are marked by crossbars: /.

lows / were killed, / and many / of those who attacked us / were killed. / *v*) They said / I was hit, / and I did not feel sick." /

w) He told it all, / and then he became quiet. / When the sun / rose / he fell down. / Something / black / came out / of his mouth. / His face / became contorted. / *x*) The people / jumped up / and cried./

y) He was dead. /

By systematically editing and emending this story, I prepared an *explicated version*,[3] the main expectation being that it would, on the whole, fare better and suffer less distortion and fragmentation than the *original version*. Examination of the two sets of reproductions might then point up some of the processes involved in recall.

The explicated version of the Ghost Story is presented below. The new and altered parts are italicized.

The Ghost Story: Explicated Version

The War / of the Ghosts /

a) One night / two / young / men / from Egulac / went down / to the river / *to fish* / and *b*) while they were there / it became foggy / and calm. / *c*) *They knew / this / was an omen / of ghosts.* / *d*) Then they heard / war-cries, / and they thought: / "Maybe this is a war-party." / *e*) They escaped / to the shore / and hid / behind a log / *f*) *But there was / no hiding / from these canoes.* / One canoe / came *straight* / up to them. / *g*) There were five / men / in the canoe, / and they said: /

h) "We are going / up the river / to make war / on the people. / *g*) We wish / to take you along. / What do you think?" /

i) "I will not go along," / one / of the young men / said. / "I might be killed. / My relatives / do not know / where I have gone. / *j*) But you," / he said, / turning to the other, / *"have no relatives,* / so you may go with them." /

k) So one / of the young men / went, / but the other / returned home. /

l) And the warriors / went on up / the river / to a town / on the other side / of Kalama. / *m*) The people / came down to the water, / and they began / to fight, / and many / were killed. / *n*)

---

[3] A detailed description and discussion of the explications is presented below in conjunction with a detailed examination of the reproductions. See pp. 33-36.

But presently / the young man / heard / one / of the warriors / say: / "Quick, let us go home: / that Indian / has been hit." /
o) Now he thought: / "*My fellows / do not call / me 'Indian.'* /
p) Oh, they *surely* are ghosts." / *q*) He did not feel sick, / but they said / he had been shot. / *r*) *Ghosts' company, / he remembered, / gives protection / from pain / and death / while the night lasts.* /
s) So the canoes / went back / to Egulac, / and the young man / went ashore / to his house, / and made a fire / to summon / everybody. / *u*) And he told them: / "Behold I accompanied / the ghosts, / and we went to fight. / Many / of our fellows / were killed, / and many / of those who attacked us / were killed. / *v*) They said / I was hit, / and I did not feel sick." /
w) He told it all, / and then he became quiet. / When the sun / rose / he fell down. / Something / black / came out / of his mouth. / His face / became contorted. / *x*) The people / jumped up / and cried. /
y) He was dead. /

The Idea of Familiarity—A Control Story with Familiar Content

The plan of the experiment was for each of two groups of subjects (*S*s) to receive one version of the Ghost Story in order to contrast their performance and ascertain what influences the explications exert. Since the two groups of *S*s are necessarily different, the experimental design requires a control story, one that is administered to both groups. Such a control story, aside from showing what differences (for example, in ability to learn and reproduce) exist between the two groups to begin with, can also be made useful in its own right by contributing a separate experiment variable. What variable can it most usefully study?

The explicated version of the Ghost Story, though more connected and somewhat less cryptic and ambiguous than the original, still seemed to retain an alien and unfamiliar ring, dealing, after all, with events and actions that are not part of our daily experience. Would this lingering quality of unfamiliarity still make it difficult for *S*s to retain the story? (Is it still something they are schematically unequipped for?)

To answer this question (and at the same time to provide a control story) I wrote a story which, while equivalent to the Ghost Story in most of its formal properties (word number, information unit number, theme number, and roughly comparable in number of episodes and plot twists), nevertheless deals with familiar characters (its main actors are secretaries and the Ss of this experiment were also secretaries) and recounts an adventure in the present day. The expectation was that such a story would fare better in recall than either version of the Ghost Story. Its title is "The Sneak Attacks" and I refer to it as the Secretary Story.

The Secretary Story

The Sneak / Attacks /

a) Two / sisters, / who graduated / from business college / in Menasser, / decided to go / overseas / and work / in foreign / embassies. / *b*) They said / to mother: / "This way / we can work / and see the world / at the same time." / *c*) They separated / and took jobs / in neighboring / countries. *d*) "Promise / you'll write to me / every day," / they said / to each other. / They agreed / *e*) and parted. /

One sister / went to Montania / *f*) which she found / in a state / of war hysteria. / *g*) Her stenographic / competence / landed her / a position / as private / secretary / to the foreign / minister. /

h) "You / will have access / to top-secret / information," / he admonished her. / "I count on / loyalty." /

i) One day / she came across / a confidential / document. / *j*) It described / a sneak / attack / by the Montania / airforce / in which they were going to bomb / all / of the government / buildings / of a small / nearby / nation. / *k*) She read / the document / with interest / until she noted / the name / of the nation. / *l*) To her horror / she realized / that it was where / her sister / was working. / *m*) "Oh, I must write / and warn her," / she thought. / But of course / censorship / was invoked / between the two countries. / *n*) She thought / desperately / how to save / her poor sister. /

o) And then / she hit on a plan. / She would stop / writing altogether / *p*) and her sister / would wonder, / then become worried, / and probably soon / decide / to come and see her / to make sure / she wasn't ill / and need her help. /

q) On the day / she put her plan / into action, / she did not receive / her sister's daily / letter. / *r*) She wondered. / The next days / she also got no letter / and she became worried. / *s*) "It is very unusual / that she shouldn't write me," / she thought. / "Perhaps / my sister is ill." /

t) So she decided / straightway / to go and see / her sister. /

u) The distance / was only / twelve / kilometers / and she figured / it would be safest / to walk. / *v*) At the border / she met, / of all people, / her sister / *w*) who was coming to visit her, / she soon learned, / for the very same / reasons. /

x) That day, / both nations / bombed / each other / and the embassies / were destroyed. /

The Serial Reproduction Method

In serial reproduction, a stimulus story is successively reproduced by a number of persons, each one of whom, except for the lead-off member, learns not the original story but rather his predecessor's reproduction of it. This technique has a number of advantages over the method of repeated reproduction, in which one S recalls a story a number of times at intervals. In repeated reproductions, to secure substantial forgetting and transformation, a relatively long time must elapse between the exposure to the stimulus story and recall, and there is no way during this period to control the activities and experiences of S which may influence his memory: for example, some might review and rehearse deliberately, others unwittingly, others not at all. Since the serial reproduction method does not require a long interval between exposure and reproduction, in my experiments I kept the time short (fifteen minutes) and occupied the S with a concentration task to prevent review.

With only minor reservations we can assume that the serial reproduction is a valid method for studying individual remembering, on the basis of Bartlett's finding that the same types of change occur in it as in the decay of individual memory, but to a magnified and accelerated extent.[4] In individual retention the forgetting curve is usually a negatively decelerating one; it begins with a steep drop and then flattens out. The serial reproduction method capitalizes on this initial drop since it uses a series of first reproductions, the point where the greatest drop occurs.

The method has a number of pitfalls, however. Since different individuals necessarily form the chain, they obviously may contribute variously to the end product. This variance can be reduced by composing the chains of persons who have been pretested and matched

---

[4] See especially his discussion on pp. 171-176, and note the corroboration of Allport and Postman who found that "... the course of individual memory and of 'social memory' are in most respects parallel. The same pattern of distortion exists in both" (1947, p. 59).

with respect to relevant characteristics (for example, retention ability, style, and background). Another pitfall is that each S needs to make sense out of the stimulus (his predecessor's reproduction) and thus understanding and interpretation enter afresh at each step in the chain. This factor has never been experimentally controlled, and must be recognized as an inherent characteristic of the method. There is, however, reason to believe that such "understanding and interpretation" also play a role in every repeated reproduction (Katona's research [1940] as well as Bartlett's support such a position).

Learning and Recall Procedures

In all of the experiments to be described the stories were learned in the following way: S (always in the presence of one or more other Ss) silently read the story[4a] twice in succession. This procedure, adopted from Bartlett, permits each person to learn at his own rate. But it has the shortcoming that review and rehearsal are not controlled during the exposure of the text. To counteract this, the instructions emphasized that S should read no slower than his usual reading pace.

The learning instructions (preceded by informal remarks describing the research and emphasizing that no "testing" of the Ss either as individuals or as a group was intended) were:

> You each have a typewritten sheet before you face down. It contains a story. Please read the story through twice at your usual reading speed. Later on I'll ask you to reproduce it from memory to the best of your ability. As you already know, this is not a test. What I am studying is the story and how easily it can be remembered. It is quite impossible, I think, to remember it completely. But it is important that you do the best you can without straining yourselves. Try to relax and read it through twice in succession, carefully, but at your usual reading pace. Turn the sheet over again when you're through and look up. Okay? Any questions? Remember: read it carefully but at your usual speed and do this twice. *Please try your best.*

Reproductions were not made until approximately fifteen minutes, "filled" with a concentration task, had elapsed after the end of the

---

[4a] His stimulus copy did not, of course, show the information-unit markings or theme letters.

reading. For the Exploratory Experiment I devised a concentration task appropriate to the *S*s, who were secretaries: they were required to proofread a manuscript into which various errors had been systematically inserted.

Recall was solicited by these instructions:

> Thanks. Would you now please write out the story you read at the beginning *as accurately as you can*. Try to write it at your usual writing speed. If you want to add anything at the end, go ahead and do so, for instance, if some details come back to you later. *Please try to do the very best you can.* Any questions?

The Exploratory Experiment

Ten female secretaries working at the Austen Riggs Center volunteered to be *S*s. I divided them into two groups of five *S*s. One group (labeled the O-group) serially reproduced the original version of the Ghost Story and the other (the E-group) reproduced the explicated version. Both groups also serially reproduced the Secretary Story.

Each *S* participated in two forty-five minute sessions during the same day, one in the morning and one in the afternoon. I tested *S*s in pairs, one member of the O-group with one of the E-group. I administered one of the stories at each session and switched the order at each step (i.e., the first members of each chain had the Ghost Stories first, the Secretary Story second; on the following day the second pair began with the Secretary Story, and had the Ghost Stories second; and so on). The stimulus text was always presented to the *S*s in typewritten form.

I knew each *S* personally and tried to create a relaxed, yet formal and businesslike atmosphere. I read all instructions, noted all comments, and recorded time intervals. The *S*s sat at opposite ends of a large table. After the session I strongly urged them not to speak about the experiment to anyone.

Quantitative Analysis

METHODS OF ANALYZING AND SCORING THE REPRODUCTIONS

The usual way to divide a verbal text into scorable parts is to separate it into so-called "idea units." The size of each unit has, in the past, varied rather widely from study to study, and criteria have usually been quite arbitrary. Levitt (1956) studied the influence on experimental results of various breakdowns of connected verbal texts, and found that, while different breakdowns do affect the absolute value of Ss' mean recall scores, they have little effect on their relative scores or rankings. Nevertheless, it would seem desirable that choice of the units of analysis be based upon linguistic considerations and information theory wherever available and applicable.

In each of many exploratory analyses, I tried to formulate objective criteria based as far as possible on simple linguistic considerations. I made separate analyses of the word and group of words, of the sentence, of the paragraph, and of the story as a whole. I will not present here those that were cumbersome to apply and did not, in the long run, seem to contribute uniquely to the results. The following are the analyses, and the scoring, for the procedures that I finally adopted.[5]

1. *Word count:* All words, including "a" and "the," were counted.

2. *Information units:* The texts were divided into "idea" or Babcock units (Babcock, 1930) following the rule that each unit should furnish a piece of information which is not redundant, that is, not superfluous or repetitive in its context. Each reproduction was scored as follows: a word or series of words in the reproduction which corresponded to an information unit of the story, even if slightly altered (in tense or by substitution of synonyms), was scored *1*; a unit which was significantly altered yet preserved the sense of the original received a score of ½; errors, distortions, and units with no correspondence to the original received *no* score. The sum of these scores for each reproduction (*information score*) was taken to represent the amount of information accurately reproduced.

3. *Themes:* The stories were divided into themes with the guidance of the following two rules of thumb: (1) each theme should embrace a relatively independent part of the story—a separate episode, event, or major piece of information; and (2) a theme should be equivalent to an "ideal" sentence and no longer (that is, a theme should be stateable in one grammatically complete, simple English

---

[5] The redundancy analysis—a story-as-a-whole measure—is discussed and presented separately below on pp. 23-25.

sentence). Each reproduction was scored for the *presence* of the themes, regardless of the accuracy of detail or sense, by means of a list of questions.[6] Thus, for the first theme of the Ghost Story, I asked myself "Does the reproduction tell of some sort of hunting or fishing expedition or task upon which the men were engaged?" If "yes," then full credit for that theme was given even if *every single detail of the content was wrong*. The *theme score* is the total number of themes contained in a reproduction.

RESULTS OF THE ACCURACY MEASURES

The results of these three measures are presented in Table 1. The results support both of the major expectations:[7] (1) the explicated version of the Ghost Story fared better on all three measures than did the original version, being consistently more accurate and complete through the five links of the reproduction chains. (2) The Secretary Story, for the most part, was recalled better than the Ghost Story by both groups of Ss. In the case of the O-group it was unequivocally better recalled. However, in the E-group the findings are equivocal: for information score, and in all but one case (No. 1) for word count, the Secretary Story was superior, but the Ghost Story was superior (in all except reproduction No. 4) with respect to theme score.

Since the E-group recalled the Ghost Story better than the O-group, it must be asked whether this superiority is due in fact to the difference between the two versions (the stimuli), or whether this group of Ss was superior in retention ability to begin with. A comparison of performances on the Secretary Story can help answer this question.

In forming the two groups I attempted (on the basis of acquaintance with the Ss and with their secretarial ability) to equate them with respect to retention ability. Nevertheless, I felt that one of the groups did have an edge over the other, and so assigned to this group the more difficult original version of the Ghost Story so that an initial superiority in retention ability, if present, would be work-

[6] The complete list of themes for the Ghost Story is presented below on pp. 35-36.

[7] A comprehensive series of statistical tests that yielded positive results was carried out on these data after a replication of the experiment had been conducted with another and larger group of Ss (Experiment III). These results are presented below on pp. 106-111. At this point, however, no tests of statistical significance were made, but the data spoke clearly in favor of the efficacy of the variables.

Table 1

ACCURACY RESULTS OF THE ORIGINAL AND EXPLICATED VERSIONS OF THE GHOST STORY AND THE SECRETARY STORY

	Original group			Explicated group		
	Word count	Information score	Theme score	Word count	Information score	Theme score
The Ghost Story	333	130	23	339	132	24
Reproduction No. 1	216	59.5	17	417	74.5	23
Reproduction No. 2	202	44	16	216	44.5	20
Reproduction No. 3	102	27.5	14	146	31	17
Reproduction No. 4	66	18.5	9	97	27	14
Reproduction No. 5	55	15.5	7	66	21.5	11
Mean of the Ghost chains	128.2	33.0	12.6	188.4	39.8	17.0
The Secretary Story	338	141	24	338	141	24
Reproduction No. 1	278	87	22	304	86	20
Reproduction No. 2	202	56.5	19	221	64.5	18
Reproduction No. 3	161	43.5	15	162	40.5	16
Reproduction No. 4	163	34.5	14	154	40	16
Reproduction No. 5	138	30	12	93	23	10
Mean of the Secretary chains	188.4	50.4	16.4	186.8	50.8	16.0

ing against the hypothesis. On the whole, the O-group did show a small superiority on the Secretary Story, doing slightly better on both word count and theme score, although on information score the E-group did better. However, compared with the large and consistent differences between the reproductions of the original and explicated versions of the Ghost Story, the small differences between the groups on the Secretary Story seem quite insignificant. We may still conclude that the explicated version was more accurately and completely reproduced than the original version because of the differences in the texts, not in the Ss.

The serial reproduction method permits only the lead-off members of each group to see the story proper, and Table 1 shows that the differences among their reproductions of the four chains are impressively in the expected direction. The question can therefore be raised: Were the effects of the explication and of familiarity confined to reproduction No. 1—i.e., are the differences between the groups due only to the effect on the lead-off members, or did the experimental variables continue to influence the reproductions throughout the chains?

To decide this question, I again scored each reproduction for accuracy, this time using as the standard of comparison not the original stimulus, but each reproduction's own stimulus story, the preceding reproduction. This analysis was done for themes and for information units. Table 2 presents the results.

If the effects of the experimental variables were confined to reproduction No. 1, we would expect to find no significant difference between the groups for reproductions No. 2 to No. 5 when each of them is compared with its stimulus story. However, Table 2 shows that reproductions No. 2 to No. 5 continue to show the expected differences. While the differences are not as consistent as are those in Table 1, the explicated version of the Ghost Story continues to be recalled more accurately and completely than the original version. A somewhat surprising finding appears in Table 2: the difference between the Secretary Story and the Ghost Story obtains only for the O-group; for the E-group the differences, though very slight, are in the opposite direction. This reversal, however, is wholly attributable to reproduction No. 5; in Nos. 1 to 4 the differences are in the expected direction.

Table 2

ACCURACY SCORES OF EACH REPRODUCTION, COMPUTED AS PERCENTAGES BASED ON EACH REPRODUCTION'S OWN STIMULUS STORY

	Ghost Story				Secretary Story			
	Original group		Explicated group		Original group		Explicated group	
	Theme score	Information score	Theme score	Information score	Theme score	Information score	Theme score	Information score
Reproduction No. 1	69	46	88	56	100	62	83	61
Reproduction No. 2	94	74	86	60	79	65	90	75
Reproduction No. 3	75	63	78	70	79	77	89	63
Reproduction No. 4	67	67	93	89	93	79	100	99
Reproduction No. 5	75	84	85	78	93	87	63	58
Mean of Reproduction No. 2 to No. 5 (omitting No. 1)	77.8	72.0	85.5	74.3	86.0	77.0	85.5	73.8

Analyzing the Text as a Whole

Any connected text has properties based not only on its parts (e.g., number of words, correct information units, themes), but also on the text as a whole. For example, a story has a structure which seems analogous to the form of a figure[8] (i.e., a story can be symmetrical, its "line" can be circular, linear, or multiply looped by digressions, and so forth). Since discontinuity can also be considered a property of the text as a whole, the structure of the Ghost Story must have been changed by explication. A thorough analysis should include an appraisal of the over-all structure and form of the texts and reproductions because such molar measures may reveal important parameters of retention. The analyses I have used so far, to show the relative accuracy and completeness of each reproduction, are molecular measures. A method had to be devised for scoring the texts and reproductions as wholes.

A story's redundancy—the degree to which its parts are repeated or duplicated in the test—is undoubtedly one of its important characteristics. Contemporary information theory emphasizes the role of redundancy in communication: it can easily be shown that a text with no redundant lexical elements is disconnected and meaningless. On the other hand, redundancy cannot be indefinitely increased without destroying movement and therefore continuity. Within these broad limits, however, texts can vary a great deal in redundancy, and this variation will reflect their over-all coherence and continuity. There is probably no one-to-one relationship between redundancy and coherence, because such factors as the complexity and familiarity of the text undoubtedly play a part—a simple familiar text requires and "tolerates" less redundancy than a complex unfamiliar text. This can be attributed partly to the presence of implicit or connotative redundancy: the fact that, for certain readers, certain words and ideas imply (are associated with) other words and ideas. This redundancy, which is so difficult to assess adequately, limits the validity of any objective method for measuring redundancy. However, with complexity and familiarity held relatively constant, it seems a plausible contention that, within wide limits, the greater the redundancy of a connected text, the greater its coherence and continuity.

[8] See Werner and Kaplan (1956). In her studies of retention Harrower (1933) also explored some of the figural properties of texts.

Since redundancy can quite easily be measured by objective quantitative procedures, it seemed to me to provide a foothold on which to begin an exploratory analysis of the structure of the stories and of the reproductions: to see what differences in redundancy can be detected between the original and explicated versions of the Ghost Story, and between the reproductions of the serial chains. If redundancy and coherence are indeed related, we may expect to find that the explicated version is more redundant than the original version, and that the serial reproductions grow progressively less redundant—especially in the original version chain. Since the Secretary Story is more familiar and hence less complex than the Ghost Story, it might be expected to be less redundant. The two stories differ in many respects, however, and we cannot draw valid conclusions about their relative coherence from their redundancy. We can, however, formulate expectations about changes in redundancy along the serial reproduction chains: namely, that the Secretary Story will show less of a redundancy decline as it goes through the reproduction chains than will either version of the Ghost Story.

MEASURING REDUNDANCY

No work has been reported on ways to analyze the redundancy of connected texts, so I improvised a technique for estimating the redundancy of word units. Redundancy is here synonymous with repetitiousness or frequency of occurrence, and word unit is akin to lexical unit.[9]

The first step in the redundancy analysis was the preparation of a distilled version of the text which omits all empty grammatical forms (e.g., weak conjunctions, articles, impersonal pronouns), changes the impersonal and passive constructions, where possible, to personal and active forms, and reduces the words to common lexical forms (e.g., "arrive" to "came-to," "returned" to "came-back-to"). In some instances this required the expansion of an ab-

---

[9] A lexical unit comprises a word and all of its dictionary equivalents, as well as its mood and tense variations (e.g., "amazement" and "surprise" may be the same lexical unit, so are "was amazed" and "will be surprised"). Furthermore, a predicate or verb with its prepositional form is a single lexical unit (e.g., "went-with," "smiled-at," "drove-toward," etc.), and abbreviated constructions are the same lexical unit as their expanded forms (e.g., "simultaneous" and "at the same time"; the latter therefore comprises a single lexical unit), and vice versa (e.g., "every day" equals "daily," "at that moment" equals "then," and so on).

breviation. For example, "warriors" was changed to "war-men"; since both "war" and "men" occur elsewhere in the test, such a transformation is necessary so that "warrior" does not stand as a unique lexical unit but is counted together with "war" and "men."

This redundancy analysis, then, is a special kind of *type-token*[10] analysis, since it reduces various types to common lexical meanings. It may be labeled a *lexical type-token* analysis. Moreover, it broadens the concept of a lexical unit beyond the grammatical and dictionary realm in that it links certain reflective and intransitive predicate forms ("become," "is," and the like) with their complements into single lexical units. For example, "became foggy" was considered the single lexical form "become-foggy," similarly "become-quiet," "is-dead," and so on, following the rule that such condensations are permissible when the complement itself can take a predicate form. Moreover, when active predicates seemed dependent upon their complement I condensed them—e.g., "made fire" into "make-fire," similarly "feel-pain."

In this analysis a number of words presented difficulties, and some *ad hoc* and perhaps arbitrary decisions had to be made. Pronouns, for example, offered a special problem. Since a pronoun usually represents a subject in an incomplete way, conveying only gender and number, it is difficult to know how much of the subject is being repeated (or made redundant). Moreover, the linguist speaks of a "zero pronoun" where one is not present but is implied by the grammatical structure. (Again the thorny problem of implicit redundancy.) Should these be counted? After some trial and error, I decided to count each pronoun as a full repetition of its referent and to ignore zero pronouns.

Once the distilled version was prepared, I counted each lexical unit and assigned a score to it, the numerator of which is 10 (arbitrarily chosen), the denominator the frequency of occurrence (e.g., since the lexical form "young" occurs five times in the text, each occurrence is scored 2). The sum of these scores for each text is its total *redundancy score*; dividing this score by the number of lexical units yields the average *redundancy score*. Finally, to derive an index that varies directly (rather than inversely) with redundancy, I subtracted the average redundancy score from 10 and called the result the *redundancy index*. I analyzed and scored each stimulus story and each reproduction in this way.

---

[10] The *type-token* ratio of a text is the number of different words in it (types) divided by the total number of words (tokens).

The redundancy index of the original version of the Ghost Story is 6.45, and of the explicated version, 6.73. Therefore, as expected, one of the results of the explication is increased redundancy. The Secretary Story has a smaller redundancy index than either version of the Ghost Story—6.11. This is not an unexpected finding, since a more familiar and less complex text probably needs less redundancy to maintain its coherence and continuity.

Redundancy Analysis of the Original Version of the Ghost Story

Underneath each lexical unit is its redundancy score: the number of times it occurs in the text divided into 10 (see pp. 28-29).

Redundancy Analysis of Serial Reproductions

Now we turn to a redundancy analysis of the reproductions to see whether there were any systematic differences along each serial chain as well as among the four groups. These results are presented in Table 3 (see p. 30).

A progressive decrease in redundancy index occurred in the serial reproductions of both versions of the Ghost Story. Only one of the ten serial reproductions failed to score lower than its precursor. No clear-cut progressive change occurred for the Secretary Story reproductions and their redundancy indexes varied within a narrow range; in the O-group there was a small steady drop in four of the five cases, while in the E-group there was a drop in three instances and a rise in two.

Of the two versions of the Ghost Story, the original version was consistently less redundant than the explicated version. Moreover, the differences between the reproductions of the two versions all exceeded the difference in the original texts. The difference between the redundancy indexes of the explicated and original versions of the Ghost Story itself was 0.28, while the average difference of the five reproductions was 1.06.

Before we can draw conclusions concerning structure from these findings, an extraneous relationship—the correlation between redundancy index and size—must be taken into account. Since the redundancy index is mathematically dependent upon the number of lexical units, the findings in Table 3 might be attributable simply to changes in the number of lexical units of the reproductions. The data, however, reveal no parallel relationship between the redundancy index and the number of lexical units; indeed a decrease in the number of lexical units frequently accompanied an increase in the redundancy index. This was conspicuous in the reproduction of the Secretary Story, where, even though the number of lexical units steadily decreased through the chains, yet the redundancy indexes did not. Therefore we can tentatively conclude that the difference in redundancy index between the Ghost Story and the Secretary Story reproductions represents a difference in their redundancy structure independent of their size, and, similarly, that the difference between the reproductions of the original and explicated versions of the Ghost Story also represents a real difference in structure.

What is the structural change reflected by the redundancy decrease? I have proposed that redundancy is related to coherence and continuity: for texts that are similar in complexity and familiarity, the greater the coherence of text, the higher will be its redundancy index. I checked this proposition by examining each reproduction, deriving an impression of its coherence and continuity, and comparing it with its redundancy index. This analysis (presented below on pp. 36-47) confirmed the close relationship between redundancy and coherence.

Thus the findings of the redundancy analysis fit nicely with the expectations, and complement the accuracy analyses in an important way, by showing that both versions of the Ghost Story, especially the original one, suffered a steady loss of coherence as they passed through the serial reproduction chains, while the Secretary Story did not. In other words, taking all of the quantitative analyses together, the Ghost Story reproductions lost steadily in accuracy and completeness as well as in coherence, while the Secretary Story lost in accuracy and completeness but maintained its coherence.

The accuracy analyses (Tables 1 and 2) were equivocal with respect to the differences between the reproductions of the explicated version of the Ghost Story and those of the Secretary Story— reproductions of the latter were not clearly superior to the former. However, the redundancy analysis reveals a clear-cut difference: the Ghost Story reproductions steadily lost coherence, while those of the Secretary Story did not.

Ghost's War
                3.3   1.4

one-night two young men from-Egulac went-to river to-hunt seals
    5   5   2   .3   5   .6   10   10

then became-foggy calm (men)* stopped work hearkened
  5   10   10   .3   10   10   10

(men) heard war cries (men) thought maybe war men**
 .3   3.3 1.4 5   .3   3.3   10   1.4 .8

(men) went-to shore hid-behind log
 .3   5   10   10

canoes came-up (men) heard paddles-noise saw one-canoe coming-up (to-men)
 2.5   .6   .3   3.3   10   10   2.5   .6   .3

five men in-canoe (men) said how-about-it (men) wish to-take-along (men)
 10   .8   2.5   .8   1.0   10   .8   10   .6   10   .3

(men) going-up river to-war-on the-people
 .8   .6   2.5 1.4   2.5

one-young man said (man) go-along-not
  2   .3   1.0   .3   .6

(man) might-be-killed (man's) relatives know-not where-gone (man)
  .3   2.5   .3   10   10   .6   .3   .3

(other man) may-go-with (men) (man) said turning-to other
  3.3 .3   .6   .8   .3   1.0   10   3.3

one-young man went other went-back home
   2   .3   .6   3.3   .6   3.3

(war men) went-up river town-Kalama's other-side
 1.4 .8   .6   2.5   10

the-people came-to river (the-people) began-to-war many killed

young man heard presently (war men) say let-us-go home quick
2   .3 3.3   5   1.4 .8 1.0   .6 3.3   10

that-Indian hit (man) thought (men) ghosts
     10   3.3 .3   3.3   .8   3.3

(man) not-feel-sick (men) said (man) was-hit
 .3   5   .8   1.0 .3   3.3

canoes went-back-to Egulac young man went-to shore house
2.5   .6   5   2   .3   .6   5   3.3

made-fire (man) rested (man) ate (man) thought (man) must-tell adventure
  10   .3   10   .3   10   .3   3.3   .3   1.0   10

(man) told said (man) went-with ghosts (men) warred
 .3   1.0 1.0   .3   .6   3.3   .8   1.4

many-enemy killed many fellows killed
   3.3   2.5 3.3   10   2.5

(men) said (man) was-hit (man) not-feel-sick
 .8   1.0   .3   3.3   .3   5

(man) told-all (man) became-quiet (man) fell /end-night/
 .3   1.0   .3   10   .3   10   5

something-black came-out-of (man's) mouth
      10   10   .3   10

(man's) face became-contorted the-people jumped-up cried
  .3   10   10   2.5   10   5

(man) was-dead
 .3   10

---

* Pronouns are represented by their referents in parentheses.
** The "canoe men" were considered distinct from the "two young men," and therefore are not connected. The former "men" are italicized in the analysis.

Table 3

REDUNDANCY ANALYSIS OF THE STORIES AND EACH REPRODUCTION

	Original group			Explicated group		
	No. Lexical Units	Redundancy Score	Redundancy Index	No. Lexical Units	Redundancy Score	Redundancy Index
The Ghost Story	169	600	6.45	168	550	6.73
Reproduction No. 1	118	480	5.93	204	670	6.72
Reproduction No. 2	102	440	5.69	113	380	6.64
Reproduction No. 3	62	300	5.16	85	360	5.76
Reproduction No. 4	35	260	2.57	60	320	4.66
Reproduction No. 5	34	220	3.53	41	230	4.39
Mean of the Ghost Chains	70.2	340	4.58	100.6	392	5.64
The Secretary Story	162	630	6.11	162	630	6.11
Reproduction No. 1	140	610	5.64	160	740	5.37
Reproduction No. 2	98	430	5.61	114	530	5.35
Reproduction No. 3	85	380	5.53	85	380	5.53
Reproduction No. 4	81	400	5.06	82	350	5.73
Reproduction No. 5	75	370	5.07	52	260	5.01
Mean of the Secretary Chains	95.8	438	5.38	98.6	452	5.39

Discussion and Conclusions

The quantitative analyses show that connected and extended verbal material, of the kind used in the present study, tends to undergo progressive skeletonization as it passes from reproducer to reproducer along a serial reproduction chain, i.e., as it goes through successive stages in a hypothetical mnemonic series. Whereas Bartlett often used as many as twenty links in his chains (continuing them until the reproductions finally became fixed and "conventionalized"), the present experiment shows that five serial reproductions, obtained under certain conditions, are enough to yield substantial skeletonization.

One of the goals of the experiment was to devise and test procedures for objectively appraising connected and extended verbal material. The two measures finally used, information and theme analyses, were selected from a group of measures all of which reflected the progressive skeletonization along the chains as well as the differences between the experimental groups. They showed that the original version of the Ghost Story lost in accuracy and completeness, of information units as well as of themes, at a greater rate than did the explicated version; and that both versions lost at a faster rate than did the Secretary Story, though at some points the explicated version was retained slightly better than the Secretary Story. These results, together with those of the redundancy analysis, show a clear-cut pattern: both versions of the Ghost Story became skeletonized with regard to content and structure, the original version to a greater extent, while the Secretary Story underwent only skeletonization of content with no marked change in structure.

Thus a familiar[11] story, even though it loses a good deal of its content, maintains a coherent structure in reproduction, while an unfamiliar, strange, and sometimes cryptic story loses both content and coherence. Furthermore, explications, while they increase the coherence of a stimulus story to begin with, apparently cannot pre-

---

[11] It should be pointed out that, since the two stories differ in a variety of respects (despite efforts to equate them), it cannot be concluded with complete assurance that the property of "familiarity" is the efficacious variable here. Nevertheless, it seems safe to conclude, on the basis of this result as well as on the findings of other experiments—see, for example, the experiments of Tressel and Spragg (1941) and Noble (1955)—that familiarity of character, setting, and event does facilitate retention.

vent its progressive loss in reproductions, though they do appreciably slow its course.

Explication and familiarity both refer to properties of the stimulus material that arouse appropriate schemas; these in turn, after some modification and organization, integrate a new schema which serves as the basis for recall. The extent to which subjects already have appropriate schemas, and the degree to which they are well or poorly articulated, will determine the organization of the new schema. If the material is familiar, as is the case for the Secretary Story, then the pre-existence of appropriate schemas is assured—the person is schematically equipped for the stimulus. If the material is strange, then schemas are not assured and the burden of organizing them is left largely to the stimulus material.

If the material is explicated, then schemas are, in a sense, furnished in the fabric of the stimulus. Perhaps the explications set in motion certain mobilizing schemas which assemble and organize the material whose schemas are primitive or poorly articulated. In turn, gaps or discontinuities in the structure of the material may interfere with the course of schema formation precisely because the missing information is necessary to facilitate the integration and organization of a new schema. When these links are missing, the corresponding steps in schema mobilization and organization do not occur, and we can expect little resistance to fragmentation. The present findings suggest that to the extent that a schema depends upon such mobilizing links, especially when they are weak or poorly articulated, it stands less chance of maintaining its integrity.

But it may be too early for this much speculation, and we will return to a consideration of these mobilizing or explicatory links and their role in schema formation after we have examined the reproductions themselves, an exercise that may throw further light on their functions. At this point we can conclude that schema formation and integrity depend upon at least two variables, explication and familiarity, and these variables may correspond, on the one hand, to those properties of the stimulus which facilitate mobilization and integration of new schemas, and, on the other hand, to the existence of already well-articulated appropriate schemas.

Qualitative Analysis

Direct Examination of the Reproductions

With the completion of the quantitative analyses our job of appraisal is not yet finished, for a careful look at the reproductions themselves must be taken. One of the questions such an examination may answer is whether the qualities and organization of the reproductions seem congruent with the various quantitative analyses, particularly the redundancy analysis—in other words, whether these measures have succeeded in capturing a tangible property of the texts.

A second goal of direct examination is to search for further hypotheses concerning modes and processes of schema functioning in reproduction. By tracing certain parts of the stories as they are transmitted through the chains (paying particular attention to those themes and information units which drop out somewhere along the chain, which come to be distorted, or which give rise to elaborations and importations), we may get hints concerning underlying schema processes and a better understanding of the role of gaps and explications in remembering. The serial reproduction method is peculiarly suited to this kind of investigation because it "freezes" the mnemonic process at a series of consecutive points. When a particular part of the story is omitted (forgotten) in, say, the fifth reproduction of a chain, it is often instructive to observe the changes which this part had undergone in the previous reproductions.

Since the direct examination will deal mainly with the Ghost Story reproductions, focusing on gaps, ambiguities, and explications, it is necessary first to discuss the original version and the manner in which I edited and emended it in the explicated version.

Explication of the Ghost Story

My first problem in editing the Ghost Story was to locate its important gaps. Having no objective way to define a "gap," I had to rely on subjective and "common sense" judgment. I located two major gaps in the texts: (1) In theme p) the young man suddenly and inexplicably comes to the dramatic conclusion that his companions "are ghosts"; (2) theme q) contains the enigmatic phrase "he did not feel sick, but . . . he had been shot."

To "fill" these gaps, I wrote two new themes: (1) The fact that he is called "Indian" is made to explain how it is that the young man realizes that the warriors are not like his fellows (incorporated into theme o) in the explicated version); (2) the fact that he is with ghosts is made to explain his insensitivity to pain and protection from death [this became theme r) of the explicated version]. This second explication, by saying that the protection is supposed to last only through that night, also prepares for the climax of the story: the death of the young man at sunrise.

In the version of the story which Bartlett used, theme c) is not present: the mention of "foggy and calm" is followed immediately by the war-cries, and the young men react by fleeing and hiding. There seems to be an implicit gap here because it somehow *feels* as if the "foggy and calm" is an omen of some sort. Therefore an explication seemed in order following theme b), to spell out the omen implied by the "foggy and calm" and therefore account for the men's flight. This explication could also help to prepare for the man's later realization that the warriors are ghosts. Theme c) in the explicated version was designed to fulfill these two purposes. In order to make the text of the original version equivalent, a new theme needed to be added there, and so for the original version I wrote another theme c) which added verbal material but not explication.

These were the three major alterations of the story. In addition, I made the following smaller changes and additions:

1. In theme a): "*to hunt seals* in the river" seemed unfamiliar, so I substituted "*to fish.*"

2. Theme f) gave another opportunity to emphasize the supernatural nature of the war party. Why is it that the hiding is to no avail? Because from "*these*" canoes there is no way to conceal oneself.

3. Themes g) and h) seem to join better when h) precedes g), and were therefore reversed in the explicated version.

4. In theme j): why the other man can go is unexplained in the original. A possible reason, suggested in part by the excuse which the first man makes, is that he has no relatives.

5. In theme p): the word "surely" is inserted for added stress.

6. Since theme r) adds fourteen words and six information units to the explicated version, it was necessary to add some text to the original version in order to make it equivalent. Therefore theme t), which also contains fourteen words and six information units but does not seem to explicate the story, was added to the original version.

Finally, in order to reduce the two versions to the dimensions of the story as Bartlett used it (to make the study an approximate replication of his), I omitted a part of the original story in which the young men protest that they have no arrows and the warriors answer that there are arrows in the canoes.

Theme Analysis of the Ghost Story

Since the unit of observation was the theme, here are the titles and the scoring criteria of the themes of the two versions of the Ghost Story. Those which are unique to the original version are marked with asterisks (*), and those unique to the explicated versions with daggers (†).

THEME ANALYSIS OF GHOST STORY

Theme a)	THE HUNT:	Does the reproduction tell of a hunting or fishing expedition by the men?
Theme b)	ATMOSPHERE:	Is some mention made of the atmospheric conditions?
**Theme c)*	CEASE WORK:	Is it mentioned that they stop and/or listen?*
†*Theme c)*	SOMETHING UP:	Is there some portent given of something pending?†
Theme d)	SOMETHING HEARD:	Does the reproduction mention that they heard something approaching (war-cries or sounds of canoes)?
Theme e)	HIDING:	Do the men hide in some way?
Theme f)	ACCOSTED:	Is there some description of the canoes approaching the men?
Theme g)	INVITATION:	Is there mention of an invitation?
Theme h)	WAR-PLANS:	Are the plans of the men in the boat mentioned?
Theme i)	REFUSAL:	Is one man's refusal mentioned?
Theme j)	PERMISSION:	Does he in some way allow or encourage the other to go?
Theme k)	SEPARATION:	Is it mentioned that one goes and not the other?

Theme l)	WAR-TRIP:	Is the traveling in the canoes mentioned?
Theme m)	FIGHT:	Is the battle mentioned or described?
Theme n)	"RETREAT":	Is it described that someone cries for the battle to cease (it is sufficient that someone cries out to bring attention to the casualty)?
†*Theme o)*	"INDIAN":	Is it mentioned that he is never called "Indian" by his people or that there is something noteworthy about it?†
Theme p)	REALIZATION:	Is it mentioned that the man realizes he is in the company of ghosts?
Theme q)	ENIGMA:	Is it mentioned that he is wounded yet feels no pain?
†*Theme r)*	PROTECTION:	Is his knowledge of ghosts' protection mentioned?†
Theme s)	HOME:	Is the return home or to his people mentioned?
**Theme t)*	DECISION TO TELL:	Is there some mention of his decision to tell his adventure?*
Theme u)	REVELATIONS:	Is it described how he tells everyone about his adventure?
Theme v)	ENIGMA AGAIN:	Is the enigma recounted?
Theme w)	SOMETHING BLACK:	Is there a description of the morning events (any one of the strange afflictions will do)?
Theme x)	REACTION:	Is the reaction of sorrow and/or horror by the people mentioned?
Theme y)	DEATH:	Is the man's death mentioned?

Quality and Structure of the Reproductions

My first examination was to gain an impression of qualitative and structural aspects of each reproduction as a whole, beginning with the reproductions of the two versions of the Ghost Story which are presented below. Themes are lettered according to the theme

EXPLICATION AND FAMILIARITY

analysis of the stimulus story, and noteworthy changes, distortions, and importations are italicized.

SERIAL REPRODUCTIONS OF THE ORIGINAL VERSION OF THE GHOST STORY

REPRODUCTION NO. 1
The War of the Ghosts

a) One night two young men from Ebaga went hunting for seals. *b*) While they were there the night became foggy and calm. *d*) They heard the sound of muffled oars. They said, "Perhaps this is a war party." *e*) They went ashore and hid behind a log. *f*) Soon a boat appeared. *h*) The men in it said, "We are going to make war on the people up the river." *The two men discussed who should go, k*) finally one went with them and the other went home.

When they reached the place, *m*) many men came down to the shore. Many on each side were killed. *n*) Finally, someone said, "That Indian is shot." *q*) The man did not feel anything, though told he was hit.

s) When the young man reached home he went ashore and lit a fire. *t*) He said to himself, "I must tell everyone about my adventures." *u*) He called his friends and told them about the battle, saying that many men on both sides had been killed *p*) and that *he had discovered that the men he was fighting on the same side as, were ghosts. v*) He told them he had been shot but not hurt.

w) When the morning came the young man grew pale. Something black came out of his mouth. *y*) He fell down. He was dead.

REPRODUCTION NO. 2

a) Two men *were fishing. d*) Suddenly they heard the sound of oars *b*) *through the fog.* One said, "Maybe it is a war party." *e*) They hid behind a log *f*) and saw the men in the boat. *h*) One man said, "We are going to attack another village up the river." *k*) One man decided to go and the other went home.

The first man traveled with the men in the boat *m*) and when they landed a lot of men came down to the river's edge and there was a terrific battle. A lot of men were killed on both sides. *n*) Suddenly one man said, "The Indian has been shot." *q*) The man didn't feel any pain.

s) He went home, built a large fire, *u*) and called all his friends to tell them of his experiences. He said there was a big battle, a lot of men were killed, *v*) and the men said he was shot. He didn't believe it because he couldn't feel anything. *p*) *He said, "They must have been ghosts!"*

w) The next morning he woke up and was sick. Black stuff fell out of his mouth, *y*) He fell down. He was dead.

(*The men were from the village of Aboga.*)

REPRODUCTION NO. 3

a) Two men were fishing. *d*) They heard a boat come up the river *b*) in the fog and saw men in it. *e*) They hid behind a log. *h*) The men in the boat were going to attack a village up the stream. *k*) One of the fishermen joined them.

m) They attacked a village and several people were killed. *n*) Suddenly one said, "The Indian is shot."

s) He returned home *u*) and told his friends about his experience. *v*) They told him he was shot but he didn't believe them.

w) In the morning he was sick and spit up black stuff. *y*) He died.

p) *"They must have been ghosts,"* he said.

REPRODUCTION NO. 4

a) Two men were fishing. *f*) A boat full of men came up the river. *e*) The men hid behind a log. *m*) The men in the boat attacked a village upstream. *k*) One of the men joined them.

In the attack some people were killed. *n*) Someone said: "The Indian is shot."

w) He was sick the next morning and spit up some black stuff *y*) and died.

p) *"They must have been ghosts."*

REPRODUCTION NO. 5

a) Two men were fishing. *f*) They saw a canoe approaching. *e*) The two men hid behind a log.

m) The men went up river and attacked a town. *k*) One of the fishermen joined them.

Someone said, *"They must be Indians."*

w) The next day the man grew ill and bled some black stuff.

p) *"He must have been a ghost."*

SERIAL REPRODUCTIONS OF THE EXPLICATED VERSION OF THE GHOST STORY

REPRODUCTION NO. 1

The War of the Ghosts

a) One night two men of Egulac went to the river to go fishing. *b*) While they were there the night became foggy and calm *c*) and they knew that this denoted that ghosts were nearby, *as this was the sort of night on which they would appear.*

d) Suddenly from out of the fog they perceived canoes approaching and in terror *e*) hid behind a log on the shore. *f*) They soon realized that there was no hiding, for one of the canoes came steadily toward them. *g*) From the canoe stepped a man who said, "You two *must* come with us, *h*) as we are about to make war on *your neighbors.*" The two fishermen then noted that the canoe held five men. *i*) On hearing this remark from the man in the canoe, one of the fishermen cried out, "Oh, no, I cannot go with you, I have a family and relatives *whom I must care for.*" *j*) He then turned to his companion and said, "But you can go, you have *no one dependent on you.*" *k*) So the second of the two fishermen entered the canoe with the five men.

l) After some traveling they reached the land of Kalama, which they had been told was their destination. *m*) A great battle ensued, many people on both sides being killed. *n*) Suddenly the fisherman heard one of his companions shout, "We must leave at once! The Indian has been hit!" *o*) This was heard with considerable surprise by the fisherman as *he knew he was not an Indian. q*) Also *he was amazed* that he had felt no pain, though he knew he had been hit and that his companions meant him when they mentioned "Indian." Then he realized that he felt no pain because *p*) he was with ghosts *and not men, r*) that explained his inability to feel pain. Also that this *magic* was good only for the night and that in the morning he would die.

s) Whereupon his companions took him back to his people and he made a great fire that called them all together. *u*) He rose amidst them and told them the story of the battle. "I was taken to a neighboring land where a great battle took place. *v*) I was called Indian and was wounded, but felt it not. Many, many people were killed on both sides."

At that moment the sun rose. The man who had told the story stood. *w*) He began to shake and fell upon the ground. Something black poured from his mouth.

y) He was dead.

REPRODUCTION NO. 2

Two men *were on the beach. b*) The night was foggy and calm— *c*) a night on which ghosts were likely to appear. *d*) Suddenly the two men heard something approach *e*) and they ran up onto the beach and *tried* to hide behind a log. *f*) They soon found there was no hiding as the canoes continued to approach. *g*) A man stepped out of the canoe and asked the two men to accompany him. *i*) The first fisherman replied that he could not go as he had a wife and relatives for whom he was obliged to care. *j*) He urged the second fisherman to go as he had no one dependent upon him. *k*) The second fisherman went. *l*) They journeyed to Kalama. *m*) War ensued. *n*) The fisherman heard one of the men say. "The Indian has been hit." *o*) He could not understand this as he was not an Indian and yet he knew they referred to him as he had been hit. *q*) Further, *he was puzzled* because he felt no pain from his wound. *p*) Then he recalled he was among ghosts and, *r*) therefore, felt no pain. He realized, however, that when morning came, the ghosts would leave and he would die. *s*) He returned to his people *u*) and told them his story. *w*) He fell over, something black poured from his mouth—*y*) he was dead.

REPRODUCTION NO. 3

Two men were sitting on a beach. *d*) They heard a noise *but couldn't see anything b*) because of the fog. *f*) The canoe came up to shore and a man got out. *g*) He asked the two fishermen to come to Tralama with him. *i*) The first fisherman refused because he had a wife and relatives to support. *k*) The second fisherman was independent and he went with him. *l*) They went away in the boat to Tralama. *m*) War ensued. *n*) He could hear somebody say, "The Indian has been hit." *o*) He couldn't see any Indian and he knew they must be talking about him. *q*) He didn't feel any pain *p*) but then remembered that he was *in a land of ghosts r*) so that he wouldn't feel anything. *s*) He came back to his friends *u*) and told them the story. *w*) All of a sudden something black came out of his mouth *y*) and he fell over—dead.

REPRODUCTION NO. 4

a) Two fishermen *were fishing off shore.* *f*) A boat came to shore and a man got out. *g*) He asked them to come with him to Tralama. *i*) The first fisherman refused, since he had a wife and children *waiting for him.* *k*) The second fisherman was independent and so went with him *l*) to Tralama. *m*) War ensued. *n*) He heard someone say "The Indian has been hit." *q*) He felt no pain *p*) but knew he was in a land of ghosts. *s*) He returned to his friends *u*) to tell them the story. *w*) Something black came out of his mouth *y*) and he dropped over—dead.

REPRODUCTION NO. 5

a) Two fishermen were fishing off shore. *f*) A man came up *g*) and asked them to go out with him. *i*) One refused because he had a wife and children. *k*) The other went with him because he had no one. *l*) They went to Tralama. *m*) War ensued. *n*) Someone cried, "The Indian *is dead.*" He was hit and *p*) *there were ghosts.* *w*) Something black fell out of his mouth *y*) and he was dead.

To begin with reproductions No. 5, and proceed backward along the chains (later we will retrace our steps to follow particular themes and information units as they are transmitted along the chains): The first impression about the two final reproductions is that the reproduction of the explicated version is more coherent and continuous. This impression is reflected in the redundancy indexes of these two reproductions as shown in Table 3: the explicated version reproduction is substantially more redundant than the original version reproduction (4.39 to 3.53). The explicated version reproduction, though only eleven words longer, is comparatively tight and retains the core of the Ghost Story, while the original version reproduction is fragmentary and has lost the core of the story. It is easy to detect three large gaps in this reproduction: theme *m*) is entirely disconnected; and the sentence, "Someone said, 'they must be Indians,' " is isolated both from what precedes and what follows it. On the other hand, No. 5 of the explicated version contains only a minor gap at theme *p*), which, although joined in a sentence with "he was hit," seems to stand apart.

The difference in structure between reproductions of the original and explicated versions is especially conspicuous in reproductions

EXPLICATION AND FAMILIARITY

No. 4. The largest difference in redundancy index between any pair of reproductions exists between these two: 2.57 to 4.66. Explicated version reproduction No. 4 is quite coherent and flowing, and tells the story well in spite of the reduction in content. Theme p), though not quite as isolated as in No. 5, is nonetheless poorly integrated. Original version reproduction No. 4, on the other hand, is disjointed: there are major breaks in the story line, particularly between themes o) and m) and between themes n) and w), and theme p) is merely tacked on at the end.

The beginnings of the fragmented character of the original version reproductions become apparent in No. 3, a choppy and staccato account which contains a number of ambiguities. For example, theme v): who "told him he was shot," his "friends" or the warriors? And why was it that "he didn't believe them"? Theme p), which is merely appended to the text, is unconnected and ambiguous—who "must have been ghosts"? And how could "he" say this when "he died" in the previous sentence? Gaps are also present between themes e) and h) and s). On the other hand, explicated version reproduction No. 3 is coherent, rather tightly constructed, and relatively free of ambiguity. Its redundancy index, however, does not seem fully to reflect this difference (it is 5.76 compared to original version reproduction No. 3 of 5.16, the smallest difference between any pair of reproductions).

In reproduction No. 2 of the original version a measure of the staccato and disjointed character is clearly discernible. For example, themes h) and k) appear abruptly without any preparation, and themes n), q) and s) are quite disconnected. Nevertheless, the account as a whole is an adequate rendition of the story, though far less so than reproduction No. 2 of the explicated version which is smoother and earns a higher redundancy index (5.69 to 6.64).

There are two prominent gaps in reproduction No. 1 of the original version: between themes q) and s), and between f) and h). It is noteworthy that theme p) stands out from the rest of the text as an essentially unconnected theme: how had he made the discovery that they "were ghosts"? Yet, in spite of its spareness, this is a rather faithful and complete account of the story.

The most complete and accurate of all is reproduction No. 1 of the explicated version which is seventy-eight words longer than its stimulus story, has lost only one theme, and has a redundancy index practically identical with that of its stimulus. It is free of any evident gaps; in fact, it contains a number of importations and amplifications which seem to cement the story further, reducing its minor gaps and further clarifying its ambiguities. It is especially noteworthy that each of the explication themes of the stimulus story is further amplified and embellished in this reproduction. Here we see, in part, a propensity of this particular S; her reproduction of the Secretary story (see below pp. 44-45) is also highly embellished and amplified. In fact, the two reproductions by this S gave rise to the idea of an importation style of remembering, and led me to study this tendency in later experiments.

At this point, the findings of the direct appraisal of the Ghost Story reproductions can be summed up by noting the high correspondence between impressions of the relative coherence and continuity of a reproduction and its redundancy index.[12] In only one case (reproduction No. 3) was the redundancy index not fully compatible with the impression.

SERIAL REPRODUCTIONS OF THE SECRETARY STORY BY THE O-GROUP

REPRODUCTION NO. 1
The War Attacks

a) Two sisters graduated from the same business school. They decided to go abroad to work at embassies; because that way, *b*) they said, "We can work and still see the world." *c*) So they went to neighboring foreign countries. *d*) They agreed to write to each other every day.

g) One sister's secretarial skill got her a job at the ministry of Montania. *f*) The country was in the grip of war hysteria. *h*) The minister told her that she would have access to much top-secret information; he said, "I expect loyalty."

i) One day she came across a document *j*) describing a sneak air attack to be made on a small neighboring nation. *k*) She read it with interest until she noticed the name of the country and *l*) saw with

---

[12] Since the texts differ in lexical content, it is not possible to demonstrate that the extent of the difference in redundancy indexes is traceable in each case to the gaps detected upon direct examination. Nevertheless, my impression of a gap regularly arose where a new lexical element (or group of elements) entered the text unheralded, and when it remained disconnected by virtue of being unrepeated elsewhere in the text. Such unprepared and isolated lexical elements add substantially to the redundancy index of a text, and, in the case of two texts that are equivalent in size and content, it is these elements which make the difference in redundancy.

horror that it was the country where her sister worked. *m*) She immediately wanted to write to her sister and warn her of the danger, but censorship prevailed between the two countries and she could not.

o) She therefore decided to stop writing to her sister. *p*) "If I do not write, she will worry, think I am ill, and come to find out."

q) On the same day that she put her plan into effect, her sister stopped writing to her. *r*) She began to worry and to fear *s*) that her sister was ill *t*) and decided to go and to see her. *u*) Since the distance was only twelve kilometers, she decided that walking would be the *simplest* way. *v*) When she got to the border whom should she meet but her sister, *w*) *and discovered that the other nation was planning a similar attack on her country.*

x) The same day both attacks were carried out and both embassies destroyed.

REPRODUCTION NO. 2

a) Two girls, sisters, graduated from business school and decided to get jobs abroad *b*) so they could "see the world" and "earn while doing so." *c*) They got jobs in adjoining countries in the embassies. *d*) They decided to write each other every day.

g) One girl got a job with the air minister. *h*) He said the job was very important and highly confidential.

i) One day the girl came across a secret document *j*) on the plans for a sneak air attack on a neighboring country—*l*) it was the same one where her sister worked. *n*) *She wanted to save her sister but didn't know how.*

m) All mail was censored. *o*) She finally decided not to write, *p*) then her sister would think she was sick and come to visit her.

q) The day she stopped writing so did her sister. *r*) After a while she became worried about her sister *t*) she decided to walk over to the neighboring country to see her. *u*) It was only twelve kilometers away.

v) When she got to the border who should she see coming toward her but her sister.

x) Both countries attacked the other that day and both embassies were destroyed. *Both sisters were saved because they weren't at their jobs in the embassies.*

REPRODUCTION NO. 3

a) Two girls, sisters, graduated from business school and decided to live and work abroad.

c) They each had a job in an embassy of two adjoining countries. *i*) One sister discovered one day the plans *j*) for a sneak air attack on the adjoining country *l*) where her sister worked.

m) The mail was censored and *n*) she couldn't figure any way to get a warning to her. *o*) She finally decided to stop writing to her *p*) so she would think she was ill and would come to see her. *q*) At the same time the sister in the adjoining country stopped writing also.

r) When she received no mail from her sister she became worried *t*) and decided to walk to the next country to see her. *u*) She walked to the border, *about* twelve kilometers off, *v*) and met her sister coming to her.

x) The next day each country attacked each other and both embassies were destroyed, but both girls were safe, as they were not at work in the embassies.

REPRODUCTION NO. 4

a) Two sisters, *recently* graduated from business school, decided to live in and work in a foreign country.
c) The girls secured positions in two adjoining countries.
i) One girl learned of the plans *j*) of a sneak air attack on *the* adjoining country.
m) She could not write to her sister of this because of *heavily* censored mail, *n*) so wondered how she could warn her sister *of impending disaster*.
o) She decided to stop writing to her sister *p*) *in the hope* that she would be thought ill, and her sister would then come to see her.
q) However, at the same time the sister stopped writing.
r) Concerned for her sister's *safety*, *t*) she decided to walk to the country where her sister was. *u*) After she had walked toward the border, *approximately* twelve kilometers, *v*) she was met by her sister who had started to walk toward that country.
x) The air attack did occur—many lives *were lost,* but the *sister* was safe because she *was not where she should have been.*

REPRODUCTION NO. 5

a) Two sisters went to business college. They wanted to get jobs in foreign countries.
c) Each got a job in *another* country.
j) One sister heard of a sneak air attack. *m*) She wanted to tell her sister but could not write about it due to heavy censure of mail.
o) She finally decided not to write, *p*) hoping her sister would figure she was ill and come to her.
q) She stopped writing but at the same time she received no letters from her sister.
r) Fearing for the *health* of her sister, *u*) she started walking to see her sister. *v*) She met her sister part of the way *w*) *as she, too, had started to find why mail had stopped coming.*
x) The attack took place—many people were killed, but the girl was safe as she was not where she should have been.

SERIAL REPRODUCTIONS OF THE SECRETARY STORY BY THE E-GROUP

REPRODUCTION NO. 1

The Sneak Attack

a) Two sisters, who had graduated from a business college named Menassa, decided to seek employment in foreign countries. *b*) They told their mother, "In that way we will obtain work and still see the world."
c) So they departed into separate countries. *e*) One sister went to

the country of Montania *g*) and because of her excellent stenographic training, was made secretary to the foreign ambassador. *h*) "You will have access to the *most* secret documents," he warned the girl. "I will expect *utmost* loyalty from you," he further told her.

i) One day somewhat later *in the pursuance of her duties* she came across a document *j*) which revealed a plan for attacking, by bombing, a nearby smaller nation. *k*) She read this with considerable interest until, to her horror, she noted the name of the small nation to be bombed. *l*) She discovered it to be the country where her sister was residing.

n) She wondered, *with great fear*, how she could warn her sister of the impending attack *o*) and then thought of the following plan. She would desist from writing her usual daily letter to her sister, *p*) her sister would become alarmed and come to visit her, to see if she were sick or in need of something. *q*) On the *very* day she proceeded to put her plan into operation, the daily letter she usually received from her sister did not arrive. *r*) She noted this with great disturbance and in the days that followed, when no more letters from her sister were forthcoming, *t*) she decided to act.

u) She proceeded toward the border of Montania, which was a distance of twelve kilometers. *v*) *To her amazement*, at the border she met her sister *w*) who was on the way to see her, telling her an identical story.

x) That day both countries were bombed and both embassies were destroyed.

REPRODUCTION NO. 2

a) Two sisters graduated from a business school, Menassa. They decided to take jobs in foreign countries. *b*) They told their mother that in this way they could work and "still see the world." *e*) One sister went to Montania. *g*) Because of her stenographic skill she obtained the job as secretary to the foreign ambassador. *h*) She was told that she would be handling secret documents and that absolute loyalty was expected of her. *i*) One day, in the pursuit of her duties, she came upon a document *j*) which told of plans for an attack on a nearby nation. *k*) She read this plan to bomb the nation with considerable interest until she realized *l*) it pertained to the nation wherein her sister resided. *n*) She tried to think of some way to warn her sister *o*) and finally evolved the following plan: she would not write her customary daily letter to her sister. *p*) Her sister would become alarmed and visit her to see if she were sick. *q*) She did not write the letter but noted with alarm that she did not receive a letter from her sister either. *r*) As the days passed with no word from her sister she became more concerned and *t*) decided to visit her sister. *v*) She met her sister at the border *w*) and the sister told *of a similar plan to bomb Montania*. *x*) Both embassies were destroyed.

REPRODUCTION NO. 3

a) Two girls had graduated from business college—Manessa. They both wanted to be secretaries to foreign ministers. *e*) One of the girls went to Montania *g*) where she became the secretary to the foreign ambassador. Her sister went to another nation. *h*) The first sister was told that she would handle a lot of secret documents and she must keep them absolutely to herself. *i*) One day she came across a plan *j*) to bomb a neighboring country. *k*) As she read it through, *l*) she realized it was her sister's nation. *n*) She tried to think of a plan to let her sister know about the bombing. *o*) She decided not to write her customary letter to her sister *p*) whereupon her sister would become alarmed and come to visit her. *q*) She did not receive a letter from her sister *r*) and became alarmed herself. *v*) She went to meet her sister at the border *w*) and found out that the sister's nation also had made plans to bomb Montania. *x*) Both nations were destroyed.

REPRODUCTION NO. 4

a) Two sisters graduated from *the same* secretarial school—Manessa. Both wanted to obtain jobs as secretaries to foreign ministers. *c*) Both sisters received positions in foreign nations. *g*) The first sister got a job as secretary to the foreign minister in the country Montania. *h*) She was told she would handle many papers which were to be kept secret. *l*) One day she received a paper *j*) which gave information concerning a plan to bomb another nation. *k*) Upon reading it she realized that it was the country in which her sister worked. *n*) She wanted to warn her sister *o*) and decided that, instead of writing her usual letter to her sister, she would not write. *p*) If her sister did not receive the letter, she would come to see her. *q*) The first sister did not receive a letter *r*) and became worried. *v*) She met her sister at the border *w*) and discovered that Montania was to be bombed. *x*) Both nations were destroyed.

REPRODUCTION NO. 5

a) Two sisters went to secretarial school. Both wanted to be secretaries to foreign ministers. *g*) The first sister became secretary to the minister of Montania. *c*) The other sister was in another foreign country. *h*) The first sister was *sworn to secrecy*. *j*) Later she learned a bomb was to be dropped on the country *l*) her sister was in. *She could not break her oath o*) and decided if she did not write, *p*) her sister would come to see what was wrong. *r*) The sister did worry *v*) and met her sister at the border of Montania. *Both were killed*.

Starting again with the ends of the chains, it is noteworthy that the degree of collapse in both reproductions No. 5, though appreciable, is not as great as in those of the Ghost Story. The collapse is more evident in reproduction No. 5 of the E-group than in that of the O-group.[13] The former is more fragmented, contains a few gaps especially from theme *r*) on, and has a noteworthy dis-

---

[13] The superiority of the O-group in their reproductions of the Secretary Story contrasts with the superiority of the E-group in their reproductions of the Ghost Story. It shows that the O-group was superior in recall ability, and thus the difference between the groups in their recall of the Ghost Story must have been due to the explications.

tortion at the end. The latter, on the other hand, though also rather spare and staccato, contains no major gaps, and is a quite faithful and complete account. Their redundancy indexes are almost identical.

Both reproductions No. 4 of the Secretary Story are coherent and complete accounts. In fact, reproductions No. 1, No. 2, No. 3, and No. 4 of both groups seem remarkably coherent in spite of their progressive loss of themes and information units. This impression tends to corroborate the redundancy analysis, which showed that the redundancy indexes of the Secretary Story reproductions vary only within a narrow range (5.73 to 5.01), without any really systematic decreases. The difference between the redundancy indexes of the two No. 4 reproductions, which is the largest of any pair (5.73 to 5.06), is reflected clearly in the texts: the E-group reproduction is conspicuously smoother and more flowing.

Reproduction No. 1 of the O-group presents an especially faithful account of the Secretary Story. In theme w), there is an amplification of the original phrase "for the same reason" into a full-blown explication. This importation of explications is especially conspicuous in reproduction No. 2 of the O-group, where the closing sentence is added to drive home the denouement of the story.

The lead-off member of the E-group—whose account is not as complete as her opposite number's—shows the same tendency to amplify and embellish here that she showed in her reproduction of the Ghost Story. Many of her importations in this case seem more to highlight the events of the story, to furnish emphasis and color, than to provide cohesiveness. (It is as though the familiar content needs no explication.) These importations are, for the most part, unprepared for and unrepeated, and hence they reduce the over-all redundancy of the text. Whereas this S maintained the redundancy level of the Ghost Story in her reproduction of it, in the case of the more familiar Secretary Story she reduced it substantially (6.11 to 5.37). The lead-off member of the O-group, on the other hand, reduced the redundancy of both stories by approximately the same amount (about 0.50).

The Fate of Content in Serial Reproductions

I will now trace certain themes and information units through the serial reproductions of the Ghost Story, paying particular attention to the vicissitudes of the explications in the explicated version chain, and to the gappy and ambiguous parts of the original version. Explications—both those inserted by the experimenter and those that *S*s introduced in the course of reproduction—should prove to play a pivotal role in influencing the course of reproductions. In the present analysis I also pay special attention to those parts of the story which dropped out or became the locations of distortions and importations.

Reproduction No. 1 of the original version loses six themes. Three of these were associated with the ambiguities and gaps that I ameliorated in the explicated version. For example, consider the gap between themes *b*) and *d*) (I "closed" it in the explicated version by emphasizing the omen): theme *c*), SOMETHING UP, which I added simply for word count, drops out completely in reproduction No. 1. Following this, the account of the one man's refusal to go and his reason for not going (again a point I had explicated in the explicated version) is condensed into "the two men discussed who should go." Finally, theme *p*), REALIZATION, is displaced from its original central position in the story and occurs instead at the end with REVELATIONS. Moreover, the account now merely says that "he had discovered that the men . . . were ghosts" and omits the part that suggests how he did so (another of my major explications).

If we compare this reproduction with the lead-off reproduction of the explicated version (it is discussed more fully below), we can appreciate the prominent part played by those gaps and ambiguities in the original version that I ameliorated. Reproduction No. 1 of the explicated version loses only one theme and that a relatively minor one: REACTION OF THE PEOPLE. On the other hand, reproduction No. 1 of the original version clearly shows the disintegrative influence of the gaps and ambiguities: some of the themes associated with them are lost entirely, others are changed and fragmented in such a way that they cause further fragmentation and loss in subsequent reproductions. For example, the deficiency in handling the ghost element of the story is probably responsible for the conspicuous vicissitudes of this theme in the later reproductions.

In reproduction No. 2 of the original version only one theme is lost and that is theme *t*), which I had added to the original version merely to equate it to the explicated version; it was not intended to contribute to the text, and, like theme c) in its stimulus, proved itself to be expendable. There are, however, a number of changes in this reproduction which seem to "prepare for" or initiate thematic losses and distortions in subsequent reproductions. These are changes in emphasis and order, abbreviations of content, rejuxtapositions of themes, and the like, and will be discussed later. At this point it may be worth noting that this S's tendency to skeletonize leads, in addition to the loss of the peripheral theme t), to a change from "hunting for seals" to the more familiar "fishing" (I was prompted to do the same in preparing the explicated version); that the discussion between the men concerning who should go is dropped out completely; and that the REALIZATION is reduced to the statement that "they must have been ghosts." This tendency to render the story in a sparer, leaner, more abbreviated form is worth bearing in mind, for it crops up again and struck me as an important individual propensity that contrasts with importation, perhaps its polar opposite.

Reproduction No. 3 of the original version loses two more themes, each ambiguous and gappy in the original story and made even more so in reproductions No. 1 and No. 2. The ENIGMA theme disappears, leaving a residue in the form of an importation via a noteworthy sequence: in reproduction No. 1, "the man did not feel anything, though told he was hit"; in reproduction No. 2, "the man didn't feel any pain" and "he didn't believe it [that he had been shot] because he couldn't feel anything" (here the theme is distorted—not only does he not feel pain, but he does not believe he was hit); now, in reproduction No. 3 the fact that he does not feel anything is omitted and what remains of the theme is only the new statement, "he didn't believe them." A complete distortion has occurred here with only the rationalized component remaining (it is a kind of explication); the gap has been "closed" at the expense of the ENIGMA theme. Finally, theme p) has become utterly unintelligible and disconnected. Now the ghost element, made progressively more ambiguous and disconnected in the previous reproductions, has disappeared from the body of the story and hangs on at the end as an isolated fragment.

Five more themes are lost in reproduction No. 4. Theme b), ATMOSPHERE, which was given an explicit significance in the explicated version that it lacks in the original, disappears after being contracted and subordinated in the preceding reproductions: in reproduction No. 2 it occupied minor position in the sentence, "they heard the sound of oars through the fog"; it was retained as "in the fog" in reproduction No. 3; it is now squeezed out completely. This sequence of contraction, subordination, and finally omission seems important because it occurs frequently in the chains. Theme h), WAR-PLANS, drops out in a similar way: in reproduction No. 2, "one man said, 'we are going . . .' "; in reproduction No. 3, "the men were going to attack . . ."—here the "saying" drops out and only the men's intentions are included, but these intentions are apparently superfluous since the narrative proceeds right away to describe the battle; and so it is not surprising that in reproduction No. 4 the statement of plans is absent. Similarly theme s): in reproduction No. 1 it is a clause of another sentence—"when the young man reached home he went ashore, lit a fire," etc. In reproduction No. 2 it is further contracted to "he went home, built a large fire," etc. In reproduction No. 3 it is reduced to "he returned home and told . . ."; since the "fire," the "resting," and the "decision to tell" (the etc.'s) have all dropped out, "home" is left bare (nothing happens there), superfluous, and of only minor significance in the narrative. In reproduction No. 4 it is omitted. Finally, theme u) is squeezed out in a similar way.

The ghost element undergoes further modification in reproduction No. 4 which partly strips it of an incongruity, the "he said." This was incongruous in reproduction No. 3 because the previous sentence had said that "he died." Nevertheless, it still retains ambiguity (i.e., who are the "they" who "must have been ghosts"?) which is resolved in reproduction No. 5, where "they" is changed to "he"—a neat bit of rationalization!

Reproduction No. 5 loses two more themes; the man's DEATH and the sounding of the RETREAT, and in the process furnishes some interesting "case material." Beginning with theme n): in reproduction No. 2, "the Indian has been shot. The man didn't feel any pain" is accurate but disconnected; in No. 3, "the Indian is shot," and the enigma aspect is split away and is mentioned later in the text; in No. 4, "the Indian is shot," now the enigma is nowhere stated, leaving this theme wholly isolated; and so finally in reproduction No. 5 it becomes "they must be Indians"; the RE-

TREAT has been transformed and two themes have fallen by the wayside. In the case of theme y), this is the sequence: reproduction No. 2 tells that he "fell down" and then "he was dead"; No. 3, "he died," and the superfluous falling down is omitted; in No. 4 the death is no longer afforded a separate sentence but becomes "... and dies"; finally in reproduction No. 5 this important theme is left out entirely. It is reasonable to suppose that this loss was caused largely by the earlier mishandling of the ghost element. The statement " 'they must have been ghosts' he said" was tacked on at the end in reproduction No. 3, and in reproduction No. 4 persisted in the disconnected statement "they must have been ghosts." Who says this is a mystery; and indeed, in this account, it appears that somehow the man dies and *then* makes the statement. This contradiction is apparently resolved in reproduction No. 5 by sparing him! It may be that the reason he did not die is that "he must have been a ghost." This is an illuminating sequence of successive opening and closing of gaps, of creating and solving ambiguities, of rationalizing and explicating—processes of schema functioning in recall that seem to merit careful and systematic study.

The serial reproductions of the explicated version contain similar, though fewer, such sequences; there is considerably less thematic loss—a direct result, the evidence attests, of the relative absence of gaps and ambiguities in the stimulus story. In reproduction No. 1 there is only one loss: theme x), the REACTION OF THE PEOPLE, a patently inconsequential part of the story. I have already discussed the fact that this reproduction embellishes the story; at this point it is worth noting that *these amplifications occur at just those points where I had already explicated the text*! For example, in theme c) (an explication) there is a major importation which, while it is largely redundant, solidly links themes b) and c). Similarly, themes i) and j) contain importations that add emphasis and clarity. Finally, a group of importations and changes cluster around themes o) and r). Incidentally, the explication I offered in theme o) of the explicated version is on the face of it not satisfactory. It purports to explain the REALIZATION, but is labored and unclear. Reproduction No. 1 simplifies and distorts it with the sentence "he knew he was not an Indian." The part that follows, however, is quite tortured, and therefore it should not be surprising that the subsequent reproductions show a disturbance at this point.

Reproduction No. 2 loses three more themes, none of which seems essential to the structure of the story.[14] Theme a), which tells of the expedition, is changed so that the men simply "were on the beach"; WAR-PLANS is omitted and the two men are merely asked to accompany the men in the canoe; and the ENIGMA is not repeated during the REVELATIONS. The entire character of this reproduction seems to reflect this S's unwillingness to repeat what she has already written. Her stimulus, reproduction No. 1, was a highly elaborated and redundant narrative and it seems that she wants to boil the story down to its essential and nonredundant parts. This attempt, even though it does not entail much loss of accuracy, seems to create gaps and ambiguities that may be responsible for loss of accuracy in the subsequent reproductions.

Reproduction No. 3, while it drops only three more themes, loses considerably in structure and coherence. Theme c), SOMETHING UP, drops out after a sequence of progressive contractions: in reproduction No. 1, ". . . night becomes foggy and calm and they knew this denoted . . ."; in reproduction No. 2, ". . . night was foggy and calm—a night on which . . ." (note how the terms "becomes," "knew," and "denoted," which focus attention on what follows, drop out); in reproduction No. 3, ". . . couldn't see anything because of the fog"—here the omen is completely lost. Moreover, "fog" has become subordinate, and is lost in the next reproduction. The other two themes, HIDING and PERMISSION, drop out with apparently no preparation.

Reproductions No. 4 and No. 5 each lose three more themes, although the former theme a) reappears, probably because the men are repeatedly called "fishermen" in the previous reproductions and, while they were "sitting on the beach," they might well have been "fishing off shore." In reproduction No. 5, theme p) has become disconnected and ambiguous, and it is a reasonable guess that, if there were a reproduction No. 6, we would see either a distortion or a complete deletion of the ghost element.

---

[14] In general, loss of information was greatest for peripheral parts of the story. I did not, however, systematically study this phenomenon; other researchers (e.g., Newman, 1939) have, and found that it could be reliably demonstrated.

General Discussion and Conclusions

Three general findings emerged from the direct examination of the reproductions. (1) Impressions of the quality and structure of the reproductions were congruent with the quantitative indices; particularly important was the correspondence between impressions of over-all coherence or continuity and the redundancy indexes. (2) Some recurring sequences of skeletonization, transformation, and importation were revealed; these may prove to be among the basic schema processes. (3) Certain Ss favored one of these processes—some imported new content and elaborated the story, others stripped away material and pared the story. An important individual differences parameter pertaining to style of remembering may be reflected in these propensities.

In this section I will take up each of these three general findings separately and discuss them at some length by referring to relevant literature and theory. The object is to place the findings in the conceptual framework that directed this program of research.

1. *Validity of the Quantitative Indices*

Those reproductions which scored lowest in the accuracy and redundancy measures were those which seemed, on direct examination, to be the most fragmented and disconnected: they lacked over-all coherence and failed to convey the core of the story. These impressions confirmed the results of the objective measures —the rapid decline in both accuracy and structure of the original version of the Ghost Story, the less rapid decline of the explicated version, and the least decline of the Secretary Story. The Secretary Story did not undergo a systematic decrease in redundancy index as the others did, and, upon examination, this corresponded to its relatively well-maintained coherence and continuity.

Therefore, by using the three indices together (information unit, theme, and redundancy index) we can appraise a reproduction in terms of how accurately it maintains the information, completeness, and over-all structure of the stimulus story. This appraisal, however, will not be complete. For one thing, the redundancy measure is not ideal for locating and assessing gaps and ambiguities, since it is affected by other factors as well (e.g., a repetitive style of writing will artificially, though not grossly, increase the redundancy index). Moreover, the measure cannot be used to compare texts that differ substantially in content and complexity. What is needed for this purpose is a technique which will analyze the structure of an extended and connected text without being influenced by its particular content and level of complexity. A linguistic method, called Discourse Analysis, has been devised by Zellig Harris (1952, 1954) for just such problems of assessing structure. I have begun some preliminary work with it, have found it promising, and plan to investigate memory data with this tool.

2. The Schema Processes of Explication, Importation, and Skeletonization

The direct examination highlighted the role of explications: they seemed to play an important integrative role in reproductions. Whether experimentally introduced into the Ghost Story or imported by the S, explications enhanced continuity by closing gaps, forming transitions, and solving contradictions; they ameliorated ambiguity by transforming the unfamiliar into the familiar, the unlikely into the likely, and so forth. Frequently, explications functioned by anticipating, preparing for, or merely repeating story material and thereby increased the redundancy and coherence of the reproductions.

Lost or distorted themes, traced through the serial reproductions, frequently followed a course of progressive contraction of content together with shifts of interrelationships. In the process of skeletonization, the eventually lost or distorted theme often became secondary and subordinate to another theme. This process resulted in the theme's becoming either redundant or peripheral before it was lost. Gaps were opened and themes became disconnected and isolated. Such gaps were usually closed in one of two ways: (1) by importations of new material (usually explicatory), (2) by the "squeezing out" of old material. That the latter occurred more often is perhaps because in this experiment accuracy was emphasized and lengthy and complex stimulus material was given limited exposure. Nevertheless, the pattern of skeletonization regularly included reshuffling of emphasis, rejuxtaposition of parts and relationships, and a steady tightening of structure around gaps and ambiguities, as well as a stripping away of redundant and ambiguous parts.

Importation, on the whole, occurred less frequently than skeletonization. Though it was not possible in every instance to pin down the function of an importation, usually its explicatory nature was conspicuous—it smoothed gaps, solved ambiguities and contradictions, and enhanced redundancy. Indeed, *only those importations which were patently explicatory went on to influence subsequent reproductions.*

Importation—sometimes called "invention" or "intrusion"—is a regular finding in studies of the retention of extended verbal material[15] and it is usually taken to highlight the functional, rational, and constructive aspects of memory. Davis and Sinha (1950), for example, reported that intrusions play a big part in people's recall of a story after the interpolation of a picture that is relevant to the story. Belbin (1950) similarly reported importations in recall, and showed how they tend to "fill the gaps" in the text. Kirkpatrick (1932) found a good deal of gap-filling when rumors were spread among students. And, under the category of *assimilation,* Allport and Postman (1947) spoke of importations which "fit" and improve the Gestalt of a remembered experience. Importation is related to the difficulty of the stimulus material, at least in children, who invent and substitute more in recalling difficult than simple poetry (Northway, 1940). Northway also found that younger children import more than older ones.

I tentatively conclude, therefore, that importation and its opposite, skeletonization, represent basic processes of schema formation and utilization. These processes can be conceptualized in terms of Hebb's neuropsychological theory (1949), which also provides an appropriate model for the schema concept. Since there may be some important advantages in applying his theoretical model, it will be spelled out here in some detail.

Schema, Phase Sequence, Fractionation, and Recruitment

Hebb attempts a reconciliation and integration of connectionism and configurationism. He begins by proposing that learning (which, in his view, lies at the heart of all psychological functioning) early in the life of an organism differs fundamentally from later learning.

---

[15] Intrusions also occur in the learning of nonconnected material. Deese and Hardman (1954) report that up to two thirds of the errors in paired-associate learning are likely to be intrusions from interpolated material.

Early learning follows association principles mediated by simple connections between the cortical representations of perceptual and motor elements. Once this stage of learning has established circular networks called *cell assemblies*, the organism no longer makes such connections between cortical representations of discrete stimuli; behavior modifications are then accomplished by realignments and repatternings among these cell assemblies. But Hebb does not imply a simple trace theory even for this first stage of learning. Experience at no point becomes internalized by an automatic isomorphic process; rather, from the very first it becomes internalized in an essentially schemalike way. The theory specifies the way this schema formation might conceivably occur.

The first misconception to discard, Hebb says, is the idea of a passive brain which requires external excitation to activate it. There is considerable evidence that the cortex is largely self-activating and that nerve cells frequently fire spontaneously. This means that sensory excitation feeds into an already active cortex. A repeated pattern of stimulation, according to Hebb, can slowly gain control over the spontaneous firing and give rise to widespread reverberating circuits that will subsequently be triggered by this pattern of stimulation. In this way simple and repeated experience gradually results in the formation of rudimentary reverberatory cell networks—the cell assemblies.

These structures are fundamentally like concepts. For example, the superordinate cell assembly which corresponds to the perception of a triangle is the product of stimulations by a variety of different-sized and -colored triangles from various angles and in various perspectives. Hebb describes the process by which, in the course of the development of the cell assembly, the neural correlates of irregular or sporadic stimulations are stripped away until finally only those which correspond to the invariant common features of *triangle* remain: the cell assembly then represents the concept triangle. Two processes are responsible for forming the cell assembly in this way: *fractionation* and *recruitment*. The former refers to the stripping away or the weakening of those connections and networks that are only sporadically reinforced (the variable aspects of the stimulation); the latter refers to the strengthening or facilitation of recurring aspects of the stimulation (the commonality of the stimulation).

Once cell assemblies reach a certain stage of development they become relatively closed and relatively autonomous. That is, they become relatively independent from sensory excitation, and are capable of spontaneous firing due to intracerebral metabolic conditions, or triggered by other cell assemblies. From this point on, a new kind of integration becomes the rule: cell assemblies link themselves together into higher-order temporal-spatial organizations. Such linkages—Hebb calls them phase sequence—differ fundamentally from the relatively permanent binding that formed the cell assembly.

The phase sequence is a temporally extended, relatively flexible, complex integration of widespread cell assemblies. Hebb stresses the relative autonomy of these central structures—their growing independence from external stimulation, their growing dependence on internal conditions (especially on the neural correlates of need, motivation, and emotion) and on the activity of other structures, and their ability to be self-triggering. Most important, in relation to stimulation they are essentially conceptlike—abstractive and skeletal. Fractionation and recruitment continue as basic processes in phase-sequence development and operation. The former refers to the stripping away (by short-circuit mechanisms) of cell assemblies, the latter to the incorporation of new assemblies.

The phase sequence has most of the properties that have been assigned to the schema. Like the schema, it is an internalized, relatively autonomous, potentially self-active, conceptual representation of experience which at once grows out of experience and is the basis for experience.

The schema processes that were inferred from direct examination of the serial reproductions in the present study centered on the two ways in which gaps and ambiguities were solved: by importation and skeletonization. The former may be considered a behavior correlate of recruitment, the latter of fractionation. The correspondence between the phenomena and the concepts may, in a strict sense, be crude; nonetheless it is striking and provocative.

I propose that the system that forms the basis for learning and retaining an extended and connected experience, such as a story, is not a rigidly bound, passive, and static structure. Rather it is a temporally integrated group of widespread and relatively autonomous cortical organizations—schemas. In order to execute a reproduction of the story, this temporally extended pattern is "run off." It must be assumed that this "running off" will partly reflect the manner in which the organization was originally formed, and two basic processes which they share are fractionation and recruitment.

His use of such concepts as schema and phase sequence reflects, I believe, a theorist's willingness to place greater emphasis on the *emitted* nature of behavior, on the lack of uniform correlations between stimuli and responses, and on the importance of relatively autonomous structures, conceived as internal to the organism, which arise as a product of the organism's history in commerce with its environment. Such structural concepts can be applied to all aspects and modes of cognition (memory is certainly continuous with perception and learning). For example, following Woodworth's formulation (1938, pp. 73-77), perception can be conceived of as schema "with correction," and the role of external stimulation can be understood as the facilitation, control, and steering of cognitive behavior rather than as the direct determination (stimulation) of response.

This view is supported by a variety of sources, and such studies as the one reported by Granit (1921) provide basic evidence. He found that children do not remember a figure unless they find it similar to a familiar object. Furthermore, children apparently do not conceive of the figure as being formed by lines—they are objects. Granit concluded that the child draws a schema of what he knows about the figure and not what he sees. Of course, we would have to take it further and argue that "what he sees" is in fact determined largely by "what he knows" about the stimulus.

There is a trap in this line of thinking—the trap of solipsism and tautology—if it is not realized that such a formulation is necessarily a first approximation, and must eventually be followed by careful specifications and definitions. But these specifications and definitions can open the problem up rather than prematurely stifle it. One can take the same position as Wolters (1933), who writes: ". . . the schemata can only be deduced from the actual behavior, but probably we should conceive of them as existing continuously, as characters of the organism, but not as entities which the organism 'possesses' " (p. 136). Wolters shows that schemas are the means of thinking rather than the objects of thought, using as an example the way we use numbers in mathematical thinking. The fact that we are also able to think about the particular numbers means, to Wolters, that the organism can somehow "turn round upon, or react to, *itself as schematized*." Wolters, incidentally, presents a definition of schema that is identical to McDougall's famous definition of instinct (". . . an innate psychophysical disposition which determines its possessor to perceive, and to pay attention to, objects of a certain class, . . . and to act in regard to [them] in a particular manner."), except that the term "innate" is omitted.

3. *Individual Differences in Remembering: Importing and Skeletonizing as Cognitive Styles*

Individual differences in recall can be demonstrated, according to Gomulicki (1956, p. 400), ". . . with a degree of statistical significance that makes it perilous to ignore them when designing experiments in recall." The differences he refers to are of ability as well as quality and manner of recall. The high price of ignoring individual differences is illustrated by the confusion in the literature regarding the influence of affective and motivational factors on cognition.

Though it is now generally accepted that such relationships and influences exist and are important (especially for an understanding of everyday learning and retention), many experiments still fail to discover any influence of needs and affects upon retention—for example, see Williams (1950). There seems to be an element of "now you see it, now you don't" in the phenomena.

Rapaport (1942), reviewing the experiments on the influence of emotions on memory, suggested that the reason for the fickleness of the phenomena is that experimenters usually overlook a central component of the relationship: the subject's stable and enduring features which mediate between motivation and cognition.[16] Klein (1954) supports this point of view, and has effectively demonstrated the mediating and directing role of cognitive styles (sometimes called "system principles") in the relationship between need and perception. The subject's style can sometimes determine in which of two opposite ways he will react to frustration and deprivation, for example. When groups of subjects are studied and their reactions are pooled, such interactions may be completely obscured

---

[16] Rapaport (1957) has recently presented a thorough discussion of this point.

and any systematic influences of motivations and affects become obliterated.

The exploration of the influence of motivation on retention therefore requires a systematic study of mediating structures by means of a study of individual differences. If there are in fact styles of remembering, they must be studied and implicated in any research on memory. The concept of style refers to the extended mode of operation of a schema organization, and embraces such properties as its complexity, stability, and temporal-sequential patterning. A new parameter can be added to this list, fractionation and recruitment, which may embrace an important dimension of cognitive style and hence point the way to a basic area of individual differences.

I decided to study this parameter, and began by hypothesizing that a style dimension is implicit here, one which can be described as a propensity to import and elaborate versus a tendency to skeletonize and fragment. Individuals in whom the recruiting process is particularly pronounced will make importations to a greater extent than those in whom the fractionating process is dominant.

A series of experimental questions immediately arose: can groups of Ss be distinguished with respect to this tendency? Is it a stable aspect of an individual's performance on retention tasks? Will the fate of stories recalled by groups of importers and skeletonizers be different? Will explication and familiarity exert different effects upon such groups? These questions form the basis of the experiments which are presented in the following chapter.

3

RETENTION STYLE AND RETENTION ABILITY

The closing discussion section of Chapter 2 focused on the complementary processes of recruitment and fractionation—whose empirical correlates are importation and skeletonization—and raised some questions about their roles in schema formation and function. The present chapter reports three interlocking experiments designed to answer the following questions pertaining to them: (a) Can groups of Ss be distinguished with respect to these propensities? (b) Do they represent stable properties of an individual's performance on retention tasks, i.e., cognitive styles? (c) Will these contrasting styles be reflected by the divergent fates of stories passed serially through groups of importers and nonimporters? (d) Will explication and familiarity have different effects upon such groups of Ss?

Experiment I was designed for two purposes: (1) to answer questions (a) and (b) about individual differences; and, if the answer was positive (as it was), (2) to permit the selection of separate groups of Ss, each homogeneous with respect to retention ability and style, to form into serial reproduction chains which would then yield data pertaining to questions (c) and (d). Experiment II consisted of the serial transmission of explicated and original versions of stories through these groups of Ss. Experiment III—an integration and replication of the foregoing experiments with a fresh group of Ss—consisted of the serial transmission of the Ghost Story (in its original and explicated versions) and the Secretary Story through chains of good retainers who were grouped into importers and nonimporters.

Experiment I: Individual Differences in Retention Ability and Importation

Purpose

The major purpose of the first experiment was to explore systematically the subject variables *ability* and *style*, to find out whether they do in fact represent stable individual differences which can be reliably measured. My original purpose was to devote as much study to skeletonization as to importation, having conceived of them as opposites along a single continuum. However, after preliminary exploration and analysis, difficulties arose with respect to the assessment of skeletonization. As a result, the major emphasis was limited to importation versus nonimportation. Study of the data also led me to explore another variable: the use and retention of imagery.

Methods and Procedures

ASSESSING RETENTION STYLES

A technique for assessing importation and skeletonization should evoke and enhance these tendencies and provide for their easy measurement. To this end, I devised a procedure modeled on retroactive interference: The S first learns a set of verbal statements, next he performs an independent though related verbal task, and then he recalls the original set of statements. This recall is examined both for importations—the infiltration of material from the intervening task—and for evidence of skeletonization.

The technique in detail is as follows. A list of seven sentences was prepared, each a terse statement of one of the seven major themes of an Indian folk tale called "The Balanced Rock." S's first task is to learn this list of themes. His next task is to make up a story based upon the theme list (the instructions urge him to use different words and try to compose a good story). Finally, S is asked to reproduce the original theme list (the instructions urge word-perfect accuracy).

The assumption underlying this technique is that a comparison between the original theme list, S's story (his *composition*), and his reproduction of the theme list will yield a valid and reliable index of his tendency to import. We can observe what new information appears in the reproduction of the theme list and see whether this new material is derived from the composition. Furthermore, since the original theme list was already skeletonized, Ss who tend to skeletonize and fragment can be expected to make their reproduction even briefer and more terse than the original.

This is the theme list:

THEME LIST FOR THE STORY "THE BALANCED ROCK"

Theme 1: Indian boys /[1] are playing / at testing / their strength. /
Theme 2: The winner / is vain / and boastful. /
Theme 3: A strange lad / appears / who is mocked / and challenged. /
Theme 4: The stranger / wins / every feat. /
Theme 5: He turns into / the / Stone Giant. /
Theme 6: The boys / are reprimanded / and shamed. /
Theme 7: He turns into / a rabbit. /

The instructions for learning the theme list were:

I am passing out a sheet which contains a list of themes of a story called "Balanced Rock." I would like you to read this list of themes carefully and get to know them. Read the list through three or four times. When you are through, turn this sheet face down and look up. Please go ahead now, read the list carefully three or four times and get to know it.

After the sheets were collected, the instructions to compose a story were given:

Now I would like each of you to compose a story which is based on the theme list you just studied. That is, *in your own words*, write out the story. Add things as you wish—make it a good story-narrative based on the list of themes. Make it about 150 words long, and take at least ten minutes to do it in. Any questions? Do you all understand what I want you to do? Remember: about 150 words and try to write at your usual writing pace. This is not a test of you, or anything like that, but do a good job anyway. When you finish, read your composition through once.

[1] The crossbars mark off the information units; they were not shown on the stimulus copies.

After the compositions were handed in, reproductions of the theme list were requested:

> Now I would like for you to write out, as accurately as you can recall, the theme list which was on that sheet—the list of themes that you read three or four times. Try to be as precise as you possibly can in reproducing what was on that sheet. Any questions? Remember, be as precise as you can.

ASSESSING RETENTION ABILITY

I expected that individuals would differ not only in style of recall, but in the efficiency with which they learn, retain, and reproduce.[2] Aside from being itself of some interest, such a factor must be controlled in order to isolate the style variable (to separate the *how* from the *how well*) and to study the effects of explication and familiarity. Therefore, some way to assess S's retention ability was needed.

The theme-list technique, described above, in addition to measuring importation and skeletonization, can also measure accuracy. However, this measure may not be a pure one since it will probably be contaminated by the interpolated task. Therefore, to assess retention ability I used a straightforward story retention task, employing the method of successively repeated reproductions, which requires S to give several reproductions of a stimulus at various time intervals from the original exposure.[3] An interval of approximately fifteen minutes (filled with an unrelated concentration task) was interposed between the initial learning and the first reproduction.

For the test of retention ability, I selected a Korean tale titled "The Bedbug, Louse, and Flea" (called here the Bedbug Story).

---

[2] Is there a generalized learning factor? Even though recent studies (e.g., Woodrow, 1940) have found low correlations among learning tasks, nevertheless in such tasks as serial-list learning the ability of Ss has proved to be an important parameter (slow learners recall better after massed practice and fast learners after spaced practice [Estes, 1956]). The failure of researchers to uncover individual differences in recall may be due to their failure to distinguish between the retention of detail and the retention of meaning, or what has been called "substance" memory. In the latter category Winch (1911) reported substantial individual differences.

[3] This method has occasioned a good deal of controversy concerning both the so-called "trace fate" issue (see Woodworth [1938], Hanawalt [1937], Hebb and Foord [1945]) and the phenomenon of "reminiscence" (see Estes [1956]). The essential point is that it has frequently been overlooked that each of the reproductions may serve as an additional learning trial.

It is approximately the same length as the Ghost and Secretary Stories. Although its events have an unfamiliar ring, it does not have gaps and ambiguities of the sort that the original version of the Ghost Story has.

In addition to being measured for retention ability, the reproductions of this story were also examined for the presence of importations. These reproductions along with the theme-list results supplied independent measures of style as well as of ability.

The instructions for learning and reproducing the Bedbug Story were the same as those used for the Ghost and Secretary Stories in the Exploratory Experiment.

The Bedbug Story

The Bedbug, / Louse, / and Flea

a) Long, long ago / a bedbug / reached the age / of sixty, / *b*) and to celebrate / the occasion / held the customary / party, / known as Hwangab, / that marks / the completion / of a whole / sexagenary / cycle. / *c*) He invited / his two / closest / friends, / a louse / and a flea. /

d) The louse / and the flea / set out together / to go to / the party. / *e*) The sprightly / flea / leapt ahead / without regard / for the louse / and before long / had left him far behind. / *f*) The louse / could not walk very fast, / for he was a portly / creature, / and his legs / were very short. / *g*) So he shouted / to the flea, / "Wait for me, / my friend!" /

h) So the flea / walked a little slower / for a time, / *i*) but before long / he lost patience / with the tardy / louse, / for by now / he was feeling rather hungry. / *j*) So he ran / straight / to the bedbug's /house. / *k*) The tables / were heavily laden / with delicious / food / and drink, / *l*) so the flea / said to / the bedbug, / "I am very thirsty, / please let me have a bowl / of wine." / *m*) So the bedbug / filled a bowl / with wine. / *n*) Then / he went out to meet / the louse / on the way. /

o) While the flea / waited for them to arrive / he refilled / his bowl / several times / from the bottles / on the table, / and soon / got very red / in the face. / *p*) When the bedbug / arrived at last / with the louse / the flea / was quite drunk / and was humming / a tune. / *q*) All / the bottles / were empty. / *r*) The louse / was already / annoyed / at the flea's behavior, / and now / he lost his temper / completely / and slapped / his face. / *s*) Then /

there was a rumpus indeed. / The flea / and the louse / grappled / fiercely with one another. / *t*) Their host, / the bedbug, / tried to get between them / to part them, / but they fought on / *u*) and in the end / fell / on top of him, / so that he was squashed / quite flat. /

v) So to this day / the bedbug / is still / a flat / creature, / *w*) the flea / has a tipsy / red face, / *x*) and the louse / has a mark / on his back / where the flea / kicked him. /

CONDUCT OF THE EXPERIMENT

The senior class of a private preparatory school, fifty boys ranging in age from fifteen to sixteen and a half, served as Ss.[4] The experiment was conducted in three sessions.

Session I: In the initial session the Ss as a group were given the Bedbug Story and the theme-list task. They were administered in one sixty-minute period in the following sequence: (1) the Bedbug Story was administered; (2) the theme list was administered; (3) the composition based on the theme list was written; (4) the Bedbug Story was reproduced; (5) the theme list was reproduced; (6) the composition was reproduced. Almost twenty minutes elapsed between steps (1) and (4), and between steps (2) and (5). Since it intermeshed the two tasks, the experimental procedure probably invited retroactive and proactive interference, thereby probably maximizing the possibilities of importation and skeletonization, though possibly more the former.

The experiment was not conducted as if it were an examination; the atmosphere seemed more like a class in English Composition. The boys appeared to apply themselves earnestly, and the procedure went smoothly.[5] Some of the boys later commented that they enjoyed the experience although the task of reproducing their own story at the end (step 6) was an arduous one.

Sessions II and III: At no point during sessions I and II were Ss told that at a future date they would be asked for further recall

[4] The mean I.Q. of these boys was above average. On Form B of the Otis Self-Administering Tests of Mental Ability, Higher Examination, their I.Q.s ranged from 95 and 145 (*mean* of 115, *mode* between 120 and 125).

[5] The problem of individual differences in time taken for the various tasks was handled in the following way. When I observed that a majority of the Ss were finished, I made a short statement pressing the others to finish up as quickly as they could. It frequently happened, however, that several boys were still working when all of the others were through. At such a time I made a second announcement urging those few to finish up quickly.

of the material. Nevertheless, they were asked for reproductions fourteen days after session I and again forty-nine days after that. In this way reproductions of all the experimental material were obtained on three separate occasions: approximately twenty minutes following exposure to the stimulus, fourteen days later, and sixty-three days later. One S was absent at session II, and four more were unable to attend session III. Therefore the data reported in Experiment I are based on an N of 45.

During these sessions the Ss, in spite of some complaining and joking, continued to be interested and cooperative. The following is the order in which reproductions were obtained during sessions II and III and the instructions used to obtain them:

1. The theme list

You recall that list of themes upon which you composed a story? Please write out, as best as you can right now, that list. Remember, this is not a test of you, so don't worry about it too much. But try to do the best you can. Any questions?

2. The Bedbug Story

Thanks. Now you recall you wrote a story based on those themes. But you dealt also with *another* story, one which was typed out, which you read through and later reproduced. That is the story I want you now to reproduce for me to the best of your present ability. Do you all have a clear picture of which story it is I want you to work on? [They all did.] Fine, then go ahead. Try to write at your normal writing speed, don't stop for long periods trying to recollect something, go right on and come back to these points later on.

3. The composition

Now the final thing I want you to do is to reproduce the story which you yourself wrote.

The final step took place six days after session III, when a questionnaire was distributed to all Ss. In addition to a number of general questions about various aspects of the experimental procedure, the questionnaire consisted of a multiple-choice recognition test on the Bedbug Story. It contained twenty-five questions: eighteen asked for a detailed fact of the story, and seven asked for recognition of a particular imagery word or phrase.

Treatment of the Data

MEASUREMENT OF RETENTION ABILITY

The following three measures were used as indices of retention ability:

1. *Theme score:* The theme score represents (as it did in the Exploratory Experiment) the number of correctly reproduced themes. Theme scores were obtained of the Bedbug reproductions, as well as of composition reproductions (the latter were computed as a percentage based on the number of themes contained in the composition itself).

2. *Theme-list score:* Each of the S's three theme-list reproductions was scored at the information-unit level in the following way: each word-perfect replica of an information unit was given 3 points; 2 points went to a unit which was roughly equivalent; and 1 point to one which had some measure of comparability to the original. A bonus of 5 points was given when the reproduction was complete (seven themes).

3. *Questionnaire score:* The sum of the number of correct choices.

I extracted from each composition a fourth index—called an integration score—which may, at least partly, reflect an ability. The extent to which an S can use all seven themes in his composition might be considered an ability variable. To get an estimate of this variable I assessed each composition for the degree to which it integrated or assimilated the original themes, scoring 1 point wherever an information unit of the theme list was accurately mentioned and in some way used in the composition. (I made no attempt to judge the extent to which each unit was successfully or inventively organized into a good story.) The sum of these scores is called the integration score.

MEASUREMENT OF RETENTION STYLES

I derived indices of importation from two sources:

1. *Theme importation:* I counted the number of new themes (i.e., those with no direct counterpart in the stimulus story) in each of the Bedbug Story reproductions as well as in the composition reproductions. I paid no attention to the extent to which a new

theme might have been related to some part of the stimulus material (i.e., how extraneous it was).

2. *Theme-list importation:* Importation of information units into the three theme-list reproductions was assessed by noting those units which were original to the reproduction. These importations were assessed in two ways: in an initial analysis I simply counted them; in a second analysis I made a subjective judgment about the magnitude of the importation (including how extraneous it was). A "major" importation was scored 2, a "minor" importation scored 1, and the total was the importation score for each reproduction.

I found that importations were quite easy to identify and to assess. The Bedbug Story reproductions contained many parts which were patently importations, and, in the case of the theme list, most of them could be traced to the composition that intervened between learning and reproduction. However, my attempt to assess skeletonization encountered difficulties. One source of difficulty lay in the fact that I felt a distinction needed to be made between an omission of a theme and a fragmentation of a theme independent of theme loss. I had anticipated that skeletonization could be detected in a reduction of information units per theme, without loss of theme.

However, the findings did not permit such a distinction. Omission and diminution seemed, for the most part, to overlap, and unmistakable fragmentations of the themes were quite rare—not nearly as common as importations of new information units and themes.

These difficulties of assessment, and the fact that a simultaneous study of four variables (importation, ability, explication, and familiarity) already complicated the experimental design, led me to abandon a systematic study of skeletonization in the present series of experiments. Nevertheless, it was possible to select a few Ss whose theme-list reproductions were conspicuously fragmented. They were formed into a serial reproduction group in Experiment II, and were studied separately.

I also explored the use and retention of imagery. On examining the reproductions, I was struck by the fact that certain Ss reproduced many of the vivid and colorful words and expressions of the Bedbug Story, while other Ss leveled the imagery to simple narrative. Moreover, some Ss used vivid imagery in their compositions and others did not. Therefore, I decided to explore this tendency to see whether it was a stable and independent one. I studied the Bedbug Story and labeled certain words as "imagery words." Then I examined each reproduction of the Bedbug Story for the presence of these words, counted them up, and labeled their sum the *imagery score*. I did the same for each composition as well.

Results

The results of the various measurements are less interesting than those intercorrelations among them which can reveal the presence or absence of stable individual differences in ability and style. Nevertheless, Table 4, which presents the *means* and *standard deviations* of all of the quantitative measures,[6] contains a number of findings that are important in their own right and need to be examined before their intercorrelations can be evaluated. These findings are of two kinds: those that point up the differences between serial reproductions and repeated reproductions; and those that point up a relationship between coherence of stimulus and accuracy of reproductions.

The word count and theme count of the Bedbug Story and the composition reproductions[7] reveal that the loss of material from the first to the third repeated reproductions was surprisingly small compared to the sizable loss which regularly occurs in the same number of serial reproductions. In the repeated reproductions, a majority of *S*s showed a steady, though comparatively small loss, while a noteworthy minority, about 30 per cent, showed some gain. It is also worth noting that the differences between reproductions II and III were, on the whole, smaller than between I and II. This difference in loss is more conspicuous in the accuracy measures, particularly of the theme-list reproductions.

These findings highlight the difference between the methods of repeated and serial reproduction. Why does the latter wreak such havoc with stimulus material, while the former shows remarkable

[6] Frequency distributions of each of the measures reported in Table 4 were prepared, and they closely approximated the normal distribution.

[7] It is noteworthy that the group complied with the instructions to write a composition of about 150 words. Only three *S*s wrote stories shorter than 120 words, and none wrote less than 90. On the other hand, fifteen *S*s wrote stories that exceed 200 words. The average story consisted of 16.5 themes; the smallest number of themes in any composition was 9, the greatest, 25.

Table 4

SELECTION DATA FROM EXPERIMENT I

Productivity

<u>a</u>. Original Compositions: Word Count 179.5*(43.5);
Theme Count 16.5 (3.77)

<u>b</u>. Repeated Reproductions: Word Count

Bedbug I	235.8 (36.9)	Composition I	153.6 (45.3)
Bedbug II	220.7 (45.5)	Composition II	144.4 (47.4)
Bedbug III	213.2 (58.7)	Composition III	137.0 (57.3)

Theme Count

Bedbug I	22.2 (2.23)	Composition I	15.3 (4.02)
Bedbug II	21.3 (3.33)	Composition II	14.3 (3.71)
Bedbug III	20.8 (4.11)	Composition III	14.5 (4.75)

Accuracy

<u>a</u>. Repeated Reproductions: Theme Score

Bedbug I	21.4 (3.76)	Theme List I	26.2 (7.29)
Bedbug II	20.0 (3.69)	Theme List II	20.7 (8.13)
Bedbug III	19.2 (4.02)	Theme List III	19.4 (8.04)
Total	60.6 (9.04)	Total	66.3 (21.8)

<u>b</u>. Theme Loss of the Three Composition Reproductions
19.4% (12.51)

<u>c</u>. Questionnaire Score 18.2 (2.8)

Style

<u>a</u>. Imagery Count: Original Compositions   4.53 (3.66)
Three Bedbug Reproductions   13.27 (4.87)

<u>b</u>. Importation Score: Three Theme List
Reproductions   13.84 (6.18)
Three Bedbug Reproductions   7.29 (4.29)
Three Composition Reproductions   3.91 (2.71)

* Each entry is a mean based on an N of 45, its standard deviation is in parentheses.

stability? One possible answer is that, in repeated reproduction, retention is affected by unique factors, among which reminiscence and relearning at each reproduction may be the most important. These renewed contacts with stimulus material undoubtedly go far in stabilizing the structure of schema. On the other hand, the serial reproduction method not only limits each individual's contact with the stimulus but also requires that he make sense out of it at each successive step. That the structure of stimulus material is better maintained when repeated reproductions are permitted is an unequivocal conclusion.

In the course of the three reproductions, Ss lost an average of 20 per cent of the themes from their own compositions, whereas they only lost 16 per cent of the themes in the Bedbug Story. Though this difference falls short of statistical significance, the opposite result can be predicted on the basis of the fact that not only did each S have more exposure to his own story, but his own story was on the average considerably shorter than the Bedbug Story. The explanation for this finding may be that the Bedbug Story was a more coherently organized as well as a more vivid stimulus, and hence created a more solid and cohesive schema.[8]

To explore the possible relation between coherence of structure and retention, I made the following analysis of the composition data. Without prior knowledge of how it fared in reproduction, I examined each of the original compositions for its over-all coherence and judged, on an impressionistic and quasi-literary basis, whether it had a "loose" or a "tight" construction. I then compared the mean integration score and mean percentage of theme loss of the "loose" and "tight" compositions.

These results are presented in Table 5. The "tight" group reproduced their compositions better than the "loose" group and also attained higher integration scores. Furthermore, there was a significant inverse relationship between integration scores and percentage of theme loss—for the entire population $r = -.33$. It is apparent that structural coherence and the degree to which the theme list is assimilated are both related to retention, and also related to each other. An S who used most of the theme list and

---

[8] The factor of fatigue, however, cannot be ruled out, since in all of the sessions the composition was reproduced last.

Table 5

THEME LOSS IN REPEATED REPRODUCTIONS
AND INTEGRATION SCORE OF
"TIGHT" AND "LOOSE" COMPOSITIONS

	% Theme Loss		Integration Score	
	"Tight"	"Loose"	"Tight"	"Loose"
Number of Ss	24	15	24	15
Mean	14	26	17.8	15.6
Standard Deviation	10	12	2.4	3.2
Difference between means	t = 3.27, P < .01		t = 2.58, P < .02	

wrote a compact story retained it better than one who either used less of the theme list or organized it into a loose story.

A CORRELATIONAL STUDY OF ABILITY AND STYLE

Now we turn to the main analysis of the data summarized in Table 4: a study of the intercorrelations between the various measures which will test the presence and extent of individual differences in ability and style.

1. *Retention ability:* Eight product-moment correlation coefficients were computed among the accuracy measures of the various tests and reproductions. They are all positive, significantly greater than zero, and rather substantial. Correlations of +.44, +.44, and +.37 for the three reproductions respectively were obtained between the theme score of the Bedbug Story and the theme-list score. The total theme score (across the three reproductions) of the Bedbug Story correlated +.63 with the total number of themes correctly reproduced of the compositions. The total theme-list score correlated +.50 with the questionnaire score.

The integration score of the original composition correlated with both the theme-list score of the first session and the total theme-list score: the r's are $+.59$ and $+.57$ respectively. These two correlations, however, probably reflect more than simple retention ability; they also reflect the finding that the extent to which S was able to integrate the theme list into his story was positively related to his ability to reproduce the theme list. By being used and rehearsed in the composition, the information of the theme list was organized into a coherent schema.

This group of unanimous significant positive correlations, along with the fact that retention ability subsequently held up throughout Experiments II and III, speaks strongly for the presence of an ability factor in the reproduction of such material as stories and lists of related themes.

2. *Importation tendency:* Three correlation coefficients were computed to test whether Ss who imported in one task also imported in the others: they are each positive, significant, and quite substantial. The total number of importations in the three reproductions of the Bedbug Story correlated $+.52$ with the total number of importations in the reproductions of the composition. The importation score derived from the three theme-list reproductions correlated $+.62$ with the importations in the Bedbug reproductions, and $+.45$ with the importations in the composition reproductions.

These correlations attest to an importing tendency that cut across the various retention tasks used in this experiment. Experiments II and III also gave strong testimony to the stability and generality of this tendency to import.

Is this tendency independent of retention ability? The present data revealed no correlation between them. In the course of selecting Ss for the serial-reproduction groups of Experiment II, I carried out a number of further analyses of the present data and analyzed the accuracy and importation of the Bedbug reproductions at the information-unit level. These analyses showed, among other things, that there was no significant correlation between importation tendency and retention ability. These further analyses will be presented and discussed below when the selection procedures for Experiment II are described.

3. *Use and retention of imagery:* Ss used an average of only 4.5 imagery words in their compositions, whereas they reproduced, in their first reproductions, an average of 5.8 of the 18 imagery words of the Bedbug Story. In both their use and retention of imagery words Ss showed individual consistency: the imagery count derived from the original composition correlated +.60 with the imagery score from the Bedbug reproductions.

There was also, however, a substantial positive correlation between the imagery and accuracy scores—the imagery score of the Bedbug reproductions correlated +.50 with the theme score of that story, and +.59 with the percentage of correct themes of the composition. This indicates that retention of imagery words went along with retention ability in general; the good retainers used and retained imagery more than did the poor retainers. On the other hand, they imported neither more or less.

4. *Productivity:* The correlations among the various measures of productivity are of some interest since they attest to the task specificity of reproducing. A comparison between the size of the first Bedbug reproduction and the original composition yielded small and statistically insignificant correlations: in word count, $r = +.18$; in theme count, $r = +.04$. For the second and third reproductions, however, the correlations between the size of the Bedbug reproductions and the compositions became significantly positive: they are +.45, +.42, +.48, and +.48. In view of the fact that these four significant correlations apply to a mnemonic task, while the former nonsignificant ones do not, these results indicate that when S *remembers* a good deal of the Bedbug Story, he is also likely to *remember* a good deal of his own composition. But remembering a good deal of the Bedbug Story does not insure the production of a long composition—these tasks are dissimilar, and, according to the correlations, quite independent.

Finally, individual consistency with regard to the size of the reproductions was revealed by the following: the word count of the Bedbug reproduction No. 1 correlated +.83 with the word count of the Bedbug reproduction No. 2. Similarly, $r = +.47$ for the theme counts. Moreover, the word count of the composition correlated +.84 with the word count of the first reproduction of the composition, and, for the theme counts, $r = +.93$.

Summary and Conclusions

The main purpose of this experiment was to ascertain whether there are significant individual differences in ability and style of retention. The experiment used a number of techniques, including the learning and repeated reproduction of a story, the learning and repeated reproduction of a connected but terse list of themes, the composing of a story based on this list, and the repeated reproduction of this composition.

These methods, singly and in combination, showed the presence of an ability variable and two style variables. All of the measures of accuracy, efficiency, importation, and imagery were substantially and positively correlated. The indices of accuracy, whether of themes or of the more molecular information units, were highly intercorrelated, attesting to the presence of a relatively stable retention-ability variable that cut across the experimental asks. The indices of importation, also at both the level of themes and information units, were highly intercorrelated, indicating that an S who imported in his theme-list reproductions was also likely to import in his repeated reproductions of the Bedbug Story and of his composition. While there was no correlation between retention ability and importation, there was a positive correlation between retention ability and the tendency to use and retain imagery words —which also proved to be a source of consistent individual differences.

In addition to these results on individual differences, the experiment also showed that the degree of coherence of a text seems to be related to subsequent reproduction of it. Ss reproduced the Bedbug Story better than they did their own compositions, and this may have been because of its greater coherence and vividness. Furthermore, those compositions which best integrated or assimilated the theme list were best recalled, and the "tight" ones were subsequently better recalled than the "loose" ones.

An additional finding was that, in a period of over two months, remarkably few themes were lost in these repeated reproductions. This finding contrasts quite sharply with the results of serial reproduction, and shows how strong a stabilizing or structuralizing effect a repeated contact with a stimulus can have.

After Experiments II and III of this series have been presented, all of the conclusions will be drawn together and some of the theoretical issues and concepts that I have already discussed will be joined with them. Experiment I can briefly be summed up as follows. Three relatively independent variables emerged: importing style, retention ability, and text coherence. The first may be especially relevant to the concept of recruitment as a process of schema formation and operation; the second and third may be related to the processes underlying schema structuralization and stability, the one approached from the subject side, the other from the stimulus side.

They have been isolated; their consistency, generality, and interdependence have been assessed. The next step is to pursue the study of these variables with the technique that magnifies forgetting and distortion, while teasing out the threads of process and function—namely, serial reproduction.

Experiment II: Importing in Relation to Retention Ability and Explication

Purpose

One of the goals of Experiment I was to provide information for arranging a population of Ss into chains for the serial reproduction of original and explicated versions of stories. The present experiment applies the magnifying glass of the serial reproduction technique to two of the variables that were isolated in the preceding experiment: importation tendency and retention ability. These two variables now became the basis for forming four experimental groups out of the Ss who participated in Experiment I: (1) good retainers who are importers; (2) good retainers who are nonimporters; (3) poor retainers who are importers; (4) poor retainers who are nonimporters.

Two goals underlay this experiment. The first was to replicate the foregoing experiments, and to show that (1) the explicated versions of each story will be retained better than the original versions; (2) the good retainers will preserve the story better than the poor retainers; and (3) the importers will import more than the nonimporters.

The second goal was to explore the relationships between these variables, particularly between explication and importation. It was evident, especially in the qualitative study of the reproductions in the Exploratory Experiment, that certain importations were similar to explications, in that they were attempts to close gaps and reduce ambiguities. This function of importations—which, incidentally, also appeared conspicuously in Ss' reproductions of the theme list in Experiment I—was interpreted as revealing one of the functions of recruitment in schema formation and operation. The effects of both explication and importation seemed to converge in this recruitment process, the first providing organizing (i.e., recruitable) material in the stimulus, the second reflecting its presence in the individual as a cognitive style. Experiment II, along with the next one, offered an opportunity to study these two influences in conjunction, and to discover whether and how they interact—e.g., will they be additive or substitutive?

One expectation, based both on the findings of the foregoing experiments and on theoretical considerations, was that the importers will do better than the nonimporters on the original versions but not on the explicated versions. In the original versions importations may serve a valuable function (i.e., the same function that the experimental explications serve), while in the explicated versions they are likely to be superfluous because the text is already structured.

The present experiment was designed to yield answers to the following three empirical questions: (1) Will the importers import more in their reproductions of the original versions than in their reproductions of the explicated versions? (2) Will even the nonimporters show some importation in their reproductions of the original versions? (3) Will these differences in importation, if present, affect the accuracy and completeness with which the stories emerge from serial reproduction?

Methods and Procedures

A factorial design was planned in which each of the three main variables was to be symmetrically balanced off against the others. Therefore not one but two stimulus stories were required, each of them in both an original and explicated version. In order to achieve a fully symmetrical design, each of the four groups of Ss needed to be divided into two equivalent chains: one chain to receive the original version of story A and the explicated version of story *B*, the other to receive the explicated version of story *A* and the original version of story *B*. In this way each of the four major experimental groups (good retainers, importers; good retainers, nonimporters; poor retainers, importers; poor retainers, nonimporters) dealt with both of the stimulus stories in both versions, and comparisons were then possible between each of the main variables taken singly and in combination.

STEP 1. SELECTING GOOD AND POOR RETAINERS

Six measures (derived from Experiment I) were used as indices of retention ability: (1) the theme score of the first Bedbug reproduction (Bedbug I); (2) the number of themes lost in the course of the three Bedbug reproductions (Σ Bedbug loss); (3) the percentage of themes (based on the original composition) lost in the course of the three composition reproductions (Σ composition loss); (4) the theme-list score of the first theme-list reproduction (theme list I); (5) the total theme-list score for all three reproductions (Σ theme-list score); (6) the score on the Bedbug questionnaire.

A separate distribution for each of the six measures was prepared. It was then divided into five parts, each containing approximately the same number of Ss, so that each of Experiment I's forty-five Ss could be assigned a quintile score on each of the measures. A score of 5 on, say, Bedbug I meant that S fell in the top quintile on that measure. Obviously, anyone who had 5's on each of the six measures was one of the good retainers; one having 1's was among the poor retainers. Each S's six quintile scores furnished a composite index of his retention ability.

Fortunately, because of the substantial positive correlations between the six accuracy measures, it proved relatively easy to isolate a group of Ss who consistently fell in the top quintiles on all of the measures and a group that consistently fell in the bottom ones. Since the present experiment called for the reproduction of a story after a fifteen-minute interval, and this task is similar to the Bedbug I task, the two Bedbug measures were given the most weight among the selection criteria.

These are the criteria that I used to segregate the Ss with respect to retention ability: (1) *Good retainers:* on the two Bedbug measures the individual must have received quintile scores of 4 or 5; on the other four measures, not more than one should have been less than 3. (2) *Poor retainers:* on the two Bedbug measures the individual must have received quintile scores of 1 or 2; on the other four measures, not more than one should have exceeded 3.

By these criteria fourteen Ss qualified as good retainers and seventeen Ss qualified as poor retainers. The remaining fourteen Ss fell toward one or the other of these poles; however, they could not meet either of the above criteria.

STEP 2. SELECTING IMPORTERS AND NONIMPORTERS

Three measures were used as indices of importation tendency: (1) the total importation score on the three theme-list reproductions (theme-list-importation score); (2) the number of themes imported in the three Bedbug reproductions (Σ Bedbug importations); (3) the number of themes imported in the three composition reproductions (Σ composition importations).

The same procedure used for assessing retention ability was used for separating the Ss into importers and nonimporters. Separate distributions were prepared for each of the three measures and each distribution was divided into five parts. Again, the substantial positive correlations between the three measures made it possible to isolate two groups: one in which no S received lower than a quintile score of 3 on any of the measures; the other in which he never exceeded 3. Nineteen Ss qualified as importers, and fourteen as nonimporters.

STEP 3. FORMING THE EXPERIMENTAL GROUPS

The procedure for 'forming the four experimental groups was complicated by the fact that, among the fourteen Ss who qualified as good retainers, six were importers, six were nonimporters, and two could not be classified as either; among the seventeen who qualified as poor retainers, nine were importers, only six were nonimporters, and two were unclassified. Therefore, according to the criteria for inclusion in one of the four experimental groups, only twenty-seven Ss qualified.

The experimental design, however, called for eight separate chains of Ss, two each in the four experimental groups. I had originally hoped that each chain would consist of five Ss because the Exploratory Experiment showed that such a series collapses a story adequately. The selection results just reported, however, did not provide ten qualified Ss for each of the four major groups: a strict adherence to the criteria would have provided only six Ss for three of the groups and nine for the fourth.

As a compromise, I selected six Ss among those who did not qualify on the strict basis of the criteria. They were selected on the basis of next best qualification; each fell just short of meeting the criteria. This made it possible to form the four groups with eight Ss in each, and each of the eight serial reproduction chains having four Ss.

The next task was to divide each group of eight Ss into two equivalent groups of four and to schedule them. In order to maximize the preservation of the stories through each chain, the Ss in each were ordered with respect to their retention ability: the Ss with the highest accuracy scores were put at the heads of the chains.

Most of the conclusions drawn from the present experiment must depend on the relative success of the selection and grouping of the Ss. Consequently, I made a careful assessment of this part of the procedure, some analyses done before the gathering of the serial reproduction data, some afterwards. Though my main purpose was to check the selection, some subsidiary findings emerged that are of interest in their own right.

Table 6 presents selection data on all members of the eight serial reproduction chains. The I.Q. scores are included, and show that on the average the good retainers had higher I.Q.'s than the poor retainers. This finding suggests that retention ability is related to a more general intellectual ability. On the other hand, I.Q. was not related to importation tendency: the importers achieved a mean I.Q. of 112.2, the nonimporters 112.7.

Table 6, containing the selection data from Experiment I, can reveal whether there were any unwanted differences between the four groups. For example, was there a systematic difference in accuracy scores between the two good retainer groups (were the importers, say, better than the nonimporters)? No differences of this kind appear. In only one respect was there a difference between the groups: among the importers, the poor retainers did significantly more importing than did the good retainers (among the nonimporters a small trend in this direction is also evident). This difference, therefore, will have to be taken into account in later analyses of the data. Fortunately, this relationship in itself was not of central interest, unlike the relationship between importing and explication. Since each group dealt with both versions of each story, the relationship between importation and explication was not contaminated by retention ability.

Table 6

SELECTION DATA ON THE EXPERIMENTAL GROUPS

Group	Order	I.Q.	Retention Ability						Importation		
			Bedbug I Theme Score	Total Bedbug Theme Loss	Total Composition Theme Loss'	Theme List I Score	Total Theme List Score	Questionnaire Score	Total Bedbug Theme Importations	Total Composition Theme Importations	Total Theme List Importation Score
Good Retainers, Importers	No. 1	120	23	5	5%	30	88	20	9	1	17
	No. 2	105	21	3	7%	27	80	20	7	2	14
	No. 3	143	24	2	18%	25	66	18	5	5	13
	No. 4	100	21	9	12%	30	88	19	5	2	15
	Mean of Chain	117.0	22.3	4.8	8.8%	28.0	80.5	19.3	6.5	2.5	14.8
	No. 1	123	23	3	9%	32	77	20	4	4	16
	No. 2	104	22	3	10%	31	80	18	8	4	13
	No. 3	115	23	2	20%	19	51	21	12	10	14
	No. 4	123	22	8	22%	37	102	20.5	9	4	15
	Mean of Chain	116.3	22.5	4.0	15.3%	29.8	77.5	19.9	8.3	5.5	14.5
Good Retainers	No. 1	120	22	0	9%	33	89	21	1	2	8
	No. 2	115	23	3	5%	35	101	21	6	2	8
	No. 3	114	22	4	4%	19	35	22	3	5	6
	No. 4	123	20	10	5%	33	93	22	6	1	6
	Mean of Chain	118.0	21.8	4.3	5.8%	30.0	79.5	21.5	4.0	2.5	7.0

Table 6 (Continued)

Nonimporters	No. 1	116	22	1	3%	35	88	21	2	5	6
	No. 2	112	19	5	23%	29	82	21	4	5	9
	No. 3	123	22	5	16%	37	105	19	1	5	6
	No. 4	112	22	7	9%	30	76	21	3	3	12
	Mean of Chain	115.8	21.3	4.5	12.8%	32.8	87.8	20.5	2.5	4.5	8.3
Poor Retainers, Importers	No. 1	107	21	10	21%	23	70	17	10	7	26
	No. 2	102	30	11	17%	10	37	16	10	4	19
	No. 3	119	20	14	16%	18	34	20	15	5	16
	No. 4	111	14	32	19%	20	48	15.5	12	2	24
	Mean of Chain	109.8	18.8	16.8	18.3%	17.8	47.5	17.1	11.8	4.5	21.3
	No. 1	102	20	10	39%	25	62	19.5	17	9	25
	No. 2	105	18	19	40%	19	46	17	9	5	24
	No. 3	106	21	16	43%	37	74	15	7	9	18
	No. 4	110	16	22	19%	17	40	11.5	19	7	18
	Mean of Chain	105.8	18.8	16.8	35.3%	24.5	55.5	15.8	13.0	7.5	21.3
Poor Retainers, Nonimporters	No. 1	123	23	14	20%	32	78	18.5	3	3	10
	No. 2	113	19	11	30%	27	74	18	5	2	12
	No. 3	115	16	35	23%	32	84	14.5	1	1	12
	No. 4	102	18	28	51%	13	20	11	7	3	10
	Mean of Chain	113.3	19.0	22.0	31.0%	26.0	64.0	15.5	4.0	2.3	11.0
	No. 1	124	22	9	32%	28	69	16	2	2	5
	No. 2	93	20	8	5%	25	69	17	9	3	8
	No. 3	96	21	17	30%	20	45	17.5	6	4	8
	No. 4	102	20	24	40%	25	33	16	3	4	8
	Mean of Chain	103.8	20.8	14.5	26.8%	24.5	54.0	16.6	5.0	3.3	7.3

84 I. H. PAUL

Some further checks of the selection data were made to see what differences existed among the eight groups, particularly on those tasks that most resemble the serial reproduction task. The relevant tasks in Experiment I were Bedbug I and theme list I, since they each involved the reproduction of a text fifteen minutes after two perusals (which is exactly what each member of the serial chains does in the present experiment). In addition to a theme analysis, I also made an information-unit analysis of the Bedbug I reproductions. These results, and the result of an information-unit analysis of the theme-list I reproductions, are presented in Table 7.[9]

With respect to retention ability and explication, the results are unequivocal: in all three measures the good retainer chains were clearly superior to the poor retainer chains; and each of the four experimental groups was successfully divided, so that the chain which received the original version of the Ghost Story was not significantly different from its counterpart which received the explicated version. Moreover, a measure of success was achieved in the scheduling procedure: at least the first members of each chain were the best retainers, even though the second and third positions were reversed.

However, with respect to importation the results are somewhat ambiguous, even though only one of the three measures (the information-unit analysis) achieved any degree of statistical significance. Nevertheless, since the nonimporters were somewhat superior to the importers in five of the six comparisons (the theme analysis in the case of the good retainers is the sole exception), one must conclude that, in this experimental sample, the nonimporters started with an edge in retention ability over the importers.[10]

I also made a further check on importations in these selection

[9] Since each chain received only one version of both stories (the original version of one, the explicated version of the other), Table 7 locates the chains only with respect to the Ghost Story (with respect to the second story the table is simply duplicated). The Ss were scheduled in the order of their retention ability, and, since it is necessary to know how successfully this ordering was done, Table 7 presents the mean for each position in the chains in addition to the mean of the chains.

[10] Whereas the nonimporters were superiors to the importers, this difference was greater among the good retainers than among the poor ones, while, in the subsequent serial reproductions, the reverse was true (see below, pp. 90-92). It is difficult to know whether this edge was big enough to account for the subsequent superiority of the nonimporters in many of the serial reproduction measures. However, it should be noted that the serial repoduction technique usually enhances and exaggerates retention processes and thus a small edge may prove efficacious.

Table 7

EXPERIMENTAL GROUPS' MEAN ACCURACY SCORES ON BEDBUG I AND THEME LIST I

		Theme Score	Information Score	Theme List Score
Ghost Story	Original Group	20.5	62.2	25.5
	Explicated Group	20.8	61.4	27.8
Good Retainers	Importers	22.4	63.8	28.9
	Nonimporters	21.5	74.9	31.4
Poor Retainers	Importers	18.8	51.6	21.1
	Nonimporters	19.9	56.9	25.3
Serial Order	Position No. 1	22.0	66.3	29.6
	Position No. 2	20.3	55.6	25.4
	Position No. 3	21.1	66.1	25.9
	Position No. 4	19.1	59.1	25.6

ANALYSIS OF VARIANCE

Source	D.F.	F-Ratio			P		
		Theme Score	Information Score	Theme List Score	Theme Score	Information Score	Theme List Score
Explication	1:25	—	—	1.21	—	—	—
Retention Ability	1:25	19.51	20.70	9.78	.001	.001	.01
Importation	1:25	—	6.11	2.23	—	.05	—
Serial Order	3:25	4.28	2.54	—	.05	.05	—

data by scoring each S's Bedbug I reproduction for importations at the information-unit level to see what differences existed between the Ss who formed the eight experimental chains. Table 8, which presents this analysis, shows that only one difference between the main groups is significant: it is the built-in difference—the importers imported more than did the nonimporters. The groups which later received the original version of the Ghost Story (the O-groups)—who did more importing in it than did those who got the explicated version—showed a slightly smaller tendency to import on Bedbug I than did the latter. However, this initial difference between the O- and E-groups is not of significant proportions.

Table 8

EXPERIMENTAL GROUPS' MEAN

IMPORTATION SCORES ON BEDBUG I

Ghost Story	Original Group	8.1
	Explicated Group	10.8
	Total	9.5
Importers	Good Retainers	15.5
	Poor Retainers	13.8
	Total	14.7
Nonimporters	Good Retainers	4.0
	Poor Retainers	4.6
	Total	4.3

ANALYSIS OF VARIANCE

Source	D.F.	F-Ratio	P
Explication	1:25	1.76	—
Retention Ability	1:25	—	—
Importation	1:25	25.86	< .001
Serial Order	3:25	—	—

One may conclude that, in all respects but one, the eight experimental groups differed from each other only in those respects upon which they were segregated. The only unwanted difference existed between the importers and nonimporters in retention ability. The difference was neither substantial nor consistent enough to attain statistical significance; nevertheless, since the serial reproduction method magnifies trends, it may prove efficacious in the present experiment. Therefore the superiority of the nonimporters must be borne in mind in assessing the results of the present experiment.

STEP 4. A SECOND STIMULUS STORY: THE POTLATCH STORY

The design of the present experiment called for a second story, in both an original and explicated form, to be used in conjunction with the Ghost Story. I selected another Indian folk story, called "The Origin of the Potlatch," which is roughly equivalent in size and character to the Ghost Story. It has the foreign ring, the gaps and ambiguities. It has 326 words (compared to the Ghost's 333), twenty themes (compared to the Ghost's 23), 128 information units (compared to the Ghost's 130), and a redundancy index of 6.40. This is the original version of the story.

The Potlatch Story: Original Version

The Origin / of the Potlatch /

a) A strange / bird / once appeared / in the ocean / in front / of the village. / *b*) All the young men / of the Quillayute / went out and tried / to shoot it, / but no one could hit it. / *c*) Every day / Blue Jay, / a slave / of Golden Eagle, / watched / the hunters / try to shoot / the strange bird. /

d) One day / Golden Eagle / said to / Blue Jay, / "Eh, my children / can catch / that queer-looking bird." /

e) "Oh, no," / replied / Blue Jay. / "They are girls." /

f) Golden Eagle's / daughters / overheard the two. / *g*) Next day / the two / younger / sisters / went into the woods / and stayed / all day. / Many days / they spent / in the woods, / telling no one / what they were doing. / *h*) Although they were girls, / just imagine / —they were making arrows! /

i) One morning, / before daylight, / they went to the forest / and brought in / the arrows they had made. / When they returned / to the village, / all the hunters / had gone out / in their canoes /

to try again / to shoot / the strange-looking bird. / *j*) The two sisters / tied / their hair / in front. / No one / could recognize them. / *k*) Then they paddled / their canoe / in a zigzag line / until they were near the bird. / *l*) The older / of the sisters / killed it / with her third / arrow. /

m) That evening / the girls / said to their father, / "We caught / the bird / and then we hid it / in the woods. / *n*) We want to use / its feathers / as presents, / for the feathers / are of many colors. / *o*) Will you tell / Blue Jay / to invite / all the birds / to come to our lodge / tomorrow?" /

p) Next morning / all kinds / of birds / were gathered / in the lodge / of Golden Eagle. / *q*) "My daughters / caught / the strange bird," / the host / explained, / "they want to give / each of you / a present." / *r*) The girls / gave / certain colors / to different birds. / They gave / to each bird / the colors / it was to have. /

s) Ever since then, / certain birds / have had / certain colors. / And since then, / there have been potlatches. / *t*) This was the first / potlatch, / the first giving / of gifts / from the people who invite / to the people who are invited. /

STEP 5. THE POTLATCH STORY EXPLICATED

I prepared an explicated version of this story, following roughly the procedure used for the Ghost Story explication. However, in the Potlatch Story, I attempted a more thoroughgoing yet piecemeal explication. I made many changes in wording to remove ambiguities, inserted many new clarifying and simplifying clauses, and changed the word order at several places. On the other hand, I added only one wholly new theme [to replace theme *o*)]. In order to equalize the two versions for word count, I omitted a number of parts of the Potlatch Story which seemed to be superfluous [primarily in themes *c*) and *i*)].

This version has a redundancy index of 6.30, which is slightly lower than that of the original version (6.40), and reveals that the extensive piecemeal explication and the omissions had the effect of reducing the redundancy of the story.[11] This is the explicated version of the Potlatch Story; the changed as well as new parts are italicized.

---

[11] Some possible consequences of this are discussed below on p. 98.

The Potlatch Story: Explicated Version

The Origin / of the Potlatch /

a) A strange / bird / appeared once / *over* the ocean / *near* / the bird-village / *where all the birds* / *of the earth* / *lived* / *once upon a time.* / *b*) All the young *hunters* / of the Quillayute, / *the bird-people*, / went out and tried / to shoot it, / but no one could hit it. / *c*) Every day / Blue Jay / watched / the hunters / try to shoot / the strange bird. /

d) One day / Golden Eagle / said to / Blue Jay, / "Eh, my children / can catch / that queer-looking bird." /

e) "Oh, no, / they are girls," / replied / Blue Jay. /

f) Golden Eagle's / daughters / *were nearby* / and overheard / *the conversation.* / *g*) Next day / the two / young*est of them* / went into the woods / and stayed *there* / all day. / Many days / they spent / in the woods, / telling no one / what they were doing. / *h*) They were making arrows—*but they were special* / *ones*! /

i) One morning, / before daylight, / they went to the forest / *to bring home* / the *special* arrows. / *j*) When they returned / to the village, / the two sisters / tied / their hair / in front / *to disguise themselves.* / *k*) Then they paddled / their canoe / in a zigzag line / so the bird wouldn't / notice / that they were approaching. / *l*) The older / of the sisters / killed it / with her third / arrow. /

m) That evening / the girls / said to their father, / "We caught / the bird / and then we hid it / in the woods. / Its feathers / are of many colors. / *n*) *Since we all in the village* / *have only* / *grey* / *feathers,* / let us all take / of these feathers / *and we shall be beautiful.* / *o*) *This will be a real* / *present* / *to everybody* / *and our people* / *will know* / *that giving presents* / *is a great virtue."* /

p) Next morning / all the birds / were gathered / in the lodge / of Golden Eagle. / *q*) "My daughters / caught / the strange bird," / the host / explained. / "They want to give / each of you / a present." / *r*) The girls / gave / to *each* bird / different-*colored* / feathers. / They gave / to each bird / the colors / it was to have. /

s) Ever since then, / certain birds / have had / certain colors. / And since then, / there have been potlatches. / *t*) *which are ceremonies* / *in which the host* / *gives presents* / *to his guests.* / This was the first / potlatch. /

STEP 6. CONDUCT OF THE EXPERIMENT

The serial reproductions were obtained by the same procedure used in the Exploratory Experiment. The *S*s participated in groups of ten: one member from each of the eight chains plus a member from each of the "residue" chains of importers and skeletonizers. I administered both stories—the Ghost Story always preceding the Potlatch Story—in one sixty-minute session. A concentration task requiring S to strike out the vowels in a typewritten text was interpolated between each learning and reproduction.

The boys continued to be cooperative. In view of the fact that the task was quite arduous, and that each had already spent three hours performing similar tasks, it seemed remarkable that there was only an occasional expression of exasperation and weariness.

Results

The measures used in the Exploratory Experiment and Experiment I were applied to the serial reproductions of Experiment II. The differences between stories and between groups were statistically assessed by the analysis of variance technique,[12] separate analyses for each of the main measures.

1. ACCURACY ANALYSES

The first analysis is of the total theme score of each chain[13] and is presented in Table 9 along with the results of the analysis of variance. It shows that three of the variables made significant differences: the explicated versions of both stories were reproduced more accurately than the original versions; the good retainers did better than the poor retainers; and the Potlatch Story was reproduced better than the Ghost Story. When the results of good and poor retainers were combined, there was no difference between the importers and nonimporters; when they were separated, however, a significant difference did emerge:[14] among the good retainers, the

---

[12] This technique reveals the level of significance of differences between means derived from a balanced design. It is described and discussed in most standard textbooks on statistics (see, for example, McNemar, 1949).

[13] The raw data upon which this and the subsequent analyses are based are too cumbersome for presentation here. Moreover, for purposes of the present analyses it was often necessary to transform each raw score to a percentage based on the stimulus stories since they contain different numbers of themes and information units.

[14] The double-interaction Retention Ability X Importation represents this finding. Only those few higher-order interactions that proved significant are included in the tables. It should be noted that the comparatively small number of cases in each cell along with the fact that each independent variable is represented by only two values (hence has only one degree-of-freedom) made it difficult for any higher-order interaction to attain significance.

Table 9

MEAN THEME SCORES OF THE CHAINS, COMPUTED AS PERCENTAGES
BASED ON THE ORIGINAL STIMULUS STORIES

Groups		Stories						
		Original Version			Explicated Version			Total
		Ghost	Potlatch	Total	Ghost	Potlatch	Total	
Good Retainers	Importers	54.3	73.8	64.1	67.7	71.3	69.5	66.8
	Nonimporters	61.9	58.8	60.4	70.8	71.3	71.1	65.7
	Total	58.1	66.3	62.2	69.3	71.3	70.3	66.2
Poor Retainers	Importers	41.3	56.3	48.8	47.9	56.3	52.1	50.5
	Nonimporters	51.1	66.3	58.7	63.5	67.5	65.5	62.1
	Total	46.2	61.3	53.8	55.7	61.9	58.8	56.3
Total		52.2	63.8	58.0	62.5	66.6	64.6	

ANALYSIS OF VARIANCE

Source	D.F.	F-Ratio	P
Explication	1:10	6.81	< .05
Retention Ability	1:11	10.52	< .01
Importation	1:11	2.96	—
Stories	1:10	9.84	< .05
Retention Ability X Importation	1:5	9.90	< .05

importers did slightly, though not significantly, better than the nonimporters; among the poor ones, the nonimporters did considerably and significantly better than the importers.

The relationship between explication and importation, though it falls short of statistical significance, is worth inspecting because of its theoretical importance. Table 9 shows that, among the good retainers, the importers did better than the nonimporters on the original versions of the stories, while on the explicated versions the reverse was true. Among the poor retainers, the nonimporters exceeded the importers on both versions but they did so to a greater extent on the explicated versions (they were 9.9 per cent better on the original, and 13.4 per cent better on the explicated). Combining both groups, explication seems to have made almost twice as much difference to the nonimporters as it did to the importers (17.5 per cent to 8.9 per cent).

The analysis of the more molecular information scores,[15] presented in Table 10, follows the theme analysis quite closely. All of the main variables exerted significant effects: both explicated versions were reproduced more accurately than the original versions; the good retainers were superior to the poor ones; the nonimporters of both groups did better than the importers; and the Potlatch Story fared better than the Ghost Story. In this analysis, as in the first, the positive effect of explication was greater on the nonimporters than on the importers. This was true primarily of the good retainers: for the importers, explication made an average difference of 7.9 units; for the nonimporters it resulted in a 10.9 average improvement. Among the poor retainers the relationship is much smaller: it made a 6.1 unit difference for the importers and a 6.8 difference for the nonimporters.

To sum up: The two main accuracy measures yielded results that are in line with expectation and corroborate the effects of explication and retention ability. The nonimporters did somewhat better than the importers in accuracy of reproduction, and the Potlatch Story was superior to the Ghost Story. Finally, explication had a different influence upon importers and nonimporters. The fact that explication made less difference to the importers is in line with

---

[15] This analysis dealt with the raw scores. A separate analysis was also made on the percentages, with identical results.

Table 10

MEAN INFORMATION SCORES OF THE CHAINS

Groups		Original Version			Explicated Version			Total
		Ghost	Potlatch	Total	Ghost	Potlatch	Total	
Good Retainers	Importers	38.25	48.75	43.50	48.75	54.00	51.38	47.44
	Nonimporters	45.25	46.25	45.75	52.50	60.50	56.50	51.13
	Total	41.75	47.50	44.63	50.63	57.25	53.94	49.29
Poor Retainers	Importers	26.25	35.00	30.63	36.00	40.25	38.13	34.38
	Nonimporters	32.50	43.25	37.88	42.00	46.00	44.00	40.94
	Total	29.38	39.13	34.26	39.00	43.13	41.07	37.67
Total		35.57	43.32	39.45	44.82	50.19	47.51	

ANALYSIS OF VARIANCE

Source	D.F.	F-Ratio	P
Explication	1:11	46.32	< .001
Retention Ability	1:11	96.29	< .001
Importation	1:11	18.72	< .01
Stories	1:11	30.69	< .001

the expectation based on the overlapping functions of these two variables.

In addition to these two main accuracy analyses, I made a number of others that merit presentation here. Separate examination of the lead-off reproductions of each chain is important, because each of them had the experimental stimulus story as its stimulus rather than a second- or third-hand version of it. Table 11 presents both the theme and information unit analyses of the eight No. 1 reproductions. In both measures the good retainers were superior to the poor ones, and the nonimporters did better than the importers. Both explicated versions were reproduced more accurately than were the original versions. In the theme analysis, however, this was true only for the Ghost Story. The Potlatch Story was reproduced better than the Ghost Story, particularly in the information-unit analysis.

Further analysis of the lead-off reproduction failed to corroborate the finding, which the analysis of the total chains pointed up, that explication had a greater effect on the nonimporters. Nevertheless, Table 11 shows that there was a small difference in line with this relationship, and it may be that this small initial difference was progressively magnified by the subsequent serial reproductions. The difference had become pronounced in the final reproductions of each chain, which I also analyzed separately.

Analysis of the final reproductions yielded virtually identical results, except that the nonimporters were only slightly (and not significantly) superior to the importers, and the relationship between explication and importation, which was slight in the lead-off reproductions and quite noticeable in the chains as a whole, is now substantial. A comparison of the theme scores of the final reproductions showed that the importers reproduced the explicated versions on the whole neither better nor worse than the original versions, while the explicated versions of the nonimporters were superior to the original versions by eleven themes. Similarly, in information score, the nonimporters exceeded the importers by an average of four units in the amount they favored the explicated versions.

Following the procedure I used in the Exploratory Experiment, I rescored each reproduction against the standard of its own stimulus text (the previous serial reproduction). Since this kind

Table 11

MEAN ACCURACY SCORES OF THE NO. 1 REPRODUCTIONS, COMPUTED AS PERCENTAGES BASED ON THE STIMULUS STORIES

		Theme Score	Information Score
Ghost Story	Original Version	77.0	46.7
	Explicated Version	93.8	60.2
	Total	85.4	53.6
Potlatch Story	Original Version	88.8	61.4
	Explicated Version	88.8	65.7
	Total	88.8	63.5
Good Retainers	Importers	87.5	56.0
	Nonimporters	97.5	68.9
	Total	92.5	62.5
Poor Retainers	Importers	77.0	51.5
	Nonimporters	86.2	57.6
	Total	81.6	54.5

ANALYSIS OF VARIANCE

Source	D.F.	F-Ratio		P	
		Themes	Information	Theme	Information
Explication	1:11	—	7.89	—	< .05
Retention Ability	1:11	15.51	6.29	< .01	< .05
Importation	1:11	12.15	8.99	< .01	< .05
Stories	1:11	1.49	10.11	—	< .01
Stories X Explication	1:5	7.16	—	< .05	—

of analysis appraises each reproduction on its own merits and does not compound errors (i.e., if No. 1 committed an error, and if the rest of the chain accurately reproduced this error, this single error was quadrupled in the final score), it can be expected to show whether the experimental variables exerted their influence throughout the chains. I made two separate analyses of these data, the first including all Ss, the second excluding the lead-off member of each chain. The results of both these analyses proved wholly corroborative and, since they are largely identical to those already reported, I will not repeat them in detail. They revealed that the three main variables continued to exert significant effects in the expected direction, and that the effect of explication was greatest on the nonimporters.

Word-count analyses of the serial reproductions are of minor interest. The only statistically significant finding was that the good retainers' reproductions were longer than those of the poor retainers. Among the former, the importers' reproductions were longer than the nonimporters'; among the latter, this was reversed. For all groups the explicated versions exceeded the original versions, but this finding failed to attain statistical significance.

2. IMPORTATION ANALYSIS

Did the importers do more importing than the nonimporters? Did all Ss import more in their reproductions of the original versions of the stories than of the explicated versions? These were the main questions for an importation analysis of the serial reproductions.

The analysis was done as follows. Every information unit and theme that appeared in a reproduction and was not present even in the form of a synonym in the original stimulus story was counted as an importation. Each of these importations was then judged as "major" or "minor," on the basis of its degree of departure from the original text.[16] Since the judgment of major and minor is largely a subjective one, the following analyses were done both on this importation score (which is computed by scoring each major importation 2 points and each minor importation 1 point) and on the number of importations, disregarding the major-minor assessment.

Table 12 presents the mean importation score and the mean number of importations in each of the serial reproductions, and the results of an analysis of variance. Only one of the main variables

---

[16] A more complete description of this procedure is presented on p. 69. The present scoring was carried out by a trained assistant who worked without access to any information that might indicate from which group any reproduction came and hence prejudice the scoring.

Table 12

MEAN NUMBER OF IMPORTATIONS AND MEAN IMPORTATION SCORE OF EACH REPRODUCTION

		Ghost Story				Potlatch Story				Total	
		Original Version		Explicated Version		Original Version		Explicated Version			
		No.	Score	No.	Score	No.	Score	No.	Score	No.	Score
Importers	Good Retainers	4.8	7.5	4.0	6.3	4.3	6.5	5.0	8.3	4.5	7.1
	Poor Retainers	4.0	6.3	3.0	4.5	3.0	4.8	4.0	6.8	3.5	5.6
	Total	4.4	6.9	3.5	5.4	3.7	5.7	4.5	7.6	4.0	6.4
Nonimporters	Good Retainers	2.0	2.8	1.0	1.3	1.5	2.3	2.0	3.5	1.6	2.5
	Poor Retainers	3.3	5.0	2.5	3.5	3.8	4.8	3.5	5.3	3.5	4.6
	Total	2.7	3.9	1.8	2.4	2.7	3.6	2.8	4.4	2.6	3.6
Total		3.6	5.4	2.7	3.9	3.2	4.7	3.7	6.0		

ANALYSIS OF VARIANCE*

Source	D.F.	F-Ratio	P
Importation	1:11	15.01	<.01
Stories	1:11	—	—
Explication	1:11	—	—
Retention Ability	1:11	—	—
Story X Explication	1:5	93.10	<.001
Importation X Retention	1:5	158.38	<.001

* Based on the Importation Score Data.

exerts a significant effect, the expected one: the importers did more importing than the nonimporters.

Two interesting results emerge in the form of interactions between the variables. First, while the original version of the Ghost Story was subjected to more importation than was the explicated version on the part of importers *and nonimporters,* this was completely reversed in the case of the Potlatch Story—here the explicated version underwent more importation than did the original version. Second, among the importers, the good retainers did more importing (on both stories, in both versions) than the poor retainers; among the nonimporters, it is the poor retainers who did more importing. (Though it failed to attain statistical significance there, this finding was also present in the selection data; see Table 8.)

Summary and Conclusions

The Exploratory Experiment revealed a congruent relationship between explication and importation that could be understood in terms of their convergence on the process of recruitment. Therefore, one of the expectations underlying the present expriment was that more importing would occur on the original versions of the stories than on the explicated versions. This expectation was confirmed, but only in the case of the Ghost Story. On the Potlatch Story it was the explicated version that underwent more importation. Why should the explication in one case favor importation, and in the other case not?

The answer may lie in the fact that my explication of these two stories differed in some important respects, as already described. Of these, the different effect of explication of the redundancy indexes may be of particular importance. It may be that redundancy is a major determinant of the degree to which a text tends to undergo importation during serial reproduction. This possibility is worth further exploration, since it points to an important function that importation may be serving: namely, the enhancement of redundancy—a possibility that was already suggested in the Exploratory Experiment. The following experiment, Experiment III, offered a good opportunity to examine this relationship in detail.

The importation variable itself stood up very well in the present experiment: the chains of importers showed more importation than those of the nonimporters. The accuracy results were also in line with expectations: the explicated versions of both the Ghost and Potlatch Stories[17] were more accurately reproduced than the original versions; and the good retainers consistently showed their superiority over the poor retainers. This held true for the chains as a whole, for the chains minus the lead-off reproduction, separately for the lead-off and final reproductions, and whether accuracy was scored on the basis of the original stimulus stories or on each reproduction's own stimulus text. All in all, the results of Experiment II provide further support for the efficacy of the stimulus variable explication, and speak strongly for the stability and relative generality of both retention ability and importation style.

Two important relationships between variables emerged: between retention ability and importation, and between explication and importation. The first, contrary to the impressions gained from the Exploratory Experiment and also to the results of Experiment I, suggests that the ability and style variables are not wholly independent from each other, but that there is a small negative relationship between them. The fact that, particularly among the poor retainers in the present experiment, the nonimporters did better than the importers can probably be traced to the small but consistent difference between the groups (revealed by careful analysis of the relevant selection data) which the serial transmission method magnified. This relationship is further explored in Experiment III.

The second relationship has noteworthy theoretical implications. Explication had a greater effect upon the nonimporters than upon the importers. This was especially true among the good retainers and became particularly apparent at the ends of the chains, though to some extent this relationship also occurred among the poor retainers and was also detectable in the lead-off reproductions.

This finding may be viewed as another testimony to the congruence or overlapping functions of explication and importation. The importer does not benefit as much from text explications be-

---

[17] The fact that the Potlatch Story was reproduced better than the Ghost Story is only of minor interest, and is probably due to the various properties of the stories in addition to the possibility that its contents were more familiar to the Ss. Since the order of administration of the two stories was not alternated (the Potlatch came second), it is not possible to rule out position and fatigue effects,

cause he himself, in importing, furnishes such explications. His schemas normally build up and function with a heavier emphasis on recruitment, so that the explications that are provided in the story in order to serve this function are superfluous or redundant. To the nonimporter, however, these organizing and integrating parts of the story are far from superfluous because of the absence in him of reliance on recruitment. In a way, the explicated version of the story contains within it materials for recruitment which compensate for the relative absence of it in the nonimporter's schema formation. Both explication and importation serve to enhance redundancy and assure the coherence and continuity of schema structure.

But before discussing these theoretical implications further let us go on with the final experiment in this series, which continues to explore and examine the relationship among the variables, and also includes the familiarity variable.

Experiment III: Importing in Relation to Explication and Familiarity

Purpose

The present experiment, which introduced importation style into the design of the Exploratory Experiment, was designed mainly to study the relationship of importation to familiarity, and to re-examine the relationship between importation and explication. Essentially, this experiment was a final replication and integration of the foregoing studies, which can be summed up briefly in the following way:

The Exploratory Experiment demonstrated the efficacy of two stimulus variables, explication and familiarity; it also brought into relief the phenomenon of importing, which occurred particularly in the reproductions of the less familiar and unexplicated stories. Experiments I and II isolated two subject variables, importation style and retention ability, and also revealed that explications had a greater effect on nonimporters than on importers. This finding, together with the results of a detailed examination of the reproductions of the Exploratory Experiment, suggested that importation and explication play overlapping or congruent roles in the formation and functioning of schemas—both converging on the schema process of recruitment. Familiarity of text and importation are also related, in a reciprocal way; there was less importing on the more familiar story. I therefore proposed that familiarity with the content of a stimulus, by assuring the presence of appropriate schemas, should, like explication, facilitate schema formation.

All of the findings made clear that importation, explication, and familiarity are closely related and that each contributes to the coherence and continuity of schemas underlying learning and retention. Experiment III was a final test of this general proposition and another attempt to explore the relationship among the variables.

Methods and Procedures

The design of Experiment III, since it was borrowed from the foregoing studies, can be stated briefly. In order to assure and enhance the familiarity of the Secretary Story (which was designed in the first place for Ss who were secretaries), secretarial students at the end of their final year of training were chosen to serve as Ss. The experiment was divided into two parts. The first part corresponded to Experiment I, and consisted of a procedure to test a population of Ss for retention ability and importation style. The second part corresponded to Experiment II, and consisted of a serial reproduction procedure with relatively homogeneous groups of importers and nonimporters selected from the larger population.

The design called for two groups of Ss (one of importers, the other of nonimporters), each to be divided into two subgroups of five Ss each, one subgroup of each main group to receive the original version of the Ghost Story, the other to receive the explicated version. All four groups were composed of good retainers, were equated for retention ability, and were scheduled so that the best retainers led off each chain.

MODIFIED THEME-LIST TECHNIQUE FOR ASSESSING IMPORTATION

I modified the theme-list technique somewhat for this experiment. In Experiment I the theme list was first learned by S in a free manner (he was told merely to "get to know" the list of themes); the next step was the composition based on the theme list, after which the theme list was reproduced. This procedure does not assess the original learning of the theme list, and so does not provide a way to detect what the S imported into the reproduction of the theme list from the composition in order to distinguish it from what he merely failed to learn in the first place. Therefore, I modified the technique to include a reproduction of the theme list *before* the composition as well as a reproduction following the composition. A comparison of these two reproductions provides for the detection of importations that are directly attributable to the composition—each of the differences between the pre- and post-theme-list reproductions can be referred directly to the composition to see whether it is reflected there or not. Only new material that is contained in the composition is scored as an importation.

This is the modified first instruction (the other instructions were unchanged):

> You have each been handed a typewritten sheet. It contains a list of themes of a story called "Balanced Rock." I would like you to read this list of themes carefully and get to know the themes of this story. Please read the list through twice, carefully but at your usual reading speed. When you are through, turn this sheet face down and look up. Are there any questions? Remember, get to know the list of themes by reading through the material carefully twice in succession. When you are finished, turn the sheet over and look up. Please go ahead now.

This method also provides an assessment of each S's retention ability: the accuracy and completeness of the first reproduction of the theme list which is uncontaminated by any relevant interpolated task. The two measures necessary for forming the groups of Ss were thus derived from a single procedure.

STEP 1. TESTING FOR IMPORTATION STYLE AND RETENTION ABILITY

Approximately one month before their graduation from a public high school, the senior class of female secretarial students—110 girls ranging in age from fifteen and a half to seventeen—was assembled for a fifty-minute period, and I administered the modified theme-list technique. Each S provided three pieces of data: a composition based on the theme list, and two reproductions of the theme list, one before and the other after the composition. A coding technique was used to assure anonymity.

STEP 2. SELECTING IMPORTERS AND NONIMPORTERS

The data that emerged from the selection procedure were treated in essentially the same way as in the foregoing experiments.[18] First I scored each theme-list reproduction I for accuracy and completeness at the level of information units. This score served as the main index of retention ability.

I ranked the Ss with respect to their theme list I scores and selected the twenty-four top-ranking Ss to serve as experimental Ss.[19] Next, I scored these Ss' theme-list reproductions II for importations (i.e., new information units traceable to the composition) and separated them into two equal groups: the twelve having the highest number of importations and the twelve having the lowest.

It turned out that those Ss who showed the greater importing tendency fell in the lower part of the rank ordering with respect to retention ability. Among the five best retainers, only one was an importer; among the next eight, only three were importers. Therefore it was not possible to select a group of twelve importers who were equivalent in retention ability to a group of twelve nonimporters. However, it was possible to divide up each group into two parts which were equivalent in this respect. Four groups of six Ss each were thus provided: two groups of importers matched in retention ability, and two groups of nonimporters also matched to each other but superior as a group to the importers.

In order to maximize the preservation of the stories during serial reproduction, I tried, as before, to schedule the Ss so that in each chain the best retainers came first. Even though absences, and the like, prevented this scheduling from being fulfilled completely, nevertheless, as Table 13 shows, the scheduling was fairly successful.

Table 13 shows the four groups, their selection data, and the way they were scheduled. It also shows each S's score on the Terman-McNemar Test of Mental Ability Form D, which was administered at the beginning of the semester by the school psychologist. The table includes the number of *new* importations in each S's third reproduction of the theme list, which was obtained after she had participated in the serial reproduction chain, between seven and

---

[18] The scoring techniques are described on pp. 68-70.
[19] I selected four more than the twenty called for by the experimental design, so that each of the four subgroups would have a substitute in the event of absence or defection.

Table 13

SELECTION DATA ON THE EXPERIMENTAL GROUPS

Order	Original Group				Explicated Group			
	I.Q.	Theme List I Score	No. Importations in Theme List II	No. Importations in Theme List III	I.Q.	Theme List I Score	No. Importations in Theme List II	No. Importations in Theme List III
Importers								
No. 1	110	67	5	0(2)*	119	59	2	0(1)
No. 2	121	51	3	3	125	59	3	4(3)
No. 3	110	42	2	3	107	37	7	2
No. 4	116	46	5	0	108	47	4	0(1)
No. 5	108	32	6(1)	0(2)	110	35	4(2)	2
Mean of Chain	113.0	47.6	4.2	1.2	113.8	47.4	4.0	1.6
Nonimporters								
No. 1	112	66	2	0(2)	104	67	0	3
No. 2	100	54	1	2(2)	99	61	0	—
No. 3	104	62	1	1	105	54	0	0
No. 4	105	52	2(2)	0	126	67	1	2
No. 5	92	51	1	1	89	57	0	2
Mean of Chain	102.6	57.0	1.4	0.8	104.6	61.2	0.2	1.4

*Those importations which cannot be traced to the $\underline{S}$'s composition are in parentheses.

nine days following the selection procedure. Included in parentheses are those importations that could not be located in S's composition and so were not counted in the main score.

In order to see whether the modified method of assessing importation resulted in scores significantly different from those obtained by the original method, I also scored each theme list I for importations in the original way. This analysis showed the methods to be highly congruent, since those Ss who were assigned to the importer groups on the basis of the modified method had more importations in their theme-list I reproductions than those who were assigned to the nonimporter groups (the means were 3.5 and 1.7 respectively). However, the lead-off members of the two importer chains each gave only one importation in their theme-list I reproductions, a fact that may be important in evaluating their performance on the serial reproductions. Incidentally, it is noteworthy that there are more instances of nontraceable importations in theme list III than in theme list II, indicating that a relatively long interval results in increasing recruitment of distant or unrelated material.

Table 13 shows that the nonimporters were significantly superior to the importers in their theme-list I accuracy scores. The former achieved a mean score of 59.10 and the latter 47.50.[20] The question arose: does this relationship contradict the finding of Experiments I and II that importation style was not significantly correlated with retention ability? To answer this question, I scored the theme-list reproductions of the entire population from which these twenty Ss were selected, and found that the nonimporters scored a mean of 38.57 against the importers' 35.58. The difference between these means is considerably smaller than that between the experimental groups, and it fails to achieve statistical significance ($t = 0.25$). Moreover, the correlation between number of importations and theme-list I scores based on the entire population of Ss (including those selected) proved small and without statistical significance.[21]

It is noteworthy that the nonimporters of the experimental groups, who were superior to the importers in their theme-list I accuracy scores, had *lower* I.Q. scores. However, this negative relationship between I.Q. and retention ability held only for those Ss who were selected for the second part of the experiment, the upper end of the total distribution. In the entire population a substantial positive correlation, $+ .36$, was found between retention ability and I.Q.,[22]

---

[20] This difference achieves a t of 2.79 and is significant at the .02 level.

[21] *Biserial* $r = .12$, with a *C. R.* of 0.83, and is not significant. The question of the relationship between importation tendency and retention ability is also discussed above on p. 74.

[22] This correlation is significant beyond the .01 level. A negative relationship between I.Q. and importation tendency was also found (*biserial* $r = .21$), but it is too small and unreliable to attain statistical significance. The nonimporters in the total population achieved a higher mean I.Q. than the importers: 97.3 to 93.7 ($t = 1.17$), again not significant. Probably the main relationship is between I.Q. and retention ability, while importation relates to I.Q. only via its small negative relationship to retention ability.

corroborating the finding of a positive correlation between them in Experiment I.[23]

Table 13 shows that the original group (the group which later received the original version of the Ghost Story) and the explicated group of the importer chains earned almost identical theme-list I accuracy scores, and were also quite similar with respect to the amount of importation on theme list II and III. Of the nonimporters, however, the explicated group had a slight superiority over the original group in their theme-list I scores, and the original group showed a small edge in importations.

STEP 3. SERIAL REPRODUCTION OF THE TWO VERSIONS OF THE GHOST STORY, AND THE SECRETARY STORY

Seven days after the selection experiment, I administered the Ghost Story, in both its original and explicated versions, along with the Secretary Story,[24] to the lead-off members of the four chains. As in the Exploratory Experiment, I varied the order in which the stories were given: the No. 1 Ss received first the Ghost Story and second the Secretary Story; the No. 2's began with the Secretary Story; and so on. The No. 2's were tested in the afternoon of the same day that their predecessors were tested in the morning. The No. 3's were tested the following morning, No. 4's that afternoon, and No. 5's the following day.

At the end of each session I asked the Ss (using the standard instructions) to reproduce the theme list (theme list III in Table 13). After this I strongly urged them not to speak about the experiment to anyone until it was over.

Quantitative Results

I applied the same quantitative measures to the serial reproductions as in the foregoing experiments. In view of the fact that the present experiment was essentially a replication of the Exploratory Experiment (with the importation variable added and retention ability controlled), and since the Ss were secretaries in both cases, I analyzed the results from both experiments together wherever possible, in order to increase the precision of the statistical analyses. Tables 1 and 2 should be consulted for the raw data wherever such combined analyses are reported.

[23] See above, p. 74.
[24] The procedure was identical with that of the Exploratory Experiment; it is described above on p. 17.

1. ACCURACY ANALYSIS

Table 14 presents the theme score, the information score, and the word count of each of the serial reproductions. It reveals that the two stimulus variables made a conspicuous difference: the Secretary Story was better reproduced than either version of the Ghost Story, and the explicated version of the Ghost Story was superior to the original version.

It is interesting that both lead-off members of the importer chains did better than those of the nonimporter chains in their reproductions of the Secretary Story. In fact, in spite of their initial superiority in retention ability (on the selection tasks), the chains of nonimporters did no better than the chains of importers on the Secretary Story (although on the Ghost Story the nonimporters, on the whole, did better). This suggests that the familiarity factor may have benefited the importers more than it did the nonimporters. Moreover, the relationship between importation and explication that emerged in Experiment II (i.e., explication had a greater effect on nonimporters) did not appear here. In the present findings, explication affected importers as well as nonimporters.

The present analysis focuses on the effects of explication and familiarity upon accuracy of reproduction; therefore, in order to gain statistical precision, the results from the importer and nonimporter chains were pooled for the following accuracy analyses, and were studied in conjunction with the results from the Exploratory Experiment chains (see Tables 1 and 2).

Table 15 presents an analysis of the theme and information scores in each of the chains. The raw scores were converted into percentages based on the number of themes and information units in the original stimulus stories.[25] This analysis reveals the efficacy of familiarity and explication. The Secretary Story was superior to the Ghost Story on both measures of accuracy. The other variables attain statistical significance only on the information-score analyses, though the differences are all in the expected directions. The explicated version of the Ghost Story was superior to the original version, whereas there was no significant difference between the two groups of the Secretary Story.

[25] A similar analysis was done on the unconverted raw scores and yielded identical results.

Table 14

ACCURACY RESULTS OF THE ORIGINAL AND EXPLICATED VERSIONS OF THE GHOST STORY, AND THE SECRETARY STORY, BY IMPORTERS AND NONIMPORTERS

	Original group			Explicated group		
	Word Count	Theme Score	Information Score	Word Count	Theme Score	Information Score
			Ghost Story			
Importers						
Reproduction No. 1	175	15	55.5	244	21	76.5
Reproduction No. 2	104	9	26	206	18	50
Reproduction No. 3	89	8	23.5	149	13	34.5
Reproduction No. 4	60	6	14.5	117	11	25
Reproduction No. 5	37	5	11.5	107	10	17.5
Mean of Importer Chains	93.0	8.6	26.2	164.6	14.6	40.7
Nonimporters						
Reproduction No. 1	191	19	56	217	21	60
Reproduction No. 2	117	13	36.5	135	14	34.5
Reproduction No. 3	105	12	34	130	14	33.5
Reproduction No. 4	97	10	30	98	14	26
Reproduction No. 5	51	7	15.5	81	11	22
Mean of Nonimporter Chains	112.2	12.2	34.4	132.2	14.8	35.2
Mean of Ghost Chains	102.6	10.4	30.3	148.4	14.7	37.9

	Secretary Story					
Importers						
Reproduction No. 1	288	21	78.5	230	23	79
Reproduction No. 2	214	18	61	243	20	50
Reproduction No. 3	182	16	53	171	17	38.5
Reproduction No. 4	146	12	39.5	106	11	26
Reproduction No. 5	106	9	24.5	115	11	25
Mean of Importer Chains	187.2	15.2	51.3	173.0	16.4	43.7
Nonimporters						
Reproduction No. 1	248	19	74.5	233	22	75.5
Reproduction No. 2	145	15	43	194	20	56.5
Reproduction No. 3	127	14	36.5	190	19	48
Reproduction No. 4	108	13	34	154	15	40
Reproduction No. 5	115	11	33	140	14	36.5
Mean of Nonimporter Chains	148.6	14.5	44.2	182.2	18.0	51.3
Mean of Secretary Chains	167.9	14.9	47.8	177.6	17.2	47.5

Table 15

MEAN ACCURACY SCORES OF THE EXPLORATORY EXPERIMENT AND EXPERIMENT III CHAINS, COMPUTED AS PERCENTAGES BASED ON THE STIMULUS STORIES

		Theme Score	Information Score
Ghost Story	Original Version	45.6	24.3
	Explicated Version	61.7	29.5
	Total	53.3	26.9
Secretary Story	O-Group	66.3	34.8
	E-Group	69.1	34.9
	Total	67.7	34.8
Experiment III Chains		58.3	39.9
Exploratory Experiment Chains		63.0	41.9

ANALYSIS OF VARIANCE

Source	D.F.	F-Ratio		P	
		Theme	Information	Theme	Information
Stories	1:4	10.19	39.13	.05	< .01
Chains	1:4	1.14	95.13	—	< .01
Stories X Explication	1:3	3.85	156.4	—	< .01

A word-count analysis revealed that the reproductions of the Secretary Story were longer than those of the Ghost Story; that the reproductions of the explicated version were longer than those of the original versions; and that the reproductions of the importers were longer than those of the nonimporters. However, only the first of these findings attains statistical significance ($F = 7.60$, $d.f.$ of 1:4; significant at the .05 level).

I made a separate analysis of the first reproductions in each of the chains. Table 16 presents these results which, on the whole, are similar to those in Table 15, although only the information scores yield statistically significant differences. The Secretary Story was reproduced better than the Ghost Story from the start. It is noteworthy that, whereas the first member of the O-groups did better than those of the E-groups on the Secretary Story, on the Ghost Story it is the explicated version which was superior to the original version, indicating that it was the influence of the text rather than an initial superiority.

Several analyses of the final reproductions in each of the chains revealed that, while the above findings were all present in direction, only one of the differences attains statistical significance: the Secretary Story was reproduced better than both versions of the Ghost Story (for information score $F = 26.87$, $d.f.$ of 1:4; significant at the .01 level).

Analyses of all the reproductions on a successive stimulus basis also revealed that the explicated version fared better than the original version, and that the Secretary Story was retained better than either version of the Ghost Story. Moreover, this was also the case when only the last four reproductions of each chain were considered.

2. IMPORTATION ANALYSIS

Table 17 presents the importation score as well as the number of importations in each of the serial reproductions. It reveals, first, that the importers did more importing on both stories than the nonimporters did. A case-by-case comparison shows only one conspicuous case in which the reverse was true: the first member of the E-group (whose importations in the selection tasks, as shown in Table 13, were also quite low.) In spite of this case, the means for each chain clearly reflect the importation variable.

Table 16

MEAN ACCURACY SCORES OF THE NO. 1 REPRODUCTIONS, COMPUTED AS PERCENTAGES BASED ON THE STIMULUS STORIES

		Theme Score	Information Score
Ghost Story	Original Version	71.5	44.3
	Explicated Version	88.0	54.2
	Total	79.8	49.3
Secretary Story	O-Group	92.0	58.0
	E-Group	88.5	57.8
	Total	90.3	57.9
Experiment III Chains		85.0	50.9
Exploratory Experiment Chains		85.0	56.2

ANALYSIS OF VARIANCE

Source	D.F.	F-Ratio		P	
		Theme	Information	Theme	Information
Stories	1:4	3.29	10.87	—	$< .05$
Chains	1:3	—	28.25	—	$< .05$
Stories X Explication	1:3	2.99	25.13	—	$< .05$

Table 17

TOTAL NUMBER OF IMPORTATIONS AND TOTAL IMPORTATION SCORE OF EACH REPRODUCTION

	Ghost Story				Secretary Story				Total	
	Original version		Explicated version		Original group		Explicated group			
	Number	Score	Number	Score	Number	Score	Number	Score	Number	Score
			Importers							
Reproduction No. 1	10	15	6	7	8	12	1	1		
Reproduction No. 2	10	14	5	8	4	5	4	7		
Reproduction No. 3	3	5	2	3	2	2	2	3		
Reproduction No. 4	4	4	6	10	2	1	3	6		
Reproduction No. 5	1	2	5	7	2	3	2	2		
Total Importer Chains	5.4	8.0	4.8	6.4	3.4	4.8	2.4	3.8	4.0	5.8
			Nonimporters							
Reproduction No. 1	13	15	6	9	5	6	4	6		
Reproduction No. 2	6	8	7	8	3	3	4	5		
Reproduction No. 3	2	4	1	1	1	2	2	3		
Reproduction No. 4	2	4	1	2	0	0	0	0		
Reproduction No. 5	0	0	3	4	1	1	0	0		
Total Nonimporter Chain	4.6	6.2	3.6	4.8	2.0	2.4	2.0	2.8	3.1	4.1
Total	5.0	7.1	4.2	5.6	2.7	3.6	2.2	3.4		

The original version of the Ghost Story underwent more importations than did the explicated version, and this was true in the reproductions of both importers and nonimporters. However, since the importers of the O-group also did more importing on the Secretary Story, we cannot, on the basis of this finding alone, be sure that explication had a special effect on the amount of importing that the importers did. Nevertheless, in the case of the nonimporters, the fact that the E-group did slightly more importing on the Secretary Story and less on the explicated version of the Ghost Story does point to a special effect of explication. Therefore, we can conclude that, certainly for the nonimporters and probably for the importers, explication was inversely related to importation, in that explication diminished the amount of importation.

Finally, Table 17 shows that both versions of the Ghost Story underwent more importation than did the Secretary Story. Of the twenty possible comparisons of importation score as well as number of importations, in only three does the Secretary Story exceed the Ghost Story.

In order to make a comprehensive test of the importation variable, I made a statistical analysis of the importation scores of all the reproductions of the Ghost Story in Experiments II and III. This combined analysis, presented in Table 18, shows that the importation variable was highly significant—the importers did the most importing—and that the original version of the Ghost Story underwent significantly more importation than the explicated version.

Finally, I counted all the importations which occurred in the serial transmission chains of Experiments II and III. A comparison of the mean number of importations per chain, presented in Table 19, shows that the importers exceeded the nonimporters at a very high level of statistical significance.

3. REDUNDANCY ANALYSIS

Following the technique devised for the Exploratory Experiment, I assessed the redundancy of each serial reproduction. These results, presented in Table 20, are noteworthy first for the fact that they corroborate the main findings of the redundancy analysis from the Exploratory Experiment as presented in Table 3. The reproductions of each chain showed a fairly steady decline in the re-

Table 18

MEAN IMPORTATION SCORE ON THE GHOST STORY IN THE CHAINS OF EXPERIMENTS II AND III

Ghost Story	Original Version	5.9
	Explicated Version	4.5
Importers	Experiment III Chains	7.2
	Experiment II, Good Retainers	6.9
	Experiment II, Poor Retainers	5.4
	Total	6.5
Nonimporters	Experiment III Chains	5.4
	Experiment II, Good Retainers	2.1
	Experiment II, Poor Retainers	4.3
	Total	3.9

ANALYSIS OF VARIANCE

	D.F.	F-Ratio	P
Importation	1:7	17.19	< .01
Explication	1:7	5.87	< .05
Chains	2:7	3.46	—
Chains X Importation	2:2	199.25	< .01

Table 19

NUMBER OF IMPORTATIONS IN THE 28 CHAINS OF EXPERIMENTS II AND III

Groups	Mean	S.D.	t	P
Importers	17.1	4.3	3.45	< .01
Nonimporters	10.9	5.2		

dundancy indexes of both versions of the Ghost Story; but there was no comparable change in the redundancy indexes of the Secretary Story. Figure 1 shows the course of the redundancy indexes for the Ghost Story as a whole compared with that of the Secretary Story. The former shows a remarkably even and steady decline, while the latter is relatively flat.

The present study further confirmed the Exploratory Experiment in the finding that the original version of the Ghost Story suffered, in each of the two importer groups, a sharper decrease in redundancy than did the explicated version. It is also true that the differences between these two groups of reproductions were greater than the initial difference between the two versions of the stimulus story (which is 0.28). This was particularly true for the importers where the mean difference was 1.30, while for the nonimporters the mean difference was only 0.47.

The relationship between importation and redundancy is ambiguous. In their reproductions of the Secretary Story, the importers generally showed greater redundancy than the nonimporters. However, on the Ghost Story, the reverse was true. Figure 1 shows this graphically.

SUMMARY AND CONCLUSIONS

In this final experiment—a replication and integration of the foregoing ones—the main variables stood up well. The explicated version of the Ghost Story emerged from serial reproduction more intact than the original version, and the Secretary Story was much better recalled than either version of the Ghost Story. These find-

Table 20

REDUNDANCY ANALYSIS OF EACH REPRODUCTION

	Importers						Nonimporters					
	Original Group			Explicated Group			Original Group			Explicated Group		
	No. Lexical Units	Redundancy Score	Redundancy Index	No. Lexical Units	Redundancy Score	Redundancy Index	No. Lexical Units	Redundancy Score	Redundancy Index	No. Lexical Units	Redundancy Score	Redundancy Index
Ghost Story												
Reproduction No. 1	97	390	5.98	119	470	6.05	104	450	5.67	121	440	6.36
Reproduction No. 2	60	320	4.67	99	380	6.16	71	320	5.49	76	320	5.79
Reproduction No. 3	50	300	4.00	72	320	5.55	65	300	5.38	74	320	5.68
Reproduction No. 4	32	230	2.81	60	310	4.83	59	280	5.25	55	260	5.27
Reproduction No. 5	21	150	2.86	57	330	4.21	32	190	4.06	53	260	5.10
Mean of the Ghost Chains	52.0		4.06	80.1		5.36	66.2		5.17	75.8		5.64
Secretary Story												
Reproduction No. 1	125	520	5.84	113	490	5.66	108	540	5.00	113	470	5.84
Reproduction No. 2	102	450	5.59	94	430	5.43	71	380	4.65	96	390	5.94
Reproduction No. 3	91	410	5.50	73	320	5.61	62	340	4.52	92	340	6.30
Reproduction No. 4	66	270	5.91	52	250	5.19	56	330	4.19	74	270	6.35
Reproduction No. 5	48	250	4.79	53	230	5.66	49	270	4.49	73	260	6.44
Mean of the Secretary Chains	86.4		5.53	77.0		5.51	69.2		4.57	89.6		6.17

Figure I

Redundancy Indexes of the Serial Reproductions

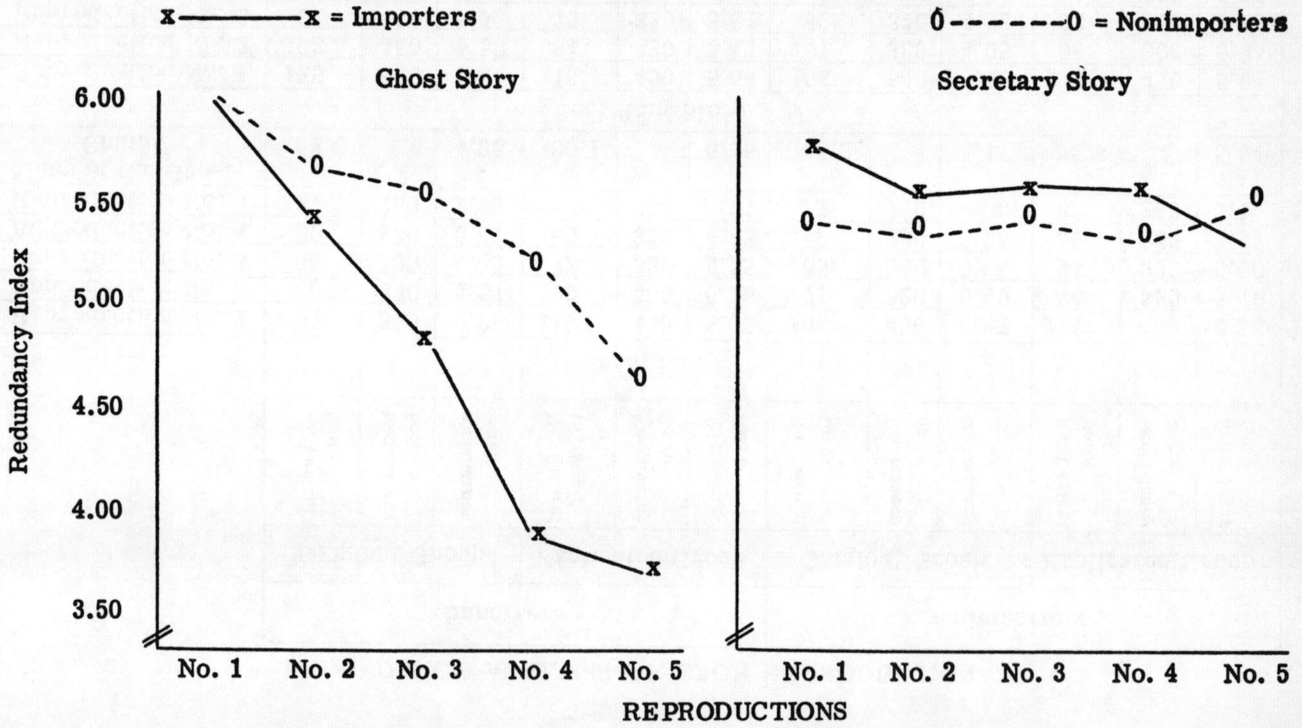

x———x = Importers
0------0 = Nonimporters
Ghost Story
Secretary Story
Redundancy Index
6.00
5.50
5.00
4.50
4.00
3.50
No. 1
No. 2
No. 3
No. 4
No. 5
REPRODUCTIONS

ings applied to the reproductions' accuracy and completeness as well as to their over-all redundancy structure. Moreover, the importation tendency proved once more to be a stable property of Ss. The importers (selected solely on the basis of the modified theme-list technique) consistently did more importing in their reproductions than the nonimporters did, justifying the designation of "importing" as a cognitive style, and lending support to the idea that recruitment is a basic schema process.

As in the earlier experiments, the original version of the Ghost Story underwent more importation than the explicated version. This finding was particularly conspicuous in the case of the nonimporters, though it also occurred to some extent among the importers. Moreover, as in the Exploratory Experiment, both versions of the Ghost Story underwent more importation than did the Secretary Story. These findings together suggest the following interpretation: when an organization of schemas is not adequate to deal with (i.e., interact with, integrate, and articulate) an extended experience, an intensification of the recruitment process occurs, resulting in recruitment from more or less related schemas. The Ghost Story, since it is largely unfamiliar and hence did not meet with adequate schema organizations in our Ss, gave rise to the importation of material more congruent with their schemas. This proposition can best be substantiated by directly examining the reproductions (see below, pp. 121-134).

The redundancy analysis of the present reproductions replicated the analysis made in the Exploratory Experiment, and reflected the differential collapse in structure of the stories: the original over the explicated version, and the Secretary over the Ghost Stories. The redundancy of the importers' reproductions was greater than those of the nonimporters, however, only in the case of the Secretary Story; this finding, paradoxically, did not emerge in the Ghost Story reproductions. The explanation may be that the importations, in the case of the alien Ghost Story, were unsuccessful because they failed to enhance redundancy. The detailed study of the reproductions may help to establish this relationship.

Because Experiment II showed that explication had a greater effect on nonimporters than on importers, I was led to propose that explicating and importing were overlapping or congruent functions. But in the present experiment, both explication and familiarity seemed to have had a greater facilitating influence on importers: the importers did better on the explicated than on the original version to a greater extent than did the nonimporters; and the importers (in spite of achieving lower accuracy scores in the selection task) did better on the Secretary Story than the nonimporters. So we have an important contradiction between the results of Experiments II and III. In one case the explications seem to have been *substitutive* with respect to importations, in the other they seem to have been *additive* or mutually facilitating.

The findings of Experiment III suggest an alternative interpretation of the relationship between explication and importation, one that focuses on the *fit* between text structure and schema structure rather than on the similarity between processes. The explicated and familiar material may have been easier for the importers to assimilate since it fitted in with their schema organization. It is as though they were more at home with stimulus material that was more like what they would do to it anyway; a highly explicated story suits their style and so is easier to apprehend and retain. However, further experimental exploration is necessary to determine under what conditions explication favors importers and when it favors nonimporters.

Qualitative Analysis

My examination of the serial reproductions in the Exploratory Experiment accomplished more than merely pointing up how much more coherent were the reproductions of the explicated version than of the original version of the Ghost Story, and how much more coherent than both of them were the Secretary Story reproductions. It revealed the pivotal integrating role played by explications: they closed gaps, formed transitions, solved contradictions, reduced ambiguity, and enhanced over-all coherence. Moreover, distortion and forgetting seemed to occur especially at those places where the original version contained gaps and ambiguities which my explicated version was designed to reduce—each of the serial reproductions seemed to tighten and reorganize the account around these points.

In addition, by tracing themes that were lost or conspicuously distorted somewhere along the chain, I could observe that they ". . . frequently followed a course of progressive contraction of content . . . gaps were opened and themes became disconnected and isolated . . . the pattern of skeletonization regularly included reshuffling of emphasis, rejuxtaposition of parts and relationships, and a steady tightening of structure around gaps and ambiguities, as well as a stripping away of redundant and ambiguous parts" (see p. 54). Many importations played a role that paralleled that of explications in that they also solved ambiguities and contradictions, and enhanced coherence—in fact, ". . . only those importations which were patently explicatory went on to influence subsequent reproductions" (see p. 55).

My detailed examination of the reproductions of Experiment III was undertaken first to see whether they concur with these observations and thus support the conclusions about schema functioning that I based on them; and second, to make a comparison between the importers' and the nonimporters' reproductions to see whether differences in their structure can be discerned that may teach us more about the role of importations.

My present examination will be briefer and more sketchy than it was in the Exploratory Experiment, since most of the ideas have already been spelled out there. The four chains of reproductions are presented below. The lettering of themes in all reproductions follows that of the theme analysis of the stimulus story,[26] and noteworthy changes, distortions, and importations are italicized. Following each chain's reproductions of the Ghost Story is its final (No. 5) reproduction of the Secretary Story.

EXPERIMENT III
SERIAL REPRODUCTION OF THE ORIGINAL VERSION OF THE GHOST STORY BY THE IMPORTERS

REPRODUCTION NO. 1
The War of the Ghost

a) Two men from Egulac *decided* to go up the river to hunt seals. *f*) They heard a *splash* and they saw a canoe coming toward them. *g*) "What do you think? We want to take you with us, *h*) we are going to war *with the Indians*." *i*) "I will not go" said one of them. "My relatives *will* not know where I have gone." *j*) "But, you may go," he said turning to the other. *k*) So his *friend* went with the warriors and he returned home. *l*) They went up the river to a place called Kalama.

[26] The theme analysis of the Ghost Story is presented above on pp. 35-36.

Some returned p) *and he thought they were ghosts, but he was not frightened. m*) Many warriors were killed and *many injured. u*) The warrior went back and told of his great fight. *v*) "They said I was hit," he said, "but I didn't feel anything." He told his story and *then went to sleep.* In the morning the *people found him*; *w*) something black came out of his mouth, his face was contorted, *x*) the people stood up and cried. *y*) He was dead.

REPRODUCTION NO. 2
War *and* Ghosts

a) Some *hunters* were going up *to* Egulic to hunt seals. *f*) They heard a splash in the water and saw some *warriors* coming. "*What shall we do*." *i*) I can't go because my relative won't know where I am. *m*) Many warriors were killed but some returned *u*) and told of the great fight. *v*) "They said I was hit, but I don't feel hurt." After that the warrior went *back to* sleep. When morning came they found him *w*) with something black *sticking out* of his mouth, his face was *distorted. y*) He was dead. *p*) *The people thought the warriors who came back were ghosts.*

REPRODUCTION NO. 3
Warriors and Ghosts

a) Some men went to the Auglic to hunt seals. *f*) They heard a splash in the water and saw *many* warriors coming. *i*) "I can't join them because my relative will not know where I am." *m*) Many of the warriors were killed, but some returned *u*) to tell the story. *v*) "They said I was hit, but I don't feel hurt." The warrior went back to sleep. The next morning he was found *w*) with something black sticking out of his mouth, and his face *deformed. y*) The warrior was dead.

REPRODUCTION NO. 4

a) Some men went to the Auglic to hunt seals. *f*) They heard a splash in the water and saw warriors. *i*) "I can't come because my relatives won't know where I am." *v*) They *thought* I was hit, but it *didn't seem* to hurt. The warrior fell asleep. *When he awoke w*) there was a black thing in his mouth—*y*) he was dead.

REPRODUCTION NO. 5

a) Some men went to the Auglic to hunt. *f*) They heard a splash and there were warriors. *i*) "I can't come my relatives won't know." He was hit. *w*) *They found* a black thing in his mouth, *y*) he was dead.

REPRODUCTION NO. 5 OF THE SECRETARY STORY

Two sisters graduated from college. They both wanted to work in foreign countries so they could see the world. One sister was good in stenography and she got a job with a minister. *It was secrecy.* One day she came across a letter which said a city was to be bombed. Her sister lived in that city. She wanted to tell her sister, but she wanted to be loyal to the minister. *So she thought she would wait a few days and write to her and tell her to visit her.* Her sister started to walk to visit her and she met her sister on the road.

EXPERIMENT III
SERIAL REPRODUCTION OF THE ORIGINAL VERSION OF THE GHOST STORY BY THE NONIMPORTERS

REPRODUCTION NO. 1
Ghosts

a) One night two men went to the river *in* Egulac to hunt seals. *b*) It became *very* foggy. *c*) The men ceased their work. *d*) They heard *faint* war cries. *e*) They *quickly* headed toward shore and hid behind a log. *f*) They then heard the paddles of canoes. One canoe appeared in which there were five men. *g*) These men wished for a man to *help* fight. *i*) The first man did not wish to go, for, he said "I might be killed." This man who had not wanted to go returned home, *j*) after he said "You may go" to the other. *l*) Now these *six* men went up the river to Kalama to fight. *m*) They *came upon* the village and started *firing*. Many men from both sides were killed. *n*) The men shouted, "*Cease fire*, the Indian has been shot—*he is not sick.*" *s*) This man now *ventured* toward home. *t*) He must tell everyone about his adventure, he thought. *u*) I was *fighting with ghosts* at Kalama when I was shot. *v*) I was not sick. When daylight came *w*) this man fell to the ground. A black substance was *pouring forth* from his mouth. *x*) People *called to him*. *y*) He was dead.

REPRODUCTION NO. 2

a) Two *hunters* were seal hunting in the river Egulac. *f*) They heard the paddle of canoes. *e*) They hid behind a log. They saw one canoe in which five men were. *g*) The man said they wanted *another* man to go to Kalamo and fight. *i*) The first *was afraid* and said, "I might be killed." He returned home, *j*) telling the other man, "You may go." *l*) The six men went to Kalamo *m*) and fought. *n*) Someone said, "Cease fire!" "*That Indian is not sick.*" *When the first man left* he thought "I am not sick. *t*) I must tell my friends about fighting ghosts at Kalamo." *s*) When he arrived home he *lay down w*) with black *froth* coming from his mouth. *y*) He was dead.

REPRODUCTION NO. 3

a) Two hunters were hunting seals at the river Egulac. *f*) They heard the paddles of canoes. *e*) They hid behind a log. There were five men in the canoe. *g*) They wanted six men to come to Kalamo and fight. *i*) The first man said, "I may be killed," and he returned home, *j*) telling the other man, "You may go." *m*) The six men fought at Kalamo. *n*) Someone cried, "cease fire." "The Indian is not sick." "I am not sick," said the man. *t*) I must tell my friends about fighting ghosts at Kalamo. *s*) When he got home he lay down and *w*) black froth *foamed* from his mouth. *y*) He was dead.

REPRODUCTION NO. 4

a) Two men were hunting seals in the river Egulac. *f*) They heard the paddling of a canoe. *e*) They hid behind a log. There were five men in the canoe. *g*) They were going to fight at Kalamo. *i*) "I am not going," said one man, "*I will die*." "The Indian *is sick*." "I am not sick," said the man. So he went home. *m*) The other six men went to Kalamo to fight. *t*) "I am going home to tell the people about fighting the ghosts at Kalamo." *s*) He went home, lay down and *w*) black foamed at his mouth. *y*) Then he died.

REPRODUCTION NO. 5

f) They heard the paddling of a canoe. *e*) They hid behind log. There were five men in the canoe. The Indian is sick. *i*) "I am not going I will die." *g*) They were going to fight at *s*) He went home. When he reached home *w*) black froth foamed at his mouth. *y*) Then he died.

REPRODUCTION NO. 5 OF THE SECRETARY STORY

Two sisters who graduated from a business college at Massar decided to become foreign secretaries so they could see the world together. They promised to write to their mother often. One sister who was a competent secretary, got a job with a prime minister. "You must always be loyal," the prime minister said, "because many important documents pass through this office." One day a declaration of war from another nation passed through the office where the girl was working. She decided to walk to that nation which was only twelve kilometers away to warn her sister. When she got there, her sister was already there to warn her. The next day both nations were destroyed.

EXPERIMENT III

SERIAL REPRODUCTION OF THE EXPLICATED VERSION OF THE GHOST STORY BY THE NONIMPORTERS

REPRODUCTION NO. 1

The War *with* the Ghosts

a) One night two men from the *city* of Euglac went fishing down by the river. *b*) The night was foggy and *dark*. *c*) *A good night* for ghosts. *d*) As they were fishing they heard sounds of a war party. *e*) They tried to hide *f*) but they could not and one of the canoes came straight up to them. *h*) "We are going to fight," they said. *g*) "You *are* going with us." *i*) One man said he couldn't go because he had a family *to take care of,* *j*) but he said to the other, "You go, *there is no one waiting for you.*" *k*) So one man went with the party and one went home. When they reached the *city* of Kalama *m*) they began to fight. *n*) Then someone shouted, "We better go, the Indian is shot." *q*) I did not feel any pain but they said I was shot. *r*) That was because when you are with ghosts at night you feel no pain. Many people were killed and *a great number injured. Yet, the Indian felt no pain.* *s*) When the man went

RETENTION STYLE AND RETENTION ABILITY 125

home to Euglac *u*) he told the people he went fighting with the ghosts, *v*) and that he was shot but had felt no pain. *w*) Then the man fell, something black rolled out of his mouth. *x*) The people all got up and cried. *y*) He was dead.

REPRODUCTION NO. 2

a) One day two men were fishing *in the Euglac River*. *b*) The night was dark and foggy. *c*) It was a good night for ghosts. *d*) Suddenly they *saw* a *group* of canoes. One canoe was heading toward them. *h*) "We have come to fight. *g*) You *must* come with us." *i*) "But I have a *wife* and family," said one man. *j*) "You have no one, you go." *l*) They went to the city of Kalama. *m*) There they fought. *q*) *One man was wounded*, but he did not feel it. That was because he was fighting *with Indians*. Many *Indians* were killed and a great number wounded. But the man felt no pain. *s*) He went back to his town in Euglac and *v*) said to *his* people, "I have been shot, but I feel no pain." He then fell to the ground. *y*) He was dead.

REPRODUCTION NO. 3

a) One day two men were fishing in the Euglac River. *b*) It was dark and foggy. *c*) It was a good night for ghosts. *d*) Suddenly they saw a group of canoes. One canoe was coming toward them. *h*) "We are going to fight. *g*) Come with us!" *i*) "I have a wife and family," said one man. *j*) "You have no one. You go." *l*) They went to *the* Kalama *m*) to fight. *q*) One man got wounded but he could not feel the pain. This was because he was fighting with Indians. Many Indians were wounded and dead but the man couldn't feel the pain of his wound. *s*) He went back to the Euglac *River* where he lived and *v*) he told everyone, "I have been wounded, but I cannot feel the pain." He fell to the ground. *y*) He was dead.

REPRODUCTION NO. 4

a) Two men were fishing on the Eglac River. *b*) It was dark and foggy. *c*) It was a good night for Ghost. *d*) They saw canoes coming toward them. *They were Indians*. *g*) "Come *h*) we are going to fight." *i*) "*No* I have a family. *j*) You have none. You go." *l*) They went to the Kalamac *m*) to fight. *q*) The man was wounded but could not feel the pain because they were fighting Indians. A lot of Indians were wounded and dead. *s*) The man went home. *v*) He said, "I am wounded but I can not feel the pain." Then he dropped. *y*) The man was dead.

REPRODUCTION NO. 5

a) Two men went fishing on the Eglac River. *b*) It was dark and foggy. *Then a ghost came*. *d*) They saw *boats* coming. They were Indians. *l*) They went to the Kalamac *River*. *m*) They came to fight. *h*) They said, "We are going to fight. *i*) No I have a family. *j*) You have none. You go." Many Indians were wounded and dead. *q*) The man was wounded but did not feel pain because he was fighting the Indians. *s*) When he went home *v*) he said he was wounded but didn't feel pain.

REPRODUCTION NO. 5 OF THE SECRETARY STORY

There were two sisters. Business school graduates. They said to their mother one day, we are going to a foreign country to work. This way we can see the world and work at the same time. One sister worked for a foreign minister. They decided to write to each other every day. One sister worked for a minister. One day he said to her you are working for me. You should be loyal to me. He told her of an attack of a city. She remembered that, that was the city her sister was working in. She decided to write to her sister but then remembered her loyalty. She wouldn't write but her sister would think she was sick. She didn't get a letter from her sister the next day. She went to see if she was sick. They met halfway. The next day both cities were bombed because both had planned an attack.

EXPERIMENT III
SERIAL REPRODUCTION OF THE EXPLICATED VERSION OF THE GHOST STORY BY THE IMPORTERS

REPRODUCTION NO. 1

The War of the Ghost

a) Two men of Eluca went fishing one night. *b*) While they were there the *air* became foggy and calm. *c*) Then they *remembered* it was the omen of *the ghost*. *d*) They heard some cries *that were like war cries* and *e*) ran to the shore to hide behind a log. *f*) But they could not hide from these canoes. One canoe came right toward them. It had five men in it. *h*) They told the men that they were going to a *town outside of Kalama* to fight *g*) and they wanted them to go. *i*) One of the men said, "I can't go. I have not told my relatives where I am. *j*) But you" he said to the other man "have no relatives. You can go." *k*) So the man went with them. *l*) When they reached the shore the people *were there* and *m*) they began to fight. Many people were killed. *n*) Then he heard one of the men say, "That Indian has been hurt, we must leave." *o*) His fellows had never called him an Indian *q*) and he felt no pain. *r*) Then he remembered that when you are in the company of the ghost you feel no pain as long as the night last. *s*) When he got back he started a fire to summon the people. *u*) He told them of his *experience* and how many *of their people* had been killed. *w*) In the morning he fell, something black came from his mouth. His face was contorted. *y*) He was dead.

REPRODUCTION NO. 2

a) Two men from Eluca were *out in a boat* fishing when *b*) the *sea* became foggy and calm. *c*) They remembered that *when the ocean became like this* it was the omen of the ghost *to appear*. *d*) They saw some men coming in a *boat* and *e*) they went to shore and hid behind a log. *It was a canoe that they had seen* and there were five men in it. *h*) The men told the two men that there *was a war going on* at Kalama and *g*) they wanted *their help*. *i*) One man said that he had relatives and *they were expecting him back home. j*) *The men turned to the other fellow and said*, "You have no relatives, come with us." *k*) He left with the five men and *m*) began to battle at the place spoken about. *He became wounded* and *n*) the *five men* said, "*Let us take this Indian away*, he is wounded." *q*) The man could feel no pain and *r*) he remembered that the night you were with the ghost you felt no pain. *s*) He got back to *his* people and *u*) told them that many of their people had been killed at the battle. *w*) The next morning something black came from his mouth. His face was contorted. *y*) He was dead.

REPRODUCTION NO. 3

a) There were two men fishing in a boat when *b*) the sea got foggy and *stormy*. *c*) The men had *always heard* that when the sea got that way a ghost would appear. *e*) The men *rushed back* to land and hid behind a log. *d*) They saw a canoe coming with five men in it. The men came up to them and *h*) told them that there was a war going on in Kalama and *g*) they *needed* help. *i*) One of the men said that his relatives were expecting him home. *j*) The men from the canoe told the other man that he had no relatives and that he was to come with them. The man was wounded in the battle *s*) and went home and *u*) told his people that many of their people were dead. *w*) The next morning they found the man with something black coming out of his mouth. *y*) The man was dead.

REPRODUCTION NO. 4

a) There were *three* men fishing in a boat one day when *b*) the sea became foggy and stormy. *c*) The men had *been told* that when the sea gets stormy a ghost appears. *They became frightened e*) and went into shore and hid behind a *large rock*. *d*) Soon a boat with some men in it came *into the island* and *h*) they told the fisherman that there was a war on Kamara. They were going and *k*) they took the man with no relatives with them. When the fighting was over *s*) one of them went home and *u*) told his *family* that *all their relatives* had been killed. *w*) Next morning they found him with black stuff coming out of his mouth. *y*) He was dead.

REPRODUCTION NO. 5

a) There were three *fishermen* in a boat when *b*) the sea *started to get* foggy and stormy. *c*) They were told that whenever the sea gets stormy a *big white* ghost appears. *e*) They went ashore and hid behind a large rock.
d) Some men came to the island in a boat. *h*) They said that a war *had started* on Karma, *and that they were taking all single men with them*. After the fighting was over *s*) one man went back to his family and *u*) told them that all of their relatives had been killed. *He got up* the next morning, *w*) black rolled out of his mouth and *y*) he fell dead.

REPRODUCTION NO. 5 OF THE SECRETARY STORY

There were two girls who went to Europe after graduating from business college. One worked for the Ambassador of Maintailin. She wrote her sister letters. The Ambassador told her not to write anything about his business in her letters. One day she found a letter on his desk that said the city in which her sister lived was going to be bombed. She had already written some letters to her sister so she couldn't write any more. So she decided to walk to see her sister because she was only fifteen kilometers away. So she walked to her sister and met her *in the middle of* the path while their two countries were being bombed.

1. IMPORTERS' REPRODUCTIONS OF THE ORIGINAL VERSION OF THE GHOST STORY

Reproduction No. 1 is a rather poor account of the story, and, even though it achieves a high importation score (see Table 18), it is quite disconnected, especially the first half of it. Nevertheless, it is not as disconnected as its counterpart, the nonimporters' reproduction No. 1 of the original version, which, in spite of achieving the same high importation score, has a lower redundancy index (see Table 20). This suggests that here the importers' importations enhanced redundancy to a somewhat greater extent than nonimporters' importations.

The major importations, in the present case, cluster in the second half of the story, whereas the first part suffers more from theme loss [themes b) and c) are wholly absent]. Theme g) enters abruptly and fails to indicate who made the INVITATION. After theme l), WAR-TRIP, the account becomes confused: there is no RETREAT, REALIZATION is confused, and "he was not sick" is transformed to "he was not frightened," thereby leveling the ENIGMA. Also conspicuous are the change from "rested" to "went to sleep," and the importations "splash" and "the people found him."

The title of reproduction No. 2, "War and Ghosts," hints that this account has lost the point of the story. Theme p), the important REALIZATION, is merely tacked on at the end, just as in the original version reproductions in the Exploratory Experiment. Here, however, it is not wholly disconnected; this S tries to make sense of the ghost element by means of a major importation that integrates the ghost idea into the body of the story: "The people thought the warriors who came back were ghosts." This is strikingly explicationlike or rationalized (in Bartlett's sense).

The first half of reproduction No. 2 is highly fragmented, and a marked decrease in accuracy and redundancy is apparent—six additional themes are lost, and, in spite of a high importation score, its redundancy index dips to 4.67. In this case, therefore, the importations fail to sustain the account's redundancy. Themes *g*) and *h*), INVITATION and WAR-PLANS, both drop out completely, perhaps because of the abrupt way they were introduced in the previous reproduction, and the ambiguity that lay in their being enclosed in quotation marks yet not attributed to any actor. The importation "what shall we do" is interesting because it seems, more than anything else, to express this *S*'s perplexity with the story.

In spite of the bad beginning, in the post-BATTLE part of the story this *S* begins to tie things together and make some sense out of the confusion in her stimulus story. For example, she introduces conjunctions to organize the material: "many were killed *but* some returned *and* told . . ." This use of conjunctions (which, incidentally, the redundancy analysis fails to capture) was most characteristic of the importers.

Although the title of reproduction No. 3 connects the "warriors" with the "ghosts," the body of the account fails to include this idea. In fact, it makes no mention of ghosts at all. Aside from this loss of theme *p*), REALIZATION, there is no further theme loss in this reproduction, and, on the whole, it seems to tighten up the account somewhat. The importation "what shall we do"—which did not seem to serve any purpose in No. 2 except to reflect the *S*'s perplexity—drops out.

Reproduction No. 4 further abbreviates the account. The remnants of theme *m*), the BATTLE, drop out (the only allusion to any fighting in No. 3 was "many of the warriors were killed"). Similarly theme *u*), REVELATIONS, which had become a minor issue in No. 3, is squeezed out entirely. The title also drops out; it had ceased to have a relation with the story since REALIZATION was missing. A striking contradiction occurs at the end: "he awoke" is followed by "he was dead." It would be surprising indeed if this strange sequence survived in the subsequent reproduction.

In reproduction No. 5 theme *v*), the ENIGMA, drops out. In No. 4 it was certainly incongruous since, although "it didn't seem to hurt," he died nonetheless. In No. 5, *S* simply accepts that he must have been hit. On the whole, this account is only a remnant of the story—compare it with this *S*'s reproduction of the Secretary

Story. It is striking how relatively well the Secretary Story survived serial reproduction and how well the redundancy analysis reflected this differential collapse (see Table 20).

2. NONIMPORTERS' REPRODUCTION OF THE ORIGINAL VERSION OF THE GHOST STORY

The lead-off member of the nonimporter chain gives a more accurate and complete reproduction of the original version than does the lead-off member of the importer chain, and it undergoes the same degree of importation. Nevertheless, a stylistic difference is clearly detectable that corresponds to its lower redundancy index. Notice how staccato and choppy the account is, how much shorter are its sentences, how abrupt its flow. On the whole, the nonimporters tended toward a sparer, more telegraphic style even where they imported. This characteristic did not always show up, as it did in the present case, in the redundancy analysis.

In reproduction No. 1 theme h), WAR-PLANS, is missing, as is theme p), the vital REALIZATION. Theme n), the RETREAT, is stated along with part of the ENIGMA, but in a very disconnected and ambiguous way that led to difficulties in subsequent reproductions.

The choppiness of No. 1 is also conspicuous in No. 2. Just as in the importers' reproductions of the original version, themes b) and c), ATMOSPHERE and SOMETHING UP, are dropped completely. (These ambiguous and gappy themes were ones that I had explicated in the explicated version.) Theme d), WAR-CRIES, also drops out. These three themes were stated very abruptly with no preparation or redundancy in No. 1, and this may have contributed to their present loss. The BATTLE episode is sharply abbreviated here, and theme n), the RETREAT, is changed in such a way as to reduce the confusion created in No. 1: the shooting of the Indian is omitted completely and the ENIGMA is separated off and repeated. Finally, theme x), the REACTION OF THE PEOPLE, which in No. 1 was transformed from "cried" to "called to him," drops out.

Reproduction No. 3 is a very faithful reproduction of No. 2; remarkably little is lost and nothing is added. Only one information unit is changed: "coming" becomes the more graphic "foamed."

Aside from the rather incongruous displacement of theme m), the BATTLE, reproduction No. 4 is a fairly good account of its predecessor, although its relationship to the Ghost Story itself is rather tenuous. The RETREAT drops out, and what remains is a concentration on the ENIGMA in the form of a debate as to whether "the Indian is sick" or not.

In reproduction No. 5 the opening theme drops out, as does theme v), REVELATIONS. (In No. 4 the latter, instead of appearing in a separate sentence as it did earlier, had become reduced to a minor part of the "going home" decision.) Theme m), BATTLE, also drops out, perhaps because of the confusing way in which it was displaced in No. 4 following its marked abbreviation in No. 2. This final reproduction of the chain is a very choppy and disconnected account in which the original story (or, in fact, any story at all) is hardly discernible. On the other hand, how coherent and relatively complete an account of the Secretary Story this No. 5 S gives!

It may be emphasized that, aside from the occurrence of importations, stylistic differences between importers and nonimporters were observable. The importers showed more importation; this did not, however, result in superior reproductions nor did it consistently enhance their redundancy indexes. It should be borne in mind that the two groups were not equal in retention ability—the nonimporters were clearly superior.

3. THE NONIMPORTERS' REPRODUCTIONS OF THE EXPLICATED VERSION OF THE GHOST STORY

Reproduction No. 1 of the explicated version by the nonimporter chain gives a quite complete, accurate, and coherent account of the story—much better than either lead-off member of the original version. It is interesting to observe that this nonimporter abbreviates and condenses and that the abbreviations and condensations occur largely in the themes that I had explicated: e.g., theme c), the OMEN, is reduced to "a good night for ghosts," and theme r), the PROTECTION, is similarly cut down. This account loses theme l), WAR-TRIP (which, however, it implies so well that it returns in reproduction No. 2, theme t), DECISION TO TELL, and theme p), REALIZATION, which drops out cleanly, leaving a gap at that point in the story.

Reproduction No. 2 markedly reduces the story and gives quite a choppy account of it—its sentences are conspicuously brief. This is only partly revealed in the extent of its redundancy-index loss (6.36 to 5.79). This reproduction also contains quite a few importations, but they fail to alleviate its choppiness or enhance its redundancy. Theme *e*), HIDING, drops out (in No. 1, instead of commanding its own sentence, it had become connected with a long sentence: "they tried to hide but could not and . . ."). Theme *n*), the RETREAT, is omitted, PROTECTION idea of theme *r*) is essentially lost, and the ghosts are changed to Indians.

Reproduction No. 3 is an almost word-perfect replica of No. 2, loses no thematic material, maintains the redundancy index, and contains only one minor importation. A few minor changes in it will be mentioned below, because they seem to have had interesting consequences in Nos. 4 and 5.

Like No. 3, reproduction No. 4 loses no thematic material, but it tells the story in a more telegraphic way, omitting some redundancies—e.g., the repetition of the ENIGMA between themes *q*) and *s*). There is an interesting importation at the beginning: "they were Indians." Apparently this is S's attempt to deal with the fact that, although the ghost element is introduced in the OMEN, the previous reproduction does not speak of ghosts again. The ghost omen therefore can only be explained as a kind of false alarm, and this is apparently what S thought, since the importation, coming right after the OMEN, implies "(but they were not ghosts) they were Indians."

The final reproduction is quite confused. It loses only three themes, but they are important ones: theme *c*), OMEN, theme *g*), INVITATION, and theme *y*), DEATH. The first one is replaced by a conspicuously disconnected distortion, "then a ghost came." This may partly result from the fact that No. 4 had written "ghost" in the singular ("it was a good night for ghost"), which is hard to understand. The INVITATION drops out via an interesting sequence of progressive contraction, so common in the Exploratory Experiment's reproductions: in No. 1, "you are going with us"; in No. 2, "you must come with us"; in No. 3, "come with us!"; in No. 4, simply "come . . ."; No. 5 merely goes one step further. Finally, it is instructive to compare this No. 5 reproduction with that of the Secretary Story, which is much more complete and coherent and achieves a very high redundancy index (6.44).

4. THE IMPORTERS' REPRODUCTIONS OF THE EXPLICATED VERSION OF THE GHOST STORY

Even though inferior in retention ability to begin with, the lead-off member of this chain gives the best reproduction of all, not only attesting to the efficacy of explication, but also indicating that explication had a greater effect upon importers. This is a faithful rendition of the story, a flowing narrative with many connectives retained and many added. "Ghosts" is made singular throughout —"the ghost." It seems that, for this S, the Indians are not equated with the ghosts, but rather the ghost is somehow *with* the men. This interpretation would have been contradicted by the line in the stimulus story "oh, they surely are ghosts" which represents the REALIZATION theme, and so this theme is omitted from the reproduction. The account also loses theme v), ENIGMA REPEATED, and theme x), REACTION OF PEOPLE. Theme o), the "INDIAN," though retained, is essentially disconnected, and a gap has been created here. It is not surprising that this theme quickly becomes lost.

Reproduction No. 2 contains many importations and changes, yet the line and sense of the story are well preserved and the structure of the account is even more coherent than its stimulus (the redundancy index rises from 6.05 to 6.16, the only instance in which a Ghost Story reproduction showed an increase in redundancy). Many of its importations seem to add emphasis (as was also true of the lead-off member of the explicated group in the Exploratory Experiment, who was so conspicuously an importer); others serve to tighten the connections of the themes. For example, in theme c), OMEN, "it" (from No. 1) is expanded to "when the ocean became like this," and "to appear" is added to "the ghost"; in theme i), REFUSAL, "I have not told my relatives where I am" (from No. 1) is probably considered too weak and so it is changed to a stronger excuse, "they were expecting him back home"; the RETREAT is expanded from "we must leave" to "let us take this Indian away, he is wounded." Theme l), WAR-TRIP, is lost (in No. 1 it had been reduced to a clause of the BATTLE). Finally, as expected, "INDIAN," theme o), which was so disconnected anl ambiguous in No. 1, drops out.

Reproduction No. 3 loses a number of themes, but, aside from the RETREAT and ENIGMA parts of the story, it remains a rather good account. In theme b), ATMOSPHERE, an interesting transformation occurs: "calm" becomes its opposite, "stormy." This S apparently associates storm rather than calm with a bad omen. "*The* ghost" (of No. 2) becomes "*a* ghost" and then ceases to figure in the story. The BATTLE episode is reduced to one statement about the man getting wounded, and theme q), the ENIGMA, is dropped. It is difficult to understand this major loss except in the light of the fact that it is often this portion of the story for which these Ss are least likely to have appropriate schemas.

More importations are introduced in reproduction No. 4: a third man is added; "they became frightened" is added (this S's schema apparently dictates that people are afraid of ghosts); and an "island" is introduced in the ocean. Theme g), INVITATION, which had become quite minor in the previous reproductions, drops out, and with it goes theme h), REFUSAL.

Aside from two changes, reproduction No. 4 is well preserved in No. 5. The ghost becomes "a big white" one (white is, after all, the color of ghosts), and "they took the man with no relatives" from No. 4 becomes "they were taking all single men." On the whole, however, the story is still discernible in this final reproduction, though it is not as intact as the Secretary Story is.

SUMMARY AND CONCLUSIONS

On the whole, direct examination of these reproductions revealed many of the same phenomena as did the Exploratory Experiment and supported many of its conclusions. The following five general conclusions may be drawn from the present examination.

1. Explication and familiarity clearly proved to be effective variables: both original version chains underwent a rapid and conspicuous collapse in content and structure, while the explicated versions remained comparatively intact. A comparison with the final reproductions of the Secretary Story highlighted this difference, and at the same time showed how much more accurate and coherent than both were the Secretary Story reproductions.

2. The reproductions of nonimporters and importers were stylistically different: the former were generally leaner in structure,

more disconnected, and more abbreviated than those of the importers; the latter seemed more continuous and coherent. The redundancy analysis sometimes failed to reflect this difference, a failure which seems largely due to the fact that it does not deal adequately with conjunctions and connecting clauses. The use of conjunctions was most characteristic of the importers.

3. A high importation score did not always result in increased connectedness and coherence. However, importation increased redundancy more for the importers than it did for the nonimporters. This finding suggests that importers' importations differ from nonimporters' in that they enhance structural coherence. This corresponds to the finding that some importations seemed like explications, others did not. The importers' importations in the explicated version chain for the most part resembled explications (and thereby seemed to facilitate understanding and retention); in the original version their importations were less like explications (e.g., the importation that merely expressed S's perplexity), and therefore often failed to cement the story by reducing gaps and ambiguities, and enhancing redundancy. Their importations sometimes leveled away an important theme (e.g., the ENIGMA theme). Paradoxically, it was the nonimporters' importations which, though they were less frequent, most often seemed truly like explications.

The originally gappy and ambiguous themes were, as in the Exploratory Experiment, the main loci of distortion and loss. It was interesting to observe that, in the explicated version, my explications were abbreviated and condensed *by the nonimporters*. On the other hand the importers seemed to use my explications to good advantage, and their reproductions benefited and were superior to the nonimporters'. This supports the idea of a congruence between the explicated version and the importers' schema functioning that facilitated their assimilation of the story, and accounts for the fact that explication benefited the importers more than the nonimporters.

4. Many of the importations and transformations in the present reproductions seemed clearly to reveal and express the Ss' personal schemas in terms of their understanding of the events in the story based upon their own conceptions and experiences. This occurred more frequently and much more flagrantly than it did in the Ex-

ploratory Experiment. Perhaps this was due to the fact that the Ss were younger and less sophisticated; hence they relied more on recruitment in their schema formation and functioning, and were less critical of their own cognitions. For the same reasons, perhaps, it was more characteristic of the present chains that peripheral and unrelated material, contradictions and incongruous sequences, quickly dropped out.

5. The sequences of thematic loss following progressive contractions of content, shifts in emphasis and rejuxtaposition of themes, creation of ambiguities and opening of gaps, were conspicuous, and followed the same pattern as in the Exploratory Experiment.

4

CONCLUSIONS AND IMPLICATIONS

This study opened with three broad questions: (1) What processes underlie people's reproductions of a story? (2) Which properties of stories facilitate and hinder recovery? (3) Do people differ systematically in the way they retain and reproduce stories? The experiments reported in Chapter 3, taken together with the Exploratory Experiment, permit some answers. This closing chapter, which is organized into three parts according to the three questions, summarizes the main findings, formulates a number of general conclusions and tentative hypotheses set in the theoretical framework that guided the research, and discusses further lines of research. Like the Discussion and Conclusions section of Chapter 2, it also reviews some relevant literature and takes up some theory.

PROPERTIES FACILITATING AND HINDERING REMEMBERING

Explication, familiarity, and coherence emerge as the main stimulus variables in this study. All three proved to facilitate learning and remembering; their absence led to fragmentation, distortion, and forgetting.

The serial reproduction findings suggest that familiarity exerted a greater facilitating effect than did explication. Familiarity with content was most effective in maintaining structural coherence even when it did not prevent substantial loss of content. Moreover, it occasioned less importation and fewer transformations. On the other hand, explication could not prevent the eventual decline of structural coherence, though it did significantly slow its rate. Explication also occasioned less importation and transformation than did the gappy and ambiguous original stimulus. These findings suggest the following theoretical propositions:

1. When a stimulus experience creates a schema organization which is made up of already well-articulated and stable schemas, that schema organization is likely to be well structured and stable (in that it can function to reconstruct the experience more completely, accurately, and coherently; and it does so with less recruitment of extraneous schemas and less transformation of its parts).

2. Schemas which are already present in the individual assure an adequate schema organization, and are more effective than those which have to be mobilized by explicatory links in the stimulus material; i.e., when a schema organization depends upon explications, it has less chance of surviving than if it depends on already present schemas. Nevertheless, such explicatory links go far in assuring an adequate schema organization.

Do explications function by inserting familiar material at unfamiliar and ambiguous places? Is explication wholly a matter of promoting familiarity, or does another factor also underlie its effectiveness as a focus of schema influence? It seems valid to view explication from a structural vantage and to propose that, by reducing gaps or discontinuities, explications enhance connectedness and thereby enhance *meaningfulness*. For, according to many theorists, connectedness is an essential ingredient in meaningfulness. Perhaps a brief digression will sharpen this point.

Learning theorists have, in general, viewed meaningfulness in terms of familiarity, i.e., previous learning which results in associations and expectations. Miller and Selfridge (1950), for example, argue that ". . . the significant distinction is not to be drawn between meaning and nonsense, but between materials that utilize previous learning and permit positive transfer and materials that do not . . . meaningful material is easy to learn, not because it is meaningful per se, but because it preserves the short-range associations that are familiar to the Ss" (p. 183).

However, there is an important difference between such meaningful material as poetry and prose, which have been found to yield relatively small amounts of retroactive inhibition (McGeoch and McKinney, 1934), and lists of discrete meaningful words, which paradoxically give rise to a great deal of interference (Mc-

Geoch and McDonald, 1931; McGeoch and McGeoch, 1936).[27] Newman (1939) concluded, from these findings as well as from his own research, that what is crucial here is the factor of *connectedness*. He rejects such associationistic notions as "verbal pigeonhole" and verbal trace system, and contends that ". . . some concept other than that of associations, bonds, identical elements or the like must be supplied . . . such a concept would require that meaning reside in the structure of organization of the material to be learned, in the organized 'sense' of the story, in a 'context' of meaning which does not consist of indifferent bonds" (1939, p. 70). In other words, meaning is largely a function of the structure of a stimulus experience, with connectedness as its major condition.

This formulation fits well with my findings that when a stimulus story starts out with major gaps, content and structure soon collapse. Such a story also gives rise to efforts on the part of Ss to recruit material to forestall this collapse. To the extent that S has appropriate schemas at his disposal, his attempt will be successful. If he is without them, then his attempts may entail considerable fractionation.

Experimentation on this proposition can take the form of using as Ss experts with varying amounts of knowledge relevant to a stimulus situation.[28] A relevant study would be to examine differences among Ss with equivalent knowledge and interests to see along what other parameters their schema functioning still varies: are there differences in recruitment and fractionation, in stability and coherence? A second experimental approach, which I have recently used, is to try to teach Ss about a relevant topic—to make them expert—to see whether and how such knowledge affects their

---

[27] A recent experiment by Postman and Rau (1957), comparing the recall of lists of nonsense syllables and lists of words, failed to find any difference between them when differential rate of acquisition (words were learned faster than nonsense syllables) was taken into account. The conclusion was that ". . . it appears that nonsense materials are retained at least as well as are meaningful materials. In fact, there are strong indications that free recall is higher for nonsense syllables than for meaningful words" (1957, p. 266).

[28] Allport and Postman found that proper names tended to be leveled out except that ". . . if the Ss' interest or training predisposes them to pay especial attention to proper names, these may be retained" (1947, p. 61). I have recently carried out an experiment which demonstrates this point and at the same time shows the influence of already present highly developed schemas on selective recall.

retention. In view of the fact that I conceive of schemas as concepts rather than as elements of content, in my experiment I taught the Ss concepts rather than contents. One of my expectations was that such concepts would enhance connectedness more than content would.

One of the structural variables that emerged in the present studies is lexical redundancy, which is an index to connectedness. That redundancy plays an important role is reflected in the finding that importations (particularly those that were explicatory) served to enhance redundancy. Moreover, it seemed at times to be specifically the redundancy rather than the fact of explication that was efficacious in inviting importation. The explicated version of the Ghost Story underwent less importation, but the explicated version of the Potlatch Story underwent more. The fact that my explication of these stories had the opposite effect, in the former case increasing redundancy and in the latter case decreasing it, seems to have been the crucial factor. In both cases, it was the less redundant version that suffered more importation. Since redundancy proved to reflect coherence, in which connectedness is an essential ingredient, these findings may simply reflect the fact that many importations served to enhance connectedness and, in that sense, meaningfulness.

Processes Underlying Reproductions of a Story

There was ample evidence in the present findings of the active schema processes which Bartlett considered so important. There was evidence of "rationalization," of "effort after meaning," and of "fit," which seemed directed by the Ss' preconceptions and attitudes (and, I would add, their styles). Many importations, transformations, rejuxtapositions, and changes of emphasis clearly fell into these categories. However, many, if not all, of these changes might also be conceptualized in the Gestalt terms of leveling, sharpening, and assimilation.

These three Gestalt categories were sufficient for Allport and Postman (1947) to classify the changes they found when they transmitted rumors verbally. Their predisposition toward learning theory was revealed in their emphasis on the third category; they concluded that ". . . the dominant prong in the process seems to be assimilation, for in all these experiments it is evident that past experience, linguistic habit, cultural forms of thought, and personal motives and attitudes set the stage for the pattern of distortion that occurs and determine just what shall be leveled out and what sharpened" (p. 144).

However, it seems to me that such phenomena can be better conceptualized as active constructions *based upon* a schema organization rather than as the reproduction *of* a trace system even with widespread assimilation. The emphasis is thus placed more on the articulating, abstracting, and comprehending aspect of the process.

What sort of concept is schema? Where does it fall in psychological theory?

Zangwill (1937) has shown that the concept of schema overlaps with the concept of "set." This fact, however, does not make the concept very precise, since, in spite of the fact that set is a ubiquitous concept in psychology, Gibson (1941), after thorough study, found that any common core of meaning was surprisingly difficult to isolate. The concept of set arose in the Würzburg school of psychology because, in their studies of such simple phenomena as reaction time, it was clear that S's reaction was frequently determined by his aim rather than by the stimuli or their associative tendencies. The idea of set, propounded to account for this finding, was conceived of as distinct from association, from reaction, and from ordinary "conscious contact." However, as Gibson points out, the concept has subsequently been defined and used in many ways, and ". . . the assumption that attitudes are determinants which are *external* to learning and also to action has persisted for forty years side-by-side with the contradictory assumption that attitudes are products of learning and are forms of action" (1941, p. 783).

It becomes clear in Gibson's study that the concept, however it is defined and used, refers to the process of thinking. Hebb (1949) has pointed out that the element common to all of the uses of set ". . . is the recognition that responses are determined by something else besides the immediately preceding sensory stimulation" (p. 5). Bartlett made just this point in developing the concept of schema. Hebb calls his "something else" the *autonomous central process* and says it is similar to Morgan's (1943) *central motive state*, Beach's (1942) *central excitatory mechanism*, and Kleitman's (1939) *interest*. Each of these concepts refers to a relatively autonomous component of behavior: a process that must somehow be conceived of as internal to the organism, as having a degree of autonomy from external stimulation, and as playing a more or less central determining role in behavior.

The virtue of Bartlett's schema concept lies in its emphasis that such internal dispositions (which are steadily implicated in behavior) function in neither a passive nor a piecemeal way. Rather their influence takes the form of such active processes as seeking "meaning" (i.e., connectedness), striving after "fit" (i.e., context), and the like. The term set, since it connotes a preparatory activity, seems at once less active and too general and all-embracing, referring as it often does to postures of a purely muscular and physical kind. The term schema, on the other hand, is more dynamic while also more limited, and designates only cognitive factors that not only prepare but, by means of fractionation and recruitment, also shape and assimilate experience.

I have borrowed the terms fractionation and recruitment from Hebb (1949) and, as I have used these concepts, they correspond roughly to the Gestalt processes of sharpening, leveling, and assimilation respectively. In spite of the fact that they are still vague and ill-defined conceptions, I found them useful for understanding the reorganization and rearticulation of schemas as revealed in the reproductions—a way of conceptualizing the many importations, substitutions, fragmentations, and skeletonizations which clustered around the gaps, ambiguities, and less familiar parts of the story. The relationship that emerged between explication and importation is instructive in this regard, because both had the general effect of enhancing redundancy and both frequently seemed to converge on the recruitment process.

Some importations seemed to serve no other function than to *sharpen*; i.e., those which merely emphasized, added color, or the like, without explaining, clarifying, or relating the material. Nevertheless, the majority of importations seemed clearly to have an explicatory function. I would stress the finding that only those importations which were explicatory seemed materially to influence subsequent reproductions and play a conspicuous facilitating

Individual Differences in Retention and Reproduction

role. The role of importations, the conditions under which they will take one form or the other, and the way they coordinate with fractionation to serve the economy of schema formation and operation, need further study.

I systematically studied two individual difference variables—retention ability and importation tendency—both of which proved to be relatively stable and relatively independent properties of Ss. At the beginning of this monograph, I contended that Bartlett's failure to concern himself with the "detailed workings" of schemas was related to his lack of concern with veridicality and with fundamental individual differences. To what extent, then, has my concern with these variables revealed such "detailed workings"?

The main result of my search for individual differences was the attention I came to pay to processes which revealed fractionation and recruitment, and to the over-all structural coherence of stimuli. An S's ability to form, use, and maintain the structure of schemas seemed only partly an outcome of his access to appropriate schemas in the form of knowledge about the stimulus experience; it also depended on his mode of schema functioning. On these questions, however, my findings are no more than suggestive and further experiments are needed to learn whether individuals may vary independently with respect to content and style, and how the two are interrelated.

Retention ability is, without doubt, a highly complex variable. Many parameters will need to be studied before we have a fuller understanding of it. Research may need to take into account the possibility that, in addition to different memory modalities (Wallach and Auerbach, 1955), there are various kinds of memory, e.g., digit span—the individual's ability to retain experience for a brief time span to which James applied the concept of short-term memory which ". . . comes to us as belonging to the rearward portion of the present space of time, and not to the genuine past" (1890, p. 647). The genuine past is the province of long-term memory where the effects of experience are learned and retained.

There has also been some recent speculation that a fifteen-minute variety of memory also exists as an independent ability.

A number of experimental and theoretical questions arise: (1) Does the same ability underlie these types of memory? (2) How are they related to each other, e.g., what learning principles are involved in the development of long-term memory from short-term memory? With regard to the first question, the present studies pointed up a positive correlation between retention ability and I.Q., suggesting that there is a broad ability parameter which underlies retention ability. One may speculate that such variables as ability to image and fantasy, available vocabulary, willingness to cooperate in an intellectual task, and the like, are also related to retention ability.

With regard to importation, my findings were unequivocal in their testimony to its validity as a parameter of individual difference. However, with regard to two subsidiary questions, they were inconclusive though highly suggestive: (1) concerning the function of importing in importers and in nonimporters; and (2) concerning the relationship between importation style and the presence of explication in a stimulus.

As I have repeatedly indicated, importing sometimes was clearly explicatory in function (assimilating and connecting), at other times merely decorative and extraneous (sharpening). Interestingly enough, for the nonimporters it rarely seemed to be the latter; most of the decorative importations were contributed by the importers. Moreover, though for the most part the importations that occurred on the unfamiliar and unexplicated stimulus stories were explicatory in nature, the importers' importations on the original version in Experiment III were largely decorative.

Experiments II and III produced conflicting results concerning the relationship between importation and explication: in one case explication benefited the nonimporters more than the importers, while in the other case the reverse was true. The former finding suggested that importation and explication are congruent and overlapping—the importers benefited not as much because their own importations were explicatory. The latter finding suggested that a differential assimilation may have occurred as a result of the "fit" between the importers' schema organization and the organization of the stimulus. To resolve this contradiction, further research is needed to determine when explication will favor importers, and when it will favor nonimporters.

I have conceived of cognitive style as the temporal-sequential and structural patterning of schemas—broadly, as their ongoing processes of operation. It follows therefore that styles are not all-or-none affairs, present in some and absent in others; rather they represent varying degrees of reliance upon what are basic cognitive processes. Styles are used by all individuals under certain extreme stimulus conditions, while in other situations individual differences will emerge. Most Ss did some importing when the stimulus story was gappy, ambiguous, and too long to be memorized. Most of them also showed skeletonization. However, only with respect to importing was I able to devise a test that can maximize the process, provide quantifiable indices of it, and so permit individual differences to be assessed reliably. A technique needs to be worked out which can do the same for skeletonization.

What other cognitive styles may be involved in remembering? I explored the use and retention of imagery, and this too may deserve further study. In addition, the reproductions also gave indications of another possible style: certain Ss seemed to strive after the meaning or structure of the stimulus, while others strove primarily for detail.[29] It might be profitable to study good retainers who grasp and capture the character and essence of the stimulus material, and compare them with good retainers who do not. Perhaps a style is reflected here that is partly independent of importation-skeletonization, one that might be termed a global versus

[29] Gomulicki (1956) recently conducted a systematic study of qualitative individual differences in the recall of meaningful material. He succeeded in isolating two recall types: he calls them *changers* and *condensers*. The one tends to alter material in recall, the other tends to omit material. The former probably overlaps significantly with my importation category. In this respect note Gomulicki's finding that ". . . one effect of the changers' efforts not to omit anything of consequence was that they introduced extraneous material, or repeated themselves half again as often as did the condensers . . ." (1956, p. 395).

Gomulicki, incidentally, presents a review of the various dichotomies and categories psychologists have suggested to differentiate people with regard to their manner of recall. Among them are Binet's "describers" versus "observers," Stern's "preservers" versus "reorganizers" (Stern observed that certain individuals are inclined to give a simple enumeration of disconnected features of their experiences, while others spin a yarn in which explanation and evaluation are all mixed up in the report itself), and Katona's persons who rely on "individual traces" of discrete items versus those who rely on "structural traces" of organized idea systems.

specific style. There was also a suggestion in the reproductions of some individual differences in how Ss dealt with the emotional components of the stimulus; some syncopated and distorted it, others leveled and erased it.

This leads to the final problem: the relationship between schemas, cognitive styles, and personality as a whole. It seems likely that certain personality types will be found to accompany certain styles.[30] When a psychologist turns his attention to problems of personality theory today, he is likely to think in psychoanalytic terms. Psychoanalytic practice and theory—a theory that has unquestionably exerted a profound influence upon psychology as a whole—offers the most comprehensive as well as the most challenging body of ideas in this field. It might therefore be a step in the direction of theoretical richness and completeness if we could integrate the concept of schema with some of the central psychoanalytic concepts and show how cognitive style may fit into its framework. It will be my aim to show that schemas may profitably be conceived of as *ego apparatuses*, or as structures in the realm of conflict-free ego functioning, in Hartmann's sense of the term (see Rapaport, 1951). To do this necessitates a discussion of some recent ideas in psychoanalytic theory.

Although psychoanalysis gives a central position to memory, nowhere in its vast literature is there an attempt to advance a systematic theory of remembering.[31] There is good reason to suppose that such a theory had to wait for the development of psychoanalytic ego psychology. Before ego psychology, the emphasis of psychoanalysis was more on forgetting than on remembering—its concepts were best suited for this task; e.g., the concepts of censorship and defense, of unconscious impulse and conflict.

Hartmann (1939) was the first to recognize that a comprehensive theory of remembering must take into account the conflict-free sphere of the ego which functions with structured and

---

[30] Stern (1938), for example, claims that there are countless people in whose consciousness the past has little temporal organization, and so mixture and blurrings occur. It can be conjectured that these people are hysterics who rely heavily upon recruitment.

[31] Lewy and Rapaport (1944) come closest to undertaking this task in a paper that set out to clarify the psychoanalytic conception of memory and show its relationship to "academic" memory theories. See also Rapaport's more recent contributions (1951, 1957, 1958).

stable apparatuses. On the whole, one can associate psychoanalytic ego psychology with a growing emphasis on the role of relatively stable and autonomous intrapsychic structures. For example, Klein's intention (1951, 1954) is to show how the effect of drives and needs upon perception is channeled by structures—what he calls styles or system-principles—even though many of these structures are themselves probably crystallizations of recurring motivational states.

This process of crystallization or structure formation is a central and crucial learning phenomenon. Hartmann has described it in these words: "An attitude which arose originally in the service of defense against an instinctual drive may, in the course of time, become an independent structure, in which case the instinctual drive merely triggers this automatized apparatus . . . but, as long as the automatization is not controverted, [the drive] does not determine the details of its action. Such an apparatus may . . . through a change of function turn from being a means into a goal in its own right" (1939, p. 26).

Hartmann has proposed the concept of *automatization* to denote the process by which ego apparatuses in general and cognitive structures in particular are formed. The term is most directly applicable to motor activities, where, with increasing exercise of an action, the intermediate links disappear from consciousness. Hartmann assumes, however, that automatization applies not only to the motor apparatus, but also to perception and thinking as well.

The term automatization seems to have unfortunate connotations. For example, it suggests the mechanical and static properties of learned behavior. Nevertheless Hartmann's formulation may be applicable to the process of schema formation, and may serve to give us a sense of how these internal structures are genetically and topographically related to motivations and to drive dynamics in general.

By conceiving of schemas as ego apparatuses, we provide ourselves with a conceptual tool that can deal with changes in cognitions along the entire scale of transformations: from flagrant distortions of an autistic kind at one end to reality-oriented (i.e., "good") changes of a rationalizing and explicating kind at the other. At the former end of the scale is a loss of autonomy with a corresponding invasion (recruitment) into schema structure of drive and drive-related schemas—perhaps a regression to an earlier developmental stage. At the other end are schemas functioning with a minimum of intrusion from drive and drive-related schemas, but with a recruitment of conceptually related schemas. The distinction is between drive-related and conceptually related schemas.

Klein's structural concept, "style," also has overtones which the alternate term "system-principle" does not. Nevertheless I have used it in this monograph because it is less unwieldy and because some of the extra connotations seem desirable at this point. The concept provides a way to conceptualize an important dimension of schema operation, namely, the temporally extended mode of operation of schemas. Moreover it may provide a way to understand the roots and functions of this parameter.[32]

In addition to these concepts and ideas, there are two general and basic ideas in psychoanalysis which might profitably be applied to learning theory in general and to memory in particular. One is the basic distinction between structure and cathexis, the other is the assumption of a hierarchical layering of all psychic functioning. With regard to the latter, Rapaport has stressed two fundamental kinds of organization: a drive organization and a conceptual organization. He writes: "Memories are originally (early in the life of an organism) organized around drives and arise in consciousness as representations of these drives when drive-tension rises. Later on, as the pertinence of the memory to partial drives is established, this drive-organization yields to the conceptual organization" (1951, p. 630).

These two organizations are related to Freud's concepts of *primary* and *secondary process* (1900). The drive organization of memory operates by the primary process, where the laws of logic do not apply, and ". . . ideas belong with a drive and all of its representations." Then the secondary process comes into play and

[32] Dr. R. R. Holt has raised the issue of whether style is properly a term for a "specific type of defense" or refers to "conflict-free modes or qualities of adaptation." In a personal communication he writes: "This distinction cannot always be made, and no doubt styles sometimes have the effect of keeping something conflict-free. But one can look at the outcome and ask if there is still evidence of not-wholly-integrated conflict in it—can you distinguish between structurally motivated importations and projective ones? Anyone with some projective inclination and pressing-enough material to project might be expected to do a little, but, as a conflict-free style, importation would be more clearly demonstrated if you could rule out the projective function (via a study of content)." This point has also been made by Klein (1954).

leads to a transition from a drive organization of cognition to a conceptual organization. Rapaport writes: "This transition is parallel to, and an aspect of, the emergence from drive-sources of attitudes, interests, and strivings as one of the implications of reality-testing and the reality principle. Attitudes, interests, etc., are cathectic processes derived from drive cathexes; their regulation . . . [is determined by] the reality principle and . . . defensive ego formations which arise when drive demands meet reality demands" (Rapaport, 1951, p. 630).

An important idea that permeates psychoanalytic thinking is that the various psychological forces and modes of organization do not replace one another, but rather in some fashion exist side by side. For example, Rapaport writes that, while the conceptual organization itself becomes progressively more autonomous and comes to consist of a hierarchic layering of organization in which the laws of drive organization are balanced against each other, and while this balance progressively shifts with the rising level of hierarchy toward preponderance of the laws of realistic logical organization, nevertheless an ideal purity of these is never achieved. According to Rapaport, the balance achieved between the two memory organizations is an internalized expression of the balance between the needs of the organism and the potentialities of the environment. It is also the balance between neutralized cathexes (i.e., energy distributions which have become autonomous from their drive source) and cathexes of partial or no neutralization.

While all of these ideas and formulations provide a framework for a learning theory, it must be reiterated that no explicit principles of learning or of structure formation exist in psychoanalytic theory. Hartmann shows how automatization may be fitted into the psychoanalytic framework and has a good deal to say about the conditions under which automatisms are suspended or fixated. But as for the principles which govern the formation and specific operation of automatisms and how automatisms function in their relatively conflict-free condition, he does not specify. Klein's styles can be demonstrated in perceptual research, and prove to be crucial to understanding the influence of needs and motives upon perception. However, just like Bartlett's schemas, their particular mode of operation is still unspecified, and is a promising and important subject for research.

BIBLIOGRAPHY

Allport, G. W. & Postman, L. (1947), *The Psychology of Rumor*. New York: Holt.
Babcock, H. (1930), An Experiment in the Measurement of Mental Deterioration. *Arch. Psychol., N.Y.*, No. 117, pp. 105.
Bartlett, F. C. (1932), *Remembering*. Cambridge: Cambridge University Press.
Beach, F. A. (1942), Analysis of Factors Involved in the Arousal, Maintenance and Manifestation of Sexual Excitement in Male Animals. *Psychosom. Med.*, 4:173-198.
Belbin, E. (1950), The Influence of Interpolated Recall upon Recognition. *Quart. J. Exp. Psychol.*, 2:163-167.
Brain, W. R. (1950), The Concept of the Schema in Neurology and Psychiatry. In D. Richter (Ed.), *Perspectives in Neuropsychiatry*. London: Lewis.
Clark, K. B. (1940), Some Factors Influencing the Remembering of Prose Material. *Arch. Psychol., N.Y.*, No. 253, pp. 1-73.
Davis, D. R. & Sinha, D. (1950), The Effect of One Experience upon the Recall of Another. *Quart. J. Exp. Psychol.*, 2: 43-52.
Deese, J. & Hardman, G. W. (1954), An Analysis of Errors in Retroactive Inhibition of Rote Verbal Learning. *Amer. J. Psychol.*, 67: 299-307.
Estes, W. K. (1956), Learning. *Ann. Rev. Psychol.*, 7: 1-38.
Freud, S. (1900), *The Interpretation of Dreams*. New York: Basic Books, 1955.
Gibson, J. J. (1941), A Critical Review of the Concept of Set in Contemporary Experimental Psychology. *Psychol. Bull.*, 38:781-813.
Gomulicki, B. R. (1953), The Development and Present Status of the Trace Theory of Memory. *Brit. J. Psychol., Mongr. Suppl.*, 29:1-94.
——— (1956), Individual Differences in Recall. *J. Pers.*, 24:387-400.
Granit, A. R. (1921), A Study on the Perception of Form. *Brit. J. Psychol.*, 12:223-247.
Hanawalt, N. G. (1937), Memory Trace for Figures in Recall and Recognition. *Arch. Psychol., N.Y.*, No. 216, pp. 89.
Harris, Z. S. (1952), Discourse Analysis. *Language*, 28:1-30.
——— (1954), Distributional Structure. *Word*, 10:146-162.
Harrower, M. R. (1933), Organization in Higher Mental Processes. In *Smith College Studies in Psychology*, No. 4. Northampton, Mass., pp. 381-444.
Hartmann, H. (1939), *Ego Psychology and the Problem of Adaptation*. New York: International Universities Press, 1958.
Head, H. (1920), *Studies in Neurology*, 2 Vols. London: Hodder & Stoughton and Oxford University Press.
Hebb, D. O. (1949), *The Organization of Behavior*. New York: Wiley.
——— & Foord, E. N. (1945), Errors of Visual Recognition and the Nature of the Trace. *J. Exp. Psychol.*, 35:335-348.
Hilgard, E. R. (1948), *Theories of Learning*. New York: Appleton-Century-Crofts.
James, W. (1890), *The Principles of Psychology*. New York: Holt, 1950.
Katona, G. (1940), *Organizing and Memorizing*. New York: Columbia University Press.
Kirkpatrick, C. (1932), A Tentative Study in Experimental Social Psychology. *Amer. J. Sociol.*, 38:194-206.

Klein, G. S. (1951), The Personal World Through Perception. In *Perception: An Approach to Personality*, eds. R. R. Blake & G. V. Ramsey. New York: Ronald Press, pp. 328-355.
——— (1954), Need and Regulation. In *Nebraska Symposium on Motivation*, ed. M. R. Jones. Lincoln, Nebr.: University of Nebraska Press, pp. 224-274.
Kleitman, N. (1939), *Sleep and Wakefulness*. Chicago: University of Chicago Press.
Koffka, K. (1935), *Principles of Gestalt Psychology*. New York: Harcourt.
Köhler, W. (1929), *Gestalt Psychology*. New York: Liveright.
Lashley, K. S. (1930), Basic Neural Mechanisms in Behavior. *Psychol. Rev.*, 37:1-24.
——— (1952), Comments on W. Penfield's: Memory Mechanisms. *Arch. Neurol. Psychiat.*, 67:178-198.
Levitt, E. E. (1956), A Methodological Study of the Preparation of Connected Verbal Stimuli for Quantitative Memory Experiments. *J. Exp. Psychol.*, 52:33-38.
Lewy, E. & Rapaport, D. (1944), The Psychoanalytic Concept of Memory and Its Relation to Recent Memory Theories. *Psychoanal. Quart.*, 13:16-42.
McGeoch, J. A. & Irion, A. L. (1952), *The Psychology of Human Learning*. New York: Longmans, Green.
——— & McDonald, W. T. (1931), Meaningful Relation and Retroactive Inhibition. *Amer. J. Psychol.*, 43:579-588.
——— & McGeoch, G. O. (1936), Studies in Retroactive Inhibition: VI. The Influence of Relative Serial Positions of Interpolated Synonyms. *J. Exp. Psychol.*, 19:1-23.
——— & McKinney, F. (1934), Retroactive Inhibition in the Learning of Poetry. *Amer. J. Psychol.*, 46:19-33.
McNemar, Q. (1949), *Psychological Statistics*. New York: Wiley & Sons.
Miller, G. A. & Selfridge, J. A. (1950), Verbal Context and the Recall of Meaningful Material. *Amer. J. Psychol.*, 63:176-186.
Morgan, C. T. (1943), *Physiological Psychology*. New York: McGraw-Hill.
Newman, E. G. (1939), Forgetting of Meaningful Material During Sleep and Waking. *Amer. J. Psychol.*, 52:65-71.
Noble, C. E. (1955), The Effect of Familiarization upon Serial Verbal Learning. *J. Exp. Psychol.*, 49:333-338.
Northway, M. L. (1940), The Concept of the "Schema." Parts I & II. *Brit. J. Psychol.*, 30:316-325; 31:22-36.
Oldfield, R. C. (1954), Memory Mechanisms and the Theory of Schemata. *Brit. J. Psychol.*, 45:14-23.
——— & Zangwill, O. L. (1942/43), Head's Concept of the Schema and Its Application in Contemporary British Psychology. Part I: Head's Concept of the Schema. Part II: Critical Analysis of Head's Theory. Part III: Bartlett's Theory of Memory. Part IV: Wolter's Theory of Thinking. *Brit. J. Psychol.*, 32:267-286; 33:58-64; 33:113-129; 33:143-149.
Postman, L. & Rau, L. (1957), Retention as a Function of the Method of Measurement. *Univ. Calif. Publ. in Psych.*, 8:217-270.
Rapaport,. D. (1942), *Emotions and Memory*, 2nd ed. New York: International Universities Press, 1950.
——— (Ed.) (1951), *Organization and Pathology of Thought*. New York: Columbia University Press.
——— (1957), Cognitive Structures. In *Contemporary Approaches to Cognition*. Cambridge: Harvard University Press.
——— (1958), The Theory of Ego Autonomy: A Generalization. *Bull. Menninger Clin.*, 22:13-35.

Stern, W. (1938), *General Psychology from the Personalistic Standpoint.* New York: Macmillan.
Tresselt, M. E. & Spragg, S. D. S. (1941), Changes Occurring in the Serial Reproduction of Verbally Perceived Materials. *J. Genet. Psychol.,* 58:255-264.
Wallach, H. & Auerbach, E. (1955), On Memory Modalities. *Amer. J. Psychol.,* 68:249-257.
Werner, H. & Kaplan, B. (1956), The Developmental Approach to Cognition: Its Relevance to the Psychological Interpretation of Anthropological and Ethnolinguistic Data. *Amer. Anthrop.,* 58:866-880.
Williams, M. (1950), The Effects of Experimentally Induced Needs upon Retention. *J. Exp. Psychol.,* 40:139-151.
Winch, W. H. (1911), Some Relations between Substance Memory and Productive Imagination in School Children. *Brit. J. Psychol.,* 4:95-125.
Wolters, A. W. (1933), On Conceptual Thinking. *Brit. J. Psychol.,* 24:133-143.
Woodrow, H. (1940), Interrelations of Measures of Learning. *J. Psychol.,* 10:49-73.
——— (1946), The Ability to Learn. *Psychol. Rev.,* 53:147-158.
Woodworth, R. S. (1938), *Experimental Psychology.* New York: Holt.
Wulf, F. (1922), Über die Veränderung von Vorstellungen (Gedächtnis und Gestalt). *Psychol. Forsch.,* 1:333-373.
Zangwill, O. L. (1937), A Study of the Significance of Attitude in Recognition. *Brit. J. Psychol.,* 28:12-17.

ON PERCEPTION, EVENT STRUCTURE,
AND PSYCHOLOGICAL ENVIRONMENT

PART 3

ON PERCEPTION, EVENT STRUCTURE, AND PSYCHOLOGICAL ENVIRONMENT

Selected Papers

by

FRITZ HEIDER

CONTENTS

A Note to the Reader   vii

Author's Introductory Remarks   xi

1   THING AND MEDIUM   1

2   THE FUNCTION OF THE PERCEPTUAL SYSTEM   35

3   THE FUNCTION OF ECONOMICAL DESCRIPTION IN PERCEPTION   53

4   ENVIRONMENTAL DETERMINANTS IN PSYCHOLOGICAL THEORIES   61

5   THE DESCRIPTION OF THE PSYCHOLOGICAL ENVIRONMENT IN THE WORK OF MARCEL PROUST   85

6   ON LEWIN'S METHODS AND THEORY   108

Bibliography   121

A Note to the Reader

Fritz Heider's work has belatedly been attracting a steadily growing circle of admirers. It has had over the years a significant, if relatively unobtrusive, impact on some of the most important theorists of our time, notably Kurt Koffka, Kurt Lewin, and Egon Brunswik. More recently, Heider's influence has been detectable in perception theory, for example, in the work of James Gibson. Still, his writings cannot be called "popular."

The paradox of the relative obscurity of Heider's work among psychologists generally and the esteem in which it is held by those familiar with it is perhaps in keeping with the contemporary psychological scene. These are restless years in psychology's history, with quick infatuations, equally rapid disenchantments, and an unscholarly impatience for dramatic returns. There is, moreover, the tidal wave of published words, pressing relentlessly on one's professional conscience, and allowing barely time enough for scanning the immediately relevant, let alone more. It is natural enough, I suppose, for so many of us to take refuge in the easiest means of survival, of reading little at all or only the most easily read. In the general skirmish for readers, it is understandable that author and reader alike fall victim to Flesch counts, promotional zeal, the eye-catching metaphor, and the high-sounding Intervening Variable. In the general din, what fate can we expect for one scholar's grudging output of papers, widely separated in time, tightly—even difficultly—written, bone-dry of polemic and of the dazzling metaphor, and disinclined to promote the potential significance of his ideas beyond the immediate context? It is to be hoped that Heider's influence will be broadened and accelerated by the recent publication of his book, *The Psychology of Interpersonal Relations* (New York: Wiley, 1958). This latest and most ambitious of his works brings to fruition, in a theory of how people perceive other people, germinal ideas that were formulated more than thirty years ago in "Thing and Medium" and "The Function of the Perceptual System."

These two papers, recognized by specialists as classics in the literature on perception, appear in the present monograph for the first time in English. One would have to look far and perhaps unavailingly to match them for their detailed exposition of the differences between the "things" or "objects" of perception and the carriers or "mediators" of things, considerations that help deepen understanding of Koffka's and Brunswik's more popular distinction between "distal" and "proximal" stimuli. The two papers contain the most probing analysis of the nature of "stimulus" to be found anywhere. These and other papers in the present collection have an obvious relevance to a variety of current issues in the fields of perception and thinking, and are an indispensable background for an understanding of Heider's book.

A few further words of introduction are in order for the psychoanalytic reader.

The papers in the present monograph are particularly relevant to some of the least investigated yet most pressing problems of psychoanalytic ego psychology—reality testing, adaptation, and structure. Anyone who ponders the concept of "reality testing," with its implication that reality *can* be perceived on its own terms, quickly runs up against paradoxes and dilemmas that are very much unresolved in psychoanalytic theory. For one: if reality is a subjective structure, what does it mean to say that we can effectively contact the *environment's* structure? For another: How can drives play so pervasive a role in the organization of psychic structures and yet our perceptions be as *effective* as they are? Is it not remarkable that perceptual processes *can* reproduce the environment's structures relatively uncontaminated by wish and drive? The starting point for all such questions is a conception of what the structure of the environment itself is, a problem which psychoanalysis is only now beginning to face as it emerges from its preoccupation with the internal environment. Similar problems of specifying environmental structure bedevil psychoanalytic efforts to come to grips with the issue of adaptation.

This very issue of environmental structure stands at the center of Heider's work, and that is why the editors felt it so important to bring this work to the attention of the psychoanalytic reader. Heider's emphasis on the *"macro*physics" of things (in contrast to the reductionist emphasis on *micro*physics), the important distinctions he develops between those parts of the environment which mediate ("medium") and those which are mediated ("thing"), his analysis of how we may distinguish behavioral events attributable to the structure of the environment and those attributable to the structure of the perceptual system—all of these merit close study. It may be mentioned that these considerations are uncommon to most contemporary theories of perception.

Throughout the papers the composition of a "unit"—whether spatial, temporal, or causal—is of central importance to Heider's distinction between "thing" and "medium." The defining properties of a "unit," therefore, come in for extended and penetrating analysis. For the psychoanalytic reader there are implications of great importance to be derived from this discussion of the structure of units. In psychoanalytic ego psychology the concept of structure and the structural point of view have taken the center of the stage. Many problems first tackled by Freud in a dynamic and economic (energy) framework seem, in his own later writings and in those of others, to be essentially structural in nature. And yet the concept of structure itself, for all its currency in contemporary psychoanalytic vocabulary, has not yet been subjected to thorough theoretical scrutiny. Perhaps a necessary preface to such scrutiny is an attempt such as Heider has made to penetrate the essential nature of the concept of structure. The general properties of physical macrostructures which he describes may apply to their subjective counterparts in ego organization.

A unique feature of Heider's approach is his attempt to fathom environmental structure not from the response side—from the inside outward, as it were, as is common in psychological theories—but from the outside inward, that is, by specifying the architectural rules of the extrapersonal world of physical object and event units. The result, then, is an extraordinarily fresh confrontation of the external structures which are assumed but never specified in psychoanalytic notions of reality testing and adaptation.

George S. Klein

Author's Introductory Remarks

The first paper which is presented here in translation is mainly concerned with the problem of how information about the vitally relevant environment reaches the perceiving person. In other words, it deals with the process which starts at the perceived object (the distal stimulus) and which ends with the stimuli impinging on the sense organs (the proximal stimuli). This process lies entirely in the environment and goes on whether or not there is an organism affected by the proximal stimuli. It belongs to what Brunswik has called the ecological phase of the causal sequence. It precedes the phase which occurs within the organism and which so far has been the focus of attention in most studies of perception. Since perception is adapted to the environment, it is obvious that we must be familiar with the environmental structures to which it is adapted if we are to get a comprehensive understanding of it.

In working on this problem it soon became clear to me that in order to describe the processes which link proximal with distal stimuli in a way that is relevant to perception, one has to go beyond the mere statement that the proximal stimulus is caused by the distal stimulus. One has to use concepts which have to do with the coordination of manifolds, with order and disorder, with the domination of one system by another, and with constraints: that is, one has to use the concepts which have been elaborated and sharpened in recent years by the new developments of information theory and cybernetics.

However, at the time when I wrote this paper a layman could not get much help from physics and my attempts to get relevant references from physicists were not very successful. In offering this paper at the present time I have to apologize for its amateurishness, and I can only hope that some day its ideas will be expressed in a more exact language.

The second paper, which deals with the function of perception, is a continuation of the first. It is mainly concerned with the processes in the organism, and with the adaptation of these processes to the ecological phase of the whole causal sequence of the perceptual event. Some of these problems had been touched upon in "Thing and Medium"; here they are elaborated, though the basic concepts used are again those having to do with transmission of variety.

The third paper was written recently. In it Russell's theory of perception is brought into relation with the ideas expressed in "Thing and Medium," and in addition the function of economical description in perception is considered. The following question is raised: if it is true that perception often exhibits a tendency toward "Prägnanz" or toward "economical description," how can we relate this feature of perception to the fact that perception, on the whole, leads to veridical results? What properties of the structure of the environment correspond to this general tendency of the perceptual apparatus toward economical description so that the adaptation of perception to the environment is assured?

In the paper on "Environmental Determinants in Psychological Theories" an attempt is made to relate a number of theories to each other. Some of the concepts developed in the two first papers, especially the distinction between proximal and distal stimuli, and the relation between core events and offshoots, provide the background for these considerations. One might say that the results of the analysis of perception were helpful for the comparison of theories in two ways: on the one hand, perception and theory building are both cognitive activities, and one may therefore expect that they will show some similarities. For instance, the data on which theories are built would be analogous to the proximal stimuli in perception, and the theories analogous to percepts. On the other hand, the difference between proximal and distal stimuli (and distal effects) will provide different possibilities for the organization of data: either proximal or distal variables can be considered as the focal variables.

The fifth paper is only indirectly related to the previous ones. In reading Proust one is struck by his excellent phenomenological descriptions and by the fact that in many cases these descriptions are apt illustrations of phenomena pointed out by Gestalt psychology and developmental psychology. A number of these descriptions are presented and discussed.

The paper "On Lewin's Methods and Theory" was given as the Kurt Lewin Memorial Award Address at the meeting of the American Psychological Association in Cincinnati in 1959. Starting with a discussion of some early publications of Lewin, this talk is mainly concerned with his ideas on the role of psychology and his concept of life space.

1

THING AND MEDIUM

We are aware of our environment, but not everything that surrounds us is of equal value for the processes of perception or cognition involved in this awareness. We perceive things that are in immediate contact with our skins and we are often aware of one thing through something else. For instance, we see stars through empty space; we hear the sound of a bell through the air; we measure the pressure of air by means of a barometer; a person's expressive movements tell us something of what he is, etc. These cases are not entirely equivalent, but what they have in common is that the object of perception or cognition does not affect the sense organ directly but by means of some kind of mèdiation.

All this is well known and has been investigated extensively, but only in so far as the subjective side is concerned. Studies have been made of the psychological processes intervening between "sensations" and "images"; but in exploring this psychological aspect the objective physical aspect has been entirely neglected. The question has never been raised whether something that serves mainly as a mediator has not, from a purely physical point of view, characteristics which are different from those of an object of perception. When the ticking of a watch is the object of perception, the vibrations of the air mediate between the watch and the ear. Are the

---

This paper was published in 1926 in the German journal *Symposion* (Verlag der Philosophischen Akademie, Erlangen, 1:109-157). In the following translation a few sections have been shortened. The only change that has been made in the content is a terminological one. In the original text the terms "thing" and "medium" are sometimes used to indicate the distinction between mediated and mediator, sometimes the distinction between solid bodies and intervening space. In this translation we have used the terms "object" and "mediator" for the first distinction, "thing" and "medium" for the second.

The author is greatly indebted to his wife, Grace M. Heider, for help in translating this paper.

two processes, i.e., the ticking and the vibrations, equivalent? Could they exchange their roles in regard to the process of perception? Does the one process act as mediation only because it is closer to the ear than the other process? Or are there differences in the physical structures themselves (regardless of the possible relation to a perceiving organism) which determine whether they play the role of objects or mediators?

We shall see that such structural differences actually exist in the physical world, and try to find out to what extent the nature of the processes of perception and cognition are determined by them.

Distance Perception

The examples cited above have in common the fact that mediation is involved in all of them; but the way in which this mediation is represented in consciousness is very different in the different cases. The barometer which informs us of the air pressure appears in consciousness as something in its own right. The vibrations of the air, on the other hand, are not represented phenomenally in this way. They spend themselves, so to speak, in the process of mediation so that we believe that we hear the ticking directly. In this case we are ordinarily not aware that mediation exists. The mediation of light waves is of the same nature. We do not perceive light waves as things that touch our eyes and refer to something else. We seem to see the mediated object directly.

In order to comprehend fully what distance perception achieves, let us assume that there exists a thinking being to whom the processes in a small limited region of the causal texture of the world are known, and who tries, by scientific methods, to deduce from these processes the nature of the wider world which surrounds him. This task seems to be almost impossible; yet this is actually the task that our organs of perception perform to a considerable degree. It is the process in a very limited region that is at their disposal and that affects them immediately, and on the basis of this process they are often able to report on a very wide environment.

How is it possible that the region of perception does not end with our skin, that we obtain knowledge not only about the small narrow part of the world near us but that we live in a wider world that extends far beyond us? This question, of course, brings us back to our first question about the characteristics of objects and mediators.

Coordination Between Stimulus Pattern and Object Process

Let us consider an example. For instance, I see a stone. The light rays which are reflected by the stone go through the medium until they meet my eyes. It is obvious that the stimulus pattern, that is, the configuration of light rays which meets my eyes, is coordinated to the object, the stone, in a special way. Even a very small change on the surface of the stone changes the stimulus configuration. It is not coordinated to any specific properties of the mediator, i.e., what is in the space between stone and eyes, as long as one can see through this space without obstruction. One cannot recognize from the stimulus pattern how the molecules of the air move, whether wind carries different masses of air, etc., and this is not the fault of the sense organs. There is actually almost nothing in the stimulus pattern that is coordinated to the changes in the mediator.

The Process and Its Substratum

We gain more understanding of these facts when we consider the relation of the process to its substratum. Medium and stone are the substrata of the process; they stay at the same place and the energy wanders through and over these substrata and takes on different forms. The effect of this energy on the substratum varies from case to case. At one extreme is the case in which the process is coordinated to the substratum at a certain place. In whatever form the energy arrives, the process always assumes, at this place, the specific form of the substratum. We might say that such a substratum has a "strong individuality." Outside influences affect it only to a small degree. At the other extreme are cases in which the process is coordinated to what impinges on the substratum from the outside. Everything is taken over and carried on by the substratum. Many different events are possible in it. External rather than internal conditions determine the possibilities which are realized.

Thus we find that the relation between process and substratum can vary. The process may be internally conditioned and coordinated to the substratum; or it may be externally conditioned and coordinated to the impinging events.

For example: three little sticks can be moved independently of each other. If unequal forces are exerted on the sticks, then the three will move in different ways. This motion of the sticks is conditioned externally. However, if I make a rigid connection between the three sticks, they will all move together, and the fact that they move together is conditioned internally. In this case, it is irrelevant how the pressure is distributed. The three sticks will always move in the same way.

The process on the surface of the stone, which reflects the light rays, is a process which is conditioned by the substratum. What happens on the stone and how it happens is but slightly dependent on the particular properties of the impinging light rays, though the event is, of course, caused by them. From the moment at which the sun disappears, no further wave processes occur. But the fact that this particular kind of process occurs, namely, one which contains waves of particular lengths arranged in certain patterns, is determined by the properties of the stone.

The process in the medium, on the other hand, is conditioned externally. What happens in it is dependent on the form of the impinging process; the special state of the medium is to a high degree irrelevant for the form of the process in it.

Composite and Unitary Events

Vibrations whose form is conditioned externally are called "forced vibrations," those whose form is conditioned internally are called "free vibrations." Forced vibrations have, besides the fact that they are conditioned externally, another characteristic, one which they have in common with most externally conditioned processes. Let us consider two cases of movements of a ball.

In one case a ball is pushed so that it rolls across a plane. In another case, the ball is guided by a hand and its movements are dependent at each moment on the movement of the hand. We are certainly justified in saying that the movement of the ball is more externally conditioned in the second case.

The difference between these two cases is the following: in the first case, an influence from the outside is active once, at the beginning of the event, and then the event takes place. Only the fact that the ball stays on the surface is conditioned externally, "forced upon it." In other respects the ball is "free." In the other case, when the ball is guided during the whole movement, the course of events is continuously influenced from the outside.

In the one case, the event forms a unit, that is, one part causes the next and is caused by the previous one. The parts of the movement are dependent on each other and cannot be separated from each other. In the second case, on the other hand, the event is a composite one, the single parts are to a high degree independent of each other, and there is no causal connection between the parts of the event since each part is caused separately from the outside.

All forced vibrations are such composite events in which a continuous influence is exerted from the outside. The vibration is guided by the external cause in each small section.

Free vibration is a unitary event. It is released by an external influence and then takes its course. The process which follows the striking of a tuning fork does not consist of parts that are independent of each other. With a forced vibration one wave could be missing, if the external influence were interrupted for a short time, and the vibration then start anew. With a free vibration, the dropping out of a part is impossible.

Here we can again use the example of the three sticks. If the three sticks are not connected, we can speak of a composite event. The movements of the single sticks are independent of each other. The movement of each stick is caused from the outside and there are three separate influences. If the three sticks are connected, their movement is unitary. In general we can say: a process which is to a great extent externally conditioned (i.e., coordinated to the influence from outside) often consists of parts which are independent of each other.

This holds not only for processes but also, for instance, for the position of parts of a body. The smaller the links of a chain, that is, the less the single parts of the chain are dependent on each other, the more closely it can follow a curve. A stick does not follow a curved line at all because it moves as a whole. A string can follow a curve even more closely than a chain because the position of its parts is largely determined by external conditions. In general, the parts of a pliable body are to a high degree independent from each other, the parts of a solid body dependent on each other.

We can experience this difference directly. We can feel a solid body through a soft one. In a certain sense, cloth is a mediator like the air-filled space through which we hear and see.

One can easily understand that composite events, whose single parts are influenced separately from the outside, are coordinated to external factors to a high degree. Each single element of the composite event has to be produced separately by the external factor and is therefore a messenger which tells about a property of the cause. And the more independent it is from its neighbors, the other messengers, the less is the message altered in the course of transmission. Since there is a multitude of messengers, each of which carries within itself something of the cause, they indicate the cause with a high degree of exactness and point univocally to it. A single wave impact could have been produced in its specificity by any one of many different causes; but the configuration of a manifold of waves could have been produced only by causes of particular properties.

The Spurious Units

The wave which is enforced upon the mediator by the tuning fork shows still another characteristic. We have seen, first, that it is conditioned by external factors, and, secondly, that it is a composite event. But how is it possible to speak about the vibrations as a whole at all if it is really a composite event? We can do this because a forced vibration has the same geometrical characteristics as a free vibration. It appears to be unitary. The beats which are independent of each other nevertheless group themselves at regular intervals. They are arranged in a definite order, something which otherwise occurs only with things whose elements are dependent on each other and not with composite entities. Externally conditioned events often form spurious units because they are produced by a unitary cause. If each beat had an independent cause, it would be very improbable that the beats would show this kind of regularity.

Mediator Processes As Signs

Now we can understand why certain processes can serve as mediators. The light rays which meet the eyes are messengers from the object and represent it. This representation of one entity by another is brought about by the close coordination between the two. The mediator processes which meet our sense organs are spurious units; they have unitary form not because of their own character but because they are coordinated to objects. If one does not refer them to their unitary cause, they are unexplainable. A manifold of light rays which has been produced by a source of light cannot be compared to an event, such as the fall of a stone, which also had its causes but which stands, so to speak, by itself. The light rays have no "reality" without their cause. They contain a strict order which cannot be attributed to the waves themselves since they are independent of each other. The situation is very similar in the case of the order in time of sound waves.

Language Mediation

In this connection it is interesting to examine the properties of the different kinds of language mediations. In writing, for instance, a multitude of forms is produced by different combinations of relatively few elements, the twenty-six letters of the alphabet. The letters can be combined in many different ways because they are independent of each other.

This great number of symbols could also be produced in other ways. There could be, for each word or for each concept, a single sign which would form a unit and not be composed of different elements. Ideographic writing is an example of this method. Most systems of signs, however, use the device of combination in order to produce the necessary number of symbols. The principle of combining independent elements is also used in flag signals or in telegraphic codes. In these cases, the combination of units occurs not in space but in time.

The telegraphic code represents an extreme case. Its manifold of signs is produced by different combinations of just two elements. It is a script which employs only two letters. Again, the elements, that is, the dots and dashes, have to be independent of each other. If they were dependent on each other, if, for instance, an apparatus were employed which could send dots only in groups of four, or in any other fixed combination, the transmission of messages would be greatly restricted. The arrangement of dots and dashes must be determined by the sender, not by the means of transmission. If a combination in time is used, the temporal position of one element has to be independent of the temporal positions of the other elements.

Behavioral Significance of the Environment

We have explained why some physical structures appear as objects of perception and some as mediators. The question now arises of how the perceptual significance of physical entities is related to their behavioral significance.

Not all parts of the environment are of equal significance for our action. We do not have to know how the particles of the air move, but the fact that a chair stands here and a table there is important and can determine our behavior. We have to be able to perceive a car that passes us in the street, the staircase of the house that we are entering. We need to know only a few of the infinite number of possible determinations of the environment in order to be adequately oriented about the possible relationships of our bodies to it. We live only in one particular level of this world; we have no relationship to many of the facts or events of our surroundings, they are not "real" for us. In order to gain more understanding of the significance for behavior of the structures in the environment, we must start with a discussion of the solid units among which we live.

The Units

A chair consists of many parts. How is it possible that it is nevertheless a unit? It is not a matter of subjective apprehension that we combine this multitude of molecules in a certain way. It would hardly be feasible to apprehend one portion of the chair and a part of the adjacent air as a single object. Such a unit would have no meaning. On purely physical grounds the chair is distinguished from its surroundings. If a corner of the chair is pulled, the whole chair follows, but not the air in contact with it. There is a dependence between the parts of the chair which does not exist between the parts of the atmosphere. This dependence consists of the fact that a solid body does not easily yield to external influences. Its parts do not change their positions in relation to each other. Such a unit remains constant to a high degree. The particles of the air separate easily and constantly change their spatial arrangement. Even a swarm of mosquitoes can change it completely.

A change of the same extent in the parts of a solid object would mean its complete destruction. To be sure, a unit can also be taken apart, but this usually takes more energy than is required to move it as a whole. Not all these units are rigid. A coat, a hat, or a rope are units which are not rigid; but they too are things which stand out from the surrounding medium.

The Properties of Wholes

These large units have specific properties as wholes. For instance, a string is something soft. If I take it and lift it, it will change its form in a certain way. If I take the two ends of the string and pull them, the string will be taut; it is then impossible to pull the ends further apart, but I can still bring them closer to each other and put them together. I can cut the string or unravel it—all these possibilities, and many more, are examples of properties of wholes.

Between these properties there exist laws and coordinations which are to a high degree invariant in regard to the properties of the elements. For instance, sphericity is such a whole property. It can be realized with an infinite number of combinations of particles. Each of these combinations has the further property that it can be rolled. A solid ball can always be rolled regardless of the material of which it is made. There are therefore correlations between different properties of wholes beyond the smaller parts and their properties. The exact determination of the relation of the units, which Köhler (1929) calls physical Gestalten, to the units which are discussed here will not be attempted in this paper. The stationary Gestalt in Köhler's sense is a system in equilibrium in which each part changes if another part is changed. Whether this is true in the same sense of a solid body is questionable. In any case, there are physical Gestalten which are not solid bodies. As Köhler emphasizes, these physical Gestalten are of great importance in the physiological processes; but structures like solid units play a more important role than these processes in the world which surrounds us and affects our behavior, and in the conditions of perception outside of the organism.

Parts and Hierarchy

What units actually exist objectively? There are, first of all, tables, houses, and trees; furthermore, there are said to be molecules, atoms, electrons, etc. Then there are the astronomical units, the sun, the moon, etc.

These units are not all of equal rank. The many single tables, chairs, etc., belong to the larger unit of the earth. The objects which form units on the surface of the earth are of a different order of magnitude than the earth itself. The earth belongs to a higher order of unit, that is, the order of the heavenly bodies. Objects such as tables, chairs, and so forth, are subordinate to these units. A unit the size of a table is in turn superordinate to the smaller units of which physics treats. There is thus a hierarchy of bodies, the larger ones containing the smaller ones.

In other words, there are parts in the world. One could very well imagine a world which contains no parts, in which two units never stand in the relation of part to whole. Each unit of this world would be an irreducible element. There would be no superordinate units, that is, several units would never unite to form a complex for even a short time. But this is not the case with our world. It possesses a different structure with larger and smaller units; the larger units have parts. The things among which we live on the surface of the earth, to which we ourselves belong, and the laws of which are so important for our lives belong to one particular stratum within this hierarchy. They have their properties, which, as we have seen, are invariant in regard to the units of smaller orders. Thus there exists a stratum of relationships which contains only things of a certain order and which, on the whole, is without relation to the higher and lower orders. It is not particularly important for the larger units how the smaller units behave. There are few coordinations which connect the lower strata with the upper strata; we can find very few events involving the smaller units which have coordinated consequences among the thing units. A releasing process would be an example of such an event; for instance, a case in which an effect is released in the stratum of things by processes in the stratum of molecules. What would it mean for our world if such cases were frequent? It would mean that events of our everyday life could originate in a region that is below the threshold of our senses, in a stratum which is inaccessible to us. Influences from a mysterious nothing would produce changes in the objective scene. Suddenly a table which the moment before was entirely at rest would fall down, a chest would explode, or a hole would be burned in a piece of paper. We would say, "Things have the property of burning up or falling down easily without any perceptible reason." Properties like "explosiveness" would be much more frequent.

Fortunately, however, our world is much more exposed to our view, and for the most part it is possible to perceive the causes of events. A chest does not usually move unless there is a visible cause for its movement, that is, unless the cause belongs to the order of things. Causations which ascend from the stratum of smaller units into that of larger units are relatively rare. That is also the reason why man is without power to influence the planets and the stars. However much we move around, change or burn the things on the surface of the earth, none of the planets will be affected.

To be sure, collective events of a lower order can have effects on a higher order as in the case of wind, burning of gasses, etc. But then it is an aggregate that has the effect and not the single individual events. These processes really belong to the higher order.

One could easily suppose that the opposite case, in which causations descend from a higher order to a lower one, is of frequent occurrence, but this also is very rare. If the earth shakes, then the things in the rooms of men shake with it and fall; if I move my hand through the air, the molecules are pushed aside. But then the effects in the region of the smaller units are again mass processes, and it is difficult to find coordinations which connect a particular event of the lower order with a particular event of the higher order. There may be certain movements of the earth which have only the effect of making a specific chest or table fall down. However, they are not characterized as special events in other respects. The fall of objects during earthquakes is only an accidental part of a mass event. In the same way, it is not probable that I could produce definite molecular events by the movements of my hand, for instance, make a certain molecule move in a particular way.

One could suppose that in the case of freely falling bodies there is a causation in which a larger unit affects the region of things. But as in the previous examples, terrestrial gravitation, too, produces only mass events in the lower stratum. The bodies are all more or less heavy, and again there is no coordination between particular events. Moreover, gravitation shows a special property: it is constant for the things on the surface of the earth, and therefore it cannot be a true cause of events, even for collective mass events. In naïve thinking, the effect of this constant condition is not felt and is therefore neglected. Because it remains constant the relation to the earth is treated as a property of things, and in daily life a sufficient interpretation is that the fall of a stone is caused by the fact that its support is removed.

If we consider how difficult it is for the physicist to produce individual molecular events, and that in the end he is able to bring about only collective events in the lower order, we realize again the rarity of causal connections between events of two different orders of magnitude.

The Things on the Surface of the Earth

Between the astronomical units there exist "simple relations," that is, relations which can be easily represented: the spatial-temporal framework is recognizable in the changes and laws of these units. The same is more or less true for the relationships between units of atomic and subatomic orders.

The things on the surface of the earth behave differently. They almost never move in regular curves. The gross simple relationships in which they stand to each other as gravitational bodies do not play an important role. The movements of these objects are never determined by the gravitational relation between them. The effects of this relation are nullified by the strength of the earth's gravitation, which, however, only rarely determines the movement of the objects; namely, when they are falling freely.

The movement of a freely falling body is one of the few events within our behavioral world in which the geometry of the free interaction of two units becomes evident. It exists as a latent property in the weight of the body. However, we have seen that the movements of freely falling bodies cannot be considered as a causal coordination between events of two different orders of magnitude.

Since the simple gravitational relationships between the units are nullified, it is possible that the more subtle and more manifold relationships, which come into play when bodies come into contact with each other, are of much greater importance. A ball is not very different from a cube in regard to its effects as a gravitational mass; however, if both of these units are held by gravitation to a larger unit, the difference between their forms is essential for their actual movements.

The organism lives and shapes its world among these smaller units, which we shall call "things." The things acquire manifold relations few of which are of a simple geometrical nature; for example, one can cut a string with scissors, but not with a rubber tube; and a coat can be cleaned better with a brush than with a knife. Of course these infinitely manifold relationships are produced by the organism; but it is probable that they are only possible with units which exist on the surface of a much larger unit. If there were an organism the size of the earth, it would be unable to create so many relationships within a system of planets of the same size, and therefore it would be impossible for it to create a livable environment.

Processes in Thing and Medium

Examples of thing events are easy to find. A stone falls, a car moves, etc. Each movement of such a thing unit is an event of this sort. These are the events that are important for our lives and of which we must be aware.

In the medium we find wave events and also movements of the small units, but we know that these events are irrelevant for the things of our order of magnitude. Therefore, where there are only these units, there is "nothing" as far as we are concerned; a room which is only filled with air is called empty. If a stone falls, it falls until it hits a thing; if I let a ball roll over a surface, it rolls until it collides with a wall or another solid body. A stick moves through the air until it hits the ground.

Thus not all events are of importance for us. Much occurs in our physical surroundings which is irrelevant for our behavioral world. The media are filled with units of a lower order, but empty as regards our order. Only thing events are of importance for us

Behavioral Significance of Wave Events

The wave events within the medium are significant for behavior only in so far as they are coupled with something important. Whether light rays pass through the medium in which we move about or not, and what kind of light rays, is irrelevant for our movements through these media. The light rays are important only in so far as they inform us of things. Otherwise they are unimportant. We do not collide with them; they do not hurt us in any way. They do not suddenly produce a motion of a paper or obstruct the course of a ball. Within the order of things we can usually assume that there are no events which are brought about by light rays, and exceptions, such as the radiometer, startle us. Sound waves, too, usually produce no effects among things. However long one shouts at a stone, it does not move. It is unusual for walls to fall at the sound of a trumpet, as happened at Jericho. While the thrusts of air waves set the larger units into vibration, they do not produce any events of thing order among them. Thus neither molecular events nor wave events have coordinated effects within the thing order. With the exception of collective events, there is nothing in the medium that is of importance for our behavioral world.

At the same time, the medium is of direct biological importance for physiological processes and the form of the organism. Water animals are built differently and move differently than air animals. But this is an effect resulting from a constant environment and is usually not represented in the behavioral world of the organism. We perceive only the differences of the environment which affect the organism directly, and not the medium as a constant surrounding.

This statement, like many in this paper, only holds in general, and one could certainly find single cases that are exceptions. These statements do not represent laws but only regularities which hold in most cases.

Wave Events

Let us consider more closely the significance of wave events. The wave beats in the medium ride through the units: the molecules retain the same positions, the waves move on. What we have to consider as an identical event is not coupled to an identical molecular unit. On the other hand, when things vibrate, the event is bound up with the static unit. Identity of event and identity of thing go together. Because things can vibrate freely, wave events are coordinated to the order of things; they are not coordinated to the order of molecules. Wave beats ride through the molecular events without being affected by their particular properties. The free vibration of a thing, on the other hand, possesses a certain wave length which is characteristic of that thing. The waves which go through the medium are therefore coordinated to the things.

The fact that free vibration occurs in things, forced vibration in media, and that the wave events are coupled with our behavioral world, is of great importance. Thus things can easily be the objects of perception, since they are internally conditioned; and the externally conditioned media can serve as mediators. This is demonstrated by the exceptions. There exist nontransparent media and transparent things. The fog is something which has no importance for us as a thing. One can move in it as in "empty air"; but the coordinations of the light waves to the things are destroyed by it. Another exception is glass. It does not impress its own characteristics on light waves; it lets them pass through and transmits them like a medium. But it is a thing unit, a solid body. These exceptions are of behavioral importance. Sailors and mountain climbers perish in the fog and birds die when they dash themselves against a window.

The Light Waves

It has been said above that there exists in the mediator a multitude of events that are independent of each other. What does this imply for light waves? It implies, first, that the events that follow each other at a certain place are not coupled. Vibration c does not follow b in a way which is characteristic of the place, as it would in vibration. An external influence has to produce each successive vibration. If the impact stops, a few vibrations still follow because of inertia, and inertia makes for a certain amount of free vibration in the medium. If the vibration were completely coordinated to the external influence, it would stop at the moment when the influence stopped. It is this remnant of free vibration which impairs the efficiency of the mediator, but it does not alter the fact that the frequency of the vibration is completely determined from the outside and that the better and the more transparent the mediator, the more completely the properties of the vibration are conditioned by the impact. If, for instance, the mediator is blue, then the frequency is conditioned to a greater extent by the mediator than when it is completely transparent.

Furthermore, the waves in two adjacent places of the mediator are likewise independent of each other to a great extent. If a red ray goes through the mediator, this does not imply that the neighboring ray is likewise red. Wave frequencies and other determinations are coupled only to a small degree, if at all. To be sure, there is a dependency in the mediator; what occurs at one place is dependent on what occurred the previous moment at the neighboring place. This kind of dependency is what makes the mediator capable of transmitting impulses.

Let us now consider wave events which occur on the surface of things. To what extent do they form units with parts which are dependent on each other? Certainly the temporal succession of vibrations on a given point of the object is caused by the behavior of the light source. The beginning or cessation of illumination tells us nothing about the object. However, the kind of vibration and its frequency are characteristic of the thing. To be sure, it can be influenced by differences in illumination, but not as completely as the vibration of a mediator. One cannot illumine vermilion in such a way as to make it look green.

It is very important that the order of the direction of light rays is changed at the surface of an object. All rays, whatever directions they come from, are absorbed to produce the one vibration which conforms to the surface of the object at each point. The rays are not reflected independently of each other as far as direction is concerned. In the case of the mirror, however, they are reflected independently of each other. A mirror changes the direction of light rays; but it changes the direction of all rays in the same way so that the configuration is preserved. At each point there is a multitude of rays of different directions, and the composition is determined externally. With an object which has not the properties of a mirror, however, the kind and direction of incoming light rays are more or less irrelevant, if only enough energy reaches each point to set its own free vibrations in motion. There is a similar difference between a colored object and a piece of colored glass. A piece of colored glass acts as a filter. Only one particular kind of light wave can pass through, but it does so without being changed. A colored object changes the directions of the rays too, so that the directions of the reflected rays are not coordinated with the directions of the arriving rays.

However, a solid thing has not one but many points. Can we consider the sum of wave events at all these points as a unit? No. It is a composite event. It is possible to illuminate each single point separately and, by using different illuminations, to force upon the thing entirely arbitrary configurations. For example, consider what appears upon the motion picture screen simply as the result of selective illumination. In these cases, the screen serves as a mediator. We do not see the screen; we see something else. And that again is only possible because the single events on the screen are independent of each other. But such complicated illuminations are the exception. In spite of the fact that the waves at the single points of a solid body are independent of each other, nevertheless in a certain sense they form a unit, because the points themselves are part of a unitary object. The substrata of the many separate events form a unit; and, in this sense, the vibrations, too, are dependent on each other. If an illuminated body moves, all the vibrations on it move in a certain order. Here again we find this important relation: freely vibrating points form a static unit and they are dependent on each other; or, in other words, things show free vibration, media show forced vibrations.

We can also put it in this way: not only is the manifold of light rays which are reflected from single points a spurious unit, but so is the much more complicated manifold which is reflected by the many points of a solid body. At first sight, one might question this statement and ask: what order or regularity is in this manifold? A spurious unit is an ordered manifold made up of units which are independent of each other. The order exhibited by the manifold of light rays which are coordinated to a thing is not of such an obvious spatial or temporal kind. Nevertheless, the light rays are coupled because they are reflected by coupled points. These light waves always appear together, although somewhat changed as a result of their illumination, position, etc. They contain an order which becomes meaningful only if one refers them to the corresponding object.

Sound Waves

If we consider these relationships as regards sound waves, we find that things often serve as mediators for sound. One can hear through a wall. In this case the wall assumes mediator characteristics: it transmits unchanged the vibrations which are forced upon it by the source of sound. Therefore the whole event is coordinated to the source of sound or to what happens at the source of sound. Only a few changes occur which are characteristic of the mediator; for instance, when a sound is damped. Damping can be produced by mediation, but it is very improbable that the mediation creates new spurious units.

We find not only cases in which a thing mediates sound waves, but also cases in which the air, which usually acts as a mediator, apparently vibrates freely. The sound of a whistle is produced by the vibration of a column of air. However, these vibrations are not coordinated to the units of the air, that is, to the air molecules. It is not characteristic of these particles of the air to vibrate in such a way. The vibration is determined by the form of the column of the air and this form is forced upon it by the shape of the solid whistle. Therefore the free vibration is characteristic only of the solid body, the whistle.

Olfactory Mediation

So far, we have only considered distance perception which is made possible by waves. But we perceive distant things also by the olfactory sense where waves are not involved. In this case, too, there are messengers, particles diffused in the air which refer to and are signs of something else. In this case, too, one can easily show that the messengers can act as signs only because they are independent of each other. A single particle, or many particles coupled to each other, can tell us very little about the distance of the body from which they are released. However, if there are many independent particles in a medium which usually does not contain these particles, then they disclose the nearness of the body in question. A single feather floating in the air does not tell us that there is a bird close by, nor do several feathers which cling together, because a single feather or a cluster of feathers remain a unit even when they are carried to a distance by the wind. The case is different when many single feathers float in a group. The more distant they are from the solid unit from which they came, the bird, the more they distribute themselves over a wide area, since their movements are independent of each other. Therefore we can infer from the presence of a cloud of feathers that the bird is not very far away.

Olfactory perception functions best in the open air (tracking of animals) because there the greatest independence of parts is possible. When the diffused particles are enclosed in a room, they do not refer so unequivocally to their source. The more tightly the room is closed, and the longer the odor remains in it, the less it tells about the nearness of the source. The cloud of independent particles which remains around an odorous body can be compared to the spurious units of wave configurations. The particles behave as if they were coupled or as if they were a unit. Actually they are independent of each other, and their clustering in one place would be highly improbable if this spurious unit were not conditioned externally by a true unit, the solid odorous body.

The Tactual Object

One often hears the following argument: it is arbitrary to assume that a body is located where it affects the sense of touch. Why is it not also present where it affects the visual or auditory sense? A body consists essentially of its ability to produce effects, and it can do this through a wide area by means of light waves. Therefore a distant thing is also present right in front of the eyes through which it is perceived. However, if one accepts this line of reasoning and takes existence as equivalent to the possibility of producing effects, the resulting concept of boundary is very different from that which is used in ordinary experience, and which probably is the only meaningful one. Our perception sets the boundary of a unit at the point where the parts which are related to each other as interdependent parts of a solid body meet those other parts that are not dependent on the parts of the solid body in this sense. We not only touch the boundary of an object there, we see it there and not just before our eyes. Thus the eye localizes in the same way as the sense of touch.

One must not forget the difference between direct and mediated effects. The sense of touch is affected directly by the unitary thing whose parts are dependent on each other. The eye is affected by an atomistic manifold, a spurious unit, which is coordinated to the thing, but which itself can produce no effects in the realm of things. The light waves are messengers which have separated themselves from the unit and whose characteristics have been derived from it, but whose further fates are entirely independent from each other and from the source. A thing is not necessarily present wherever there are effects which are coordinated to it, and we are entirely correct when we do not localize the thing wherever it produces mediated effects. The epistemological significance of the sense of touch comes from the fact that the thing units affect it directly and not through a mediation. Therefore we always believe that we are closest to the thing when we touch it.

Mediating Things

Within the things themselves we find internally conditioned events, core events, and externally conditioned events, which are composed of the offshoots of a central event. The offshoot event can always stand as a sign for the core event. This is the case, for instance, when one sees a mole digging through the earth. The thing that we see directly serves itself as a mediator. What we hear, too, can be the mediator for something still more distant. For example, in the woods one can tell from the snapping of the branches that something alive is approaching.

Measuring instruments, such as thermometers, barometers, electrical measuring instruments, etc., function as mediators and inform us of data which are important to us. The less internally conditioned the position of the parts which indicate something else, the better mediators will they be. In an apparatus which serves as an indicator, there must be a flexible element which yields to influences from outside, that is, a mediatorlike element. To be sure, measuring instruments are not common mediators which simply transmit the influence which affects them. They are to some extent internally conditioned; they abstract certain properties of the influence and change them into forms which can be perceived with a greater degree of exactness. The transposition has to occur in a strictly coordinated way. That means that changes of the position of the pointer must be coordinated exactly to changes of the influence. Such a coordination is typical of mediators: the successive positions of the pointer are not connected in a way which is characteristic of the pointer itself, but they are externally conditioned.

Traces As Mediators

Something static, too, can serve as a mediator, and such mediators are generally called traces. Changes in the position of parts of solid bodies, or changes on the surfaces of soft materials are traces through which we can recognize their causes. Again we find the same relationships. The trace is the more characteristic of the source the more possibilities of change the mediator had at the moment at which the trace is produced, that is, the more it pictures that which produced the trace. If internally conditioned solid units such as stones are present in clay, the impressed traces are relatively less characteristic of the cause than traces in pure clay. If the substratum of the trace loses its mediator characteristics and becomes a rigid body, the trace becomes permanent and the material cannot serve for further mediation. This is what occurs in every "fixation," whether applied to a photographic film or a drawing; the hardening of a plastic mass in casting serves the same purpose.

Reproduction

If one models a piece of clay so that it resembles a thing, it is plausible that the offshoots of this piece of clay are similar to those of the original, and that we recognize the original in the reproduction. The reproduction consists, in this case, of a unit which is similar to the original. A photograph is a square piece of paper with black and white spots. Nevertheless, it can be made to represent an infinite number of things. Thus a manifold of offshoots corresponding to the original is sent out by a thing which is entirely different from the original.

The light rays which proceed from a thing are conditioned by its form, its surface characteristics, and the illumination. If one wants to produce the representing light rays by form alone, one obtains a plastic reproduction, a form imitation of the original. If one excludes the factor of form (by using a plane surface), and of illumination (by equalizing the illumination), and wants to produce the representing light rays by changes of the surface characteristics, one obtains a picture in the narrower sense of the word. If one uses only the factor of illumination with the exclusion of the factors of form and surface characteristics (by using a plain white wall), one obtains a projected image. Illumination and surface characteristics are usually not coupled with the behavioral significance of a thing, as is the case with its shape. Therefore, by changing these two conditions, one can change, to a great extent, the light rays which are reflected by a thing, and one can give them an order which imitates a light-ray manifold characteristic of another thing.

If the reproduction is produced by an apparatus, the process is essentially as follows: one lets the offshoots produce a trace. This trace must be such that of itself it sends out offshoots which are similar to the trace-forming offshoots. In this way the offshoots are fixated, for the substratum of the trace can become a rigid body: the position of its parts is not changeable, and it retains its characteristics in a changing environment. It is a fixation of spurious units, that is, a fixation of the mediation.

A phonograph fixates a multitude of offshoots which are temporally distributed. With such a fixation, each point in time has to be coordinated to a point of the trace. Thus the temporal manifold is transformed into a spatial manifold of traces which are independent of each other—independent in so far as the form of one point of the record does not condition the form of a neighboring point. A temporal multitude cannot be fixated immediately, that is, be made into a unit which remains constant in the face of changes of the environment. If one wants to make it static, one must transform it into a spatial configuration which is bound up with a rigid unit. To be sure, there are static units, rigid bodies, to which are coordinated temporal successions and which can be reproduced at any time without the presence of a spatial configuration corresponding point for point to the temporal one. That is the case with a freely vibrating body; an event is coordinated to it and can be reproduced at any time. This event is a unit, not a composite which consists of externally conditioned elements, as is the case with the vibrations of a phonograph needle. Actually, however, it is impossible to find bodies whose free vibrations consist of a piece of music which is reproduced when one strikes the body. It is therefore necessary to use composite coordination if one wants to fixate a temporal manifold, that is, to attach an event to a solid body. When a spatial manifold unfolds into the temporal one, it has to be collected into a unit, which, in the case of the phonograph, consists of the needle and the sound box.

With moving pictures, also, the temporal manifold is transformed into a spatial manifold, and an event is preserved as a solid body. The properties of the solid body, that is, the film, are forced upon it by the core event, i.e., the event which is represented in the pictures. The spatial manifold can again be unfolded and the screen functions as a collecting unit, corresponding to the phonograph needle.

Expression of Personality by Movement and Action

This process of transmission appears in its most striking and complicated form in connection with human personality. Each personality radiates a multitude of significant offshoots and is surrounded by a halo of traces and events which have taken on the characteristics of the unity of the person.

The single actions of a person can be thought of as the parts of this spurious unit; they are independent of each other in the sense in which light rays issuing from one source are independent of each other. When a person raises his arm, the sequence of the arm movements is not determined by the properties of the arm itself. The person may lift it still further or may let it down. To this extent, the single movements are not directly dependent on each other. As the light rays become meaningful only by reference to the unitary source, so actions become intelligible only if one refers them to the underlying objective unit, that is, the person or the performer and the sequence of psychological events within his person. The case is made more complicated by the fact that the achievement of the action acts back upon the person, so that there is an indirect dependence of the single actions on each other. But this dependence does not lie in the internal conditions of the executing organ.

Expressive movements, too, are the more significant the less they are internally conditioned. Therefore facial expression is especially important because the anatomical structure is such that many different combinations of movement are possible. Traces can also serve as mediators for inner-personal processes. From footprints to the most complex traces, such as handwriting or artistic or scientific creations, there are manifold mediations through which we can recognize the personality and the intentions of a person.

The Functions of Perception

We have considered the structure of the environment in regard to perception and cognition. Now we can try to understand the meaning of the perceptual apparatus. We shall first consider the physiological event which corresponds to the final product of a perceptual process. This event must be coordinated in some way to the stimuli or the stimulus pattern. If that were not so, the organism would live in an imaginary world. On the other hand, this event must have effects as a unit. It must stand as a whole in the chain of causal connections, and it must be possible to stimulate it as a whole from different regions (for instance, the image of a table can be aroused not only peripherally but also centrally). It can be aroused as a whole from different regions only if it is unitary; the more composite it is, the less is that possible—and on this fact is based the coordination of the composite events in the mediators to events in the objects. Thus the perceptual apparatus makes the object again into a unit at a place where its effects are only spurious units, which are coordinated to the object. The perceptual apparatus transforms these spurious units again into true units which have physical effects within the order of magnitude of things.

The light rays proceed from the things; they form a composite event, which, although it is coordinated to the unit of the thing, is not itself a true unit. The organism gathers these effects together and thus they become effective in the region of things; for instance, the organism moves around in a way which conforms to the solid bodies of the environment. The effect of the things remains latent and physically unreal in the medium. It appears again in the organism. Thus in the brain there is again something which is coordinated to the thing and which at the same time is physically unitary.

The fact that there is a perception apparatus in the world structure allows the things to have more characteristic effects. One can say that they become real to a greater extent, since they obtain new possibilities of having effects. For instance, what effect does a knife have on inorganic connections of thing order? It certainly acts as a whole, as a physical unit. It acts by means of its weight, it even acts by means of its form; that is, it can cut. But when does its form as a whole have a unitary coordinated effect on another body? One is tempted to say that this happens only when an organism is involved which recognizes its form.

The Synthesis

The organism has to reconstruct the coordinated core event from the offshoots. That is the function of perception. We can now try to relate these considerations to the more familiar treatment of perceptual processes. The sensations, as they were understood by the older psychology of perception, are the immediate effects of the offshoots on the sense organ. They correspond to the events which make up the composite mediation. Their structure is atomistic because the mediation to which they are supposed to be correlated is atomistic, that is, composed of parts which are independent of each other. The reconstruction of the core events on the basis of the offshoots is a process of "synthesis of images out of sensations," of "Gestalt production," etc. The structure of the environment shows that such a synthesis is necessary; we can say that any being that is to recognize its environment by means of mediators has to avail itself of it. And if we want to construct an apparatus which would react to distant things through a medium in a coordinated way, we would have to build one that gathers into units the composite effects which have their source in the distant units. In this sense the synthesis is conditioned by the structure of the physical world.

Resonance

In the mediator the wave events are mixed. The effects of waves proceeding from the single points of objects interfere with each other. If one holds a photographic plate in front of an illuminated object, it will be exposed more or less equally at all points. No coordinations are formed between points of the plate and points of the object. The combination of light rays coming from a chair is certainly different from one coming from a table, but the plate cannot register this difference. A certain order of light rays exists in the medium, but it does not become physically effective. The case is different if I hold a cardboard with a little hole which serves as a pinpoint lens in front of the plate. Coordinations are formed. The plate is now exposed in a specific way which is dependent on the nature of the object. The order that is latent in the medium is made physically effective, and this is the first step toward a meaningful unification of the effects conveyed by the mediator. This unification requires, first, that the mixture existing in the mediator be decomposed and the single effects be segregated so that they can become effective individually. Only after such an analysis can the real synthesis into meaningful units begin. This analysis of the manifold of events is performed by the more mechanical apparatus at the entrance of the sense organs, for instance, the lens, the compound eye, or the cochlea with its resonance apparatus. They respond only to a limited range of stimuli and exclude interfering events. Thus the single event is segregated. The single point on the film of a pinhole camera responds only to light rays of a certain direction. So do the facets of an insect's eye. The lens has an even more important effect in that it not only excludes what comes from other points of the object but also collects the composite event which comes from one point. This is the beginning of the synthesis. Of course it is only the beginning, for, although the lens reinstates the order of the points from which the light rays are reflected, it does not produce units which correspond to things. On the plate or just in front of the retina, neighboring points are all equivalent in atomistic order.

General and Special Apparatuses

If the wave mediator were not homogeneous, and the waves did not proceed according to a general scheme, such a generally useful combining apparatus as the lens would be impossible. One can imagine an apparatus which would combine the rays proceeding from one point through an unhomogeneous mediator. In such a case where the medium was not uniform, a special apparatus would be necessary for each point of space. A duality which is of greatest importance begins in the lens. There is, first, the event itself, but secondly also its "meaning." The rays in some way refer to, or are coordinated to, the points from which they come. If the rays which proceed from one point are again combined into one point, they are guided "correctly," "meaningfully." This is analogous to the relationship of physiological to mental events. Two layers of functionally related processes are superimposed. The offshoots have to be combined into units, that is, the kind of combination is determined by laws according to which the offshoots are coordinated to the distant objects. But the physiological processes which perform this unification have their own laws also, regardless of what they achieve.

If a special apparatus were provided for each single case of the unification of offshoots, then the laws of the dynamics of the organism itself would play no part; a discrepancy could never arise between the two different layers if only the right apparatus were employed. Of course an infinite number of apparatuses would be necessary. However, the two levels could be related in another way: the laws of the physiological processes could agree in their structure with the laws of the level of meaning. An apparatus could, on the basis of its own dynamics, react meaningfully to many different stimulus configurations; that is, it could react by reconstructing the distant objects. Two different manifolds of stimuli would have as their effects two different central processes, not because they set into action two different fixed apparatuses, but because the same apparatus reacts in two different ways. As we have said, the lens of the eye is just such a general apparatus. In contrast to the more central nervous processes, its function is more or less rigid and it does not depend on previous experience or exercise. At the same time, we can improve our perception based on bodily equipment with manufactured instruments such as glasses, microscopes, and telescopes. As we have mentioned, this is possible because the light rays proceed according to a general scheme. Although they do not form a physical unit, they form a spatial unit. With spurious units whose parts follow a definite order in time or space, it is possible that a mechanically rigid apparatus performs the unification according to a general method. The case is different when we are dealing with spurious units whose spatial or temporal order shows no regularity. That is the case with the light-ray manifold which proceeds from a solid body. To be sure, there are some regularities that characterize the manifolds that are coordinated to things, but they are to be thought of only as typical occurrences and not as laws. The more special the coordination of offshoots to core events, the less probable it is that there exist physiological apparatuses which react meaningfully to different stimulus configurations. One might mention that Köhler has suggested that there exist physiological apparatuses which react meaningfully on the basis of their own dynamics to many different stimulus configurations.

Sensory Qualities

The ideal case of such reconstruction of underlying units from the offshoots would appear thus: we open our eyes and see the room full of objects; we see the units of the thing order which are important for us. We see a table and we see that it is something solid which, however, can be moved as a whole. We see that one can put something on it. In short, the light rays mediate to us everything that is important for our behavior. We see the unit and its place within all possible relations and functions; nothing else is given to consciousness, the mediator does not appear to the subject.

On the whole, this is what actually occurs. However, this ideal case is never completely realized. It is not irrelevant for the phenomenon how the knowledge about the object is mediated. Light rays and sound waves which serve as mediators appear phenomenally as colors and sounds. Not only does the kind of mediation influence the images of objects; it is even possible to focus perception on the mediator itself. Although we can produce conditions in which it is impossible to refer the waves to some entity of the object world, they are nevertheless perceived as something specific and they are recognized. Even if the mediation transmits object units to us, we can disregard them (reduction).

We are not trying to solve the problem of why mediation appears at all phenomenally. Instead we turn to the discussion of another question. The mediation, that is, what affects the sense organs directly, is perceived as color, sound—in general, as sensory quality. Is it possible to relate the special character of sensory qualities to the role which the physiological correlates play in the whole process of mediation?

It is first of all characteristic of sensations that they are unitary in a special sense, which is different from that of a Gestalt. The quantitative aspect is important, and they are somehow "subjective"; a wave is perceived as color or sound. Does the physical structure in any way correspond to these facts? The waves affect the sense organ directly and as units. It is not possible to separate the crest of a wave from the trough in such a way that they have specific effects. They are the true units out of which the medium manifolds are composed. This may explain that such special phenomenal units are coordinated to the light waves. But does the subjectivity follow from this property? Let us compare the image of a "correctly" perceived movement with the sensory quality which is an "incorrect" subjective representation of movement. I see how a black dot moves. I can perceive this movement as a unit. Nevertheless, this unit is objective to a much greater degree than if the movement were perceived only as a special sense quality. We can assume that this objectivity consists in the relations to other objective events somehow being represented in this image. If I see a black point moving, I know immediately that this event belongs to the large class of events where something moves. And if, at another time, I see the movement of a big white cloud, I know immediately that this event has something in common with the movement of the dot. Thus I perceive the position of the event in relation to other events. If I perceived these two movements only as two different sensory qualities, the relationship between the two would not be directly given in perception.

What distinguishes the more objective perception from the more qualitative? The movement of a point can be something unitary. However, I can distinguish parts in it which also correspond to something objective. I see how it is composed of parts; I can see the different positions of the point, or at least these different positions are somehow embedded in the whole movement. That is not the case with color. I cannot recognize parts in it. For the corresponding physical event this means that there are part correlations with the point movement; not only the movement as a whole but also the parts of the movement have specific effects.

The kind of unification is entirely different in the two cases. The transformation of vibration into nervous excitation is a unification which has more the character of a summation, for instance, like the summation into a unitary vibration of strokes on a solid object. The individual effects of the single impact are entirely lost. One cannot segregate any part coordinations.

With the perception of thing movement, on the other hand, the direct effect on the sense organ is manifold. The retina is stimulated at many points. Even if interaction occurs at once between the points, this interaction does not make coordination to the single excitations impossible. The event which corresponds to the movement is, when it enters the sense organ, an externally conditioned event; it is composed of parts, which are coordinated to the single parts of the perceived movement. Starting with this manifold, the unification occurs within the nervous system in such a way that the single parts are to some degree preserved in the end product. One sees the whole and at the same time one perceives the way in which it is composed out of parts. It is then understandable that the one movement is seen in a way which corresponds much more to the objective movement than the other. If something objective corresponds to the parts of the whole, and if the way in which the whole is built up of parts is phenomenally represented, then the whole is recognized much more correctly. One could also represent these relationships in the following way: all influences which belong to an order of magnitude below a certain threshold are received as units; those which are above this threshold produce, as a first step within the sense organ, a composite event which allows for the possibility of analysis.

To be sure, the sense qualities, too, contain many traits which correspond to objective relationships. Light obtains its phenomenal value first of all from its function as a condition of perception. Light means "clearness" and "brightness," in contrast to darkness whose phenomenal value refers to the difficulty of getting about. Those characteristics of light which lie above the order of magnitude of the threshold of analysis are, of course, perceived correctly. To these characteristics belong the relationship of the source of light to a reflector, the fact that light always proceeds in straight lines, etc. We do not claim that all this is seen at once without previous experience, only that these characteristics are adequately represented in the direct experience of the adult. Only the finer structure below the threshold of analysis is inadequately perceived, and this finer structure is irrelevant for our behavior because it lies below the order of magnitude of things.

Figure and Ground

The single offshoot, that is, the single unitary event proceeding from an object, can be coordinated to many different causes, or many different core units. We have seen that only a multitude of independent offshoots gives a more univocal coordination. If there are too few offshoots, they remain ambiguous, and they can be coordinated to different phenomenal units. Different core events can be meaningfully derived from them.

As an example of such "equivocality" we shall discuss the difference between figures and ground, about which there exists a considerable body of research. One can perceive a spot either as something which lies on supporting ground, or as a hole. What is the relationship of core unit to offshoots in the two cases? "Figure" refers to a solid body which is in front of something else. "Ground" is something that is unitary only in regard to the figure; it is what is behind the figure regardless of whether it consists of a multitude of objects or a white wall. Let us consider the coordinated light-ray event as it meets the retina. It is a spatial configuration of events which are equivalent as processes, although they represent entities of different values in the thing world. No specific characteristic exists which would distinguish all light rays which come from an object. The significance of one ray is only determined by its position among the other rays. The single ray becomes univocal only in relation to the surrounding pattern. Thus it can happen that with a change of surrounding field the significance of the single part changes. In such a case, if only the objects were represented and not the mediation, we would see only unrelated phenomenal objects following each other. It would be impossible to recognize any identity in this change, for only the mediation would remain the same. But the mediation can have its own phenomenal representation: the colors, and also the form in so far as it is not yet interpreted as figure or ground. This makes it possible for us to speak of something as being phenomenally identical in figure-ground reversals.

Thus the difference between figure and ground refers to objects, and if we see a black spot on a white paper as a figure, it means that we see it as a picture. For this reason, most ornaments have some object meaning. It is impossible to ask how it would be if we were to interpret the offshoots differently, that is, reverse figure and ground. That would be asking, "How would it be if we were to perceive solid bodies as air and the air as a solid body?" Figure and ground belong to the phenomenal qualities whose object significance is more or less known to us. One could, however, imagine such exchanges in regard to qualities; one could ask how it would be if red appeared as blue, because red and blue are not anchored in the thing world like solid bodies or figure and ground.

Mediation in the Motor System

In discussing expressive movements, we compared the single motor impulses to the light rays which proceed from a source. We have seen that the comparison does not hold exactly. Nevertheless it throws some light on the process of motor mediation. The organs of the body which affect things directly must be as nearly as possible perfect mediators for the action impulses coming from the brain. We know what that demands. The coordination of the movements of the single parts must not be internally conditioned but must be determined entirely by external influences. The hand is the most perfect action mediator, and we recognize in it the general characteristics of the mediator. It is the more perfect the more the single fingers are independent of each other and the less rigid they are. If, instead of the hand, we had a solid body whose form were entirely internally conditioned, we could not grasp anything. The piano player or the mechanic notices the least deterioration in the mediator characteristics of the hand. When the hand is cold, it is internally conditioned to a greater extent and can no longer transmit slight impulses.

But not only the organs of one's own body serve to mediate action. Tools, machines, and even other people can transmit the impulse which comes from the acting person to the place where the essential event of the action occurs. As we see the thing through the medium, so we act through tools and are concerned only with the core event of the action without regarding the special kind of mediation. For the driver of a car, driving is not simply a turning of the wheel. This immediate effect of the movements of his hands loses its own meaning entirely, since it serves only as mediation for the further effect which is the core event of the action; namely, that the car at one time goes straight on, then turns toward the right, etc. The fact that he feels he can control this core event is again conditioned by the medium characteristics which the steering apparatus must possess. It must obey each slight pressure, it must not be internally conditioned to too great an extent. Other examples: a person who is writing does not think of himself as making black marks on a piece of white paper; he makes thoughts or feelings "objective." He makes them into something that one can carry around, in short, into a thing. If a painter puts oils on a canvas, he works through these mediations on the intention of his picture even if it is to be only an abstract painting.

Thus the organism does not stand in the causal texture like a thing that is pushed and pushes other things; it lives between two spurious units of composite process. This peculiar kind of causal connection makes possible new events in the world of things. It could happen, for instance, that from a heap of colored stones all the round blue ones were suddenly pushed aside into a separate group, but such an event would be most improbable if only the usual causal connections were effective. It is likely only if a human organism is involved. This kind of causal connection involving two spurious units, one on the perceptual and one on the motor side, frees the organism from gross physical relationships.

Summary

Are there structural characteristics of the physical world which are important for perception? This was our first question. In order to answer it, we began by analyzing distance perception. We found that there exist mediators and the mediated objects. There exist cores, or units, which are internally conditioned and which are in some way centers of the causal texture of the world. These units are surrounded by something whose forms and processes are molded by them and which is thus externally conditioned. The centers are unitary, while that which is externally conditioned is mostly composite, built up of many parts which are independent of each other. These parts sometimes form spurious units, which become intelligible only by reference to the unitary cause. This structure makes it possible for events in the externally conditioned regions to inform us of the internally conditioned centers; thus it underlies the distinction between objects and mediators.

It is important that the mediated objects are at the same time usually thing units. The object-mediator structure agrees with the thing-medium structure in regard to its centers, and coordinates wave events to the world of things which is important for us. If one can see through something without hindrance, one can, in most cases, also put one's hand through it without meeting resistance. That which is "something" for the eye is usually also "something" in regard to relationships between things. Therefore it is possible that waves serve as mediators in the cognition of things. The relationship of mediator to mediated, which we found in the case of wave events, holds in general for mediation in cognition. In most cases, there exists a core event which is unitary, internally conditioned, and sends out offshoots which are mostly composite and atomistic. Through these offshoots, through traces, pictures, expressive movements, writings, etc., we apprehend the underlying units.

It is the task of the apparatus of perception to construct out of the manifold of impinging offshoots something that is coordinated to core events. This has been called the synthesis of images out of sensations. We have made the attempt to explain some characteristics of the "sensations" on the basis of the characteristics of their correlates among physical events. Finally, such mediation by means of a composite process exists for action as well as for processes of cognition. From our analysis one can say that the processes in the organism take place between two spurious units.

2

THE FUNCTION OF THE PERCEPTUAL SYSTEM

I

The purpose of this paper is to consider perception in regard to its adaptation to the environment, or, to use a term of K. Bühler's (1929), to analyze that "aspect of function" of perception. A start in this direction has been made in "Thing and Medium"; the present essay attempts to bring out more clearly the way in which these considerations can be helpful to a theory of perception.

Everybody will concede that the perceptual apparatus belongs to an organism which is adapted to the environment; nevertheless, in discussions of perception the structure of the environment is often completely neglected, and only the proximal stimuli (for instance, the wave length of the stimuli impinging on the organs) are taken account of. It is not asked whether these stimuli possess a certain meaning in themselves which can be understood only if their objective role in the environment is considered.

The description of this environment to which the perceptual apparatus is adapted is a problem of physical science and as such not part of psychology. The fact that it has been neglected is due to the present state of physics, which so far does not offer suitable concepts. In considering the environment in its relation to perception, one has to analyze its macroscopic structure, the meaning of the single process in greater wholes, and the interaction of causal chains—and these are questions which the physicist has so far avoided.

Translated from: Die Leistung des Wahrnehmungssystems. *Zeitschrift für Psychologie,* 114:371-394, 1930.

We shall make use of a structural analysis in order to find out what in the environment is vitally important for the organism. There is always danger that this way of looking at things may lapse either into microscopic or into psychological concepts; we must make it clear that we are concerned neither with atomic physics nor with the environment "as it appears to the organism."

One might have misgivings about treating such a description as part of physics. But since no better word is available, the word "physics" will be used here as also referring to such a macroscopic description.

In "Thing and Medium" we tried to describe the structure of the environment which is essential for distance perception. If an organism is to perceive the environment, the mere possession of perceptual organs is not sufficient; it is also necessary that the perceiving organism and the objects of perception are in a certain way causally connected. Without this physical, extraorganismic connection, distance perception is impossible. In the analysis of the causal structure two concepts are of importance: the concepts of "internally conditioned" and "externally conditioned," which correspond to the concepts of "free" and "forced" vibrations in wave mechanics. That certain parts of the environment have the meaning of mediators through which we perceive something else, that we hear and see things "through air," that we recognize meaning through letters in reading, cannot be attributed entirely to the properties of our perceptual equipment. Something can be a mediator only if it occupies a particular place in the structure of the environment, and if it possesses the characteristics of a mediator independent of whether or not it is used by an organism as such.

A mediator is distinguished by the fact that its processes are conditioned from the outside: they cannot be explained without reference to something beyond the mediator. Thus physical nature contains the conditions for distance perception. A contrary role is played by the centers, the "cores" of the environment, of which the solid things are examples. These cores determine processes which are internally conditioned; they impose their form on the surrounding medium, which is permeated by causal offshoots coming from the cores. The cores as such can never serve as mediators in the cognition of the environment; they are the objects of perception and contain the vitally relevant processes.

Usually only the mediator processes impinge directly on the perceptual organs, and the vitally relevant core processes have to be reconstructed from them. The relation between stimulus and perceptual image corresponds in mirror fashion to the relation between core and offshoot. This correspondence is an instance of the adaptive function of the perceptual apparatus: a task which is set by the environment is solved in an efficient way. Just as thinking corresponds in some way to the logic of relations, the perceptual organs correspond to the environment which is to be perceived. Though the analogy must not be overstressed, it is permissible to say: just as it is impossible to analyze the thinking process without referring to its content, it is a mistake to study the psychology of perception without considering the tasks which originate outside of the organism but which the organism solves in a meaningful way.

II

A good starting point for the discussion is furnished by an experiment of Rubin:

> In Figure 1, R represents a ring; A represents a wheel, the diameter of which is exactly half of the diameter of the ring. The wheel can move in the ring. One can demonstrate mathematically that all the points on the periphery of the wheel perform straight pendulum movements through the center of the ring if the wheel moves. Five positions of the wheel . . . are shown in the figure; the square and round marks indicate the five positions of two points. The apparatus makes it possible to illumine one to six points of the periphery. If the apparatus is set up in a dark room and only one point is visible, one sees it perform a pendulum movement; the speed is greatest in the middle. If two points are visible one can see two intersecting pen-

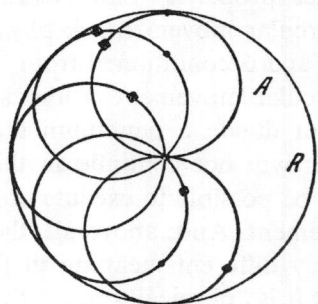

FIGURE 1

dulum movements. However, if all six points are visible, one does not see six straight movements. One sees six points which all move uniformly in circular paths, these being defined by the six points; at the same time the whole system of six points performs another uniform circular movement the center of which is the center of the ring [Rubin, 1927, p. 388f.].

That means that the phenomenon which corresponds to a single stimulus is completely changed if one adds other single stimuli. If the single stimulus is given by itself, one sees a pendulum movement; if the same stimulus is surrounded by other stimuli, one sees a double circular movement.

We shall now consider the structure of the perceived object and the kind of mediation. Rubin seems to imply that the difference between the two phenomena—pendulum movement and double circular movement—has to be attributed completely to the perceptual apparatus, and he states expressly: "One or two movements are mathematically only two *façons de parler,* but psychologically they are two different realities" (1927, p. 390). However, a mathematical description which determines path and speed of a point is not sufficient for the description of the movement of a point on a thing if we want to describe the movement in terms of macroscopic physics as it is envisaged in the present paper. Though pendulum movement and double circular movement of a thing point are identical mathematically, they play very different roles within the macroscopic structure. Kurt Lewin has made this clear by referring to a similar example, and said, in this connection: "Processes which are closely related phenotypically can belong to very different conditional-genetic types" (1927, p. 398). A true macroscopic pendulum movement has properties and possibilities different from those of a double circular movement. A physically real pendulum movement is unitary and is conditioned from the inside to a greater degree; a double circular movement is imposed from the outside. Therefore one cannot divide a pendulum movement into pieces; if it is interrupted, it will not continue in the same way. On the other hand, it would be possible to execute only a small part of the double circular movement. And, above all, the rectilinearity of the path has a completely different meaning in the two cases. In the pendulum movement it is "physically real," that means it has physical significance, while in the double circular movement it is an unreal component of two movements and the rectilinear path is not a distinguished case, it is only one possibility among other not rectilinear paths. What Lewin says of his example can also be applied here: "The same mathematical function means epistemologically something different according to whether it is supposed to describe the process phenotypically, or whether one contends that it is a description of the genotype of the process. The mathematical representation by itself is ambiguous in this regard, unless the context makes it clear what is supposed to be described" (Lewin, 1927, p. 399, note). Our perception, therefore, does not produce a difference where objectively we find no such difference; to the two different psychological realities correspond two different environmental realities. If we call a physically real pendulum movement (i.e., an oscillation of a body produced by forces directed toward a midpoint) P, and an imposed double circular movement (i.e., the movement of a body attached to a wheel in a ring) K, then we can say:

P is mathematically equal to K
P is physically not equal to K
P is phenomenally not equal to K.

Under normal circumstances the phenomenal appearance corresponds to a high degree to the macroscopic physical processes, that is, one sees from the whole arrangement what significance the movement possesses; Rubin justly states that this perceptual analysis of movements is important, and classifies it with the constancies (1927, p. 391).

However, as the experiment of Rubin shows, K is seen as P in certain cases. One can show that the source of this "mistake" does not lie in the perceptual apparatus, but that the physical mediation is responsible for it. P and K are macroscopic thing processes from which offshoots issue; these offshoots impinge on the sensory organs and from them perception reconstructs the underlying processes. The mediating offshoots in this case are light rays, and it is obvious that these rays, coming from the single points, are determined only by the paths and the speed of the points, i.e., what can be mathematically described and what is equal in P and K. If the offshoots coming from the neighboring points do not reach the retina, the perceptual apparatus has no criterion by which to decide between

P and *K*. This is the reason for this "mistake"; we see one phenomenon instead of the other if the offshoots of *P* and *K* are given without the offshoots of the other points which are necessary for a complete determination of the real process.

To be sure, that does not yet solve the further question: why do we always see *P* if the offshoots of *P* or *K* are given alone? Why are offshoots which could have been produced by *K* as well as by *P* always interpreted as coming from *P*? If *P* and *K* are objectively equivalent, then it seems that we have to ascribe this tendency toward the *P* phenomenon to the perceptual apparatus; we may at last have found a fact which we cannot explain by an analysis of the structure of the objective environment. However, *P* and *K* are not equivalent and their relation to the mathematical determination, which is the only one given in the single point experiment, is not the same. The mathematical determination is an essential characteristic of *P*, it belongs to *P*'s real physical structure. In other words: these offshoots could have been caused by a great number of different thing movements and one can imagine any number of complicated machines which could carry a point in this pendulum movement. However, only one of these movements is unitary in itself and conditioned internally to a high degree, and that is *P*. Therefore, if only the mathematical determination of a movement is given, the offshoots will be interpreted as coming from that movement which belongs to these determinations in its unitary structure, and is correlated to them in an objectively physical though not in a psychological sense.

Three questions arose in the analysis of this experiment: (1) why are *P* and *K* two psychologically different realities; (2) why, with the single stimulus, is *P* always seen; and (3) why does the phenomenon change into *K* if the other stimuli are introduced? These three questions find answers if one investigates the structure of the perceived objects and the mediation. Any apparatus whose task it is to present an adequate picture of the environment would be misled in this case by the mediation, just as the human perceptual organ is.

III

As is the case with many problems of the psychology of perception, the ambiguity of the single local stimulus is central in the

THE FUNCTION OF THE PERCEPTUAL SYSTEM

analysis of this experiment. By investigating the physical processes one can distinguish between several cases of ambiguity. To the statement, "The meaning of a 'sensation' is determined by the whole in which it is placed," corresponds another statement which refers to the physical environment: "An offshoot can be caused by different core events, and usually only a manifold of offshoots is univocally coordinated to the core."

One can classify into two groups the cases in which the single offshoot is ambiguous: the offshoot can contain too much, or too little: too much, because it is also determined by other events, not merely by the perceived object; too little, because not all properties of the object are represented in it.

The constancies belong to the first group. The offshoot, for instance, a light ray, depends partly on the properties of the thing, partly on the illumination. The illumination disturbs the univocal correspondence between offshoot and thing. Things of the same color can have different offshoots, differently colored things can have similar offshoots. Within the offshoot manifold, things belonging to different illumination levels are referred to one level; things belonging to different coordinate systems are, as it were, referred to one system. Similarly, the arrangement of light rays may be the same whether they come from an object that is large and distant or from one that is small and near. The reconstruction of the correct levels is the task of the perceptual apparatus, which solves this task by considering other nonlocal data. The essential meaning of the constancies lies in this reconstruction which is required by the physical conditions of perception. Therefore the fact that the so-called perceptual constancies exist, is based on a feature of the environment—though this does not yet explain how these constancies are brought about in the human perceptual apparatus.

In other cases the offshoots are not univocal because they are coordinated only to a part aspect of the core. The light rays are correlated to the form and color of a thing but not to its possibilities of movement. As was said before, these possibilities depend on whether the piece of matter perceived is a unitary object by itself, or, if it is a part of a bigger thing, on the properties of that bigger thing. A piece of wood of a certain color and form does not have the same possibilities of movement if it is part of the handle of a hammer that it has if it is part of the leg of a table. Since the offshoots are taken to represent the complete object (the piece of wood with all its properties, even its possibilities of movement), but are coordinated univocally only to form and color, they are ambiguous. Two-dimensional figures belong to a special group among these cases, whether they are drawn on paper, projected on a wall, or produced in some other way. With them we find particularly often that the significance of a part is determined by the whole. This does not seem to be true for the objective physical thing, a fact which points in this case to a difference between the phenomenal appearance and the physical relationships. For it is obvious that the physical possibilities of a piece of paper covered with black ink will not be changed if the surrounding pieces are made black. It must be asked whether this difference between phenomenon and object is due to the peculiarities of the perceptual apparatus.

In this connection it is important to realize that these plane figures which are produced by ink and paper are treated by our perception as if they were pictures of objective things. If one accepts this point of view one can again explain many ambiguities by referring to the objective structural significances, especially by referring to the fact that form does not imply a univocal determination of the possibilities of a thing. One can then easily understand why the ambiguities are especially striking in these cases. Subjective differences are produced to which no macroscopic physical differences correspond. What is objectively identical imitates what is different.

As mentioned above, the perception of complicated movement is similar to the cases of the constancies. The concepts which have been discussed allow us to determine more exactly the relationships involved. We are dealing with combinations of movement; for instance, a point executes a physically real movement X, which may be a true pendulum movement. The whole process can occur on a body y with the movement Y. The offshoots of X are then not univocally coordinated to the movement X, they are rather a function of X and Y; they change if Y changes. This motion is, so to speak, the level, in the sense that illumination is a level; the motion X belongs to the thing, it is presented to us by the offshoots and corresponds to the object color. The factors X and Y, which are thrown together in the offshoots as comparable magnitudes, have to be separated by the perceptual apparatus and referred to the correct level.

Thus we see that in many cases the ambiguity of a single local stimulus originates in the physical structure of the environment.

IV

Figure 2 represents in a schematic way the relation between the perceptual system and the environment.

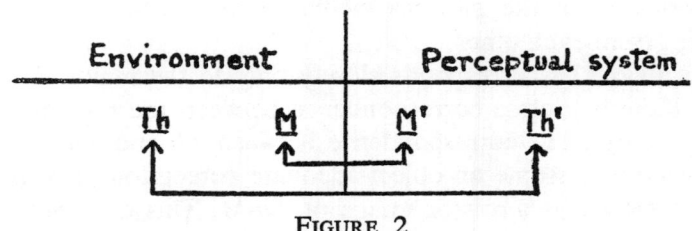

FIGURE 2

Th: The vitally relevant environment (we often call it "the world of things," but people, events, etc., also belong to it).

M: The mediating events, the stimuli which directly impinge on the organism.

M': The processes in the organism correlated to the stimuli; they can be experienced under certain conditions, e.g., as reduction color.

Th': Experiences which refer to things.

Ambiguity of the local stimulus means: to a certain segregated part of the region *M'* correspond different events in region *Th'*. This is still an inexact formulation. It would be better to say, in a more general way: the regions *MM'*, the regions of mediation, do not exactly correspond to the two regions *ThTh'* which are correlated to each other and which, so to speak, hold hands across the mediation region.

In order to get a better understanding of these relations, let us assume that we can order the entities of the mediating region *M* according to their similarities to each other. We would then obtain a manifold of points, and each point of this manifold would symbolize a certain stimulus pattern, e.g., a certain combination of light rays. Neighboring points would symbolize patterns which are similar to each other, and two points which are distant from each other would represent patterns which are very different from each other. The *Th* region could be ordered into a manifold in a similar way.

Let us now relate these two manifolds. Since one particular object can be mediated by a great number of different stimulus patterns, one point of the *Th* region has to be coordinated to many points of the *M* region. Further, these points in the *M* manifold are not located in one small connected region but are often far from each other since the patterns mediating one object can be very different from each other.

The region *Th* corresponds closely only to the region *Th'*; similarly, there is a close correspondence between the regions *M* and *M'*. Of course, this correspondence between *Th* and *Th'* is perfect only when we assume an object-adequate perception, in which the relation *M'-Th'* is a mirror image of *Th-M*. This does not always hold. When a melody is perceived, the object is not simply coordinated to the Gestalt character of the melody. Thus in this case there exists an incongruence between the systems which has nothing to do with the reference to the vitally relevant environment. Here we will not discuss the problem of the reality status of Gestalt characters. The objections which von Kries and Becher raised against an association theory of perception are based on the incongruence between the regions *Th* and *Th'* on the one hand and the regions *M* and *M'* on the other hand. Von Kries (1901) says: ". . . processes and patterns which are similar in a psychological sense, and which both lead to the same verbal symbol and are subsumed under the same general image, can be completely different" (p. 23). "One will always have to emphasize that two impressions which are similar according to their psychological effect have nothing in common if one considers them as a sum of stimuli arranged spatially in a certain way. The optical stimuli which a horse produces, one time seen from the front and from a small distance, another time from the side and from a greater distance, have nothing in common with what the designation 'horse' could be connected according to the association principle" (p. 25). Many examples demonstrating the same point can be found in Becher (1911), and in the literature of Gestalt psychology.

In general, the fact of mediation incongruence has been demonstrated, in a perhaps too one-sided way, only with figural and simple melodic forms. It certainly exists there, and may be especially impressive in these cases. But it must be emphasized that this mediation incongruence does not concern only figural perception. The same thing can "express" itself in many different stimulus patterns which are different from a figural point of view as well; and we can recognize it through these different mediations. This is shown, for instance, by von Kries's example of seeing a horse from the front and from the side.

Perhaps one can assume that there exist a number of different systems which connect the incongruent regions M' and Th'. The system of figural Gestalt units might be such an intermediate region. It is neither simply coordinated to the region of stimulus patterns, nor coordinated to the region of object meanings. Within the figural region there is no principle of identification according to which all figural structures representing the same meaning are included in one class.

This can be shown with the well-known illusion which consists of a picture of three men, drawn in equal size, walking away from the spectator down a hallway with perspective indicated by converging lines. The man who appears to be farthest away is seen as the tallest. True enough, the lines surrounding the men and the figural organization of these lines are the cause of this illusion. But it would be impossible to define the cause as something identifiable figurally. The basic reason for the illusion is the fact that the three men are, by means of the surrounding lines, put into different apparent distances, and that could have been achieved by many different line structures which have nothing in common figurally. Thus, if one considered only the figural region, one would make an error which could be called a skipping of meaning. One would be overlooking the fact that the effect from figure to figure does not occur within the figural region but in a region of meaning.

This example is analogous to that of the double-circle motion which was discussed before. There too the effect of the apparent motion of the surrounding points on the motion of one point does not occur in the figural region: the motion in the surrounding points refers, so to speak, the motion of a point to a different level of motion. Again, this level of motion is not identifiable figurally, but only as the "physical meaning of the motion."

Of course, one has to assume a certain correspondence between the regions Th and M in spite of this lack of simple congruence, because otherwise the region M could not serve as mediation. But this correspondence is not rigid and immediate; it is brought about by the intermediate systems.

To a certain extent, the M regions can be considered as irrelevant. The essential invariance in the perceptual process concerns the relation of the regions Th and Th'. The organism lives with and among things, and the specific mediation is to a large extent variable and allows substitution. If something new appears in the mediation, the processes will be reorganized in such a way that the coordination Th-Th' is re-established.

Since the essential process occurs between the regions Th and Th', it does not seem quite adequate to consider only the processes connecting M' and Th', and to try to find general laws concerning these processes. It is true that one may be able to show how a specific stimulus pattern gives rise to a specific meaning, but the factors which make possible a coordination between the regions Th and Th' seem to be more basic.

V

Thus we see that the performance of the perceptual apparatus is to a great extent determined by the structure of the environment. The next question to be discussed is the following: we find many cases of veridical perception, i.e., cases in which the perceptual apparatus functions adequately. What role do these cases play in the investigation of perception? One could defend the position that the environment-adequate cases of perception are less apt to reveal the structure of the perceptual system than the cases of illusions or distortions.

In order to understand better the meaning of this possible answer to our question, we must try to determine more exactly this "dependence" of the perceptual system (P) on the environment (E). We shall begin by analyzing not the dependence of P on E, but simpler examples in which one system is, so to speak, the "leader" and another system is the "follower." These examples may show us some general features of this relation of dependence. We want to find lawful relationships which would hold in every case of such a coupling of systems. These relations can also be studied in simple physical examples. We need not be afraid of "physicalism." We shall use some concepts which have been employed in Chapter 1. It will be noted that we are not beginning with an analysis of the object of our investigation itself—the perceptual system—but with an analysis "from the outside." We use this procedure not because we think it is the only correct one, but because there are cases in which the method of beginning "from the outside" may be fruitful.

The following physical example may serve to present the relevant concepts. An iron ball is placed on a horizontal surface, and is fastened by a thread to a point of the surface. A magnet moves around above the ball. The magnet is the "leading" system, the fastened ball is the "following" system. The magnet system will be called X, the ball system Y. In Figure 3 the path of the magnet is

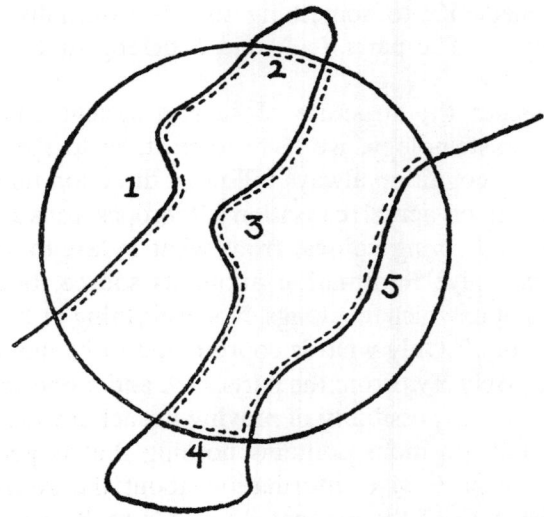

FIGURE 3

shown by a continuous line, the path of the ball by a dotted line. The parts of the path of the ball are not equal in meaning. In some parts ($1, 3, 5$) the ball follows the magnet. In other parts ($2, 4$) the form of the path of the ball is determined by the ball system itself, that is, in those parts in which the ball, held by the taut thread, cannot completely follow the magnet. Thus in some parts of the path the form has its source in Y (ball system) itself, in others the source of the form lies in X (magnet system).

The concept of the source of an event is important. A process can belong to a system Y but be centered, or have its source, in system X. This is possible if system Y has a great range of possibilities, while X determines which one of these possibilities will be actualized in a concrete case. Then the order in which the different actualizations follow each other has its source in X. Related to the concept of source is the concept of being internally or externally conditioned. In so far as an event has its source in the system to which it belongs, it is an internally conditioned event. It is externally conditioned if belonging and source are separated. Thus the form of the pieces 1, 3, and 5, which has its source in X, is externally conditioned. If we designate belonging by a capital letter, and source by a small letter, then Yy refers to something that is internally conditioned, Yx to something that is externally conditioned within system Y. The parts 1, 3, and 5 belong to Yx, the parts 2 and 4 to Yy.

If we consider the structure of such a system coupling in its relevance to epistemology, we have to start, so to speak, from the other end, since cognition always follows a direction that is opposed to the direction of actual causation. It gropes forward from the effect to the underlying causes, from what is last to what is first. Everything can give information about its source, but not necessarily about that to which it belongs. Not everything in Y is helpful for the cognition of Y. Only what is coordinated to its inner conditions is helpful, i.e., only Yy. From the parts 1, 3, and 5 one can infer only that the ball has the possibility of moving in such a way. The special sequence of ball positions contains nothing that is peculiar to Y. However, these parts give information about the system X, since they copy the path of the magnet. In so far as Y contains a Yx it is a medium and one can cognize X through Y.

The properties of Y, on the other hand, can only be found out from Yy. In other words: if one wants to cognize the properties of Y from a process in Y, then one has to exclude everything which agrees with X, disregard the features which can be resolved or explained by reference to X. Only those parts in which Y does not completely follow X, in which it makes "mistakes" in copying X, only those parts can serve to give information about Y. This thesis,

THE FUNCTION OF THE PERCEPTUAL SYSTEM

which concerns the cognition of the system Y, is of special importance for the considerations that are to follow.

Let us consider a tuning fork which is struck in a certain rhythm with a stick. The stick—and, of course, what guides the stick—is the leading system in this coupling, the tuning fork the following system. Again, we can separate two features in the process going on in the tuning fork. The wave frequency is proper to the tuning fork, but the rhythm of successive sounds is externally conditioned and is not characteristic of the system; it is forced on the system. If we apply the letters again, we can call the stick X, the tuning fork Y, the frequency Yy, and the rhythm Yx. If one wants to find out the properties of Y, one again must rely on Yy. One must subtract from the whole event the Yx which belongs to Y but copies X. Those features which cannot be understood as a copy of the leading system have to have their source in Y itself. One could also say: the more an object is a medium—i.e., the more the Yx predominates—the less can one find out about it from its actual state. One cannot get much information about a transparent pane of glass as long as one lets it act as a medium. One can look through it as if it were clear air. Only if one touches it with one's hand—that is, only when it does not simply mediate what comes from the outside but rather acts as an internally conditioned object—can one get information about the pane itself. This is also the case when it is possible to see its edge, or when one sees it from the side and notices a thin glittering line. In all these cases it does not act as a pure medium. The space which lies between us and the objects could be filled with many objects; it would be impossible for us to cognize them from optical data if they always were pure media for light rays. One could say, this part of space has the property of being a medium, and that is all one could say about it.

Thus, if one knows a feature of a system Y—a system that is influenced by a system X—one has to consider this feature first in relation to X in order to find out whether it is a characteristic of Y. Where Y disagrees with X, there are the points of "inadequacy" (inadequacy in regard to copying X) which are characteristic for Y. One must not refer these features to system X, but rather they must be ordered in a way which corresponds to the properties of Y. The taking into account of X has only the purpose of avoiding a wrong conceptual centering.

This danger of a wrong centering and wrong unit formation is especially great where we are confronted with an enduring coupling of two systems. One is then easily induced to ascribe properties to Y which in reality are forced upon Y by X. Through constant coupling, features and units which are foreign to a system acquire the appearance of features proper to it. The wrong application of achievement concepts is a case of this kind of unit formation, which is foreign to the system one wants to describe.

Now we can attempt to treat the relation between E (environment) and P (perceptual system) in terms of the discussed concepts. E is the leading system, it is a case of X; P follows, it is a case of Y. The events in P have their source partly in P itself, partly in E. One can separate Pp from Pe. Pe is not symptomatic of P, it contains features which are foreign to P. In other words: E is mirrored in P. Where the mirror copies E exactly, it does not give information about P itself; only where the mirror distorts E can one get information about properties of P from the mirror image. This means that only when our perception is mistaken, only when it does not correctly reproduce the objects, can one obtain useful data for the study of the properties inherent in the perceptual system.

We have discussed the thought model which is characterized by the concepts of "leading" and "following" systems, "X-determined" and "Y-determined" features in Y, with two examples; this approach has been used to gain a better understanding of the relation of the environment to the perceptual system. Now we ought to consider whether the relation of E to P is actually analogous to the couplings which we found in the physical examples. We are especially concerned with Yx, those features of the system Y which have their source in X. In the physical examples it is simply X-adequate; it consists of the properties of Y which agree with X. They agree because in direct causation X induces the Yx in Y.

However, obviously the E-adequate features of P are not induced through a direct influence of E. This is indicated by general considerations which can be summarized as follows: object-adequate percepts are not directly enforced on P by E. Stimulus adequacy is not environment adequacy, and the more the receiving system elaborates and organizes the direct influences from the environment (i.e., the stimulus patterns, the raw data), the more it approaches the environment, and the more it offers an adequate picture of E. This can be demonstrated with every simple perception. If a tree is perceived, what is adequate to the tree does not consist of what is enforced on the retina by the stimuli but rather of what P makes out of these stimuli according to its own structure. Precisely the way in which P modifies and elaborates what is directly forced upon it proves to be very object-adequate. In other words, the P system functions purposefully. Therefore, with P, we have to distinguish between (1) what is forced on P by E directly, and (2) what is E-adequate in P.

As long as we consider only the regions M and M' (the region of stimuli and the region of "sensations"), we can maintain with a certain justification—though strictly speaking, it does not even hold there—that everything in P which is adequate to E (in this case to the stimuli) is forced on P by the direct influence of E. We still can use the analogy with the physical examples. But it is different with the regions Th and Th', between which the two adjacent regions M and M' lie. Region Th, the objects, is the leading system; it is followed by region Th', the region of percepts; these give a picture of Th and are more central psychical structures. Thus one finds E-adequacy in region Th', but one cannot talk about direct enforcing.

One could also say that one finds adequacy of two different kinds. The one concerns only actual processes which belong to M' and which are enforced on M' by M. The other kind concerns dispositional characters and refers to the functions of P which connect M' with Th'. As we saw previously, these functions must to some degree correspond, like a mirror image, to the relation Th-M.

In the physical examples, there exists in Y an X-adequacy only as long as X influences Y directly; when X is absent, there is no Yx. With P it is different. E-adequacy lies in the structure and in the functions of P. This adequacy is also present when E does not influence P. It is something dispositional and it concerns the possibilities and properties of P.

This is a fundamentally new relation. It represents a higher level of adequacy. Instead of adequate actual processes it consists of adequate dispositions and functions. Dispositions of a system, which are adequate to something foreign to this system, are doubly centered; they seemingly have their home both inside and outside of the system. With these considerations we have found an approach to the concept of "purpose." A function is called purposeful if it can be meaningfully referred to two different systems—or, if we want to use a more cautious formulation, to two systems which at first sight seem to be separate. It is not contended that the essence of purposefulness consists of this property, only that it shows this feature when it is analyzed "from the outside." However, our thinking revolts against attributing such a double home to any part of reality. We cannot conceive of correlations which hang in the air, so to speak. We try to derive the separate but nevertheless corresponding facts from a unitary source.[1] This can be done in two ways: (1) One can assume that both facts have their source in one of the systems. In doing this, one is also assuming, along with this dispositional correspondence, a forcing upon, a leading and a following system. (2) One can assume that the corresponding facts have a common source outside the two systems. It may be mentioned that association theory and related theories make use of the first possibility. We can conceive of these theories as attempts to explain the correspondence by the assumption that one system forces dispositions upon another system.

But here we want only to consider some methodological questions, primarily whether, taking into account dispositional correspondence, we can still maintain the thesis stated above: i.e., that only inadequate perception reveals the properties of the perceptual system. One could contend that this proposition is also justified in regard to functions. As long as a function is adequate in reference to something foreign to the system, it tells us only just this fact, namely, that it follows the other system. But how this adequacy is brought about, and on which more fundamental possibilities it is based, one can find out only by observing inadequacies.

Thus the method of studying the properties of the perceptual system can be characterized as follows (and this method is probably valid in all similar cases of system coupling): the features which are adequate to the environment must be determined first, and then facts must be referred to an immanent order, which is made possible by taking into account the inadequate features.

[1] See Bühler (1929, p. 148ff.). The theory of system coupling is of great importance for many philosophical and scientific problems. The correspondence of two seemingly independent systems appears to man as a problem and points to some underlying causes (e.g., the body-soul problem).

3

THE FUNCTION OF ECONOMICAL DESCRIPTION IN PERCEPTION

The purpose of this paper is (1) to relate some of the ideas expressed in the paper on "Thing and Medium" to Russell's theory of the role of causal lines in perception, and (2) to discuss the function of economical description in veridical perception.

The starting point of "Thing and Medium" was the puzzle which arises when one considers the causal antecedents of the stimuli impinging on the organism. Let us take the case of a visual perception of a distant object. Tracing the process back from the proximal stimulus we find the following stages: (1) light waves between the organism and the object, (2) an event involving the object, (3) light waves between the object and the light source, and (4) a process in the light source.

If one says that the percept is directed toward the object because the object causes the proximal stimulus, the following question must be posed: why is the object the target of perception and not any of the other stages which are all causal antecedents of the proximal stimulus? (Cf. Meinong [1906, p. 107]; the section dealing with this question in "Thing and Medium" has been omitted.)

Russell says in discussing this problem: "In the daytime, practically all the light that reaches the eye comes ultimately from the sun, but we do not say that we are seeing only the sun. We are seeing the last region after which the course of light was virtually unimpeded until it reached the eye. When light is reflected or scattered, we consider, as a rule, that it makes us see the last object from which it is reflected or scattered . . ." (Russell, 1948, p. 207).

This essay has been especially written for this volume and has not been published before.

Thus the fact that the distal stimulus "causes" the proximal stimulus cannot be the only basis for the possibility of our seeing objects. In order to solve the problem of why we do not say that we see the source of light when we look at illuminated objects, one has to consider the relation of the light process to the different systems ("substrata") through which it passes. Some of these systems show a high degree of restraint, their parts are mutually dependent, and they impose their order on the process. These systems are, by and large, the vitally relevant things of our environment, the distal stimuli. Opposed to them are systems which show a low degree of restraint; their parts are mutually independent, and they take on any order imposed on them. These systems can serve as mediators. When proximal stimuli impinge on our sense organs, we say we perceive the things of the environment, that is, the systems which imposed their order on the mediation and through the mediation on the perceptors. We do not say we perceive the source of illumination because it is not responsible for the order contained in the proximal stimuli.

Russell, who as we saw is concerned with similar questions, says: "When I see a table or a chair or a page of print there are causal lines from its parts to the eye. We can carry the chain of causation further back, until we reach the sun—if we are seeing by daylight. But when we go further back than the table or chair or page of print, the causes have no longer any close resemblance to their effects. . . . Consequently, the experience that I have when I 'see a table' can give me much knowledge concerning the table, but not much knowledge concerning earlier parts of the process that ends in my experience. For this reason I am said to be seeing the table, not the sun" (Russell, 1948, p. 459). By "causal line" he does not mean a line connecting any cause and effect, but a line which preserves variety: "A 'causal line,' as I wish to define the term, is a temporal series of events so related that, given some of them, something can be inferred about the others whatever may be happening elsewhere" (p. 459). He also refers to the mutual independence of mediating events: "If percepts are to allow inferences to objects, the physical world must contain more or less separable causal chains. . . . The theory of light assures us that this is the case. Light waves emanating from a source will, in suitable circumstances, pursue their course practically unaffected by other light waves in the same region" (p. 206).

An imposed order can therefore function as a sign for the imposing order; it cannot be explained in terms of the system which contains it because this system has few restraints and any order arising in it would be highly improbable. In "Thing and Medium" these imposed orders are called "spurious units"; they make cognition in depth possible; they are responsible for the fact that our world extends beyond what touches our skins. They are the manifolds of "offshoots" from which we infer the core systems and core events.

When a manifold of offshoots is interpreted as coming from one causal center, and if this manifold is thus taken as a sign of the causal center, the interpretation is "economical." It seems worth while to spell out in greater detail the relation between economical interpretation on the one hand, and the probability of the connection linking offshoot and center on the other hand.

Let us think again of the schematic representation of the total perceptual event (see "The Function of the Perceptual System"). It contains two parts: the environmental part, extending from object to proximal stimulus, and the part extending from proximal stimulus to phenomenon. Brunswik (1955b, p. 9) called them the ecological and the organismic phase.

The first part is characterized by the relation between causal center and offshoot manifold. One specific offshoot manifold x could have been caused by a great number of causal centers c_1, c_2, ... c_n, though with unequal probabilities. That is, the probability that x has been caused by c_1 may be .001, by c_2 .003, and so on, but that it has been caused by a certain c_3 is .99. We find one c with a probability very much higher than that of any other c, if we disregard the possibility of an ambiguous x. These probabilities we could obtain by a frequency count of actual coordinations between x and the different centers. They are given by the structure of the environment and are independent of the perceptual system.

Now let us consider the organismic part of the perceptual event. It is ruled by the law of *Prägnanz,* which has recently been reformulated as the law of economical description. A certain pattern of stimuli is linked to a number of theoretically possible phenomena or "interpretations." The one that usually occurs is distinguished by being an economical description. Thus, Hochberg and McAlister (1953) suggest the hypothesis that "the probability of a given response to a stimulus is an inverse function of the amount of information required to define that pattern" (p. 364). Using a slightly different approach, Attneave (1954) says: "It appears likely that a major function of the perceptual machinery is to strip away some of the redundancy of stimulation, to describe or encode incoming information in a form more economical than that in which it impinges on the receptors" (p. 189).

Thus the offshoot manifold, the x, is coordinated on the environmental side to the most probable cause, and on the organismic side to a response which is economical of information. How is it possible that by "stripping away the redundancy of stimulation" a representation of the object that caused the stimulation is obtained? Why does the law of economical description furnish a general rule for the decoding of the stimulus pattern?

Russell says that "when a group of complex events in more or less the same neighborhood all have a common structure, and appear to be grouped about a central event, it is probable that they have a common causal ancestor" (Russell, 1948, pp. 464-465). In this formulation he has in mind especially cases like that of one object seen from different points of view. The proximal stimulus patterns are approximately identical and they are all referred to the same causal center.

The first part of the quoted sentence implies the possibility of economical description. When several complex events have a common structure, they can be described economically "by describing one and specifying the positions of the others and the fact that they are identical (cf. *similarity* as a grouping law)" (Attneave, 1954, p. 190). Though Attneave refers to somewhat different examples, his statement is relevant here.

The second part of the sentence refers to the probability of the common causal ancestor, and Russell says that he is using the word "probable" in the sense of frequency. He suggests that there exists an underlying law of nature which he formulates as follows: "Any complex event tends to be followed by other complex events identical, or approximately identical, with it in structure, and distributing themselves from next to next throughout a certain region of space-time" (Russell, 1948, p. 467).

Thus we see that possibility of economical description (in this case similarity) and probability of the common causal ancestor are considered as belonging together. Essentially the same idea is expressed in "Thing and Medium" by the concept of "spurious unit," by which is meant a regularity which points to a "unitary cause," that is, to a common causal ancestor. In regard to forced vibration, which is taken as an example of a manifold produced by a common source, it is said that "if each beat had an independent cause, it would be very improbable that the beats would show this kind of regularity" (see p. 6).

The role of probability and parsimony in perception were considered by Ernst Mach (1897). He took as an example the case of a straight line. He says that, on the one hand, it is an instance of economy of description which he formulates in the following way: "Thus the straight line in space represents a minimum of departure from the mean of the depth-sensations; and the assumption forthwith presents itself that the straight line is seen with the least effort" (p. 96). This formulation is similar to that of Attneave (1954, p. 191).

It may be mentioned that in Mach's theory the "deviation of a sensation from the mean of the neighboring sensations" plays an important role. We are reminded of Helson's theory of adaptation level and of Attneave's discussion of it (1954, p. 191). Mach says that "The deviation of a sensation from the mean of the adjacent sensations is always noticeable, and exacts a special effort on the part of the sense-organ" (1897, p. 97). He applies this idea also to light "sensations."

To return to the straight line: it also illustrates Mach's "principle of probability," in that "The most probable object . . . answering to a perspective straight line, is a spatial straight line" (Mach, 1897, p. 95). What is meant is that a straight line in the environment, for instance, the edge of a table, will always produce a straight line in the perspective plane in whatever position it lies, except when it is directed toward the receptor and its projection is a point. A straight line in the perspective plane could also have been produced by a curved line in space, but only by one lying in a plane in which also the receptor lies. Therefore, it is much more probable that the perspective straight line is produced by a straight line than by a curve in space. "The visual sense acts therefore in conformity with the principle of economy, and, at the same time, in conformity with the principle of probability, when it exhibits a preference for straight lines" (Mach, 1897, p. 96).

Obviously, Mach here introduces something like the principle of inverse probabilities. In this connection it is interesting to see how Laplace (1814) states the "fundamental principle . . . which consists in passing from events to causes." He says: "Each of the causes to which an observed event may be attributed is indicated with just as much likelihood as there is probability that the event will take place, supposing the event to be constant. The probability of the existence of any one of these causes is then a fraction whose numerator is the probability of the event resulting from this cause and whose denominator is the sum of the similar probabilities relative to all causes; if these various causes, considered *a priori,* are unequally probable, it is necessary, in place of the probability of the event resulting from each cause, to employ the product of this probability by the possibility of the cause itself" (p. 1331). Laplace states that this principle expresses the reason why we attribute regular events to a particular cause: "If we seek a cause wherever we perceive symmetry, it is not that we regard a symmetrical event as less possible than others, but, since this event ought to be the effect of a regular cause or that of chance, the first of these suppositions is more probable than the second" (p. 1331). These considerations certainly seem highly relevant to our problem. Again we find a connection stated between the possibility of economical description (symmetry), and attribution to a causal center.

As a last example we take the attribution of relative motion, which has been studied by Duncker (1929) and Johansson (1950). Hochberg (1957) summarizes Johansson's findings as follows: "In Johansson's motion studies, those components in a complex moving stimulus which are common to all members of a group are 'partialled out' and form a single framework in relation to which the residual motions appear" (p. 82). He adds that "such unification achieves an 'informational' economy since, for any given stimulus, the perception entailing the least number of changes is obtained" (p. 82). It is illuminating to compare with this formulation of the relation between the proximal stimulus and phenomenon another treatment of essentially the same case, which is, however, more interested in the relation between proximal stimulus and the actual environmental changes, that is, in the ecological phase. Cournot (1838) states that if we observe a manifold of points and notice that all points except one had preserved their relative position, "we should consider it very probable that this single point was the only one which had moved, unless, indeed, all the other points were so connected that the movement of one would involve the movement of all" (p. 1204). He uses this principle to obtain the most probable hypothesis regarding the attribution of relative changes of values of commodities, and he comes to the conclusion that "among all the possible hypotheses on absolute variations some explain the relative variations more simply and more probably than others" (p. 1205). Thus simplicity of organization and probability of reconstructing the actual environmental process are again coupled.

These quotations, taken from different sources, do not yet give us a formal and exact description of the relations between economy and probability in perception. However, they seem to indicate that in using the principle of economy of description our perceptual apparatus succeeds in decoding the stimulus pattern in an adaptive and realistic way. A causal center is responsible for a number of offshoots spreading out in different directions. When this offshoot manifold is defined with reference to the center, then, in most cases, it is defined more economically than without this reference.

However, we must ask whether it is really necessary to assume that the perceptual apparatus "uses" the principle of economy as a general method of decoding the stimulus input. Here we can apply the considerations which were presented in "The Function of the Perceptual System." One point that was made there was that not everything that happens in a system has to be ascribed to the restraints of this system.

The very fact that the principle of economy is adapted, that is, that it implies a correspondence with the environment, is a reason to be cautious in believing that it is embodied in the functioning of the perceptual system. So far we have found out only that the principle of economy leads to results that conform to the environment, and that we can describe the "outputs" of the perceptual apparatus as if they followed that principle. But we have thus only described the achievements, the end results of the perceptual system; we do not know how they are attained. Maybe they are attained without the help of this principle by a sort of rote memorizing of all the different cases of offshoot-center connections.

For example, a person may know how to write down the correct answers to a number of puzzle questions, and an observer could describe the answers as being in accord with a general method of solution. But that does not prove that this general method was used in obtaining the answers; they may have been learned by heart. Again, one might be able to produce a machine which gives the response "cube" to a limited number of perspective views of an actual cube, and which similarly gives correct responses to views of a pyramid or a cone. The responses could be described as following the principle of economy of description of the stimulus pattern, though they are actually the result of specific connections and the principle of economy has played no part in the functioning of the machine.

Fortunately, we have ample evidence about the role of the principle of economy in perception. The percepts which can be described in terms of this principle are not all adapted, they do not all point to the true causal center. They are often "errors" of the perceptual system. To use the analogue of the person who "solves" puzzles: as long as he gives answers which are correct solutions, we do not know whether he has just memorized the solutions or whether he produced them with an understanding of the operations involved. But if he makes an error, and we are able to trace this error to the wrong application of a principle, we can conclude that this principle plays a role in his thinking. In the same way, we do not know whether we are justified in attributing the principle of economy to the perceptual apparatus as long as it leads to veridical perception. But since it often leads to nonveridical perception, we can assume that it is a characteristic of the perceptual processes.

4

ENVIRONMENTAL DETERMINANTS IN PSYCHOLOGICAL THEORIES

Numerous attempts have been made to bring about discussions in which the basic concepts of different psychological theories can be brought into relation with each other. But such attempts have usually failed to yield fruitful results, and they have failed largely because the basic terms in which the data are organized by the different theories are not fully analyzed and because discussion is often based on concepts that are not directly comparable. In order to bring together the different theoretical approaches to psychological problems and to discuss them, we must recognize that it is often possible, especially in sciences dealing with the organism, to organize data in several different ways, at least in a first approximation. The way in which data are organized and the method by which the identity of focal unities or focal variables is determined are significant characteristics of a theory. Until we understand clearly what a given theory considers essential for the description of phenomena and in what terms it describes a given process in order to connect it with what has preceded and to predict its future, we cannot try to bring that theory into relation with others.

The purpose of this paper is to consider some general problems of determination and of the derivation of subordinate systems. The distinction between proximal and distal determinants is treated in detail and an attempt is made to analyze several psychological theories in terms of this distinction.

Originally published in *Psychological Review*, 46:383-410, 1939.

General Remarks about Determination of Focal Variables

Relevant Determination

In order to discuss the determination of focal variables we can do no better than to begin with a quotation from Holt (1915):

> ... It is inaccurate to say that a river flows toward the sea ... while it is fairly accurate to describe it as always flowing towards the next lower level of the earth's surface, and this is a law describing flow as a constant function of the earth's crust and the position of the earth's center. The test is, of course, whether this or that could be removed *without changing* the river's course. ... So in behavior, the flock of birds is not, with any accuracy, flying over the green field; it is, more essentially, flying southward; ... the sole question which we need ever ask is, "What is it doing?" [p. 166].

Or again:

> ... the man is walking past my window; no, I am wrong, it is not past my window that he is walking; it is *to* the theater; ... the functional view ... admonishes us to keep the man whole (if it is *behavior* that we are studying) and to study his movements until we have discovered *exactly what* he is doing, that is, until we have found that object, situation, process ... of which his behavior is a *constant function* [p. 161f.].

Koffka (1935), in explaining the meaning of relevant and irrelevant description, uses almost the same example:

> ... a ball runs down an incline and finally falls into a hole. Now there may be water in the hole or not, and therefore I can say the ball falls into a hole with water or without water. But this difference does not affect the motions of the ball until it has reached that position in space where the water begins in the one case and not in the other. For the rest of the motion the presence or absence of water is wholly irrelevant; similarly, the statement that the rat does not run towards food when the experimenter has just removed it, is quite irrelevant to the run of the rat until it is near enough to notice the absence of food [p. 37].

Of course the inquiry, "What are the objects doing?" is not so simple as Holt makes it out. Each theory uses a different set of concepts as the only valid and legitimate one. But we learn from these quotations, first, that there exist a great number—as a matter of fact an infinite number—of possibilities of determining an event. We can determine the motion of the water in a river as toward the sea or toward the next lower level of the earth's surface; we can describe the motion of a flock of birds as "over the green field," or as "southward." Besides the determinants mentioned in the quotations, a great number of other determinants are possible.

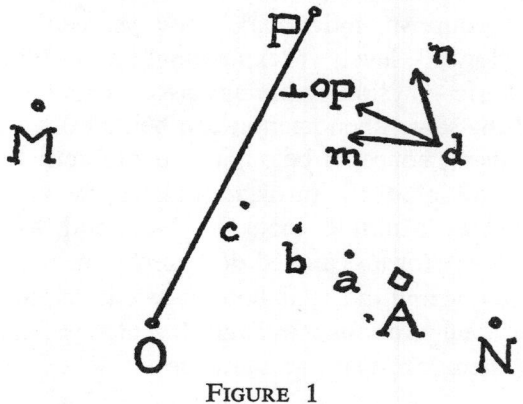

FIGURE 1

Secondly we learn that only a few determinants are relevant; i.e., there are only a few determinants that can be used to describe the events in a simple way. The test for this relevancy consists in finding constant functions. We may add another example which demonstrates the same facts in a more abstract way. Let us assume that one can observe that particle A in Figure 1 moves through points a, b, c. We are free to determine this motion in many different ways. We can say A is moving toward M, or away from N, or that it is moving toward the line OP in a direction perpendicular to it. Which determination is relevant? That is to say, what is A "really" doing? We find the answer if we remove A to point d. If A then moves in direction m, it is moving toward M. If it moves in direction n, it is moving away from N, and so on.[1]

Rival Determinants

However, the task of determining the variables in a relevant way is not always so simple. It is often made difficult by the possibility

[1] In regard to methods for finding relevant determinations, see the important studies of Heinrich Klüver (1933, 1936).

of rival determinants. Usually only one determinant will be successful, that is to say, will make a simple description of events possible and will yield constant coordinations for different situations. However, it often happens that determinants which belong to different regions seem to yield constant functions. Wherever we find two or more contending theories there exists such a situation. Examples are: description in terms of the whole or in terms of the parts (gas vs. molecule, group vs. individual, body vs. cell); in terms of "higher" or "lower" levels ("explaining" and "understanding" psychology, physics-physiology-biology-psychology). In all of these cases one and the same phenomenon can be described more or less relevantly by using concepts belonging to different focal regions.

The fact of multiple focus furnishes philosophy with many of its classical problems. Multiple focus is distasteful to thinking; it blocks the tendency toward unified determination. It is as if it were possible to read one and the same book in two ways; once by organizing the letter configurations into English sentences, and then again by organizing them into German sentences.

Types of Derivation of Subordinate Systems of Determinants

In order to escape the dilemma of rival determinants different devices are used. Thus many theories say: "Yes, it is true that one can find more or less constant functions if one chooses the terms of region B. However, using these determinants, one will never attain a complete description of the cases in question. The seemingly constant functions one finds in this way are the product of a combination of functions which can only be determined adequately if one applies the terms of region A." The derivation of subordinate systems of functions becomes, therefore, a main problem for many theories.

This derivation follows certain patterns. A typical kind of derivation is, for instance, derivation by selection. Let us assume that a given manifold of processes or objects can be determined more or less relevantly in terms of two different regions, A and B. This is a case of multiple focus. Let us now assume that one theory, in order to reduce this multiple focus to single focus, declares A to be the focus, the independent system, and B to be the derived system.

The theory contends, then, that originally there were an infinite number of processes or objects, and they were all relevantly determinable in system A. The fact that we find a few processes which show constancy when determined in system B is due to chance. If there is an infinite number of items available we can arbitrarily choose any determinants and we shall always find a certain number of items which show constant functions in regard to those determinants. Furthermore, the theory contends that there is a selection going on which works in such a way that in the end only items conforming to system B are left over, and all items not conforming to B are eradicated. Since all items conform to A, the items which are left over conform to both A and B. It is assumed that the selection itself can also be explained in terms of system A alone. Thus it can be shown that only determination in system A is inherently relevant. Determination in B is not independently relevant; it is an outgrowth of determination in A.

Darwin's theory of selection uses this method in establishing the system of teleological determination as a dependent system. An infinite number of possibilities is realized, all conforming to system A, which is in this case the system of causal explanation. Some of them possess characteristics which "make sense" in system B also; that is to say, they can be determined as having some use for the organism. Natural selection then works in such a way that only these possibilities are left over.

Other cases of derivation by selection are offered by the theories which explain the teleological properties of perception or thinking, namely the fact that in some way they show a correspondence to the "real" world, in terms of experience. The problem is very similar: double determination, that is to say, determination in causal and in teleological terms, has to be reduced to single determination in causal terms. An infinite number of possible bonds is realized, all conforming to causal system A. Some of them also fit the teleological system B, and a law of effect, for instance, takes care of the selection. Theories of association, of conditioned reflex, positivistic and pragmatistic theories of the derivation of logical forms, all make use of this type of derivation.

Often the defenders of system B use counterarguments, which again follow typical patterns. They can say, first, that the assumption of an originally infinite number of possibilities is untenable. In observation we find only a small number of items $A\bar{B}$ (conforming to A but not to B); most of the items are AB. It cannot be due to chance, therefore, that B's appear.

Or they can say that the B's are of such great complexity that the probability of B's coming into existence among the A's through chance is infinitely small.

Or they can say that there exist B's in regions where the process by which B's were selected from the infinite number of A's never occurred.

To this last argument the defenders of A can retort by using the device of extrapolation. They assume that selection worked so often on items conforming to system A that these items, in time, got used to conforming to B and so exhibit B-characteristics even in regions where the selection was not directly active.

Tendencies Affecting the Selection of Determinants

One might assume that the question as to which region shall be used as the primary system of determination is always answered on the basis of empirical findings. However, this assumption does not always seem to hold. General *a priori* tendencies are often responsible for the choice of a certain region as a focus. A few of these tendencies may be enumerated.

1. A tendency to use regions close to the observer as the focal region.—This tendency results from a reluctance to make theories and from an inclination to measure prematurely. Surface processes or surface characteristics are taken as relevant determinants and correlations are computed. Both the psychology of personality and of social functions provide many examples. This tendency is supported by positivism. The important principle which states that every concept should be anchored in observations or "operations" is often misunderstood. It is thought that one should take the directly observed entities themselves as the focus and that one should be satisfied with a language of data. Cruder forms of behaviorism thus find an ally in a misunderstood positivism.[2]

2. A tendency to use the same focus for different regions of a science.—One does not want the science to be broken up into regions with different determinants. There will always be attempts

[2] See Koffka's concepts of achievement and performance (1935, p. 530), and Lewin's confrontation of historic-geographic and systematic concepts, phenotypic and genotypic language (1935).

ENVIRONMENTAL DETERMINANTS

to find constancies of a higher order and to put the focus into a deeper layer so as to combine the different regions.

3. *A tendency to use proximal determinants and to avoid distant determinants.*—No change should be determined by something which is distant in time or space. More will be said about this point later.

Psychological Fallacies

In determining the focus of a psychological theory one must always keep in mind the possibility of a disguised focus. The relevant variables may be assumed to be in region *A;* however, since there often exists a confusion between regions, or an unwarranted assumption of equality of regions, the relevant variables are really described in terms of another region *B*. By means of a disguised focus sham solutions of many problems are possible. This fact has often been noticed, and it has been discussed in a more general way under the name of "fallacy" or "error."

Some of these confusions (see Table I) are:

1. James' "psychologist's fallacy."—The "mental state" is determined in terms of the coordinated object. "Equal to" is substituted for "referring to."

> The *great* snare of the psychologist is the *confusion of his own standpoint with that of the mental fact* about which he is making his report. I shall hereafter call this the "psychologist's fallacy" *par excellence.* . . . Now when it is a cognitive state (percept, thought, concept, etc.), he ordinarily has no other way of naming it than as the thought, percept, etc., *of that object*. He himself, meanwhile, knowing the self-same object in *his* way, gets easily led to suppose that the thought, which is *of* it, knows it in the same way in which he knows it, although this is often very far from being the case [1890, Vol. I, p. 196].

TABLE I

SOME OF THE PSYCHOLOGICAL "FALLACIES"

The arrows start in the region the terms of which are supposedly used; they end in the region the terms of which are actually used.

	images	sensations	stimuli	objects
James' fallacy	—————————————————→			
Stimulus error (Titchener)		——————————————→		
Constancy hypothesis		—————→		
Experience error			—————→	

2. *Titchener's stimulus error.*—The psychological "elements" (sensations, etc.) are described in terms of the physical environment. "The psychologist commits the stimulus-error when he lapses from the psychological point of view into some other, like the physical" (Boring, 1929, p. 410).

3. *Köhler's constancy hypothesis.*—"Sensations" are hypothesized and described in terms of the stimuli (1929, p. 96).

4. *Köhler's experience error.*—Stimuli are described in terms of the experiential or distant object.

> In psychology much has been said about the stimulus-error which consists in our confusing our knowledge about the physical conditions of sensory experience with experience as such. But another mistake, which I propose to call the *experience-error,* is not less unfortunate. It occurs when we unintentionally attribute certain properties of sensory experience to the actual constellation of stimuli, properties which are so very common that we tend to apply them to whatever we are thinking about. This is the case primarily, wherever we have not yet learned to see the *problem* contained in those common properties of experience. No wonder, then, that neurologists and some psychologists still talk about "the retinal stimuli" corresponding to an object, as though there were something like detached functional units on the retina [Köhler, 1929, p. 176].
>
> Because the distant object is a thing by itself, the assumption is tacitly made that the retinal image corresponding to it is also [Koffka, 1935, p. 97].

Distal and Proximal Determinants in Several Psychological Theories

A consideration of relevant description and its relation to a manifold of regions is important for psychology because, as the discussion of the fallacies has shown, there are so many regions involved in each psychological process. And not only are there many regions involved, but determination in terms of each region seems to make sense; that is to say, leads to relatively constant functions. This makes for the multiplicity of psychological theories, each of which places the focal concepts in a different region.

In the following an attempt is made to describe a few psychological theories in regard to the place of focus. We shall, for the most part, consider only the outer field, that is to say, environmental determinants, and shall only occasionally refer to internal, inner-organismic determination.

Of prime importance for all theories is the question whether distal or proximal data are used as the focus in the determination. One can treat perception and action either in terms of the distant object (perception functions in such a way that the distant object is "attained"; the organism moves toward the food, etc.); or one can treat it in terms of proximal influences and effects, that is to say, in terms of processes close to the skin, stimuli, muscle contractions or movements of the limbs.[3]

Theories in Terms of Proximal Influences and Effects

These theories fall into two groups. One group stresses perception; to it belong the older theories of perception which emphasized the stimulus-oriented sensations. The other group treats the psychological processes more from the point of view of action and motor phenomena; to it belong the stimulus-response theories.[4]

It is easy to see that these theories get their vitality from the general tendency to use proximal determinants and not from observation; observation favors distal determinants much more. The exponents of these theories want to relate psychological processes to the actual concrete influences which organism and environment exert on each other.

The most important arguments against these theories can be reduced to a single point: observation shows that often distal determination is possible where proximal determination is impossible. Von Kries, Becher, Ehrenfels, and the Gestalt theory used this argument against the older theories of perception; different teleological systems (McDougall, etc.) used this argument against stimulus-response theories.

Indeed, the most important problem for all theories using proximal determinants is to show that it is possible to establish that system of determination as the independent one, and further that it is possible to derive from that system the existence of relevant distal determinants, which are found in observation, and to treat them as only apparently relevant determinants. The device which

[3] See Koffka's use of the terms proximal and distant stimuli (1935, p. 80).
[4] That these two groups of theories belong together has been shown, for instance, by Köhler (1929).

is almost exclusively used for this derivation is selection. There is the infinite number of possibilities of bonds of association or conditioned reflexes between any stimuli and any responses. Contact with the environment establishes or strengthens only a limited, selected number of these bonds. Selection works in such a way that distal determination, that is to say, correspondence to the objects of the environment, is brought about.

However, very often the derivation of distal from proximal determination is effected by the surreptitious substitution of distal for proximal terms.[5] The following cases are examples of disguised focus. We quote here from a study in which distal determinants are quite openly introduced into a "stimulus-response" theory.

> Suppose that we are studying the behavior of such an organism as a rat in pressing a lever. The number of distinguishable acts on the part of the rat that will give the required movement of the lever is indefinite and very large. Except for certain rare cases they constitute a class, which is sufficiently well-defined by the phrase "pressing the lever." Now it may be shown that under various circumstances the rate of responding is significant—that is to say, it maintains itself or changes in lawful ways [Skinner, 1935, p. 44].

We note that the author starts out to study "the behavior of such an organism as a rat in pressing a lever," that is to say, a phenomenon which is from the beginning defined by distal determinants. It is conceded that it is impossible to find coordinated proximal events: "The number of distinguishable acts on the part of the rat that will give the required movement of the lever is indefinite and very large." Therefore, instead of proximal events, there is substituted a "class which is sufficiently well defined by the phrase 'pressing the lever,'" a phrase which of course denotes distal determination in its purest form. And, placing the focus in the distant environment, one can find that "the rate of responding is significant—that is to say, it maintains itself or changes in lawful ways," namely, distal determination yields constant functions.

That distal determination is forced upon us by the observed facts is also stressed in the following quotation:

---

[5] See especially the keen analysis of stimulus-response theories by Arthur F. Bentley (1935).

The uniformity of the change in rate excludes any supposition that we are dealing with a group of separate reflexes and forces the conclusion that "pressing the lever" behaves experimentally as a unitary thing [Skinner, 1935, p. 45].

We should like to add one more quotation from the same paper, in which the principle of finding the relevant determination is clearly expressed:

> It is then possible to test the irrelevance of a non-defining property by showing that two responses, one of which possesses the property, the other not, contribute equally well to a total number [of elicitations of a reflex] [1935, p. 44].

Not always is the change in focus as patent as in this paper. It is much more difficult, for instance, to find in Hull's theory of habit-family hierarchy the place where distal determinants are substituted for proximal determinants. The problem that this theory attempts to solve comes from the fact that "habits" which are determined distally, by the achievement, represent a confusing variety in proximal terms. "Instead of presenting a single unvarying and undistinguishable sameness, as is too often assumed, habits . . . present remarkably varied series of patterns" (Hull, 1934, p. 33).

According to Hull, some mechanism has to be found which gives identity to this "family" of patterns in terms of action sequences. The problem is essentially the same as that which von Kries stated for perception: Is there anything identical in the different stimulus patterns that correspond to an identical object? If the analogous problem were solved for action, it would be a decided advance toward an explanation of goal-directed behavior. "It [the principle of habit-family hierarchy] is operative in all situations wherever there is more than one distinct action sequence which will lead to the attainment of a particular goal or subgoal. It is believed, for example, that the habit-family hierarchy constitutes the dominant physical mechanism which mediates such tests of truth and error as organisms employ—that it provides the basis for a purely physical theory of knowledge" (Hull, 1934, p. 40f.).

We do not have to go into the details of this interesting and ingenious theory in order to show why we believe that it, too, achieves the solution by means of a disguised focus. The critical point is the definition of the identical element which makes the different action sequences belong to one family and thereby interchangeable. This identical element is the "same" goal reaction which is brought forward in the action sequence as the "fractional anticipatory goal reaction." "It thus seems probable that the fractional anticipatory goal reaction is the major mechanism which brings about the integration of the habit-family hierarchy" (Hull, 1934, p. 43).

The whole theory depends on the terms in which the goal reaction is defined. If it is possible to define it in real stimulus-response terms, that is to say, proximally, and without including environmental determinants, then the theory has solved its problem.

It seems, however, that the goal reaction is not defined in this way. This fact becomes especially clear if we examine the case of "purposeful" locomotion and orientation in space which Hull discusses in terms of this theory. Which determinants do we have to use in order to be able to say that goal reactions belonging to different action sequences (action sequences which correspond to different paths to the same goal in the environmental space) are all one and the same goal reaction? According to Hull, these goal reactions seem to be distinguished from other goal reactions only in that they all occur at a certain place in the environment, which lies in a specified (again environmentally determined) direction from the starting point. But are these goal reactions identical from the point of view of proximal determination? That would be the case only if, for instance, the movements of the rat in eating the food (i.e., the real response) varied when the rat approached the food from different points of the environment, and were the same when it approached from the same place. In other words, we could make this assumption only if there were a differentiation in the movements corresponding to the differentiation of the environmental space, and in some way coordinated to the spatial relation between starting point and goal. Actually, however, the identity of goal reactions is not determined proximally: two occurrences of goal reaction are called the same goal reaction when they occur at the same place in the environment. Thus we find that in this theory also the identical element conceals distal determinants behind apparent proximal determinants; it is a case of disguised focus.

Many critics have objected to the use of environmental (distal) determinants in stimulus-response theories. The following quotations are examples of such objections:

> ... the conditioned response formula seems to me inadequate in that the two stimuli and the two responses which are picked out in the above example by the conditioned response formula are not, it must be observed, stimuli and responses in any strict physiological sense. They are not physiologically, but environmentally defined affairs. Thus food and string, as visual, olfactory, and tactual stimuli patterns, may be quite different from occasion to occasion. They retain their respective identities from time to time only by virtue of their environmental "meanings." And eating and string-pulling, as responses, do not correspond to specific and invariant sets of muscle contractions, but are only identifiable through successive times in terms of environmentally nameable "manipulations" ... the conditioned response formula ... must be loosened so as to allow both "stimuli" and "responses" to be identifiable in terms of relatively gross and meaningful characters and not in terms of any precise or necessarily constant sense-organ and muscle processes [Tolman, 1937, p. 200].
>
> These supplementations do more than call attention to the complexity of stimulus-response relationships in conditioning experiments; they introduce terms such as direction, organization, means-end relationships, which are foreign to the logic of stimulus-substitution. To confess that the bold statement of association by contiguity is unsatisfactory because we oversimplify the items which are contiguous is one thing; to supplement the concept with heterogeneous organizing principles not coherent with it is another [Hilgard, 1936, p. 550].

Sometimes it is believed that the variations in the stimuli and responses, which are meaningful if they are determined environmentally, can be explained away by pointing out that there are random variations in every stimulus-response experiment (see Hilgard, 1936, p. 373). However, distal order cannot be derived from proximal disorder. A demonstration of the variations in the stimuli and responses shows only that the function between them is more complex than originally assumed; but it does not explain why it is possible to find distal constants in these proximal variations. Tolman has stated:

> ... there is a big difference between admitting that stimuli or responses probably vary from time to time and being able to give any account of (in truly stimulus-response terms) why they can

nonetheless be called identical with their former selves. It is this latter requirement which I think both Guthrie and Skinner have failed to satisfy [1937, p. 201, note].[6]

"Why they can nonetheless be called identical with their former selves"—that, indeed, is the central problem for any theory using stimulus-response terms. It is the problem of reducing distal terms to proximal terms.

Thus we see that all the theories that employ proximal determinants, whether in terms of perception or of stimulus-response, are faced with the problem of explaining the existence of relevant distal determinants. The weak point of these theories seems to be that they end up by substituting distal for proximal determinants without realizing the change of focus.

Theories in Terms of Distal Determination

Distal determination of the entities to be coordinated to the processes in the organism seems at first sight to be entirely possible. Hobhouse, for instance, comes to the conclusion that the organization of observations in distal terms is as legitimate as the organization in terms of proximal determination.

> If a philosopher from another planet, ignorant of all forms of life as they exist upon this world, were to watch a stone rolling downhill and a man running to catch his train, he would come to the conclusion that the stone and the man were actuated by very different principles. He would, for example, see the man go round the obstacle which caught up the stone, and if he proceeded to compare their behavior under many circumstances and in different relations, he would arrive at the result that the broad difference could be most easily formulated by conceiving the stone's action as determined always by the reaction of its inherent qualities upon the forces directly impressed upon it without regard to the ultimate issue, while the man's action would be, in the majority of cases, determined by its relation from moment to moment to some result more or less remote. . . . That is to say, proceeding purely by inferences based on comparison of behavior, he would discover two fundamentally distinct types of correlation, one in which each element of behavior is conditioned by its relation to its result, the other in which no such relation is operative although the result is in fact produced. Now he might ultimately decide that these two types are reducible to one.

[6] See also Köhler (1929, p. 122) and Klüver (1933, p. 344ff.).

... But even in the latter alternative he would still acknowledge two clearly distinct types of correlated behavior, in one of which the bearing of act on result is operative, while in the other it is not. He would now hold that this relation is made operative by a mechanical arrangement. But operative it still would be, and this would generically distinguish the type of correlation from the type in which there is no such element operating [Hobhouse, 1926, p. 15].

Hobhouse means that, even if we are able to reduce distal to proximal determination, we have to acknowledge that we find in observation cases which give constant coordinations in distal terms. And that is perfectly true, if one limits oneself to a "majority of cases"; however, there is no distally determined process or movement of the organism which could not be disturbed or made impossible by processes coordinated with proximal events. Pure distal determination is an absurdity; it would mean perception without sense stimulation and action without muscle contraction. And worse still, it would be a logical impossibility, because distal determination without coordinated mediating processes could give, in the last analysis, no definite determination at all. If perception is entirely determined by the distant environment, what determines which object is perceived in a concrete situation? Distal determination seems to imply the impossibility of complete determination, and that may be the real cause for the general distrust of distal determinants.[7]

Without doubt, the most imposing system using distal determination is Brunswik's psychology in terms of objects. It is important not only because it stresses distal determinants, but also because it offers concepts and methods which allow systematic experimentation. It seems to be the ideal fulfillment of Holt's program, to find "that object, situation, process of which . . . behavior is a constant function" (1915, p. 161). At first sight, this psychology seems to combine distal and proximal determination, since the "real objects" of perception or action are determined both in terms of the environmental objects and in terms of stimuli.

[7] The impossibility of complete determination in distal terms is clearly expressed by Brunswik, although his own theory is based on distal determinants: ". . . we are dealing with casually distant effects, for which all conditions are not yet ascertained. The relation is therefore not one which is univocally determined in advance but only a more or less probable one. For, it is always possible that unexpected 'marginal' causal chains interfere, or that conditions are absent which one can expect in a normal environment" (1938, p. 18f.).

However, we find that the role of the stimuli in mediation and their place "between" objects and the organism is more or less disregarded. Brunswik writes:

> All of the above facts concerning the functioning of the organism in perception suggest a general way of consideration which would seem to be the one most profitable for psychology. Thus, both for reception and for action, it turns out that the special manner in which anything is mediated (or done) is not especially essential or significant. One and the same means-object may be represented at different times by very different stimulus configurations. And one and the same goal may be reached equally well by very different kinds of movements and means-object manipulations. The focal-points of life occurrences, *i.e.*, means-objects and final goal-effects, lie, respectively: relatively far away in time and space, backward (in cognition), or forward (in action). They are removed from the actual stimulus conditions and the actual body movements, so that the really significant question always is: What are the kinds of such objects and final goal-effects which the organism is able to attain independently of all varying circumstances with a relatively large degree of accuracy and probability; achieving them by perception, on the one hand, and by action, on the other. In short, questions of "what" are much more important in psychology than questions of "how." And thus to seek to describe the abilities and performance of an organism, by giving an inventory of the kind of objects attained by it, may be called "Psychology in Terms of Objects." In principle, this viewpoint need not have any concern with the organism's actual sensory, nervous, or motor conditions—*i.e.*, with mere mediation problems, as studied in traditional behaviorism, psychophysics, and physiological psychology [1936, p. 125].

As we can see, mediation problems, or problems of proximal determinants, have no place in a psychology in terms of objects. At best, mediating entities are considered in their role as good or bad cues for the distant objects (see especially Tolman and Brunswik, 1935).

What kind of psychology can be built upon such foundations, what determination-tendencies can it satisfy? It is true that it is flawless from the point of view of a positivistic program, and that it is carefully grounded in observation and is verifiable by experiment. It blocks, however, the tendency to unified determination and it fails to make possible complete determination. Unified determination is not attempted, since its goal is an "inventory," a multitude of coordinations which it cannot, and does not, strive to reduce to coordinations of a higher order. Because it only asks "what" and not "how," it cannot achieve complete determination. If it were to ask "how," and if it wanted to describe completely the processes involved in a single concrete case of behavior, it would have to consider proximal and interior determinants; it is, in the end, even questionable whether it is possible to give a complete answer to the question "what" without doing so.[8]

These remarks are not intended to belittle the importance of the theory. It is a substantial contribution to the development of psychology, since in theories which emphasize proximal determinants many distal coordinations have been neglected, even when, in principle, the fact of relevant distal determinants has been taken into account. There are many fields of psychology in which we are still ignorant of the distal coordinations of behavior, and often the problem has not even been properly stated. The psychology of the mental development of the child, or of language, offers many examples. An experimental method of determining the "attained objects" of behavior can certainly contribute much to the body of psychology.

A Theory in Terms of Orientation

The theory of tropism, as it is presented by Crozier and Hoagland (1934), coordinates "stimuli" with "orientation," that is to say, direction which is determined in relation to the environmental space. Not what is closest to the skin-muscle contractions or movements of the limbs is taken as the focus, but an effect, an achievement of the movement of the limbs. Thus this theory goes a step beyond pure proximal determination. Determination by orientation lies between determination by the movements of the organs and distal determination in terms of the objects of the environment.

From the following quotations it will be clear that the authors distinguish sharply between proximal determination and determination in terms of orientation, and that they do not think that the second can be reduced to the first.

[8] Brunswik himself recognizes that "what" and "how" problems are intimately connected: "Since the ways of mediation will always determine the achievement, the highly abstracted type of object-critical analysis as outlined above would lead, ultimately, to a statement of all psychologically relevant types of "how"-problems and -findings in terms of "what," *i.e.*, of objects attained" (1937, p. 251, note).

Since the anatomical basis for such actions is quite different in diverse organisms, but the behavior element dynamically identical, it is clear that the quantitative formulations arrived at refer to the *behavior,* and not to specific accidents of structure . . . [Crozier and Hoagland, 1934, p. 6].

The "anatomical basis" and "accidents of structure" are proximally determined entities; the "dynamically identical behavior element" refers to orientation.

Gestalt Theory

In order to describe the focal terms of Gestalt theory, we do best to present first the reasoning we find in Chapter III of Koffka's *Principles of Gestalt Psychology* (1935). The question, in what terms should one describe perceptual processes, is put in the form: why do things look as they do? (p. 76ff.).

1. Distal determinants.—"A first answer would be: things look as they look because they are what they are." The method of finding out whether this answer is adequate is to "single out a few aspects of behavioral things and compare them with real ones." That is to say, one may determine how constant the coordinations between perceptual phenomena and distant objects are. Of course, it is easy to find cases in which there are no constant coordinations, such as the moon illusion where there is no constancy. Distal determinants are therefore discarded, because there are cases of disagreement.

2. Proximal determinants.—We have to distinguish between (*a*) local proximal determinants and (*b*) nonlocal proximal determinants.

a. Local proximal determinants.—A second possible answer is: "Things look as they do because the proximal stimuli are what they are" (p. 80ff.). Again, we find many cases in which there is no correspondence between the local proximal stimulus and the perceptual phenomenon. For example: "The constancy of real things is to a great extent preserved in the constancy of the *phenomenal* things despite variations in their proximal stimuli" (p. 83).

b. The principle of nonlocal proximal determination has to be accepted. For example: "If, without a table and even without a light . . . , we could produce the same pattern of excitation . . . which is ordinarily produced on our retinæ when we fixate a table, then the person on whose retinæ these excitations were produced should and would see a table" (p. 79). That means, in such an experiment we would find the perceptual process coordinated only to proximal events, not to objects.

Thus both distal and local proximal determinants are discarded; that distal determination is possible in many cases is recognized but used only in the refutation of local proximal determination. Only nonlocal proximal determinants are accepted, and that means for Gestalt theory that external determination is made in terms of stimulus patterns, internal determination in terms of fields and Gestalt processes. Koffka (1935) states:

> All we intend to do is to replace laws of local correspondence, laws of machine effects, by laws of a much more comprehensive correspondence between the total perceptual field and the total stimulation ... [p. 97]. Things look as they do because of the field organization to which the proximal stimulus distribution gives rise [p. 98].

Thus we find the program of Gestalt psychology to be: perceptual processes have to be defined in terms of stimulus pattern and field organizations; the question, "Why do things look as they do?" should be answered in these terms.

Gestalt theory has found a new device for the derivation of distal from proximal determination. As we have seen, several forms of conditioned reflex theory take into account both proximal and distal determinants. They make use of local proximal determination and from it derive distal determination by the device of selection. For Gestalt theory, too, it is possible to take into account both kinds of determinants. However, it does not derive the one from the other in a way which makes the derived focus a spurious one.

Let us consider, as an example, visual fixation and pursuit (Koffka, 1935, p. 311ff.). As long as we determine the coordinations proximally and locally, in terms of peripheral movements and sensations (or local stimuli), we find a bewildering confusion without constancy. Distal determination is in many cases easy: the eye is tuned in on the object world, it follows moving objects, etc. The problem is: how can we anchor distal determination in proximal determination, how can we exclude teleology?

The solution proposed by Gestalt psychology is the following: it is wrong to start with an identification of muscle movement *qua* movement (local determinants), and then hook on to these entities connections which are forced upon the organism by the contact with the environment. Muscle movements and stimuli are of course there and play their role in the process, but they can be determined only as parts of an organization. And this organization takes care of the distal determination at the same time. According to Koffka (1935), "... a stimulus inhomogeneity [starts the movement] and the movement takes place in such a way that this stimulus inhomogeneity is brought into the center of the retina" (p. 313).

The organization in which the local stimulations and the local movements are embedded is of such a kind that it gains its equilibrium when the requirements of distal coordination are fulfilled; that is to say, when the eye is directed toward the object, which is coordinated to the stimulus inhomogeneity. In this way proximal and distal determinants, the local events and their "achievement," are brought into harmony. The model of this combination is taken from physics. In physics, too, an event can often be described in both proximal and distal terms.

> We may best visualize the relationship between the responses that make up the so-called purposive behavior category by the raindrop analogy. We may start with the assumption that every drop of rain in some way or other gets to the ocean.... Anthropomorphizing this condition, we may say that it is the *purpose* of every drop of rain to get to the ocean. Of course, this only means that virtually every drop *does* get there eventually. How it gets there depends upon where it falls.... Each stage, each fall from one leaf to the next, may be designated as a *means* toward the final end, the sea, and a number of the intermediate stages may be grouped together and the terminal stage designated as the purpose of the antecedent stages.... Human behavior is merely a complication of the same factors. Instead of only a few physical forces such as gravity, temperature, humidity, surface tension, friction, that act on the drop of rain, the stimuli which act on the sensori-motor system of man are much more numerous [Weiss, 1925, p. 346f.].

Gestalt psychologists can agree essentially with these statements of Weiss. They show that distal determination in physics is in principle identical with that of behavior, and that physics makes use of a device which resolves distal into proximal determination. Thus it does not leave teleology hanging in the air. However, the most important concept by which physics achieves this end is not given enough credit in the above quotation. It is the gravitational field and not leaves, ground, or arbitrarily arranged forces which make the movement of the drop of water one which can be determined distally. Field and equilibrium are the concepts by which in physics the distal determination is made congruent with the proximal. The field brings together the end of the movement and the forces which affect the moving body directly and makes them actually one and the same thing. The "goal" is a unique place within a field at every point of which there are forces directed toward this place. Field determination is really neither distal nor proximal determination; both these determinants are merely aspects of field determination.

The total process of a psychological organization is, of course, much more complicated than the organization of these simple physical examples. Several regions often take part in the total process, regions which have more or less autonomous organizations.

In the actual work of Gestalt psychology, we find a discrepancy between the treatment of perceptual problems and that of behavioral problems. The coordination of the organism to the object world, that is to say, distal determination in terms of the objective environment, is considered and "explained" in the treatment of the psychology of action. In the treatment of perception, however, the fact of correspondence to the object world is often neglected and the goal, or final state toward which a process is directed, is determined in terms of figural properties.

It is significant that Koffka (1935) introduces his discussion of action with a section which is headed: "The Results of Behavior" (p. 306). In this chapter we read:

> ... if we want to explain behaviour, behaviour which has been such a powerful agent in the world, can we ever hope to succeed if, right at the outset, we forget what behaviour has accomplished? That is to say, must we not, in order to explain behaviour, first gain some knowledge about those universal aspects of behaviour which have been responsible for its success? Will it do to introduce explanatory principles indifferent to the results of behaviour, principles which would explain as well, or better, utter chaos ... ? [p. 307].

However, in the chapter on the constancies, we read:

> ... the connection between this uniqueness of one set of conditions and its cognitive value should not be used in any sense as

explanatory of the uniqueness ... the constancy problem should be re-formulated in this way: What shape, size, brightness, will correspond to a certain local stimulus pattern under various total external and internal conditions? Once we have answered this question we shall know when to expect constancy, when not. Indeed some effects of non-constancy are just as striking as the effects of constancy which have been so much emphasized ... [1935, p. 227].

Does that not mean that we should "introduce explanatory principles indifferent to the results" of the perception?

Thus we find an inconsistency in the attitude toward distal determinants. Especially in perceptual problems, Gestalt theory has limited itself to an investigation of figural organizations, and has more or less disregarded the original program of taking into account the "achievements" in terms of equilibria. The original program was to make "meaning" dynamically real and to give a solution of the problem of the coordination of the organism to the object world.

This is also the meaning of the claim of Gestalt psychology to make the "order" in the psychological processes understandable. Order always refers to some particular kind of determination. Something can be orderly in regard to one determination and disorderly in regard to another. The order about which Gestalt psychology talks in its general program is mainly the order we find when we determine the events distally. As Köhler (1929) has said: "All this order is as remarkable as it is necessary for our response to the objects which, in the form of bodily movement, must be adjusted properly to the physical world" (p. 115). That other systems of psychology failed to explain adequately the coordination of the organism to the environment is again and again pointed out by Gestalt psychologists.

However, as we have seen, in the psychology of perception the environmental distal determination is disregarded. The focus is placed in the figural, geometrical properties of the stimulus pattern, and the distal determinants which are used are figural-distal determinants; i.e., the fact is pointed out that we can often describe perceptual processes as tending toward a certain configuration.

We have seen that distal determination does not order the events in the same way as local proximal determination; we have to add it does not order them in the same way as figural determination.

That means that when we determine in terms of figural properties we have not yet solved the problem why environmental distal determination is possible. This fact has been pointed out by several authors:

> The same thing can "express itself" in many different stimulus patterns, which are different from a figural point of view as well; and we can recognize it through these different mediations [see Chap. 2, p. 40ff.].
> One can call this multitude of possibilities a transposibility—perhaps "sign transposibility." This is different from the gestalt or sum-transposibility and plays, so far, only an unimportant role in gestalt psychology. For, the different equivalent possibilities do not show common form (figural) properties... but only common empirical significance (*Bewährung*) ... they have in common their character as a sign of something that is causally more distant than they are [Brunswik, 1934, p. 228].

Thus we see that Gestalt psychology has developed a new device for the solution of the problem of the discrepancy between proximal and distal determination. However, it has not made use of this device consistently, and in some cases it has lost sight of the environmental distal determinants. Connected with this is the fact that it has not yet developed a theory of experience in terms of organization; it does not account for the fact that contact with the environment makes the organism more coordinated with it. Of course, the limitation to an intense study of figural processes was probably very wise; one might only raise the question whether the psychology of perception in its present stage would not be advanced greatly by a more extensive consideration of distal environmental coordinations.

Summary

In organizing any data one can apply an infinite number of determinants. Scientifically fruitful and relevant determinants are those that yield constant coordinations. This empirical test may lead to rival determinations: at least in a first approximation the same group of data can sometimes be determined relevantly in two or more different ways.

In order to escape the dilemma of multiple determination one kind of determinant is often selected as primary and the attempt is then made to derive the fact that other relevant determinants exist from this primary determination. These derivations follow certain patterns; derivation by selection is a common type. Empirical findings are not always responsible for the selection of a particular determination. We find *a priori* tendencies which favor certain determinants.

Questions of determination are especially important in psychology because there are several regions involved in every psychological process. The rivalry between proximal and distal determinants is one of the most significant for psychological theories. Theories using proximal determinants as the primary ones are faced with the problem of explaining the existence of relevant distal determinants. In the attempts to solve this problem use is often made of the device of derivation by selection. It can be shown, however, that the apparent success of these derivations is brought about by the unnoticed introduction of distal determinants into the assumptions from which these determinants are supposedly derived.

Theories using distal determinants as the primary ones are faced with the problem of what to do with the fact of relevant proximal determinants. They often state explicitly that this fact has no place in psychological theory. Thus the way to complete and unified determination is cut off.

Gestalt theory offers a framework of concepts which makes it possible to take both distal and proximal determinants into account and which resolves the dilemma of deciding between them. Gestalt theory, however, has not yet made consistent use of these concepts.

5

THE DESCRIPTION OF THE PSYCHOLOGICAL ENVIRONMENT IN THE WORK OF MARCEL PROUST

Novelists who have the reputation of being good psychologists can give evidence of their knowledge of human nature in different ways. A Dostoyevsky amazes us by convincing descriptions of persons on or beyond the borderline of normality; others reveal to us man's hidden motives, like vanity, egoism, and will to power; with still others psychological insight is more implicitly woven into the fiber of the story. Proust uses all these approaches in his analysis of people and social atmospheres; but he is unique in one respect: in the way in which he sifts and dissects each little event to try to describe the subjective environment of that moment. He wants to know how we perceive reality and how our subjective impressions are different from the objective world laid out in measurable time and space. His preoccupation with these questions leads him on and on in his descriptions of the French society of his day.

These problems belong to the field of perception in its broadest sense. Since this field is one which has been most thoroughly investigated by psychologists, it is not surprising that in Proust's work we find many points of contact with academic psychology. It is difficult to translate Dostoyevsky's insights into psychological terminology. But in Proust we find pages that seem to be written almost for the purpose of illustrating the laws that are found in psychological treatises. As the psychologist reads Proust, he is reminded especially of two somewhat related approaches to psychological problems. One is the theory of perception as Gestalt psy-

Originally published in *Character and Personality*, 9:295-314, 1941.

chology has elaborated it; the other is developmental psychology as it is represented in the works of Piaget and Werner. Gestalt psychology, in its experimental studies, has dealt largely with perception in the normal adult. Developmental psychology is concerned with the mental processes in the undeveloped or regressed mind; it attempts to describe the perception, thought, and emotion of children, so-called primitive people, or psychotics.

A few remarks about developmental psychology may be in place. When we want to describe the psychological environment of children, we compare it with that of more logical and objective adults who possess a high degree of "object constancy." We then find in children "syncretic" and "diffuse" perception and thought (Werner, 1926). Their world shows a lack of differentiation between ego and objects. "Intelligence thus begins neither with knowledge of the self nor of things as such but with knowledge of their interaction, and it is by orienting itself simultaneously toward the two poles of that interaction that intelligence organizes the world by organizing itself" (Piaget, 1937, pp. 354-355). "For it is characteristic of primitive mental life that it reveals a relatively limited differentiation of object and subject, of perception and pure feeling, of idea and action, etc." (Werner, 1926, p. 59).

These conclusions are based on the observation of the behavior of animals, children, primitives, and psychotics. There are relatively few introspective reports available to complete the picture. The reason for this lack is obvious: persons of primitive mentality are usually not capable of that "objectivity" toward their own subjectivity which introspection demands.

Only in poets or writers of fiction do we sometimes find this combination of primitivity and intellectuality; and in no work of literature is it as perfect as in Marcel Proust's *Remembrance of Things Past,* which abounds in illustrations for a psychology of mental development.

That Proust has, in some respects, the mentality of a primitive has been noted by several of his critics, especially Dandieu (1930): "The confusion between present and past, subject and object, . . . are corrected or rather completed by what the sociologists call the sentiment of participation, which is the key to all magic operations and also the origin of Proust's metaphor" (p. 48; see also Ellis, 1935).

PSYCHOLOGICAL ENVIRONMENT IN PROUST'S WORK

In what follows a few quotations are collected which show how Proust's descriptions of the psychological environment illustrate the analyses of Gestalt psychology and developmental psychology. But we do not attempt, of course, to give a complete picture of the psychology of Proust's personality, or of the many psychological insights which are contained in his writings.

REGION, WHOLE SITUATION

When we examine the way in which Proust describes the properties of the psychological environment we find, first of all, that he is aware of the role played by greater units, regions,[1] and whole situations. He describes these units very convincingly when he talks of the two regions of the "Guermantes way" and the "Méséglise way":

> Since my father used always to speak of the "Méséglise way" as comprising the finest view of a plain that he knew anywhere, and of the "Guermantes way" as typical of river scenery, I had invested each of them, by conceiving them in this way as two distinct entities, with that cohesion, that unity which belongs only to the figments of the mind; the smallest detail of either of them appeared to me as a precious thing, which exhibited the special excellence of the whole. ... But, above all, I set between them, far more distinctly than the mere distance in miles and yards and inches which separated one from the other, the distance that there was between the two parts of my brain in which I used to think of them, one of those distances of the mind which time serves only to lengthen, which separate things irremediably from one another, keeping them for ever upon different planes. And this distinction was rendered still more absolute because the habit we had of never going both ways on the same day, or in the course of the same walk, but the "Méséglise way" one time and the "Guermantes way" another, shut them up, so to speak, far apart and unaware of each other's existence, in the sealed vessels—between which there could be no communication—of separate afternoons [1913, p. 172f].

The view of Bergson or James, namely, that our consciousness consists of a continuous stream of ever changing happenings, is not

[1] The terms "psychological environment" and "region" are not used in a narrow perceptual sense. In regard to the concept of psychological environment see Koffka (1935, p. 27ff.), and Lewin (1936, p. 18f.). Lewin, whose usage of the term *region* we follow, gives, among others, these examples for it: "region of a forest; a region within which one may be seen from a certain point; . . . the sphere of influence of a person; a social group; an occupation . . ." (Lewin, 1936, p. 94).

held by Proust. This becomes especially evident when he describes a change from one whole situation to another. In this case we are likely to become aware of the existence of regions in our psychological environment, and of their sometimes sharply defined boundaries:

> [Approaching home after a happy walk,] I would know that in half an hour we should be at home, and that there ... I should be sent to bed as soon as I had swallowed my soup, so that my mother ... would not come upstairs to say good night to me in bed. The zone of melancholy which I then entered was totally distinct from that other zone, in which I had been bounding for joy a moment earlier, just as sometimes in the sky a band of pink is separated, as though by a line invisibly ruled, from a band of green or black. You may see a bird flying across the pink; it draws near the border-line, touches it, enters and is lost upon the black. The longings by which I had just now been absorbed, to go to Guermantes, to travel, to live a life of happiness—I was now so remote from them that their fulfillment would have afforded me no pleasure. How readily would I have sacrificed them all, just to be able to cry, all night long, in the arms of Mamma! ... and this state would persist until the morrow, when ... I would leap out of bed to run down at once into the garden, with no thought of the fact that evening must return, and with it the hour when I must leave my mother. And so it was from the "Guermantes way" that I learned to distinguish between these states which reigned alternately in my mind, during certain periods, going so far as to divide every day between them, each one returning to dispossess the other with the regularity of a fever and ague: contiguous, and yet so foreign to one another, so devoid of means of communication, that I would no longer understand, or even picture to myself, in one state what I had desired or dreaded or even done in the other [1913, p. 235f.].

This description reminds us of topological psychology (Lewin, 1936), in which terms like "region" ("zone" is used by Proust as equivalent to "region"), "sharpness of boundaries," "communication," etc., play a basic role. We may note at the same time that Proust uses both of the concepts which are, in topological psychology, fundamental for the determination of relationships between regions; that of locomotion ("entering the zone of melancholy," the analogy of the flying bird), and that of communication ("the sealed vessels—between which there could be no communication," "devoid of means of communication").

The effect of these regions on behavior is especially noticeable with persons of primitive mentality whose life space is less object-adequate.

> The fact that the primitive world may be built up out of different spheres, each of which is a self-contained unity, is of special importance for developmental psychology. These diverse spheres are determined by different drive patterns among which there is little intercommunicability. One sphere succeeds the other like scenes on a revolving stage .. since an object is reacted to according to its attachment to a certain sphere, it is to be assumed that the meaning of the "same" object changes from sphere to sphere. Only when ... things can be grasped on the basis of different distinct aspects ... is it possible to have an identity and constancy of things [Werner, 1926, p. 381].

We also want to call attention to another point in Proust's observation, namely, the fact that the forces and goals (desires, wishes, "drive patterns" in the quotation from Werner) may change with a change of region.

That the parts of a region exhibit the quality of the whole is also expressed clearly by Proust ("the smallest detail of either of them appeared to me as a precious thing, which exhibited the special excellence of the whole"). Gestalt-psychological experiments with abstract forms have proved that the appearance of the parts often depends on the characteristics of the whole. Werner (1926) points out that this dependence of the part on the whole is more pronounced in primitive perception. Object-constant perception presupposes independence, to a certain degree, of the appearance of the object from the setting. "The embedding of things in the concrete situation demonstrates clearly what is meant by a relatively global, or diffuse, type of organization" (p. 135). "In this diffusely organized, homogeneous perception it is fundamental that each constituent part contain some of the quality-of-the-whole, and that these parts be instinct with the situative meaning, the broader meaning of the totality" (p. 113).

In many places Proust explicitly describes the influence of embeddedness. A case which is taken from more peripheral perception and in which a veritable optical illusion resulted is the following:

> Her black eyes gleamed, and I did not at that time know, and indeed have never since learned how to reduce to its objective ele-

ments any strong impression, since I had not, as they say, enough "power of observation" to isolate the sense of their colour, for a long time afterwards, whenever I thought of her, the memory of those bright eyes would at once present itself to me as a vivid azure, since her complexion was fair; so much so that, perhaps, if her eyes had not been quite so black—which was what struck one most forcibly on first meeting her—I should not have been, as I was, especially enamoured of their imagined blue [1913, p. 180].

The influence of embeddedness in a setting is also apparent in the following example:

Every few minutes the little train brought us to a standstill in one of the stations which came before Balbec-Plage, stations the mere names of which ... seemed to me outlandish, whereas if I had come upon them in a book I should at once have been struck by their affinity to the names of certain places in the neighborhood of Cambray. But to the trained ear two musical airs, consisting each of so many notes, several of which are common to them both, will present no similarity whatever if they differ in the colour of their harmony and orchestration. So it was that nothing could have reminded me less than these dreary names, made up of sand, of space too airy and empty and of salt, out of which the termination "ville" always escaped, as the "fly" seems to spring out from the end of the word "butterfly"—nothing could have reminded me less of those other names ... which, because I had heard them pronounced so often by my great-aunt at table, in the dining-room, had acquired a certain sombre charm in which were blended perhaps extracts of the flavour of "preserves," the smell of the fire of logs and of the pages of one of Bergotte's books, the colour of the stony front of the house opposite, all of which things still to-day when they rise like a gaseous bubble from the depth of my memory preserve their own specific virtue through all the successive layers of rival interests which must be traversed before they reach the surface [1919, Part I, p. 335f.].

Proust shows in this description that he is fully aware of the fact that recognition failed to occur because the place names were imbued with the whole quality of the old setting. "A trace strongly 'embedded' in a trace system is less available for a new process than a trace loosely embedded" (Koffka, 1935, p. 623).

We add a few quotations which show how the home in which a beloved person lives, the things with which she is connected, form a region which stands out significantly from its background. The quality and the value which are attributed to the object of love, and even the history of that love give this region its specific coloring. These passages illustrate the fact that the needs of the person are factors in the organization of the life space into regions, and that needs can be responsible for figure-background relationships:

> My imagination had isolated and consecrated in the social Paris a certain family, just as it had set apart in the structural Paris a certain house, on whose porch it had fashioned sculptures and made its windows precious. . . . Just as my father and mother looked upon the house in which Swann lived as one that closely resembled the other houses built at the same period in the neighborhood of the Bois, so Swann's family seemed to them to be in the same category as many other families of stockbrokers . . . in order to distinguish in all Gilberte's surroundings, an indefinable quality analogous, in the scale of emotions, to what in the scale of colours is called infra-red, a supplementary sense of perception was required, with which love, for the time being, had endowed me; and this my parents lacked [1913, p. 536f.].
>
> All the ideas that I had formed of the hours, different from those that exist for other men, passed by the Swanns in that house which was to their life what the body is to the soul, and must give expression to its singularity, all those ideas were rearranged, amalgamated —equally disturbing and indefinite throughout—in the arrangement of the furniture, the thickness of the carpets, the position of the windows, the ministrations of the servants. When, after luncheon, we went in the sunshine to drink our coffee in the great bay window of the drawing-room, while Mme. Swann was asking me how many lumps of sugar I took, it was not only the silk-covered stool which she pushed towards me that emitted, with the agonising charm that I had long ago felt—first among the pink hawthorn and then beside the clump of laurels—in the name of Gilberte, the hostility that her parents had shewn me, which this little piece of furniture seemed to have so well understood, to have so completely shared that I felt myself unworthy, and found myself almost reluctant to set my feet on its defenceless cushion. . . . [1919, Part I, p. 158f.].[2]

---

[2] The following passages are also relevant to the topic of this section. In regard to the concept of psychological environment in general: 1924, p. 255; 1925, p. 217. In regard to regions: 1913, p. 400f. (social regions in Swann's life); 1920, Part I, p. 31 (psychological boundary); 1925, p. 187f. (zones of substitute satisfaction). Closely related are the cases where he speaks of different "selves" instead of regions: 1919, Part II, p. 346; 1925, p. 17ff. For descriptions of physiognomic characters: 1919, Part II, p. 342 (faces); 1920, Part I, p. 103 (landscape); 1920, Part I, p. 69 (clothes). Needs as factors in the organization of the environment: 1919, Part I, p. 141 (region of loved person); 1919, Part II, p. 348 (face); 1919, Part II, pp. 55, 102f. (time). Embeddedness: 1920, Part I, p. 4f. (names); 1920, Part II, p. 123 (landscape).

Resuscitation of Situations

That a situation with all its original forces can be reinstated after a long interval during which other situations were dominant is shown by what Proust calls "intermissions of the heart." The narrator of the novels had always loved his grandmother dearly, but it was during a visit to Balbec, when he spent a vacation alone with her, that he had been most dependent on her. She died when they were in Paris again. The realization of what her death meant came to him only a whole year later when he was again in Balbec and when the situation of the previous summer was reinstated.

> ... if the setting of sensations in which they [our joys and sorrows] are preserved be recaptured, they acquire in turn the same power of expelling everything that is incompatible with them, of installing alone in us the self that originally lived them. Now, inasmuch as the self that I had just suddenly become once again had not existed since that evening long ago when my grandmother undressed me after my arrival at Balbec, it was quite naturally, not at the end of the day that had just passed, of which that self knew nothing, but—as though there were in time different and parallel series—without loss of continuity, immediately after the first evening at Balbec long ago, that I clung to the minute in which my grandmother had leaned over me. The self that I then was, that had so long disappeared, was once again so close to me that I seemed still to hear the words that had just been spoken, albeit they were nothing more now than illusion, as a man who is half awake thinks he can still make out close at hand the sounds of his receding dream. I was nothing now but the person who sought a refuge in his grandmother's arms, sought to wipe away the traces of his suffering by giving her kisses, that person whom I should have had a great difficulty in imagining when I was one or other of those persons which, for some time past, I had successively been, as the efforts, doomed in any event to sterility, that I should now have had to make to feel the desires and joys of any of those which, for a time at least I no longer was [1921-23, Part I, p. 218ff.; see also 1925, p. 176f.; 1920, Part I, p. 104].

In this situation the reinstatement of the old situation was produced by the environment which was, with the exception of the absence of the grandmother, more or less the same as that of the original situation. In other cases situations are revived by a mere fragment of the original environment, and these play a central role in Proust's work.³ The savour of a small cake (the famous *madeleine*), the sound of a spoon striking against a plate, the stepping on uneven flagstones, the starchy stiffness in a napkin, give rise to the experience of whole situations in which these fragments played a part.

> ... in stepping back, [I] struck my foot against some unevenly cut flagstones leading to a carriage house ... immediately all my discouragement vanished before a feeling of happiness.... A deep azure blue intoxicated my sight, impressions of coolness and dazzling light hovered near me and, in my eagerness to seize them, not daring to move—just as when I tasted the flavour of the *madeleine* and tried to bring back to my mind what it suggested to me—I stood there, swaying back and forth, as I had done a moment before, one foot on the higher stone and the other on the lower, indifferent to the possible amusement of the large crowd of chauffeurs. Each time that I merely repeated the action physically, the effort was in vain; but if I forgot the Guermantes reception and succeeded in recapturing the sensation I had felt the instant I placed my feet in that position, again the dazzling, elusive vision brushed me with its wings ... almost immediately I recognized it; it was Venice ... which was brought back to me by the sensation I had once felt as I stood on two uneven flagstones in the baptistry of Saint Mark's, and with that sensation came all the others connected with it that day, which had been waiting in their proper place in the series of forgotten days, until a sudden happening had imperiously commanded them to come forth. It was in the same way that the taste of the little *madeleine* had recalled Cambray to my mind [1927, p. 191f.].

> What happened was that a servant, trying in vain to make no noise, struck a spoon against a plate. The same kind of felicity as I had received from the uneven paving stones now came over me; the sensations were again those of great heat, but entirely different, mingled with the odour of smoke, tempered by the cool fragrance of a forest setting, and I recognized that what seemed to me so delightful was the very row of trees ... which, in a sort of hallucination, I thought now stood before me.... I wiped my mouth with the napkin ... immediately ... a fresh vision of azure blue passed before my eyes; but this time it was pure and saline and it rounded upward like bluish breasts. The impression was so vivid that the moment I was reliving fused with the real present and ... I thought the servant had just opened the window toward the beach and everything called me to go down and stroll along the embankment at high tide; the

---

³ Proust's ideas of the involuntary memory play an important part in his own thinking about these phenomena. To discuss these would be beyond the scope of this paper; see Blondel (1932).

napkin which I had taken to wipe my mouth had precisely the same sort of starchy stiffness as the towel with which I had had so much trouble drying myself before the window the first day of my stay at Balbec.... [1927, p. 192f.]

In the next quotation, the noise of a hot-water pipe reminds him of "blasts we sometimes heard of a summer evening from pleasure boats of Balbec."

... it was not merely an echo or a duplication of a past sensation which the sound of the hot-water pipe had just made me experience, but that very sensation itself. In that case, as in all the preceding ones, the sensation common to both occasions had sought to re-create about itself the former setting, while the present setting, which was occupying its space, opposed with all the resistance of its mass this invasion of a Paris residence by a Normandy beach or a railway embankment. The dining-room by the sea at Balbec... had sought to shatter the solidity of the Guermantes mansion and force open its doors, and it had for an instant made the sofas rock about me.... Always, in these resurrections of the past, the distant place, evoked about the common sensation, had grappled for a moment, like a wrestler, with the present scene [1927, p. 200].

It seems to us that the passages taken from Proust support Werner's analysis rather than an interpretation based on associationistic principles. Werner explains the arousal of whole-situations from a fragmentary part in children by the diffuse character of the child's experience of the situations. "The common, global significance of a situation in which any part may represent the whole ... acted again to occasion an identical reaction in a similar version. It is because of this that a child often tries to complete a situation on the basis of a fragmentary part which, for the adult, might not necessarily show any relation at all to the whole, but which, for the child, may be shot through with the same coloration as the previously experienced total situation" (Werner, 1926, p. 114).

It is always the "coloration," the physiognomic quality of the total situation, which is first aroused ("impressions of coolness and dazzling light," "sensations of great heat mingled with the odour of smoke, tempered by the cool fragrance of a forest setting," "azure blue—rounded upward like bluish breasts"). Only further search discloses the more objective properties of the original situation.

Another interesting feature of these experiences is their hallucinatory character. It reveals that the differentiation into ego and environment is not fully developed and that the boundary between them is not laid out in the same way as it is in a more "objective" person. "Everywhere in primitive society we find that visionary appearances not only are accorded an objective value, but are also invested with a superior significance, in that they may even supersede the common reality of life from day to day" (Werner, 1926, p. 146). For Proust these visionary remembrances are certainly "invested with superior significance." In the first sixty pages of the second part of *Past Recaptured* he explains how his whole philosophy of life and art and his attitude to reality is based on them.

Framework

The influence of spatial and temporal framework is described by Proust in several places. This framework, which determines where in time and space we "are" phenomenally and dynamically, is (cf. Koffka, 1935, Chap. V-VII), although it has far-reaching psychological effects, often not manifest, probably because it corresponds so often to the measurable reality. Proust catches it at the one moment when in everyday life its reality is most easily observed, at the moment of awakening in an unusual situation, which has disturbed the smooth working of the framework mechanism.

> When a man is asleep, he has in a circle around him the chain of the hours, the sequence of the years, the order of the heavenly host. Instinctively, when he awakes, he looks to these, and in an instant reads off his own position on the earth's surface and the amount of time that has elapsed during his slumbers; but this ordered procession is apt to grow confused, and to break its ranks. Suppose that, towards morning, after a night of insomnia, sleep descends upon him while he is reading, in quite a different position from that in which he normally goes to sleep, he has only to lift his arm to arrest the sun and turn it back in its course, and, at the moment of waking, he will have no idea of the time, but will conclude that he has just gone to bed. Or suppose that he gets drowsy in some even more abnormal position; sitting in an armchair, say, after dinner: then the world will fall topsy-turvy from its orbit, the magic chair will carry him at full speed through time and space, and when he opens his eyes again he will imagine that he went to sleep months earlier and in some far distant country. But for me it was enough if, in my own bed, my sleep was so heavy as completely to relax my

consciousness; for then I lost all sense of the place in which I had gone to sleep, and when I awoke at midnight, not knowing where I was, I could not be sure at first who I was; I had only the most rudimentary sense of existence, such as may lurk and flicker in the depth of an animal's consciousness; I was more destitute of human qualities than the cave-dweller; but then the memory, not yet of the place in which I was, but of various other places where I had lived, and might now very possibly be, would come like a rope let down from heaven to draw me up out of the abyss of not-being, from which I could never have escaped by myself: in a flash I would traverse and surmount centuries of civilization, and out of a half-visualised succession of oil-lamps, followed by shirts with turned-down collars, would put together by degrees the component parts of my ego [1913, p. 3f.; see also 1920, Part I, p. 112; 1921-23, Part II, p. 175].

In this description the role of the framework in the constitution of the ego is stressed. In the following paragraphs we find an observation of a reorganization of the framework; it had been, from memory, erroneously constructed and was set right as soon as an outside stimulus affected the organization.

It is true that, when morning drew near, I would long have settled the brief uncertainty of my waking dream, I would know in what room I was actually lying, would have reconstructed it round about me in the darkness—and fixing my orientation by memory alone, or with the assistance of a feeble glimmer of light at the foot of which I placed the curtains and the window—would have reconstructed it complete and with its furniture, as an architect and an upholsterer might do, working upon an original, discarded plan of the doors and windows; would have replaced the mirrors and set the chest-of-drawers on its accustomed site. But scarcely had daylight itself—and no longer the gleam from a last, dying ember on a brass curtain-rod, which I had mistaken for daylight—traced across the darkness, as with a stroke of chalk across a blackboard, its first white correcting ray, when the window, with its curtains, would leave the frame of the doorway, in which I had erroneously placed it, while, to make room for it, the writing-table, which my memory had clumsily fixed where the window ought to be, would hurry off at full speed, thrusting before it the mantelpiece, and sweeping aside the wall of the passage; the well of the courtyard would be enthroned on the spot where, a moment earlier, my dressing-room had lain, and the dwelling-place which I had built up for myself in the darkness would have gone to join all those other dwellings of which I had caught glimpses from the whirlpool of awakening; put to flight by that pale sign traced above my window-curtains by the uplifted forefinger of day [1913, p. 240f.].

Aspects

We shall now quote a few examples in which it is the history of the approach or the mediation which determines the appearance of an object. This case shows effects similar to those of embeddedness in a whole situation. One and the same object, when embedded in two different whole situations, can appear as two different objects; similarly, one and the same object, perceived from two different sides, can appear as two different objects. This happens when the aspects are not considered only in their role as mediators of objects; in other words, when the aspect, which includes a relationship between person and real object, is interpreted as a property of the object. When an object is given us in two different aspects we often hardly recognize it as the same; or, when it is recognized, we are confronted by the problem of two things being the same and not the same. Usually we are not aware that only certain aspects of objects are given to us. However, when two aspects of the same object conflict, we realize the fact that the appearance of objects can depend on, among other things, the history of our approach and on the particular circumstances of mediation.

Proust's ideas about the role which aspects play in our perception are most articulately expressed when he deals with the "perception" of personalities. Often, in order to demonstrate the general validity of his observations, he takes analogies from the field of visual perspective, where the influence of the point of view on the appearance of objects is most obvious:

> The good and bad qualities which a person presents to us, exposed to view on the surface of his or her face, rearrange themselves in a totally different order if we approach them from another angle—just as, in a town, buildings that appear strung irregularly along a single line, from another aspect retire into a graduated distance, and their relative heights are altered [1919, Part II, p. 241].
> Apart from the most recent applications of the art of photography —which set crouching at the foot of a cathedral all the houses which, time and again, when we stood near them, have appeared to us to reach almost to the height of the towers ... bring into actual

contact the two columns on the Piazzetta which a moment ago were so far apart, thrust away the adjoining dome of the Salute, ... I can think of nothing that can so effectively as a kiss evoke from what we believe to be a thing with one definite aspect, the hundred other things which it may equally well be since each is related to a view of it no less legitimate. In short, just as at Balbec Albertine had often appeared to me different, so now, as if, wildly accelerating the speed of the changes of aspect and changes of colouring which a person presents to us in the course of our various encounters, I had sought to contain them all in a space of a few seconds so as to reproduce experimentally the phenomenon which diversifies the individuality of a fellow creature, and to draw out one from another, like a nest of boxes, all the possibilities that it contains, in this brief passage of my lips towards her cheek it was ten Albertines that I saw; this single girl being like a goddess with several heads, that which I had last seen, if I tried to approach it, gave place to another [1920, Part II, p. 76f.].

How the picture of a person must be reorganized when a new aspect has to be integrated into our concept of a personality is shown in the description of the scene in which the narrator learns that M. de Charlus is homosexual:

From the beginning of this scene a revolution, in my unsealed eyes, had occurred in M. de Charlus, as complete, as immediate as if he had been touched by a magician's wand. ... Those of my readers who do not care to refer, for examples of this law, to the Messieurs de Charlus of their acquaintance, whom for long years they had never suspected, until the day when, upon the smooth surface of the individual just like everyone else, there suddenly appeared, traced in an ink hitherto invisible, the characters that compose the word dear to the ancient Greeks, have ... only to remind themselves how many times ... they have found themselves on the point of making a blunder. Nothing upon the blank, undocumented face of this man or that could have led them to suppose that he was precisely the brother, or the intended husband, or the lover of a woman of whom they were just going to remark: "What a cow!" But then, fortunately, a word whispered to them by someone standing near arrests the fatal expression on their lips. At once there appear, like a *Mene, Tekel, Upharsin,* the words: "He is engaged to," or, "he is the brother of," or, "he is the lover of the woman whom we ought not to describe, in his hearing, as a cow." And this one new conception will bring about an entire regrouping, thrusting some back, others forward, of the fractional conceptions, henceforward a complete whole, which we possessed of the rest of the family. In M. de Charlus another creature might indeed have coupled itself with him which made him as different from other men as the horse makes the centaur, this creature might indeed have incorporated itself in the Baron, I had never caught a glimpse of it. Now the abstraction had become materialised, the creature at last discerned had lost its power of remaining invisible, and the transformation of M. de Charlus into a new person was so complete that not only the contrasts of his face, of his voice, but, in retrospect, the very ups and downs of his relations with myself, everything that hitherto had seemed to my mind incoherent, became intelligible, brought itself into evidence, just as a sentence which presents no meaning so long as it remains broken up in letters scattered at random upon a table, expresses, if these letters be rearranged in the proper order, a thought which one can never afterwards forget [1921-23, Part I, p. 18ff.].

In the next example we see how conflicting aspects can make us skeptical of our ability ever to approach the reality of a person through his aspects. It is essentially the case of Locke's temperature illusion: the same water, when approached under different conditions, appears different. We derive from such situations arguments for the subjectivity of aspects.

When Françoise, in the evening, was polite to me, and asked my permission before sitting down in my room, it seemed as though her face became transparent and I could see the goodness and honesty that lay beneath. But Jupien ... revealed afterwards that she had told him that I was not worth the price of a rope to hang me, and that I had tried to insult her in every possible way. These words of Jupien set up at once before my eyes, in new and strange colours, a print of the picture of my relations with Françoise so different from that on which I used to like letting my eyes rest, and in which, without the least possibility of doubt, Françoise adored me and lost no opportunity of singing my praises, that I realised that it is not only the material world that is different from the aspect in which we see it; that all reality is perhaps equally dissimilar from what we think ourselves to be directly perceiving; that the trees, the sun and the sky would not be the same as what we see if they were apprehended by creatures having eyes differently constituted from ours, or, better still, endowed for that purpose with organs other than eyes which would furnish trees and sky and sun with equivalents, though not visual. However that might be, this sudden outlet which Jupien threw open for me upon the real world appalled me. So far it was only Françoise that was revealed, and of her I barely thought. Was it the same with all one's social relations? And in what depths of despair might this not some day plunge me, if it were the same with love? ... At any rate I realised the impossibility of obtaining any direct and certain knowledge of whether Françoise loved or loathed me. And thus it was she who first gave me the idea that a person does not (as I had imagined) stand motionless and clear before our eyes with his merits, his defects, his plans, his intentions with regard to ourself exposed on his surface, like a garden at which . . . we gaze through a railing, but is a shadow which we can never succeed in penetrating, of which there can be no such thing as direct knowledge, with respect to which we form countless beliefs, based upon his words and sometimes upon his actions, though neither words nor actions can give us anything but inadequate and as it proves contradictory information—a shadow behind which we can alternately imagine, with equal justification, that there burns the flame of hatred and of love [1920, Part I, p. 82ff.].

That one and the same person can be seen by different people from different points of view is also discussed in the description of Swann's personality. The role Swann plays in the eyes of the narrator's relatives differs widely from that which he plays in the aristocratic circles of Paris (1913, p. 19ff.). Certainly we find many works of other writers in which aspects or the "angle of vision" plays an important part. But hardly anywhere do we find such detailed analysis and abstract formulations of the facts involved as we find in Proust's work.

We may also add here a few examples of egocentricity in which the role of aspects is exemplified by the difference between the picture that we form of ourselves, our actions, and words, and that which other people form of them:

Each of our actions, our words, our attitudes is cut off from the "world," from the people who have not directly perceived it, by a medium the permeability of which is of infinite variation and remains unknown to ourself; . . . What we actualy recall of our conduct remains unknown to our nearest neighbor; what we have forgotten that we ever said, or indeed what we never did say flies to provoke hilarity even in another planet, and the image that other people form of our actions and behaviour is no more like that which we form of them ourself, than is like an original drawing a spoiled copy in which, at one point, for a black line, we find an empty gap, and for a blank space an unaccountable contour [1920, Part I, p. 373f.].

We imagine always when we speak that it is our own ears, our own mind that are listening [1919, Part I, p. 264].

That our words are, as a general rule, filled, by the person to whom we address them, with a meaning which that person derives from her own substance, a meaning widely different from that which we had put into the same words when we uttered them, is a fact which the daily round of life is perpetually demonstrating [1919, Part II, p. 252].

The most important application of this doctrine of aspects we find in Proust's theory of erotic fixation. At the same time this theory is illuminating in regard to his attitude toward reality. Often, the situation of the first encounter determines the role a woman plays in a man's life (Proust does not describe women in a corresponding situation). A man falls in love with a woman when he is separated from her by a great psychological distance, and when he thinks, erroneously or not, that the goal of his love is difficult to attain. Then he lets his imagination loose, he starts dreaming about her, and he fashions around a small core of reality a picture of his ideal. Just as in a Rorschach test, he projects his whole ego and attaches it to a kernel of reality. Only the fact that he knows very little about the real woman makes this possible; the "stimulus conditions" are weak.

> I realised also then all that the human imagination can put behind a little scrap of face, such as this girl's face was, if it is the imagination that was the first to know it; and conversely into what wretched elements, crudely material and utterly without value, might be decomposed what had been the inspiration of countless dreams if, on the contrary, it should be so to speak controverted by the slightest actual acquaintance. I saw that what had appeared to me to be not worth twenty francs when it had been offered to me for twenty francs in the house of ill fame, where it was then for me simply a woman desirous of earning twenty francs, might be worth more than a million, more than one's family, more than all the most coveted positions in life if one had begun by imagining her to embody a strange creature, interesting to know, difficult to seize and to hold. No doubt it was the same thin and narrow face that we saw, Robert and I. But we had arrived at it by two opposite ways, between which there was no communication, and we should never both see it from the same side. That face, with its stares, its smiles, the movements of its lips, I had known from outside as being simply that of a woman of the sort who for twenty francs would do anything that I asked. And so her stares, her smiles, the movements of her lips had seemed to me significant merely of the general actions of a class without any

distinctive quality. And beneath them I should not have had the curiosity to look for a person. But what to me had in a sense been offered at the start, that consenting face, had been for Robert an ultimate goal towards which he had made his way through endless hopes and doubts, suspicions, dreams. He gave more than a million francs in order to have for himself, in order that there might not be offered to others what had been offered to me, as to all and sundry, for a score. That he too should not have enjoyed it at the lower price may have been due to the chance of a moment, the instant in which she who seemed ready to yield herself makes off, having perhaps an assignation elsewhere, some reason which makes her more difficult of access that day. Should the man be a sentimentalist, then, even if she has not observed it, but infinitely more if she has, the direst game begins. Unable to swallow his disappointment, to make himself forget about the woman, he starts afresh in pursuit, she flies him, until a mere smile for which he no longer ventured to hope is bought at a thousand times what should have been the price of the last, the most intimate favours [1920, Part I, p. 213f.; see also pp. 235, 246].

Variance of a belief, annulment also of love, which, pre-existent and mobile, comes to rest at the image of any one woman simply because that woman will be almost impossible of attainment. Thenceforward we think not so much of the woman of whom we find difficulty in forming an exact picture, as of the means of getting to know her. A whole series of agonies develops and is sufficient to fix our love definitely upon her who is its almost unknown object. Our love becomes immense; we never dream how small a place in it the real woman occupies. And if suddenly . . . we cease to be uneasy, to suffer pain, since it is this pain that is the whole of our love, it seems to us as though love had abruptly vanished at the moment when at length we grasp the prey to whose value we had not given enough thought before. What did I know of Albertine? One or two glimpses of a profile against the sea. . . . Since my first sight of Albertine I had meditated upon her daily, a thousandfold, I had carried on with what I called by her name an interminable unspoken dialogue in which I made her question me, answer me, think and act, and in the infinite series of imaginary Albertines who followed one after the other in my fancy, hour after hour, the real Albertine, a glimpse caught on the beach, figured only at the head, just as the actress who creates a part, the star, appears, out of a long series of performances, in the few first alone. That Albertine was scarcely more than a silhouette, all that was superimposed being of my own growth, so far when we are in love does the contribution that we ourselves make outweigh—even if we consider quantity only —those that come to us from the beloved object. And the same is true of love that is given its full effect. There are loves that manage not only to be formed but to subsist around a very little core. . . . [1919, Part II, p. 218ff.].

It is the terrible deception of love that it begins by engaging us in play not with a woman of the external world but with a puppet fashioned and kept in our brain, the only form of her moreover that we have always at our disposal, the only one that we shall ever possess, one which the arbitrary power of memory, almost as absolute as that of imagination, may have made as different from the real woman as had been from the real Balbec the Balbec of my dreams; an artificial creation to which by degrees, and to our own hurt, we shall force the real woman into resemblance [1920, Part II, p. 84f.].

. . . a certain similarity exists . . . between all the women we love, a similarity that is due to the fixity of our own temperament. . . . They are, these women, a product of our temperament, an image inversely projected, a negative of our sensibility. . . . We understand the characters of people who do not interest us; how can we ever grasp that of a person who is an intimate part of our existence, whom after a little we no longer distinguish in any way from ourself . . . our curiosity as to the woman whom we love overleaps the bounds of that woman's character, which we might if we chose but probably will not choose to stop and examine [1919, Part II, p. 270f.].[4]

Proust's Personality

We have seen that many of the quotations which we selected describe the functioning of a primitive mind. How can we combine this finding with the fact that Proust's intellect was extremely subtle and differentiated, and his sensitiveness oversophisticated? We cannot solve this problem; we can only state it in more explicit terms.

Two tendencies are discernible in Proust's attitude toward the

[4] The following references are also relevant to this section. In regard to aspects of persons: 1913, p. 525f.; 1919, Part I, p. 28; 1919, Part II, p. 242; 1921-23, Part II, p. 230; of faces: 1919, Part II, p. 301f.; 1920, Part I, p. 77; of a landscape: 1921-23, Part II, p. 207f. In regard to the egocentric image of ourselves: 1920, Part I, p. 373f; 1921-23, Part II, p. 268. There exist also a few beautiful passages in which the interaction of traces and "stimuli conditions" is treated: 1913, p. 21; 1920, Part I, p. 187f. We add these references here since they are related to the subject of this section. In regard to erotic fixation and the illusory picture of the loved person, see also: 1919, Part II, p. 243; 1920, Part I, p. 388; 1920, Part II, p. 73; 1921-23, Part I, p. 318f; 1921-23, Part II, pp. 218, 379.

world.[5] On the one hand he strives constantly to represent persons, situations, and social groups with the utmost objectivity and he attempts to construct their essential core by rational means. He tries to overcome the subjectivity of perspective aspects, observes the typical traits in persons and is interested in general laws. Not only is this tendency patent throughout his work, but he himself testifies to it.

> ... it is the feeling for the general which in the future writer automatically selects what is general and can therefore enter into a work of art. For he has listened to the others only when, however mad or foolish they were, by repeating parrot-like what people of like character say, they had thereby become the prophet-birds, the spokesmen for a psychological law [1927, p. 230f.].
>
> I was not unmoved by these last examples, as always when, beneath the particular instance, I was afforded a glimpse of the general law [1920, Part I, p. 154].
>
> Like a geometrician who, stripping things of their perceptible qualities, sees only their linear substratum, what people said escaped me because what interested me was not what they wanted to say, but the way they said it insofar as it revealed their characters or their ludicrous traits; or, rather, there was one thing which had always been the object of my investigation because it gave me a very special pleasure, and that was the point that two human beings had in common. It was only when I caught sight of this that my mind . . . suddenly took up the chase joyfully, but what it then pursued—for example, the identical recurrence of the Verdurin salon in various times and places—was located halfway down, below the range of vision, in a zone somewhat recessed. . . . It was of no use for me to go out to dinner, I did not see the guests because, when I thought I was looking at them, I was looking through them as with an X-ray. The result was that, when I came to put together all the notes I had been able to make on the guests at a dinner, the pattern of the lines I drew represented a collection of psychological generalisations in which the special interest of the guests' remarks occupied hardly any place [1927, p. 24f.].

Opposed to this scientific tendency is a Bergsonian tendency in Proust. He is convinced that true reality can only be found in the

---

[5] See Blondel (1932). We, however, do not agree with Blondel's solution of this problem.

sphere of subjective impressions, of the totality of experience; that is to say, only in organizations in which the ego elements are given full scope.

> Only the subjective impression, however inferior the material may seem to be and however improbable the outline, is a criterion of truth and for that reason it alone merits being apprehended by the mind, for it alone is able . . . to lead the mind to a greater perfection and impart to it a pure joy [1927, p. 207].

Proust's difficulty in getting satisfaction out of contact with objective reality is related to this attitude.

> . . . I came to realise clearly that disappointment in a journey and disappointment in a love affair were not different in themselves but merely the different aspects assumed in varying situations by our inability to find our real selves in physical enjoyment or material activity [1927, p. 204].

> How many times in the course of my life had I been disappointed by reality because, at the time I was observing it, my imagination, the only organ with which I could enjoy beauty, was not able to function, by virtue of the inexorable law which decrees that only that which is absent can be imagined [1927, p. 197].

Havelock Ellis (1935) says of Proust: "We are thus led to various manifestations of ruptured vital contact with reality, marked in Proust as well as in Rousseau, the extreme sensitiveness, the morbid susceptibility, the aptitude for suspicion . . . which made relations with friends, and sometimes even with strangers, so difficult" (1935, p. 431).

His theory of art is based on this attitude to reality. At the beginning of the second book of *Past Recaptured* he explains in detail how he came to the conviction that the true task of the writer is to rediscover the subjective reality

> . . . from which we live so far removed and from which we become more and more separated as the formal knowledge which we substitute for it grows in thickness and imperviousness [p. 224].

> This work of the artist . . . is exactly the reverse of the process which, during every minute that we live with our attention diverted

from ourselves, is being carried on within us by pride, passion, intelligence and also by our habits, when they hide our true impressions from us by burying them under the mass of nomenclatures and practical aims which we erroneously call life [p. 225].

We are reminded of a statement by Koffka (1935), who, in talking about physiognomic characters, says:

> We conclude that objects in the field may possess characters which can be expressed in terms neither of shape and colour nor of practical use, and which are apt to exert a powerful influence on our behavior. . . . Our preoccupation with practical use and scientifically classifiable properties has robbed our world of a good many of them. . . . On the other hand, if we can abandon our practical or scientific attitude, we become aware of more and more such characteristics. Among us the poets and artists are those who are most free from the craving for efficiency. And truly, for them the world is richer in such characters than it is for us [p. 359].

This attitude toward reality, which results in a suppression of the segregation into ego and environment, lies at the basis of the so-called primitive phenomena which abound in his work. We called this attitude Bergsonian, and, indeed, Bergson could have written the paragraphs we have quoted. Proust, however, is not at all a consistent Bergsonian.[6] Even in the description of the immediate data of consciousness we can discern his scientific tendency. He is not afraid of describing his findings by general concepts and he very often uses even spatial terms (see Dandieu, 1930, p. 190). And the first quotations we presented in this paper show that he did not see the "stream of consciousness" as a Heraclitean flux in Bergson's sense. He holds with modern psychology that often the sequence of phenomena is divided by sharply defined boundaries. Furthermore, a person who is totally immersed in his subjective experiences would not be able to bring out so clearly in what way they are subjective. Only by contrasting them with a differentiated environment is it possible to describe them. Most of the concepts of developmental psychology, as Piaget, Werner, and others have applied them, contain such a reference to an "objective" reality.

[6] See Dandieu (1930, p. 35n.), and Blondel (1932, p. 166ff.).

Proust, too, can give us an adequate picture of his experiences only by comparing them with a more object-constant reality.

We cannot explain this duality in Proust's ego-environment relationship. But we can understand that the coexistence of these two attitudes made it possible for him to give these beautiful descriptions of diffuse and syncretic phenomena.

6

ON LEWIN'S METHODS AND THEORY

I want to talk about two aspects of Lewin's theory:[1] first, about his ideas on the relative autonomy of psychology, and second, about the notion of life space. Both conceptions appeared very early in Lewin's publications, and I thought it might be of interest if I described briefly the contents of his first book and first paper in which these ideas are foreshadowed.

I begin with the principle of the autonomy of psychological concepts, which has its roots in certain notions belonging to the philosophy of science, or "metatheory." A number of Lewin's early publications deal with this field, among them the book which he published in 1922. Its title might be translated as "The Concept of Identity in Time in Physics and Biology." The subtitle is "A Contribution to the Comparative Science of Science." In this book he compared different sciences and tried to define the basic differences between them. He dealt mostly with physics and biology, giving less attention to psychology. The central concept he used is "genidentity," by which he meant the identity of objects over time. It is a unit formation which allows appearances of an object at different times to be treated as identical. For instance, physics considers its objects as extending over time; one speaks of one and the same stone or star although it has been observed at different times. Again, when we talk of the motion of an object, we imply gen-

---

Kurt Lewin Memorial Award Address given at the Annual Meeting of the American Psychological Association, Cincinnati, Ohio, September, 1959. Also published in *Journal of Social Issues,* Supplement 13, 1960.

[1] I acknowledge my indebtedness to Leeper (1943), Deutsch (1954), and Cartwright (1959), who have given us excellent presentations of this theory.

identity, that is, we imply that at different times the same object is at different places.

One of the main theses of the book is that physics and biology use the concept of genidentity in different ways. Let us consider an egg and the two-year-old chicken that grew out of this egg. Egg and chicken are biologically genidentical, they represent different stages of development of the same biological object. However, physically they are not genidentical, because the molecules composing them have changed. In the same way a person at the age of forty is biologically identified with the same person at the age of twenty, though physically only a small number of the molecules may be the same. He may have changed as a biological entity, but the fact that we can speak of a change means that we refer what happened to one organism.

Thus, Lewin tries to show that there is an essential difference between physics and biology in the basic units of description used. This leads him to the view that a fundamental incommensurability separates sciences from each other; each science is a closed unit of systematically connected concepts. Paths of derivation lead along the lines of this network, but the propositions or laws of one science cannot be derived from those of another. Going from one science to another means to change completely the way of dividing up reality into units.

In a later paper (1926) he says there is a tendency in the development of sciences which leads to a sharpening of the differences between them. Each science gradually purifies its concepts and segregates itself more and more from its neighbors. In line with these ideas he says: "The yearning for meaning and unity of life must not look for an illusory satisfaction in the idea of a philosophical unit of science" (p. 73). In other words, he believed that the idea of an eventual unification of all sciences is wishful thinking. Of course, he was well aware of the fact that there are many bridges between the sciences, and he was all for building more of them, for instance, in intermediate fields like biochemistry, or physiological psychology. Nevertheless, from his point of view, they were bridges between regions whose concepts and propositions are basically different.

These ideas form the background of his conviction that psychology should strive to build up a more or less autonomous realm of concepts which form a closely knit system, and that as it develops it should become more aware of its own proper nature, that it should segregate itself from other sciences, for instance, physiology, and that it should, in this way, purify itself. Deutsch says about Lewin: "He takes the stand that psychological phenomena must be explained in psychological terms just as physical phenomena must be explained in physical terms" (1954, p. 183).

Another aspect of this conception of psychology is the emphasis on the central region and the relative neglect of peripheral input and output. Brunswik, who especially has stressed this feature in his descriptions of Lewin's theory, says "Lewin's system and its laws remain confined to a post-perceptual, yet prebehavioral . . . field in the central area" (1955a, p. 736). This is true—but as we state it we should add two points: first, Lewin did take perception and behavior into account as belonging to the boundary of the life space, though he never succeeded in formalizing the relation of this boundary to the life space itself. Second, in his experiments stimuli and action outcomes play important roles as observables.

Maybe we can make this last point somewhat clearer if we ask ourselves what is the point or the goal of a Lewinian experiment. In trying to answer that question we will do well to recall the physicist Lenzen's notion of the partition between observer and object. He says that

> If one touches a desk with a finger, the partition is between them. An observer, however, may be extended by mechanical devices. Bohr has cited the following example: If one firmly grasps a long stick in one's hand and touches it to a body, the body touched is the object of observation, and the stick is an apparatus that may be viewed as part of the observer. . . . If a physicist is looking at a pointer on a scale, its status depends on the purpose of observation. If he is using the instrument to measure an electric current, the pointer is an extension of the observer; the object is the electric current. If the physicist is calibrating his instrument, the pointer is part of the object of observation; the light by which the pointer is seen is then an instrument which belongs to the observer [Lenzen, 1955, 308-309].

That is, the instruments used in observation and measurement belong to the observer, they are the mediation and not the focus of observation, unless the reliability and validity of the instrument are in question. The difference between object and mediation is as important for the scientific gathering of data as it is for perception. We can try to set up the observables themselves as the focal points of our theoretical system and try to find the laws which may obtain between them; or we can consider the observables as something that will, under certain conditions, give us information about constructs lying beyond them. In Lenzen's terms, we can put the observer-object partition between observer and the directly observable, or between the directly observable and the construct.

I think one can say that for Lewin the partition between observer and object is at the life space; his primary concern is with what goes on in this life space; that is where he expects to find the relevant variables, the nodal points which will follow exact laws without exceptions.

In contrast to Lewin's concern with the life space, psychology today often considers input and output as the primary object of study; true enough, there are also intervening variables, but they play only an ancillary role. The psychologist deals with them somewhat reluctantly and then only because otherwise the relations between input and output become unmanageable.

For Lewin these so-called intervening variables are the focus from the start, and input and output are relegated to a secondary role; they are the tools of observation which make it possible for us to get a glimpse of the processes in the life space which are the ultimate object of observation. Only by referring these manifestations or offshoots to the central layer can one obtain laws related to each other in a wider system. In themselves they are surface phenomena, phenotypes, each of which is determined by a multitude of factors and therefore cannot be expected to have stability and invariance.

The difference between this centralist position of Lewin and a peripheralist position is shown, for instance, by Spence's (1944) clearly formulated and therefore valuable description of Lewin's theory. Spence says that Lewin is not concerned with laws linking stimuli with responses but with laws mediating between two different responses, one being what the subject says about the situation, the other, what the subject does in the situation. However, my own feeling is that this does not describe what Lewin was really doing. According to the tenor of Lewin's theory, the goal of psychological investigation is not to find response-response laws. Both behavior and description of the situation must be referred to constructs belonging to the life space; they must be used as indicators of the contents or processes of the life space. Lewin was studying the laws which obtain in the life space, and for him the partition between the observer and the object was located at the life space and not at the behavior.

In the same way, the physicist uses the pointer readings of his volt meter and his other meters as manifestations of properties of the electric current; he studies the laws of electricity and is not concerned with the motions of the pointer as such. Or, the astronomer does not study the very complicated light processes in front of his telescope; these light processes only mediate information about the true objects of his inquiry—stars and planets.

This concentration on the processes in the life space has, of course, its disadvantages, for example, the relative neglect of peripheral input or output which I have already mentioned. But in spite of these disadvantages, the gains from this kind of approach are very great. Brunswik, who as I mentioned before was certainly very much aware of the defects of Lewin's system, also stressed its positive aspects. He says:

> Encapsulation into the central layer . . . may be the least harmful of all the limitations which possibly could be imposed upon psychology: It may actually mean concentration upon the most essential phase in the entire process of life and of its ramifications. It may be the thing psychology has always been really after throughout its history [1943, p. 266].

I come now to the second part of this discussion, which deals more specifically with Lewin's notion of life space. Let us try to observe this notion *in statu nascendi,* so to speak, and to find out what were the primary experiences which led Lewin to develop it and to express it, at a later stage, in terms of topological concepts. I am aware of the fact that I am disregarding here the considerable influence Wertheimer and Köhler had on Lewin's thinking.

What I want to talk about is Lewin's first publication, a short paper in which he applied the concept of life space in a very interesting way, though the term is not used and *topology* does not yet appear. This paper was published in 1917 in the *Zeitschrift für angewandte Psychologie,* and it is entitled "Kriegslandschaft": "War Landscape." Lewin states that it deals with the phenomenology of landscape, and in it he describes how the environment appears to the soldier in trench warfare. He himself had served and had been wounded in the First World War.

This paper is fascinating to read in view of the later development of topological psychology. Many of the concepts which afterwards were defined in a systematic way appear here as descriptive concepts, for instance, boundary, direction, and zone.

To review this paper briefly: Lewin begins by saying that as the soldier approaches the front lines he experiences a peculiar transformation of the appearance of the landscape. The landscape at a greater distance from the front, which Lewin calls the peace landscape, seems to extend evenly on all sides almost to infinity. This landscape is without direction. Near the front the landscape seems to be bounded, the environment suddenly comes to an end. It has a direction, a front and a back, and this direction is not referred to the marching soldier but belongs to the environment itself. This transformation cannot be described simply as an awareness of increasing danger and eventual inaccessibility; it is experienced as a feature of the objective landscape.

Along the front lines there is a boundary zone whose characteristics become intensified as the enemy lines are approached. This boundary zone is to be distinguished from regions of danger. For instance, there may exist isolated danger islands, which are relatively distant from the front but exposed to enemy fire.

He then talks about the difference between peace things and battle things. By this he means not the difference between, for instance, a farmhouse and a cannon; he means that the same objects may be experienced in a different way according to whether they are seen in the context of peace or in the context of battle. He says:

> What lies within the battle zone belongs to the soldier as his legitimate property, not because he has gained it by force of arms, but because in the context of battle everything is seen as something to be used for military purposes. Even such barbaric acts as the burning of furniture in war cannot be compared to the same acts in peace time [1917, p. 445].

He describes the impression of incongruity he felt when he had to get straw for bedding or coal to warm his supper from a village in the battle zone. It seemed absurd to have to use battle things suddenly as peace things. The main characteristics of battle things have to do with protection against being seen or shot at by the enemy.

These samples may give an idea of this paper on the war landscape, about which Koffka (1935) writes that it is an

> exceedingly good and instructive description of a field with a very simple kind of inhomogeneity. [It is] a field which has a polar structure in one direction: the enemy's land on the one side and home and safety on the other. This vectorial property is a primary characteristic and determines the entire field, no other characteristic being entirely free from it [pp. 43-44].

Let us take a closer look at the notion of phenomenal field or life space as it is applied in this description of the war landscape. There are a great many puzzles and unsolved problems hidden in it. Whenever one tries to formulate what is really meant by it or what its implications are, one is led deeper and deeper into significant questions. Some of them are, I suppose, characteristic of every kind of cognitive psychology, others seem to be more specific to Lewinian theory.

Let us begin with the relation of the environmental part of the life space to the objective environment, or, to use Koffka's terms, the relation of the behavioral environment to the geographical environment. The geographical environment is the environment as described by physics or geography. Certainly the geographer would describe the war landscape in a way which is very different from Lewin's phenomenological description. He would characterize the hills and villages as to their location, extent, altitude, and so on, but not as to their function in giving protection from the enemy. Nevertheless, one cannot say that the "phenomenal" landscape which Lewin portrayed as representing the experiences of a typical soldier is entirely subjective. Though it includes more than the purely physical features of the environment, it still has a certain kind of objective existence. It contains the *functional possibilities* of the environment which do not vary according to the personal needs or biases of a subject in a particular situation. It refers to what a typical soldier can do and what he may suffer in this environment. These functional possibilities are objective in the sense that they are more or less valid for all persons in this environment. For instance, when a soldier enters a danger island, there exists a certain probability of his being wounded or killed, regardless of whether he is aware of the fact or not. Of course, whether or not he goes to a certain place will depend on this awareness; however, the concept of danger island can also be used in an objective sense though it is not a geographical or physical concept. It has to do with causal relationships existing in the environment. Could it be that this description of the war landscape does not after all describe the behavioral environment or life space, but something between the behavioral environment and the geographical environment?

Chein, in an interesting article (1954), has talked about a geo-behavioral environment, by which he seems to mean the environment as it would affect an average person, or even as it would affect a person typical of a certain group.

It appears that here we get into a problem which Floyd Allport (1955) has characterized as the inside-outside problem. We are dealing with an interaction between the person inside and the environment which is outside. Of course, we can leave it at that and talk about some kind of transaction and refuse to get involved in further analysis, but this does not lead very far. We usually attribute such an interaction more to one or more to the other of two poles, and that is what we do with the person-environment interaction.

When we talk about the person as opposed to the geographical environment, we attribute a minimum to the outside entities, that is, we attribute to the outside only those properties which it shows in interactions with the widest possible range of other objects, regardless of whether they are persons or inorganic objects. When we confront the person with the geo-behavioral environment we attribute to the outside a great deal more, namely, everything that persons have in common in the interactions with the environment. In a way, the average person is then attributed to the outside. In this way we can enter more and more on the accounts of the environment until the person shrinks to an undifferentiated point: the environment is then characteristic for one particular person at one particular moment.

However, the geographical environment is still with us, and the problem now arises of relating this physicalistic environment to the different, other, "enriched" environments. And we have not given up entirely the attribution to the person. We have to characterize these environments by saying: this is the environment for this group, or for this person. And why do we still call it environment when it is in some way attached to a particular person?

These questions have to do with the problems of intention or representation which every cognitive psychology has to meet in some way. Something belonging to the inside part, the person, is described in terms of the outside part, the environment. The so-called intervening variables can be related to environmental variables in two different ways: causally, or through intentionality. In stimulus-response theories the intervening variables are defined by the causal relation; in cognitive theories they are defined both by the causal relation and by the relation of intention or reference. When we think about mentalistic concepts we are apt to be so occupied with the difficulty of anchoring them in observables that we forget that they also have this characteristic of intentionality which places them somewhat apart from other scientific concepts.

Lewin does not treat this problem systematically. However, he comes into contact with it, for instance, when he talks about the life-space dimensions of time and reality. He says that one has to distinguish psychological facts from their referents. A present psychological fact can refer to something that lies in the future or in the past, and an existing psychological fact can refer to something unreal. He proposed the following general formulation: "The existence or nonexistence and the time index of a psychological fact are independent of the existence or nonexistence and time index of the fact to which its content refers" (1936, p. 38). The fact that I will get on a train for Kansas tomorrow morning affects my behavior today: it is part of my present life space although it will not happen until tomorrow.

This duality of psychological fact and its referent has sometimes been treated as a case of symbolic reference. Thus Angyal says in his book *Foundations for a Science of Personality:* ". . . the function of the so-called mental process is essentially a semantic one. By this we mean that 'psychological contents' function as symbols and that psychological processes are operations with these symbols" (1941, p. 56). There is no question that the concept of symbol is useful here as a thought model, but it is not entirely satisfactory. A word can be called a symbol for a thing. In this case both symbol and referent are present in awareness. The concept is used in this way by Cassirer (1944) when he says that man is the symbolic animal and that the world of man is shaped by the symbolic systems of language, religion, science, and so on. When Angyal talks about symbolic reference he means the relation between a life-space content and something outside the life space, for instance, something belonging to the geographical environment. Though this relation is similar to the relation between word and thing, it has to be distinguished from it. However, in spite of this difference I will go on using the terms symbol or symbolic reference in the way Angyal uses them.

Before the advent of cognitive field theory, association theory employed concepts involving symbolic reference, as, for instance, "idea," or "image." These concepts have two homes, so to speak. On the one hand they have a place as psychological facts in a network of causal relations; that is, they are functionally related to each other in such a way that the presence of one idea tends to evoke another idea. But on the other hand, they are also connected with the environment, by this peculiar relation of representation: each idea stands for something, often for a content of the objective world. It seems to be a characteristic of this theory that it is the single idea that shows a representational function, while the relations between ideas do not symbolize the environment. The fact that two ideas are associated does not in itself refer to a relation existing in the environment.

With the idea of field representation we come to an entirely new notion. Not only single entities but also the relation between entities, for instance, part-whole or neighboringness relations, have a representational function. Instead of a collection of symbols we find something like a map. Or instead of a list of words as in a dictionary, we find something which includes grammar.

This new notion is, of course, implicit in the Gestalt-psychological concepts of cognitive structure. But one might say that its most consistent elaboration is found in Lewin's construct of life space. The parts of the life space are identified by their referents, they are usually characterized by the words we use to describe the objective environment. And not only the parts, but the relations between the parts, have this representational function. For instance, the fact that two regions of the life space are adjacent refers to, or symbolically represents, the fact that the referents of these regions stand in some neighboringness relation.

Since the life space is involved in this relation of intentionality, it is a kind of construct that is not found in other sciences. Angyal says: "The symbolic relationship is quite unique in that it does not occur, as far as we know, outside the psychological realm" (1941, p. 58). Maybe the reason why many psychologists shy away from using mentalistic concepts is not only the difficulty of operational definition but also this uniqueness.

A word may be added about the concept of "field" as Lewin uses it. Critics have pointed out that there are important differences between it and the field as the physicist understands it (London, 1944). Lewin himself noted this difference, which shows in, for instance, the definition of direction in the life space (Lewin, 1938, p. 40). This direction depends not only on the state of the immediate surroundings, but on the field at large, a conception which is not in harmony with the physical field concept, at least not with the classical one. I feel that this difference between life space and physical field is also connected with the fact that the life space shows this feature of intentionality.

I want to add a few further questions which arise when we consider the life-space contents as symbols. Words are symbols of things, and they can be classified in two different ways: on the one hand according to their own properties, their length maybe, or their first letter, and on the other hand according to their meaning. Thus they belong to two orders, they have two homes. Is that also true of life-space contents? And how about causal connections: words as such do not really interact causally, even if we put them on paper. They are not like chemical substances which interact when one mixes them, they do not spontaneously group themselves in certain ways. But the life-space contents do interact, and if they are symbols, they are symbols that influence each other. Should their interaction be understood in terms of their meaning, or in terms of their own properties, whatever those are? These are some of the questions we are faced with when we conceive of the life space as something having symbolic reference.

I must append one more remark here. So far I have considered only the environmental part of the life space. According to Lewin there exists another part, the person, and he uses basically different theoretical notions in treating it. The representation of the person is not a map: structurally it is more similar to association theory. Each single region of the person can be considered to be a symbol of an activity, but the relations between them do not show symbolic reference in the sense in which this is true for the relations of neighboringness between regions of the environment. As in association theory, they stand for functional relations between psychological facts, especially for possibilities of tension communication.

In this paper I have dealt mainly with the relation of the person to the environment in Lewin's theory, and also with the manifold problem of intentionality which is implied in it. I have tried to communicate an impression I get whenever I try to understand Lewin's basic notions, and that is that they are, so to speak, visions, not at all completely formulated and explicated; that they have a wealth of implicit meaning which has not yet been exhausted, and that they are therefore still full of promise for further development.

Bibliography

Allport, F. H. (1955), *Theories of Perception and the Concept of Structure.* New York: Wiley.
Angyal, A. (1941), *Foundations for a Science of Personality.* New York and Cambridge: The Commonwealth Fund and Harvard University Press.
Attneave, F. (1954), Some Informational Aspects of Visual Perception. *Psychol. Rev.,* 61:183-198.
Becher, E. (1911), *Gehirn und Seele.* Heidelberg: Winter.
Bentley, A. F. (1935), *Behavior, Knowledge, Fact.* Bloomington, Indiana: Principle Press.
Blondel, C. (1932), *La Psychographie de Marcel Proust.* Paris: Vrin.
Boring, E. G. (1929), *A History of Experimental Psychology.* New York: Century.
Brunswik, E. (1934), *Wahrnehmung und Gegenstandswelt.* Leipzig & Wien: Deuticke.
—— (1936), Psychology in Terms of Objects. *Proc. 25th Anniversary Celebration of the Inauguration of Graduate Studies at the University of Southern California,* ed. H. W. Hill. Los Angeles, pp. 122-126.
—— (1937), Psychology as a Science of Objective Relations. *Phil. Sci.,* 4:227-260.
—— (1938), Die Eingliederung der Psychologie in die exakten Wissenschaften. *Einheitswissenschaft,* 6:17-34.
—— (1943), Organismic Achievement and Environmental Probability. *Psychol. Rev.,* 50:255-272.
—— (1955a), The Conceptual Framework of Psychology. In *International Encyclopedia of Unified Science,* 1:655-760. Chicago: University of Chicago Press.
—— (1955b), Scope and Aspects of the Cognitive Problem. In *Contemporary Approaches to Cognition.* Cambridge: Harvard University Press, 1957, pp. 5-31.
Bühler, K. (1929), *Die Krise der Psychologie,* 2nd ed. Jena: Fischer.
Cartwright, D. (1959), Lewinian Theory as a Contemporary Systematic Framework. In *Psychology: A Study of a Science,* Study I, Vol. 2, ed. S. Koch. New York: McGraw-Hill, pp. 7-91.
Cassirer, E. (1944), *An Essay on Man.* New Haven: Yale University Press.
Chein, I. (1954), Environment As a Determinant of Behavior. *J. Soc. Psychol.,* 39:115-127.
Cournot, A. (1838), Mathematics of Value and Demand. In *The World of Mathematics,* ed. J. R. Newman. New York: Simon & Schuster, 1956, pp. 1203-1216.
Crozier, W. J. & Hoagland, H. (1934), The Study of Living Organisms. In *A Handbook of General Experimental Psychology.* Worcester, Mass.: Clark University Press, pp. 3-108.

Dandieu, A. (1930), *Marcel Proust, sa révélation psychologique*. Paris: Firmin-Didot.
Deutsch, M. (1954), Field Theory in Social Psychology. In *Handbook of Social Psychology*, ed. G. Lindzey. Cambridge, Mass.: Addison-Wesley, pp. 181-222.
Duncker, K. (1929), Über induzierte Bewegung. *Psychol. Forsch.*, 12:180-259.
Ellis, H. (1935), Marcel Proust. *Atlantic Monthly*, 156:421-432.
Hilgard, E. R. (1936), The Nature of the Conditioned Response. *Psychol. Rev.*, 43:366-385, 547-564.
Hobhouse, L. T. (1926), *Mind in Evolution*, 3rd ed. London: Macmillan.
Hochberg, J. E. (1957), Effects of the Gestalt Revolution: The Cornell Symposium on Perception. *Psychol. Rev.*, 64:73-84.
——— & McAlister, E. (1953), A Quantitative Approach to Figural "Goodness." *J. Exp. Psychol.*, 46:361-364.
Holt, E. B. (1915), *The Freudian Wish*. New York: Holt.
Hull, C. L. (1934), The Concept of the Habit-Family Hierarchy and Maze Learning. *Psychol. Rev.*, 41:33-54, 134-142.
James, W. (1890), *Principles of Psychology*. New York: Holt.
Johansson, G. (1950), *Configurations in Event Perception*. Uppsala: Almquist & Wiksell.
Klüver, H. (1933), *Behavior Mechanisms in Monkeys*. Chicago: University of Chicago Press.
——— (1936), The Study of Personality and the Methods of Equivalent and Non-equivalent Stimuli. *Character & Pers.*, 5:91-112.
Koffka, K. (1935), *Principles of Gestalt Psychology*. New York: Harcourt, Brace.
Köhler, W. (1929), *Gestalt Psychology*. New York: Liveright.
Laplace, P. S. (1814), Concerning Probability. In *The World of Mathematics*, ed. J. R. Newman. New York: Simon & Schuster, 1956, pp. 1325-1333.
Leeper, R. W. (1943), *Lewin's Topological and Vector Psychology*. Eugene, Ore.: University of Oregon Press.
Lenzen, V. F. (1955), Procedures of Empirical Science. In *International Encyclopedia of Unified Science*, 1:279-339. Chicago: University of Chicago Press.
Lewin, K. (1917), Kriegslandschaft. *Z. ang. Psychol.*, 12:440-447.
——— (1922), *Der Begriff der Genese in Physik, Biologie und Entwicklungsgeschichte*. Berlin: Springer.
——— (1926), Idee und Aufgabe der vergleichenden Wissenschaftslehre. *Symposion*, 1:61-93.
——— (1927), Gesetz und Experiment in der Psychologie. *Symposion*, 1:375-421.
——— (1935), *Dynamic Theory of Personality*. New York: McGraw-Hill.
——— (1936), *Principles of Topological Psychology*. New York: McGraw-Hill.
——— (1938), The Conceptual Representation and Measurement of Psychological Forces. *Contr. Psychol. Theory*, 1 (4). Durham: Duke University Press.
London, I. D. (1944), Psychologist's Misuse of the Auxiliary Concepts of Physics and Mathematics. *Psychol. Rev.*, 51:266-291.
Mach, E. (1897), *Contributions to the Analysis of the Sensations*, tr. C. M. Williams. Chicago: Open Court.
Meinong, A. (1906), *Über die Erfahrungsgrundlagen unseres Wissens*, 6. Sonderheft der Z. physikal. chem. Unterricht. Berlin: Springer.
Piaget, J. (1937), *The Construction of Reality in the Child*. New York: Basic Books, 1954.
Proust, M. (1913), *Swann's Way*, tr. C. K. Scott Moncrieff. New York: Modern Library, 1928.

―――― (1919), *Within a Budding Grove,* Parts I & II, tr. C. K. Scott Moncrieff. New York: Modern Library, 1925.

―――― (1920), *The Guermantes Ways,* Parts I & II, tr. C. K. Scott Moncrieff. New York: Modern Library, 1925.

―――― (1921-23), *Cities of the Plain,* Parts I & II, tr. C. K. Scott Moncrieff. New York: Modern Library, 1927.

―――― (1924), *The Captive,* tr. C. K. Scott Moncrieff. New York: Boni, 1929.

―――― (1925), *The Sweet Cheat Gone,* tr. C. K. Scott Moncrieff. New York: Boni, 1930.

―――― (1927), *The Past Recaptured,* tr. F. A. Blossom. New York: Boni, 1932.

Rubin, E. (1927), Visuell wahrgenommene wirkliche Bewegung. *Z. Psychol.,* 103:384-392.

Russell, B. (1948), *Human Knowledge: Its Scope and Limits.* New York: Simon & Schuster.

Skinner, B. F. (1935), Generic Nature of Stimulus and Response. *J. Gen. Psychol.,* 12:40-65.

Spence, K. W. (1944), The Nature of Theory Construction in Contemporary Psychology. *Psychol. Rev.,* 51:47-68.

Tolman, E. C. (1937), The Acquisition of String-Pulling by Rats—Conditioned Response or Sign-Gestalt? *Psychol. Rev.,* 44:195-211.

―――― & Brunswik, E. (1935), The Organism and the Causal Texture of the Environment. *Psychol. Rev.,* 42:43-77.

von Kries, J. (1901), *Über die materiellen Grundlagen der Bewusstseinserscheinungen.* Tübingen & Leipzig: Mohr.

Weiss, A. P. (1925), *A Theoretical Basis of Human Behavior.* Columbus, Ohio: R. G. Adams.

Werner, H. (1926), *Comparative Psychology of Mental Development,* rev. ed., 2nd printing. New York: International Universities Press, 1957.

COGNITIVE CONTROL

PART 4

COGNITIVE CONTROL

A Study of Individual Consistencies in Cognitive Behavior

by

RILEY W. GARDNER
PHILIP S. HOLZMAN
GEORGE S. KLEIN
HARRIET B. LINTON
DONALD P. SPENCE

Toward a
Science of
Psychoanalysis

"**If** *psychoanalysts are themselves to make a science of their knowledge, they must be prepared to follow the standard rules of science."*

This combined *caveat* and sign-post to new directions — pronounced by the distinguished psychologist Ernest Hilgard — illuminates the remarkable ferment that is now shaping the future of psychoanalysis as a *scientific* endeavor. Only the most intractably optimistic practitioner or patient would deny that the foundations and techniques of the psychoanalytic process must ultimately be rooted in the very real and observable facts of human behavior.

And this critical need to anchor psychoanalysis to the rigorous and self-adjusting requirements of a truly scientific discipline is both the driving force and point of departure of PSYCHOLOGICAL ISSUES. The objective of this unusual monograph series is simple and direct: *to implement the development of a general "psychoanalytic theory of behavior."* It has done so by drawing from the most pertinent and meaningful controlled studies of either an experimental or clinical character. These studies represent the most important effort to erase the unhappy fact that, for many years, the only common association between *psy*choanalysis and *psy*chology was a Greek prefix. The purpose and promise of this volume is to bridge that gap.

Just as PSYCHOLOGICAL ISSUES makes stringent demands of the two fields from which its contents are drawn, it makes serious demands of the reader. But the attentive reader will be amply rewarded. The structure and subtleties of the human mind, reflected in these monographs, are enormously complex and challenging.

And the basic concepts and "transactions" of an effective psychoanalytic approach must mirror these awesome complexities. The four contributions and the introduction included in PSYCHOLOGICAL ISSUES richly demonstrate the great variety of subjects that form the framework of a psychoanalytic science. They range from a careful, serial study of remembering, to a brilliant systematic commentary on the psychosocial stages of the life cycle of man.

Two of these studies, in particular, represent the most impressive aspects of this growing movement to provide sound, scientific credentials for the psychoanalytic movement. Both of these contributions — one by Erik Erikson and the other by the late David Rapaport — demonstrate the intellectual explorations of psychoanalytic psychology at its very best. In Erikson's hands the scope of psychoanalysis extends beyond individual pathology to encompass a broad view of growth in human society. It suggests the depth of work yet to be done to relate psychoanalysis to a scientific psychology of development and maturation.

David Rapaport's historical survey of "ego psychology" — a foundation stone of psychoanalytic theory — provides a significant setting for Erikson's comments and also points the way for future areas of productive merging beween psychoanalysis and psychology. With all of its conceptual immaturities and inconsistencies, the psychoanalytic process stands as one of the most remarkable achievements of modern man.

For those who wish to "participate" in the movement of psychoanalytic thought towards a rigorous, scientific base, PSYCHOLOGICAL ISSUES is a vital stepping-stone.

Extra Selection:
Psychological Issues
by Erik H. Erikson, David Rapaport, I. H. Paul, Fritz Heider, Riley Gardner, Philip S. Holzman, George S. Klein, Harriet Linton, and Donald P. Spence

Publisher's Price $12.00
Member's Price $8.95
plus one bonus credit towards the four required for your next free Bonus Book

Contents

I IDENTITY AND THE LIFE CYCLE *Selected Papers by* ERIK H. ERIKSON *Introduction: A Historical Survey of Psychoanalytic Ego Psychology by* DAVID

1. Ego Development and Historical Change — *Clinical Notes*
2. Growth and Crises of the Healthy Personality
3. The Problem of Ego Identity

II STUDIES IN REMEMBERING. *The Reproduction of Connected and Extended Verbal Material by* I. H. PAUL

1. Some General Considerations Regarding Learning and Remembering
2. Explication and Familiarity in Serial Reproduction of Stories: An Exploratory Experiment
3. Retention Style and Retention Ability
4. Conclusions and Implications

III ON PERCEPTION, EVENT STRUCTURE, AND PSYCHOLOGICAL ENVIRONMENT. *Selected Papers by* FRITZ HEIDER

1. Thing and Medium
2. The Function of the Perceptual System
3. The Function of Economical Description in Perception
4. Environmental Determinants in Psychological Theories
5. The Description of the Psychological Environment in the Work of Marcel Proust
6. On Lewin's Methods and Theory

IV COGNITIVE CONTROL. *A Study of Individual Consistencies in Cognitive Behavior by* RILEY W. GARDNER, PHILIP S. HOLZMAN, GEORGE S. KLEIN, HARRIET B. LINTON, *and* DONALD P. SPENCE

1. Aims and Theoretical Perspectives
2. Plan of the Study
3. The Leveling-Sharpening Control Principle
4. The Control Principle of Tolerance for Unrealistic Experiences
5. The Equivalence Range Control Principle
6. The Focusing Control Principle
7. The Constricted-Flexible Control Principle
8. Field Dependence-Independence
9. Factor Analyses
10. Control Principles and Styles
11. Cognitive Controls and Defenses
12. Retrospect and Prospect

PSYCHOLOGICAL ISSUES, *the Alternate Selection of The Behavorial Science Book Service, is available in addition to or instead of the Main Selection.*

CONTENTS

1	**AIMS AND THEORETICAL PERSPECTIVES**	1
	The Behavioral Units in Cognitive Control and Cognitive Styles	4
	Systematic Conceptions of Personality	6
	Relationship to Psychoanalytic Theory	9
	Some Considerations of Measurement	14
	Design of the Present Study	17
2	**PLAN OF THE STUDY**	18
	Subjects	19
	A Look Ahead	21
3	**THE LEVELING-SHARPENING CONTROL PRINCIPLE**	22
	The Schematizing Test	23
	Kinesthetic Time Error Test	27
4	**THE CONTROL PRINCIPLE OF TOLERANCE FOR UNREALISTIC EXPERIENCES**	31
	Apparent Movement Test	32
	Aniseikonic Lenses Test	35
5	**THE EQUIVALENCE RANGE CONTROL PRINCIPLE**	39
	Object Sorting Test	40
	Size Constancy Test	42
6	**THE FOCUSING CONTROL PRINCIPLE**	46
	Size Estimation Test I	48
	Picture Sorting Test	50
7	**THE CONSTRICTED-FLEXIBLE CONTROL PRINCIPLE**	53
	Color-Word Test	54
	Incidental Recall Test	58
	Size Estimation Test II	59
	Free Association Test	63
8	**FIELD DEPENDENCE-INDEPENDENCE**	67
	Rod and Frame Test	70
	Embedded Figures Test	72
	Rorschach Test	76

9	FACTOR ANALYSES	77
	Statistical Technique	77
	Method of Analysis	78
	Tests of the Purity of the Factorial Structures	79
	Results for Men	79
	Results for Women	94
	Discussion of Results	109
10	CONTROL PRINCIPLES AND STYLES	115
	The Person Clusters	117
	Clusters of Men	118
	Clusters of Women	118
	Clusters vs. Single Control Principles: Consensus in Response to a Personal Inventory	121
	Discussion	123
11	COGNITIVE CONTROLS AND DEFENSES	127
	Leveling and Repression	129
	Scanning and Isolation	132
	Discussion	136
12	RETROSPECT AND PROSPECT	137
	Future Studies Needed	140
	Summary	146
	APPENDICES	149
	A. Intercorrelation of Major Scores	150
	B. Results of 33-Score Factor Analyses	155
	C. Tests of the Purity of the Factor Structures	159
	D. Factor Scores	162
	E. Cluster Analyses	164
	F. Replication Study of Relationships between Rorschach Signs and Basic Measures of Field Dependence-Independence	168
	G. Order of Presentation of Squares in the Schematizing Test	176
	H. Method of Computing Increment Error Score for Schematizing Test (Score 3)	177
	I. Method of Computing Assimilation Score for Kinesthetic Time Error Test (Score 4)	178
	BIBLIOGRAPHY	180

Acknowledgments

This study and the studies of cognitive controls that preceded it were made possible by research grants #MH-25 and #M-1182 from the National Institute of Mental Health, U.S. Public Health Service, and generous additional support from The Menninger Foundation. Dr. Gardner Murphy, Director of Research, The Menninger Foundation, was in many ways instrumental in providing means for the completion of the study. The authors are indebted to Dr. Murphy and to Drs. David Rapaport and Robert Holt for careful readings of the manuscript. Special credit should also be given to Mrs. Diana Siegal, who did much of the laboratory testing, and to Miss Lolafaye Coyne, who contributed greatly to the analyses of the data.

1

AIMS AND THEORETICAL PERSPECTIVES

The present study of individual consistencies in cognitive behavior is one of a series dating back to 1948. The premise of this work has been that the wide range of behaviors with which an individual encounters reality may be encompassed by relatively few dimensions of organization. Presumably, these dimensions concern modes of coping with particular situational frameworks of task, stimulus-constraints, and intentions for which the modes are especially relevant and suited. They manifest themselves through perceptual, recollective, and other functions. To emphasize their orientation toward reality and environmental structures, we have thought of such organizing tendencies as *adaptive controls,* and of their behavioral consequences as *adaptive solutions.*

The theoretical understructure of the concept of cognitive control has been developed in a series of papers: in relation to *personality theory* (Klein and Schlesinger, 1949; Klein, 1951; Klein and Krech, 1952); in relation to *clinical diagnostic testing* (Klein, 1949b, 1949c; Klein, Holzman, and Laskin, 1954; Holt, 1954); in relation to *psychophysics and Gestalt theory* (Holzman, 1954; Holzman and Klein, 1954); in relation to *drives and motivational concepts* (Klein, 1954; Holzman and Klein, 1956b; Klein, 1958); and in relation to the *psychoanalytic concept of defense* (Klein, 1954, Holzman and Gardner, 1959; Klein, 1959). In this chapter only a few of these theoretical considerations will be briefly developed.

In its focus on those stable features of organization that we call cognitive controls, the present study takes its place within the long history of personality theory. The work of Gordon Allport, Thurstone, and Angyal is especially relevant to the concepts of cognitive controls and styles. Allport and Vernon's studies (1933) of expressive movement were a pioneering effort to define structural constants of personality in cognitive processes. Allport's (1935) later distinction between "motivational" and "instrumental" attitudes influenced our attempts to relate cognitive controls to drives. Thurstone's (1944) exploration of perceptual behavior was also based upon the assumption that perception depends in part upon enduring organizations superordinate to the perceptual system itself.

Investigations of such organizational constants stand astride two major trends of cognitive research: (a) the search for generalized effects of motivation on behavior, and (b) the study of psychophysical correspondences between response and stimulus. The present study draws attention to structural constants—cognitive controls and styles—that condition and limit the influence of environmental forces and of tensions provoked by motives. Too often, perception-motivation studies have tended to overlook the fact that motivational effects do have limits, that there are restrictions on how much a drive can distort reality, and that motivational variables will not alone account for these limits. The opposite is also true—needs sometimes make perception especially faithful to reality. Presumably there are also limits to this direction of influence. Alleged distortions of cognition by drives or needs (e.g., effects on the estimation of size) have been difficult to confirm, partly, in our opinion, because the formal or structural components of cognition, and differences among individuals in these respects, are often neglected. Our studies have demonstrated that people differ in the emphasis they give to one or another of the configurational qualities of objects, e.g., figure-ground differentials, contour formation, etc. (e.g., Holzman, 1954). It has seemed to us important to consider that differences of this kind in perceptual organization may also constitute *structural* restraints on the effects of drives. In psychoanalytic terms, such structural components of perception may determine the extent to which primary-process determinants will dominate thinking. Most perception-motivation studies have tended to overlook a point that is ever obvious to the clinician—that there are different means of controlling drives, different ways of accomplishing the same end.

Similarly, demonstrations of a highly precise psychophysical coordination of stimulation and response will not by themselves account for individual differences in the slopes of such psychophysical functions (see Johansson, Dureman, and Sälde, 1955; Holzman and Klein, 1954). If we think of response as coerced not by stimulus alone or by motives alone, but also by the organizational dispositions of the responding system, then universal as well as varying responses can be accounted for within a conception of organismic controls. The concept of cognitive control is offered as one means of ordering persons' variations in responses to both environmental stimuli and drives.

Individual differences in cognitive behavior have been variously interpreted by personality theorists. Some have seen in such differences evidence of "distortion" or "autism" produced by drives, needs, wishes, and conflicts. Taking some single standard of accuracy or effectiveness, these investigators have tended to regard deviations as indicative of projective influences on thought. The present study and its precursors were guided by the possibility that such variations among people arise from a different source. It did not seem to us that wishes pressing to override reality are a major factor in producing such differences. Not all motivated processes which produce deviations from some standard of veridicality are ineffective from the standpoint of adaptation. Nor do all motivated processes reflect projections of a wish or a need. On the contrary, it seemed to us that differences among people could simply reflect different adaptive approaches to reality, all effective (if not equally accurate) as ways of coping with reality. "Effective perception does not mean uniform perception among people; conversely, individual differences in perception do not necessarily imply 'distorting' mechanisms" (Klein, 1958, p. 106). For the subjects involved, either *leveling* or *sharpening,* for example, may be an adequate way of taking hold of reality.

In this respect, the present research is closely linked to a fundamental premise of psychoanalytic theory: the organism must not only bring needs, impulses, and wishes into continual harmony; it must also resolve the many independent claims of reality. A person is always in a state of motivation, i.e., never without purpose. But while much of his behavior is concerned with reaching satisfying and desirable objects or states, his attempts at need satisfaction are molded by an even more central requirement of survival: that of allaying his strivings without sacrificing effective adaptation to external conditions. Effectiveness in this respect must not be confused with standards of accuracy. For instance, a compulsive regard for accuracy which reaches obsessional intensity may carry with it the price of slowing down the categorizing and appraising of relevant stimuli, and seriously cut into the small interval of time available for adjusting effectively to changing stimuli.

Freud recognized the adaptive characteristics of behavior by postulating an arrangement of structures concerned with such matters as (a) the gratification of drives, (b) the modulation and delay of drive consummation, (c) appraisal of reality and reconciliation of environmental forces and internal tensions. He conceived of cognitive development as following a course intimately linked to, and partly determined by, developmental changes in the drives themselves. He considered perceiving, remembering, and thinking to involve a matrix of structures which limit and mediate motivational influences. In our view, a cognitive control describes an organizational tendency that relates the functioning of these structures to each other within the person. It is an intervening structural condition accounting in part for the *particular* impact of a need on cognition.

The Behavioral Units in Cognitive Controls and Cognitive Styles

In earlier reports, we referred to superordinate dimensions of cognitive control as "perceptual attitudes," "syndromes," "cognitive attitudes," "*Anschauungen*," and "system principles." None of these terms quite suited our definitions of them. It now seems inappropriate to consider these principles as pertaining only to perceptual events. Since perception is certainly not an isolated function, it is descriptively inexact to refer to the organization of adaptive encounters only in terms of perceptual response. From the perspective of the whole adaptive sequence which unfolds when a person "intends" an action, the perceptions that occur are intimately linked to the larger effort to take hold of the situation. Michotte's dictum seems to us indisputable:

> Perception should be regarded as a phase of action and the activity of the individual both motor and intellectual . . . [Perception] influences

behavior only insofar as it has a signification that is given to it by the relations that unite it to other objects, relations in space and time, relations of causality and finality, etc. [1952, p. 221].

The *scores* obtained in a test situation reflect much more than a perceptual response. Assessing perceived information against some standard, reperceptions, rechecking, etc., are involved in the sequence of events condensed in the subject's "score." It seems to us now that the total sequence implementing an adaptive intention—not simply the perceptual, memory, or motor segment of it—constitutes the proper unit of analysis of a control principle. As one of us stated elsewhere:

> The integrating factor in an adaptive behavior unit is the goal-set—the objective or aim, e.g., to judge size in an experiment, or to look for food when one is hungry. Within this orientation determined by goal-sets, the [cognitive control] unfolds *in* the reaction. Cognitive [controls] refer to the organizing principles that guide this interplay of action and transaction and determine what will be an *adequate* perceived result [Klein, 1958, p. 99].

In the behavior segment that discloses a control principle, perceptions and actions are united by the requirements of an intention. Both contribute to the intention and hence both are commensurate with it. In this total sequence, action and thought are not conceived of in any rigidly sequential relation, and consequently it is difficult to refer the workings of controls to particular functional components of the sequence.

The term "cognitive attitude," previously used to designate these generalized dispositions, also carries undesirable implications, and "system principle" does not quite convey their regulative aspect. The term "control" seems to imply more clearly the embeddedness of cognitive functions in a structural arrangement geared to regulation, and is therefore more precisely suited to our definitions.

Cognitive controls are conceived of as slow-changing, developmentally stabilized structures: (a) they are relatively invariant over a given class of situations and intentions; (b) they are operative despite the shifts in situational and behavioral contexts typical of cognitive activity from moment to moment. Cognitive controls refer to a level of organization that is more general than the specific structural components underlying perception, recall, and judgment. The invariant which defines a control has to do with the manner of coordination between a class of adaptive intentions and a class of environmental situations. They are the individual's means of programming the properties, relations, and constraints of events and objects in such a way as to provide an adaptively adequate resolution of the intentions which brought him into an encounter with reality.

Certain aspects of cognitive organization may be secondary consequences of a cognitive control, following upon continual and repeated reliance upon it (Klein, 1958). Conceivably, a leveling disposition (see Chapter 3) could in time lead to a relatively impoverished conceptual structure because of the blurring of temporally extended stimuli that is characteristic of levelers. Associated qualities of ingenuousness and naïveté may also be secondary consequences of this control principle.

Since a number of cognitive controls are assumed to coexist within a personality, the possibility arises that the composition of controls within a person may itself have consequences for behavior that cannot be deduced from the individual controls alone. We shall see in Chapter 10 that extreme *scanning* can appear in a context of low *field-articulation, contricted control,* and *intolerance for unrealistic experiences.* We have referred to such arrangements of controls as *cognitive styles.* The importance of style is that it may provide a basis for predicting behaviors that cannot be inferred from the characteristics of individual controls.

It is our hope that definitions of the regulative tendencies of controls and styles will eventually specify the component processes and structures involved in them, rather than their behavioral, phenomenological, and adaptive outcomes. Pending clarification of the process components of these dimensions, our definitions have emphasized the classes of adaptive situations to which the different controls and styles seem to be linked.

Systemic Conceptions of Personality

At the heart of the present study and its precursors lies an assumption fundamental to any personality theory: that the objective of a theory of behavior is to discover the most general regulatory principles that determine a person's responses and account for individual differences among people. Our approach to behavior may be illustrated in the way we would try to understand the responsiveness of a mobile to wind currents. We would stress the structural characteristics of the *mobile*—its organization as a system. We would not be content with stimulus-response coordinations alone, but would seek to relate responsiveness to general properties of the mobile's over-all structure. Our "laws" would be those of mobiles rather than of wind currents.

Similarly, a systemic conception of personality assumes not only that the organism is well stocked with purposes, directional tendencies or motives, and instrumental means (percepts, motor responses), but that these are arranged in a hierarchical organization of structures, function linked to function. Most diagnostic statements in clinical testing constantly lean upon a belief in such an over-all regulatory system. Conceptions of systemic organization are little advanced, however, beyond the stage of analogy and metaphor. Only the skimpiest theory exists as to how the processes in the organism partake of such an order, and in what forms, and what the most efficient model would be for envisioning a total system of regulation and control.

In general, a systemic theory must address itself to (a) considerations of structural manifolds; (b) order and disorder within and between these manifolds; (c) relative dependence and independence of subsystems; (d) constraints within and between subsystems; (e) a conception of a hierarchy of constraints within the system, ranging from lower-order to higher-order ones; (f) the problem of the relative autonomy of lower-order and higher-order subsystems; (g) the problem of the relationship of lower systems to higher systems, e.g., the manner in which the lower subsystems may become implicated in the workings of the higher-order structures.

While such a systemic conception assumes a hierarchy of regulations, it also assumes that the lower subsystems preserve and the higher subsystems attain a certain relative autonomy. Behavior is determined both by structures specifically linked with certain responses or experiences (e.g., in perception, retinal gradients determine experiences of texture or slant) and by superordinate structures which may temporarily draft a particular subsystem to their service. A crude analogy is the relationship of a bay to the ocean of which it is an integral subsystem. The relative independence of the bay is vouchsafed by its land outlines, which give its water currents distinctive qualities, although these may be overruled by insistent events of the larger system, e.g., a storm occurring in the larger ocean body. Autonomy is relative here in the sense that the bay reflects—in fact, owes its structure in part to—properties of the larger ocean structure. *Particular* behaviors of the bay water, however, are referable to the properties of both the bay and the ocean.

In the personality, organizational characteristics of superordinate structures are imposed upon the lower-order systems (e.g., specific perceptual and cognitive processes) and become manifest in the achievements of these processes. In this sense the latter serve as mediating subsystems; the higher-order structures serve as leading systems. The organizational coherence of the lower-order systems assures them a certain measure of autonomy from the superordinate structures. For instance, perception of size involves motor adjustment in equating a standard and comparison field. Whether a subject is capable of refined motor adjustments or only of crude ones is a relatively autonomous factor in his response. To take another example, retinal structure—like the bay in our analogy—has its own local laws. The constraints of both the local system and the superordinate controls are reflected in a particular behavioral product of vision. It is to be expected that such relatively autonomous structures (e.g., those of perception) reduce the predictive power of a control. Thus, cognitive controls are by no means the only or necessarily the crucial determinants of behavior in a test situation. The relative autonomy of lower-order systems limits the influence of cognitive controls on response.

Special skills are also examples of highly autonomous structures lower in the organizational hierarchy than cognitive controls. They seem to be linked to specific properties of situations. In efficient aircraft recognition, for example, sensitivity encompasses a large number of cues. Christensen and Crannell (1955) have found, however, that transfer from this specific discriminative skill to acuity in other contexts is very slight. Obviously, predictions from cognitive controls to performance on tasks in which subjects have already developed such isolated, well-practiced skills would not be very efficient.

Relationship to Psychoanalytic Theory

Psychoanalytic theory provides a useful framework for a conception of organismic controls. The present study, in its emphasis on the organism's efforts to coordinate behavior with environmental structures, and on internal controlling structures as the stabilized derivatives of these efforts, has a particularly close tie with recent developments in psychoanalytic theory, especially the work of Hartmann (1939) and of Rapaport (1957, 1959). Beyond its sketchily conceived notion of "character defense," however, the traditional form of psychoanalytic theory is relatively poor in structural concepts that can account for individual differences in mental processes. For example, the possibility that "conflict-free" cognitive functions are *idiosyncratically* organized in individuals has not yet been explored by psychoanalysis. It is precisely in this respect that the concept of cognitive control, with its provision for adaptively adequate yet various modes of encountering reality, may prove a useful addition to the theory.

In the following pages, we shall draw attention to a few points of contact between the present study and some major premises of psychoanalytic theory.

Relationship to Psychophysical Coordination

Hartmann has emphasized that an adaptation involves not only means of conflict resolution (e.g., defense), but also processes pertaining to a relatively "conflict-free" sphere of ego functioning. He assumes a genetically determined psychophysical organization, very much in the manner of Jakob von Uexküll's (1934) assumption of a species *Umwelt,* which guarantees a state of adaptedness between the individual and his drives on the one hand and his environment on the other. Hartmann conceives of adaptive events (e.g., object comprehension; thinking; language; perceptual and recall phenomena; motor development, including grasping, crawling, and walking) and of the maturational and learning processes implicit in all of these activities as indicating the presence from the first of an ensemble of functions that exert their effects outside the region of mental conflicts. Though they are closely linked to drive development (as mediating structures), the relative autonomy of the conflict-free functions is assured by characteristics which make them especially suited to represent and deal with environmental forces. Cognitive controls refer to precisely those processes which Hartmann has termed conflict-free. Specifically, they describe the characteristic ways in which reality-adaptive events have become organized in the person; each constitutes for the person his optimal adaptational level in the particular class of environmental situations to which it is suited.

To say that controls are adaptive does not mean that they provide an accurate translation of reality; it means that they provide a "workable fit." The most accurate grasp of reality is not necessarily the most effective one. Cognitive controls involve individually varying standards of adequacy within intention-guided encounters that include perceptual, cognitive, and motor activities. There is great elasticity in human adaptiveness; there are usually several alternative means of mastering an environmental relationship. One man's frustration is another man's solution, meaning the more or less steady state an individual reaches in the face of a task, a problem, or stimulus, as he resolves it in his own way. For example, even in the seemingly simple operation of adjusting the size of one object to that of another, the matching process is no easy matter. It offers ample opportunities for people to take different routes to the same ends, e.g., "big enough" or "small enough." Complex processes are invoked to make possible perceptual contact with the sizes, slants, and colors of things. These processes are themselves part of a larger process of search, informational return (feedback), and re-search that includes conceptual and motor activity. Cognitive controls describe the generalized tendencies which typify the organization of one or another or all phases of this total adaptive effort.

In short, several adaptive functions are assumed for cognitive controls: (1) They govern the extent of informational *feedback*— the degree and extent of renewed encounter with stimuli or ideas before an adaptive intention is deemed met and an adaptive behavioral sequence is terminated. (2) They involve the application of *automatized standards of adequacy* to behavior or experience. If the behavioral outcome does not meet these standards of adequacy, perceptual or ideational activity is renewed to a point reflecting the inherent requirement of the control. (3) The outcome of a cognitive control is a pattern of *attribution,* in which stimulus events and ideas are brought into a relation to each other as relevant and irrelevant, experienced and nonexperienced, segments of a stimulus field. Controls are not identical in respect to these adaptive functions. We have by no means been able to trace the details of these functions in all the controls we have studied so far. We are not sure that all of these functions *are* in fact involved in every cognitive control, or that the controls are equivalent with respect to these functions. For instance, *leveling-sharpening* seems to pertain mainly to the formation of memory schemata; *equivalence range,* to adequacy of "fit" (criteria of satisfactory equivalence); *scanning,* to extent of feedback.

Relationship to Drive

Needs are subject to modulation and enforced postponement. Defenses are, of course, especially prominent means of effecting such delay, but it must be emphasized that psychoanalysis does not assume that delay is exclusively accomplished by defense. In psychoanalytic theory, all structures are conceived of as having a delaying function. Since cognitive controls have an organizing influence on behavior, they must also be assumed to have a hand in delaying need discharge.

Klein et al. (Klein and Salomon, 1952; Klein, 1954; Klein, Salomon, Smith, and Mandler, in preparation) have demonstrated the modulating effects of one cognitive control in a temporary need state. In an investigation of the ways in which thirst is expressed in the behavior of people at opposite extremes of *constricted and flexible control* (see Chapter 7), they found large differences in responses of the two thirsty groups to thirst-related objects in a variety of test situations. Although the study pointed strongly to the role of cognitive controls in drive-imbued thinking, it only touched the general problem of relationships between these controls and reality adaptation in drive or need states. The types of drives themselves, the place of the need state in the hierarchy of drives (ranging from instincts to highly refined attitudes), and the conflicts provoked by arousal of the need, all require more detailed study.

It may be noted that the action of cognitive controls under special conditions is not essentially different from their established function in ordinary encounters with reality. It is not that of defense, in one sense in which defense is sometimes meant: as a special characteristic of response to conflict and anxiety. The thirsty subjects dealt with the tasks confronting them in ways that clearly reflected the need, but their behavior was essentially consistent with how they could be expected to deal with similar situations with the need absent.

Relationship to Defense

As control structures, cognitive controls do, however, serve a function similar to defenses, and it would not surprise us if similar structures were involved in both. That this may be the case is suggested by Hartmann's (1939) point that behavior patterns invoked to resolve conflict are often retained as favored means of adaptation after the conflict subsides. They may, in fact, serve the organism well in this respect, producing effective encounters with reality, even while continuing to serve whenever necessary in their original capacity of resolving intrasystemic conflicts. If our vantage point is that of how cognitive controls affect drives, we may well be impressed by the degree to which cognitive controls are coordinated with specific environmental conditions; if our vantage point is that of how motivational conditions produce variations in the control of reality, we are likely to appreciate more the utility of cognitive controls *and* defenses as means of delaying drive tensions.

It is therefore doubtful that two sets of controls are involved, each invoking different mediating structures. It seems more likely that defenses and cognitive controls involve the same signal and action apparatuses. Both defenses and controls can expedite or complicate drive discharge. The concept of control only draws attention to the extent to which drive discharge is appropriately attuned to reality.

To summarize: (a) both cognitive controls and defenses are considered to be structures; (b) they provide instrumental means through which drive discharge takes place; (c) they modulate drive-discharge processes to accord with established modes of confronting the reality context in which consummation is sought.

Relationship to Development

Psychoanalytic theory assumes that drives and controls develop from a common matrix of structures and processes. In the course of development and through repeated environmental encounters, enforced delays of gratifications are internalized as controls:

> The controlling countercathectic energy distributions, once arisen, differentiate affective and ideational instinct representations and thus liberate the new conscious qualities of ideation from the rule of affective pleasure-pain regulation [Rapaport, 1950, p. 165].

Though originating in part from drive-environment interaction, control organizations have a degree of independence from drives. Developmental momentum includes a continuous process of internalizing reality through the building of models of reality—what Hartmann (1939) calls the "inner world." These models are constructed under the impetus of drives which themselves change in character as the models of the environment continue to serve in the programming of stimuli and in the channeling of drives into certain directions of satisfaction and not others. Changes in control structures and modification of drive aims go hand in hand. But just as structures in general and cognitive controls in particular are means by which an individual achieves a certain autonomy from his drives, cognitive controls seem especially important in attaining for the individual a similar autonomy from the environment (see Rapaport, 1951b, 1958). Reactions that originally occurred in relation to the external world are increasingly displaced into the interior of the organism in the form of generalized programming arrangements, so that similar adaptive situations eventually become equivalent with respect to the organism's modes of response.

Some Process Considerations

As yet not much can be stated confidently about the process components of cognitive controls. A few interesting possibilities arise, however, when we view the workings of controls from the standpoint of the availability, mobilization, and deployment of attention (Klein, 1958; Gardner, in preparation). Since the influence of cognitive controls is very much a matter of highlighting certain environmental features and reducing the effectiveness of others, it is precisely in the regulation of attention that the influence of cognitive controls may be most apparent.

In speaking of attention, we are referring to Freud's conception of a fixed quantity of hypercathexis that may be deployed or mobilized in a variety of patterns. Presumably, a critical quantity of such cathexis must be attracted by an idea or stimulus for it to become part of the field of consciousness. The availability of attention hypercathexis and its patterning are presumably vital matters in the development and maintenance of cognitive structures (Rapaport, 1950). The concept of attention hypercathexis focuses upon the conditions of competition for this fixed supply.

It is possible to account in part for some of the properties of several cognitive controls in these terms. For instance, the control principle we call *scanning* implies a distinctive patterning of attention. Extensive *scanning* reflects deployment of attention hypercathexes over widespread segments of a stimulus field. In *field-articulation*, we have a pattern of attention deployment in which attention hypercathexes are mobilized upon the most *relevant* segments of an informational array. The *leveling-sharpening* control principle raises the problem of attention *availability*. It is possible that the fixed amount of attention hypercathexis is relatively low in levelers, so that their capacity for concentration is limited. It may be this limitation that accounts for the relatively great interaction between percepts and traces in levelers.

Some Considerations of Measurement

Since coordination with reality looms large in our understanding of cognitive controls, their empirical definition must specify situational contexts. The present study separates itself from those conceptions of traits which seem to imply an encapsulated personality structure and which look for trait consistency alone, without regard for the adaptational setting or situational specificity of "traits." It would be misleading, for example, to define *leveling-sharpening* or *scanning* solely in terms of response properties or in terms of the physical specifications of different tasks. It is necessary to be clear about what is meant by the generality of a cognitive control. The generality refers to the range of situations which pose similar adaptive requirements and similar situational characteristics. It does not refer simply to the physical characteristics of stimuli nor to identities of behaviors. In this sense, a control principle like *scanning* represents the way a person may typically cope with circumstances which allow him the option of deploying attention to any preferred degree. The *significance* of behaviors for the adaptive requirements of a situation is the all-important consideration in specifying the control principles contributing to responses.

In order to detect these regulative constants, one must know a person's explicit intentions, as well as the circumstances he must adapt to. An intention is aroused when one is set to discriminate, to remember, to image, etc. Also tied up with the intention are standards of adaptive adequacy which tell a person that the intention has been met and which serve as termini for his behavior.

From the standpoint of measurement, the intentions evoked by a task are all important in any attempt to account for a person's behavior. For instance, in one study in which we sought to investigate *tolerance for unrealistic experiences* (see Chapter 4), it was important to make the subject understand that the apparent motion of the stimuli he would be exposed to was really an illusion—that two actually stationary objects were being shown. The manner of creating the illusion by varying the rate of alternation of two figures was demonstrated to him. In the test proper, the stimuli were presented in a wide range of speeds of alternation, and the subject's range of experienced movement was determined. This subjective range expressed the option accepted by the subject in organizing his responses: either to base his responses on his knowledge that the stimuli were *not* actually moving, or to base them on the impressiveness of the experience of motion. Thus the intention created by instructions was for the subject to judge movement. Beyond this, however, implicit intentions modified the explicit one, depending on the subject's choice of one or the other option in organizing his response.

The antecedent conditions of cognitive controls must be sought in the task-sets, expectations, and options provided for response; these define the conditions for isolating and defining cognitive controls experimentally. The tendency to ignore the adaptive context of a task is perhaps one reason it has been so difficult to establish the predictive generality of responses in different test conditions. Experimenters have been either too response-centered or too stimulus-centered, and have ignored the *intentions* provoked by a task.

Viewed in these terms, the control-principle conception avoids the traditional pitfalls of typologies which define personality consistency solely in terms of response characteristics. In focusing upon antecedent conditions of situational contexts, we increase the possibility of operational control in predicting behavior from control principles. The very same stimulus situation can become a very different adaptive task when the instructions are changed, thereby precluding the operation of certain control principles.

An important assumption in the operational definition of control principles concerns their dimensional properties. We assume a continuous variation in the process components of a control principle. Thus, with *scanning,* we imply that people vary in respect to the extensiveness of attention deployment. In this way we again avoid a common pitfall of typologies by implying that more or less *scanning* behavior or more or less *leveling* behavior can occur. Furthermore, no encapsulated traits are implied. To say that one is a strong leveler does not mean that performance is independent of the situation or of adaptive intention.

In general, our means of specifying control principles utilizes different tests as if they were "items" of a questionnaire. By massing "items," i.e., different test situations, and looking for relationships among them, we hope that a control principle will stand out in relief. By working with an expanding circle of experimentally defined phenomena it is therefore possible to include a wider range of behaviors and situations that are unified by a single organizational principle and to sharpen our understanding of the principle. Inferences about the control principle can then be drawn which allow prediction to congruent behaviors in different regions of the personality.

Design of the Present Study

Five previously defined controls, conceived of as dimensions, form the core of the present study: *leveling-sharpening* (Holzman and Klein, 1951, 1954; Holzman, 1954; Holzman and Gardner, 1959; Gardner, Jackson, and Messick, in preparation); *focusing* or *scanning* (Schlesinger, 1954; Holzman and Klein, 1956b; Holzman, 1957; Klein, 1958; Gardner, 1959; Gardner, in preparation); *constricted-flexible control* (Smith and Klein, 1953; Klein, 1954; Loomis and Moskowitz, 1958); *equivalence range* (Gardner, 1953; Sloane, 1959); and *tolerance for unrealistic experiences* (Klein and Schlesinger, 1951; Klein, Gardner, and Schlesinger, in preparation). Also represented in the study is Witkin's *field dependence-independence* dimension (see Witkin et al., 1954), because of its apparent similarity to principles which we isolated and because it seemed to fit nicely into the present concepts of cognitive control.

The present study was designed primarily to test the adequacy of the previous formulations on a single group of sixty subjects (thirty of each sex) and to develop more precise descriptions and operational definitions of these dimensions. These control principles were previously studied in different groups of subjects and, in some instances, in narrow ranges of test situations. Earlier definitions of some of the principles seemed to overlap. *Constricted-flexible control* and *field dependence-independence* are two of the dimensions that seemed closely similar in their initial descriptions, in spite of the fact that each had been defined in different test situations. An important aim, then, was to bring the different control principles under tighter operational rein in order to clarify still more the tasks and adaptive intentions to which they are specifically linked. It was our hope that the study would also add precision to predictive applications of these principles.

Our tool for investigating commonalities of test situations with respect to control principles is factor analysis. It is here employed simply as a quantitative tool for testing predicted congruences of performance. Our *interpretations* of these commonalities are guided solely by assumptions concerning the adaptive significance of the factors in individual behavior.

2

PLAN OF THE STUDY

The five control principles were measured by fourteen experimental tasks. Two of Witkin's procedures (see Witkin et al., 1954) —the Rod and Frame and Embedded Figures Tests—were used to measure the field dependence-independence dimension, which was considered an additional control principle. In addition, we administered the Rorschach test. Rorschach administration and scoring followed the procedure suggested by Rapaport et al. (1946). The records were also scored by the Klopfer method, so that we could compare our findings directly with those of Witkin and his collaborators. A Personal Inventory of 234 items was also administered to all subjects.

The total testing time for each subject was approximately nine hours, in one- or two-hour sessions. The testing was conducted primarily by one assistant (Mrs. Diana Siegal) and supplemented by two of the authors (RWG and PSH). The division of testing was not sufficiently systematic to permit exploration of examiner-test interactions.

Great care was taken to insure full understanding of the instructions, and testing did not proceed until this was clearly obtained. All subjects found most of the procedures interesting and brief enough to minimize fatigue and boredom. Conspicuous exceptions were the Schematizing and Kinesthetic Time Error Tests. The former, although not unpleasant, required forty minutes of judging sizes and was quite monotonous. The latter required three twenty-minute sessions, on separate days. Many subjects, particularly the women, found repeated lifting of the weights fatiguing and boring. It was our general impression, however, that all subjects were highly motivated to do their best in the experiment and that the effects of these features of the two tests, which might have been major handicaps with another group of subjects, were minimal.

Subjects

Although paid $10 for participating, the sixty subjects were of necessity volunteers who were self-selected for persistence, interest in this general type of work, and willingness to add nine hours of testing (often in the evening and on week ends) to otherwise busy schedules. The volunteer subject in this type of experiment is probably not very defensive about exposing himself to study by psychologists; on the contrary, he is probably less "on guard" than the traditional college sophomore who is required to participate in experiments.

Because of the difficulty in getting subjects it was not practicable to control such variables as age, education, intelligence, occupational and economic status. All subjects were of middle-class background. They spanned a variety of occupations and differed widely in education. Their educational levels and occupations are presented in Table 1 (see p. 20). Their ages ranged from 17 to 39.

There were a number of conspicuous differences between the men and women of our sample. The women were significantly older than the men; the average age for the women was 27.4 as compared to 23.7 for the men. Twelve of the thirty men and twenty-one of the thirty women were married. Twelve of the women were wives of professional staff members of The Menninger Foundation, three were skilled secretaries, and two were nurses. Eighteen of the women were friends or acquaintances of the experimenters. Only three women subjects were total strangers to the research staff. On the other hand, the experimenters knew personally only three of the thirty male subjects. Seventeen men were volunteers from the local university. Two were members of the adjunctive therapy staffs of local psychiatric hospitals. Three held professional degrees. In addition to these differences, the experimenters shared the impression that the women subjects were generally more sophisticated and had a broader range of cultural interests than the men.

The men and women also differed significantly in performance on certain tests, namely, the Rod and Frame Test, the Embedded Figures Test, the Picture Sorting Test, the Object Sorting Test, and the Apparent Movement Test. These disparities were not anticipated except for the first two tests, in which Witkin also found noticeable sex differences (Witkin et al., 1954).

Table 1

SAMPLE CHARACTERISTICS

Education		Occupation	
Men	Women	Men	Women
2 Some college	2 High school students	17 College students	19 Housewives
17 College students	8 High school graduates (4 with additional work in business college)	3 State civil service	3 Secretaries
9 College graduates		2 Adjunctive therapists (psychiatric)	2 Nurses
2 Postgraduate work	8 Some college (2 with additional nurses training)	2 Engineers	2 High school students
	8 College graduates	1 Newspaper reporter	1 Teacher
	4 Postgraduate work	1 Salesman	1 Dance teacher
		1 Public relations man	1 Newspaper reporter
		1 Recreation director	1 Unemployed
		1 Bookkeeper	
		1 Lawyer	

In addition to the differences in individual tests, the general level of correlations between scores and the patterning of correlations were quite different for men and women (Table 6, Appendix A). Therefore, it seemed to us advisable to do separate factor analyses for men and women. It is likely, however, that some of these sex differences reflect sampling disparities rather than basic differences between the sexes.

A Look Ahead

In the chapters to follow, we will describe each of the six control principles and their constituent measures: *leveling-sharpening, tolerance for unrealistic experiences, equivalence range, focusing, constricted-flexible control,* and *field dependence-independence*. The definition of each control principle will be followed by a description of the relevant tests, the rationale of these tests, and a brief description of the test scores. All scores are numbered consecutively throughout the monograph.

Relationships between control principles were explored in two sets of factor analyses, described in Chapter 9. From a total of 40 measures, we selected 33 and factored them separately for men and women. Five factors were extracted for men and three were extracted for women. Because the samples of men and women were small, additional factor analyses were done with 16 scores, in order to determine the stability of the 33-score factor structures.

In Chapter 10 we summarize our data from another vantage point, looking this time at relationships between subjects rather than between tests. We computed $\triangle^2$ values between subjects' factor scores, and grouped men and women into principal clusters that may represent a higher level of cognitive organization.

In Chapter 11, we discuss the relationship between each of two controls and a defense mechanism.

Chapter 12 includes a summary of our present thinking about control principles in the light of the factor analyses and a discussion of further studies that have been done or that could be done, based upon the findings of the present study.

3

THE LEVELING-SHARPENING CONTROL PRINCIPLE

The terms "leveling" and "sharpening" were used by Wulf (1922) and by Carmichael, Hogan, and Walter (1932) to describe systematic changes in memory traces, and by G. W. Allport and Postman (1947) to describe alterations in rumor. It is necessary to distinguish these uses from our own conception. Leveling-sharpening here refers to a principle of personality organization and is applied to the problem of explaining consistent individual differences in perception and cognition.

Previous studies (Holzman and Klein, 1951, 1954; Holzman, 1954) were designed to show a general leveling-sharpening tendency in a variety of modalities. Leveling was first defined as a low degree of articulation of stimulus fields. Such a tendency might manifest itself in: (a) difficulty in extracting figures embedded in larger contexts; (b) easy assimilation of new stimuli into dominant organizations, so that a gradual change in the stimulus field would go unrecognized for a relatively long period. In general, leveling was used to mean maximal dedifferentiation of the cognitive field; and sharpening to mean the opposite, i.e., maximal complexity and differentiation of the field. Thus a leveler should have difficulty in extracting figure from ground, whereas a sharpener should not.

Performance in embedded figures tests, however, was not reliably related to leveling-sharpening (see also Krathwohl and Cronbach, 1956). Results, while always in the predicted direction, hovered around the 10 per cent level of significance. Relations between measures of leveling-sharpening and performance on assimilation tests, such as time error tests (Holzman and Klein, 1954; Holzman, 1954), however, were stronger and pointed to the value of defining leveling and sharpening as modes of organizing a *sequence* of stimuli. It seemed most likely, in view of these findings, that leveling implied a low level of articulation in a *sequence* of stimuli, whereas sharpening implied a high level of articulation.

THE SCHEMATIZING TEST

Apparatus and Procedure

The Schematizing Test, adapted from a procedure used by Hollingworth (1913), requires judgments of a series of 150 squares which gradually increase in size. The fourteen sizes of squares range from 1.2 to 13.7 inches on a side. They were projected individually from a 35-millimeter film strip onto a screen approximately 15 feet from the subjects, who were tested in groups of five. They sat at desks, mounted with small lamps, to record their judgments. An electromagnetic shutter, operated by a mechanical timer, exposed each square for three seconds, with an interval of eight seconds between exposures. Two-minute rest periods were given after trials 40 and 75.

At the beginning of the test, the five smallest squares were shown first in ascending order and then in two random orders. These 15 judgments constituted Series 1. Without interruption, the smallest square was then removed and a new square, larger than any previously seen, was added. This new cluster of five squares (Series 2) was then presented three times, first in ascending order and twice more in random order. By subtracting the smallest square and adding a new, larger square after each series of 15 judgments, the procedure was repeated ten times and the complete range of sizes gradually traversed.

The difference in size between adjacent squares averaged 20 per cent, well above the differential limen of a sample of pilot subjects. The squares were (in inches): 1.2, 1.6, 2.0, 2.4, 2.8, 3.2, 3.8, 4.6, 5.5, 6.6, 7.9, 9.5, 11.4, 13.7. The order of presentation is given in Appendix G.

The instructions, which were projected on the screen and read to the subjects, were as follows:

> We wish to see how well you can judge the size of squares. We're going to show you a number of squares on the screen and we want you to tell us how big they are. The squares may range anywhere

between 1 inch and 18 inches. This doesn't mean you will necessarily get a square which is 1 inch or 18 inches, though you may. The squares will always be somewhere within this range.

To help you judge the size of the squares, we will show you what a 1-inch square looks like—the smaller end of the range—and what an 18-inch square looks like—the larger end of the range.

The 1-inch and the 18-inch squares were then exposed individually for approximately five seconds.

We will show them to you again. You will see 150 squares during the course of the hour and you have 150 numbered spaces on your sheet. Write your estimation of the size of each square in its own numbered space. Thus, for square number one record its size in inches next to number one, etc.

Don't go back over your judgments to change them. In changing them you are more likely to be inaccurate. Please don't compare your estimates with anyone or make any comment during the hour. Make your judgments independently.

Now to remind you once again of the range in which the squares will fall, we will show you again the smaller and the larger end of the range.

The 1-inch and 18-inch squares were then exposed twice, with five seconds allowed for each exposure.

Now we are ready to begin. You will see each of the following squares for only a few seconds. Look at it all the time it is on the screen and make your estimation when it disappears. The next square you will see will be number one.

Rationale

Two aspects of the subject's response must be distinguished: (a) his discriminative sensitivity (his "perception"), and (b) his means of reporting or communicating it to the experimenter (e.g., the crudity or refinement of the yardstick he uses, his preference for certain scaling units rather than others, and the range of scale values covered by his judgments). It is entirely possible for two subjects of equal sensitivity to adopt markedly different scaling units. Indeed, a pilot study indicated that scaling preference is not related to discriminative accuracy. One group of subjects was required to employ fixed scale units (1 to 32), while the other group used the "free report" method of the present study. Measures of discriminative accuracy within each series of 15 trials and between series were applied to the data of both groups. The mean accuracy of the two groups was almost identical. Helson (1947) also reports a low relation between scaling preference and discrimination. We used free report in the present study because it might give us additional data about individual preferences.

The degree to which the subject keeps pace with the progressive increase in size is a major aspect of his performance on this test. Analysis of this facet of response must take into account the anticipations induced by the instructions. The subject is told three times to expect squares within a range of 1 to 18 inches. He proceeds without any information about how quickly changes in size will be made, in what order the squares will appear, or how often the same square will be repeated. Some subjects may expect large squares to appear early; others may expect small squares.

The instructions alone, with their incomplete information about the order in which the stimuli will appear, are not the only source of anticipations. The first series of 15 trials—in which all the squares are small—may itself create a powerful bias. Because he has seen only small squares, the subject may ignore the instruction that larger squares may appear, and allow his judgments to be swayed by the more tangible perceptual evidence. As a result, he may fail to shift appropriately.

Failure to reproduce the progressive increase in size can also be understood as an assimilation effect (see the summary of assimilation studies by Koffka, 1935). That is, lagging behind the trend of increase in size may result from assimilation between the perceptual processes representing new squares and the trace aggregate representing the smaller squares seen previously. This interpretation is supported by the fact that gross deviations from the trend of increase usually take the form of extreme underestimation. The leveler, then, may be the subject who is characterized by large assimilation effects.

The second major facet of response in this test is the accuracy with which the subject ranks the sizes of the successive stimuli. Low accuracy may mean either that the subject is not able to discriminate small stimulus differences, or that he has no consistently stable conception of the previous stimuli, and hence cannot assign the new stimuli to correct positions in the series.

Low ranking accuracy may also stem from relatively unsustained, spotty attention, which results in inexact registration of individual squares. The subject's attention may vary over any block of 15 squares, and his conception of some preceding squares may be sharper than others. The squares which registered more vividly will have a disproportionate influence on the ranking, resulting in low ranking accuracy.

Ranking accuracy can also be conceived of in terms of assimilation effects. Maximal assimilation between processes representing new squares and memory traces of preceding squares should lead to low accuracy.

In spite of the previously mentioned differences in determinants of the two major aspects of response, the repeated low but significant correlations between increment error and accuracy scores in earlier studies suggests that assimilation proneness is an important factor in both.

Scores

On the basis of the preceding rationale, three separate scores were developed.

1. *Ranking accuracy.* This score was obtained by dividing the number of stimuli correctly ranked by the maximum number (150). Two stimuli given the same rank were considered equally inaccurate. Corrected odd-even reliability coefficients were .90 for men and .84 for women.

2. *Increment error (regression).* This score compared the *estimates* of size increase with the *actual* rate of increase. It was identical with Score 3 except that it was based on the regression of mean increment error on the mean of Series I. It is highly correlated with Score 3 (.84 for women and .90 for men).

3. *Increment error.* This score was the raw mean increment error value. Detailed computation procedures are described in Appendix H.

Kinesthetic Time Error Test

In the earlier discussion of the leveling-sharpening control, it was pointed out that the leveling effects may stem from relatively great assimilation between new experiences and traces of preceding experiences. Two studies (Holzman, 1954; Holzman and Klein, 1954) have supported this assumption by demonstrating relationships between the measures of leveling-sharpening described above and other measures of assimilation. The present Kinesthetic Time Error Test was one of the tests used in these early studies.

Apparatus and Procedure

In this test, the subject judges the weight of a comparison stimulus in relation to that of a standard. In two of the three conditions used, the comparison is made more difficult by interpolation of a third weight which is much lighter or heavier than the standard or comparison stimuli.

The comparison stimuli were five black circular metal pill boxes, each three inches in diameter. The boxes were loaded with lead shot embedded in paraffin; they weighed 184, 192, 200, 208, and 216 grams. The weights were arranged on a revolving circular platform. The standard weight (200 grams) was presented first, followed (in two conditions) by the intervening weight, followed in turn by the comparison weight. The subject compared each of the five weights with the standard, reporting whether it felt lighter or heavier than the standard. A "no difference" response was not allowed.

The subjects were tested individually, seated in a comfortable chair directly in front of the revolving platform and blindfolded to prevent visual recognition of the weights. There were three conditions.

Condition I (light intervening stimulus). The subject first lifted the standard weight for three seconds; then a light intervening stimulus (132 grams) for ten seconds; and then one of the five comparison weights for three seconds. After giving his judgment, he picked up the light stimulus again for twenty seconds, then picked up the standard to start a new series. Each weight was compared with the comparison weight seven times, for a total of 35 judgments. The subject was instructed as follows:

I am going to blindfold you. [The blindfold was put in place.] This is an experiment to see how you judge weights. Rest your elbow on this pad. [The elbow of the subject's preferred arm was put on the pad.] When I tap my pencil like this [demonstration] I want you to lift up the weight that will be right in front of your hand. [The subject's hand was then directed to the weight.] Grasp the weight with all five fingers like this [demonstration] and lift it this high twice [demonstration] and at this rate of speed [demonstration]. Keep your elbow on the pad at all times. When I tap my pencil again, and this will be just after you put the weight down, you will pick up another weight. But this time I want you simply to *hold* the weight for a few seconds. Then, I will tap my pencil again, and you will put the weight down. I'll then give you another tapping signal, and you will pick up a third weight. This weight you will lift twice, just as you did the first one, and then put it down. Now after you put this third weight down, I want you to tell me if that third weight was lighter or heavier than the first weight you picked up. Ignore the middle weight, which you will hold for a few seconds. After you give me your judgment, I'll tap my pencil again and you'll pick up that middle weight again and hold it for a while. Then, we'll start the cycle again. Remember, judge only the third weight, and tell me if the third one is heavier or lighter than the first weight. Let's have two practice runs.

Two practice trials were given to the subject at this point. The following stimuli were used in practice runs: 200 grams, interpolated 132 grams, 184 grams; 200 grams, interpolated 132 grams, 216 grams. When these practice trials were completed, the experimenter continued:

All right, now we're ready to begin. Remember, lift the weights only at my signal, and tell me if the third is lighter or heavier than the first. Try to ignore the middle weight.

Condition II. The same standard and comparison weights and the same instructions were employed as in Condition I. After the standard weight was put down, however, the subject lifted a weight heavier than any in the stimulus series (290 grams). He held this weight for ten seconds, put it down, and then lifted the comparison weight. After the comparison weight was put down, he lifted the 290-gram weight again and held it for twenty seconds. A new series was then begun.

Condition III. No interpolated weights were employed in this condition. The intervals between presentations of stimuli were ten and twenty seconds.

Rationale

The instructions encouraged the subject to be as accurate as possible in judging the relative weights of the standard and the comparison stimuli. He was told to try to ignore the middle, interpolated weight. Time error is traditionally computed as the difference between the objective mid-point and the subjective mid-point (point of subjective equality, or PSE) of the series of comparison stimuli. It is fairly well established that when the interpolated stimulus is more intense than the comparison series, PSE shifts toward the intervening stimulus and is higher (positive time error, or TE). When the interpolated stimulus is less intense than the comparison pair, PSE is lower (negative TE). The closer the interpolated stimulus to the comparison series, the greater is its effect on the PSE. With very few exceptions, these trends have proved reliable not only for motivated experimenters serving as subjects but for those who find the task boring and tedious. Thus TE seems unrelated to motivation. It appears to be directly related to the way the subject experiences the progression of different weights. Köhler (1923), Lauenstein (1932), and Kreezer (1938) have suggested that this progression may best be conceived of as a series of gradients. The intervening stimulus acts as an intrusion into the comparison process, and the subject experiences a series of "ups" and "downs" in intensities. He is required to attempt to ignore or suppress the influence of the interpolated field, a task which is impossible to fulfill completely, since it provides a quality of stimulation similar to that of the other two stimuli. The degree to which the subject can partial out this intervening stimulus is reflected in his TE score, and seems to be a function of his proneness to assimilation effects.

The influence of the intervening stimulus seems also to be related to the subject's initial adaptation level. The 200-gram standard weight may feel subjectively light or heavy. Its position on his scale of subjective equality influences the level of his PSE.

Scores

4. *Assimilation.* This score was the difference in time error between Conditions II (heavy interpolated weight) and I (light interpolated weight). The procedures for determining PSE and time error are described in Appendix I.

5. *Time error.* This score was the algebraic sum of the subject's time errors for the three conditions.

4

THE CONTROL PRINCIPLE OF TOLERANCE FOR UNREALISTIC EXPERIENCES

A control principle related to tolerance for unrealistic experiences was proposed in a 1951 report (Klein and Schlesinger) of a study in which range of apparent movement was successfully predicted from ratings of Rorschach protocols. Since both the Rorschach and Apparent Movement situations seemed to measure "the degree to which 'reality testing' rigidly requires the 'holding on' to forms as they are known to be" (Klein and Schlesinger, 1951, p. 301), it was presumed that one principle of control applied to both situations. Tolerance for instability (here called tolerance for unrealistic experiences) was defined as acceptance of experiences which do not agree with what one knows to be true. Tolerant subjects were assumed to take their experience at face value and to have relatively little need to mold it in terms of "usual" or "expected" reality. Intolerance for instability was defined as resistance to perceptual or cognitive experience in which ideational or immediate sense data controvert conventional reality.

In a second study (Klein, Gardner, and Schlesinger, in preparation), the range of apparent movement for three stimulus figures was used as a criterion measure of the control principle. Successful predictions were made (a) to experienced reversals of a figure in which one aspect conformed to and one "defied" conventional reality; (b) to the length of time during which the more conventional phase of this reversible figure was experienced; (c) to the time required to recognize the distortion induced by aniseikonic lenses; (d) to the amount of distortion induced by these lenses; and (e) to acceptance of Rorschach test requirements, as indicated by a relaxed and imaginative approach to the test. The range of apparent movement was *not* correlated with the number of reversals of a "windmill" figure, in which neither organization was more in accord with conventional reality. Other results of this study suggested that intolerance may be related to avoidance of affect experiences. Relatively "intolerant" subjects responded to the Rorschach test as if they were discomfited by the emotional evocativeness of the stimuli. These subjects seemed to prefer confirmable perceptions, rather than variations in affective experience, as bases for response.

Jeffreys (1953) found that "form-bound" (intolerant) Rorschach performance was associated with a narrow range of apparent movement and a tendency to form conceptual groups with a high potential for public prediction of group limits. "Form-labile" (tolerant) response to the Rorschach was associated with grouping on the basis of private meanings.

Kaplan (1952) showed that this mode of control may also be relevant to memory, by demonstrating a relationship between performance on the Aniseikonic Lenses Test and recall of equivocally structured stories. Subjects who "resisted" the distortion induced by the lenses were characterized by efforts to "rationalize" and by relative poverty in their recall of contradictory or loosely linked story elements.

Martin (1954) showed that this control principle, as measured in the aniseikonic lenses situation, was related to reactions to three ambiguous interpersonal situations. Subjects who asked many questions to clarify these situations were slow to report the distortion induced by the lenses.

Taken together, these results suggest that tolerance for unrealistic experiences may apply to widely disparate tasks, involving perception, memory, and concept formation, including response to stimulus ambiguity of the kind found in the Rorschach. Unrealistic (nonconfirmable) as well as realistic (confirmable) response-options are offered by these situations.

Apparent Movement Test

Apparatus and Procedure

The apparatus was a Dodge tachistoscope modified to provide three fields. In each of two fields was a horse with feet astride, approximately ½ x ½ inch and drawn in black India ink. In the third field was a blank white cardboard. Illumination provided by "daylight" fluorescent tubes was of the same intensity in the three fields, which were exposed in ACBC order. Each stimulus was exposed for 22 per cent of the cycle length. The mechanism consisted of an ⅛ horsepower constant-speed motor driving a dual-controlled Graham variable-speed transmission. Noise-making parts of the apparatus were isolated in an adjacent room and were controlled by means of flexible shafts running through the laboratory wall. The subject looked into the eyepiece of the tachistoscope to see the figures, which were 27 inches from his eyes. The test was administered in a normally lighted room.

Before the actual test, the operation of the apparatus was explained to the subject. He was shown the two separate stimulus cards, and was told that, although he might later experience "movement," no actual movement would occur.

In pretest trials, care was taken to insure that each subject could recognize the aspects of the experience which he was expected to report in the test trials. In each of three test trials the experimenter slowly increased the alternation rate until the subject reported that his experience changed from that of one figure alternately succeeding the other to that of a single figure moving back and forth. After recording the alternation rate at which this occurred (in cycles per second), the experimenter continuously increased the rate until the subject reported that his experience changed to that of two figures "flashing on and off" simultaneously. The difference between the two alternation rates was the basic score.

Rationale

Although Wertheimer's (1912) epoch-making study of apparent motion and Koffka's (1935) summary of findings concerning it included general theoretical accounts of the phenomenon, we are still unable to explain the marked individual differences observed in a situation of apparent motion. In our relatively simple test, subjects show notable differences (a) in the alternation rates at which they first perceive "motion," and (b) in the *range* of alternation rates over which "motion" persists.

This situation can be made "unrealistic" if the experience of movement occurs in a context of conflicting information. If the subject understands that he is actually seeing two stationary figures appearing alternately, he is confronted with an issue of "tolerance." The conflicting information is introduced by the increasing speed of alternation which leads to the illusion of movement. To some degree, individual differences in range of apparent movement may depend upon how tenaciously subjects hold to their knowledge that the horses do not actually move. As the alternation rate increases, each subject reaches a point at which he compromises with this knowledge and makes his perception consistent with the paradoxical movement. He maintains the movement experience until the alternations reach a point at which the two horses again appear as separate entities. At this point, the horses appear to flicker simultaneously, rather than move.

In spite of the fact that a conflict is set up between the known and the apparent, both the instructions and the nature of the stimuli bias the subject toward perceiving movement. Perhaps this in part explains the fact that for many subjects the lower threshold of apparent movement was below that at which any of the experimenters themselves experienced movement.

The *range* of apparent movement is a complicated datum. The first experience of apparent movement (the lower threshold) and the experience of flicker (the upper threshold) are rather strikingly different. In general, subjects are confident in the transition from alternation to movement. In contrast, the transition zone between apparent movement and flicker is much more unstable; either "movement" or flicker can be experienced, and subjects express much more doubt about judgments of this upper threshold. We can assume that the range offers a rough representation of the degree to which the subject allows himself to compromise with the known, but the meaning of his range is partly confounded because the upper threshold does not represent a return to his original experience but rather a transition to a new and very different experience. The degree to which any subject clings to his knowledge of the actual nature of the stimuli is partially obscured by this fact. It suggests that the lower threshold itself may be an important datum because it indicates the point at which the subject originally "compromises" with the known state of affairs.

Scores

In keeping with the rationale, two scores were selected for this test:

6. *Mean movement threshold.* In the present study, three judgments of the "horse" figures were used. As in the preceding experiment (Klein, Gardner, and Schlesinger, in preparation) only ascending trials were used. This score consisted of the mean alternation rate, in cycles per second, at which the subject first reported a shift in his experience from that of two horses to that of one horse moving back and forth. The corrected reliability coefficients were .97 for men and .94 for women.

7. *Mean range.* This score consisted of the mean interval, in cycles per second, between the alternation rates at which the subject first reported the experience of one horse moving back and forth and the higher alternation rate at which he experienced two horses flickering simultaneously. While there is a substantial correlation between the lower and upper thresholds (.53 for the whole sample), the *range* is negligibly correlated with the lower threshold (—.10) and highly correlated with the upper threshold (.79). It can be considered, therefore, as a measure of the upper threshold, with the effect of the lower threshold partialed out. The corrected reliability coefficients were .96 for men and .93 for women.

Aniseikonic Lenses Test

A set of lenses developed by Ames alters in specific ways the size and shape, but not the focus, of images transmitted through them. These lenses simulate a visual aberration called aniseikonia. Excellent descriptions and illustrations of the various effects produced by several types of aniseikonic lenses have been provided by Ames (1946) and Kilpatrick (1952). In the present experiment, we used a pair of 2 per cent meridional sized lenses, the axes of these lenses being positioned obliquely at 45° in one lens and 135° in the other.[1]

[1] These lenses were supplied by the Institute for Associated Research, Princeton, N.J.

Apparatus and Procedure

Condition I. In this condition, the 135° lens was placed over the right eye and the 45° lens over the left eye. The floor of the room then appears to slant sharply downward; the experimenter appears extremely tall, as if on stilts; and the wall in front of the observer seems to slant away and to assume a trapezoidal shape, wide at the top and narrow at the bottom. The experience of distortion is not immediate, but rather develops gradually.

The subject was seated in a chair in the center of a large room, one wall of which was covered with a "camouflage" curtain printed with numerous "leaves" in various shades of green. The subject was about eight feet from the uncurtained side walls and about twenty feet from the wall he faced. He was asked to close his eyes and the glasses were put on, over his own glasses if he wore them. He was instructed as follows:

> When you open your eyes, you will see the wall and the floor of the room just as they were before you closed them. I want you to look around through the glasses. Now some people, when they look through these glasses, find that things look different. Other people find that the glasses don't make any difference at all. I would like you to describe to me all the time that you are looking about just how the floor and the wall look to you. Things may suddenly look different to you either as soon as you open your eyes or after a few moments. On the other hand, nothing may happen. Please describe whatever you see as you look about the room, especially if you should notice any change. Now open your eyes.

The subject's comments were recorded and the time of each remark was noted.

A minute or so after the subject reported recognition of tilt, he was seated at a student's desk chair, the desk portion of which was covered with a white cloth. A black wooden stick 15 inches long and 1 inch square, with rounded ends, was fastened by a friction hinge to the far end of the desk at a viewing distance of about fifteen inches. An expanse of white cloth covered the wall facing the subject at a distance of about six feet. The subject was instructed as follows:

> The object of this test is to adjust this bar until it is just exactly vertical—straight up and down. You will notice that this bar can be

moved to any position in this plane [demonstration]. If you should overshoot the mark, feel free to readjust the bar until it seems exactly vertical. All right, go ahead.

Five adjustments were made. The angle of deviation from the vertical was measured with a bubble-level protractor.

Condition II. In this condition, the 45° lens was placed over the right eye and the 135° lens over the left eye. The general effect is then opposite to that of Condition I. The floor slants sharply up, the experimenter appears short, and the opposite wall appears wide at the bottom and narrow at the top. The procedure was the same as Condition I. After the subject had recognized tilt, he made a second series of five rod adjustments.

Rationale

According to Ames (1946), all persons with normal binocular vision have a similar visual experience when wearing the aniseikonic lenses. The effect has been explained in terms of disparities between monocular and binocular cues produced by the glasses. Viewed monocularly through one lens, the environment appears undistorted; viewed through both lenses, it becomes distorted. The amount of distortion depends on the amount of binocular disparity produced by the lenses. It also depends on at least three other factors: (a) properties of the stimulus object: rectilinear objects are subject to less distortion than irregular forms; (b) distance from the stimulus object; (c) familiarity of the stimulus object: familiar stimuli appear to resist distortion.

Given these general considerations, there are sharp individual differences in the *speed* with which subjects recognize distortion, which seems to be an appropriate measure of tolerance for unrealistic experiences. Some subjects experience the effects immediately after putting on the glasses, whereas others do not report distortion even after wearing the glasses for five minutes or more. It seems possible for a subject to facilitate the experience of distortion by focusing on distortion-prone objects, or to delay the distortion by focusing on distortion-resistant objects. If a person tends to experience discomfort in an unfamiliar field, he may attempt to stabilize the field, for example, by focusing on familiar objects or by favoring monocular over binocular cues. Thus, recognition of distortion depends in part on where the subject chooses to focus attention.

An additional determinant may be the extent to which small changes or disparities are noticed by the subject (the leveling-sharpening control principle described in Chapter 3). Some subjects may not be aware of small changes in appearance because these changes are assimilated to the dominant and immediately preceding experience of rectilinearity. For this reason, we would expect performance with the lenses to be related to performances in the Schematizing and Kinesthetic Time Error Tests (Scores 1, 2, 3, 4). Results of the study by Klein, Gardner, and Schlesinger suggested that both tolerance for unrealistic experiences and leveling-sharpening are determinants of performance in the Aniseikonic Lenses Test.

In adjustments of the rod, a motor response replaces verbal reporting. Some subjects (Klein, Gardner, and Schlesinger, in preparation) never report experiencing change but make predictable errors in adjusting the rod. Awareness of distortion may be bypassed in this condition. For this reason, rod adjustment is not necessarily related to the recognition of tilt.

Scores

Two scores were developed to represent the two main features of response to the lens situation: awareness of change, and sensitivity to change.

8. *Log recognition time.* This score was the logarithm of the time in seconds required to report recognition of tilt in Condition I.

9. *Mean deviation.* This score was the mean difference (in degrees) between the subject's adjustments of the rod and the true vertical. Only Condition I was used; the position of the lenses in Condition II leads to adjustments of the rod close to the subject's face, which imposes an artificial limit on the amount of distortion.

The reliability of this score was .97 for men and .98 for women (corrected coefficients).

5

THE EQUIVALENCE RANGE CONTROL PRINCIPLE

The control principle of equivalence range springs in part from Klüver's (1936) suggestion that the method of equivalent stimuli may provide useful data concerning personality organization. In support of this notion, Gardner (1953) found that subjects who spontaneously sorted objects into relatively many groups (narrow equivalence range) made more accurate retinal and object matches in two size-constancy situations, were better able to match shapes in a shape-constancy test and to equate the brightnesses of two light patches. A narrow equivalence range seemed to imply detailed categorization of certain aspects of experience. "Narrow-range" subjects had relatively exact standards for judging similarity. "Broad-range" subjects on the other hand, were less finicky about fine stimulus differences, and grouped stimuli into broader categories.

Qualitative analysis of the findings suggested that sensitivity to differences per se was not responsible for the variations in categorizing behavior. Some "broad-range" subjects noticed many subtle differences in the objects in the Sorting Test. The essential difference between subjects at the opposite poles seemed to lie in the degree to which they were impelled to act upon or ignore an *awareness* of differences.

Marrs (1955) extended the demonstrated generality of this control principle by showing consistent individual differences in equivalence range in (a) the Object Sorting Test (described below) used in the original study (Gardner, 1953); (b) an alternate form of this test developed by Dickman (1954); (c) grouping of 69 statements describing a variety of everyday behaviors; and (d) grouping of 69 Chinese ideographs. Sloane (1959), who also used the Object Sorting Test, extended the applicability of the equivalence range principle to situations in which the subject categorizes (a) the names of objects;[1] (b) descriptions of people; (c) photographs of human faces; and (d) drawings of objects.

Studies of "category width" by Bruner and Rodrigues (see Bruner, Goodnow, and Austin, 1956, p. 28; Pettigrew, 1958), and a recent study by Fillenbaum (1959) showing "a general tendency toward coarseness-fineness in categorizing" (p. 193) appear to offer further support to the hypothesis that individuals can be characterized by consistent differences in equivalence range in a wide variety of situations.

OBJECT SORTING TEST

Apparatus and Procedure

Seventy-three objects of varying familiarity were used in this test. They were selected with an eye to variations in material, color, shape, size, and content. They were presented in a fixed, random arrangement. The following objects were used:

(1) Red cardboard circle; (2) red and white oilcloth, roughly rectangular; (3) half bar soap; (4) yellow pencil; (5) small glass jar; (6) white jar lid (fits small glass jar); (7) flashlight bulb; (8) small light bulb; (9) and (10) small blue candles; (11) and (12) blue plastic candle holders; (13) dime; (14) penny; (15) metal fork; (16) metal knife; (17) metal spoon; (18) small red plastic spoon; (19) small blue plastic spoon; (20) small red plastic knife; (21) white plastic button; (22) cigarette; (23) cigar wrapped in cellophane; (24) jar rubber; (25) red paper rectangle; (26) white leatherette doll shoe; (27) padlock and key (green design); (28) block of wood with nail; (29) block of wood painted yellow; (30) block of plywood with red paper pasted on one side; (31) medicine dropper; (32) small printed picture, colored—Western scene; (33) ping-pong ball; (34) piece of white chalk; (35) black and yellow fishing fly; (36) green wooden spool with roll of fine wire; (37) hairpin; (38) pipe bowl; (39) pipe stem (fits pipe bowl); (40) bottle of mercurochrome; (41) nail; (42) rubber stopper with metal ring; (43) picture postcard, black and white—wood scene; (44) piece of large white candle; (45) and (46) small corks; (47) orange lollipop with paper handle; (48) orange vitamin pill; (49) metal

[1] These tests were developed by Martha Clayton, of Pennsylvania State University.

staple with paper on head; (50) sugar cube; (51) olive drab whistle with white star design; (52) small pebble; (53) mothball; (54) putty knife with red wooden handle; (55) blue plastic comb; (56) metal thimble; (57) metal pulley with white porcelain wheel; (58) white rectangular card; (59) two German stamps, one red and one green, attached; (60) whiskbroom; (61) toy hammer with red wooden handle; (62) toy metal saw; (63) bicycle bell; (64) piece of chamois skin; (65) rubber nipple; (66) green plastic earring with metal clip; (67) bow tie on cardboard holder; (68) suede brush, metal and wood, with paper price tag; (69) piece of fine sandpaper; (70) plastic dark glasses with metal clip; (71) red lipstick container; (72) screwdriver; (73) piece of red crayon.

The subjects were first asked to examine the objects and inquire about any they were not familiar with. They were then instructed as follows:

> First of all, I want you to know that there is no *answer* to this test. Everyone does it in his own way. I want you to do it in the way that seems most natural, most logical, and most comfortable to you. The instructions are simply to put together into groups the objects which seem to you to belong together. You may have as many or as few objects in a group as you like, as long as the objects in each group belong together for a particular reason. If, after you have thought about all the objects, a few do not seem to belong with any of the others, you may put those objects into groups by themselves. Please sort all the objects.

During the sorting, the experimenter made notes on qualitative features of the subject's performance, such as his comments, regroupings, questions, etc. After all objects had been grouped, he determined the subject's reason for including objects in each group by asking "Why do these objects belong together?"

Rationale

This test is purposely permissive in order to encourage spontaneous categorizing behavior. The instructions are designed to allow each subject to reveal his categorizing propensities. He is deliberately and explicitly "put on his own," the only requirement being that he must have an explanation for each group. The lack of restriction was repeatedly emphasized so that subjects would not assume that they were supposed to sort in a particular way (e.g., form as many groups as possible).

The objects can, of course, be sorted in several different ways: e.g., on the basis of material, persons to whom they might belong, situations in which they might appear, etc. Inasmuch as many of the objects are common and familiar, it is not surprising that they are frequently organized in terms of use.

Many of the objects have multiple characteristics that allow them to be categorized in a number of different ways. For example, the *pencil* and the *picture postcard* may be grouped together, or the *pencil* may be grouped along with other wooden objects, such as the *block of wood* and the *green wooden spool*.

Score

10. *Number of groups.* This score is the number of groups each subject formed from the 73 objects. When one large group contained definitive subdivisions, each of the subdivisions was scored as a separate group. Each object put by itself was scored as an additional "group."

Size Constancy Test

Apparatus and Procedure

This situation was modeled after one used by Thouless (1931; 1932a, b; 1934). All figures were viewed through a reduction screen with a 5.1 x 1.9 cm. viewing aperture, 48.5 cm. above the table. The standard figure was a circle of white cardboard, 39.7 cm. in diameter. It was placed at right angles to the subject's line of vision at a distance of 230 cm. The subject compared the standard with each of 23 circles, ranging in diameter from 29.7 cm. to 39.7 cm. in steps equal to 1.25 per cent of the diameter of the standard. Each comparison circle was shown to the left of the standard at a distance of 172 cm. All judgments were monocular and were made with the dominant eye.

Prior to the experiment proper, the subject was trained to recognize the difference between real and apparent size in a small pilot demonstration. He was given the following instructions:

> Before we actually do this part of the experiment, I want to make sure it is clear to you just what kind of a judgment is called for. First of all, I would like to have you *imagine* that you are looking

at a house which is a mile away. You will realize that at that distance it will *look* very, very small. If you put your thumb up in front of your eye [experimenter demonstrates], your thumb might "cover" the house. That is, your thumb might *look* larger than the house, although you know perfectly well that the house is actually many times larger. That is what we mean by *apparent* size or *seeming* size. And that is the kind of judgment we are going to make here. We are not interested in how large the objects actually are, but in how large they appear or seem to be.

Following this explanation, the experimenter instructed the subject to close one eye and to observe the smallest figure (29.7 cm.) as he gradually brought it closer to the subject's eye. When the subject reported that it seemed to grow larger as it was brought closer, he was asked to compare its apparent size at approximately 15 cm. from his eye to that of the standard at 230 cm. When he reported with confidence that the nearer circle *seemed* larger, the reduction screen was placed on the table and the experiment begun. The subject made an ascending and a descending series of comparisons. The ascending series was presented first, with these instructions:

> Now I am going to present a series of figures, gradually increasing in size, here [experimenter points to black wooden stand]. After I place each figure here, I want you to compare it with the one at the end of the table and tell me if the apparent size of the one I place here is larger or smaller than the one at the end of the table. If a figure looks exactly the same, you may say "same." You will look through the slit in the cardboard here [experimenter points]. Take your time and rest your eye at any time you wish. You may look back and forth between the two figures as many times as you need to in order to decide if the one I place here is larger, smaller, or the same in *apparent* size as the figure at the end of the table.

In this series, the comparison stimuli were then presented in order of increasing size, beginning with the smallest. Following the ascending series, the subject was given a descending series with the following instructions:

> Now we are going to do the same thing exactly, except that I will begin with the largest of the figures and gradually decrease the size of these circles. Tell me each time whether the figure I place here

is larger, smaller, or the same in apparent size as the figure at the end of the table.

To many subjects, *several* of the comparison stimuli appeared the same apparent size as the standard. Whenever this occurred, the largest figure called "the same" in the ascending trial and the smallest in the descending trial were used in the scoring.

Rationale

Effective retinal matching requires the subject to reflect critically and analytically upon his own experience. Subjects usually are in conflict between two tendencies: (a) the overlearned response to actual object size; and (b) the experimental demand to respond in terms of retinal size. Effective retinal matching in this test seems to require facility in adopting the unfamiliar retinal set. The preliminary training was done to control this factor by helping the subject to distinguish between real and apparent size. It was assumed that once he had clearly recognized the experience of apparent size in the training period, his equivalence-range proclivities would determine his judgments of retinal equivalence. For this reason, the Size Constancy Test seemed to provide an apt measure of equivalence range. Such an assumption is partly supported by an earlier study (Gardner, 1953) in which retinal matching was correlated with two other types of matching performance. In view of the fact that the studies by Sloane (1959) and Gardner, Jackson, and Messick (in preparation) did not confirm this earlier finding, however, future studies could well employ the Object Sorting Test and other *direct* tests of categorizing as criterion situations for equivalence range.

Scores

Three scores were developed on the basis of this rationale. The first measure is the primary one, and it is the one used in previous experiments.

11. *Mean diameter*. This score indicates the accuracy of the subject's matching of comparison with standard in terms of apparent size. It is the mean diameter of the figures judged the same apparent size as the standard. The lower the score, the more accurate the retinal match. The corrected r's between ascending and descending series were .80 for men and .84 for women.

12. *Improvement*. This score indicates change in matching accuracy from the ascending to the descending trial. It consists of the difference between the comparison figure judged "the same" as the standard in trials one and two. A high score indicates relatively great improvement in retinal matching.

13. *Area of uncertainty*. This measure is based on the notion that fluctuation in judgments may represent equivalence range. It consists of the average number of judgments intervening between an unbroken series of "smaller" and "larger" judgments in the two trials. In the ascending trial, for example, the subject might call the first ten comparison stimuli "smaller," the next stimulus "the same," the next "smaller," and the remaining stimuli "larger." His area of uncertainty would be 2. Extremely narrow categorizing might show itself in zero scores; broad categorizing might be reflected in greater ambiguity at the borderline between apparent and real size, leading to larger area-of-uncertainty scores.

6

THE FOCUSING CONTROL PRINCIPLE

The original formulation of the focusing control (Schlesinger, 1954) was derived in part from Freud's (1926) observation that the defense of isolation separates an idea from other ideas in consciousness, and from its emotional attributes. In addition, Freud proposed that "concentration is utilized to keep at a distance not solely matters of indifference, things that are irrelevant, but in particular things that seem inconveniently counter to the matter at hand" (1926, p. 56). As a consequence, Schlesinger's original conception of focusing had two aspects: (a) a tendency to narrow awareness and to keep experiences discrete; and (b) a tendency to separate affect from idea.

The first aspect of focusing—narrowed awareness—was presumed to be measured by a size-estimation test in which subjects were required to cope with distractions or irrelevancies that could interfere with accurate performance. Extreme focusers were expected to be highly accurate in estimating the size of disks containing distracting cues, i.e., to narrow attention to the relevant datum. Focusing was assumed to be "not only the ability to take and maintain such a set for accuracy when it is appropriate to do so, but also an underlying preference for experiencing the world in a narrowed, discriminating way, even when the task does not demand such an approach" (Schlesinger, 1954, p. 356). It was further hypothesized that large errors are characteristic of "persons who are inclined to experience the world far more inclusively. . . . Such people would be less intent upon checking their inner experiences against some objective standard and would be more prone to accept them uncritically" (p. 356).

The second aspect of focusing—separation of affect from idea—was approached through a Picture Sorting Test consisting of sexual, aggressive, and neutral pictures. It was assumed that focusers would not commit themselves to a clear-cut affective experience and would therefore sort relatively many pictures into an "Indifferent" category.

As expected, performance on the Size Estimation Test was related to performance on the Picture Sorting Test. Low-error subjects in the Size Estimation Test (focusers) made an average number of 25.5 "Indifferent" choices, whereas high-error subjects (nonfocusers) made an average number of 15.3 "Indifferent" choices. The difference was significant ($p < .01$). Schlesinger also found differences between extreme groups on a personality inventory, with focusers more attuned to "objective" features of a situation and less aware of feeling.

Further analysis of the Size Estimation Test, subsequent to the original experiment, suggested that it measures the *extent of attention deployment*. Following Piaget's centration hypothesis—that the magnitude of an object in the center of the attentional field is overestimated as a function of its actual size and the duration of centration (summarized in Piaget, Vinh-Bang, and Matalon, 1958)—we assume that subjects who deploy attention extensively will tend toward relative underestimation, whereas subjects who attend primarily to the obvious and interesting standard stimuli will tend toward relative overestimation. In a recent paper, Gardner (1959) described results that confirm this interpretation.

This new possibility led to a reformulation of the control principle. The earlier definition implied that in extreme focusing irrelevancies are "shut out" of experience. The reinterpretation of the principle suggests, in contrast, that subjects originally called "focusers" may actually deploy attention to relatively many aspects of stimulus fields. The focuser is broadly aware of many aspects of the stimulus field because he is constantly scanning the field, whereas the nonfocuser is more narrow in his deployment of attention. For these reasons the dimension of individual consistencies originally observed by Schlesinger may be more aptly described in terms of a scanning control principle.

Size Estimation Test I

Apparatus and Procedure

The apparatus that produced the variable comparison field was originally described by Bruner and Rodrigues (1953). A double-ground glass screen 5 inches square was mounted on the 9-inch square end of a box facing the subject. A 10-watt concentrated arc lamp (Western Electric) was focused on the screen from inside the box to produce a smooth-edged circle of uniform brightness that could vary in diameter from 1.2 to 6.5 cm. without substantial loss of sharpness in the contour and without penumbra. The subject adjusted the size of the circle by turning a crank. Three disks were used: (a) a 10-gram "neutral" gray disk, 48.5 mm. in diameter; (b) a 65-gram gray disk, otherwise identical to the "neutral" disk; (c) a 10-gram disk covered with black velvet, 50 mm. in diameter. The size difference was introduced to counteract possible tendencies toward perseveration in judgment.

The subject was required to adjust the variable circle of light, 14 inches from his eyes, to the sizes of the disks which he held in his left hand, 15¼ inches from his eyes. Constant checking of adjustments was possible and was encouraged by the instructions. No time limit was specified, and, since there was no mention of time in the instructions, the subject was not forced to sacrifice accuracy for speed. Normal room illumination prevailed. A total of 12 judgments was made in four series, with a random order of disk sizes in each series. The order of ascending and descending judgments was D, D, A, A. No rest periods were provided unless the subject requested them.

The experimenter first switched on the light producing the comparison stimulus. He then turned the crank to vary the size of this circle of light. The subsequent instructions were as follows:

> You see how I can make this circle larger or smaller by turning this crank handle. I want you to adjust this circle of light to be equal in size to some disks. Here is the first disk. [The subject was shown how to hold the disk between his forefinger and little finger. He was also shown how not to obscure any part of the disk with his fingers.] When the circle of light looks to be the exact size of the disk, stop and tell me.

Rationale

The task itself is not difficult. It requires no special skill and does not tax the limits of the average subject's ability. Furthermore, the distractors are not obviously intrusive, although they have discernible effects upon apparent size. Holzman and Klein (1956a) showed that the heavy gray disk was overestimated more than the lighter gray disk, while the black velvet disk was overestimated less. Presumably, the black velvet disk is seen as a sharply defined circle against the hand. The sharp contrast may produce an "impressiveness effect" or a "Liebmann effect," similar to that reported by Koffka and Harrower (1931).

It seems likely, however, that distractors are not the primary source of individual differences in accuracy in this test. This assumption is supported by the significant correlations observed by Schlesinger between average-error scores for plain disks and disks covered by pictures. In the present study, correlations between the neutral gray, black, and heavy gray disks were above .70, $p < .001$, for both men and women. This finding also suggests that error in this test is not primarily attributable to the presence of distractors.

Accuracy in this kind of size estimation may be a function of the degree of attention deployment. Practically all subjects' errors take the form of overestimation, and one basis of overestimation in such situations could be an imbalance in relative centration, i.e., looking longer at the standard stimuli than at the comparison stimulus, or looking for relatively long periods at the standard stimuli in individual centrations. Low error could stem from balanced centration, including short individual centrations upon the standard stimuli. Thus, overestimation in the present test might represent an "error of the standard" (see Piaget, 1947). Those who characteristically deploy attention broadly could be expected to overestimate little in this test; those who characteristically limit their scanning largely to the most obvious and interesting objects in the field (in the present situation, the standard stimuli) should overestimate much more.

Scores

Two scores were derived from this test. The first is the primary measure and was used by Schlesinger (1954) in his original study.

14. *Average error.* This measure consisted of average error in 12 judgments of the three disks. Corrected odd-even reliability coefficients were .95 for men and .92 for women.

15. *Heaviness effect.* This measure represents the increase in apparent size resulting from the heaviness of one of the disks. It was computed by subtracting each subject's constant error score for the neutral disk from his constant error for the heavy disk, and dividing by his constant error for the neutral disk.

Picture Sorting Test

Apparatus and Procedure

Materials for this test were sixty pictures of varied content, emotional loading, and artistic quality. They included photographs of hungry Korean children, reproductions of modern students' paintings, children's drawings, monochromatic lithographs, nudes, portraits, etc. The pictures were mounted individually on 7 x 7-inch white cardboard mats. Schlesinger noted that "No picture was chosen consistently as indifferent and it appears unlikely that the particular pictures used are of great significance for the problem or the results" (1954, p. 362).

The subject was given the following instructions:

> I have here a stack of cards which I want you to place in three piles in front of you. It is most important that you understand the basis on which you are to sort these pictures into three piles. I want you to look at each picture and put it into one of the three piles depending on the instantaneous feeling the picture inspires in you. If the feeling is one of *liking,* put the picture in the pile on your right. If it is one of *dislike,* put it in a pile to your left. And finally, if the picture creates *no feeling* in you *at all,* one way or the other, put it in the middle. There are no standards for this test; the only thing that matters is the immediate feeling which each picture may arouse in you. I specifically do not want you to make any judgment about the picture's artistic quality, style, or technique, the artist, should you recognize him, or anything else of the kind. This is not to be an artistic or critical evaluation of any kind of the pictures. I merely want you to *react* to each picture in terms of the *first feeling* which it arouses. Only if it *arouses no feeling at all,* are you to place it in the middle pile. You do *not* have to justify your sortings. There are no right and wrong answers, and it does not matter which picture ends up in which pile or how many end up in any pile. This is not a

test of speed, either. Work only as quickly as is comfortable for you. Don't interrupt yourself for questions or for anything else until you are finished. Please hold the cards in your lap and sort them one at a time into the three piles.

Questions were answered, when possible, by repeating appropriate portions of the instructions. An electromagnetic pen connected to a continuous-feed kymograph recorded the time taken to sort each card. The subject was told that this would occur, but that it was not intended to hurry him. Each subject was asked whether or not he experienced time pressure in this test, and no one reported that he did. Signs of indecision were also noted, as were changes in sortings, spontaneous remarks, gestures, etc. Following the test, the subject was asked to describe his experience. Inquiry was conducted into the degree of difficulty he experienced in the sorting, how he conceived of his sorting, how natural the task seemed to him, and whether or not he experienced the pictures in the terms required by the instructions.[1]

Rationale

The original hypothesis for the Picture Sorting Test was that people who avoid or circumvent experiences of affect should sort relatively many pictures into an Indifferent category. When the test is examined more closely, however, several other possibilities emerge. Some subjects may not wish to *express* feelings and may use the Indifferent category for those pictures which they feel are "too hot to handle." Thus, a high Indifferent score might well represent denial and avoidance, as well as isolation. Other subjects may be slow to react to the card, and place it in the Indifferent category because they have no feeling at the moment; slow reac-

---

[1] Special stress was placed in the inquiry upon how the subject experienced the process of making "indifferent" choices. Particular attention was paid to whether these choices were indeed accompanied by "no feelings at all," by "equal but opposite feelings," or by "slight feelings." The subject was then asked if he placed pictures in the Indifferent category not because he had no feeling about them but because he would prefer not to *express* any feeling about them. He was also asked if he placed any pictures into the Like category not because his immediate feeling was one of liking, but because he felt he ought to put the picture into that category. Similar questions were asked about the Dislike category. If the subject indicated he had made decisions on these bases, all the individual cards were reviewed with him and the basis for each sorting noted. Responses of the few subjects who showed marked indecision were reviewed with particular care.

tion time is not necessarily related to isolation. Finally, some subjects may place pictures in the Indifferent category simply because it is provided. This may be especially true for subjects who are relatively unmotivated. In general, an Indifferent sorting may have several sources and is by no means a pure test of proneness to avoid affective experiences.

Score

16. *Number Indifferent.* This measure is the number of pictures placed in the Indifferent category.

7

THE CONSTRICTED-FLEXIBLE CONTROL PRINCIPLE

The terms "constricted control" and "flexible control" were first used by Klein (1954) to describe differing reactions to stimulus fields containing contradictory or intrusive cues. The criterion task was a Color-Word Test, modeled after Stroop's (1935), in which subjects were required to read the color of a word and ignore its content. Performance in this test was related to a variety of tasks (including Size Estimation Test II and the Free Association Test, described in this chapter) in which the subject was faced with a field of conflicting cues. Consistencies of behavior over the several tasks suggested a dimension of constricted-flexible control.

Constricted-control subjects resorted to counteractive measures in their attempts to overcome the disruptive effect of intrusive cues. When possible, their responses were guided by the most central or obvious aspect of a field; i.e., they coped with distracting stimuli by ignoring them in favor of a salient, easily confirmable stimulus attribute. When external cues seemed to contradict internal cues, the conflict was resolved in favor of the most obvious external ones. These subjects tended to avoid using feelings or emotional reactions as a source of information. Constricted-control subjects also seemed resistive to change, preferring to maintain sets long after they were appropriate, another indication that they could not take advantage of all available cues.

Flexible-control subjects seemed relatively comfortable in situations that involved contradictory or intrusive cues. They were not overimpressed with a dominant stimulus organization if the instructions rendered another part of the field more appropriate. Thus, they were capable of differential response to specified aspects of a field in the face of explicitly interfering cues. In addition, their responses to a personal inventory suggested that they did not tend to suppress feeling and other internal cues.

Two recent studies support Klein's (1954) finding that constricted and flexible control differentially mediate the effects of a need upon cognitive behaviors. Using an interference score from the Color-Word Test, Lazarus, Baker, Broverman, and Mayer (1957) found evidence "that high interference-prone individuals are less able to modulate their behavior and impulse expression when strong motive states are aroused" (p. 570). Hardison and Purcell (1959), who used the Color-Word Test with measures of independence, found "that the effects of stress upon performance did not appear if individual difference variables were ignored" (p. 257).

In another recent study employing the Color-Word Test, Loomis and Moskowitz (1958) explored relations between the constricted-flexible control principle and response to stimulus ambiguity.

In many respects, the descriptions of constricted-flexible control are similar to descriptions of field dependence-independence by Witkin et al. (1954). Tests representing both variables were included in the present study to explore their similarity. The modes of handling affect described above are similar to those Schlesinger (1954) observed in relation to a focusing or scanning principle.

Color-Word Test

First used by Jaensch et al. (1929), the Color-Word Test was introduced in this country by Stroop (1935) and modified by Thurstone (1944).

Apparatus and Procedure

The Color-Word Test used in the present study consists of three parts. Part I is a "warm-up" page of color names: "red," "green," "yellow," and "blue." The names are printed in black in random order, ten words to a line, ten lines to a page. Part II is a page of color strips, rows of red, green, yellow, and blue asterisks which match the arrangement of words in Part I, and the length, position and color of words in Part III. In Part III, the four colors and the four color names appear in contradictory combinations; e.g., "green" printed in blue, etc. No color name is printed in its own color.

Subjects were first screened for color blindness on the Ishihara Test. The instructions for Part I of the Color-Word Test followed:

> This page consists of names of colors. I'd like you to read the page out loud as fast and as accurately as you can. For instance, read this top line [the subject reads the practice line]. Now, when I turn the page, start reading as fast and as accurately as possible.

Total reading time in seconds was recorded.

A thirty-second interval separated Parts I and II. Instructions for Part II were:

> Now I am going to show you another page consisting of colors. I want you to name the colors as fast and as accurately as possible. To make sure that you have the color names correct, read the practice line [the subject reads the practice line]. Now when I give the signal, start reading as fast and as accurately as possible.

Reading time was recorded cumulatively by pairs of lines. Errors were also recorded.

A one-minute interval separated Parts II and III. Instructions for Part III were:

> This is a different kind of page. It consists of color names printed in different colors. For instance, the word r-e-d may be printed in the color *blue*; you would read blue and ignore the word. I want you to call only the *colors* and ignore the words, and you are to read the colors off as fast and as accurately as possible. Try the practice line [the subject reads the practice line]. Now remember, at my signal read the colors off as quickly and as accurately as possible, ignoring the words. People do best when they try not to squint or to use artificial devices for ignoring the words.

Cumulative reading times and errors were recorded as in Part II.

Rationale

Reading time is invariably longer for Part II (reading color strips) than for Part I (achromatic words) because the perception of the color must be followed by verbal communication of its name. This communication is often difficult and leads to aphasia-like blocking in which the subject clearly "sees" the color but momentarily cannot produce the correct name for it. The blocking is especially pronounced in levelers (see Chapter 9, Factor II for women).

In Part III, two contradictory, familiar, easily available response tendencies are pitted against each other: the overlearned inclination to read words, and the more adaptively relevant but unfamiliar requirement to concentrate on the colors. Both sets of stimuli—color and word—are always present; it is physically impossible to separate the competing stimuli. The ever-present conflict between response tendencies probably contributes to the restlessness, body tension, and exaggerated postures which frequently accompany performance in this part of the test. The subject will often try to point (which is not allowed) or speak more loudly in an attempt to isolate the color more effectively. The test also seems to arouse self-critical attitudes, particularly among persons who are self-conscious about the impressions they give of maturity, poise, self-control and "status."

Rapid color-naming in Part III seems to depend upon two related processes: (a) relative restriction of attention to the relevant colors; and (b) active inhibition of the more readily available response to the incongruous color words. Both of these processes may be important in this test because of the physical inseparability of the two sets of cues, which makes the words unusually powerful distractors. Although Part III seems to require the selective direction of attention in a way similar to laboratory tests of field dependence-independence (see Chapter 8), performances in the latter procedures may be affected less by the subject's capacity to "hold back" response to distracting cues.

Efficiency in overcoming the interfering effects of the words may be enhanced if the subject can quickly surmount the initial tension created by the difficulty of the task, and if he can discard previous responses quickly and approach each new color-word combination in its own right.

In the earlier study (Klein, 1954), high-interference subjects performed best on tasks in which they dealt with simplified stimulus organizations; they found it difficult to detect smaller stimulus units when they were embedded in a context having one dominant scheme of organization. Smith and Klein (1953) found that high interference was also associated with inability to discard a "search set" in the Gottschaldt task when it was no longer appropriate.

By analyzing the sequence of responses in Part III of the Color-Word Test, Smith and Klein isolated four distinctive patterns of variability.

a. *Cumulative* pattern. In this pattern, response becomes increasingly slowed as the subject progresses through the ten lines of Part III. Smith and Klein showed that, when tested in other situations, individuals with cumulative reactions did not shift easily from a previously well-practiced set.

b. *Dissociative* pattern. In this pattern, reading speed increases and decreases erratically. It was found to occur in both high- and low-interference subjects. Subjects with dissociative performances are apparently capable of relinquishing previous sets, but only within certain limits. Because their capacity to shift sets is limited, they tend to resort to familiar sets, i.e., reading *words,* when attention falters.

c. *Stabilized* pattern. In this pattern, reading tempo is relatively constant. Subjects with this pattern seem consistently poised for change. This pattern is usually associated with a low level of interference.

d. *Cumulative-dissociative* pattern. This pattern combines elements of patterns (a) and (b).

Scores

17. *Interference.* This measure was based on the regression of reading time for Part III on reading time for Part II (the two time scores were correlated .58, $p < .001$, one-tailed test). Each subject's interference score was computed as the difference between his actual reading time for Part III and his predicted reading time, based on the regression of reading time, Part III, on reading time, Part II. Although reading errors were infrequent, they were penalized by multiplying the reading time per unit by the number of errors and adding this value to the reading time for the page.

18. *Reading time, colors alone* (Part II). This measure reflected the amount of blocking on reading colors alone. It consisted of the reading time for Part II plus penalty for reading errors.

19. *Temporal patterns of response.* Methods of deriving these scores are fully described by Smith and Klein (1953). The scores are based on two measures: the slope of the regression line (Z'), and residual variability (V). $Z' + V =$ total variability. Subjects

were assigned to one of four groups according to their positions on the Z' and V distributions, as follows:

a. *Cumulative*—above median on Z', below median on V (6 men, 9 women).

b. *Dissociative*—below median on Z', above median on V (7 men, 11 women).

c. *Stabilized*—below median on Z', below median on V (9 men, 5 women).

d. *Cumulative-dissociative*—above median on Z', above median on V (8 men, 5 women).

INCIDENTAL RECALL TEST

Apparatus and Procedure

The materials for this test are similar to those for the Color-Word Test, but the procedure was different and was administered in a later testing session. Part II of the Color-Word Test (colors alone) was readministered. Thirty seconds later, the subject was asked to read the same four colors in a page of "neutral" words. The instructions were as follows:

> I have another page of words printed in different colors. As before, I want you to ignore the words and read the *colors* as fast and as accurately as you can. [There were no practice lines in this test.]

As soon as the subject finished reading, the examiner covered the page with its face sheet. Then, after a one-minute pause, the subject was asked to read a page of colors (arranged as in Part III) printed in thirst-related words. These words were used in order to replicate part of an earlier study (Klein, 1954). The fact that these were thirst-related words had no special significance in the present study. Instructions were:

> Same thing this time. Here is another page of colors printed in different words, and I want you to ignore the words and read the colors as fast and as accurately as possible.

As soon as the subject finished reading the second page, the recall portion of the test was administered. The instructions were:

> On the last two pages you read, you know, of course, that words were printed in different colors. I realize I asked you to ignore the

words but wonder if, in passing, you did notice the words themselves. Tell me all you remember.

After the subject's first report, he was encouraged with: "Try to think. Anything else?"

Rationale

Recall of relatively many words in this test could result from: (a) a specific inability to avoid responding—in the sense of attending—to words, even though the subject was directed to call out only the colors (an inability tentatively suggested by results of the earlier study); (b) a general tendency to be aware of relatively many cues in a stimulus field. To the degree that the former predominates, we should expect to find relationships between the number of words recalled and other measures of constricted-flexible control (color-word interference, Free Association Test performances). To the degree that the latter plays a part in the number of words recalled, we should expect to find relationships between this score and amount of scanning (see Chapter 6), as measured in Size Estimation Test I.

Score

20. *Incidental recall.* The score for this test was the total number of words correctly recalled from the pages of neutral and thirst-related words.

Size Estimation Test II

In this test, the subjects judged the sizes of four symbol-bearing disks under two conditions: perceptual and memory. The type of test has been used frequently in need-perception studies and has been a favorite marshaling ground of controversial views concerning the effects of needs on perception. (See, for example, Bruner and Goodman, 1947; Carter and Schooler, 1949; Klein, Schlesinger, and Meister, 1951). It was introduced into an earlier study (Klein, 1954) to explore individual differences in response to perceived irrelevancy. The question asked was: Are there characteristic ways of coping with intrusive stimuli that will determine the impact of a need upon behavior? The aim was to show that high- and low-interference groups on the Color-Word Test would exhibit different error tendencies in response to the presence of intrusive symbols on the disks. It was found that subjects high in color-word interference tended to underestimate size.

Apparatus and Procedure

The apparatus used to provide an adjustable comparison field was the same as that used in Size Estimation Test I (see Chapter 6). The circle of light appeared at eye level and directly in front of the subject at a distance of two feet.

The four standard disks, 32 mm. thick, were painted gray and were mounted on a darker gray cardboard background 8 x 7½ inches. Disks 43 mm. in diameter bore (a) a picture of a Coke glass and (b) a picture of a movie projector; disks 42 mm. in diameter bore (c) a picture of an "old-fashioned" drink and (d) a picture of two gold coins. These thirst-related and neutral symbols were selected from the twelve pictures used in the earlier study, and were matched as closely as possible in brightness, size, and color. The content of the pictures was not significant for the present study. In addition, disks (a) and (b), and disks (c) and (d), had similar formal properties. The cards bearing the four disks were mounted, one at a time, on the wall to the subject's left, so that he could view them at eye level at a distance of two feet by turning his head 90 degrees from his original position facing the comparison field.

In the perceptual condition, the subject judged each of the four disks twice, in each of two series, for a total of 16 judgments. Before the first judgment, the experimenter adjusted the circle to a size well above or below the size of the standard and said:

> I am going to put a card with a disk on it in the frame over there and I would like you to adjust this disk [comparison] with the crank until it is exactly the same size as the disk at your left, as nearly as you can tell.

The subject was allowed to look back and forth from standard to comparison as many times as he wished, and to adjust the crank as he pleased until he was satisfied with the setting. After the first judgment, the experimenter turned the crank to the "above" (or "below") position for that judgment and said: "Now do it again from this direction."

The next disk was presented and the subject made an ascending and descending judgment. The order of ascending and descending trials was randomized for Series I and reversed for each stimulus in Series II. This order was constant for all subjects. Series I and II were separated by a thirty-second rest period. The disks were randomized within each series for size and sequence of thirst and nonthirst symbols. The order of presentation was the same for all subjects.

After two minutes, the subject was asked to judge from memory the sizes of each of the four standard stimuli. He judged each disk twice (ascending and descending trials) for a total of 8 judgments. The ascending and descending trials were randomized, in a fixed order for all subjects. Before the judgment of each disk, the subject was asked: "Do you remember the one with the coke glass?" etc. The experimenter then instructed him to reproduce the size of that disk as exactly as possible from memory.

Rationale

Perceptual Condition. Size Estimation Test II was originally employed (Klein, 1954) to explore the hypothesis that the manner of dealing with irrelevant, distracting symbols is an important factor in determining the experienced size of symbol-bearing disks.

Underestimation of these disks was accompanied by high interference in the Color-Word Test, suggesting that subjects respond in a consistent manner to irrelevant stimuli. This pattern of performance was thought to reflect a strained attempt to avoid confusion and indefiniteness that stemmed from a generalized discomfort with overlapping and ambiguous stimuli.

It was speculated that overestimation could be the product of several reaction tendencies: (a) a tendency for interesting objects (interest was enhanced by the pictures on the standard disks) to loom large in *judgment,* an interpretation suggested by earlier need-cognition studies; (b) a relaxed standard of accuracy, often accompanied by an absence of self-critical attitudes in judgments; (c) the greater attractiveness of the symbol-bearing disks, as compared to the empty circle of light. Subjects may unwittingly compensate for this difference by increasing the brightness of the comparison field and thereby increasing its size.

Under- and overestimation could also stem from two other

factors: (a) "Shrinkage" of the memory image. Since the subject must turn his head to look from the standard to the comparison field, he must adjust the comparison field to conform to his memory of the standard. Some subjects may be unable to retain the memory image faithfully. (b) The fact that the symbols were *smaller* than the disks the subjects were asked to judge. This second factor could affect apparent size in two possible ways. The presence of the smaller symbols may make the disks seem more compact (more *eindringlich*) to some subjects as a result of an "inherence effect" (see Koffka and Harrower, 1931). Or subjects who underestimate may be unable to restrict their attention to the disks themselves. Constricted-control subjects, who have difficulty attending only to relevant cues (as in the Color-Word Test), may be unable to avoid attending to the smaller symbols, with the result that they experience the disks as smaller than they are. This last possibility seems most clearly in keeping with the general inability of constricted-control subjects to attend to relevant cues and inhibit response to irrelevant cues.

Variability of judgments in the perceptual condition may arise from the qualitative difference between the standard and comparison fields. The standard stimuli are solid surfaces of objects, whereas the comparison field is an empty circle of light. Thus, the subject is asked to match a comparison stimulus to a quite dissimilar standard. In these circumstances, size constancy must be maintained in the face of a transformation of context. Failure to allow for different mediating conditions may account for variability of judgment.

If apparent size in this test is, as suggested above, a function of the deployment of attention to disk and/or symbol, variability of judgment could reflect fluctuations in attending to these sources of conflicting size impressions.

Memory Condition. Correlations between constant errors in the memory and perceptual conditions were .75 for men and .77 for women. Perhaps the size adjustments in the perceptual condition consolidate the subject's images of the disks and allow him to transfer them, relatively unchanged, to the memory condition. It is interesting that estimates of the thirst stimuli increased and estimates of the nonthirst stimuli decreased in the memory condition. We have no explanation for this difference.

Variability of judgments in the memory condition may be an

outcome of an assimilation tendency. That is, subjects with relatively undifferentiated memory schemata for the disks may show more variability in attempting to recall their sizes. If so, the variability score (#26) should be related to leveling-sharpening scores.

Scores

Seven scores were used to measure different aspects of the perceptual condition.

21. *Constant error, perceptual.* This was the error of judgment of thirst and nonthirst stimuli combined. (Their intercorrelation was .92 for all subjects.) Odd-even reliability coefficient (corrected) were .98 for men and .99 for women.

22. *Constant error, memory.* This was the error of judgment for all stimuli in the memory situation. (The correlation between thirst and nonthirst stimuli was .82 for all subjects.) Corrected reliability coefficients were .99 for men and .98 for women.

23. *Change, thirst stimuli.* This score for thirst stimuli alone consisted of the difference between constant error in the memory condition and predicted constant error (based on the regression of constant error, memory, on constant error, perceptual).

24. *Change, nonthirst stimuli.* This score was computed in the same manner as #23, using constant error values for nonthirst stimuli.

25. *Variability, perceptual.* This score was the standard deviation of size judgments for all stimuli in the perceptual condition.

26. *Variability, memory.* The standard deviation of size judgments for all stimuli in the memory condition.

27. *Variability, total test.* The standard deviation of size judgments for all stimuli in both conditions.

Free Association Test

Apparatus and Procedure

The subject was asked to report, for three minutes, everything that came to mind after hearing each of two stimulus words: "Dry" and "House."

He was placed in a comfortable chair and the room lights were dimmed to encourage reverie and minimize distraction. The experimenter sat behind the subject and gave these instructions:

I'd like you to close your eyes when we start. This isn't a test in the usual sense at all. That is, you can't be right or wrong in what you say. I am going to say a word, and after I say it you are to report everything that comes into your mind—words, sentences, thoughts, images, *anything*—after I say a certain word. My word is meant just to start you going, but it is not meant to limit you in any way. You are to say everything that comes into your mind. Now close your eyes and sit back comfortably.

The experimenter said the word "Dry" and started the stop watch and sound recorder. One encouragement was offered for any unusually long pause during the three minutes. Thirty seconds after completion of associations to "Dry," the experimenter gave the second stimulus word, "House."

Rationale

Discussions of association tests and processes comprise a bulky literature; an especially searching rationale may be found in Rapaport et al., *Diagnostic Psychological Testing* (1946). Here we shall simply emphasize two outstanding features of the test: (a) It provides two anchor words, "Dry" and "House." (b) The instructions encourage freedom of response, although the key words are given as starting points. The subject has the option of remaining with the stimulus word or drifting to more remote associations.

In the earlier study (Klein, 1954), this Free Association Test was used as a measure of constricted-flexible control. It was proposed that flexible-control subjects could widen or narrow their field of awareness according to the immediate requirements of the task. When given license to do so, this group was expected to veer toward remote associations. Constricted-control subjects, on the other hand, were expected to show various indications of "fascination" with the stimulus word, particularly the word "Dry" because of its affective charge for the thirsty subjects. These expectations were supported; flexible-control subjects proved to be less committed to the stimulus word than constricted-control subjects.

Although not tested in the original study, the assumption could also be made that constricted-control subjects would give relatively few responses, and that many of these would be highly fragmented, consisting only of single words.

Scores

Each subject's responses to "Dry" and "House" were first divided into units, defined as the least number of words that could stand alone as a single thought. These units were then divided into categories representing distance from the stimulus word. Breaking down the protocols into response units and categorizing the units were carried out independently by two of the experimenters. Their procedure was to score a small number of protocols, discuss and resolve the disagreements. Their joint scoring was then checked by two other experimenters. The same procedure was followed for successive groups of protocols until all the records had been scored. The following scores were used:

28. *Percentage distant, "Dry."* Each subject's responses to this word were classified into seven categories representing degrees of distance from the stimulus word. The categories were: I. *Direct references to dryness.* II. *Direct references to wetness and water.* III. *Implied dryness* (sand, Egypt, sun, hot, etc.). IV. *Implied wetness* (jungle, fishing, swimming, rain spout, clouds, etc.). V. *Distant but relevant* (boat, frog hunting, camel, cactus, Arabs, etc.). VI. *Word play* (dry goods, Mrs. Dry). VII. *Nondry and nonwet*. This score was the percentage of response units classified as unrelated to the stimulus word (Category VII). The interrater reliability coefficient for this score, based upon original ratings by the two primary judges, was .96.

29. *Percentage distant, "House."* Responses to the stimulus word "House" were also classified into seven categories representing distance from the stimulus word. The categories were: I. *Direct references to house.* II. *References to the interior structure of houses.* III. *Contents of houses.* IV. *Surrounding landscape* (yard, garage, swings, garden, etc.). V. *Distant but relevant* (house in the generic sense, real estate, the use one makes of a house, etc.). VI. *Word play.* VII. *Nonhouse.* This score was the percentage of responses classified as unrelated to the stimulus word (Category VII). The interrater reliability coefficient was .97.

30. *Percentage "Home" responses.* This score was the percentage of responses to the stimulus word "House" that were classified by the raters in Categories II, III, and IV.

31. *Productivity*. This score was the total number of typed lines in the subject's protocols for the two stimulus words.

32. *Average length of unit*. This score was the average number of lines per response unit.

Scores 31 and 32 are rather highly correlated (.57 for men, .71 for women), because they are partially contaminated. If the number of response units is partialed out, productivity, Score 31, is a direct function of average length of unit, Score 32.

8

FIELD DEPENDENCE-INDEPENDENCE

Field dependence-independence, as defined and studied by Witkin et al. (1954), was included in the present study because it seemed coordinate with the five preceding control principles. Its resemblance to constricted-flexible control was particularly striking. Witkin et al. invoked the concepts of field dependence and independence to account for individual differences in situations described as requiring extraction of an "item" from the field in which it appears. In a number of these tests, field-independent subjects responded to bodily cues in the face of interfering visual cues. In other tests (e.g., the Embedded Figures Test), both sets of conflicting cues were visual. In general, the principle seemed to apply to situations that contained competing sets of cues, so long as the subject perceived the "competition."

In the original study, field dependence-independence was reported to be related to three major groups of personality characteristics revealed in the TAT, Rorschach, and Figure Drawing Tests, and in interviews and case histories. Field dependence was said to be associated with (a) general passivity in dealing with the environment; (b) lack of self-awareness and relatively poor control of impulses, with accompanying fear of aggressive and sexual impulses and high anxiety; and (c) low self-esteem, including low evaluation of the body and a primitive body image. Field independence was said to be associated with (a) activity in dealing with the environment; (b) awareness of "inner life" and effective control of impulses, with low anxiety; and (c) high self-esteem, including confidence in the body, and a relatively adult body image.

The field-dependent subject's low self-esteem and his tendency to seek direction from without were further demonstrated in Linton's (1955) study of individual differences in judging the autokinetic phenomenon. When first confronted with the pinpoint of light, field-independent subjects began to work out methods of arriving at decisions concerning the apparent movement. When a "plant" was introduced, field-dependent subjects felt he must be more skilled than they and tended to follow his lead, whereas field-independent subjects persisted in the approaches they had already begun. Thus, the subject's susceptibility to influence seemed a function both of self-confidence and of development of a decision-making scheme to structure his experience in the preliminary portion of the test. In a related study, Rosner (1957) found that "high yielders" to pressures in a group situation had significantly more failures in the Embedded Figures Test than "low yielders," although time scores were not significantly different. In the same general area of relationships, Block (1957) found greater GSR reactions in a "lie-detection situation" among field-dependent than among field-independent subjects.

Gross (1959) increased subjects' errors in the Rod and Frame Test by introducing a "lens" and telling subjects that it would distort their vision in amounts they could not determine. In response to an inventory concerning their experience in this situation, field-dependent subjects stressed feelings of uncertainty, while field-independent subjects emphasized feelings of expectancy.

Wertheim and Mednick (1958) reported a positive relationship between field independence and "need-achievement" measures based on fantasy material. Using the Edwards Personal Preference Schedule, Marlowe (1958), however, found significant relationships only between field independence and "need intraception" (positive) and "need succorance" (negative).

A number of other published studies have dealt with field dependence-independence. Jackson (1957), for example, found significant correlations between speed in the Embedded Figures Test and Intelligence Test scores (the likelihood that relationships of this kind may result from high correlations with certain subtests of intelligence tests is discussed in Chapter 12). Gardner (1957) showed that field dependence-independence is predictably related to the capacity to overcome effects of certain illusions. Bieri, Bradburn, and Galinsky (1958) reported that mathematical aptitude was correlated significantly with speed in the Embedded Figures

Test for both men and women. In their sample of men, Rorschach *M* production and preference for complexity in the Barron-Welsh Art Scale were associated with speed in the Embedded Figures Test. In women, *slowness* in the Embedded Figures Test was correlated with Rorschach *M* production, as well as with the perception of others in superficial, "external" terms.

A recent study of larger scope by Crutchfield, Woodworth, and Albrecht (1958) also included measures of field dependence-independence. These authors reported the following to be associated with large displacement of the rod toward the frame (field dependence) in a Rod and Frame Test: relatively low scores in intelligence tests; low spatial reorganization ability; low ability and interest in analytical tasks; low originality; ego weakness and dependency; and a relatively intense orientation toward other people (pp. 27-28). These findings supported those of Witkin et al. (1954) in the original study of field dependence-independence. Crutchfield et al. also employed a Gottschaldt Figures Test, which was in many respects similar to Witkin's modification of the Gottschaldt procedure. They found similar, but even more extensive relationships between these performances and other assessment measures. A study by Young (1959) also confirmed several of the basic findings reported by Witkin et al. (1954) and added the Chair-Window Test (Barrat, 1955) to the list of procedures in which the field dependence-independence control principle is particularly evident.

Witkin himself (1959) has recently summarized his studies of perception of the upright in relation to personality organization, described developmental studies of field dependence-independence, and presented age curves for performance on three criterion tests. These age curves are similar to the age curve for accuracy in judging parts of the Müller-Lyer figure reported by Wapner and Werner (1957), an intriguing fact in view of Gardner's (1957) finding that field dependence-independence is a determinant of adult responses to this figure. Witkin, Karp, and Goodenough (1959) recently showed that male alcoholics tend to be more field-dependent than nonalcoholics.

At least one other large-scale research endeavor seems to have an obvious relationship to field dependence-independence. In working out developmental scores for the Rorschach, Phillips and others (see, for example, Brooks and Phillips, 1958) have suggested that the concept of "decontextualization" be employed in analyzing such Rorschach measures. This dimension was defined (see Brooks and Phillips, 1958, p. 287) in terms almost identical to those used originally to describe field dependence-independence and was based upon strikingly similar test performances (e.g., responses to the Gottschaldt Concealed Figures Test.)

Rod and Frame Test

Apparatus and Procedure

The following description of the apparatus is taken from Witkin et al. (1954, p. 25):

> The apparatus . . . consists of a square frame, its sides 1 inch wide and 42 inches long, within which is mounted a rod, 1 inch wide and 39 inches long. The frame and rod are pivoted at their centers, but mounted on separate shafts, so that they may be tilted from side to side independently of each other. A protractor, mounted on the frame shaft, moves with the frame against a stationary pointer, permitting direct readings of the position of the frame in degrees (that is, its angle with the perpendicular). A similar arrangement shows the position of the rod. Frame and rod are coated with luminous paint, and during the test are the only objects visible in the completely darkened room.
>
> A wooden chair for the subject is placed seven feet in front of the rod-and-frame apparatus. It has a high back support, an adjustable headrest, and a footrest. This chair may be placed in any one of three positions: upright, tilted 28° left, or tilted 28° right.

The subject was brought into the room blindfolded, seated in the chair, and required to adjust the rod to the vertical in each of twenty-four trials. In the first eight trials, the chair was tilted 28° to the left; in the second eight, it was tilted 28° to the right; and in the last eight, it was upright. In half of the first sixteen trials, the body and frame were tilted in the same direction; in the other half, they were tilted in the opposite direction. Further details of the procedure can be found in Witkin et al. (1954).

Rationale

In this test, two sets of cues are pitted against each other. Accurate estimation of the verticality of the rod requires (a) that the subject attend selectively to bodily cues (his only source of information concerning the true vertical) and respond to these cues effectively; and (b) that he not attend to, or in some way actively resist responding to, the misleading frame. Individual differences seem to represent variations in a general capacity to articulate stimulus fields, in the sense of responding to relevant cues while surmounting the misleading effects of irrelevant cues.

Scores

A preliminary analysis of the data failed to disclose the distinction observed by Witkin between average error in body-with-frame and body-opposite-frame trials. For this reason, and because of the increase in reliability to be gained, all trials in which the subject was tilted were grouped together. The fact that all subjects made significantly less error in the body-erect than in the body-tilted trials and that the correlation between these two error scores in men was only .20 pointed to the need for a separate score for the body-erect condition. In women, the scores for body-tilted and body-erect trials were correlated .85. Because the score distributions were skewed (due to the nature of the apparatus), average-error scores 33, 34, and 35 below were used in normalized-standard-score form, with the normalized scores based on male and female subjects taken together. This conversion was not used in Witkin's scores.

Three scores were derived from this test.

33. *Average error, body tilted.* This score was the average deviation of the subject's judgments from the true vertical in the first sixteen trials (normalized standard score). Odd-even reliability coefficients (corrected) were .99 for men and .98 for women.

34. *Average error, body erect.* This score was the average deviation of the subject's judgments from the true vertical in the last eight trials (normalized standard score). The corrected reliability coefficients were .97 for men and .99 for women.

35. *Average error, total test.* This score differed slightly from the total-test score used by Witkin. The latter score, called the "rod-and-frame index," was the average of the subject's standard scores for the body-with-frame, body-opposite-frame, and body-erect conditions. The present score consisted of the average nor-

malized standard score for the body-tilted and body-erect trials, with the resulting average normalized.

Embedded Figures Test

Apparatus and Procedure

The stimuli for this test were identical to those used by Witkin—twenty-four complex figures and eight simple figures. Each complex figure contained one of the simple figures. Additional simple and complex figures were used to demonstrate the procedure. Witkin (1950) increased the difficulty of the original Gottschaldt figures by adding colors to all but one most difficult complex figure.

At the beginning of the test, the subject was given the following instructions:

> I am going to show you a series of colored figures. Each time I show you one of these designs, I want you to describe the over-all pattern that you see in it. After you have examined each design, I will show you a simpler figure which is contained in that larger design. You will then be given the larger design again and your job will be to locate the smaller figure in it. Let us go through one to show you how it is done.

The subject was then shown the complex practice figure for fifteen seconds, after which he was shown the simple practice figure for ten seconds. The simple figure was then removed, and the complex figure presented again. The subject was instructed to outline the simple figure upon discovering it. The following instructions were then given:

> This is how we will proceed on all trials. In every case the smaller figure will be present in the larger design. It will always be in the same position as shown to you. There may be several of the smaller figures in the same design, but you are to look only for the one in the same position. Work as quickly as you possibly can, since I will be timing you; but be sure that the figure you find is exactly the same as the simple figure in size, proportion, and position. As soon as you have found the figure, let me know at once. If you ever forget what the small figure looks like, you may ask to see it again. Are there any questions?

The experimenter recorded the subject's descriptions of the complex figures verbatim.

Subjects were required to indicate the location of the simple figures by tracing them with a stylus. They were not, however, allowed to use the stylus while they were searching for the simple figures.

Time in seconds was recorded and the stopwatch was halted when the subject found the simple figure (errors were also recorded but not used in the present study). If tracing revealed that he had not found it, the stopwatch was allowed to run and he was asked to keep looking for the simple figure. Solution time thus represented the total time occupied by the subject in searching for the simple figure before finding it. A five-minute time limit was used.

Rationale

This test is similar to the Rod and Frame Test in that the subject is required to respond to certain cues in the face of competing effects of other cues. In contrast to the Rod and Frame Test, the important cues are all visual, and the subject is aware of his successes and failures. Also, the Embedded Figures Test makes it more explicit to the subjects that they are confronted with the specific task of disentangling one part of the field from its context.

Witkin's discussion of this test (1950, 1954) focuses upon the requirement of extracting item from field. Several other aspects of this test are also worth considering.

To perform effectively, the subject must maintain an adequate memory image of the simple figure while searching for it in the complex figure. The more accurate the memory image, therefore, the faster the solution time, which may explain the moderate correlation often found between measures of leveling-sharpening and solution time in Embedded Figures Tests (see Chapter 3). The ability to maintain a clear and accurate memory image may be represented in part by the number of times the subject requests to see the simple figure. These requests were not systematically recorded in the present study, but might be investigated in future work.

Before being shown the simple figure in each trial, the subject is shown the complex figure and asked to describe it for fifteen seconds. These descriptions of the figure may provide valuable data on individual differences in field-dependence-independence. The way the complex figure is first experienced may not only set the stage for later dealings with it, but may also represent individual differences in perceptual differentiation similar to those measured by solution times. In the majority of cases, the descriptions in the present study were essentially *geometrical* (e.g., "another rectangle with a rectangle on the inside; it has a vertical column going through it"); but some subjects provided *object names* for the complex figures, such as "a house," "a barn," "an ice-cream bar," etc. Besides being more abstract, the geometrical descriptions seemed to represent a higher degree of perceptual articulation than the concrete, object-naming responses. Within the geometric descriptions, there were also great differences in complexity and elaboration ("a bunch of squares," vs. "two parallel sets of trapezoids, each bisected by a diagonal to form two triangles, alternating red and orange"). To explore relations between figure descriptions and other measures, two of the authors sorted the descriptions into five categories, three of which are included in Score 39 below.

An extreme variability of item difficulty is an obvious feature of this test. The variability might in part issue from two qualitatively distinct approaches to which different items lend themselves. In some of the easier items, the simple figure can be *seen* immediately in the complex figure. In some of the more difficult items, however, such recognition is all but impossible; the subject must "figure out" the location of the simple figure since he cannot experience it as a perceptual entity in its own right. Since the more difficult, "conceptual" items contributed more than the easier, "perceptual" items to the total time score used by Witkin, it seemed likely that personality correlates of performance in the Embedded Figures Test in his study might have been related primarily to performance on the "conceptual" items. These considerations suggested that part scores might be more desirable than total scores and led us to perform an item analysis of the test.

Item Analysis

Time scores for each item were converted to logs. These log scores were then standard-scored for all sixty subjects for each item. On the basis of item intercorrelations, two major clusters of items were identified.

Cluster I contained the following eight items: A-3, C-1, C-2, C-4, C-5, D-2, F-1, and G-1. The letters refer to the simple figures, the numbers to the serial appearance of that figure. All figures are described in Witkin's (1950) original article. The average correlation among these items was .41. By and large, Cluster I contained items in which the simple figure can usually be *perceived*. The simple figures in this cluster are less completely masked by the complex figure, are not as deeply embedded in terms of form alone, and the major lines of the simple figure often form the border between different colors. Mean time for solution of these items by all sixty subjects was 15 seconds (obtained by log transformation).

Cluster II also included eight items: A-1, A-4, A-5, E-1, E-2, E-3, E-4, and E-5. The average correlation among these items was .56. Although a few easy items were included, on the average they are more difficult than Cluster I items. The mean solution time for all subjects was 42 seconds (obtained by log transformation). The figures in this cluster are similar in that they contain, or seem to contain, alternative correct solutions. For most people, the key figures defy direct perception. The subject must "figure out" where the simple figures are and trace them line by line.

The average correlation between items in Clusters I and II was .35. The fact that the clusters were correlated suggested that the ability to be perceptually analytic was an important determinant of time scores for both clusters, with Cluster II requiring more conceptual activity.

Scores

Three time scores and two auxiliary measures were derived from this test. Scores 36, 37, and 38 were based on the average of each subject's standard scores for the items. The fact that log scores were standardized for all sixty subjects on each item separately equated the contribution of each item to these three scores.

36. *Mean log time, cluster I.* The corrected odd-even reliability coefficients for this score were .68 for men and .78 for women.

37. *Mean log time, cluster II.* The corrected reliability coefficients for this score were .87 for men and .88 for women.

38. *Mean log time, total test.* The corrected reliability coefficients for this score were .92 for men and .95 for women. For

the entire group of sixty subjects, this score was correlated .90 with the mean-time-in-seconds score used by Witkin.

39. *Geometricality of descriptions.* Two of the experimenters sorted the descriptions of the complex figures into the following categories: (a) Object Names; (b) Vague, No Form (including no description); (c) Crude Geometrical Description; (d) Average Geometrical Description; (e) Analytic Geometrical Description. A weighted score expressing the complexity of geometrical description, but ignoring (a) and (b), was computed by the formula:

$$\frac{d + 2e}{c + d + e}$$

40. *Field-dependence index.* An index score was computed by averaging each subject's standard scores for the total Rod and Frame Test (Score 35) and the Embedded Figures Test (Score 38). Because of modifications of Witkin's total scores for both these tests in the present study, this index score cannot be considered identical to his, although it is undoubtedly highly correlated with it. In the case of the eighteen subjects who did not take the Rod and Frame Test, these index scores were obtained by multiplying their standard scores for the total Embedded Figures Test by 1.725 (the regression coefficient of total scores for the Embedded Figures Test on total scores for the Rod and Frame Test was .725 for the entire sample).

Rorschach Test

The fact that the Rorschach Test had been administered to the sixty subjects allowed us to test the hypothesis that relationships observed by Witkin et al. between laboratory measures of field dependence-independence and Rorschach variables would also be evident in the present study (see Appendix F). In order to do this, the Rorschachs—originally scored by the method suggested by Rapaport et al. (1946) for purposes of classifying subjects in terms of major defenses (see Chapter 11)—were rescored by the Klopfer method Hertzman used in developing Rorschach signs for the earlier study.

9

FACTOR ANALYSES

Although the samples of men and women were too small to make factor analysis an ideal way of assessing relationships between the hypothesized control principles, several facts pointed to its potential value: (a) it provides the most appropriate means available for evaluating such relationships; (b) intercorrelations among scores representing each of the control principles had been explored separately in at least one preceding study; (c) specific hypotheses were available to guide the interpretation of results. Factor analysis has the added advantage of allowing unanticipated dimensions to emerge, since the extraction of factors is a mechanical procedure that is not affected by hypotheses. The hypotheses can bias only the rotation of factors in that rotations may be made that will maximize the likelihood of obtaining the predicted factors, but the actual relationships among scores in the sample set a limit to the extent of such bias. In the present study, interpretation was confined to the factors that accounted for the largest amounts of variance and which conformed to hypothesis.

STATISTICAL TECHNIQUE

Since a preliminary analysis of the data, as well as earlier studies (see Witkin et al., 1954), indicated that the patterning of correlations might differ for the two sexes, a separate correlational matrix was obtained for each sex (Table 6, Appendix A contains the intercorrelations between all major scores). The two matrices were, in fact, quite different. The 33-score matrix used in the factor analysis for women contained generally higher r's than the corresponding matrix for men, and the patterning of r's in the two matrices was clearly different. Two separate factor analyses were therefore carried out.

METHOD OF ANALYSIS

The factors interpreted were derived from 33-score analyses (see Table 2) for each sex. These included all of the original scores except for clearly redundant ones and indices composed of several measures. It was decided to use Thurstone's multiple-group method (1947, pp. 107-175). The chief advantage of this method is that it yields factors that, before rotation, are closer to simple structure than those obtained by the centroid method. Its chief disadvantage is that results are more affected by chance error than is the case with the centroid method; pseudo factors may appear if the initial grouping of scores is not done properly.

In order to strengthen the grounds for grouping the scores, as well as to guide subsequent rotations of factors, a key group of 16 scores (indicated in Table 2) was first factored for each sex by the centroid method. For the male sample, results of this preliminary analysis were equivocal and hence not helpful as a guide in grouping the 33 scores. For this reason, and because the 33-score matrix included many low correlations (see Table 6), the centroid method was used for men. This method requires fewer assumptions than the multiple-group method and is less affected by chance error. Five factors were extracted and rotated orthogonally; the factors before and after rotation are presented in Appendix B.

For women, the preliminary analysis yielded six factors, three of them strongly in support of hypotheses. On the basis of the preliminary analysis, the 33 scores were divided into four groups and the corresponding factors extracted by the multiple-group method. The residuals significantly exceeded chance and a fifth factor was extracted by the centroid method. After the fifth factor, residuals were approximately at the chance level, and a sixth factor was extracted.[1] The six factors were rotated orthogonally; the factors before and after rotation are presented in Appendix B.

[1] As Cattell (1952, pp. 302-303) has pointed out, "it pays to extract too many rather than too few factors" and "the true patterns of the factors are better reproduced than when one tries to rotate the factors in fewer dimensions than they are actually meant to occupy."

Tests of the Purity of the Factorial Structures

In the 33-score analyses, there were several instances in which two similar scores from the same test were included and in which the correlation of the pair of scores was so high that it seemed more like a reliability coefficient than a correlation between two independent scores. This created the suspicion that the obtained factors were unduly weighted by these pairs of scores and were therefore somewhat impure. The additional factor analyses described in Appendix C were therefore performed with sets of 16 nonoverlapping scores that had high factor loadings in the 33-score analyses. Overlapping pairs of scores were eliminated by using a single score to represent each such pair. The correspondence between the sets of factor loadings in the two analyses was so great (cf. Appendix C) as to make it clear that the factors from the 33-score analysis were not seriously affected by the overlap of some scores.

Results for Men

The unrotated and rotated factors obtained from the 33-score correlational matrix for men are presented in Tables 7 and 8, Appendix B. The five factors extracted accounted for 39.6 per cent of the total score variance. Two of the factors are interpreted. Factor I accounted for the largest share (12.3%) of score variance and corresponded to the predicted control principle of scanning. Factor IV accounted for the next largest share of score variance (7:5%) and strongly resembled the control principle of tolerance for unrealistic experiences.

Of the other factors, Factor II could not be easily interpreted. Factor III resembled certain aspects of field dependence-independence, as described in Chapter 8, while Factor V seemed to include constricted-flexible control and other aspects of field dependence-independence. The appearance of two factors representing these two principles for men, in contrast to the single factor found for women (see below), may have been due to the fact that eight men did not return to take the Rod and Frame Test, and that these eight were quite different in their performance in other tests from the twenty-two men who did return. The absent eight showed

Table 2

SCORES USED IN THE PRELIMINARY AND 33-SCORE FACTOR ANALYSES

	Score	Meaning of High Score
[a]1.	Schematizing: Ranking Accuracy	High accuracy
[a]2.	Schematizing: Increment Error (Regression)	Extreme lagging
[a]4.	Kinesthetic Time Error: Assimilation	Much assimilation
5.	Kinesthetic Time Error: Time Error	Low negative time error
6.	Apparent Movement: Mean Movement Threshold	High threshold
[a]7.	Apparent Movement: Mean Range	Wide range
[a]8.	Aniseikonic Lenses: Log Recognition Time	Long recognition time
[a]9.	Aniseikonic Lenses: Mean Deviation	Large error
[a]10.	Object Sorting: Number of Groups	Many groups
11.	Size Constancy: Mean Diameter	Nonretinal match
12.	Size Constancy: Improvement	Judgment becomes more retinal
13.	Size Constancy: Area of Uncertainty	High within-trial variability
[a]14.	Size Estimation I: Average Error	Large error
15.	Size Estimation I: Heaviness Effect	Greatly affected by heaviness
16.	Picture Sorting: Number "Indifferent"	Many in "Indifferent" category
[a]17.	Color-Word: Interference	High interference
18.	Color-Word: Reading Time, Colors Alone	Slow reading
20.	Color-Word: Incidental Recall	Many words recalled
[a]21.	Size Estimation II: Constant Error, Perceptual	Great overestimation
23.	Size Estimation II: Change, Thirst Stimuli	Great increase, memory estimates
24.	Size Estimation II: Change, Nonthirst Stimuli	Great increase, memory estimates
25.	Size Estimation II: Variability, Perceptual	High variability
26.	Size Estimation II: Variability, Memory	High variability

Table 2 (continued)

[a]28.	Free Association: Percentage Distant, "Dry"	Many distant associations
29.	Free Association: Percentage Distant, "House"	Many distant associations
30.	Free Association: Percentage "Home" Responses	Many home responses
31.	Free Association: Productivity	Long protocol
[a]32.	Free Association: Average Length of Unit	Long units
33.	Rod and Frame: Average Error, Body Tilted	Large error
34.	Rod and Frame: Average Error, Body Erect	Large error
[b]35.	Rod and Frame: Average Error, Total Test	Large error
36.	Embedded Figures: Mean Log Time, Cluster I	Long solution time
[a]37.	Embedded Figures: Mean Log Time, Cluster II	Long solution time
39.	Embedded Figures: Geometricality of Descriptions	High geometrical descriptions

[a]Used in both the preliminary and 33-score factor analyses.
[b]Used only in the preliminary factor analyses.

much more interference ($p < .05$) in the Color-Word Test and were slower to find simple figures in Cluster II of the Embedded Figures Test; consequently their scores[2] on Factor V were higher ($p < .05$). These differences indicate that the male subjects who did not take the Rod and Frame Test were more field-dependent and constricted than the rest of the sample. As a result of the very restricted range of Rod and Frame Test scores, the correlations of the Rod and Frame Test scores with the Color-Word and Embedded Figures Test scores that were expected to form the core of a single factor did not appear in the male sample. Since the presence of two factors where one might be expected is apparently due to an artifact specific to the present study, Factors III and V will not be interpreted.

Factor interpretations are stated first in general terms, then in terms of the performances of subjects with extreme factor scores. Ancillary data are presented when they add to interpretation. These ancillary findings were obtained by comparing the performances of subjects in the upper and lower thirds of the factor score distribution for each factor.

FACTOR I—SCANNING
(see p. 83)

This may be described as a scanning factor. It represents the degree of attention deployment to objects, object properties, and events. This factor seems to confirm the redefinition of the focusing principle suggested in Chapter 6.

High Factor Scores

Subjects with high factor scores tended to scan the environment extensively. Their extreme scanning led to awareness of and responsiveness to many objects and object properties.

28. and *29. Free Association: Percentage Distant, "Dry" and "House."* In this test, the "field" is construed to be an internal one consisting of spheres of meanings in which the two stimulus words were embedded. High-factor-score subjects gave many associations that were distant in content from the stimulus words.

[2] The method of obtaining factor scores is described in Appendix D.

Factor I[a]

Scanning

Loading		Score	Performance of Subjects with High Factor Scores
.72	29.	Free Association: Percentage Distant, "House"	Many distant associations
-.69	26.	Size Estimation II: Variability, Memory	Low variability
-.61	11.	Size Constancy: Mean Diameter	Good retinal match
-.59	14.	Size Estimation I: Average Error	Small error
.58	28.	Free Association: Percentage Distant, "Dry"	Many distant associations
.52	20.	Color–Word: Incidental Recall	Many words recalled
-.52	25.	Size Estimation II: Variability, Perceptual	Low variability
.48	34.	Rod and Frame: Average Error, Body Erect	Large error
.46	1.	Schematizing: Ranking Accuracy	High accuracy
-.40	37.	Embedded Figures: Mean Log Time, Cluster II	Short solution time
.35	18.	Color–Word: Reading Time, Colors Alone	Slow reading

[a] Loadings of .35 and above are listed for each factor.

25. and *26. Size Estimation II: Variability, Perceptual and Memory.* High-factor-score subjects made relatively stable judgments of size in both the perceptual and memory conditions of this test; furthermore, their judgments did not become more variable in the memory condition. The stability of their judgments is presumed to be a function of their sampling of relatively many properties of objects. The sampling of multiple properties, such as brightness, texture, color, distance, background, and weight, provided many separate indications of size, and may have tended to stabilize their conceptions of size.

11. Size Constancy: Mean Diameter. Because they were generally free ranging in their attentiveness to the properties of objects, the experience of retinal size (a usually unfamiliar one) was more readily available to these subjects than to subjects with low factor scores.

14. Size Estimation I: Average Error. The average-error score for this test does not, by itself, clarify the meaning of the factor. Rather, it seems possible that the factor may produce fruiful hypotheses for understanding performances in this test. Accuracy of performance seems only a by-product of the test conditions and is therefore not particularly helpful in understanding the judgmental processes that contribute to response. This is indicated by the fact that the subjects most accurate in this test are not necessarily those most accurate in Size Estimation Test II.

Virtually all subjects tended to overestimate size in this test. This tendency appeared to a notably lesser degree, however, among the high-factor-score subjects. It thus seems more valuable to interpret average-error scores in terms of greater or lesser overestimation. If direction only is considered, the broad scanning of high-factor-score subjects may be justifiably linked to Piaget's hypothesis regarding "centration" to account for performances in this test (see Piaget, 1947; Piaget et al., 1958). Piaget assumes that centration upon an object results in overestimation of its size. It seems likely that the tendency to peruse *all* aspects of the field, the prime characteristic of extreme scanning, leads to reduced centration upon the standard disks and thus results in *less* overestimation of these disks.

18. and *20. Color Word: Reading Time, Colors Alone; Incidental Recall.* High-factor-score subjects were slow in reading in both the colors-alone and interference sections of this test, although when reading time for colors was partialed out, they did not show particularly high interference effects. Thus, their difficulty was only in reading colors. Reading colors requires not just perception of the colors, but finding the names for them as well. In the extreme scanner, this choice of appropriate names from among the possibilities was slow. This slowness may stem from a general retardation of choice and decision which has its ultimate source in the scanner's hyperawareness of many elements in a field. It seems possible that *extensive* deployment of attention has the secondary consequence of slowing down the selection of relevant details. The availability of several alternatives can prevent speedy appraisal and choice of *one only*. None of the other tests in the battery emphasizes quick decisions to the degree true of the Color-Word Test.

Another possibility is that extreme scanners respond to the color itself. If color reflects affective experience in the manner suggested by findings with the Rorschach Test, the slowed reading may indicate conflict about affective experience. Indeed, the ancillary data presented below suggest that they do tend to avoid affective experiences.

High-factor-score subjects were able to recall many words in the Incidental Recall Test, in spite of the fact that the instructions directed attention to the reading of colors and explicitly warned the subjects to ignore the words. The tendency of these subjects to recall the irrelevant words was in keeping with their general tendency to attend to many facets of stimulation, whether or not they were relevant to the task at hand.

34. Rod and Frame: Average Error, Body Erect. The relatively great error made by these subjects in the body-erect condition of the Rod and Frame Test was consistent with their tendency to attend to relatively many aspects of a stimulus field. In this test, cues are available from three major sources: the rod, the frame, and the body. Since cues from the frame are misleading, response to all three sets of cues leads to inaccuracy.

1. Schematizing: Ranking Accuracy. These subjects were accurate in ranking squares in the Schematizing Test. This finding, too, would seem to be a result of the degree of their awareness of multiple aspects of objects. Presumably, subjects with high factor scores compare their previous impressions of the sizes of squares with the currently appearing square, so that they achieve effective ranking of the squares. The appearance of this score in the scanning factor seems to suggest that ranking accuracy may have at least two major determinants: the degree to which successive experiences assimilate to each other (a process presumed to underlie Leveling-Sharpening), and the extent of scanning of the field of memories of previous stimulation.

37. Embedded Figures: Mean Log Time, Cluster II. These subjects were relatively quick to identify the simple figures in the complex designs of this test. Since effective performance requires the seeking out of one aspect of that complex field, free-ranging scanning facilitates the extraction process.

Low Factor Scores

The performance of subjects with low factor scores seemed to represent limited scanning.

28. and *29. Free Association: Percentage Distant, "Dry" and "House."* Their production of many "close" associations in the Free Association Test apparently resulted from limited scanning of the internal field of meanings surrounding the stimulus words.

25. and *26. Size Estimation II: Variability, Perceptual and Memory.* Their size judgments were unstable in the perceptual condition and became more variable ($p < .01$) in the memory condition. Presumably, awareness of many properties of an object stabilizes the conception of that object. Low-factor-score subjects may have sampled only limited properties of these objects, so that their comparisons of the disks were highly variable and became more so when the stimulus was unavailable.

11. Size Constancy: Mean Diameter. These subjects had difficulty experiencing retinal size in this constancy situation. They responded to the obvious, "object" character of the stimulus, and found it relatively difficult to "scan" their experience for indications of retinal size.

14. Size Estimation I: Average Error. They tended to overestimate size in this test. In keeping with the hypothesis that their attention was limited to the more obvious or dominant sectors of stimulus fields, their attention may have been centered on the standard stimuli, which, according to the centration hypothesis, leads to overestimation.

18. and *20. Color Word: Reading Time, Colors Alone; Incidental Recall.* They named colors quickly and smoothly and recalled few words in the Color-Word Test. Selection of the appropriate color name offered no problem, presumably because they were less aware of the multiplicity of response possibilities. They seemed to handle the color-word conflict by paying minimal attention to the words, as shown by their poor recall of them, in keeping with the suggestion above that they were relatively less attentive to incidental aspects of stimulus fields.

34. Rod and Frame: Average Error, Body Erect. Their accuracy in this portion of the Rod and Frame Test may have been the result *not* of an ability to respond differentially to various sets of cues (as was presumed for subjects with low scores on Factor I for women), but of the fact that they paid minimal attention to the misleading incidental cues.

1. Schematizing: Ranking Accuracy. Their relative inaccuracy in ranking the squares in this test is presumed to be a function of limited *scanning* of previous impressions of the sizes of squares, which hinders effective ranking of squares.

37. Embedded Figures: Mean Log Time, Cluster II. The long times required by these subjects to find the simple figures in the complex designs were presumably the result of their limited scanning of the complex designs.

Ancillary Findings

As noted above, the associations of subjects with high factor scores tended to drift far from the stimulus words in the Free Association Test. These subjects' performance also had a particular quality: the impression conveyed by their protocols was that they avoided the expression of personal feelings by producing a steady flow of impersonal intellectualized material. Thus, their tendency to "scan" their own available responses extensively seemed associated with intellectualizing. For example, they discussed such topics as the theory and history of architecture, species of animals that live in the desert, and the like. The avoidance of feelings in their performance also seemed to reflect a concern that their associations might reveal something about them.

The extreme scanners' tendency to avoid personal interpretations of experience also seemed apparent in the Object Sorting Test.

These subjects were more likely to give impersonal, objective reasons as their basis for placing objects together in a group, such as the materials of which the objects are made, or their function. Although nonscanners also gave a majority of impersonal reasons, they did so less often and were more likely to group objects in terms of their own experience with them or other personal associations (difference between groups significant at .01 level).

In an earlier study (Schlesinger, 1954), extreme scanners (formerly called "focusers") sorted more pictures of the Picture Sorting Test into the "Indifferent" category than did subjects at the other extreme. This finding suggested that they found it difficult to respond in terms of immediately available feelings, perhaps because of a general tendency to isolate affect from idea. This specific finding was not supported in the present study. It was apparent, however, that these subjects did make greater use of the "Dislike" category in the Picture Sorting Test than did the low-factor-score subjects. The pictures in this test can be divided into four groups: (a) those with sexual connotations; (b) those with aggressive connotations; (c) mood-expressive pictures (e.g., pictures showing people crying); and (d) emotionally inexpressive ("neutral") pictures. Compared to low-factor-score subjects, those with high factor scores sorted relatively more of the "mood" and "sexual" pictures into the "Dislike" category ($p < .10$). The "Dislike" reaction was elicited most clearly by pictures that most strongly depict loss of emotional control. Thus, extreme scanners in the present sample of men tended not so much to deny expression of feeling as to react *negatively*. Such a negative reaction is also an expression of unwillingness to give way to their spontaneous feelings.

In the Rorschach Test, as in the Picture Sorting Test, extreme scanners tended to produce impersonal responses. For example, a relatively great percentage of their responses concerned animals (references to birds and marine life were particularly striking, $p < .02$) and objects.

Summary

Factor I seems to confirm the redefinition of the focusing control principle suggested in Chapter 6; it is more properly labeled scanning. The extensive scanner actively peruses objects about him and is continually searching or scanning the field, becoming aware in this process not only of the field properties relevant to his present intentions but also of fringe properties. One consequence of extensive scanning of object properties is the stabilization of conceptions of objects. A second consequence of extensive scanning is a slowing of decision making. Since these subjects seemed to deploy attention to relatively many aspects of stimulation, both when the field was external and when it was internal, they took a long time to make choices. It is thus assumed that doubt and uncertainty prominently accompany extreme scanning.[3]

Factor IV—Tolerance for Unrealistic Experiences
(see p. 90)

This factor appears to represent the principle of tolerance for unrealistic experiences and represents modes of organizing behavior in respect to experiences that violate the normal assumptions of reality.

High Factor Scores

Subjects with high factor scores (tolerant of unrealistic experiences) tended to organize behavior in terms of experiences that were inconsistent with their knowledge of reality.

31. and 32. Free Association: Productivity; Average Length of Unit. In the Free Association Test, it seems likely that a tolerance for emerging ideas that might deviate from the conventional would lead to a freer rein of association, indicated by long associative units and, consequently, long protocols. The long units and long protocols produced by high-scoring subjects indicate that the absence of any guide for reality testing in this task neither inhibited them nor produced signs of tension (they had few long pauses, $p < .01$). This kind of Free Association Test performance corresponds to the finding by Temerlin (1956) that subjects who are tolerant of the autokinesis experience (which, under certain circumstances, can be thought of as another unrealistic experience) find it relatively easy to associate freely in psychoanalytic treatment. These results are also in keeping with the acceptance of

---

[3] As discussed in Chapter 6 and in the factor interpretation, extreme scanning bears an obvious relationship to the defense of isolation. This relationship is explored further in Chapter 11.

Factor IV

Tolerance for Unrealistic Experiences

Loading	Score		Performance of subjects with High Factor Scores
.62	32.	Free Association: Average Length of Unit	Long units
.61	31.	Free Association: Productivity	Long protocol
-.54	8.	Aniseikonic Lenses: Log Recognition Time	Short recognition time
.50	2.	Schematizing: Increment Error (Regression)	Extreme lagging
.44	7.	Apparent Movement: Mean Range	Wide range
.35	4.	Kinesthetic Time Error: Assimilation	Much assimilation

feeling-based responses noted by Klein, Gardner, and Schlesinger in their study of this control principle.

8. *Aniseikonic Lenses: Log Recognition Time.* These subjects were quick to recognize and accept distortion after putting on the lenses. This finding suggests that they readily accepted sense impressions at variance with the knowledge of the actual shape of the room.

2. *Schematizing: Increment Error (Regression).* The instructions for the Schematizing Test state that the squares to be seen may range from 1 to 18 inches. The appearance of many small squares early in the test, however, "lulled" nearly all subjects in this and previous experiments (cf. Chapter 3) into lagging behind as the actual sizes of the squares gradually increased. One determinant of such lagging (see Factor II for women, below) is the degree to which new experiences assimilate to preceding ones. Another determinant of lagging is apparent here: the degree to which the subject adhered to the anticipation about the range of sizes set up by the initial instructions. For "tolerant" subjects, the knowledge of the actual range given in the instructions yielded to their experience with consistently small squares in the first part of the test.

7. *Apparent Movement: Mean Range.* Since they were informed that the movement is an *illusion,* the high scorers' broad range of apparent movement experience reflected their acceptance of stimulus organizations that deviated from their knowledge of the actual state of affairs.

4. *Kinesthetic Time Error: Assimilation.* In this test, the interpolated weight tended to obscure the actual weight of the first stimulus, thus interfering with the subject's experience of it. High-scoring subjects tended to accept this violation of previous experience, as shown in their relatively high assimilation scores.

Low Factor Scores

Subjects with low factor scores (intolerant of unrealistic experiences) tended to organize behavior only in terms of experiences that conformed to conventional reality or to what they knew to be objectively true.

31. and *32. Free Association: Productivity; Average Length of Unit.* The low scorers' short associative units, short protocols, and excessive blocking of the associative stream confirmed the results of the study by Klein et al., in which "intolerant" subjects showed notable constriction when they were given a choice as to the degree to which their responses included feeling-determined productions. As before, it is assumed that their limited associative productivity in the Free Association Test results partly from a reluctance to give anything more than rather stereotyped and conventional associations.

8. *Aniseikonic Lenses: Log Recognition Time.* These subjects were slow to report tilt on the first trial with the lenses; on the second trial, however, they reported tilt as quickly as did the high scorers. The discrepancy in their behavior on the two trials suggests that the delay on the first trial did not represent an inability to see tilt, but rather a *reluctance* to accept and report an experience so much at variance with their knowledge of the actual shape of the room. Once they knew that this was what the experimenter expected them to see, they were able to report tilt readily on the second trial. (Their behavior is in contrast to that of high scorers on Factor II for women [levelers], who had long recognition times on both trials, suggesting a genuine difficulty in seeing tilt.)

2. *Schematizing: Increment Error (Regression).* The greater conformance to *actual* changes in the size range of the squares on the part of "intolerant" subjects apparently reflected (a) adherence to their *knowledge* of the nature of the stimuli, provided by the instructions, and (b) consequent resistance to the impression induced by the small squares in the first part of the test.

7. *Apparent Movement: Mean Range.* Their resistance to experiences that contradicted their knowledge of reality was also expressed in the small range of alternation rates over which they accepted the illusion of movement.

4. *Kinesthetic Time Error: Assimilation.* Low scorers showed little assimilation effect in this test. Their efforts to make their experience conform as exactly as possible to actual conditions in the external world apparently prevented them from yielding to any *apparent* changes induced by the interpolated weights.

Ancillary Findings

In the Rorschach Test, low-scoring ("intolerant") subjects tended to limit themselves to clearly defined forms. They had a smaller proportion ($p < .10$) of responses in which the form was vague (e.g., "clouds"). The difference was most marked in their whole responses. "Intolerant" subjects produced almost as many well-formed whole responses as "tolerant" subjects, but they produced less than half as many vague wholes ($p < .05$). As a result, their $W\%$ (proportion of whole responses) was lower ($p < .05$); instead, they gave more responses ($p < .01$) to the large details of the blots, which are the most clearly defined and easily accepted forms. "Intolerant" subjects, then, tend to limit themselves to rational, reality-bound responses and to utilize those parts of the blots that most easily lend themselves to such interpretation. "Tolerant" subjects were more likely to tamper with the "reality" of the blots.

While reading time and interference in the Color-Word Test were largely unrelated to this factor, the pattern of reading speed within the interference section (Part III) was related ($p = .055$). "Tolerant" subjects were more likely to have a *stabilized* pattern; that is, their tempo was relatively unvarying. This pattern is found in people who are poised for change and do not use familiarity as the sole basis for organization (Smith and Klein, 1953). "Intolerant" subjects were more likely to have *dissociative* patterns, in which reading speed increases and decreases erratically. It is suggested (see Chapter 7) that a dissociative pattern occurs in people whose capacity to shift sets is limited, so that they tend to resort to familiar sets when they are unable to sustain the attention required for this task.

Summary

Factor IV seems to represent tolerance for unrealistic experiences, as defined in Chapter 4 and in earlier studies of this control principle. The two extremes of performance represented by high and low factor scores reflected the extent to which individuals limited themselves to what they knew to be objectively true. "Intolerant" subjects seemed engaged in continual efforts to make their experience conform to the actual state of affairs in the external world. "Tolerant" subjects seemed in equally adequate contact with external reality, but were much more relaxed in their acceptance of both ideas and perceptual organizations that required deviation from the conventional. Thus, they were able to show more direct evidence of the influence of momentary feeling states on their experiencing of the external world.

Results for Women

The unrotated and rotated factors obtained from the 33-score correlational matrix for women are presented in Tables 9 and 10, Appendix B. The six factors extracted account for more of the total test variance than did the factors found for the male sample (56.1% vs. 39.6%); this follows from the fact that there were more high correlations in the matrix for women (see Table 6). Three factors are interpreted. Factor I accounted for the largest share (15.3%) of score variance and included features of the previously identified controls of field dependence-independence and constricted-flexible control. Factor II accounted for the next largest share (11.7%) of the score variance and strongly resembled the leveling-sharpening control principle. Although weaker statistically (6.8% of the score variance), Factor III is also discussed because it resembles the equivalence range control principle. Factors IV, V, and VI did not lend themselves to interpretation.

Factor I—Field-Articulation
(see p. 95)

This may be termed a field-articulation factor. It applies to situations of perceived incongruity. The nature of this factor indicates that, in the present sample at least, the variables described as field dependence-independence and constricted-flexible control may, as suggested in Chapters 7 and 8, be more economically subsumed under a single control principle.

High Factor Scores

Subjects with high factor scores tended to organize fields containing stimulus incongruities along the simplest possible lines. Because of this, they did not cope effectively with tasks in which they were required to respond selectively to *relevant* cues in fields containing contradictory and interfering cues. In situations where it was possible, they resolved the incongruity by responding only to the most compelling elements and ignoring others. When such a

Factor I
Field-Articulation

Loading		Score	Performance of Subjects with High Factor Scores
.91	33.	Rod and Frame: Average Error, Body Tilted	Large error
.84	37.	Embedded Figures: Mean Log Time, Cluster II	Long solution time
.81	36.	Embedded Figures: Mean Log Time, Cluster I	Long solution time
.78	34.	Rod and Frame: Average Error, Body Erect	Large error
-.71	32.	Free Association: Average Length of Unit	Short units
.66	17.	Color-Word: Interference	High interference
-.58	31.	Free Association: Productivity	Short protocol
.49	26.	Size Estimation II: Variability, Memory	High variability
.48	25.	Size Estimation II: Variability, Perceptual	High variability
-.43	21.	Size Estimation II: Constant Error, Perceptual	Underestimation

course was difficult, in the Rod and Frame Test, or impossible, as in the Color-Word Test, in which conflicting elements are physically inseparable, their performance was impaired.

33. and 34. Rod and Frame: Average Error, Body Tilted and Body Erect. Accuracy can be achieved in this test only by selectively directing attention to bodily cues while ignoring or actively withholding response to the compelling visual cues from the frame. These subjects' inability to articulate the stimulus field in this way led them to responses primarily determined by the impressive but misleading cues from the frame. It should be noted that the large errors typical of these subjects usually arose not from a compromise between visual and bodily cues but from an actual alignment of the rod with the frame. In 57 per cent of the body-tilted trials and in 68 per cent of the body-erect trials, they brought the rod to within 8° of the 28°-tilted frame (only one low-scoring subject was influenced by the frame to this extent).

36. and 37. Embedded Figures: Mean Log Time, Clusters I and II. High-scoring subjects had relatively great difficulty in finding the simple figures. Their inability to articulate the complex design by directing attention only to potentially *relevant* areas of the complex designs (e.g., suborganizations roughly the same as the simple figures in size and organizational properties) apparently led to their slowness in finding the embedded simple figures.

31. and 32. Free Association: Productivity; Average Length of Unit. They produced very short, clipped idea units, accompanied by much blocking of the associative stream; as a result, their protocols were short. These performances seem to reflect their inability to direct attention to *relevant* (related to the stimulus words) items in their memory schemata. Thus their inability to articulate complex fields containing revelant and irrelevant items seems as apparent when the field is an internal, memoric one as when the field includes internal and external cues, or only external cues.

17. Color-Word: Interference. When the conscious experience of incongruity was unavoidable, their difficulty in responding differentially to contradictory sets of cues produced a marked disruption in performance. This was shown in the Color-Word Test not only by a much slower reading time for Part III (color-word) than for Part II (colors alone), but also by an erratic variability of reading speed within the interference section; high-scoring subjects were more likely ($p < .05$) than low scorers to have either a dissociative or cumulative-dissociative pattern.

25. and 26. Size Estimation II: Variability, Perceptual and Memory. To perform in a stable manner in this test, the subject must preserve the *constancy* of his impression of disk size in spite of the distracting figures on the disks and the disparity between a solid disk and the circle of light used as the comparison stimulus. Unarticulated initial response to relevant *and* irrelevant cues makes for high variability in the perceptual condition and saturates the memory schema with conflicting cues. Thus, these subjects' variability was high in both perceptual and memory conditions. It might be assumed that if the preservation of constancy were not impeded by the presence of contradictory cues, these subjects would be no more variable than their low-factor-score counterparts.

21. Size Estimation: Constant Error, Perceptual. High-scoring subjects tended to underestimate disk sizes in the perceptual condition. This underestimation could be a further consequence of their inability to respond to relevant cues in fields containing cues leading to contradictory impressions. These subjects presumably underestimated because they could not withhold attention from the irrelevant, smaller pictures on these disks. A related possibility is that the presence of the smaller figures on the disks may, as suggested in Chapter 7, produce an "inherence" effect, making the disks seem smaller than they would appear without the figures on them. Subjects who directed attention to *both* the disks and the irrelevant pictures could have maximal inherence effects.

Low Factor Scores

Subjects with low factor scores were able to articulate incongruous configurations of cues by confining attention to those aspects of fields required by instructions; they either ignored or actively resisted responding to contradictory irrelevant cues.

33. and 34. Rod and Frame: Average Error, Body Tilted and Body Erect. In both conditions of this test, they responded selectively to the relevant bodily cues and therefore adjusted the rod accurately, despite the misleading position of the visually dominant tilted frame.

36. and *37. Embedded Figures: Mean Log Time, Cluster I and II.* In the Embedded Figures Test, they readily penetrated a complex figure and extracted from it the particular aspect required by the instructions. Their ability to extract the simple figures was shown in both the "perceptual" and "conceptual" clusters of the test. As in the Rod and Frame Test, effective performance coincides with differential responsiveness to competing relevant and irrelevant cues.

31. and *32. Free Association: Productivity; Average Length of Unit.* The high scorers' free association protocols were quite fluent, with long idea units, few pauses ($p < .02$), and long protocols. They were apparently at ease in selecting from complex memory schemata relevant and irrelevant responses.

17. Color-Word: Interference. In the Color-Word Test, they were able to attend effectively to the relevant color cues, avoiding response to the contradictory words in which the colors were printed. In addition, their performance did not show the erratic variability that was noted above for the high scorers.

25. and *26. Size Estimation II: Variability, Perceptual and Memory.* By virtue of their selective attention to relevant cues concerning the sizes of the disks (as contrasted to the irrelevant smaller figures on the disks), low-factor-score subjects were able to develop stable impressions of disk sizes in the perceptual condition. Presumably, their initial attentiveness only to cues relevant to the task prevented contradictory irrelevant cues from finding representation in the memory schema, so that their judgments were less variable in the memory condition as well.

21. Size Estimation II: Constant Error, Perceptual. Low-scoring subjects tended to err in the direction of overestimation. Thus, these subjects showed the kinds of "errors of the standard" (see Piaget, 1947) one would expect if they responded only to the disks —the kinds, in fact, that nearly all subjects showed (see Chapter 6) in responding to plain disks in Size Estimation Test I. A related interpretation is that their withholding of attention from the figures led them to show minimal "inherence" effects.

Ancillary Findings

Subjects with high factor scores were mostly housewives, while most of the subjects with low factor scores were involved in careers outside the home ($p < .01$). Since most of the employed women were married, this difference does not reflect a difference in marital status.

Low-scoring subjects (field independent, flexible control) tended to be active and task-oriented in the testing situations ($p = .038$), judging from the observations made of them during testing by one of the experimenters.[4] The high scorers (field dependent, constricted control) tended to display an anxious, driven talkativeness during testing ($p = .036$). These qualitative differences in the laboratory behavior of subjects at different points along the factor-score continuum suggest differences in their orientations to everyday life that are consonant with their test performances.

High- and low-scoring subjects showed many differences in the Rorschach Test, which, in general (see Appendix F), were similar to those found in Witkin's (1954) study.[5] Subjects in the high-scoring third of the factor score distribution had, on the average, more than twice as many "field dependent" Rorschach signs as those in the lower third ($p < .01$).

Summary

Low scorers on Factor I were able to penetrate complex configurations and attend selectively to features that were relevant in terms of test instructions. As a consequence of this, their performance on several of the experimental tasks was markedly stable. High scorers, on the other hand, were relatively unable to respond selectively to relevant features of stimulus aggregates containing contradictory cues.

The fact that the constant-error score for Size Estimation Test II appears in this factor has important implications for our understanding of the processes involved in all of these tests. Witkin et al. (1954) have spoken of field-dependent subjects as those who are relatively unable to extract item from field. This interpretation may be unduly limited. In Size Estimation Test II, subjects are required

---

[4] Mrs. Diana Siegal made these observations after having tested many of the subjects and before the data had been analyzed.

[5] The results reported in Appendix F were based not on the Factor I scores used here, but on basic measures of field dependence-independence drawn from the Rod and Frame and Embedded Figures Tests. However, since Factor I scores and Index scores for field dependence-independence were correlated .92, the results in Appendix F may safely be taken to apply to Factor I as well.

to *respond to the field* (the entire disk) and to *withhold response from the item* (the smaller figure embedded in the field). Thus, the individual differences observed by Witkin et al. in laboratory tests may well have even greater generality than they originally indicated. In such procedures, field-independent subjects (here called extreme "field-articulators") may be capable of differential attention to relevant versus irrelevant cues irrespective of which is item and which is field. The above finding also suggests that field-articulation can be observed whether or not the important cues in the field actually form a dominant, superordinate *Gestalt* organization.

Factor II—Leveling-Sharpening
(see p. 101)

This factor is consistent with the conception of leveling-sharpening offered in Chapter 3. Factor II is relevant to situations involving the temporal patterning of stimuli. It does *not* represent discrimination of differences per se. Rather, it pertains to differentiation in memory organization as a function of the extent to which successive stimuli assimilate to each other.

High Factor Scores

Subjects with high factor scores (levelers) showed relatively simple, undifferentiated memory organizations in a variety of situations. Perhaps the basic attribute of leveling is a relatively high degree of interaction among memories and present percepts, so that the elements lose their individuality. The following test performances reflected these tendencies.

1. and *2. Schematizing: Ranking Accuracy and Increment Error (Regression).* In the Schematizing Test, their intraserial ranking was inaccurate, suggesting great assimilation among successive impressions of the squares. When impressions of earlier squares are not discrete, the subject has no clear scale against which to judge each new square, so that his relative estimates of the sizes of the squares tend to become inaccurate. The high scorers' high increment-error score can also be understood as a product of the assimilation of new experiences to preceding ones. In this test, assimilation leads to underestimation of the sizes of

Factor II

Leveling-Sharpening

Loading		Score	Performance of Subjects with High Factor Scores
.71	21.	Size Estimation II: Constant Error, Perceptual	Overestimation
-.68	1.	Schematizing: Ranking Accuracy	Inaccuracy
.67	32.	Free Association: Average Length of Unit	Long units
.65	8.	Aniseikonic Lenses: Log Recognition Time	Long recognition time
.65	4.	Kinesthetic Time Error: Assimilation	Much assimilation
-.50	28.	Free Association: Percentage Distant, "Dry"	Close associations
.47	2.	Schematizing: Increment Error (Regression)	Extreme lagging
.45	18.	Color-Word: Reading Time, Colors Alone	Slow reading
.44	26.	Size Estimation II: Variability, Memory	High variability
-.38	30.	Free Association: Percentage "Home" Responses	Few home responses
.38	37.	Embedded Figures: Mean Log Time, Cluster II	Long solution time[a]

[a] Although solution time for Cluster II of the Embedded Figures Test had a moderate loading on Factor II (.38), the actual scores of extreme levelers and sharpeners on this measure did not differ significantly. The factor loading was apparently due to the correlation between Factors I and II and would disappear from Factor II if an oblique rotation were made. This measure was therefore not interpreted in the discussion of Factor II.

the progressively larger squares. Therefore, the leveler lags behind the trend of increase in size.

4. Kinesthetic Time Error: Assimilation. High-factor-score subjects showed considerable assimilation between their impressions of the initial weight and impressions of intervening weights in this test.

21. and 26. Size Estimation II: Constant Error, Perceptual; Variability, Memory. Unlike Size Estimation Test I, this test seems to involve an important memory component. Since the subject has to turn away from the standard disk to adjust the comparison disk, an adequate memory of the standard is needed. Perhaps the leveler, in his attempt to obtain a stable memory image of the disk, centered his regard on it longer than the sharpener, with consequent overestimation of its size. This hypothesis, which is in keeping with other indications of the comparative instability of the leveler's memories, should be tested experimentally.

The highly variable performance of these subjects in the memory condition seemed to be a direct outcome of the assimilation of their impressions of the disks to each other. In other words, their variability is assumed to reflect lack of clarity and discreteness in their memories of the individual disk sizes.

8. Aniseikonic Lenses: Log Recognition Time. These subjects were slow to experience tilt, which can also be understood as a form of high assimilation. Wearing the lenses confronts the subject with a new stimulus organization that conflicts with his previous experience that the room is rectangular. It can be assumed that subjects characterized by high assimilation among new stimuli and preceding stimulus organizations will be relatively slow to recognize and report the experience of tilt. These subjects took a long time to report tilt in the second as well as in the first trial, which strongly suggests that they were genuinely slow to recognize tilt (compare the discussion of lens performance in Factor IV for men).

28., 30., and 32. Free Association: Percentage Distant, "Dry"; Percentage "Home" Responses; Average Length of Unit. Levelers produced long units of association, but their protocols as a whole were no longer than average; this occurred because they produced a smaller number of idea units than did the sharpeners ($p < .05$). This finding suggests that their associations, drawn from their memory schemata, were organized in a rather global and undifferentiated fashion. The content of their associations was also relatively undifferentiated from the stimulus, as reflected in few distant associations to "Dry" and few responses to "House" dealing with the home (as well as relatively few distant associations).

18. Color-Word: Reading Time, Colors Alone. These subjects were slow in reading colors alone in the Color-Word Test. Rapid and accurate reading of colors is an unusual reading requirement. To do well, the subject must have ready access to the four color names. Such availability is optimal when the subject's semantic schemata are highly differentiated. Semantic schemata, like other memory organizations, are probably less highly differentiated in levelers. If so, the linking of the appropriate color name to the perceived color should be a relatively effortful and time-consuming task for them.

Low Factor Scores

Subjects with low factor scores (sharpeners) were able to maintain discrete impressions and memories of successive stimuli.

1. and 2. Schematizing: Ranking Accuracy and Increment Error (Regression). Their intraserial rankings were accurate and their increment-error scores were low, both presumably the product of minimal assimilation among perceptual processes and memory traces.

4. Kinesthetic Time Error: Assimilation. They were able to preserve an accurate impression of the weight of the standard stimulus despite the intervening stimulus, indicating that in this modality, as well, they formed discrete impressions of the separate stimuli.

21. and 26. Size Estimation II: Constant Error, Perceptual; Variability, Memory. Sharpeners tended to underestimate the sizes of the standard disks in the perceptual condition of this test and were less variable in the memory condition. A possible interpretation is that they developed a stable memory image of the standard with a minimum of fixation. According to Piaget's centration hypothesis, such a minimal fixation on the standard disks would produce the underestimation shown by the sharpeners. The characteristic clarity and discreteness of their impressions of stimuli would explain their low variability in the memory conditon.

8. Aniseikonic Lenses: Log Recognition Time. Sharpeners recognized tilt quickly in this test by responding to the new set of cues produced by the lenses as a separate experience, rather than by assimilating it to their previous impression of the room.

28., 30., and 32. Free Association: Percentage Distant, "Dry"; Percentage "Home" Responses; Average Length of Unit. Sharpeners tended to break their associations up into a large number of short units ($p < .05$), reflecting a highly differentiated memory organization. The content of their associations to both stimulus words did not remain close to the stimulus; to "Dry" they gave distant associations, and to "House" they gave associations dealing with the contents and structure of houses as well as more distant material. Their associations were not, then, bound by the initial stimuli, but were clearly differentiated from them.

18. Color-Word: Reading Time, Colors Alone. They read colors rapidly in Part I of the Color-Word Test. To do this, the subject must be able not only to recognize colors, but also to communicate their names quickly. Apparently sharpeners' more highly differentiated memory organizations facilitate ready access to the appropriate color names.

Ancillary Findings

In the Free Association Test, sharpeners showed relatively little blocking ($p = .077$). As in color reading, they seemed to have ready access to ideas and associations.

In the Color-Word Test, while levelers and sharpeners did not differ in amount of interference, they did differ in temporal patterns during the interference series. Levelers were more likely to show a progressive slowing down, a *cumulative* pattern ($p = .015$), while sharpeners were more likely to show a *stable* pattern ($p = .10$). Previous research (see Chapter 7) has indicated that a cumulative pattern is found in those who have difficulty in shifting from a well-established set, while the maintenance of a stable pattern requires alertness to change and constant effort.

Sharpeners tended to describe the complex figures of the Embedded Figures Test in more highly analytic geometric terms. This result was not statistically significant, but when the ability to solve the figures was partialed out of the description score, the difference between levelers and sharpeners reached significance ($p < .05$). In other words, sharpeners were more likely than levelers to break the figure up into its geometrical components when they described it, and the difference between the two groups of subjects was greater than could be explained by their slight difference in the analytic ability required to find the hidden figures. This was apparently another example of the sharpeners' more highly differentiated schemata.

Summary

The contrasting performances of levelers and sharpeners exemplified varieties of process-trace interaction that produces differences in memory organization. Sharpeners were characterized by small assimilation effects in a variety of situations, and their memory schemata seemed relatively differentiated. In levelers, successive perceptual impressions were assimilated to each other, so that distinctions among them were blurred. Memories of past impressions were also less available to them, presumably because of the general lack of differentiation of their memory schemata.

Factor III—Equivalence Range
(see p. 106)

Factor III corresponds to the equivalence range control. Factor scores reflect the degree to which subjects judged stimuli to be similar. This factor does not represent sensitivity to differences but pertains, rather, to the subjective criteria used to categorize experiences.

High Factor Scores

Subjects with high factor scores (broad equivalence range) showed relatively relaxed and inclusive criteria of similarity.

10. *Object Sorting: Number of Groups.* High-scoring subjects tended to sort the objects into a few large groups. These groups tended to be loose aggregates defined by their usual location, such as "objects found in the kitchen," "household things," or "things one would have in a desk drawer." They also formed groups based on personal experience, such as "things I use for sewing."

11. *Size Constancy: Mean Diameter.* In the Size Constancy Test, they were unable to make the required retinal match; their adjustment was actually much closer to the actual object size than

Factor III

EQUIVALENCE RANGE

Loading	Score	Performance of Subjects with High Factor Scores
-.80	10. Object Sorting: Number of Groups	Few groups
.59	11. Size Constancy: Mean Diameter	Nonretinal match
.57	29. Free Association: Percentage Distant, "House"	Many distant associations
.53	28. Free Association: Percentage Distant, "Dry"	Many distant associations
.43	15. Size Estimation I: Heaviness Effect	Greatly affected by heaviness[a]

[a] The heaviness effect score from Size Estimation Test I, although it satisfies the factor-loading criterion for inclusion in the interpretation, is not interpreted here because the peculiar distribution of its scores makes its usefulness doubtful. Twenty-five of the 30 female Subjects had very similar scores, all within 0.3σ of the mean, while three Subjects had very high scores and two had very low scores.

to the correct retinal equivalent. This suggests rather casual criteria for similarity.

28. and 29. *Free Association: Percentage Distant, "Dry" and "House."* Their associations ranged far from the meaning of the stimulus words. Their criteria of relevance thus appeared broad, rather than narrow.

Low Factor Scores

Subjects with low factor scores (narrow equivalence range) showed more exacting criteria of similarity.

10. *Object Sorting: Number of Groups.* These subjects divided the objects into many small groups. They seemed, in effect, unwilling to consider more than a few objects as having enough in common to belong to the same group.

11. *Size Constancy: Mean Diameter.* In the Size Constancy Test, subjects were called on to adopt an unfamiliar set: to select the comparison disk matching the retinal image of the standard and ignore the real size of the standard. Low-scoring subjects seemed able to compartmentalize the two different ways of experiencing an object, thus maintaining the distinction between retinal and actual size. In this sense, they were more exacting in what they were willing to consider similar.

28. and 29. *Free Association: Percentage Distant, "Dry" and "House."* Their associations hovered closely around the most obvious meanings of the stimulus words. It was as if the stimulus words defined categories and these subjects permitted themselves to produce (or report) only closely related ideas.

Ancillary Findings

Some of the qualitative features of their behavior suggested that broad-range subjects were aware of and acted on a richer array of connotations of objects than did subjects with a narrow equivalence range. As noted above, they often relied on the everyday meanings as bases for sorting in the Object Sorting Test. In contrast, narrow-range subjects tended to categorize on more impersonal grounds, with less of the fabulated quality that linked the groupings of broad-range subjects to personal experience. The impersonality of the groupings made by narrow-range subjects was exemplified in the fact that 63 per cent sorted two or more groups on the basis of material (e.g., "all paper"), while broad-range subjects gave no such responses ($p = .009$). All narrow-range subjects formed at least one group consisting entirely of identical or nearly identical objects (e.g., corks, brushes, coins), while only 11 per cent of the subjects at the other extreme gave any such group ($p = .0004$). Eighty-eight per cent of narrow-range subjects had groups consisting of single items, while only 11 per cent of broad-range subjects had such groups ($p = .003$). It is striking that even when these three types of groups were excluded, narrow-range subjects formed twice as many groups as broad-range subjects.

In the Rorschach, the two groups produced different content. Broad-range subjects gave more human content ($p < .05$); they differed significantly ($p < .05$) from narrow-range subjects in the number of whole human figures produced, but not in the number of parts of human figures. When human and animal content are considered together, the broad-range subjects had a larger proportion of humans and mammals, while narrow-range subjects had a larger proportion of lower-order creatures, such as birds, fish, and insects ($p < .05$). Broad-range subjects were apparently able to project human and humanlike content into the blots quite readily, while narrow-range subjects were more cautious in attributing human life to the blots, since they could often see only a part of a person rather than the whole figure, and made much more use of the kinds of creatures that are least humanlike.

Broad-range subjects also used either color or human movement in more of their responses ($p < .05$). When narrow-range subjects did see human movement, a larger proportion of it was weak or flexor movement ($p = .029$). These findings also indicate that broad-range subjects projected more life and activity into the inkblots.

Summary

Factor III scores represent individual differences in categorizing behavior. This factor is relevant to tests involving direct or implicit demands to make judgments of similarity. It is not relevant to discriminatory behavior as measured by other tests in the present study.

Subjects with low factor scores (narrow equivalence range)

were reluctant to judge disparate stimuli or distinguishable aspects of their experience as "similar." In the Object Sorting Test, which provided the richest source of ancillary observations, they tended to respond to the inherent properties of objects, rather than to their connotative implications. Subjects with high factor scores (broad equivalence range) were likely to dismiss differences in detail and to consider the objects in terms of their associated meanings, rather than in terms of their physical properties. At times, their emphasis on connotative meanings of stimuli led them to group the objects in terms of visual impressions of the places in which they had seen them in their everyday lives. At other times, their sortings reflected a tendency toward fabulation, so that objects were linked together because of their relevance to some personal activity.

DISCUSSION OF RESULTS

The Hypothesized Control Principles

In view of the inadequacies of sampling, it is striking that all of the hypothesized controls described in Chapters 3 through 8 received confirmation for at least one sex. Sampling biases may be expected to obscure relationships between test performances so that control principles would be less likely to emerge than in a better selected sample.

Leveling-Sharpening. This control principle was represented in Factor II for women. It did not appear in the male sample.

Tolerance for Unrealistic Experiences. Factor IV for men appeared to represent this control principle. A comparable factor was not found for women.[6]

Equivalence Range. Factor III for women seemed clearly to represent this control principle. An equivalence range factor was not found for men.

Scanning. Factor I for the male sample seemed to represent this control principle and to support the reinterpretation of focusing suggested by earlier results (see Chapter 6). No comparable factor was obtained for women.

---

[6] After testing was completed, it was discovered that the apparatus used to test apparent movement had changed during testing. Inspection of the trend of scores indicated that the drift in the apparatus did not affect the results for the male sample, but did invalidate results for the female sample. The inadequacy of the Apparent Movement scores for women may be one reason why a tolerance for unrealistic experiences control principle was not apparent in the sample of women.

Constricted-Flexible Control. This control principle is represented in Factor I for women, where it is merged with field dependence-independence. For men, it seems to be represented in Factor V, although not strongly enough to warrant interpretation, and to remain partially distinct from field dependence-independence. As noted above, however, the two factors might have merged for men if all male subjects had taken the Rod and Frame Test.

Further experiments are needed to verify the apparent merging of this principle with field dependence-independence in the case of women subjects and to clarify reasons for the failure of these principles to form a single factor for men.

Field Dependence-Independence. As noted above, Factor I for women coincided strongly with expectations about this variable based on previous studies. In this study, it merged with constricted-flexible control. For men, some aspects of field dependence-independence appeared in Factor III, other aspects in Factor V (constricted-flexible control), neither of which was interpreted.

Sex Differences in the Factor Analyses

The striking sex differences in results of the factor analyses for the present small samples of men and women require interpretation. On the basis of previous results, it seems safest to assume that these differences are more apparent than real. Gross sex differences were not apparent in previous studies of five of the cognitive controls. The study of field dependence-independence by Witkin et al., in which sex differences were explored more adequately, showed greater consistency in men than in women, in direct contrast to the present results. Further studies with larger and better-controlled samples of each sex are needed to explore the possibility that men and women are in fact characterized by different control principles and different relationships among control principles.

It is important to note that future attempts to learn about the nature of sex differences will necessarily include a number of additional unknowns. Little is known, for example, of the relationships between age and the kinds of behavior observed in the present study. The age at which some of the control principles emerge is still unknown. Ideally, future studies will take age into account and include samples of different ages for each sex.

Scores Used to Represent the Control Principles

One of the most intriguing products of the factor analyses is the evidence that even very simple laboratory measures (a number of which are spoken of in the classical literature as if they represented single response processes) are determined by more than one of the limited number of control principles studied here. It is a clinical truism that responses in such tests as the Rorschach (and, as indicated by results of the present study, free association tests) stem from many aspects of personality organization. It is well known, for example, that a large number of whole responses (W) in the Rorschach can be achieved by routes that have markedly different diagnostic implications. A striking finding in the present study is that such multiple determination also applies to performances in the relatively simple laboratory tests.

It seems clear that more than one control principle is involved in almost any adaptive task. The Rod and Frame Test, for example, involves the *extent* to which an individual deploys attention (scanning) as well as his ability to attend differentially to competing cues (field-articulation). As was noted in the factor interpretations, extreme scanning and extreme field-articulation may have opposite effects on the differential direction of attention to relevant and irrelevant cues. Scanning also plays a part in the Schematizing Test, although this test has provided criterion measures of leveling-sharpening.

Above and beyond the interaction of different control principles in the various tasks, the factor analyses show that two demonstrably different control principles may account for significant portions of the variance in a *single* score. One of the most striking examples of this occurs in the Free Association Test. Long associative units are typical of low field-articulators, and also of levelers. Examination of individual protocols shows that subjects who have both of these tendencies also have very long units, that subjects who are high field-articulators and sharpeners have very short units, and that subjects who are low field-articulators but who are also sharpeners have associative units of intermediate length.

The present study can be taken as an object lesson in the complexity of cognitive organizing principles involved in even the simplest procedures. In the classical literature on time error, for example, discussion has centered around such determinants as assimilation effects, as if these were *solely* responsible for the observed phenomena. In the present study, however, the tolerance for unrealistic experiences factor found for men also plays a part in time error. The primary purpose of the present study was to clarify general determinants of individual differences in test behavior, and hence contribute to an understanding of the processes involved. Beyond this, however, the fact that loadings for certain test variables appear in more than one orthogonal factor indicates that a single response end-product can be achieved by two or more independent processes.

This aspect of the results also has implications for the "purity" of specific measures in representing individual control principles. To take the most extreme example, individual measures developed for the Free Association Test had strong loadings on several of the factors interpreted. This implies that many attributes of cognitive organization play a part in this complex and open-ended task. For this reason, measures derived from the Free Association Test are not useful as specific indicators of any one control principle. For certain purposes, purer measures of individual control principles are necessary. For other purposes, however, multiply determined variables are not objectionable. In fact, some of the most profitable future studies of relationships between cognitive controls may involve predictions about the effects of two or more control principles on a single aspect of test performance.

It may be of value to list the measures that thus far appear to provide the best estimates of the control principles.

Leveling-Sharpening. In the present factor analysis, four experimental measures were strongly represented in the obtained leveling-sharpening factor. Three of them, however, were also found in other factors. The *ranking-accuracy* score of the Schematizing Test appeared in the scanning factor, although not as strongly. Both the Schematizing Test increment-error score and the Aniseikonic Lenses Test *recognition-time* score appeared in the tolerance for unrealistic experiences factor, but in directions that were opposite to each other from the standpoint of leveling-sharpening; that is, *tolerance* was associated with a leveling performance on the increment-error score and a sharpening performance on recognition time.[7] The Kinesthetic Time Error Test *assimilation* score did not have a strong loading on any other factor, although it had a moderate loading on the tolerance for unrealistic experiences factor. At the present stage of our understanding, it may be best to use both measures from the Schematizing Test. The raw increment-error score should probably be used; the regression score represents an unnecessary refinement. As a saving in testing time, the Kinesthetic Time Error Test could probably be omitted with little effect.

These results suggest the need for more definitive measures of this principle. One approach would be a tachistoscopic presentation of pairs of figures (e.g., squares or circles) of different sizes in close temporal juxtaposition, over a range of exposure and interval times. Immediately after the two exposures, the subject could adjust a comparison figure to the experienced size of the second figure. This could conceivably yield a measure of assimilation that is less contaminated by other factors than are the present measures. Such a test would tap the major process presumed to underlie performance in the Schematizing Test. The effect of the second figure on the trace of the first, which is analogous to the Kinesthetic Time Error Test assimilation score used in the present study, could also be measured in such a situation.

Tolerance for Unrealistic Experiences. From its loading in Factor IV for men, recognition time for tilt in the Aniseikonic Lenses Test would appear to be the best available measure of this principle, but the fact that this measure also appears strongly in Factor II for women (leveling-sharpening) suggests that it could not safely be used by itself. The most uncontaminated measure is probably the mean range of apparent movement, which has previously been used successfully as a criterion measure of this principle. Use of the two measures in combination would probably yield the most unequivocal results.

Equivalence Range. The very high loading of the number of groups score for the Object Sorting Test on Factor III for women,

---

[7] The recognition-time score used in the factor analysis was for the first trial only. As noted earlier, recognition time on the second trial was related to the leveling-sharpening factor, but not to the tolerance for unrealistic experiences factor. If recognition time were to be used as a leveling-sharpening measure, it would seem best to use both trials, or possibly the second trial only.

and the fact that it is represented in no other factor, indicate that it is the most direct measure of equivalence range available.[8]

Scanning. The error score for Size Estimation Test I was the only one of the three experimental measures with very high loadings on Factor I for men that was placed unequivocally in that factor on both empirical and theoretical grounds. Constant error, however, rather than average error, seems ideal for studies of breadth of scanning and its relationship to the centration hypothesis. Of the other measures represented in this factor, the incidental recall measure is the only one that may be considered a valid and unequivocal indicator of scanning. A more reliable measure of this control principle could be obtained by combining the two measures, but such a procedure is probably unnecessary.

Field-Articulation. The Embedded Figures and Rod and Frame Tests provide clear measures of this control principle, since the four measures from these tests had very high loadings on Factor I for women and not on any other factor. A single score for each of these tests would be adequate. If it is desired to measure constricted-flexible control and field dependence-independence separately, since the evidence for their identity is so far limited to the present study, the Embedded Figures and Rod and Frame Tests could be used to measure field dependence-independence, while the Color-Word Test interference score would seem the best measure of constricted-flexible control.

---

[8] Sloane's (1959) results suggest that the Paper-and-Pencil Object Sorting Tests referred to in Chapter 5 also provide satisfactory measures.

10

CONTROL PRINCIPLES AND STYLES

The factor analyses described in Chapter 9 have demonstrated that a limited number of factors, corresponding by and large to predicted cognitive controls, can describe the relationships between individual test scores. These factors make it possible to conceptualize the complex correlational matrices, presented in Appendix A, in terms of discrete dimensions, each of which cuts across a number of specific test performances.

The fact that these dimensions are independent of each other means that individual subjects may have widely different patterns of factor scores. Thus, one female subject could be low in field-articulation, high in leveling-sharpening, broad in equivalence range; another could be low in field-articulation, low in leveling-sharpening, and narrow in equivalence range. Klein (1958, p. 111) has postulated that the *cognitive styles* represented by such patternings of control principles may represent "a superordinate level of control within the personality system." Since they represent combinations of control principles, these styles are perhaps more independent of specific adaptive requirements than the control principles.

In one sense, style is our answer to the issue of typology. Although it is tempting to speak of subjects who have high scores on a leveling-sharpening measure as "levelers" and make predictions to molar aspects of their behavior in other situations, this kind of extrapolation flies in the face of the fact that leveling-sharpening is evident in response to a limited class of adaptive requirements. The other control principles, too, seem to represent relatively specific aspects of cognitive organization. Field-articulation seems most evident in the laboratory when subjects are confronted with perceived incongruity. Tolerance for unrealistic experiences is observable when the subject's adherence to conventional reality is a factor determining response. The adequacy of laboratory procedures designed to measure individual control principles can, in fact, be evaluated in terms of the unequivocality with which they sample responses to limited classes of adaptive requirements. Style, on the other hand, may allow more effective prediction to molar aspects of behavior within and outside the laboratory, some of which may not be evoked by specific adaptive requirements.

To take but one example, one might assume that because "levelers" appear to be "passive" in the Schematizing Test, they are "passive" in a variety of life situations. For purposes of discussion, let us ignore for the moment the possibility that "passivity" itself may be divisible into a variety of unrelated forms. Assuming some degree of generality in "passivity," it immediately becomes obvious that if a "leveler" is high in field-articulation, or high in scanning, he may seem very "active" in situations involving these controls. Thus, "passivity" on a more molar scale can more probably be linked not to leveling alone, but to cognitive style including leveling, low field-articulation, low scanning, and other controlling behaviors involving a minimum of activity in response to a variety of adaptive requirements.

A subject's style also has direct implications for his cognitive behavior in adaptive situations of greater complexity than our laboratory tests. For example, under certain conditions, a "leveler" who is high in field-articulation should form a memory organization distinctly different from that of a "leveler" who is low in field-articulation. If these two subjects were later confronted with an adaptive situation in which articulation of the field depended in part upon the memory organization formed earlier, their performances should show still greater divergence. In general, a more complete understanding of a subject's cognitive behavior would require information concerning his position relative to all the control principles called into play.

In order to observe some of the combinations of control principle behaviors characterizing the subjects of the present study, we undertook a clustering of persons based upon combinations of factor scores. Because of the small samples, the clusters extracted can serve only as examples of possible combinations. Some attempt was made to show that these small clusters had a unique predictive power for such complex behaviors as responses to the Rorschach Test. The results were suggestive and promising, and an analysis using the Personal Inventory will be presented below. Firm demonstrations that clusters of factor scores represent an "emergent" level of cognitive organization would require: (a) a clear factor structure in a large sample of subjects; (b) clusters large enough to allow statistical comparisons between them on other measures. The sizes of the present samples obviously made it impossible to meet these criteria. For that reason, the findings that follow are only suggestive.

The Person Clusters

Description

Clusters of persons were extracted by the $\triangle^2$ method, a modification of the D^2 method (Cronbach and Gleser, 1953). Two subjects with identical scores on all n factors would have a D^2 of zero; the less similar the factor-score patterns, the larger the D^2. For the men, the clustering was based on scores for male Factors I, III, IV, and V; for the women, it was based on scores for female Factors I, II, and III. The procedures and underlying assumptions are explained in detail in Appendix E.

Limitations and Advantages

Any clustering of the kind attempted here is open to the possibility of chance groupings. The method used to obtain clusters tended to rule out this possibility by enabling us to select only the most homogeneous clusters. For the women, the average $\triangle^2$ (see Appendix E for explanation of terms) for the six clusters shown in Table 3 falls below the 3 per cent level of all the $\triangle^2$ obtained among all possible pairs of women in the sample. The average $\triangle^2$ for the six male clusters falls below the 9 per cent level of all possible $\triangle^2$ for the men. Thus the subjects within these clusters are much more similar than pairs of subjects in different clusters.

The small samples of men and women in the present study limited the number and kinds of clusters that could be extracted. In the female sample, clusters of three subjects each were found with the following major characteristics: low field-articulation, leveling; low field-articulation, sharpening; and high field-articulation, sharpening. Only one subject was a leveler high in field-articulation. We cannot say whether such a combination is psychologically unlikely or merely poorly represented because of our small sample.

The $\triangle^2$ method takes the level as well as the shape of a profile into account. This is a decided advantage in an exploratory study. The method also takes into account curvilinear relationships between factors.

It is important to note also that the factors were weighted equally in the determination of clusters. Although this is the simplest procedure and involves the fewest assumptions, we cannot say whether it is the most valid method psychologically.

Clusters of Men

Table 3 indicates the clusters extracted from the present sample of men. The mean score of each cluster on each of the relevant factors is given, with the standard error of the mean.

Scanning is a distinguishing characteristic in six of the seven clusters; tolerance for unrealistic experiences in four; constricted-flexible control in five; and field-articulation in five. Some interesting comparisons are provided by clusters 6 and 7, which have low scanning in common, but differ on constricted-flexible control; 1 and 6, which are similar in constricted control; and 4 and 7, which are roughly similar in everything but tolerance for unrealistic experiences. In all these comparisons, the control principle(s) shared by the two clusters may be employed in quite different ways, and a thorough knowledge of how each cluster employs each control principle could help to expand our definitions of individual controls.

Clusters of Women

Among the women (Table 4) field-articulation is a distinguishing characteristic in four of the six clusters; leveling-sharpening in five; and equivalence range in five.

The interesting contrasts here are between Clusters 1 and 2, which share low field-articulation and broad equivalence range but

Table 3

PERSON CLUSTERS BASED ON FACTOR SCORES

Men

Mean Factor Scores and Probable Errors

Cluster	N	Factor I Scanning (+ = high; - = low)	Factor III Field-Articulation (+ = low; - = high)	Factor IV Tolerance for Unrealistic (+ = tolerant; - = intolerant)	Factor V Constricted-Flexible Control (+ = constricted; - = flexible)
1	3	1.11 ± .25	1.51 (1 S)	- .29 ± .36	1.84 ± .24
2	4	1.08 ± .14	.09 ± .13	- .98 ± .35	- .15 ± .38
3	5	.87 ± .15	- .69 ± .33 (4 Ss)	1.23 ± .37	- .67 ± .22
4	2	- .87 ± .24	2.05 ± .68	-1.06 ± .17	-1.01 ± .13
5	4	- .11 ± .22	- .82 ± .22	-1.00 ± .24	- .37 ± .20
6	3	-1.87 ± .32	- .94 ± .28	.20 ± .25	1.11 ± .63
7	4	- .80 ± .08	.37 ± .26	.19 ± .23	- .68 ± .19

Table 4

PERSON CLUSTERS BASED ON FACTOR SCORES

Women

Mean Factor Scores and Probable Errors

Cluster	N	Factor I Field-Articulation (+ = low; − = high)	Factor II Leveling-Sharpening (+ = leveling; − = sharpening)	Factor III Equivalence Range (+ = broad; − = narrow)
1	3	1.76 ± .51	1.01 ± .48	.68 ± .50
2	3	.98 ± .35	− .89 ± .22	.63 ± .21
3	6	− .03 ± .13	1.06 ± .11	− .71 ± .31
4	4	.25 ± .43	−1.24 ± .29	−1.16 ± .30
5	4	− .58 ± .28	− .11 ± .24	1.38 ± .21
6	3	−1.31 ± .34	−1.16 ± .52	.29 ± .46

differ in leveling-sharpening; Clusters 3 and 4, which share narrow equivalence range but differ in leveling-sharpening; and Clusters 2 and 6, which share sharpening but differ in field-articulation.

Clusters vs. Single Control Principles: Consensus in Response to a Personal Inventory

If we assume that a cluster is primarily an expression of cognitive style, it should follow that members of a cluster are more homogeneous in their reactions to certain extralaboratory situations than subjects grouped on the basis of single control principles. This follows from our assumption that the control principles refer to single aspects of cognitive organization, whereas the styles correspond to broader aspects. To test this argument, we examined patterns of responses to a Personality Inventory, a list of 234 statements administered to each of our sixty subjects along with the regular laboratory tasks. These items cover a gamut of experiences —relationships with people, awareness of feelings, work habits, favorite routines, etc. Subjects scored each item on a seven-point scale from completely true of themselves to completely false, but for the purposes of this analysis the scale was collapsed into two categories, agree and disagree, with the middle category excluded.

It was hypothesized that members of a cluster would show greater consensus (agree or disagree unanimously with more items) than an equal number of subjects who were at the extremes on each of the constituent factors. It was further hypothesized that the cluster consensus would be greater irrespective of item content. We selected the three female clusters and three male clusters with the tightest patterning of factor scores (lowest $\triangle^2$'s—see Appendix E). The number of Inventory items on which there was unanimous agreement or disagreement for each of these six clusters is presented in Table 5. Below each cluster are listed consensus values for groups of subjects at the extremes on each of the factors involved in the cluster. For example, the subjects in Group 2-A are the three women whose factor scores indicated lowest field-articulation; the subjects in 2-B are the three women at the sharpening extreme of leveling-sharpening factor scores. In some cases the consensus for two similar groups is not the same (compare Groups 1-A and 3-A for men) because different numbers of subjects comprise the groups. Such differences were necessary to make the groups equal in size to the relevant cluster.

Table 5 shows that each of the six female factor groups is less homogeneous in response to the Personal Inventory than the related clusters ($p < .02$, one-tailed sign test). Of the five male groups of extremes on factors, two show consensus on fewer items than the relevant cluster; two on more items; and one shows no difference. Thus our principal hypothesis seems confirmed for the female clusters, but not for the male. The female clusters show greater consensus on a wide variety of topics than do equal numbers of subjects characterized by similar positions in respect to single control principles.

Female Cluster 2, which shows the most impressive difference, seems to show a general response set for agreement. This cluster is, however, even more homogeneous in agreement to a particular set of items. We selected 26 items from the Inventory in which agreement seemed clearly indicative of obsessive-compulsive tendencies (e.g., "when playing a hand of cards, I like to keep the tricks in a neat, orderly arrangement"), a syndrome selected because it was relatively easy to identify. Female Cluster 2 agreed unanimously with 14 of the 26 items and disagreed with none; Group 2-A, low in field-articulation, agreed with 6 and disagreed with 5; Group 2-B, representing sharpening, agreed with 2 and disagreed with 3. The cluster agreed with significantly more of these items than either group ($p < .025$). To rule out the factor of response set, we selected another 26 items by choosing every eighth item in the Inventory and replacing all those related to compulsiveness. In this random sample of 26 "noncompulsive" items, Cluster 2 agreed unanimously with 4 items and disagreed with 4. When their agreement to the 26 "compulsive" items was tested against agreement to the 208 "noncompulsive" items, the difference was significant ($p < .05$, one-tailed test). Apparently, response set—the tendency to agree with an item regardless of content—does not account for the cluster's homogeneity of agreement to "compulsive" items.

This finding must be considered as only tentative because of the methodological limitations referred to earlier in this chapter, but it raises some intriguing questions. On the face of it, the greater consensus for the cluster on these items seems to suggest that style is a more effective basis for predicting defenses than individual control principles. The "obsessive-compulsive" items included in the inventory do not, however, provide an adequate basis on which to evaluate this behavior and the defenses underlying it. Only one of the three subjects in Cluster 2 was rated high on the defense of isolation (presumed to be one of the main defenses underlying obsessive-compulsive behavior) in the more comprehensive analyses described in Chapter 11 that were based upon Rorschach protocols. The other two subjects were rated as "mixed" and "narcisisstic" in this more elaborate analysis of major defenses.

Two possibilities suggest themselves: (a) subjects in the cluster have more homogeneous conscious self-conceptions than subjects similar along single control dimensions, above and beyond the actual predominance of particular defenses in their defensive organizations; (b) obsessive-compulsive traits, although not always predominant in members of the cluster, are present in a sufficient degree to produce the observed similarity in their inventory responses.

Discussion

Whatever relationship is ultimately demonstrated between style and the kinds of self-evaluation provided by inventory responses, the analysis described above suggests the fruitfulness of exploring such complex behaviors from the vantage point of style.

What are the implications of these findings for understanding the clusters? For one thing, large consensus on the Inventory suggests that female cluster members have similar attitudes toward a wide variety of situations. We cannot be sure from the Inventory alone that they would *behave* alike when faced with a particular set of circumstances, but their *attitude* seems to be similar. Thus we can say that the clusters of women are relatively homogeneous as to attitude, or outlook, and in this way differ from the factor-score groups.

The relative lack of agreement shown by the control principle groups in response to the Inventory argues against making assumptions about a sharpening *type,* an extensive scanning *type,* etc. The same point is illustrated in the make-up of the clusters. The appearance of sharpening, for example, in two clearly distinguishable combinations (female Clusters 2 and 6, Table 5) indicates that sharpening is relevant only to a limited aspect of cognitive or-

Table 5

INVENTORY ITEM CONSENSUS

Subjects	Distinguishing Characteristics	N	Agree	Disagree	Total
Female Cluster 2	Low Field-Articulation; Sharpening	3	91	16	107
Group 2-A	Low Field-Articulation	3	46	22	68
Group 2-B	Sharpening	3	43	30	73
Female Cluster 5	High Field-Articulation; Broad Equivalence Range	4	25	32	57
Group 5-A	High Field-Articulation	4	29	23	52
Group 5-B	Broad Equivalence Range	4	30	17	47
Female Cluster 6	High Field-Articulation; Sharpening	3	41	49	90
Group 6-A	High Field-Articulation	3	39	40	79
Group 6-B	Sharpening	3	43	30	73

Table 5 (Continued)

Subjects	Distinguishing Characteristics	N	Item Consensus		
			Agree	Disagree	Total
Male Cluster 1	High Scanning; Constricted Control	3	35	21	56
Group 1-A	High Scanning	3	20	40	60
Group 1-B	Constricted Control	3	26	30	56
Male Cluster 3	High Scanning; Tolerance for Unrealistic Experiences	5	18	8	26
Group 3-A	High Scanning	5	11	14	25
Group 3-B	Tolerance for Unrealistic Experiences	5	29	5	34
Male Cluster 6	Low Scanning; Constricted Control	3	56	24	80
Group 6-A	Low Scanning (same $\underline{Ss}$ as Cluster 6)	3	—	—	—
Group 6-B	Constricted Control	3	26	30	56

ganization; it does not dictate a subject's other factor scores, nor does it tell us much about broader aspects of his personality organization.

The proof of the style hypothesis—that the clusters represent something more than the sum of their parts—must await further experiments. The present Inventory findings should be followed up more systematically by relating cluster and factor scores to various complex behaviors. Still another possibility is to examine the performance of several people from different clusters on a particular task to see how they differ. Such an approach would require observation of the *processes* by which responses are achieved, rather than exploration of relationships between outcome scores.

11

COGNITIVE CONTROLS AND DEFENSES

In Chapter 1 cognitive controls were described as structures intervening between motivational states and response, but not tied to specific drives. In this respect they reflect a function ordinarily attributed to defenses. In psychoanalytic theory, defenses are conceived of as relatively stable organizations serving to modulate and affect the consummation of needs; and their operations are effected through such cognitive functions as memory, concept formation, perception, and judgment. Repression and denial are inferred from failure and elisions in recall and perception; regression from indicators of developmentally earlier thought modes or from qualities of thinking that characterize the primary process. Thus, control principles and defenses are somewhat alike. The two concepts came into being, however, for different reasons. Defenses were originally conceived of as modes of resolving conflict; control principles were conceived of solely as modes of coping with certain insistent configurations and events in external reality. That control principles can exercise a delaying function with respect to drives is seen as a by-product of their essential characteristics as cognitive structures.

Possible relationships between control principles and defenses were first discussed by Klein (1954) in relation to the finding that constricted and flexible control, identified in responses to relatively neutral cognitive tasks (see Chapter 7), accounted in part for individual differences in the effects of thirst in a variety of cognitive tasks. At present, five ways of looking at the control-defense problem present themselves.

A. All defenses have adaptive as well as conflict-resolving attributes. Hartmann (1939, p. 14) has pointed out, for example, that in addition to its defensive properties, intellectualization "has another, reality-oriented, aspect also, showing that this mechanism of defense against instinctual drives may at the same time be regarded as an adaptive process." It is possible, therefore, that control and defense may be the same process looked at from two different vantage points—adaptation and conflict.

B. Defenses, as they emerge in the course of development, may generalize in such a way as to extend certain schemata of organization to adaptive behaviors. That is, "character defenses" may become preferred means of adaptation (see Hartmann, 1939, p. 26).

C. Particular emphases in the employment of defenses may be occasioned by individual variations in "the maturation and exercise of the apparatuses of the conflict-free ego sphere" (Hartmann, 1939, p. 106). Cognitive control principles—representing basic schemata of organization in adaptive behavior—may thus be preconditions for the emergence of defensive structures.

D. Control principles and defenses may be distinguishable in terms of their antecedent conditions. The antecedent conditions of defense operations always include internal conflict. The conflict may be the product of a drive and one's personal set of attitudes toward its expression or a drive and society's restrictions on its satisfaction. The ensuing anxiety, guilt, or shame precedes defense. The defense serves to delay satisfaction by disguising and displacing the need, so that the subsequent behavior contains derivatives of both the drive and the prohibitions. Anna Freud's monograph (1936) contains many illustrations of this process. We assume that the antecedent conditions of cognitive control principles need not involve an internal conflict: primary among these antecedents are realistic issues, such as the solving of a problem, the satisfaction of a biological need, or the performance of a task.

E. If cognitive controls and defenses are related to each other but have different antecedent conditions, it may ultimately be most economical to conceive of repression and leveling (or isolation and extreme scanning) as two aspects of a higher-order principle governing a large segment of secondary-process functioning.

The present study provided an opportunity to test specific hypotheses concerning relationships between two sets of control principles and defenses—leveling-sharpening and repression and scanning and isolation—and to review again the relationships between the control and defense concepts.

LEVELING AND REPRESSION

In Chapter 3, we employed leveling and sharpening to describe the loss or preservation of distinctions among a series of stimuli. Levelers are characterized by maximal assimilation effects, and by memory organizations in which the fine shades of distinctions among individual elements are lost. This interpretation describes the tendency of levelers to ignore size differences in the successively presented squares of the Schematizing Test, to show large assimilation effects in Time Error Tests, and to experience difficulty in naming the colors in Part II of the Color-Word Test.

In psychoanalytic writings, repression proper, as distinguished from primal repression (Freud, 1915), is conceived of as the withdrawal of consciousness from an idea with which an unpleasant affect is associated. According to Freud, this expulsion from consciousness is assisted by the attraction exerted by an already unconscious idea. Freud wrote (1915, p. 87): "We have to consider . . . the attraction exercised by what was originally repressed upon everything with which it can establish a connection. Probably the tendency to repression would fail of its purpose [i.e., to remove a potentially dangerous idea from consciousness] if these forces did not co-operate, if there were not something previously repressed ready to assimilate that which is rejected from consciousness." Thus, the process of repression is at least analogous to the process of assimilation apparently measured in our tests of leveling. In both repression and leveling a new idea or experience assimilates to an older one by virtue of the relationship between them. As a consequence, the assimilated idea loses its individuality, and hence its availability to consciousness as a discrete entity. It seems plausible to assume that repression as a typical way of coping with internal conflict can occur most easily in persons whose memory organization is congenial to this kind of easy assimilation. Where such a process is not a natural outcome of the person's basic patterns of memory organization, other ways of dealing with traumatic material may appear.

Clinical examinations have taught us that persons in whom repression is the principal defense (hysterical neurotics or hysterical characters) possess typical and easily recognizable thought organizations. For instance, Rapaport et al. (1945) and Schafer (1948) report that it is the hallmark of such persons that they experience difficulty in extracting single ideas from memory frames of reference. It is not uncommon, for example, that when asked "Where is Egypt?" in the information subtest of the Wechsler-Bellevue Intelligence Scale, such persons say "Somewhere in the East," or when asked "Where is Brazil?" say, "In a jungle, somewhere—near Argentina."

These apparent similarities between leveling and repression led us to explore possible relationships between the two processes. The specific question we asked was: Are persons who rely on repression as their principal means of dealing with conflict-arousing ideas levelers in our laboratory tests?

Method

Repression cannot be observed directly. One cannot count the number of times in a given period a person represses, nor is it feasible to test subjects in laboratory stress situations and observe which of them repress and which do not. Repression occurs in circumstances that are highly individual; we cannot safely assume that any prearranged stress situation will trigger long-standing conflicts in a given person. Even if we could create a situation that would give rise to repressive behavior in individuals characterized by repression as a major defense, we could not surmount the problem of identifying and measuring the phenomenon. We are thus forced to infer repression from the presumed effects of lifelong reliance upon this defense: constriction of ideation, absence of intellectualizing, unreflectiveness, naïveté, relatively unmodulated affect.

Subjects were classified in terms of predominant defenses on the basis of performances in the Rorschach Test. This classification was carried out jointly by two of the experimenters (RWG and PSH), both of whom are experienced in the use of the test. It was done without reference to the performances of subjects in the laboratory tests. Each protocol was read several times. Following tentative classification in terms of predominant defenses, doubts and disagreements were reconciled. Because of the nature of the evaluation process, it is not possible to record here all the aspects of Rorschach performance that played a part in the classification of individual protocols. As aids to clinical judgment, these experimenters made use of the following specific indicators suggestive of long-standing, pervasive use of repression. It is to be understood, however, that in every instance the evaluation process went beyond the use of these indicators.

1. *Verbalizations.*

   A. Expressive reactions to the stimulus materials, such as "Oh my!" "This is pretty!" "How ugly!" etc.

   B. Phobic verbalizations, such as a "weird animal," "I have an aversion to bugs," "a nasty spider," etc.

2. *Notable lack of specificity.* This indicator includes such comments as "standing at the table or something," and extremely bare and unelaborated reports of "paints," "ink," etc.

3. *Failures.*

4. *Poor integrative efforts.* The unusually repressive person is often unable to cope with the complexity of entire blots or major portions of them.

5. *Childlike material.* Expressions of unusual naïveté, unreflectiveness, impulsiveness, and infantile content; personal references or unusually concrete references to past experience, e.g., "It looks like a bat because I've seen them in caves."

6. *Symbolic content without awareness of the significance of these responses.* This indicator is exemplified by such responses as "A small but comfortable bay. Ships could be very comfortable in that bay."

7. *Little variety in content.*

8. *Score indicators.*

   A. Fewer than twenty-five responses.

   B. Fewer than two human movement responses.

   C. Emphasis on color, unusual predominance of *CF* and *C*.

Results

Eight of the thirty men were judged to rely upon repression as their principal defense. Of these eight, six were levelers as indicated by scores in the upper half of the distribution of leveling-sharpening index scores (no factor scores could be obtained for men). These scores consisted of average standard scores for two measures (1. Schematizing: Ranking Accuracy; 3. Schematizing: Increment Error). A high-average standard score, indicating leveling, represented a low ranking-accuracy score and a high increment-error score. This result was not significant but was in the expected direction. Five of the eight men were in the leveling half of each of the scores used to obtain the index.

Repression was a prominent defense in eleven of the thirty women. Nine of these eleven women were relatively extreme levelers in the distribution of Factor II scores (see Chapter 9). This result was significant at less than the .03 point in the binomial distribution. Eight of the eleven women were in the leveling half of the ranking-accuracy scores ($p < .125$), nine in the leveling half of the increment-error scores ($p < .05$), both basic measures of leveling-sharpening in this and previous experiments. Eight of these subjects ($p < .125$) were in the leveling half of the distribution of assimilation scores (4. Kinesthetic Time Error: Assimilation) derived from performances in the other procedure used in earlier studies of leveling-sharpening.

Neither the eight men nor the eleven women "repressors" formed a significant proportion of those in the upper or lower halves of distributions of criterion scores (factor scores; average standard scores for major measures; or, in the case of scanning, average-error scores for Size Estimation Test I) for any of the *other* control principles.

Thus, although the numbers of men and women who were judged to rely upon repression as their primary defense were small, results for both sexes pointed to a close association between repression and leveling.

Scanning and Isolation

Psychoanalytic theory has paid considerably less attention to isolation than to repression. This is not surprising, since repression and hysteria held central positions in Freud's first formulations of the general psychoanalytic theory. Indeed, at one time he equated repression with all of defense. It was not until 1926 (in *The Problem of Anxiety*) that he referred to "isolation" as still another defense mechanism of the ego. He had described the defense without naming it, however, in "Notes upon a Case of Obsessional Neurosis," published in 1909.

Briefly, the defense of isolation operates to separate affect from idea, so that potentially unpleasant ideas become more tolerable. Cleavages occurring within *networks* of ideas, such that individual components are rendered tolerable, are also referred to this mechanism.

Freud speculated that isolation is accomplished by the hypercathexis of ideas, words, and things. Habitual reliance upon isolation presumably divests thought of its affective components, which produces an excessive emphasis upon the operations of logic, attentiveness to spatial and temporal attributes of objects, and deemphasis of their expressive attributes and affective reverberations. Similar qualities appear in isolators' relationships with people. Extreme isolation is exemplified by syllogistic logic, in which impulse, whim, and feeling find no direct representation. Schafer (1948) has noted that isolation and repression have almost opposite effects upon the contents of awareness. Repression narrows awareness; isolation broadens it. By keeping ideas separate from their emotional components, isolation increases the repertoire of consciously accessible ideas; even perverse, murderous, and incestuous thoughts can be admitted to consciousness without horror or disgust.

Schlesinger (1954) noted the similarity of an extreme focusing tendency to isolation (see Chapter 6). In a later paper, Holzman and Klein (1956b) reported findings which suggested a statistical relationship between the presence of isolation as a prominent defense and the scanning control (which represents a redefinition of focusing).

Method

Two experimenters (RWG and PSH) jointly selected subjects in whom isolation was apparently the major defense, by means of the Rorschach signs listed below. It is important to note, however, that classification was not based solely on these indicators, but often included other considerations.

1. *Special qualities of verbalization.*

    A. Total absence of infantile verbalizations, such as childlike comments, baby talk, etc.

B. Absence of spontaneous "expressive" comments concerning the test materials.

C. Expressions of doubt and qualification, such as "either this or that," "if you stretch your imagination," and the like.

2. *Unusual specificity*. This indicator may take at least two forms.

A. A form of specificity that would differentiate an isolator from other subjects, but that would result in no striking difference in the $F+$ percentage, is qualification and elaboration of percepts that are of poor form quality, e.g., "The irregularities around the outside of the figure remind me of a coastline with a small number of outlying islands." To be strong indicators of isolation, these elaborations must refine the reported percept. Such elaborations as the following are *not* considered indicative of isolation: "Makes me think of the Andes Mountains—maybe an Aztec temple." This elaboration detracts from the specificity and precision of the response.

B. The specificity or overspecificity may appear in the report of the percept itself, as in the following examples: "a vertebra from the lower portion of the spine," or "petals of a jonquil, looking down on it."

3. *Rumination about symmetry*. This indicator refers to verbalizations that go beyond simple comments about symmetry to more elaborate discussions of it.

4. *Intellectualizing*. When present, intellectualizing must be "on the mark" and effective. Examples are: "I can also view it medically"; "has a slight appendage at the bottom, perhaps a poorly developed foot of some sort"; and "a Mephistophelian-like profile."

5. *Content indicators*.

A. Unusual variety of content.

B. Anal content.

C. Unusual emphasis on objects.

D. The presence of mechanical content, such as "tweezers," or "nose of a pair of pliers."

E. Complex representations of balance or control, such as might appear in the response, "the governor on a motor."

6. *Score indicators*.

A. More than thirty responses.

B. Percentage of total responses in which F is the primary determinant greater than 90.

C. Number of $CF + C$ responses less than number of FC responses.

D. More than three human movement responses.

E. $F+$ percentage of all responses in which form (F) is primary greater than 90. In records in which the $F+$ percentage does not reach this level, some of the $F-$ responses of a subject classified as an "isolator" should contain elaborations or attempts at specificity which qualify the poor form quality of the response (see 2A above). For example, the response, "snake's eyes," is qualitatively different from the response, "eyes." To be considered manifestations of isolation, these qualifications should represent attempts at increased specificity, rather than simple fabulation.

Results

Isolation was conspicuous in the Rorschach protocols of nine of the thirty men. Eight of these nine men had Factor I scores in the extreme-scanning half of the distribution. This result was significant at less than the .02 point in the binomial distribution. Six of these nine men had average-error scores for Size Estimation Test I in the lower half of the distribution. This result was in the predicted direction, but not significant.

Five of the six women ($p < .11$) judged to rely principally on isolation had scores in the lower half of the average-error distribution for Size Estimation Test I (factor scores could not be obtained for women). Although this was not a statistically significant result, it was in the predicted direction and suggests that isolation and scanning may also be related in women.

"Isolators" were not significantly different from other subjects on criterion measures (factor scores or average standard scores for major measures) for any of the other control principles except constricted-flexible control. Seven of the nine men "isolators" had average standard scores in the constricted-control half of the distribution of index scores (derived from 17. Color-Word: Interference; and 21. Size Estimation II: Constant Error, Perceptual) for this control. This result is significant at less than the .10 point in the binomial expansion. The index scores of the "isolators" represented high interference in the Color-Word Test and relative underestimation in Size Estimation Test II. It seems possible that in isolation, as in scanning, extreme investment of attention in external objects may lead to unusual responsiveness to "irrelevant" and "relevant" cues alike. This could be an impediment to performance on the Color-Word Test.

Discussion

The results were consistent with our hypothesis of an association between repression and leveling and isolation and extreme scanning. The relationship of repression and leveling has been verified in a separate study by Holzman and Gardner (1959) which followed the present one.

It is important to note here that these predicted relationships beween defenses and controls are unidirectional. Extreme repressors tend to be levelers and extreme isolators tend to be broad scanners, but the converse is not true. An extreme leveler may or may not be unusually repressive; an extreme scanner may or may not be notable for isolation. Thus, a variety of defensive patterns may characterize extreme levelers or scanners. The unidirectionality of these relationships may offer some support to the hypothesis that controls provide preconditions for the emergence of defenses. That is, repression may be a likely defense in an extreme leveler, but not in an extreme sharpener. In this view, repression would emerge against a background of a *general* tendency toward maximal assimilation between present and past experiences that leads to relatively undifferentiated memory organizations. Although other conditions are necessary for the actual occurrence of repression, the tendency toward assimilation (leveling) seems to be a necessary antecedent structure.

A final answer to questions concerning the relationship between various controls and defenses is, of course, not provided by the present data. Adequate understanding of these relationships may be possible only when developmental studies of the emergence of both controls and defenses are completed.

12

RETROSPECT AND PROSPECT

Our purpose in the present study was to test several principles of cognitive consistency, observed in earlier studies, and to explore relationships between them. Each of the six principles defined in the earlier studies was evident in the cognitive behaviors of the present sample, in one or the other sex. Among men, the clear factors were scanning and tolerance for unrealistic experiences; among women, field-articulation, leveling-sharpening, and equivalence range. The interpretation of the scanning factor is a reformulation of the earlier focusing principle; field-articulation represents a composite of the earlier constricted-flexible control and field dependence-independence principles.

These dimensions of individual consistency were apparent in a broad array of test situations. They were isolated in the face of several obvious forms of extraneous variance, e.g., individual differences in variability along the dimensions; special training; and limitations imposed by the measures used (largely "error" scores). The results confirm our original assumption that the control principles are linked to specific classes of adaptive requirements (e.g., to categorize, to evaluate successive stimuli, to articulate fields containing conflicting information). That is, the activation of individual cognitive controls requires particular *adaptive intentions* and particular arrangements of stimuli, as suggested by Klein (1958). In addition, we find that the control principles are not restricted in their operation to specific sensory modalities, or even to the traditional divisions of cognitive behavior into memory, perception, learning, etc.

Perhaps the most salient new finding of the present study is that these control principles are independent of each other. To know that a person is an extreme leveler does not allow us to predict his preference for broad or narrow conceptual categories (his equivalence range), the degree to which he articulates a stimulus field inducing perceived incongruity, how widely he scans, or his tolerance for unrealistic experiences. This is an important finding. It implies that it is necessary to sample the various controls in a person's cognitive behavior if we are to understand his "cognitive style." This is particularly true since even the simplest-appearing adaptive behaviors may involve more than one cognitive factor. In terms of psychological processes, our studies of cognitive control principles have dealt primarily with major facets of (a) attention; (b) the interactions of percepts and memories; (c) concept formation; and (d) modes of dealing with unrealistic experiences.

Although the field-articulation principle could be explained in terms of the mobilization of attention (see Köhler and Adams [1958] on articulation as a function of attentional intensity), it seems probable that the actual functions involved are those employed in a differential cathexis of relevant and irrelevant cues. That is, field-articulation seems to represent facility in the *direction* of attention to certain aspects of stimulation while avoiding or actively withholding attention from other aspects. In this sense, the principle is related to, but distinct from, the scanning principle. The latter refers to the characteristic breadth of attention deployment under relatively free conditions, rather than to the capacity to concentrate attention, when required, upon certain relevant aspects of stimulation. Thus, these control principles refer to two major aspects of use of attention. Their differential employment is linked to the particular adaptive situation in which the person finds himself.

Although we have evidence only that leveling-sharpening describes the tendency toward assimilation between percepts and memory traces, this principle may also be rooted in attention. It is conceivable, for example, that a sharpener may have available large quantities of free energy for hypercathexis of new stimuli which renders them unusually clear and distinct. It is possible that levelers show large assimilation effects because they have limited amounts of energy for hypercathexis of new stimuli. Thus, extremely repressive persons could be levelers because the massive countercathexis of ideas held out of consciousness uses up large quantities of energy that would otherwise be available for hypercathexis of new stimuli. If this were true, the individual consistencies described by the leveling-sharpening principle would appear to be determined by the defensive structure.

Anticipation is another process parameter that may be essential to an understanding of the leveling-sharpening principle. Subjects who lag behind the trend of increase in the sizes of squares in the Schematizing Test may be influenced by an anticipation of smallness built up early in the test. In other situations, such as time-error tests, their slowness in changing anticipations may show itself in exaggerated experiences of contrast. For example, the anticipation of heaviness built up by experiencing the interpolated heavy weight (see Chapter 3) could lead to underestimation of the subsequent lighter weight and hence to a "leveling" response. Further studies of this aspect of leveling-sharpening are obviously called for.

The processes underlying the equivalence range principle are less clear. We observe individual consistencies in the breadth of realms subsumed under single conceptual rubrics, and we note that inclusion or exclusion of an object from a realm is based upon judgment, rather than upon perception. But the means by which these realms are formed and the relation of realm-breadth to other aspects of concept formation need to be clarified.

The processes underlying tolerance for unrealistic experiences also require further study. Although the individual consistencies observed in previous studies seemed clear in male subjects of the present study, the means by which subjects "accept" or "reject" unrealistic experiences remains unclear. Perhaps this control, in contrast to some of the others, is relevant to a relatively high level of cognitive complexity and involves a wide variety of response processes all serving to maintain the relative position of the ego in relation (a) to drives and their low-order derivatives, and (b) to external reality (see Rapaport, 1951b, 1958).

The present study has provided us with some first glimpses of relations between cognitive control principles and the structures for resolving internal conflict (defenses). Cognitive controls are evident in behaviors which do not involve internal conflict. Still, descriptively, certain control principles do seem quite similar to particular defenses, at least in the kind of adaptive consequences they lead to. A number of hypotheses concerning these relationships were proposed (see Chapter 11). Although some of the evidence seems to support the conception that cognitive controls may be preconditions for defenses, developmental studies are needed to answer questions concerning the emergence of these aspects of cognitive organization.

Further Studies Needed

The work we have described in this monograph suggests a variety of further studies. We have attempted to describe some of the most obvious of these in the sections below.

The Validity of Control Principles

Although some of the control principles observed in the present study lend themselves readily to interpretation, others are still relatively unclear. Scanning, for example, has been assumed to represent the orientation of attention in response to stimulation. Following Piaget, we have assumed that the degree of centrations in certain tests determines the relative apparent sizes of stimuli. The validity of this interpretation is now being tested directly, in a study at the Menninger Foundation. Relative centration times on standard and comparison stimuli in our Size Estimation Tests and a number of other aspects of scanning behavior are being measured by electronic recording of subjects' eye movements. These direct measures of scanning are being studied in relation to other forms of scanning and to incidental learning and noticing in a variety of situations. Gardner (1959) has shown that errors of the standard in Size Estimation Test I are related to errors of the standard in response to the inverted-T, presumably indicating the validity of the interpretation of scanning in the present study. Gardner and Long (1959) have provided further evidence concerning errors of the standard made by three samples of subjects.

To take another example, we have implied that field-articulation represents individual differences in the selective direction of attention. We have assumed that extreme field-articulators are unusually adept at directing attention to relevant portions of complex fields. As a partial test of the validity of this interpretation, a study is being conducted (Gardner, in preparation) in which measures of field-articulation and scanning—conceived of as guiding two distinct aspects of attention direction—are used to predict response to two types of visual illusions (a preliminary report on part of this study has been made by Gardner [1957]). Another possible explanation of the means by which complex fields are articulated also needs to be tested, however. Köhler and Adams (1958) have shown that the articulation of fields may be a function of the intensity of attention. What we have called field-articulation could also be the product of this aspect of response. An explicit test of this possibility is needed.

The Generality of Control Principles

Studies of individual consistencies such as we have reported lend themselves to many extensions. In the main we have confined our studies to laboratory tasks. Nevertheless, the descriptions of the control principles tempt us to explore the general hypothesis that they are important determinants of other categories of observable behavior. Murney (1955), for example, has attempted to investigate the relationship of performance in the Schematizing Test to certain specific personality traits.

Formulating hypotheses from a control principle to new situations in which the control principle may be relevant must be preceded by careful consideration of the problems confronting the subject in the new test situation. He may be described as "passive," for example, but such a global description does not specify the circumstances in which passivity may occur. Thus studies relating a cognitive control to "passivity" are unlikely to yield definitive results because the so-called "passive" subject may be quite active on the cognitive tests. Passivity and cognitive controls tap different aspects of behavior, and attempts to relate them may muddy the conception of cognitive controls and lead to unwarranted conclusions about their relation to interpersonal behaviors.

More effective generality studies are rooted in careful analysis of the functional implications of the control principles. Sloane (1959), for example, has effectively shown the relevance of equivalence range to a variety of categorizing behaviors, including the categorizing of pictures of persons. Further generality studies are now in progress at the Menninger Foundation. A large-scale study of equivalence range includes tests of concept formation in probability estimates, the homogeneity of conceptions of the self and others, categorization of descriptions of behavior, etc. The generality of leveling-sharpening is being explored in a study that includes (a) further tests of process-trace interaction (e.g., assimilation among shapes); (b) tests of interaction among traces per se (with original registration equated); (c) tests developed by Wulf (1922); (d) the quality of organization of early memories; (e) serial reproduction situations developed by Paul (1959); and (f) additional tests of proactive and retroactive interference employing meaningful story materials. The generality of the scanning principle is being explored in studies of incidental learning.

Many other studies of the generality of cognitive controls are possible. For example, tolerance for unrealistic experiences may be relevant to individual differences in response to stimulus deprivation. "Intolerant" persons may be particularly uncomfortable when many of the usual criteria of reality are removed.

A broad and largely unexplored area concerns the various compositions or stylistic arrangements in which individual control principles may coexist in the personality (see Chapter 10), and the relation of control and style to various aspects of social behavior, including the perception of the self and other persons.

The Stability of Cognitive Controls

Witkin et al. (1954) have provided evidence of the stability of field dependence-independence over time. Holzman (1954) has provided indirect evidence of the stability of indices of leveling-sharpening. The study of intellectual abilities by Gardner, Jackson, and Messick (1958; also, monograph to be published, *Psychological Issues*) provides strong indirect evidence of the stability of several control principles over a number of months. Further studies of consistency over time are obviously needed, however, both of individual measures and of factors derived from groups of measures.

A related problem concerns the elasticity of controls when a person is subjected to special training or experiences, or special motivational conditions. It is important to know, for example, whether a leveler *can* behave like a sharpener if he is highly motivated to do so. In line with this general problem of the modifiability of controls, it may be particularly fruitful to observe changes in controls in persons who are undergoing intensive psychotherapy or psychoanalysis. In these studies, it may also be possible to learn more about the relations between controls and defenses. It is conceivable, for example, that a pathologically rigid defense is employed less rigidly and pervasively following psychoanalysis, but that the control principle to which it is linked persists unchanged.

Systematic Variation of Criterion Tasks

For the most part, we have varied stimulus conditions in our search for intraindividual consistencies. One might profitably hold the stimuli constant and vary the instructions. For example, subjects in the Schematizing Test could be informed of the true range of the stimuli, or the order in which the stimuli will appear; or the inspection of sample squares during the instruction period could be eliminated. One might present the tasks as "intelligence" tests, or otherwise vary the general set under which the subject approaches the tasks. Such studies would provide further evidence concerning the generality and stability of control principles.

Controls and Defenses

The present study and the subsequent study of leveling and repression by Holzman and Gardner (1959) have shown the fruitfulness of exploring relationships between various aspects of cognitive structure (see Klein, 1954). It is now time to carry out larger studies of relations between controls and defenses. Since an adequate evaluation of defenses is difficult to achieve by other methods, it may be well to study persons who have been observed intensively in the clinic.

Cognitive Controls and Intelligence Test Performance

The study by Gardner et al. showing definite links between control principles and various "intellectual abilities" points the way to a reassessment of the independence traditionally assumed of intelligence test performance and generalized personality dimensions.

Since tests of intelligence are similar in many ways to our tests of cognitive organizing principles, to hold intelligence constant in the investigation of a cognitive control principle creates a pseudo issue. Intelligence does not involve a "g" factor that can be studied as an entity. It seems likely that the control principles are involved in responses to various subtests of intelligence scales. The Wechsler-Bellevue Intelligence Test (Wechsler, 1958), for example, is made up of eleven subtests, each of which presumably taps a separate intellectual function. As Rapaport and his coworkers have argued (1945), the Information subtest samples memory, the Comprehension subtest samples judgment, Digit Span samples attention, Similarities samples concept formation, etc. Most of these functions correspond to functions involved in our tests of cognitive control principles. Several functions may be required, however, for effective response in a single subtest. To answer the question "How far is it from Paris to New York?" in the Information subtest of the Wechsler-Bellevue Intelligence Scale—a question which presumably tests the subject's realm of previously learned material—one must first attend to the examiner so that the question is apprehended. The form of the question sets up an anticipation for response: the subject must think of distances, not climate or the name of the ocean that separates the two cities. Then he must scan his memory frame of reference for the appropriate response. Thus, like tests of cognitive controls, subtests on intelligence scales are not pure tests of specific functions.

One immediate implication of these comments is that it makes little sense to insist on controlling the "intelligence" level of subjects in studies of cognitive control principles.

On *a priori* grounds, we would expect a relationship between behavior in the criterion tasks of the control principles and behavior in certain intelligence tests. For example, such Wechsler performance subtests as Picture Completion, Block Designs, and Object Assembly are obviously weighted with the requirement to articulate complex fields. It is reasonable to expect a relationship between these subtests and the field articulation tests designed by Witkin. The learning efficiency subtest of the Babcock Test (1930) may be a good addition to the group of leveling-sharpening tests, since both presumably tap intake and recall of serially exposed material.

There is another, more conceptual, similarity between the functions underlying both cognitive controls and intellectual behaviors:

they may coincide with increasing control over action. Piaget's conception of intellectual development from its sensorimotor stages to its formal operational stage and the psychoanalytic theory of intellectual advancement from primary-process thinking to reality-oriented, secondary-process thinking both grant to intellectual functions the role of control and delay structures. They serve to channel needs and impulses by mediating between drive and reality. Their role as delay mechanisms is similar to the delay function assumed for cognitive controls. Both intellectual functioning and cognitive controls act as rudders, steering response. Thus, two apparently disparate functional aspects of personality may actually involve similar or identical structures. Studies of the origin and development of both cognitive controls and intellectual functioning are required. Piaget's attempt (1936, 1947) to investigate intellectual development represents a rich beginning that is unfettered by the constraints of standard intelligence tests.

Control Principles, Empathy, and Communication

An intriguing set of questions concerns the effects of control-principle variations on communication and empathic understanding between individuals. It is a common observation in treatment clinics that psychotherapists of equal skill and sensitivity vary in their effectiveness with different types of patients. Certain therapists are able to arrive at better results with patients having certain personality characteristics. At times this is expressed by the therapist in such terms as, "I just couldn't work with that patient"; or "I feel that I am with this patient all the way." The degrees of empathy expressed in these comments may in part be manifestations of stylistic variables in cognition. Whether two people with similar cognitive styles achieve better empathic understanding than two people with different styles is an avenue for research that has practical significance for both diagnosis and psychotherapy.

Additional Control Principles

The present group of control principles is not thought to exhaust the realm of enduring attributes of cognitive organization relevant to adaptation. Equivalence range may apply only to the breadth of categories formed in concept formation; leveling-sharpening may apply only to interactions between percepts and traces; field-articulation and scanning may be two of a larger number of organizing principles relevant to the deployment of attention in particular kinds of adaptive situations. Facets of cognitive functioning we have not yet considered may be controlled by hitherto unanticipated principles. One unexplored possibility is a tendency to organize stimuli in physiognomic terms (Klein, 1951).

Developmental Studies

When the construct validity and generality of controls have been adequately determined for adults, studies can be done of the developmental emergence of these principles. It is important to know at what ages consistent individual differences in various control principles first become apparent. It is possible that the principles vary in time of emergence and are subject to different degrees of fluctuation in the course of development. Only in developmental studies can the relations of controls to defenses or to intellectual functioning be fully evaluated. The emergence of these principles should also be explored in relation to the developmental crises described by Erikson (1950).

Summary

We have seen evidence of the operation of several cognitive structures in a wide variety of situations. We consider these structures essential aspects of ego organization. Our study has provided us with glimpses of relations between two of these structures and certain defensive structures defined earlier by Freud and observed primarily in the clinic. Although in some ways it is a long leap from the laboratory to the psychotherapist's consulting room, our studies of individual consistencies have enabled us to see links between the cognitive controls that govern adaptive behaviors and those relevant to the channeling of drives in conflict. The problem that joins the laboratory to the psychoanalyst's couch is that of personality organization, involving phenomena that cannot be adequately sampled in either of these settings alone. The essential question we have posed concerns the individual's style of adaptation—his mode of coming to terms with the world—conceived of as the patterning or arrangement of his functioning along several dimensions of cognitive control. We have sampled a vast area where the efforts of the healer and the experimenter may converge. We regard the present study as a step toward such a convergence. Our results raise more questions than they answer, but in so doing help to delineate a fertile area for further study.

APPENDICES

APPENDIX A
Table 6

INTERCORRELATIONS OF MAJOR SCORES[a]

Women

	Score	1	2	3	4	5	6	7
[b,c]1.	Schematizing: Ranking Accuracy		-41	-32	-09	12	25	-03
[b,c]2.	Schematizing: Increment Error (Regression)	-07		84	31	-06	19	15
3.	Schematizing: Increment Error	01	90		44	-04	12	24
[b,c]4.	Kinesthetic Time Error: Assimilation	16	39	49		-23	-09	17
[c]5.	Kinesthetic Time Error: Time Error	-06	-14	-17	-10		24	13
[c]6.	Apparent Movement: Mean Movement Threshold	10	-24	-16	-17	03		16
[b,c]7.	Apparent Movement: Mean Range	-18	22	15	14	25	-15	
[b,c]8.	Aniseikonic Lenses: Log Recognition Time	18	-30	-25	-07	09	15	-01
[b,c]9.	Aniseikonic Lenses: Mean Deviation	-11	11	06	-29	31	-07	06
[b,c]10.	Object Sorting: Number of Groups	06	35	21	02	05	-13	17
[b,c]11.	Size Constancy: Mean Diameter	-37	02	07	14	35	05	02
[c]12.	Size Constancy: Improvement	-05	-06	-13	-14	30	12	-04
[c]13.	Size Constancy: Area of Uncertainty	02	-01	-03	00	-03	07	-24
[b,c]14.	Size Estimation I: Average Error	-10	-12	-16	-22	23	15	05
[c]15.	Size Estimation I: Heaviness Effect	-10	-05	-05	30	-11	02	05
[c]16.	Picture Sorting: Number "Indifferent"	-13	11	08	09	-01	17	14
[b,c]17.	Color-Word: Interference	01	07	03	19	-04	-05	-16
[c]18.	Color-Word: Reading Time, Colors Alone	31	02	03	-13	06	-09	19
[c]20.	Color-Word: Incidental Recall	05	27	29	-03	01	02	-14
[b,c]21.	Size Estimation II: Constant Error, Perceptual	13	-10	-16	-32	-20	-05	-20
22.	Size Estimation II: Constant Error, Memory	08	-10	-17	-43	-05	-25	-07

		1	2	3	4	5	6	7
c	23. Size Estimation II: Change, Thirst Stimuli	-10	04	-04	-23	-01	-22	00
c	24. Size Estimation II: Change, Nonthirst Stimuli	07	-11	-11	-30	25	-34	18
c	25. Size Estimation II: Variability, Perceptual	-17	-20	-13	-05	01	42	-17
c	26. Size Estimation II: Variability, Memory	-45	-16	-22	-05	17	03	-04
c	27. Size Estimation II: Variability, Total Test	-27	-27	-26	-14	09	09	-06
b,c	28. Free Association: Percentage Distant, "Dry"	46	30	29	22	-23	13	06
c	29. Free Association: Percentage Distant, "House"	24	09	03	15	-41	07	-04
c	30. Free Association: Percentage "Home" Responses	19	-11	-18	-15	03	13	-28
	31. Free Association: Productivity	20	34	30	20	-01	08	28
b,c	32. Free Association: Average Length of Unit	-17	47	45	-04	12	-05	39
c	33. Rod and Frame: Average Error, Body Tilted	-02	15	09	06	37	20	20
c	34. Rod and Frame: Average Error, Body Erect	37	05	09	17	-01	29	12
b	35. Rod and Frame: Average Error, Total Test	21	13	11	13	12	30	21
b,c	36. Embedded Figures: Mean Log Time, Cluster I	-15	07	10	-20	20	26	16
b,c	37. Embedded Figures: Mean Log Time, Cluster II	-09	-11	-08	-08	-03	-27	13
	38. Embedded Figures: Mean Log Time, Total Test	-16	-11	-06	-12	07	-04	09
c	39. Embedded Figures: Geometricality of Descriptions	-19	16	12	26	16	07	18
	40. Field-Dependence Index	00	-05	-01	-03	18	09	24
	41. Age	-07	-12	-09	12	09	-13	23

Men

[a] Decimal points omitted. N was 30 for men and 30 for women, except for intercorrelations involving Rod and Frame Test scores, in which case N was 22 for men and 20 for women.
[b] Used (carried to three places) in the preliminary factor analyses.
[c] Used (carried to three places) in the 33-score factor analyses.

Table 6 (Continued)

Women

	8	9	10	11	12	13	14	15	16	17	18	20	21	22	23	24	25	26	27
1.	-58	17	14	-10	24	-09	-02	-03	13	-09	-12	-02	-29	-14	05	17	03	-16	-04
2.	06	-19	06	-03	00	01	16	-09	-08	20	10	12	-07	-15	-11	-18	15	22	30
3.	-03	-22	-04	-01	07	11	00	-08	03	19	-01	13	-03	-07	-01	-11	21	33	32
4.	06	00	00	06	00	-13	01	-09	25	-10	21	-06	42	19	-19	-16	-05	17	03
5.	-05	-23	03	03	39	37	27	-04	-19	-24	-26	-03	-31	-25	01	-06	00	-06	-06
6.	-16	04	07	00	40	07	16	16	-51	-04	02	22	-04	-05	-12	08	-10	-06	-03
7.	23	-34	08	-09	-03	-20	27	-23	-35	-07	29	41	31	08	-16	-26	25	14	16
8.		-31	-09	-06	-33	-16	13	25	-29	16	27	13	28	17	-03	-09	18	03	10
9.	03		22	-08	02	05	29	-15	15	31	-16	-52	07	09	04	05	01	-14	-13
10.	-08	-17		-51	-01	04	-13	-38	06	-15	-06	-15	-02	01	01	07	15	-35	-14
11.	-07	-05	-11		01	31	18	33	34	-02	26	06	32	39	25	15	-21	28	10
12.	14	14	-12	-15		46	12	-01	-35	-31	-09	16	-26	-10	28	-03	13	21	20
13.	07	-03	10	17	36		08	-03	16	-08	-06	09	-23	-10	29	-12	22	16	17
14.	07	-02	-02	-14	-04	18		-06	-10	19	04	-31	07	-18	-12	-53	32	28	34
15.	-10	06	18	-14	-14	-03	-51		-14	03	-15	-05	17	26	06	29	-02	15	18
16.	19	03	21	26	-17	-02	08	19		-06	04	-25	02	08	09	08	-06	03	-05
17.	07	-05	26	07	-08	-12	-16	27	32		04	-09	-16	-14	-07	02	33	16	37
18.	-08	20	-07	-47	05	-21	-19	-24	-10	-07		38	28	37	32	12	08	19	20
20.	14	-14	23	-34	00	-29	-28	06	-03	-02	11		-08	-02	00	10	08	05	05
21.	-01	06	12	-10	-25	18	08	-13	20	-32	21	-04		77	-03	12	-23	11	-10
22.	-10	10	29	-02	-13	19	15	-22	24	-07	21	-18	75		53	62	-15	15	01
23.	-16	13	33	03	-02	08	02	-13	20	24	02	-26	11	66		51	22	37	37
24.	-07	02	24	10	13	08	20	-18	08	20	13	-15	-03	58	61		-18	-19	-17

	8	9	10	11	12	13	14	15	16	17	18	20	21	22	23	24	25	26	27
25.	-04	07	-15	18	20	08	34	-15	13	-27	-13	-25	09	09	26	-16			
26.	02	21	-14	22	38	09	15	-12	-03	06	-34	-39	-21	02	42	08	56	38	72
27.	13	18	-14	18	25	04	32	-20	05	07	-21	-36	-11	21	53	25	69	89	84
28.	-20	-29	15	-22	-15	-18	-09	-06	-14	23	21	25	-16	-28	-29	-15	-41	-61	-61
29.	31	-28	12	-50	-02	-15	-43	23	02	31	11	40	-14	-27	-19	-25	-33	-41	-39
30.	-20	31	-17	08	-01	-02	04	01	10	09	-04	-14	08	03	-01	-07	01	-05	-08
31.	-43	-12	29	-04	-15	-10	-03	-07	05	-31	05	04	08	03	03	-10	06	-18	-20
32.	-39	07	20	20	-07	-07	08	-30	12	-34	12	05	04	15	27	08	18	-03	-02
33.	42	10	09	10	03	13	35	-02	26	-13	05	25	03	-30	-45	-41	-10	-28	-29
34.	37	-08	17	-06	-30	-32	-10	27	34	30	35	26	11	-02	-08	-10	01	-48	-23
35.	50	02	14	04	-15	09	12	12	36	08	23	31	08	-21	-38	-36	-06	-45	-33
36.	03	24	-02	38	15	28	31	-11	-14	03	-14	-26	-30	-19	-07	13	06	-01	02
37.	-02	02	17	15	-02	12	42	-19	-14	14	05	-49	-21	18	42	45	28	29	47
38.	11	03	10	30	13	23	42	-14	-17	21	-06	-38	-32	-03	14	37	19	21	35
39.	00	-09	09	-02	-13	-07	08	10	-17	-16	-12	36	-17	-35	-24	-35	-08	00	-09
40.	35	08	17	27	00	12	43	-06	11	23	12	-18	-18	-06	-04	23	09	-08	13
41.	-20	-24	-02	-08	-06	00	-04	02	23	-25	37	15	20	18	-07	15	-05	-25	-19

Men

Table 6 (Continued)

Women

	28	29	30	31	32	33	34	35	36	37	38	39	40	41
1.	29	11	37	03	-19	-03	14	06	-26	-28	-25	34	-12	14
2.	-46	-16	-28	25	27	03	00	02	14	17	16	-25	14	09
3.	-47	-15	-38	32	32	16	15	16	20	13	18	-21	18	12
4.	-24	-20	-05	15	30	21	39	32	13	13	11	-21	16	06
5.	23	19	16	-10	-24	-10	-38	-26	-18	-09	-08	-12	-19	00
6.	09	-17	23	20	13	-22	-31	-29	-24	-13	-14	02	-14	-08
7.	-05	-24	06	18	28	-25	-32	-30	-27	-05	-19	00	-22	-05
8.	-04	-16	06	-10	04	05	-05	00	03	12	01	-19	-02	-28
9.	00	01	11	-20	-13	20	21	21	27	28	28	-08	31	-10
10.	-42	-48	10	00	14	-25	-32	-30	-13	-21	-22	06	-24	-33
11.	16	08	-02	01	04	04	-03	00	06	11	19	-24	15	01
12.	-04	09	05	-08	-11	-10	-10	-11	03	-17	-03	-30	-05	43
13.	-18	-08	00	-48	-34	31	-02	12	33	14	39	-36	30	07
14.	-05	08	03	-19	-11	-02	-04	-03	12	38	30	-43	24	14
15.	04	10	-09	03	11	-06	-11	-09	-14	-09	-14	06	-16	-12
16.	-17	01	-27	-02	08	17	32	26	03	03	08	01	13	04
17.	06	-13	21	-14	-33	63	57	63	54	56	54	03	62	09
18.	20	-05	02	-08	23	-01	-02	-02	01	00	02	00	06	20
20.	05	-14	15	11	05	06	01	03	-25	-18	-19	07	-12	13
21.	-10	-25	-03	22	53	-28	-38	-35	-20	-11	-18	-13	-23	-24
22.	05	-16	-01	30	49	-19	-39	-31	-19	-26	-25	-07	-25	-21
23.	03	07	00	00	01	14	-01	07	15	-09	05	-16	10	05
24.	32	03	03	37	26	-05	-14	-11	-24	-40	-39	26	-32	-15
25.	-31	-22	07	-22	-17	33	11	24	18	21	18	-02	21	05
26.	-32	-07	-12	-03	08	39	35	39	29	47	41	-30	43	46
27.	-37	-18	-02	-13	-07	42	34	40	29	42	36	-20	41	39
28.		56	25	-02	22	-03	-07	-05	-12	-21	-15	36	-10	02
29.	50		-34	-13	-21	-04	08	02	-16	-22	-15	16	-11	24
30.	18	-20		-19	-49	41	17	30	09	12	13	17	23	-32
31.	24	-12	10		71	-46	-20	-34	-26	-28	-35	07	-35	-01
32.	00	-17	-25	57		-64	-47	-58	-34	-33	-42	04	-51	04
33.	07	-16	25	-17	-12		79	94	57	63	70	-16	88	-01
34.	15	36	-09	08	-13	32		95	56	58	60	-10	83	23
35.	13	09	10	-07	-09	86	76		60	64	68	-13	88	14
36.	07	-14	12	-06	10	18	16	21		73	90	-31	85	23
37.	-24	-23	-30	-18	07	-27	-03	-20	33		89	-39	85	20
38.	-14	-13	-21	-34	-08	-04	10	02	70	83		-44	95	20
39.	10	01	-32	30	08	13	-11	03	-24	-26	-34		-37	-20
40.	-04	-07	-08	-32	-09	61	63	76	62	59	79	-27		21
41.	-08	-07	-09	38	16	-06	01	-04	-39	-17	-31	23	-21	
	28	29	30	31	32	33	34	35	36	37	38	39	40	41

Men

APPENDICES 155

APPENDIX B

Results of 33-Score Factor Analyses

Table 7

UNROTATED FACTOR LOADINGS: MEN[a]

Score	Factor				
	I	II	III	IV	V
1	-27	-12	-06	41	-10
2	-42	-27	-05	-22	12
4	-44	13	06	-31	24
5	29	-13	-26	-06	23
6	13	22	-46	14	06
7	-16	-29	-11	-30	24
8	19	29	-10	43	33
9	29	-16	-14	06	-17
10	-23	-32	14	08	29
11	45	-20	-13	-42	38
12	30	28	06	04	04
13	38	11	12	05	15
14	55	-24	-32	-25	28
15	-29	24	23	13	15
16	05	-17	-11	23	20
17	-09	-11	41	33	44
18	-23	-30	-15	28	-28
20	-50	23	-24	21	08
21	07	-12	-15	28	-45
23	28	-42	44	08	-14
24	24	-60	49	12	13
25	50	12	-12	-20	-20
26	59	22	33	-37	-10
28	-63	-19	-14	13	11
29	-60	28	13	40	18
30	20	-13	-19	31	-25
31	-37	-35	-28	-34	-25
32	-10	-46	-22	-46	-13
33	05	03	-66	19	47
34	-30	-17	-35	39	28
36	32	-23	-13	-06	42
37	30	-33	44	-27	15
39	-31	29	-23	-40	14
Percentage of Variance Accounted for	11.9	6.8	7.3	7.5	6.0

[a] Decimal points have been omitted.

Table 8

ROTATED (ORTHOGONAL) FACTOR LOADINGS: MEN[a]

Score	Factor I	II	III	IV	V	h^2
1	46	16	09	-06	-12	26
2	20	-07	08	50	08	31
4	16	-39	-13	35	23	37
5	-27	-01	38	-03	06	22
6	-02	-26	33	-28	-19	30
7	-06	-06	21	44	14	27
8	11	-11	24	-54	22	42
9	-19	21	16	-09	-22	16
10	24	18	14	25	32	27
11	-61	-05	34	16	26	58
12	-21	-07	-08	-34	07	17
13	-27	06	01	-29	19	19
14	-59	04	51	02	07	61
15	31	-15	-22	-08	25	23
16	10	13	30	-08	11	14
17	28	24	00	-11	59	49
18	35	26	12	10	-32	32
20	52	-35	08	-01	-06	40
21	11	27	03	-15	-46	32
23	-17	64	-15	05	12	48
24	-12	72	01	14	37	69
25	-52	-01	-01	-19	-23	35
26	-69	04	-36	-19	09	65
28	58	-10	15	34	02	48
29	72	-22	-14	-12	22	65
30	03	26	18	-23	-31	25
31	08	-05	09	61	-36	52
32	-20	06	17	62	-23	51
33	07	-33	74	-17	05	69
34	48	-04	49	00	05	47
36	-29	08	42	01	28	35
37	-40	37	-13	21	36	49
39	00	-59	-02	25	00	41
Percentage of Variance Accounted for	12.3	7.2	6.7	7.5	5.9	39.6

[a] Decimal points have been omitted.

Table 9

UNROTATED FACTOR LOADINGS: WOMEN[a]

Score	Factor					
	I	II	III	IV	V	VI
1	-07	-55	02	-34	-36	-26
2	05	36	-22	24	20	19
4	04	49	-08	15	-12	42
5	06	41	13	-05	06	-66
6	26	38	07	08	-46	-47
7	-20	15	-21	60	08	-16
8	08	45	10	54	14	18
9	09	00	-15	-64	-16	14
10	-23	-11	-81	-11	-19	-09
11	05	11	57	06	-17	30
12	-02	45	10	-10	-08	-50
13	-36	20	03	-13	46	-16
14	-21	-20	06	-07	61	21
15	-05	-11	41	-04	-04	11
16	04	-36	-06	-20	-07	46
17	64	10	00	-09	19	16
18	08	21	15	51	-24	16
20	00	-28	-02	68	-14	-17
21	-34	46	13	25	-30	49
23	20	-26	09	16	-22	08
24	22	32	30	-07	-83	-18
25	43	-02	-32	16	23	-09
26	47	26	18	24	14	27
28	-12	-48	52	01	-11	-27
29	-06	-11	60	-25	13	-21
30	27	-42	-17	06	-14	-19
31	-50	13	-01	11	-28	27
32	-60	43	-07	27	-38	45
33	90	-01	06	-13	22	11
34	74	08	08	-06	27	08
36	73	06	-07	-07	36	14
37	74	35	-01	-12	41	31
39	26	29	14	-01	-59	-51
Percentage of Variance Accounted for	14.0	9.3	6.9	7.5	9.6	8.9

[a]Decimal points have been omitted.

Table 10

ROTATED (ORTHOGONAL) FACTOR LOADINGS: WOMEN[a]

Factor

Score	I	II	III	IV	V	VI	h^2
1	-22	-68	04	-06	30	-11	62
2	12	47	-23	05	-16	03	31
4	-02	65	-07	-13	12	-06	46
5	08	-08	00	-02	-03	79	64
6	04	06	-04	06	53	61	66
7	-15	28	-25	54	-16	18	51
8	13	65	08	30	-10	13	56
9	02	-19	-13	-62	18	-14	48
10	-29	-18	-80	-04	07	-13	78
11	-03	26	59	-06	18	-08	46
12	-06	01	-02	-12	06	67	48
13	-14	00	-02	-14	-57	25	42
14	07	-07	11	-04	-64	-27	51
15	-06	-04	43	-03	01	-08	20
16	00	-09	04	-18	08	-59	39
17	66	12	-01	-15	10	-06	49
18	-03	45	14	36	25	03	42
20	-06	-02	-02	75	12	-03	59
21	-43	71	15	-04	13	-10	74
23	09	-08	13	21	29	-20	20
24	-15	11	24	-12	85	38	97
25	48	00	-32	17	-03	01	37
26	49	44	18	07	07	-03	47
28	-15	-50	53	24	05	02	61
29	00	-29	57	-14	-15	21	49
30	19	-38	-15	24	24	-12	34
31	-58	29	01	-01	04	-14	44
32	-71	67	-05	-01	09	-12	97
33	91	00	07	-14	18	-08	89
34	78	08	08	-10	07	-01	64
36	81	09	-06	-12	-02	-09	69
37	84	38	00	-31	-06	-04	96
39	-02	-07	04	02	65	60	78
Percentage of Variance Accounted for	15.3	11.7	6.8	5.9	8.2	8.2	56.1

[a]Decimal points have been omitted.

APPENDIX C

Tests of the Purity of the Factor Structures

As a test of the hypothesis that the factors derived from the 33-score matrices for men and women were not affected to an important degree by the inclusion, for exploratory purposes, of some pairs of highly correlated scores (particularly true for women subjects) and some pairs of scores that were by definition correlated with each other, a smaller set of 16 scores was factored for each sex. The scores were selected from those that had high loadings in the 33-score analysis.

Scores used in the further analysis for men were:

1. Schematizing: Ranking Accuracy
2. Schematizing: Increment Error (Regression)
4. Kinesthetic Time Error: Assimilation
7. Apparent Movement: Mean Range
8. Aniseikonic Lenses: Log Recognition Time
11. Size Constancy: Mean Diameter
14. Size Estimation I: Average Error
17. Color-Word: Interference
20. Color-Word: Incidental Recall
21. Size Estimation II: Constant Error, Perceptual
27. Size Estimation II: Variability, Total Test (replacing the separate scores for the perceptual and memory conditions, which had an r of .56)
— Free Association: Percentage Distant, "Dry" and "House" (replacing the separate scores, which had an r of .50)
32. Free Association: Average Length of Unit
35. Rod and Frame: Average Error, Total Test (replacing the separate scores for body-erect and body-tilted trials, which had an r of .32)
36. Embedded Figures: Mean Log Time, Cluster I
37. Embedded Figures: Mean Log Time, Cluster II

Scores used in the further analysis of women were:

1. Schematizing: Ranking Accuracy
2. Schematizing: Increment Error (Regression)
4. Kinesthetic Time Error: Assimilation
8. Aniseikonic Lenses: Log Recognition Time
10. Object Sorting: Number of Groups
11. Size Constancy: Mean Diameter
14. Size Estimation I: Average Error
17. Color-Word: Interference
18. Color-Word: Reading Time, Colors Alone

21. Size Estimation II: Constant Error, Perceptual
25. Size Estimation II: Variability, Perceptual
26. Size Estimation II: Variability, Memory
— Free Association: Percentage Distant, "Dry" and "House" (replacing the separate scores, which had an r of .56)
32. Free Association: Average Length of Unit
35. Rod and Frame: Average Error, Total Test (replacing the separate scores for body-erect and body-tilted trials, which had an r of .79)
38. Embedded Figures: Mean Log Time, Total Test (replacing the separate scores for Clusters I and II, which had an r of .73)

A centroid analysis was performed with each matrix, and the factors were then rotated orthogonally. For both men and women, certain rotations were clearly called for by the graphic plots, and no conscious attempt was made to duplicate the factors from the 33-score analysis. Three factors were found for the female sample and four for the male sample. Each factor clearly corresponded to a factor obtained in the 33-score analyses.

In order to evaluate the similarity of these factors to the previously obtained factors, each of the new factors was matched with one of the previous ones by inspection. An index of similarity was then obtained, using the formula

$$\frac{\Sigma ab}{\sqrt{\Sigma a^2} \cdot \sqrt{\Sigma b^2}}, \text{ where } a = \text{loading on previous factor}$$
$$b = \text{loading on new factor.}$$

It can be seen that this formula is similar to a product-moment correlation coefficient, with the difference that the magnitudes of a and b are taken from a reference point of zero, rather than from a mean. When a score in the new matrix combined two previously used scores, the average of the two previous loadings was used.

The index of similarity essentially indicated the relative magnitudes and directions of the loadings in the two analyses, and could equal 1 if the loadings on a factor were, for example, all one half the loadings on the comparable factor. The regression of b on a was therefore also computed, as an index of difference in over-all magnitudes of loadings in the two analyses.

Results for Men

Factor I (scanning). The index of similarity was .948. The slope of the regression line was 1.034. All but one of the loadings previously greater than .350 remained over .350 in the same direction: Score 1, Schematizing: Ranking Accuracy, dropped from -.462 to -.307. In addition, Score 36, Mean Log Time for Cluster I of the Embedded Figures Test, rose from .290 to .378.

Factor II (tolerance for unrealistic experiences). The index of similarity was .848. The slope of the regression line was 1.095. All but one of the loadings previously greater than .350 remained over .350 in the same direction: Score 4, Kinesthetic Time Error: Assimilation, dropped from .352 to -.060. In addition, Score 1, Schematizing: Ranking Accuracy, rose from -.061 to -.359.

Factor III (constricted-flexible control). The index of similarity was .781. The slope of the regression line was 1.117. Two of the loadings originally greater than .350 remained so. The loading of mean log time for Cluster II of the Embedded Figures Test (Score 37) dropped from .358 to .160. In addition, Score 2, Schematizing: Increment Error (Regression), rose from .076 to .401 and Score 4, Kinesthetic Time Error: Assimilation, rose from .229 to .599. This was the factor with the weakest replication in the new analysis.

Factor IV (field dependence-independence). The index of similarity was .884. The slope of the regression line was 1.077. Two of the loadings originally greater than .350 remained so. Average error in Size Estimation Test I (Score 14) dropped from .506 to .323. In addition, recognition time for tilt in the Aniseikonic Lenses Test (Score 8) rose from .243 to .425.

Results for Women

Factor I (field-articulation). The index of similarity was .967. The slope of the regression line was .939, indicating that the new loadings were slightly smaller. Of the previous loadings greater than .350, all remained over .350 in the same direction.

Factor II (leveling-sharpening). The index of similarity was .974. The slope of the regression line was .846. Of the previous loadings greater than .350, all were still over .350 in the same direction.

Factor III (equivalence range). The index of similarity was .956. The slope of the regression line was 1.046. All loadings over .350 remained over .350 in the same direction. In addition, the loading of variability in the memory condition of the Size Estimation Test II (Score 26) rose from .185 to .384.

Summary

In general, when overlapping measures were eliminated and a smaller selection of scores analyzed, the factors that emerged corresponded well to those obtained in the 33-score analyses. Of the factors interpreted in Chapter 9, all three factors for women and Factor I for men were clearly apparent in the subsequent analyses. The other three factors for men corresponded fairly well to previous factors. As noted above, the new rotations were made from the graphs, with no deliberate effort to reproduce the previous factors. If such an effort had been made, it is possible that Factors II, III, and IV for men might have been duplicated more closely.

APPENDIX D

Factor Scores

Estimated factor scores were obtained by the multiple-regression method described by Guilford (1954, pp. 524-526). R was obtained between each of the factors and several test scores having the highest loadings on that factor. Regression weights were used to obtain a factor score for each subject based upon these test scores, as indicated below. To simplify the computation of factor scores, the formula actually used was obtained by substituting integers in the proper ratios to each other for the regression weights. R^2 indicates the amount of factor variance accounted for by the test scores used to estimate factor scores.

In obtaining the factor scores, the subjects' test scores were represented by z-scores, which were obtained for each sex separately. This had the effect of giving equal weight to each test score before multiplication by the appropriate weight. The resulting factor scores were converted to z-scores. The test scores are denoted by the numbers used throughout the present study.

MEN

Factor	R	R^2	Regression Formula	Formula Used
I	.918	.842	$-.480z_{26} + .290z_{29} - .281z_{14} - .224z_{11}$	$-24z_{26} + 14z_{29} - 14z_{14} - 11z_{11}$
II	.848	.719	$.514z_{24} + .180z_{23} - .397z_{39}$	$14z_{24} + 5z_{23} - 11z_{39}$
III[a]	.874	.763	$.489z_{33} + .338z_{34} + .311z_{14} + .185z_{36}$	$13z_{33} + 9z_{34} + 8z_{14} + 5z_{36}$
IV	.795	.632	$.165z_{32} + .243z_{31} - .311z_{8} + .190z_{2}$ $+.268z_{7}$	$7z_{32} + 10z_{31} - 13z_{8} + 8z_{2}$ $+11z_{7}$
V	.721	.520	$.400z_{17} - .313z_{21} + .222z_{10} + .197z_{37}$	$32z_{17} - 25z_{21} + 18z_{10} + 16z_{37}$

[a] Since a large portion of the variance of Factor III was derived from the Rod and Frame Test scores (33 and 34), factor scores were computed only for the 22 men who took the Rod and Frame Test.

WOMEN

Factor	R	R^2	Regression Formula	Formula Used
I	.907	.822	$.359z_{36} + .468z_{37} + .205z_{17}$	$7z_{36} + 9z_{37} + 4z_{17}$
II	.952	.905	$.588z_{4} - .411z_{1} + .375z_{8}$	$17z_{4} - 12z_{1} + 11z_{8}$
III	.869	.755	$-.493z_{10} + .313z_{11} + .309z_{29}$	$-8z_{10} + 5z_{11} + 5z_{29}$
IV	.826	.682	$.521z_{20} - .266z_{9} + .234z_{7}$	$18z_{20} - 8z_{9} + 7z_{7}$
V	.994	.987	$.661z_{24} - .251z_{14} - .468z_{13}$	$16z_{24} - 6z_{14} - 11z_{13}$
VI	.947	.896	$.596z_{5} + .317z_{12} - .362z_{16}$	$13z_{5} + 7z_{12} - 8z_{16}$

APPENDIX E

Cluster Analysis

Basic Principles

The basic problem is to find some way of grouping subjects so that those within each group are quite homogeneous in their total pattern of test scores and different in at least some essential respects from subjects in other groups. The method used in the present study was a modification of the D^2 method, which is based on the distance (D) between each pair of subjects in n-dimensional space, the space being defined by the n variables used to measure each subject's performance.

The distance (D) between any two subjects is measured by:

$$D^2 = d_1^2 + d_2^2 + d_3^2 + \ldots + d_n^2,$$

where d_j is the distance between their scores on variable j; this is an extension of the Pythagorean theorem into n dimensions. In order to give equal weight to all variables, all measures are converted into standard score form (z), with a mean of zero and a sigma of one for each variable; d_j for subjects p and q can, therefore, also be expressed as: $z_{pj} - z_{qj}$. The minimum D^2 possible is zero; this occurs when two subjects have identical scores on all measures (in the present sample the smallest D^2 is 0.03 times the number of measures—a root-mean-square d of 0.17). Theoretically, D^2 can range to infinity (maximum in the present sample is 10.59 times the number of measures—a root-mean-square d of 3.25).

A D^2 of any particular size other than zero can occur in a number of ways. For example, if the D^2 between two subjects is of average size, it may mean that they are an average distance from each other on all variables, or it may mean that they are very similar on some measures and very different on others. Interpretation of such a D^2 is, then, quite ambiguous. On the other hand, a small D^2 has a more clear-cut meaning; it indicates that two subjects are quite similar on the total group of measures. Since the goal in this study was to isolate groups of subjects with high within-group similarity, only small D^2's were of interest. This made irrelevant the issue of ambiguity of interpretation, which is one of the most salient criticisms of the D^2 method. Problems did arise in defining a "small D^2," and they are discussed below.

Method

1. <u>Choice of scores</u>. While the distance between two subjects is an index of their degree of similarity, it measures similarity only in respect to the particular scores used in the

analysis. The choice of scores is therefore crucial, since it limits the sphere within which we can speak of subjects being "similar" or "dissimilar" to each other once the clusters have been obtained. Since the present cluster analysis was intended as an extension of the factor analysis, clustering was based on factor scores, using only the interpretable factors. The male sample was clustered on the basis of Factors I, III, IV, and V; for the female sample, Factors I, II, and III were used.

2. <u>Selection of an index of similarity</u>. The most obvious way to isolate clusters of subjects would be to choose a cut-off point for D^2, below which a pair of subjects would be considered "similar," and develop clusters such that all subjects within a cluster were similar by this criterion. Such a method cannot be used for clustering, however, since the distributions of D^2 for different subjects are so different that any such cut-off point would define certain subjects as "similar" to most other subjects, leaving other subjects "similar" to none. Furthermore, it often happens that two subjects are "similar" to each other, and each is "similar" to several other subjects, but in no case are they "similar" to the same subject.

The reason for this is that the distribution of D^2's between any one subject and all other subjects is a function of his eccentricity (e^2), i.e., how far he is from the center of the n-dimensional space. The farther he is from the center of this space (i.e., the larger his e^2), the larger will be his range of D^2 from other subjects. It can be shown that a subject's average $D^2 = m + e^2$, where m = the number of variables on which the D^2 is based. One subject's D^2's can, then, be made comparable with those of another subject by subtracting each subject's e^2 from each D^2 between him and other subjects. When this correction is made, the distributions of D^2 for all subjects have the same mean, since m is a constant.

The index of similarity used in this study, called Δ^2, was obtained in the following way. Each D^2 was corrected twice, once for the e^2 of each of the two subjects involved in it. D_{pq}^2, corrected for S_p, became $D_{pq}^2 - e_p^2$; corrected for S_q it became $D_{pq}^2 - e_q^2$. The formula was, then:

$$\Delta_{pq}^2 = 2D_{pq}^2 - e_p^2 - e_q^2.$$

3. <u>Comparison of D^2, Δ^2, and vectors</u>. The relationships among these measures, and their dependence on e^2, can be seen (for two variables, x and y) in Figure 1. D_{ab}^2 was the same as D_{cd}^2; subjects a and b were, however, on opposite sides of the mean on both measures, while c and d were in the same general direction. Another way of expressing this difference is to say that, with the same within-pair D^2, c and d, the two subjects with extreme scores (i.e., high e^2) had vectors that were similar in direction, while a and b, both with low e^2, were in the opposite direction from each other. The profile similarity within the two

pairs was, therefore, very different; the angle between a and b was 180°, so that r_{ab} = -1.00; the angle between c and d was 39° and r_{cd} was + .78. The two subjects e and f, on the other hand, each had an e^2 as small as that of a and b, but the angle between their vectors was the same as that between c and d; this could occur only when D_{ef}^2 was smaller than the D^2 between either of the other pairs.

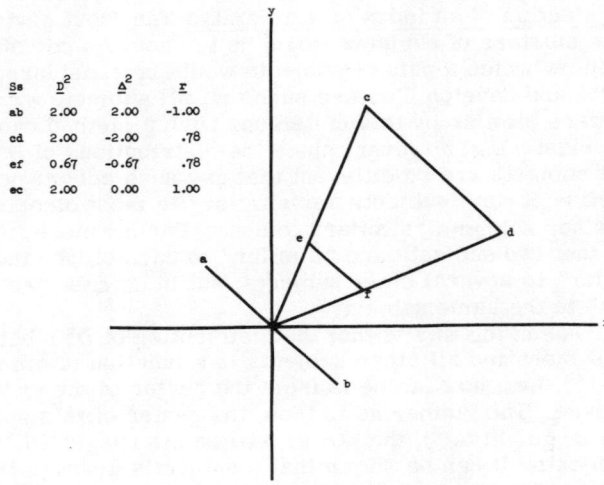

Ss	D^2	Δ^2	r
ab	2.00	2.00	-1.00
cd	2.00	-2.00	.78
ef	0.67	-0.67	.78
ec	2.00	0.00	1.00

Figure 1. Comparison of Three Methods of Clustering Subjects

In clustering subjects, it seemed desirable that subjects in the same cluster have vectors that were close, since this meant that their profiles of scores would be similar. Using vectors alone, however, would not take into account differences between subjects in the extremeness of their scores, and this also seemed important. Subjects e and c, for example, had identical vectors, but both of c's scores were three times as large as e's.

The Δ^2 method used here was a compromise between the raw D^2 and the vectors. By correcting for e^2, it gave some weight to the relative directions in space of the two subjects in a pair, without completely discounting their comparative extremeness of scores.

As a test, all three measures were computed for 30 comparisons among pairs of subjects, and then intercorrelated. The correlation between D^2 and the angle between vectors was .61, supporting the impression that they by no means measure similarity in the same way. Δ^2 correlates .94 with the angle between vectors and .83 with D^2, indicating that it takes into account both the direction of each subject's vector and his distance from the origin, but gives somewhat more weight to direction.

Δ^2 proved superior to D^2 in practice in that subjects who were thus defined as similar were much more likely to be similar to the same subjects. Not only did this make the practical work of grouping subjects easier, but it indicated that Δ^2 was a more valid basis for grouping subjects into clusters.

4. <u>The assignment of subjects to clusters.</u> The requirements for clustering subjects were: (a) that all subjects in the same cluster be similar to each other and (b) that no subject not in a particular cluster be similar to all subjects in that cluster. The frequency distribution of Δ^2 was obtained, separately for each sex. The first step was to note all pairs of subjects whose Δ^2 was in the lowest 5 per cent of all Δ^{2}'s. This produced many pairs, several groups of three subjects, and several open-ended groups in which there were several linkages among three, four, or five subjects, but not all Δ^{2}'s were in the lowest 5 per cent. Δ^{2}'s ranging up to the lowest 10 per cent were then noted, and many of these linkages were closed. While there were occasional cases where a subject who had been placed in one cluster was also close to a subject in another cluster, there was no case where a subject was close to all or most subjects of more than one group.

In this manner, 23 of the 30 women and 25 of the 30 men were assigned to clusters. When all within-cluster Δ^{2}'s are considered, 44 per cent of them were from the lowest 5 per cent of the total Δ^2 distribution (46 per cent for men, 42 per cent for women), 80 per cent from the lowest 10 per cent (80 per cent for men, 81 per cent for women), and 92 per cent from the lowest 15 per cent (94 per cent for men, 89 per cent for women).

Five of the seven women who were not placed in clusters were very close to the mean on all factors, having the five lowest e^{2}'s. While they were, therefore, similar to each other, there was nothing really distinctive about their patterns of factor scores that could lend itself to interpretation; their Δ^{2}'s are low but not extremely so. Of the remaining two female subjects, one was between two clusters, being close to half the members of each cluster, and the other was not close to any cluster. Two of the five men not placed in clusters also had consistently middle scores, having the two lowest e^{2}'s for men; each of the other three was moderately close to two clusters but not distinctively in either.

APPENDIX F

Replication Study of Relationships between Rorschach Signs and Basic Measures of Field Dependence-Independence

Rorschach Signs

In preliminary examinations of the Rorschach protocols, it was evident that Hertzman's criteria (see Witkin et al., 1954) would have to be modified for the present samples. For example, in spite of the fact that women in the present study were more field-dependent than Witkin's women subjects in perceptual tests, they had far fewer Rorschach signs (indicating field dependence) than Witkin's subjects when the original criteria were used. In the present study, we allocated two separate sets of Rorschach signs to our subjects' protocols: (a) those arrived at by use of the original criteria; and (b) those arrived at by use of modifications of those criteria based on the distributions of scores in the present study. Both sets of criteria are described below.

1. W. Since a good whole response entails dealing with the impact of the blot as a whole, it reflects the ability to cope successfully with a complex, unstructured stimulus. Whole responses were classed as adequate (good forms) or inadequate (poor forms or percepts primarily determined by color or shading). The original criteria for this sign were (a) three or fewer adequate W, or (b) more than three adequate W but an equal or greater number of inadequate W. In the present study, the chief modification was to subtract inadequate W from adequate W. The sign was given to men if adequate W minus inadequate W was equal to three or more, and to women if adequate W minus inadequate W was equal to four or more.

2. P. Since popular responses represent the images most easily seen in the blots, their use indicates an ability to deal with readily available features of the environment in an everyday, common-sense manner. In the Witkin study, field-dependent subjects gave relatively few P responses, in spite of the fact that their non-P responses were not richer or more individualized than those of field-independent subjects. P was based on a list of 20 including those given by Klopfer and Kelley (1942) and those given by Beck (1944), with the exception of "clouds" on Card VII. Nearly all these responses proved to be "populars" in the present study. The total sample (especially the women subjects) gave many more of these popular responses than did either Witkin's or Linton's (1954) sample. Only two of each sex received the sign on the original criterion of five or fewer P. The criterion for both sexes in the present study was eight and one half or fewer P, with near-popular responses scored as one half.

3. *C*. This sign indicates the extent to which emotional reactions (represented by color) are controlled by rational considerations, i.e., form. All color responses were taken into account, including those that were part of larger responses (e.g., "clowns with red hats"). The original criteria were: (a) no *FC* and one or more *CF* or *C*; (b) one *FC* and two or more *CF* or *C*; (c) two or more *FC* and *CF+C* more than twice *FC*. In the present study, the criterion was *CF+C* equal to or greater than twice *FC*. This was similar to the original criteria, but allowed us to give the sign to a few borderline cases. In addition, one male subject who gave no scorable color responses but offered many comments about color was given the *C* sign.

4. Movement is used as a measure of the richness of inner life and ideational activity. *M* was scored with the Klopfer-Kelley criteria. Some indication of motor activity was required, and clearly expressed movement in parts of human figures received the score. Marginal responses (movement tendencies) were not scored *M*. Animals in humanlike activity were scored *M* if the activity was improbable for that animal (e.g., "rabbits serving tea," but not "dancing bears"). The original criterion was two or fewer *M*. In the present study, the criteria were: men, two or fewer *M*; women, three or fewer *M*.

5. *H*. Human content is considered to reflect the self-image, and a high proportion of parts to whole human figures suggests a fragmented self-image or low self-esteem. The original criterion was an $Hd/H+Hd$ of .50 or more. In the present study, the criterion was $H-Hd$ of two or less. The effect of using the difference between H and Hd, rather than a proportion of Hd to the total, with the present sample was that the new criterion was more likely to include subjects with low total human content (e.g., a subject with two H and one Hd received the sign).

6. *F*. The *F* sign is intended as an over-all measure of constriction. The original criterion was *F* percentage of 60 or more, or sum of human movement and all color responses five or less. In the present study, the criteria were: men, *F* percentage 64 or more, or sum of *M* and color responses nine or less. Twelve subjects received the sign on the basis of *F* percentage alone, 11 on the basis of low *M* and color, and 11 on the basis of both criteria. Subjects receiving the sign on the basis of *F* percentage alone tended to emphasize quantity rather than quality (mean $R = 54$). Those having the sign on low *M* and color alone gave very sparse records (mean $R = 20$), while those without the sign gave a moderately large number of responses (mean $R = 39$).

7. Animal Type. In Linton's (1954, 1955) study, field-dependent subjects were not different from field-independent subjects in total *A* percentage, but reported different kinds of animals. They tended to see such animals as insects, birds, and sea creatures, while field-independent subjects tended to see animals

that lend themselves more easily to the projection of human emotion, such as dogs, rabbits, and bears. Thus, animal responses in the present study were divided into two groups: humans and other mammals, and nonmammals. The one exception to zoologically correct classification was the classification of bats as nonmammals, with the hypothesis that they are generally felt to be nonhuman and do not lend themselves as readily to identification as do other mammals. The criteria for the present study were: men, nonmammals 40 per cent or more of total animal plus human content; women, nonmammals 45 per cent or more of total animal plus human content. A high proportion of nonmammals, who are distant from human life, suggests that the person tends to experience his own drives as ego-alien.

8. *C* Trend. In Linton's (1954, 1955) study, the *C* sign used by Witkin did not relate highly to measures of field dependence-independence. Subjects at the extremes of the latter did not differ as much in the over-all proportion of controlled to uncontrolled color responses as they did in the trend of their color responses over the course of the test. A new sign was therefore devised for that study in which response to each color card was rated as "controlled" ($FC + C$ equal to or greater than FC). The sign was given to subjects showing a pattern of deteriorating control over the five color cards, i.e., a shift from "controlled" to "no color" or "uncontrolled," or from "no color" to "uncontrolled." In equivocal cases (e.g., +, -, 0, -, +), the decision was made on the basis of responses to the three all-colored cards, VIII-X.

Sum Scores. In the Witkin study, the Rorschach signs were divided into two main groups that were considered to represent separable though related aspects of personality.

9. *WPC*. These three signs are more concerned with the adequacy of the subject's coping with stimuli, in that they reflect his ability to integrate the blots into appropriate forms.

10. *MHF* (*-At*). These signs deal more with the self-concept, either in terms of self-awareness or self-acceptance. In the Witkin study, field-independent subjects offered a relatively large number of anatomy responses; this was interpreted as a sign of high self-awareness coupled with low self-acceptance. In the present study, the *At* sign was not significantly correlated with the perceptual measures. For purposes of comparing our results with Witkin's, *MHF* and total Rorschach sign scores were correlated both with and without the *At* sign, which is subtracted from the others (Tables 13 and 14).

11. *WPCMHF* (*-At*). The sum of all the signs provides an over-all measure of the Rorschach indicators of field-dependence. This group of signs is the same as that used in the Witkin study.

12. *WPCMHF* (*-At*). This is the same as the above group with the addition of the two signs derived from Linton's study (1954).

Results

For purposes of comparison with Witkin's results, all r's for data obtained in the present study were, whenever possible, obtained using both the original Rorschach criteria and those developed for the present study.[1] For the Rod and Frame Test, body-erect condition, r was directly comparable. For the body-tilted condition, we combined Witkin's Series 1 and 2. The correlation for the combined condition was obtained by the formula:

$$r_{x \cdot 1\,2} = \frac{r_{x1}\sigma_1 + r_{x2}\sigma_2}{\sigma 1 + 2}$$

The Rod and Frame Test Index score was obtained by averaging the z-scores for parts of the test. In Witkin's index score, the subject-tilted condition (16 trials) contributed twice as much as the subject-erect condition (8 trials), while in our study they were given equal weight. It is doubtful, however, that this greatly altered the results. For the Embedded Figures Test, Witkin used the mean raw time values for the 24 items, whereas we used the mean of z-scores made with the data from Linton's study (1954, 1955), indicated that this log time score can be expected to have higher r's with Rorschach variables than Witkin's mean time score.

Tables 11 and 12 contain biserial correlations between field dependence-independence measures and individual Rorschach signs in Witkin's study, in the present study using Witkin's criteria, and in the present study using the modified criteria that seemed more appropriate to the protocols of the present samples.

Tables 13 and 14 show product-moment correlations between field dependence-independence measures and Rorschach sum scores.

Since the direction of results was predicted on the basis of Witkin's findings, all significance tests in these tables were made using one tail of the probability distribution. Correlations for the field-dependence Index were based upon N's of 30. For the Rod and Frame Test alone, N was 22 for men and 20 for women.

Among the correlations for men, for all signs except the H sign, r's for the Rod and Frame Test were much lower than for the Embedded Figures Test. To interpret this discrepancy, it should be understood that eight men who failed to take the Rod and Frame Test received more signs than those who took the test. For the sum of eight signs, the difference was significant at the .02 level (means were 5.8 versus 3.7 signs). The differences were most marked in what Witkin called the "coping" area. The difference was significant at the .05 level (means were 2.3 versus 1.4) for the *WPC* group, but not significant for the *MHF(-At)* group (1.9 versus 1.4).

---

[1] Correlations for the Witkin study were obtained from the book "Personality through Perception" (1954).

Table 11
BISERIAL CORRELATIONS BETWEEN RORSCHACH SIGNS AND BASIC MEASURES OF FIELD DEPENDENCE-INDEPENDENCE

Standard type: Witkin sample, Witkin study criteria.
Italics: Present sample, Witkin study criteria.
Bold face: Present sample, present study criteria.

Sign	Field Dependence Index	Embedded Figures Total	Cluster I	Cluster II	Rod and Frame Total	Body Tilted	Body Erect	Percentage of Subjects with Sign
W		.37*			.54**	.49**	.53**	38
	.12	*.21*	*.14*	*.35*	*.00*	*−.07*	*.09*	*43*
	.28	**.33**	**.14**	**.33**	**.05**	**.01**	**.07**	**63**
a_p		.16			.35	.36*	.29	23
	.27	**.28**	**.41***	**.18**	**.06**	**−.18**	**.32**	**60**
C		.50**			.37*	.33*	.36*	40
	−.03	*.07*	*.16*	*−.04*	*−.01*	*−.12*	*.14*	*30*
	.24	**.30**	**.44***	**.19**	**.05**	**−.01**	**.11**	**37**
b_M		.35*			.26	.22	.30	44
	.69**	**.68****	**.64****	**.58****	**.38**	**.36**	**.24**	**47**
H		.45*			.46**	.38*	.50**	42
	.37	*.25*	*−.05*	*.20*	*.34*	*.11*	*.48*	*30*
	.60**	**.35**	**.21**	**.25**	**.68***	**.45**	**.69***	**70**
F		.03			.23	.13	.37*	46
	.44*	*.35*	*.32*	*.32*	*.28*	*.24*	*.24*	*63*
	.52*	**.40***	**.18**	**.45***	**.36**	**.34**	**.24**	**57**
Animal Type	*.58**	*.17*	*.17*	*.08*	*.76***	*.53**	*.74***	*70*
C Trend	*.36*	*.08*	*.18*	*.00*	*.50**	*.35*	*.47**	*53*

*p < .05, one-tailed test.   **p < .01, one-tailed test.

a_r's not computed for Witkin criteria, since only two subjects had the sign.

b Present study criteria the same as Witkin's.

Table 12
BISERIAL CORRELATIONS BETWEEN RORSCHACH SIGNS AND BASIC MEASURES OF FIELD DEPENDENCE-INDEPENDENCE

Standard type: Witkin sample, Witkin study criteria.
Italics: Present sample, Witkin study criteria.
Bold face: Present sample, present study criteria.

Women

Sign	Field-Dependence Index	Embedded Figures			Rod and Frame			Percentage of Subjects with Sign
		Total	Cluster I	Cluster II	Total	Body Tilted	Body Erect	
W		.26			.53**	.56**	.45*	31
	.34	*.44**	*.22*	*.41*	*.04*	*.02*	*.06*	27
	.63**	**.75****	**.70****	**.50***	**.27**	**.31**	**.21**	57
a_p		.28			.57**	.52**	.53**	27
	.21	*.18*	*.17*	*.21*	*.56**	*.50*	*.55**	30
C		.32			.02	.03	.01	51
	.24	*.27*	*.14*	*.19*	*.18*	*.14*	*.20*	20
	.36	**.38**	**.25**	**.36**	**.27**	**.22**	**.29**	27
M		.15			.04	.25	.04	29
	.21	*.14*	*.07*	*−.06*	*.33*	*.40*	*.23*	17
	.35	**.32**	**.19**	**.25**	**.33**	**.40**	**.25**	23
b_H		.29			.21	.23	.15	37
	.01	*.08*	*.22*	*−.06*	*−.19*	*.01*	*−.34*	37
	.15	**.17**	**.22**	**.00**	**−.01**	**.11**	**−.12**	67
F		.37			.24	.21	.23	37
	.14	*.17*	*.06*	*−.08*	*−.05*	*−.01*	*−.08*	23
	.50*	**.54***	**.50***	**.44***	**.31**	**.45**	**.16**	57
Animal Type	.49*	.55*	.52*	.57*	.45	.45	.41	33
C Trend	.36	.27	.23	.21	.53*	.37	.62*	57

*p < .05, one-tailed test.   **p < .01, one-tailed test.

a_r's not computed for Witkin criteria, since only two subjects had the sign.

bA criterion of $H\text{-}Hd < 3$ was correlated .56* with the Field-Dependence Index, .60* and .17 with the total-test scores for the Embedded Figures and Rod and Frame Tests. It was not used because it would have been given to 24 (vs. 6) subjects for correlations with the Embedded Figures Test scores and the Field-Dependence Index and 17 (vs. 3) subjects for correlations with the Rod and Frame Test scores.

Table 13

PRODUCT-MOMENT CORRELATIONS BETWEEN RORSCHACH SUMMED SCORES AND BASIC MEASURES OF FIELD DEPENDENCE-INDEPENDENCE

Standard type: Witkin sample, Witkin study criteria.
Italics: Present sample, Witkin study criteria.
Bold face: Present sample, present study criteria.

Men

Sign	Field-Dependence Index	Embedded Figures			Rod and Frame			
		Total	Cluster I	Cluster II	Total	Body Tilted	Body Erect	
WPC		.39**			.46**	.43**	.42**	
	.03	.15	.15	.13	−.10	−.14	−.01	
	.28	**.32***	**.29**	**.25**	**.06**	**−.07**	**.20**	
MHF		.44*			.46**	.41**	.46**	
(−At)	.52**	.50**	.45*	.42*	.28	.18	.28	
	*.58***	*.54***	*.46***	*.46***	*.35*	*.30*	*.27*	At omitted
	.58*	**.47***	**.34***	**.42***	**.45***	**.36**	**.36**	
Total [6 signs: WPC MHF (−At)]		.51**			.56**	.52**	.55**	
	.41*	.44*	.42*	.36*	.21	.12	.24	
	*.53***	*.51***	*.45***	*.45***	*.32*	*.21*	*.32*	At omitted
	.53*	**.48***	**.38***	**.41***	**.35**	**.22**	**.37**	
ªTotal [8 signs: WPC MHF(−At) An, C Trend]								
	.55*	**.43***	**.41***	**.38***	**.49***	**.33**	**.48***	At omitted
	*.57***	*.43***	*.37***	*.34***	*.53***	*.42***	*.53***	

*p < .05, one-tailed test.
**p < .01, one-tailed test.
ª For total score (8 signs) split-half r = .72, corrected r = .83.

It was noted above that male subjects not taking the Rod and Frame Test had longer than average time scores on the Embedded Figures Test. It would appear that the loss of subjects from one end of the distribution of men may have been the reason for the low correlations between the Embedded Figures and Rod and Frame Test scores. It is of interest, therefore, that even when the Embedded Figures Test scores were equated, subjects not taking the Rod and Frame Test had more Rorschach signs. Of the 15 male subjects with longer time scores on the Embedded Figures Test, those taking the Rod and Frame Test averaged 4.5

Table 14

PRODUCT-MOMENT CORRELATIONS BETWEEN RORSCHACH SUMMED SCORES AND BASIC MEASURES OF FIELD DEPENDENCE-INDEPENDENCE

Standard type: Witkin sample, Witkin study criteria.
Italics: Present sample, Witkin study criteria.
Bold face: Present sample, present study criteria.

	Field-Dependence Index	Embedded Figures			Rod and Frame			
Sign		Total	Cluster I	Cluster II	Total	Body Tilted	Body Erect	
WPC		.32*			.55**	.50**	.54**	
	.27	.30	.13	.24	.15	.10	.19	
	.48*	**.53***	**.45***	**.42***	**.40***	**.41***	**.36**	
MHF (-At)		.29*			.16	.15	.18	
	.12	.12	.13	−.04	.06	.17	−.03	
	*.33**	*.32**	*.31*	*.22*	*.28*	*.37*	*.17*	At
	.34	**.35***	**.32***	**.24**	**.21**	**.32**	**.10**	omitted
Total [6 signs: WPC MHF (-At)]		.37**			.45**	.41**	.45**	
	.25	.27	.18	.10	.16	.19	.11	
	.47*	**.49***	**.45***	**.38***	**.37**	**.42***	**.29**	At
	.46*	**.50***	**.44***	**.37***	**.34**	**.41***	**.25**	omitted
ªTotal [8 signs: WPC MHF(-At) An, C Trend]	**.54***	**.56***	**.51***	**.46***	**.47***	**.49***	**.41***	At
	.53*	**.55***	**.49***	**.44***	**.43***	**.46***	**.37**	omitted

*$p < .05$, one-tailed test.
**$p < .01$, one-tailed test.
ª For total score (8 signs), split-half $r = .66$, corrected $r = .79$.

signs (from the groups of 8 signs), those not taking it, 6.4 signs. Of the 15 subjects who had shorter time scores in the Embedded Figures Test, those taking the Rod and Frame Test averaged 3.0 signs, those not taking it, 4.7 signs.

Summary

In spite of the discrepancies noted above, the relationships observed by Witkin between performances in laboratory tests and field-dependence signs derived from performances in the Rorschach Test seemed, in general, to be confirmed for both sexes.

APPENDIX G

Table 15

ORDER OF PRESENTATION OF SQUARES IN THE SCHEMATIZING TEST[a]

1.	1.2	26.	1.6	51.	3.2	76.	3.2	101.	3.8	126.	7.9
2.	1.6	27.	3.2	52.	2.8	77.	3.8	102.	7.9	127.	6.6
3.	2.0	28.	2.4	53.	4.6	78.	4.6	103.	5.5	128.	11.4
4.	2.4	29.	2.8	54.	2.4	79.	5.5	104.	6.6	129.	5.5
5.	2.8	30.	2.0	55.	3.8	80.	6.6	105.	4.6	130.	9.5
6.	2.0	31.	2.0	56.	2.4	81.	4.6	106.	4.6	131.	5.5
7.	1.6	32.	2.4	57.	4.6	82.	3.8	107.	5.5	132.	11.4
8.	2.0	33.	2.8	58.	3.2	83.	6.6	108.	6.6	133.	7.9
9.	1.2	34.	3.2	59.	3.8	84.	3.2	109.	7.9	134.	9.5
10.	2.4	35.	3.8	60.	2.8	85.	5.5	110.	9.5	135.	6.6
11.	1.2	36.	2.8	61.	2.8	86.	3.2	111.	6.6	136.	6.6
12.	2.8	37.	2.4	62.	3.2	87.	6.6	112.	5.5	137.	7.9
13.	2.0	38.	3.8	63.	3.8	88.	4.6	113.	9.5	138.	9.5
14.	2.4	39.	2.0	64.	4.6	89.	5.5	114.	4.6	139.	11.4
15.	1.6	40.	3.2	65.	5.5	90.	3.2	115.	7.9	140.	13.7
16.	1.6	41.	2.0	66.	3.8	91.	3.8	116.	4.6	141.	9.5
17.	2.0	42.	3.8	67.	3.2	92.	4.6	117.	9.5	142.	7.9
18.	2.4	43.	2.8	68.	5.5	93.	5.5	118.	6.6	143.	13.7
19.	2.8	44.	3.2	69.	2.8	94.	6.6	119.	7.9	144.	6.6
20.	3.2	45.	2.4	70.	4.6	95.	7.9	120.	5.5	145.	11.4
21.	2.4	46.	2.4	71.	2.8	96.	5.5	121.	5.5	146.	6.6
22.	2.0	47.	2.8	72.	5.5	97.	4.6	122.	6.6	147.	13.7
23.	3.2	48.	3.2	73.	3.8	98.	7.9	123.	7.9	148.	9.5
24.	1.6	49.	3.8	74.	4.6	99.	3.8	124.	9.5	149.	11.4
25.	2.8	50.	4.6	75.	3.2	100.	6.6	125.	11.4	150.	7.9

[a] Values for squares represent inches per side.

APPENDIX H

Method of Computing Increment Error Score for Schematizing Test (Score 3)

The percentage increase of each of the nine series means over the mean of the first series was computed as follows:

A. Using the actual sizes of the stimuli and substituting these values in the formula

$$\frac{{}^M Series_2 - {}^M Series_1}{{}^M Series_1}, \quad \frac{{}^M Series_3 - {}^M Series_1}{{}^M Series_1} \quad \text{etc.,}$$

yielded a nine-point trend line (in percentage-increment terms) describing the <u>objective</u> shift in series means. (A "series mean" is the average size of a group of five stimuli; Series 1 contains the smallest figures; Series 10, the largest.)

B. This same procedure was followed using <u>judgments</u> of sizes of stimuli by each subject. (It should be noted that a subject's "series mean" is the average of 15 judgments, three for each of the five figures in the series.) This yielded for each subject a set of increment values that could be compared with the percentage-increment values of the actual stimuli.

C. Each subject's percentage increment for each series was then subtracted from the percentage increment of the stimuli for that series (signs were ignored). This yielded a set of nine percentage-increment-error values.

D. The average of these nine scores was the increment-error score for each subject.

APPENDIX I

Method of Computing Assimilation Score for Kinesthetic Time Error Test (Score 4)

Time error was computed as *PSE* minus objective mid-point (200 gms.). Thus, if the *PSE* was greater than 200 gms., time error was positive. *PSE* was computed in the following manner.

Assume the following protocol:

Stimulus, gms.	Number of judgments "Heavier"	Number of judgments "Lighter"	p
184	0	7	(1.00)
192	4	3	.43
200	5	2	.29
208	7	0	0
216	7	0	0
			.72

If the subject called 184 gms. lighter than 200 gms. seven out of seven times, his *PSE* was at least 184 gms. If he did not call 184 gms. lighter than 200 gms. seven out of seven times, it was arbitrarily assumed that if the series were carried out to one step interval below 184 gms., that is, to 176 gms., he would call 176 gms. lighter than 200 gms. seven out of seven times. Therefore, his *PSE* was at least 176 gms. After the basal *PSE* had been determined in this manner, partial credit was given for each step within the transition zone (between his basal score— 176 or 184—and his *PSE*), in proportion to the relative frequency of success at that step. Thus, if he called 192 gms. lighter than 200 gms. three out of seven times, he received 3/7 of a step interval credit, or .43. If he called 200 gms. lighter than 200 gms. two out of seven times, he was given 2/7 of a step interval credit, or .29, and so forth. To arrive at the *PSE*, the p values within the transition zone were added and multiplied by i, the step interval (8 gms.). This value, plus 1/2 step interval, was added to the basal score (184 gms.). Thus, the formula for the *PSE* was:

$$PSE = B + \frac{i}{2} + i \Sigma p$$

where B equals the basal score, i equals the step interval and p equals the proportion of successes in the transition zone. In our example:

$$PSE = 184 + \frac{8}{2} + 8\,(.72)$$
$$= 184 + 4 + 5.76$$
$$= 193.76$$
$$TE = PSE - MP$$
$$= 193.76 - 200$$
$$= -6.24$$

TE was computed in this way for all three conditions. The assimilation score was the difference in TE between Conditions II and I. This test did not include enough trials to provide an adequate test of the reliability of this assimilation score.

Bibliography

Allport, G. W. (1935), Attitudes. In *A Handbook of Social Psychology*, ed. C. Murchison. Worcester, Mass.: Clark University Press, pp. 798-844.
────── & Postman, L. (1947), *The Psychology of Rumor*. New York: Holt.
────── & Vernon, P. E. (1933), *Studies in Expressive Movement*. New York: Macmillan.
Ames, A., Jr. (1946), Binocular Vision as Affected by Relations between Uniocular Stimulus-Patterns in Commonplace Environments. *Amer. J. Psychol.*, 59:333-357.
Angyal, A. (1941), *Foundations for a Science of Personality*. New York: Commonwealth Fund.
Babcock, H. (1930), An Experiment in the Measurement of Mental Deterioration. *Arch. Psychol.*, New York, 18; No. 117.
Barratt, E. S. (1955), Space-Visualization Factors Related to Temperament Traits. *J. Psychol.*, 39:279-287.
Beck, S. J. (1944), *Rorschach's Test*. I. Basic Processes. New York: Grune & Stratton.
Bieri, J., Bradburn, W., & Galinsky, M. D. (1958), Sex Differences in Perceptual Behavior. *J. Pers.*, 26:1-12.
Block, J. (1957), A Study of Affective Responsiveness in a Lie-Detection Situation. *J. Abn. Soc. Psychol.*, 55:11-15.
Brooks, M. O. & Phillips, L. (1958), The Cognitive Significance of Rorschach Developmental Scores. *J. Pers.*, 26:268-290.
Bruner, J. S. & Goodman, C. C. (1947), Value and Need as Organizing Factors in Perception. *J. Abn. Soc. Psychol.*, 42:33-44.
────── & Goodnow, J. J., Austin, G. A. (1956), *A Study of Thinking*. New York: Wiley.
────── & Rodrigues, J. S. (1953), Some Determinants of Apparent Size. *J. Abn. Soc. Psychol.*, 48:17-24.
Carmichael, L., Hogan, H. P., & Walter, A. A. (1932), An Experimental Study of the Effect of Language on the Reproduction of Visually Perceived Form. *J. Exp. Psychol.*, 15:73-86.
Carter, L. & Schooler, E. (1949), Value, Need, and Other Factors in Perception. *Psychol. Rev.*, 56:200-208.
Cattell, R. B. (1952), *Factor Analysis*. New York: Harper.
Christensen, J. M. & Crannell, C. W. (1955), The Effect of Selected Visual Training Procedures on the Visual Form Field, WADC Technical Report 54-239, Wright Air Development Center, Air Research and Development Command, USAF, Wright-Patterson Air Force Base, Ohio.
Cronbach, L. J. & Gleser, G. C. (1953), Assessing Similarity between Profiles. *Psychol. Bull.*, 50:456-473.
Crutchfield, R. S., Woodworth, D. G., & Albrecht, R. E. (1958), Perceptual Performance and the Effective Person. Armed Services Technical Information Agency: Document No. AD 151039.

BIBLIOGRAPHY

Diamond, S. (1957), *Personality and Temperament*. New York: Harper.
Dickman, H. R. (1954), An Investigation of the Relationship between the Cognitive Organization of Objective and Behavioral Stimuli. Unpublished master's thesis. On file, University of Kansas library.
Erikson, E. H. (1950), *Childhood and Society*. New York: Norton.
Fillenbaum, S. (1959), Some Stylistic Aspects of Categorizing Behavior. *J. Pers.*, 27:187-195.
Freud, A. (1936), *The Ego and the Mechanisms of Defence*. New York: International Universities Press, 1946.
Freud, S. (1909), Notes upon a Case of Obsessional Neurosis. *Collected Papers*, 3:293-383. London: Hogarth Press, 1946.
—— (1915), Repression. *Collected Papers*, 4:84-97. London: Hogarth Press, 1946.
—— (1926), *The Problem of Anxiety*. New York: Norton, 1936.
Gardner, R. W. (1953), Cognitive Styles in Categorizing Behavior. *J. Pers.*, 22:214-233.
—— (1957), Field Dependence as a Determinant of Susceptibility to Certain Illusions. *Amer. Psychologist*, 12:397.
—— (1959), Cognitive Control Principles and Perceptual Behavior. *Bull. Menninger Clin.*, 23:241-248.
—— Cognitive Controls and Attention Deployment in Response to Visual Illusions. In preparation.
—— & Jackson, D. N., Messick, S. (1958), Personality Organization in Cognitive Attitudes and Intellectual Abilities. *Amer. Psychologist*, 13:336 (Abstract).
—— —— —— Personality Organization in Cognitive System Principles and Intellectual Abilities. To be published, *Psychological Issues*.
—— & Klein, G. S., Schlesinger, H. J. (1951), Perceptual Attitudes toward Instability: Prediction from Apparent Movement Responses to other Tasks Involving Resolution of Unstable Fields. *Amer. Psychologist*, 6:332.
—— & Long, R. I. (1959), Errors of the Standard and Illusion Effects with the Inverted-*T*. *Percept. Mot. Skills*, in press.
Gottschaldt, L. (1926), Über den Einfluss der Erfahrung auf die Wahrnehmung von Figuren: 1 Über den Einfluss gehäufter. Einprägung von Figuren auf ihre Sichtbarkeit in umfassenden Konfigurationen. *Psychol. Forsch.*, 8:261-317.
Gross, F. (1959), The Role of Set in Perception of the Upright. *J. Pers.*, 27:95-103.
Guilford, J. P. (1954), *Psychometric Methods*, 2nd ed. New York: McGraw-Hill.
Hardison, J. & Purcell, K. (1959), The Effects of Psychological Stress as a Function of Need and Cognitive Control. *J. Pers.*, 27:250-258.
Hartmann, H. (1939), *Ego Psychology and the Problem of Adaptation*. New York: International Universities Press, 1958.
Helson, H. (1947), Adaptation-Level as Frame of Reference for Prediction of Psychophysical Data. *Am. J. Psychol.*, 60:1-29.
Hollingworth, H. (1913), The Central Tendency of Judgment in Experimental Studies of Judgment. *Arch. Psychol.*, New York, 29:44-52.
Holt, R. R. (1954), Implications of Some Contemporary Personality Theories for Rorschach Rationale. In *Developments in the Rorschach Technique*, B. Klopfer, et al. New York: World Book.
Holzman, P. S. (1954), The Relation of Assimilation Tendencies in Visual, Auditory, and Kinesthetic Time-Error to Cognitive Attitudes of Leveling and Sharpening. *J. Pers.*, 22:375-394.
—— (1957), Focussing: A Style of Reality Contact. *Amer. Psychologist*, 12:388.

——— & Gardner, R. W. (1959), Leveling and Repression. *J. Abn. Soc. Psychol.*, 59:151-155.
——— & Klein, G. S. (1951), Perceptual Attitudes of "Leveling" and "Sharpening": Relation to Individual Differences in Time-Error. *Amer. Psychologist*, 6:257.
——— ——— (1954), Cognitive System-Principles of Leveling and Sharpening: Individual Differences in Assimilation Effects in Visual Time-Error. *J. Psychol.*, 37:105-122.
——— ——— (1956a), Intersensory and Visual Field Forces in Size Estimation. *Percept. Mot. Skills*, 6:37-41.
——— ——— (1956b), Motive and Style in Realty Contact. *Bull. Menninger Clin.*, 20:181-191.
Jackson, D. N. (1957), Intellectual Ability and Mode of Perception, *J. Consult. Psychol.*, 21:458.
Jaensch, E. & collaborators (1929), *Grundformen menschlichen Seins*. Berlin: Otto Elsner.
Jeffreys, A. W., Jr. (1953), An Exploratory Study of Perceptual Attitudes. Unpublished doctoral dissertation. On file, University of Houston library.
Johansson, G., Dureman, I., & Sälde, H. (1955), Motion Perception and Personality. *Acta Psychol.*, 11:289-296.
Kaplan, J. N. (1952), Predicting Memory Behavior from Cognitive Attitudes toward Instability. *Amer. Psychologist*, 7:322.
Kilpatrick, F. P. (1952), *Human Behavior from the Transactional Point of View*. Hanover, N.H.: Institute for Associated Research.
Klein, G. S. (1949a), Adaptive Properties of Sensory Functioning: Some Postulates and Hypotheses. *Bull. Menninger Clin.*, 13:16-23.
——— (1949b), A Clinical Perspective for Personality Research. *J. Abn. Soc. Psychol.*, 44:42-50.
——— (1949c), An Application of the Multiple Regression Principle to Clinical Prediction. *J. Gen. Psychol.*, 38:159-179.
——— (1951), The Personal World through Perception. In *Perception: An Approach to Personality*, eds. R. R. Blake & G. V. Ramsey. New York: Ronald Press, pp. 328-355.
——— (1953), The Menninger Foundation Research on Perception and Personality, 1947-1952: A Review. *Bull. Menninger Clin.*, 17:93-99.
——— (1954), Need and Regulation. In *Nebraska Symposium on Motivation*, ed. M. R. Jones. Lincoln: University of Nebraska Press, pp. 224-274.
——— (1956), Perception, Motives and Personality: A Clinical Perspective. In *Psychology of Personality*, ed. J. L. McCary. New York: Logos Press, pp. 121-199.
——— (1958), Cognitive Control and Motivation. In *Assessment of Human Motives*, ed. G. Lindzey. New York: Rinehart, pp. 87-118.
——— (1959), Consciousness in Psychoanalytic Theory: Some Implications for Current Research in Perception. *J. Amer. Psa. Assoc.*, 7:5-34.
——— & Gardner, R. W., Schlesinger, H. J. Tolerance for Unrealistic Experiences: A Generality Study. In preparation.
——— & Holzman, P. S. (1950), The "Schematizing" Process: Personality Qualities and Perceptual Attitudes in Sensitivity to Change. *Amer. Psychologist*, 5:312.
——— ——— & Laskin, D. (1954), The Perception Project: Progress Report for 1953-54. *Bull. Menninger Clin.*, 18:260-266.
——— & Krech, D. (1952), The Problem of Personality and Its Theory. In: *Theoretical Models and Personality Theory*, ed. D. Krech & G. S. Klein. Durham, N.C.: Duke University Press, pp. 1-23.
——— & Salomon, A. (1952), Cognitive Style and Regulation of Need. *Amer. Psychologist*, 7:321-322.

―――― ―――― & Smith, G. J. W., Mandler, J. M. Studies in Cognitive Style and the Regulation of Need. To be published, *Psychological Issues*.
―――― & Schlesinger, H. J. (1949), Where Is the Perceiver in Perceptual Theory? *J. Pers.*, 18:32-47.
―――― ―――― (1951), Perceptual Attitudes toward Instability: I. Prediction of Apparent Movement Experiences from Rorschach Responses. *J. Pers.*, 19:289-302.
―――― ―――― & Meister, D. E. (1951), The Effect of Personal Values on Perception: An Experimental Critique. *Psychol. Rev.*, 58:96-112.
Klopfer, B. & Kelley, D. M. (1942), *The Rorschach Technique*. New York: World Book.
Klüver, H. (1936), The Study of Personality and the Method of Equivalent and Non-Equivalent Stimuli. *Charact. & Pers.*, 5:91-112.
Koffka, K. (1935), *Principles of Gestalt Psychology*. New York: Harcourt, Brace.
―――― & Harrower, M. R. (1931), Colour and Organization: I and II. *Psychol. Forsch.*, 15:145-192; 193-275.
Köhler, W. (1923), Zur Theorie des Sukzessivvergleichs und der Zeitfehler. *Psychol. Forsch.*, 4:115-175.
―――― & Adams, P. (1958), Perception and Attention. *Amer. J. Psychol.*, 71:489-503.
Krathwohl, D. R. & Cronbach, L. J. (1956), Suggestions Regarding a Possible Measure of Personality: The Squares Test. *Educ. Psychol. Measmt.*, 16:305-316.
Kreezer, G. (1938), The Neurological Level of the Factors Underlying Time-Errors. *Amer. J. Psychol.*, 51:18-43.
Lauenstein, O. (1932), Ansatz zu einer physiologischen Theorie des Vergleichs und der Zeitfehler. *Psychol. Forsch.*, 17:130-177.
Lazarus, R. S., Baker, R. W., Broverman, D. M., & Mayer, J. (1957), Personality and Psychological Stress. *J. Pers.*, 25:559-577.
Linton, H. (1954), Rorschach Correlates of Response to Suggestion. *J. Abn. Soc. Psychol.*, 49:75-83.
―――― (1955), Dependence on External Influence: Correlates in Perception, Attitudes and Judgment. *J. Abn. Soc. Psychol.*, 51:502-507.
Loomis, H. & Moskowitz, S. (1958), Cognitive Style and Stimulus Ambiguity. *J. Pers.*, 26:349-364.
Marlowe, D. (1958), Some Psychological Correlates of Field Independence. *J. Consult. Psychol.*, 22:334.
Marrs, C. L. (1955), Categorizing Behavior as Elicited by a Variety of Stimuli. Unpublished master's thesis. On file, University of Kansas library.
Martin, B. (1954), Intolerance of Ambiguity in Interpersonal and Perceptual Behavior. *J. Pers.*, 22:494-503.
Michotte, A. (1952). In *A History of Psychology in Autobiography*, Vol. IV, eds. H. S. Langfeld et al. Worcester, Mass.: Clark University Press.
Murney, R. J. (1955), *An Investigation of the Cognitive System Principles of Leveling and Sharpening and Their Relationship to Selected Personality Variables*. Washington: Catholic University of America Press.
Paul, I. H. (1959), Studies in Remembering; The Reproduction of Connected and Extended Verbal Material. *Psychological Issues*, 1; No. 2.
Pettigrew, T. F. (1958), The Measurement and Correlates of Category Width as a Cognitive Variable. *J. Pers.*, 26:532-544.
Piaget, J. (1936), *The Origins of Intelligence in Children*. New York: International Universities Press, 1952.
―――― (1947), *The Psychology of Intelligence*. London: Routledge & Kegan Paul, 1950.
―――― & Vinh-Bang, Matalon, B. (1958), Note on the Law of the Temporal

Maximum of Some Optico-Geometric Illusions. *Amer. J. Psychol.*, 71:277-282.

Rapaport, D. (1950), On the Psycho-Analytic Theory of Thinking. *Int. J. Psychoanal.*, 31:161-170.

───── (1951a), Toward a Theory of Thinking. In *Organization and Pathology of Thought*, ed. D. Rapaport. New York: Columbia University Press, pp. 687-730.

───── (1951b), The Autonomy of the Ego. *Bull. Menninger Clin.*, 15:113-123.

───── (1951c), The Conceptual Model of Psychoanalysis. *J. Pers.*, 20:56-81.

───── (1957), Cognitive Structures. In *Contemporary Approaches to Cognition.* Cambridge: Harvard University Press, pp. 157-200.

───── (1958), The Theory of Ego Autonomy: A Generalization. *Bull. Menninger Clin.*, 22:13-35.

───── (1959), The Structure of Psychoanalytic Theory: A Systematizing Attempt. In *Psychology: A Study of a Science*, Vol. III, ed. S. Koch. New York: McGraw-Hill. Also to be published in *Psychological Issues*, 1960.

───── & Gill, M., Schafer, R. (1945), *Diagnostic Psychological Testing*, Vol. I. Chicago: Yearbook.

───── ───── ───── (1946), *Diagnostic Psychological Testing*, Vol. II. Chicago: Yearbook.

Rorschach, H. (1942), *Psychodiagnostics.* Bern: Hans Huber.

Rosner, S. (1957), Consistency in Response to Group Pressures. *J. Abn. Soc. Psychol.*, 55:145-146.

Schafer, R. (1948), *The Clinical Application of Psychological Tests.* New York: International Universities Press.

───── (1954), *Psychoanalytic Interpretation in Rorschach Testing.* New York: Grune & Stratton.

Schlesinger, H. J. (1954), Cognitive Attitudes in Relation to Susceptibility to Interference. *J. Pers.*, 22:354-374.

Sloane, H. N. (1959), The Generality and Construct Validity of Equivalence Range. Unpublished doctoral dissertation. On file, Pennsylvania State University library.

Smith, G. J. W. (1952), Cognitive Controls in Temporal Behavior Patterns. *Amer. Psychologist*, 7:322.

───── & Klein, G. S. (1953), Cognitive Controls in Serial Behavior Patterns. *J. Pers.*, 22:188-213.

Stroop, J. R. (1935), Studies in Interference in Serial Verbal Reactions. *J. Exp. Psychol.*, 18:643-661.

Temerlin, M. K. (1956), One Determinant of the Capacity to Free-Associate in Psychotherapy. *J. Abn. Soc. Psychol.*, 53:16-18.

Thouless, R. H. (1931), Phenomenal Regression to the 'Real' Object. I. *Brit. J. Psychol.*, 21:339-359.

───── (1932a), Phenomenal Regression to the 'Real' Object. II. *Brit. J. Psychol.*, 22:1-30

───── (1932b), Individual Differences in Phenomenal Regression. *Brit. J. Psychol.*, 22:216-241.

───── (1934), The General Principle Underlying Effects Attributed to the So-called Phenomenal Constancy Tendency. *Psychol. Forsch.*, 19:300-310.

Thurstone, L. L. (1944), *A Factorial Study of Perception.* Psychometric Monogr. No. 4. Chicago: University of Chicago Press.

───── (1947), *Multiple Factor Analysis.* Chicago: University of Chicago Press.

Tyler, L. E. (1956), *The Psychology of Human Differences.* New York: Appleton-Century-Crofts.

von Uexküll, J. (1934), A Stroll through the Worlds of Animals and Men.

In *Instinctive Behavior,* ed. C. H. Schiller. New York: International Universities Press, 1957.
Wapner, S. & Werner, H. (1957), *Perceptual Development.* Worcester, Mass.: Clark University Press.
Wechsler, D. (1958), *The Measurement and Appraisal of Adult Intelligence.* Baltimore: Williams & Wilkins.
Wertheim, J. & Mednick, S. A. (1958), The Achievement Motive and Field Independence. *J. Consult. Psychol.,* 22:38.
Wertheimer, M. (1912), Experimentelle Studien über das Sehen von Bewegung. *Z. Psychol.,* 61:161-265.
Witkin, H. A. (1950), Individual Differences in Ease of Perception of Embedded Figures. *J. Pers.,* 19:1-15.
────── (1959), The Perception of the Upright. *Sci. Amer.,* 200:50-56.
────── & Karp, S. A., Goodenough, D. R. (1959), Dependence in Alcoholics. *Quart. J. Stud. Alc.,* 20:493-504.
────── & Lewis, H. B., Hertzman, M., Machover, K., Meissner, P. B., Wapner, S. (1954), *Personality through Perception.* New York: Harper.
Wulf, F. (1922), Über die Veränderung von Vorstellungen (Gedächtnis und Gestalt). *Psychol. Forsch.,* 1:333-373.
Young, H. H. (1959), A Test of Witkin's Field-Dependence Hypothesis. *J. Abn. Soc. Psychol.,* 59:188-192.

INDEX

1—ERIK H. ERIKSON: *Identity and the Life Cycle; Selected Papers.* Historical Introduction by DAVID RAPAPORT

2—I. H. PAUL: *Studies in Remembering; The Reproduction of Connected and Extended Verbal Material*

3—FRITZ HEIDER: *On Perception, Event Structure, and the Psychological Environment.* Preface by GEORGE S. KLEIN

4—RILEY GARDNER, PHILIP S. HOLZMAN, GEORGE S. KLEIN, HARRIET LINTON, and DONALD P. SPENCE: *Cognitive Control; A Study of Individual Consistencies in Cognitive Behavior*

INDEX

INDEX

Ability, 2, 62, 74, 76, 81; see also Verbal material, retention of
Achievement concepts, 3, 50
Ackerman, N. W., 1, 123
Action, 4, 5
Activity, 1, 11, 13, 128, 133
Adams, P., 4, 138, 141
Adaptation, 1, 10-14, 40; 4, 1, 3, 4, 6, 9-17, 116, 127-128, 137, 138, 146-147
  and perceptual apparatus, 3, viii, 35-52, 59, 60
Adler, A., 1, 11
Affect, 4, 54
  and idea, 4, 46, 47, 88, 129, 133
Albrecht, R. E., 4, 69
Allport, F. H., 3, 115
Allport, G. W., 2, 15, 55, 139, 140; 4, 1, 2, 22
Ambiguity; see Verbal material
Ames, A., Jr., 4, 35, 37
Anality, 1, 66-68, 72, 154
Angyal, A., 3, 116, 117, 118; 4, 1
Anticipations, 4, 25, 139
Apparatuses, combining, 3, 26-27
Aspects, 3, 97-103
Assimilation, 2, 3, 55, 140, 141, 142, 144; 4, 25, 26, 29, 63, 100, 102, 103, 113, 129, 136, 138, 142
Attention, 4, 13, 16, 47, 49, 56, 82, 85, 89, 93, 96, 111, 138, 140, 141, 144, 146
Attitudes, 4, 2
Attneave, F., 3, 56, 57
Auerbach, E., 2, 143
Austin, G. A., 4, 40
Autokinetic phenomenon, 4, 68, 89
Automatization, 1, 13; 2, 147, 149
Autonomy, 2, 142, 147, 149
  relative, 2, 57, 58; 4, 7, 8, 9, 13
  secondary, 1, 16
  vs. shame and doubt, 1, 15, 53, 65-74, 142, 154, 155
  see also Ego, autonomy of

Babcock, H., 2, 18; 4, 144
Badeali, 1, 109
Baker, R. W., 4, 54
Barratt, E. S., 4, 69
Bartlett, F. C., 2, 1, 3-6, 9-10, 15-16, 31, 34-35, 128, 140, 141, 142, 143, 149
Basic trust vs. basic mistrust, 1, 15, 53, 55-65, 68, 134, 140, 141, 154
Bateman, J. F., 1, 139
Beach, F. A., 2, 142
Becher, E., 3, 44, 69
Beck, S. J., 4, 168
Behavior, 3, 8, 13-15, 21, 28, 81, 110; 4, 2, 4-10, 12, 15
Belbin, E., 2, 55
Benedek, T., 1, 61
Benedict, R., 1, 114
Benjamin, J., 1, 17
Bentley, A. F., 3, 70
Bergson, H., 3, 87, 106
Bettelheim, B., 1, 17, 27
Bibring, E., 1, 16, 126
Bieri, J., 4, 68
Binding, 1, 13
Binet, A., 2, 145
Biology, 3, 108-109
Bipolarization, 1, 140
Bisexual diffusion, 1, 145, 163
Block, J., 4, 68
Blondel, C., 3, 93, 104, 106
Blos, P., 1, 122
Body ego, 1, 149
  image, 1, 41
Boring, E. G., 3, 68
Boundaries, 3, 19, 88, 106, 110, 113
  ego, 3, 86, 95, 106
Bradburn, W., 4, 68
Brain, W. R., 2, 4
Brenman, M., 1, 133
Breuer, J., 1, 6
Brooks, M. O., 4, 70
Broverman, D. M., 4, 54
Bruner, J. S., 4, 40, 48, 59

Numbers in italics indicate the Monograph number.

Brunswik, E., *3*, vii, 55, 75, 76, 77, 83, 110, 112
Bühler, K., *3*, 35, 52
Burlingham, D., *1*, 137

Carmichael, L., *4*, 22
Carter, L., *4*, 59
Cartwright, D., *3*, 108
Cassirer, E., *3*, 117
Cathexis, *2*, 148, 149; *see also* Hypercathexis
Cattell, R. B., *4*, 78
Causal texture; *see* Environment
Causes, *3*, 56-58, 65, 117
Cell assemblies, *2*, 56, 57
Centration hypothesis, *4*, 47, 84, 86, 103, 114, 140
Change of function, *1*, 12, 13, 16
Character defense; *see* Defense
Chein, I., *3*, 115
Christensen, J. M., *4*, 8
Clark, K. B., *2*, 11
Clayton, M., *4*, 40
Cognition, *2*, 58, 59; *3*, 1, 2, 23, 34, 48, 55; *4*, 1-4, 8, 9, 22, 111, 145
Cognitive controls, *4*, 1-6, 9-15, 17, 77, 109, 110, 137-140, 145-147
and adaptation, *4*, 1, 3, 4, 6, 9-17, 116, 127-128, 137, 138, 146-147
and cognitive styles, *4*, 115-126
and defenses, *4*, 1, 9, 11-12, 21, 122-123, 127-136, 139-140, 143
and development, *4*, 12-13, 146
and drive, *4*, 1-4, 9-13, 127, 139
and intelligence tests, *4*, 143-145
and passivity, *4*, 116, 141
and prediction, *4*, 8, 16, 17, 137
and psychoanalysis, *4*, 9-14, 127-136, 146
and psychotherapy, *4*, 143, 145
behavioral units in, *4*, 4-6
constricted-flexible control, *4*, 6, 11, 16, 17, 21, 53-66, 79, 114, 127
  factor analyses, results for women, Factor I, *4*, 94, 99, 118, 135, 137, 161
  see also Field articulation
equivalence range, *4*, 11, 16, 21, 39-45, 94, 115, 137-139, 141, 145
  factor analyses, results for women, Factor III, *4*, 105-109, 113-114, 118, 121, 137, 161
factor analysis of, *4*, 17, 21, 77-114, 159-162
  and person clusters, *4*, 116-126, 164-167

results for men of, *4*, 79-94
  Factor I—Scanning, *4*, 82-89
  Factor IV—Tolerance for unrealistic experiences, *4*, 89-94
results for women of, *4*, 94-109
  Factor I—Field articulation, *4*, 94-100
  Factor II—Leveling-Sharpening, *4*, 100-105
  Factor III—Equivalence range, *4*, 105-109
sex differences in, *4*, 110
field articulation, *4*, 6, 14, 22, 115, 116, 138, 140, 141, 144, 146
  factor analyses, results for women, Factor I, *4*, 94-100, 111, 114, 117-118, 121, 122, 137, 161
field dependence-independence, *4*, 17, 18, 21, 54, 56, 67-76, 79, 100, 142
  factor analyses, results for women, Factor I, *4*, 94, 99, 110, 114, 137, 161, 168-175
  see also Field articulation
focusing, *4*, 16, 21, 46-52, 54, 82, 88, 133, 137, *see also* Scanning
generality of, *4*, 141-142
leveling-sharpening, *2*, 3, 140, 142, 144; *4*, 3, 6, 11, 14, 16, 21-30, 38, 63, 73, 86, 94, 115, 116, 139, 142, 144, 145
  and repression, *4*, 128-132, 136, 138, 143
  factor analyses, results for women, Factor II, *4*, 100-105, 109, 111-113, 118, 121-123, 137, 161
measurement of, *4*, 16-18
process components of, *4*, 13-14
scanning, *4*, 6, 11, 14, 16, 47, 49, 54, 79, 116, 138, 140, 142, 146
  and isolation, *4*, 89, 128-129, 132-136
  factor analyses, results for men, Factor I, *4*, 82-89, 109, 111, 112, 114, 118, 123, 137, 160
  see also Focusing
scoring of, *4*, 111-114
stability of, *4*, 142-143
tolerance for unrealistic experiences, *4*, 6, 15, 16, 21, 31-38, 79, 116, 138, 139, 142
  factor analyses, results for men, Factor IV, *4*, 89-94, 109, 112, 113, 118, 137, 161
validity of, *4*, 140-141
Cognitive styles, *2*, 7, 59-62, 65, 73, 119, 145-149; *4*, 2, 4-6, 115-126

Coherence; *see* Verbal material
Communication, *3*, 88; *see also* Language; Speech
Compulsiveness, *4*, 122-123
Concept formation, *4*, 32, 127, 138, 139, 141, 144, 145
Conditioning (determination), internal and external, *3*, 3-6, 32, 36, 38, 40, 48, 49; *see also* Vibrations
Conflict, *4*, 9, 12, 127, 128, 139
Conjunctions, *2*, 129, 135
Conscience, *1*, 80, 93
Constancy hypothesis, *3*, 68
Constricted-flexible control; *see* Cognitive controls
Control; *see* Cognitive controls; Drive
Control principles; *see* Cognitive Controls
Cores, *3*, 33, 36, 37, 55
Cournot, A., *3*, 59
Crannell, C. W., *4*, 8
Crises, normative, *1*, 53-54, 61, 75, 88, 90, 113-115, 116, 141
Cronbach, L. J., *4*, 22, 117
Crozier, W. J., *3*, 77, 78
Crutchfield, R. S., *4*, 69
Cybernetics, *3*, vii

Dandieu, A., *3*, 86, 106
Danger, *1*, 11, 114
Dann, S., *1*, 118
Darwin, C., *3*, 65
Davis, D. R., *2*, 55
Deese, J., *2*, 55
Defense, *1*, 6, 11, 48
 and cognitive controls, *4*, 1, 9, 11-12, 21, 122-123, 127-136, 139-140, 143
 autonomous, *1*, 12
 character, *4*, 9, 128
 fluidity of, *1*, 117
Delay; *see* Drive
Denial, *4*, 51
Descartes, R., *2*, 2
Determinants, distal and proximal, *3*, 61, 67-84
Determination, *3*, 61-84
 by orientation, *3*, 77-78
 see also Conditioning
Deutsch, M., *3*, 108, 110
Dickman, H. R., *4*, 39
Discourse analysis, *2*, 54
Distantiation, *1*, 95-96, 125
Dostoyevsky, F., *3*, 85
Doubt, *1*, 142-143
Drive, *2*, 148-149; *4*, 128, 145
 and cognitive controls, *4*, 1-4, 9-13, 127, 139

control of, *4*, 12-13, 145
delay of, *4*, 4, 11, 13, 145
Duncker, K., *3*, 58
Dunham, H. W., *1*, 139
Dureman, I., *4*, 3

Economical description, law of, *3*, viii, 55-60
Effort after meaning, *2*, 4, 5, 140
Ego, *1*, 5, 6, 46-49, 149
 and environment, *1*, 147-164; *3*, 86, 95, 106-107
 apparatuses, *2*, 146, 147
 of primary and secondary autonomy, *1*, 12, 13
 autonomy of, *1*, 10, 13, 14
 boundaries, *3*, 86, 95, 106
 definition of, *1*, 9
 development, *1*, 18-49
 functioning, conflict-free sphere of, *1*, 152, 154; *2*, 146-149; *4*, 9-10, 128
 ideal, *1*, 20, 39, 40, 147-150
 identity; *see* Identity
 instincts, *1*, 7
 psychology, *1*, 18; *2*, 146-147
  historical survey of, *1*, 5-17
 regression in the service of the, *1*, 13, 133
 space-time, *1*, 32-33, 41, 48
 synthesis, *1*, 42, 48, 89, 102, 116, 119
 see also Body ego
Eisenstadt, S., *1*, 159
Elimination, *1*, 37, 67, 154
Ellis, H., *3*, 86, 105
Embeddedness, *3*, 89-90, 97
Emotions, *2*, 59
Environment, *3*, vii, viii, 1, 24, 41, 50-51, 54, 56, 59, 114-119
 and adaptation, *4*, 6, 9, 10
 and cognitive controls, *4*, 12, 13
 and ego, *1*, 147-164; *3*, 86, 95, 106-107
 and organism, *3*, 24, 35-37, 69, 76, 80-83
 and perception, *3*, 35-37, 43-46, 50-52
 and person, *3*, 115-116, 119
 average expectable, *1*, 12, 151, 155
 behavioral significance of, *3*, 8
 causal texture of, *3*, 2, 33, 36
 psychological, *3*, 85-107
 structure of, *3*, 8-23, 25, 33, 35, 40
 see also Reality; Things; Wholes; Units
Epigenesis, *1*, 14, 52, 119, 121
Equivalence range; *see* Cognitive controls
Erikson, E., *1*, 2, 3, 6, 9, 11, 12, 14, 15, 16, 17, 24, 25, 27, 50, 59, 101, 102,

113, 121, 132, 133, 154, 155, 159, 160, 163, 164; *4*, 146
Erikson, J., *1*, 2
Erikson, K. T., *1*, 3, 139, 163
Escalona, S., *1*, 17
Estes, W. K., *2*, 64
Events, *3*, 23, 26, 29-31, 58
 causes of, *3*, 11-12, 48
 composite and unitary, *3*, 4-6, 17, 20, 22, 24, 26, 30
 core, *3*, viii, 20, 22, 25, 27, 30-32, 34, 41, 55
 thing, *3*, 13
 wave, *3*, 13-17, 25, 33
Experience error, *3*, 68
Explication; *see* Verbal material
Expressive movements, *3*, .23, 32, 34; *4*, 2

Factor analyses; *see* Cognitive controls
Fallacies, psychological, *3*, 67-68
Familiarity; *see* Verbal material
Federn, P., *1*, 147
Feedback, *4*, 10, 11
Fenichel, O., *1*, 16, 20
Field, *3*, 117, 118
 determination, *3*, 81
Field articulation; *see* Cognitive controls
Field dependence-independence; *see* Cognitive controls
Figure and ground, *3*, 30-31, 91
Fillenbaum, S., *4*, 40
Fit; *see* Verbal material
Focal variables, determination of, *3*, 61-68
Focus, *3*, 64, 66, 68-69, 78, 79, 111
 disguised, *3*, 67, 70, 72
 multiple, *3*, 64
Focusing; *see* Cognitive controls
Foord, E. N., *2*, 64
Fractionation, *2*, 7, 8, 55-58, 60, 61, 139, 142, 143
Fragmentation; *see* Verbal material
Framework, spatial and temporal *3*, 95-97
Frankenstein, C., *1*, 159
Fremont-Smith, F., *1*, 72
Freud, A., *1*, 6, 11, 16, 46, 118, 137; *4*, 128
Freud, S., *1*, 6, 7, 8, 9, 10, 11, 12, 13, 14, 16, 19, 20, 21, 22, 23, 24, 31, 39, 42, 48, 49, 50, 52, 76, 77, 88, 96, 101, 102, 147, 148, 153, 154, 163; *2*, 148; *4*, 4, 13, 46, 129, 132, 133, 146
Fromm-Reichmann, F., *1*, 56

Galinsky, M. D., *4*, 68

Gaps; *see* Verbal material
Gardner, R. W., *4*, 1, 13, 16, 17, 31, 35, 38, 39, 44, 47, 68, 69, 91, 136, 140, 141, 142, 143
Generativity vs. stagnation, *1*, 15, 97, 154
Genidentity, *3*, 108-109
Genitality, *1*, 40, 96, 97
Gestalt psychology; *see* Psychology
Gibson, J. J., *2*, 141
Ginsburg, S. W., *1*, 128
Gleser, G. C., *4*, 117
Goal reaction, *3*, 72
Gomulicki, B. R., *2*, 2, 59, 145
Goodenough, D. R., *4*, 69
Goodman, C. C., *4*, 59
Goodnow, J. J., *4*, 40
Gottschaldt, L.; *see* Tests
Gounod, C. F., *1*, 108
Granit, A. R., *2*, 58
Gross, F., *4*, 68
Guilford, J. P., *4*, 162
Guthrie, E. R., *3*, 74

Habit-family hierarchy, *3*, 71-72
Hanawalt, N. G., *2*, 64
Hardison, J., *4*, 54
Hardman, G. W., *2*, 55
Harris, Z. S., *2*, 54
Harrower, M. R., *2*, 23; *4*, 49, 62
Hartmann, H., *1*, 5, 6, 11, 12, 13, 14, 15, 16, 114, 147, 149, 151, 152, 153; *2*, 146, 147, 149; *4*, 10, 12, 13, 127, 128
Head, H., *2*, 4
Hebb, D. O., *2*, 3, 4, 7, 55, 56, 57, 64, 141, 142
Helson, H., *3*, 57; *4*, 25
Hendrick, I., *1*, 22, 128
Hertzman, M., *4*, 76
Hilgard, E. R., *2*, 3; *3*, 73
Historical change, and ego development, *1*, 18-49
Hitler, A., *1*, 27
Hoagland, H., *3*, 77, 78
Hobhouse, L. T., *3*, 74, 75
Hochberg, J. E., *3*, 56, 58
Hogan, H. P., *4*, 22
Hollingworth, H., *4*, 23
Holmes, G., *2*, 4
Holt, E. B., *3*, 62, 75
Holt, R. R., *2*, 148; *4*, 1
Holzman, P. S., *4*, 1, 2, 3, 16, 22, 27, 49, 133, 136, 142, 143
Horney, K., *1*, 6, 11
Hospital community, *1*, 138-139
Hull, C. L., *3*, 71, 72
Huxley, J., *1*, 122

Hypercathexis, *1*, 13; *4*, 13-14; *see also* Cathexis

Id, *1*, 11, 12, 20, 24, 25, 48, 49, 149
  psychology, *1*, 16
Idea, and affect, *4*, 46, 47, 88, 129, 133
Identification, *1*, 9, 31, 74, 82, 87, 88-90, 97, 110-121, 128, 137, 140
Identity
  and identification, *1*, 89-90, 110-121
  consciousness, *1*, 118, 142-143, 162-163
  crisis, *1*, 103, 113
  definition of, *1*, 116
  Eastern, *1*, 33-34
  ego, *1*, 19-26, 34, 36, 41, 43, 48, 89-90, 93, 101-164
  group, *1*, 19-26, 27, 42, 46, 49, 92, 102, 157, 158
  Midwestern, *1*, 35-36
  negative, *1*, 127, 129-132, 144, 161-164
  Negro, *1*, 37-38
  psychonalytic, *1*, 152-153
  resistance, *1*, 135
  sexual, *1*, 125, 145, 156
  Southern, *1*, 36-37
  vs. identity diffusion, *1*, 15, 88-94, 118, 121-146, 162
  Western, *1*, 34-35
Ideology, *1*, 110, 142, 146, 148, 153, 155-161, 162
Imagery, *2*, 62, 67, 69-70, 75, 76, 145
Importation; *see* Verbal material
Incorporation *1*, 37, 57, 59, 154
Individual differences, *2*, 5, 7, 53, 59-62, 64, 73, 76, 143, 144; *4*, 9
Industry
  diffusion of *1*, 127-129
  vs. inferiority, *1*, 15, 82-88
Information theory, *2*, 23; *3*, vii
Initiative vs. guilt, *1*, 15, 53, 74-82, 144, 154, 155
Inner world, *4*, 13
Integrity vs. despair, *1*, 15, 98-99, 154, 156
Intellectualizing, *4*, 87, 128
Intention, *4*, 5, 15
Intentionality, *3*, 116, 118-119
Intimacy and distantiation vs. isolation, *1*, 15, 123-126, 145, 154, 156
  vs. self-absorption, *1*, 95-97
Introjection, *1*, 113
Intrusion, *1*, 37, 76, 154
Irion, A. L., *2*, 3
Isolation, *4*, 123
  and focusing, *4*, 46, 51, 52
  and scanning, *4*, 89, 128-129, 132-136

Israel, *1*, 159-161

Jackson, D. N., *4*, 16, 44, 68, 142
Jacobson, E., *1*, 16, 17
Jaensch, E., *4*, 54
Jahoda, M., *1*, 51
James, W., *1*, 116; *2*, 143; *3*, 67, 87
Jeffreys, A. W., Jr., *4*, 32
Johansson, G., *3*, 58; *4*, 3
Judgment, *4*, 5, 127, 139
Jung, C., *1*, 31

Kant, I., *1*, 20
Kaplan, B., *2*, 23
Kaplan, J. N., *4*, 32
Kardiner, A., *1*, 6, 11
Karp, S. A., *4*, 49
Katona, G., *2*, 16, 145
Kelley, D. M., *4*, 168, 169
Kibbutz movement, *1*, 159-161
Kilpatrick, F. P., *4*, 35
Kinsey, A. C., *1*, 96, 145
Kirkpatrick, C., *2*, 55
Klein, G. S., *2*, 7, 59, 147, 148, 149; *4*, 1, 3, 5, 6, 11, 13, 16, 17, 22, 27, 31, 35, 38, 49, 53, 54, 56, 57, 58, 59, 61, 64, 91, 92, 93, 115, 127, 133, 137, 143, 146
Klein, M., *1*, 11
Kleitman, N., *2*, 142
Klopfer, B., *4*, 18, 76, 168, 169
Klüver, H., *3*, 63, 74; *4*, 39
Knight, R. P., *1*, 122, 133
Koffka, K., *2*, 3, 4; *3*, 62, 66, 68, 69, 78, 79, 80, 81, 87, 90, 95, 106, 114; *4*, 25, 33, 49, 62
Köhler, W., *2*, 3; *3*, 9, 27, 68, 69, 74, 82, 112; *4*, 29, 138, 141
Krathwohl, D. R., *4*, 22
Krech, D., *4*, 1
Kreezer, G., *4*, 29
Kris, E., *1*, 11, 12, 13, 14, 16, 17, 133, 152, 153

Landscape, *3*, 113-115
Language, *3*, 7, 77; *see also* Communication; Speech
Laplace, P. S., *3*, 58
Lashley, K. S., *2*, 3, 4
Laskin, D., *4*, 1
Latency period, *1*, 76, 111
Lauenstein, O., *4*, 29
Lazarus, R. S., *4*, 54
Learning, *2*, 1-2, 3, 8, 16, 55-56, 58, 59, 64, 101, 137, 138, 144, 147, 148, 149
Le Bon, G., *1*, 19

Leeper, R. W., *3*, 108
Leitch, M., *1*, 17
Lenzen, V. F., *3*, 110, 111
Leveling-sharpening; *see* Cognitive controls
Levitt, E. E., *2*, 11, 18
Lewin, K., *3*, ix, 38, 39, 66, 87, 88, 108-119
Lewy, E., *2*, 146
Lexical unit; *see* Verbal material
Liebmann effect, *4*, 49
Life cycle, *1*, 14, 15, 44, 151
Life space, *3*, ix, 89, 91, 108, 110-118
Linton, H., *4*, 67-68, 168, 169, 170, 171
Locke, J., *3*, 99
Locomotion, *1*, 22-23, 75-76, 163; *3*, 88
Loewenstein, R. M., *1*, 11, 12, 14, 152, 153
London, I. D., *3*, 118
Long, R. I., *4*, 140
Loomis, H., *4*, 16, 54

Macfarlane, J. W., *1*, 59
Mach, E., *3*, 57, 58
Mahler, M., *1*, 17
Man, mechanization of, *1*, 46
Mandler, J. M., *4*, 11
Manifolds, *3*, vii, 7, 22, 23, 27, 30, 43-44, 55, 59
  structural, *4*, 7
Mannheim, K., *1*, 142, 157
Marlowe, D., *4*, 68
Marrs, C. L., *4*, 39
Martin, B., *4*, 32
Martin, C. E., *1*, 145
Matalon, B., *4*, 47
Mayer, J., *4*, 54
McAlister, E., *3*, 56
McDonald, W. T., *2*, 139
McDougall, W., *2*, 59; *3*, 69
McGeoch, G. O., *2*, 139
McGeoch, J. A., *2*, 3, 138, 139
McGregor, G., *1*, 31
McKinney, F., *2*, 138
McNemar, Q., *2*, 90
Mead, G. H., *1*, 147
Mead, M., *1*, 145
Mediation; *see* Perception
Mediator, *3*, 1-34, 36-37; *see also* Structures, mediating
Medium, *3*, 1-34, 48, 49
Mednick, S. A., *4*, 68
Meinong, A., *3*, 53
Meister, D. E., *4*, 59
Mekeel, H. S., *1*, 21
Memory, *2*, 2, 4, 55, 58, 59, 60, 143, 144, 146, 148, 149; *4*, 4, 11, 22, 32, 102, 103, 104, 116, 127, 129, 130, 137, 138, 142, 144
Messick, S., *4*, 16, 44, 142
Michelangelo, *1*, 109
Michotte, A., *4*, 4
Miller, A., *1*, 91
Miller, G. A., *2*, 138
Modality, *1*, 58, 60, 66, 69-70, 78
Mode, *1*, 15, 37
Moratorium, *1*, 145
  historical *1*, 160
  psychosexual, *1*, 111, 145
  psychosocial, *1*, 104, 111, 119, 164
Morgan, C. T., *2*, 142
Moskowitz, S., *4*, 16, 54
Motivation, *2*, 5, 57, 59, 60, 147, 149; *4*, 3
  and cognitive controls, *4*, 1, 2, 4, 29
Murney, R. J., *4*, 141
Mutuality, *1*, 15, 58, 113, 125, 140

Narcissism, *1*, 20, 147
  infantile, *1*, 39
Need; *see* Drive
Neutral energies, *1*, 9
Neutralization, *1*, 13
Newman, E. G., *2*, 52, 139
Noble, C. E., *2*, 31
Northway, M. L., *2*, 55
Nunberg, H., *1*, 11, 25, 49

Object process, *3*, 3-4, 5
Objects, *3*, 75-76, 97
  and observer, *3*, 110-112
  aspects of; *see* Aspects
  see also Genidentity
Offshoots, *3*, viii, 20, 21-23, 25-28, 30-31, 34, 36-42, 55-56, 59, 111
Oldfield, R. C., *2*, 4
Orality, *1*, 57, 59-63, 68, 72, 154
Organism, and environment, *3*, 24, 35, 36, 69, 76, 80-83

Passivity, *1*, 10, 13, 128, 133
  and cognitive controls, *4*, 116, 141
Pathology,
  ego, *1*, 26-38
  social, *1*, 38-49
Paul, I. H., *4*, 142
Perception, *2*, 3, 58, 59, 147, 149; *3*, vii, viii, 1, 2, 8, 9, 27-30, 33, 35, 39-42, 51, 65, 69, 71, 74, 75, 78, 79, 82, 83, 85-86, 97, 110, 111; *4*, 2, 4-5, 7, 8, 10, 22, 24, 32, 127, 137, 139, 142
  adequate and inadequate, *3*, 50-52

and tactual object, *3*, 19-20
causal lines in, *3*, 53, 54
distance, *3*, 2-3, 33
economical description in, *3*, 53-60
functions of, *3*, 23-25
mediation in, *3*, 1-34, 38-40, 43-46, 54, 75, 76, 97, 110-111
   language, *3*, 7
   light waves, *3*, 15-17
   olfactory, *3*, 18-19
   sensory qualities of, *3*, 28-30
   sound waves, *3*, 17-18
objects of, *3*, 1-34
probability in, *3*, 56-59
synthesis in, *3*, 25, 26
see also Cognitive controls; Cognitive styles
Perceptual constancies, *3*, 41, 42
Perceptual input and output, *3*, 110-112
Perceptual system, *3*, 24, 34, 55, 56, 60
   adaptive function of, *3*, 35-52, 59
   structure of, *3*, 46, 52
Person clusters; see Cognitive controls, factor analyses of
Personal Inventory, *4*, 117, 121-126
Personality, *2*, 146
   aspects of; see Aspects
   growth and crises of healthy, *1*, 50-100
   theory of, *4*, 1-3, 6-8, 146
Pettigrew, T. F., *4*, 40
Phase sequence, *2*, 55, 57, 58
Phase specificity, *1*, 119
Phillips, L., *4*, 69, 70
Physics, *3*, 108-109
Piaget, J., *3*, 86, 106; *4*, 47, 49, 84, 98, 103, 140, 145
Piers, G., *1*, 130, 142
Plato, *2*, 2
Play, *1*, 84-88, 140
Pleasure principle, *1*, 45
Pomeroy, W. B., *1*, 145
Positivism, *3*, 65, 66
Postman, L., *2*, 15, 55, 139, 140; *4*, 22
Prägnanz, *3*, 55
Primary process, *2*, 148; *4*, 127, 145
Primitive mentality; see Thinking
Proactive interference, *4*, 142
Probability, *3*, 56-59
Projection, *1*, 113; *4*, 3
Proust, M., *3*, viii, 85-107
   theory of art of, *3*, 105-106
Psychoanalysis, *1*, 5-18, 43-45, 48, 49, 52, 71, 77, 96, 101, 111, 114, 150-153, 159; *2*, 146, 148, 149; *4*, 2, 3, 145

and cognitive controls, *4*, 9-14, 127-136, 146
and memory, *2*, 146
see also Ego psychology
Psychological concepts, relative autonomy of, *3*, 108-110
Psychological fallacies; see Fallacies
Psychological theories, environmental determinants in, *3*, 61-84
Psychology, *3*, 108-109
   association theories, *3*, 44, 52, 65, 70, 94, 117, 119
   conditioned reflex theories, *3*, 65, 70, 79
   configurationism, *2*, 55
   connectionism, *2*, 2, 55
   developmental, *3*, ix, 77, 86, 87, 89, 94, 106; *4*, 146
   ego; see Ego psychology
   Gestalt, *2*, 2, 140, 142; *3*, ix, 25, 28, 44, 45, 69, 78-87, 89, 117; *4*, 1
   stimulus-response theories, *3*, 69, 70, 72-74, 116
   topological, *3*, 88, 112, 113
   Würzburg school of, *2*, 141
Psychotherapy, and cognitive controls, *4*, 143, 145
see also Psychoanalysis
Purcell, K., *4*, 54
Purpose, *3*, 52
Putnam, M. C., *1*, 17

Rank, B., *1*, 17
Rapaport, D., *1*, 10, 13, 17, 133; *2*, 1, 59, 146, 148, 149; *4*, 9, 13, 14, 18, 64, 76, 130, 139, 144
Rationalization, *2*, 4, 5, 140
Rau, L., *2*, 139
Reality, *1*, 6, 10-14; *4*, 1, 3, 6, 9, 10, 12-14, 139
   and drive, *4*, 2, 4, 145
   principle, *1*, 8, 11, 45
   Proust's conception of, *3*, 101-107
see also Environment
Recognition, *1*, 111-112, 163
Recruitment, *2*, 7, 8, 55-58, 60, 61, 77, 78, 98, 100, 101, 119, 136, 139, 142, 143, 147
Redl, F., *1*, 17
Redundancy, *2*, 18, 23-26, 40, 42, 53, 54, 98, 119, 140, 142
   analysis, *2*, 26-31, 33, 114-116, 128-133, 135
Regions, *3*, 43-46, 84, 87-91
Regression, *1*, 56, 68, 133; *2*, 148; *4*, 127
   in the service of the ego, *1*, 13, 133

Religion, *1*, 64-65
Remembering, *2*, 1-5, 8, 59, 75
 style of, *2*, 53, 60, 137, 145, 146
 see also Memory; Verbal material, retention of
Repression, *1*, 7, 8; *4*, 127, 133
 and leveling, *4*, 128-132, 136, 138, 143
Resistance, *1*, 45, 133-136
Resonance, *3*, 25-26
Retention (mode), *1*, 37, 67
Retention; *see* Verbal material, retention of
Retroactive inhibition, *2*, 138
 interference, *2*, 62; *4*, 142
Riesman, D., *1*, 162
Rodrigues, J. S., *4*, 40, 48
Role experimentation, *1*, 144
Rorschach, H.; *see* Tests
Rosner, S., *4*, 68
Rousseau, J. J., *3*, 105
Rubin, E., *3*, 37, 38, 39
Rumor, *2*, 140; *4*, 22
Russell, B., *3*, viii, 53, 54, 56, 57

Sälde, H., *4*, 3
Salomon, A., *4*, 11
Scanning; *see* Cognitive controls
Schafer, R., *4*, 130, 133
Schemas, *2*, 2, 4-7, 9, 10, 32, 53-55, 57-61, 72, 77, 101, 119, 120, 135, 138-143, 145
 as ego apparatuses, *2*, 146-149
Schilder, P., *1*, 142, 147
Schlesinger, H. J., *4*, 1, 16, 17, 31, 35, 38, 46, 47, 49, 50, 54, 59, 88, 91, 133
Schooler, E., *4*, 59
Schwartz, M. S., *1*, 139
Sciences, *3*, 108-109
Secondary process, *1*, 8, 11, 12; *2*, 148; *4*, 128, 145
Self, *1*, 6, 147, 149, 150
Self-esteem, *1*, 20, 39, 40, 46, 68, 89, 147
Selfridge, J. A., *2*, 138
Senn, M. J. E., *1*, 50
Serial reproduction, *4*, 142
Set, *2*, 141, 142
Sexuality, *1*, 95
 infantile, *1*, 53, 76-77
Shakespeare, W., *1*, 107, 108
Shame, *1*, 142-143, 163
Sharpening; *see* Leveling-sharpening
Shaw, G. B., *1*, 87, 102-110, 112, 122, 142, 156, 157
Sherrington, C. S., *2*, 2
Siegal, D., *4*, 18, 99

Singer, M. B., *1*, 130, 142
Sinha, D., *2*, 55
Sioux Indians, *1*, 21-22, 24
Situations, resuscitation of, *3*, 92-95
Skeletonization; *see* Verbal material
Skinner, B. F., *3*, 70, 71, 74
Sloane, H. N., *4*, 16, 39, 44, 114, 141
Smith, G. J. W., *4*, 11, 16, 56, 57, 93
Social institutions, *1*, 15
 confirmation, *1*, 144
 initiation, *1*, 144
Space; *see* Ego space-time; Life space; Framework, spatial and temporal
Speech, *1*, 75, 115; *see also* Communication; Language
Spence, K. W., *3*, 111
Spencer, H., *1*, 84
Spitz, R. A., *1*, 17, 60
Spock, B., *1*, 64, 65
Spragg, S. D. S., *2*, 31
Stage, definition of, *1*, 59
Stern, W., *2*, 145, 146
Stimuli, *3*, 3, 38, 44, 45, 46, 51, 59, 75, 77
 and perceptual apparatus, *3*, 24, 37, 53
 distal, *3*, vii, viii, 54
 proximal, *3*, vii, viii, 35, 53, 54, 55, 56, 58, 59
Stimulus, ambiguity of, *3*, 40-43
 and response, *3*, 111; *4*, 2, 3; *see also* Psychology, stimulus-response theories
 deprivation, *4*, 142
 irrelevant, *4*, 61
Streicher, J., *1*, 32
Stroop, J. R., *4*, 53, 54
Structures, *1*, 8-10; *4*, 2, 4, 5, 7, 8, 11, 12, 13
 formation of, *2*, 2-3, 147, 149
 mediating, *4*, 8, 9, 12
Submarines, *1*, 25
Sullivan, H. S., *1*, 6, 11, 147
Superego, *1*, 9, 20, 21, 24, 25, 46, 48, 49, 80, 147-150, 158, 159, 164
Symbol, *3*, 116-118
Synthetic function, *1*, 11, 25, 49, 149, 154
System coupling, *3*, 47-50, 52
System principles, *2*, 147, 148; *see also* Cognitive controls; Cognitive styles
Systems, *3*, 59
 leading and following, *3*, 46-52; *4*, 8

Temerlin, M. K., *4*, 89
Tests
 Aniseikonic Lenses, *4*, 31, 32, 35-38, 91, 92, 102, 103, 112, 113, 159

Apparent Movement *4*, 19, 31, 32-35, 91, 92, 159
assimilation, *4*, 22, 27
Chair-Window, *4*, 69
Color-Word *4*, 53, 54-59, 62, 82, 84, 87, 93, 96, 98, 103, 104, 114, 129, 135, 136, 159
diagnostic, *4*, 1
Embedded Figures, *4*, 18, 19, 22, 67-69, 72-76, 82, 86, 87, 96, 98, 99, 104, 114, 159, 171, 174-175
Free Association, *4*, 53, 59, 63-66, 82, 86, 87, 89, 91, 96, 98, 102, 104, 107, 111, 112, 159, 160
Gottschaldt Concealed Figures, *4*, 69, 70, 72
Incidental Recall, *4*, 58-59, 85, 114
Kinesthetic Time Error, *4*, 18, 27-30, 38, 91, 92, 102, 103, 111-113, 129, 132, 139, 159, 178-179
Object Sorting, *4*, 19, 39-42, 87, 105, 107, 109, 113, 114, 159
Picture Sorting, *4*, 19, 47, 50-52, 88
Rod and Frame, *4*, 18, 19, 68-73, 76, 79, 82, 85, 87, 96, 97, 99, 110, 111, 114, 159, 171, 174-175
Rorschach, *4*, 18, 31, 32, 76, 88, 99, 108, 111, 117, 123, 130-131, 133, 135, 168-175
Schematizing, *4*, 18, 23-26, 38, 85, 87, 91, 92, 100, 103, 111, 112, 113, 116, 129, 132, 139, 141, 143, 159, 177
scoring procedures for, *4*, 26, 30, 35, 38, 42, 44-45, 49-50, 52, 57-58, 59, 63, 65-66, 71-72, 75-76
Size Constancy, *4*, 42-45, 84, 86, 105, 107, 159
Size Estimation I, *4*, 47-50, 59, 60, 84, 86, 98, 102, 114, 132, 135, 140, 159
Size Estimation II, *4*, 53, 84, 86, 97, 98, 99, 102, 103, 135, 136, 159, 160
time error, *4*, 22; *see also* Tests, Kinesthetic Time Error
Themes; *see* Verbal material
Things, *3*, 1-34
   reproduction of, *3*, 21-23
   see also Objects; Units
Thinking, *2*, 141, 147; *3*, 37, 65
   primitive, *3*, 86, 89, 103, 106
   see also Primary process; Secondary process; Thought
Thirst experiments, *4*, 11, 12, 127
Thorndike, E. L., *2*, 2
Thought, *4*, 4, 5, 133; *see also* Thinking; Idea
Thouless, R. H., *4*, 42

Thurstone, L. L., *4*, 1, 2, 54, 78
Time diffusion, *1*, 126-127, 141, 146, 162
Titchener, E. B., *3*, 67, 68
Tolerance for unrealistic experiences; *see* Cognitive controls
Tolman, E. C., *3*, 73, 76
Totality, *1*, 133
Trace, *2*, 2, 3, 4, 139, 141, 145
   theory, *2*, 3, 56
Traces, *3*, 20-21, 22, 23, 34, 90
Transference, *1*, 133-136
Tresselt, M. E., *2*, 31
Tropism, *3*, 77
Trust; *see* Basic trust
Type-token, *2*, 25
Typology, *4*, 15, 16, 115

Undifferentiated phase, *1*, 12
Units, *3*, 8-14, 16-19, 22, 24-26, 28-30, 33, 34, 45, 87, 108, 109
   spurious *3*, 6-7, 17-19, 22-24, 27, 33, 34, 55, 57
   see also Cores

Values, *1*, 154
Variables; *see* Focal variables
Verbal material,
   ambiguity in, *2*, 6, 7, 33, 48, 53, 54, 120, 135, 142
   coherence of, *2*, 23-24, 26, 27, 31, 42, 53, 54, 70, 72, 77, 120, 121, 135, 137, 139, 140, 143
   connectedness of, *2*, 138-140, 142
   explication of, *2*, 6, 7, 8, 10-13, 19, 21, 23, 26, 31-35, 48, 54-55, 60, 64, 77-121, 134, 135, 137, 138, 142, 144
   familiarity of, *2*, 13-15, 21, 31, 32, 60, 64, 100-138
   fit in, *2*, 4, 5, 55, 120, 140, 142
   fragmentation of, *2*, 8, 32, 48, 137, 142
   gaps in, *2*, 6, 7, 32-34, 48, 53-55, 120, 135, 138, 139, 142
   importations in, *2*, 7, 8, 53-55, 57, 59-62, 68-69, 74, 76-137, 140, 142-145
   information units in, 18, 31, 53
   lexical unit of, *2*, 24-27
   repeated reproduction of, *2*, 9, 15, 64, 70, 72, 76
   retention of, *2*, 3, 60, 143
   style, *2*, 61-136
      ability, *2*, 19, 61-136, 144
   serial reproduction of, *2*, 6, 9, 15-16, 21, 31, 33, 37-40, 42-46, 70, 72, 76, 77
   skeletonization of, *2*, 7, 8, 31, 53-55, 57, 59-63, 69, 142, 145

themes in, *2*, 18, 53
  analysis, *2*, 31, 35-36
  score, *2*, 68
Vernon, P. E., *4*, 2
Vibrations, forced and free, *3*, 4-6, 14-17, 22, 29, 36, 57
Vinh-Bang, *4*, 47
von Ehrenfels, C. *3*, 69
von Kries, J., *3*, 44, 45, 69, 71
von Uexküll, J., *4*, 9

Waelder, R., *1*, 11
Wagner, R., *1*, 107
Wallach, H., *2*, 143
Walter, A. A., *4*, 22
Wapner, S., *4*, 69
War casualties, psychoneurotic, *1*, 42-44
Wechsler, D., *4*, 144
Weiss, A. P., *3*, 80
Werner, H., *2*, 23; *3*, 86, 89, 94, 106; *4*, 69
Wertheim, J., *4*, 68
Wertheimer, M., *3*, 112; *4*, 33
Wholeness, *1*, 132-133
Wholes, properties of, *3*, 9

Whole situation, *3*, 87-91, 94, 97
Will, G. T., *1*, 139
Williams, M., *2*, 59
Winch, W. H., *2*, 64
Witkin, H. A., *4*, 17, 18, 19, 54, 67, 69, 70, 71, 72, 73, 74, 75, 76, 77, 99, 100, 110, 142, 144, 168, 170, 171, 172, 173, 174, 175
Wolf, K., *1*, 17
Wolter, A. W., *2*, 58, 59
Woodrow, H., *2*, 64
Woodworth, D. G., *4*, 69
Woodworth, R. S., *2*, 58, 64
Word count, *2*, 18
Work, *1*, 85-88, 104-105, 140, 145
  paralysis, *1*, 127, 155
Workmanship, *1*, 127, 155
Wulf, F., *2*, 3; *4*, 22, 142

Young, H. H., *4*, 69
Yurok Indians, *1*, 24

Zangwill, O. L., *2*, 4, 141
Zilboorg, G., *1*, 19

Erratum: Monograph 1, p. 123, Footnote 8, lines 1-2 should read Newcomb, et al. (1953), instead of G. H. Mead (1934).